The Editors

NINA AUERBACH is John Welsh Centennial Professor of History and Literature and Professor of English at the University of Pennsylvania. She is the author of *Communities of Women: An Idea in Fiction*; *Woman and the Demon: The Life of a Victorian Myth*; *Romantic Imprisonment: Women and Other Glorified Outcasts*; *Ellen Terry, Player in Her Time*; *Private Theatricals: The Lives of the Victorians*; and *Our Vampires, Ourselves*. She is co-editor, with U. C. Knoepflmacher, of *Forbidden Journeys: Fairy Tales and Fantasies by Victorian Women Writers*.

DAVID J. SKAL is the author of several books on genre cinema and fantastic literature, including *Hollywood Gothic: The Tangled Web of "Dracula" from Novel to Stage to Screen*; *The Monster Show: A Cultural History of Horror*; *V is for Vampire*; and *Screams of Reason: Mad Science and Modern Culture*. With Elias Savada, he is co-author of *Dark Carnival: The Secret World of Tod Browning*. He has also written and produced numerous video documentaries on fantastic films and literature.

DRACULA

AUTHORITATIVE TEXT
CONTEXTS
REVIEWS AND REACTIONS
DRAMATIC AND FILM VARIATIONS
CRITICISM

A NORTON CRITICAL EDITION

Bram Stoker
DRACULA

AUTHORITATIVE TEXT

CONTEXTS

REVIEWS AND REACTIONS

DRAMATIC AND FILM VARIATIONS

CRITICISM

Edited by

NINA AUERBACH

UNIVERSITY OF PENNSYLVANIA

and

DAVID J. SKAL

W • W • NORTON & COMPANY • *New York* • *London*

Copyright © 1997 by W. W. Norton & Company, Inc.

The text of this book is composed in Electra with the display set in Bernhard
Modern. Composition by PennSet, Inc. Manufacturing by Courier Companies.
Cover illustration: Portrait of Henry Irving as Mephistopheles. Courtesy of the
Victoria and Albert Museum, London.

Library of Congress Cataloging-in-Publication Data
Stoker, Bram, 1847–1912.
Dracula : authoritative text, backgrounds, reviews and reactions, dramatic and film
variations, criticism / edited by Nina Auerbach and David J. Skal.
p.   cm. — (Norton critical edition)
Includes bibliographical references (p. 000)
ISBN 0-393-97012-4 (pbk.)
1. Dracula, Count (Fictitious character) — Fiction. 2. Stoker, Bram, 1847–1912 —
Film and video adaptations. 3. Horror tales, English — History and criticism.
4. Dracula, Count (Fictitious character) 5. Stoker, Bram, 1847–1912 Dracula.
6. Vampires in literature. 7. Vampires — Fiction. I. Auerbach, Nina, 1943–
II. Skal, David J.
PR6037.T617D7   1996c
823'.8 — dc20   96-18985

W. W. Norton & Company, Inc., 500 Fifth Avenue, New York, N.Y. 10110
www.wwnorton.com

W. W. Norton & Company Ltd., Castle House, 75/76 Wells Street,
London W1T 3QT

Contents

Preface

Though *Dracula* was published in 1897, it is difficult to detach the novel from its vigorous twentieth-century life: we tend to superimpose on Bram Stoker's enigmatic monster Bela Lugosi's intonations or Frank Langella's sinuous seductiveness or Gary Oldman's tears. Stoker's vampire story is far more important to us than it was to its contemporary Victorians, who relished it as a good potboiler but never made Bram Stoker or his monster famous. A novel that seemed commonplace in its time unfurled into a legend haunting and defining the next century.

Dracula seemed commonplace in 1897 in part because it was one of many fantastic adventure stories pitting manly Englishmen against foreign monsters. Throughout the 1880s and 1890s, authors such as H. Rider Haggard, Rudyard Kipling, Robert Louis Stevenson, and H. G. Wells turned out hordes of tales—several more eloquent and sophisticated than *Dracula*—in which fabulous creatures from remote corners of the earth (or beyond) threatened the integrity of the British home and empire. Sometimes these creatures arose from within: in Robert Louis Stevenson's *The Strange Case of Dr. Jekyll and Mr. Hyde*, a hideous alien reminiscent of a monkey, a Cockney, and an overgrown boy springs out from within a doctor even more respectable than Stoker's John Seward. *Dracula*'s essential formula of invasion and appropriation was by 1897 cozily familiar to readers of adventure tales.

But unlike Rider Haggard's She or the Beast People in H. G. Wells's *The Island of Doctor Moreau*, Dracula is an adaptable monster—more so in Stoker's novel than in its many flamboyant film adaptations—and this may be why we continue to believe in him. When we meet the vampire, he has never left his native Transylvania, but his English is more elegant and lucid than that of the Englishmen he accosts, many of whom are tangled in the thickets of their own dialect.

Moreover, Dracula is a monster only to those who know him. Humans instinctively shy away from Stevenson's Mr. Hyde as an alien, though he has no visible deformity; Dracula blends into London as if he belongs there, even sporting a straw hat. When we strip away the mannerisms of movie Draculas, we meet a vampire with the potential to be at home everywhere.

Dracula may be less alien than he seems, but he is a monster of his time in that he embodies a threat that haunted *fin-de-siècle* England:

that of atavism, or reversion. At the height of domestic prosperity and imperial expansion, thoughtful Victorians were uneasily aware of the fragility of their sophisticated civilization. Technology was galloping forward and London and its inhabitants had never looked more gorgeous or conversed more stylishly, but barbarians were glimpsed at the gates, as if the inhumanity of the twentieth century dropped an ugly shadow. In this spirit, the human characters in *Dracula* surround themselves with modern gadgets and skills—shorthand, typewriters, dictating machines, cameras—but they must learn to combat an ancient enemy with ancient beliefs: wild Eastern European superstitions (several of which Stoker invented), and, with Van Helsing as medium, the Catholicism that was anathema to the enlightened secularism of sophisticated Victorians. *Dracula*'s evolution into atavism hinted that advanced civilization is itself a lie.

London's glamour may have seemed especially unreal to Bram Stoker because he gave his best energies to fortifying its illusions: between 1878 and 1898, he managed the Lyceum Theater, headed by the tyrannical actor-manager Henry Irving. Irving was Stoker's indelible inspiration, not only for his vampire, but for the noble England Dracula threatened: Irving specialized in diabolical roles, but his ornate Lyceum exuded conspicuous consumption and cultural uplift. Like England itself, Irving's Lyceum was grand, solid, and implacably patriarchal. Because of Irving's achievement, the disreputable stage found itself for the first time in the vanguard of Victorian art and culture. Yet Stoker saw the price of this cultural primacy. Irving was always overspending, never saving: his theater's appearance of solidity was built on sand. Only outsiders were surprised when, in 1898, he had to relinquish his control over the Lyceum to a syndicate.

The Lyceum family had always been a brilliant fiction. Onstage, Irving paternally engulfed his radiant partner, the beloved actress Ellen Terry. But while the Lyceum made Terry famous, it thwarted her as an artist. Irving was too solemn and stately to stage the comedies she loved; he refused, in fact, to stage any play that did not highlight his own magnificence. Throughout the 1890s, Ellen Terry aged into increasing agitation and barely suppressed rage at her diminishing roles in rickety vehicles for Irving. Stoker wrote much chivalrous gush about Ellen Terry, but he observed her as well. Like Ellen Terry, the women in *Dracula* are uneasy in their roles even before the vampire comes. Like her in her rages, they show sinister and unexpected powers once bitten. During Stoker's long career at the Lyceum, he saw the fissures in imperial British society and the hierarchical English family. His life in a powerful theatrical company imperceptibly coming apart gave him the material to articulate fears that reached beyond the stage.

In the world beyond the theater, England was losing her homogeneity, if not yet her primacy. The British Empire's penetration into

Africa and India—"the dark places of the earth," as Conrad called
them—accompanied a new penetration of England by aliens: the waves
of immigrants, especially Jewish immigrants, that began in the 1880s.
As the boundaries of England and Englishness became less clear-cut,
racial purity became a new fetish. Max Nordau's *Degeneration* (1893)
was a popular jeremiad against racial deterioration—and the deterioration of manhood as well. Jonathan Harker's dislocating journey to
Transylvania at the beginning of *Dracula*; his possible human and sexual pollution there; and Dracula's ensuing invasion of the heart of
London—all arise from a decade in which national, racial, and even
human boundaries appeared increasingly permeable. It is uncertain in
Dracula whether Jonathan's journey *beyond* England or Dracula's journey *to* it poses the greatest threat to the integrity of British male humanity. In Stoker's time, that integrity was increasingly besieged.

Englishmen were threatened not only by dark places, foreigners, and
Jews, but by their own women. Victorian patriarchy, whereby middle-
class women were, to preserve the sanctity of the family, legally, edu-
cationally, and economically dispossessed, had always been a vulnerable
institution. The 1890s saw a rising wave of feminist awareness, a wave
that would crest in the next decade with the mass movement for female
suffrage; only World War I, followed by the granting of partial suffrage
in 1918 and universal suffrage in 1928, would check it.

In 1897, a new dispensation seemed to many women an exhilarating
possibility. Their vision of new lives was incarnated in a personification
called the New Woman, about whom Stoker's Mina makes ambivalent
jokes. Celebrated and mocked in fiction and journalism, the New
Woman is an eccentric with no relation to the collective movement
feminism was rapidly becoming. Still, for most men, she was threatening enough on her own, for she refused to be satisfied with the old
Victorian definitions: economically and sexually, she was either independent of male control or aspiring to be so. Thus she was by conventional standards perverse, no longer recognizable as female. The
appellation "New Woman" itself suggests an evolutionary mutation.
The strange changes Dracula catalyzes in Lucy and Mina—seemingly,
of all London's "teeming millions," the only mortals on whom he
preys—are symptomatic of the changes men feared in all their women.
In the guise of fantasy, Bram Stoker wrote a novel true to the dislocating
experience of his bewildered contemporaries.

New Women threatened British manhood from without, but Oscar
Wilde—like Stevenson's Mr. Hyde—eroded it from within. The Wilde
trials of 1895 probably shocked Stoker into writing *Dracula* as we
know it, for Wilde's two-year imprisonment for "acts of gross indecency"
gave Victorian England a new monster of its own clinical making: the homosexual. An impertinent novelist and playwright who relished the license his fame gave him to shock the middle class, Oscar

Wilde became the test case, not only for a new statute criminalizing sodomy, but for a new medical model of homosexuality that stigmatized not acts, but essence: like the vampire, this creature was tainted in his desires, not his deeds. This pariah, more dangerous than the New Woman because more insidiously pervasive, cast a shadow not only over the theatrical community but over all men.

Stoker knew Wilde, not only through the theater: Wilde had proposed to the beautiful Florence Balcombe, whom Stoker later married. Stoker himself may, in freer days, have been involved in the homosexual community later ostracized in Wilde's person: his impassioned hero worship of Walt Whitman and then of Irving released an obsessed ardor scarcely apparent in his marriage. In *Dracula*, though, Stoker created a monster, not an alter ego.

The Wilde trials generated the terror that took the form of *Dracula*, but Stoker's humorlessly single-minded predator has nothing in common with his imprisoned former friend. If anything about his vampire suggests Wilde, Stoker did his best to expunge it, as he expunged Wilde's name from his sanctimonious memoir, *Personal Reminiscences of Henry Irving* (1906). Dracula may be closest to Wilde because he is most alive in his silences. Once Wilde was sentenced to prison, he had tried vainly to speak: "And I? May I say nothing, my lord?" But the judge only waved to the warders, who hurried Wilde to his cell. In the same spirit, *Dracula* abounds in narratives; almost every character spills out stories in diaries, letters, and monologues; but once he arrives in England, Dracula is effectively voiceless, existing only in the tales of experts who want to destroy him.

Compared to such earlier vampires as Polidori's Lord Ruthven and Sheridan Le Fanu's Carmilla, Dracula is scrupulously hygienic, even monogamous. He seems to abstain from biting his mortal guest Jonathan Harker, attacking men by destroying their women in proper British fashion. But in a passage published only in the 1899 American edition, he announces that he will feast on Jonathan; there are faint hints throughout the novel that Jonathan, like his wife Mina, is changing; but these undeveloped glimmers of a less orthodox *Dracula* subside. Dracula's official abstinence is a concession to the new taboos the Wilde trials bequeathed to the twentieth century, but repression does not destroy this terrifying novel: rather, repressive conditions probably frightened Stoker into writing it.

Later, more comfortably progressive decades would develop these faint hints of a vampire existence that eludes patriarchal categories: in the 1970s, Dracula was transformed into a poignantly androgynous liberator of trapped women, while Anne Rice's best-selling *Vampire Chronicles* are openly homoerotic. In Stoker's novel, though, the vampire is a snarling enigma, the repository of mortals' fears for themselves. He never quite lives and he never quite dies: since his final, hurried destruction is shorn of the rituals Van Helsing decrees necessary to drive vampires into the "true death," Dracula may well rise again after our heroes have returned to England. Whether he rises or not, his power has expanded beyond his time. In 1897 and today, Dracula lives in the transformations he inspires.

Acknowledgments

Certain critics with Freudian tastes have suggested that Bram Stoker wrote his novel simply by releasing the sexual monsters in his own unconscious, but Stoker's consciousness—informed, urbane, alert—pervades his story. Editing *Dracula* confronted us with the staggering range of Bram Stoker's knowledge and awareness—not only of vampires and the occult, but of the mores, the science, the art, of his own England.

Since scholarship is a cumulative enterprise, we would not have seen quite so much in *Dracula* without the many editors who came before us, explicating its arcane contemporary allusions and its larger folkloric frame of reference. Leonard Wolf's *The Essential* Dracula (Plume Books, 1993; first published by Clarkson Potter as *The Annotated* Dracula in 1975) remains the most ornately and exhaustively annotated edition; we particularly admire Leonard Wolf's pioneering work. We are grateful to have been invited speakers at his *Dracula* centenary conference "The Aesthetics of Fear," held at New York University in March 1997, and we gratefully acknowledge his *Annotated* Dracula, and *Essential* Dracula, which have informed a number of our notes.

Raymond McNally and Radu Florescu's edition, also called *Essential* Dracula (Mayflower Books, 1979), is the most historically substantive of all the editions; we learned much from it. We also benefitted from the *Draculas* edited by George Stacie (Bantam Classics, 1981), A. N. Wilson (Oxford University Press, 1983), Maurice Hindle (Penguin Classics, 1993), and Marjorie Howe (Everyman Editions, 1993).

We wish to thank the Rosenbach Museum and Library in Philadelphia for allowing both editors direct access to Bram Stoker's working notes for *Dracula* prior to our work on this edition; especially useful were Stoker's original transcriptions of Yorkshire dialect. We thank with particular warmth the Rosenbach's executive director, Stephen Urice, for his encouragement, appreciation, hospitality, and invitation to speak at the opening of the Rosenbach's *Dracula* Centenary Exhibition. Other research collections consulted include the Elmer Holmes Bobst Library of New York University; the Billy Rose Theatre Collection, New York Public Library at Lincoln Center; the Van Pelt Library of the

University of Pennsylvania; and the University Research Library of UCLA.

We thank all other Dracula-hunters who preceded us in leading the vampire out of the shadows. We wish good hunting to the many who will surely follow.

A Note on the Text

This edition of *Dracula* is based on the original British edition, published by Archibald Constable and Company in June 1897. Simple typographical errors and misspellings have been silently corrected; a few textual variations are covered in footnotes.

DRACULA

BY

BRAM STOKER

WESTMINSTER
ARCHIBALD CONSTABLE AND COMPANY
2 WHITEHALL GARDENS
1897

TO

MY DEAR FRIEND

HOMMY-BEG[1]

---

1. *Dracula* is dedicated to the novelist Hall Caine, one of Stoker's closest friends. "Hommy-Beg" is an affectionate Manx nickname meaning "Little Tommy."

How these papers have been placed in sequence will be made made manifest in the reading of them. All needless matters have been eliminated, so that a history almost at variance with the possibilities of later-day belief may stand forth as simple fact.[1] There is throughout no statement of past things wherein memory may err, for all the records chosen are exactly contemporary,[2] given from the standpoints and within the range of knowledge of those who made them.

1. An appeal to the empirically based Victorian scientific method.
2. The simulation of temporal immediacy is a familiar device in English fiction; see Samuel Richardson's epistolary novels, *Pamela* (1740) and *Clarissa* (1747–48), and Wilkie Collins's multiply narrated *The Woman in White* (1860) and *The Moonstone* (1868).

Contents

Chapter I

Jonathan Harker's Journal

(KEPT IN SHORTHAND)[1]

3 *May. Bistritz.*[2]—Left Munich at 8.35 p.m. on 1st May, arriving at Vienna early next morning; should have arrived at 6.46, but train was an hour late. Buda-Pesth seems a wonderful place, from the glimpse which I got of it from the train and the little I could walk through the streets. I feared to go very far from the station, as we had arrived late and would start as near the correct time as possible. The impression I had was that we were leaving the West and entering the East; the most Western of splendid bridges[3] over the Danube, which is here of noble width and depth, took us among the traditions of Turkish rule.[4]

We left in pretty good time, and came after nightfall to Klausen-burgh. Here I stopped for the night at the Hotel Royale. I had for dinner, or rather supper, a chicken done up some way with red pepper, which was very good but thirsty. (*Mem.*, get recipe for Mina.) I asked the waiter, and he said it was called 'paprika hendl,' and that, as it was a national dish, I should be able to get it anywhere along the Carpathians.[5] I found my smattering of German very useful here; indeed, I don't know how I should be able to get on without it.

Having some time at my disposal when in London, I had visited the British Museum,[6] and made search among the books and maps in the library regarding Transylvania;[7] it had struck me that some foreknowl-

---

1. Various shorthand systems were employed in the nineteenth century; in 1837, the Pitman method came into general use. This method of speedwriting, in which geometric shapes replace words, is difficult to learn but efficient to use.
2. Now Bistrita, Romania.
3. Count Széchenyi's bridge over the Danube linking Buda and Pest was completed in 1849.
4. Transylvania passed from Turkish dominion to the Austro-Hungarian Empire in 1711.
5. A heavily forested, V-shaped mountain range separating Transylvania proper from the other Romanian provinces: Moldavia to the east and Wallachia to the south.
6. Established 1753. The British Library Reading Room with its majestic dome, a haven for self-improving Victorians, opened in 1857. Like Jonathan Harker, Stoker learned most of what he knew about Eastern European history and legend in the British Museum.
7. In western Romania; about 43 percent of the territory. In essence, fittingly for vampires, the history of Transylvania is a history of whom it belongs to. From the second to the fourth centuries, Dacia, as it then was, was incorporated into the Roman empire. In the tenth century, the Hungarians (Magyars) conquered it, colonizing it through the fifteenth century with German settlers. In 1526, the Turks overran the Hungarian kingdom; Transylvania, still ruled by Hungarian princes, became a semi-independent province of the Turkish Empire. In 1691, the Hapsburgs reconquered it; in 1867, the Austro-Hungarian Empire placed Transylvania under Hungarian rule. After World War I, Transylvania became Romanian, though Hitler briefly returned it to Hungary in 1940.

 Bram Stoker gave to Transylvania vampires and notoriety, but he did so at the last minute: Dracula's homeland was originally Styria, like that of Joseph Sheridan Le Fanu's languidly loving vampire in *Carmilla* (1872). When he changed *Dracula*'s setting, Stoker drew freely on Emily Gerard's *The Land Beyond the Forest* (1888), a popular Victorian account of Transylvanian history and legend.

edge of the country could hardly fail to have some importance in dealing with a noble of that country. I find that the district he named is in
the extreme east of the country, just on the borders of three states,
Transylvania, Moldavia, and Bukovina,[8] in the midst of the Carpathian
mountains; one of the wildest and least known portions of Europe. I
was not able to light on any map or work giving the exact locality of
the Castle Dracula,[9] as there are no maps of this country as yet to
compare with our own Ordnance Survey maps;[1] but I found that Bistritz, the post town[2] named by Count Dracula, is a fairly well-known
place. I shall enter here some of my notes, as they may refresh my
memory when I talk over my travels with Mina.

In the population of Transylvania there are four distinct nationalities:
Saxons in the south, and mixed with them the Wallachs, who are the
descendants of the Dacians;[3] Magyars in the west, and Szekelys in the
east and north. I am going among the latter, who claim to be descended
from Attila and the Huns.[4] This may be so, for when the Magyars
conquered the country in the eleventh century they found the Huns
settled in it. I read that every known superstition in the world is gathered
into the horseshoe of the Carpathians, as if it were the centre of some
sort of imaginative whirlpool; if so my stay may be very interesting.
(*Mem.*, I must ask the Count all about them.)

I did not sleep well, though my bed was comfortable enough, for I
had all sorts of queer dreams. There was a dog howling all night under
my window, which may have had something to do with it; or it may
have been the paprika, for I had to drink up all the water in my carafe,
and was still thirsty. Towards morning I slept and was wakened by the
continuous knocking at my door, so I guess I must have been sleeping
soundly then. I had for breakfast more paprika, and a sort of porridge
of maize flour which they said was 'mamaliga,' and eggplant stuffed
with forcemeat,[5] a very excellent dish, which they call 'impletata.'
(*Mem.*, get recipe for this also.) I had to hurry breakfast, for the train
started a little before eight, or rather it ought to have done so, for after

---

8. Moldavia was a province of Romania, which had become a kingdom in 1881. In the 1890s,
   Bukovina was an autonomous duchy within the Austro-Hungarian Empire; it too is now part
   of Romania. The wild border country through which Jonathan travels teeters on the edge of
   fragile national independence.
9. Despite the claims of various tour directors, and some critics as well, Castle Dracula does not
   exist on any map.
1. Military maps.
2. A town with a post office or post-horses.
3. Dacia, whose area corresponds roughly to twentieth-century Romania, became a province of
   the Roman Empire under the Emperor Trajan in A.D. 105. As late as June 1995, a Romanian
   patriot boasted in a letter to the *New York Times* of his Roman inheritance, scrupulously
   differentiating Romanians from the "Romanay Gypsies" who, in *Dracula*, prove to be treach-
   erous allies of the vampire.
4. Attila was king of the Huns from 434 to 453. These Asian nomads invaded and devastated
   China, Italy, and the Roman Empire. Dracula's Szekelys claim descent from these enemies
   of Western civilization.
5. Finely ground and highly spiced meat, fish, or poultry that is served alone or used in stuffing.

rushing to the station at 7.30 I had to sit in the carriage for more than an hour before we began to move. It seems to me that the further East you go the more unpunctual are the trains. What ought they to be in China?

All day long we seemed to dawdle through a country which was full of beauty of every kind. Sometimes we saw little towns or castles on the top of steep hills such as we see in old missals; sometimes we ran by rivers and streams which seemed from the wide stony margin on each side of them to be subject to great floods. It takes a lot of water, and running strong, to sweep the outside edge of a river clear. At every station there were groups of people, sometimes crowds, and in all sorts of attire. Some of them were just like the peasants at home or those I saw coming through France and Germany, with short jackets and round hats and homemade trousers; but others were very picturesque. The women looked pretty, except when you got near them, but they were very clumsy about the waist. They had all full white sleeves of some kind or other, and most of them had big belts with a lot of strips of something fluttering from them like the dresses in a ballet, but of course petticoats under them. The strangest figures we saw were the Slovaks, who are more barbarian than the rest, with their big cowboy hats, great baggy dirty-white trousers, white linen shirts, and enormous heavy leather belts, nearly a foot wide, all studded over with brass nails. They wore high boots, with their trousers tucked into them, and had long black hair and heavy black moustaches. They are very picturesque, but do not look prepossessing. On the stage they would be set down at once as some old Oriental band of brigands. They are, however, I am told, very harmless and rather wanting in natural self-assertion.

It was on the dark side of twilight when we got to Bistritz, which is a very interesting old place. Being practically on the frontier—for the Borgo Pass[6] leads from it into Bukovina—it has had a very stormy existence, and it certainly shows marks of it. Fifty years ago a series of great fires took place, which made terrible havoc on five separate occasions. At the very beginning of the seventeenth century it underwent a siege of three weeks and lost 13,000 people, the casualties of war proper being assisted by famine and disease.

Count Dracula had directed me to go to the Golden Krone Hotel, which I found, to my great delight, to be thoroughly old-fashioned, for of course I wanted to see all I could of the ways of the country. I was evidently expected, for when I got near the door I faced a cheery-looking elderly woman in the usual peasant dress—white undergarment with long double apron, front, and back, of coloured stuff fitting almost too tight for modesty. When I came close she bowed, and said, 'The Herr Englishman?' 'Yes,' I said, 'Jonathan Harker.' She smiled, and

_____
6. This mountainous elevation, beginning in Tihucza (Bistrita), is less sublime than Stoker's imagination makes it.

gave some message to an elderly man in white shirt-sleeves, who had followed her to the door. He went, but immediately returned with a letter:—

MY FRIEND,—Welcome to the Carpathians. I am anxiously expecting you. Sleep well tonight. At three tomorrow the diligence[7] will start for Bukovina; a place on it is kept for you. At the Borgo Pass my carriage will await you and will bring you to me. I trust that your journey from London has been a happy one, and that you will enjoy your stay in my beautiful land.

Your friend,
DRACULA.

4 May.—I found that my landlord had got a letter from the Count, directing him to secure the best place on the coach for me; but on making inquiries as to details he seemed somewhat reticent, and pretended that he could not understand my German. This could not be true, because up to then he had understood it perfectly; at least, he answered my questions exactly as if he did. He and his wife, the old lady who had received me, looked at each other in a frightened sort of way. He mumbled out that the money had been sent in a letter, and that was all he knew. When I asked him if he knew Count Dracula, and could tell me anything of his castle, both he and his wife crossed themselves, and, saying that they knew nothing at all, simply refused to speak further. It was so near the time of starting that I had no time to ask any one else, for it was all very mysterious and not by any means comforting.

Just before I was leaving, the old lady came up to my room and said in a very hysterical way.

'Must you go? Oh! young Herr, must you go?' She was in such an excited state that she seemed to have lost her grip of what German she knew, and mixed it all up with some other language which I did not know at all. I was just able to follow her by asking many questions. When I told her that I must go at once, and that I was engaged on important business, she asked again:

'Do you know what day it is?' I answered that it was the fourth of May. She shook her head as she said again:

'Oh, yes! I know that, I know that! but do you know what day it is?' On my saying that I did not understand, she went on:

'It is the eve of St George's Day. Do you not know that tonight, when the clock strikes midnight, all the evil things in the world will have full sway? Do you know where you are going, and what you are going to?' She was in such evident distress that I tried to comfort her, but without effect. Finally she went down on her knees and implored me not to

7. A large stagecoach.

go; at least to wait a day or two before starting. It was all very ridiculous, but I did not feel comfortable. However, there was business to be done, and I could allow nothing to interfere with it. I therefore tried to raise her up, and said, as gravely as I could, that I thanked her, but my duty was imperative, and that I must go. She then rose and dried her eyes, and taking a crucifix from her neck offered it to me. I did not know what to do, for, as an English Churchman,[8] I have been taught to regard such things as in some measure idolatrous, and yet it seemed so ungracious to refuse an old lady meaning so well and in such a state of mind. She saw, I suppose, the doubt in my face, for she put the rosary round my neck, and said, 'For your mother's sake,' and went out of the room. I am writing up this part of the diary whilst I am waiting for the coach, which is, of course, late; and the crucifix is still round my neck. Whether it is the old lady's fear, or the many ghostly traditions of this place, or the crucifix itself, I do not know, but I am not feeling nearly as easy in my mind as usual. If this book should ever reach Mina before I do, let it bring my goodbye. Here comes the coach!

5 *May. The Castle.*—The grey of the morning has passed, and the sun is high over the distant horizon, which seems jagged, whether with trees or hills I know not, for it is so far off that big things and little are mixed. I am not sleepy, and, as I am not to be called till I awake, naturally I write till sleep comes. There are many odd things to put down, and, lest who reads them may fancy that I dined too well before I left Bistritz, let me put down my dinner exactly. I dined on what they call 'robber steak'—bits of bacon, onion, and beef, seasoned with red pepper, and strung on sticks and roasted over the fire, in the simple style of the London cat's-meat.[9] The wine was Golden Mediasch, which produces a queer sting on the tongue, which is, however, not disagreeable. I had only a couple of glasses of this, and nothing else.

When I got on the coach the driver had not taken his seat, and I saw him talking with the landlady. They were evidently talking of me, for every now and then they looked at me, and some of the people who were sitting on the bench outside the door—which they call by a name meaning 'word-bearer'—came and listened, and then looked at me, most of them pityingly. I could hear a lot of words often repeated, queer words, for there were many nationalities in the crowd; so I quietly got my polyglot[1] dictionary from my bag and looked them out. I must say they were not cheering to me, for amongst them were 'Ordog'—Satan, 'pokol'—hell, 'stregoica'—witch, 'vrolok' and 'vlkoslak'—both of which mean the same thing, one being Slovak and the other Servian for some-

---

8. After the Oxford Movement of the 1830s and early 1840s, which sought to revitalize the Church of England by reviving certain Roman Catholic practices, Victorian Anglicanism was particularly suspicious of anything that smacked of Catholic relics and rituals.
9. Jonathan compares his meals to the horsemeat fed to animals in London.
1. One dictionary definition, "a mixture or confusion of languages," anticipates the linguistic cacophony that threatens to overwhelm *Dracula*'s characters.

thing that is either werewolf[2] or vampire. (*Mem.*, I must ask the Count about these superstitions.)

When we started, the crowd round the inn door, which had by this time swelled to a considerable size, all made the sign of the cross and pointed two fingers towards me. With some difficulty I got a fellow-passenger to tell me what they meant; he would not answer at first, but on learning that I was English he explained that it was a charm or guard against the evil eye. This was not very pleasant for me, just starting for an unknown place to meet an unknown man; but every one seemed so kind-hearted, and so sorrowful, and so sympathetic that I could not but be touched. I shall never forget the last glimpse which I had of the inn-yard and its crowd of picturesque figures, all crossing themselves, as they stood round the wide archway, with its background of rich foliage of oleander and orange trees in green tubs clustered in the centre of the yard. Then our driver, whose wide linen drawers covered the whole front of the box-seat—'gotza' they call them—cracked his big whip over his four small horses, which ran abreast, and we set off on our journey.

I soon lost sight and recollection of ghostly fears in the beauty of the scene as we drove along, although had I known the language, or rather languages, which my fellow-passengers were speaking, I might not have been able to throw them off so easily. Before us lay a green sloping land full of forests and woods, with here and there steep hills, crowned with clumps of trees or with farmhouses, the blank gable end to the road. There was everywhere a bewildering mass of fruit blossom—apple, plum, pear, cherry; and as we drove by I could see the green grass under the trees spangled with the fallen petals. In and out amongst these green hills of what they call here the 'Mittel Land'[3] ran the road, losing itself as it swept round the grassy curve, or was shut out by the straggling ends of pine woods, which here and there ran down the hillside like tongues of flame. The road was rugged, but still we seemed to fly over it with a feverish haste. I could not understand then what the haste meant, but the driver was evidently bent on losing no time in reaching Borgo Prund.[4] I was told that this road is in summertime excellent, but that it had not yet been put in order after the winter snows. In this respect it is different from the general run of roads in the Carpathians, for it is an old tradition that they are not to be kept in too good order. Of old the Hospadars[5] would not repair them, lest

2. Werewolves and vampires are often allied in Romanian folklore. They are natural as well as linguistic kin—both are hybrids, prone to nocturnal transformation into animals—but Dracula, with nineteenth-century faith in his own supremacy, treats wolves merely as his servants.
3. Middle or central.
4. Anglicized variant of Borgóprund, the Hungarian name for the Romanian village and rail junction Prundul-Bârgăului, located 13 miles NE of Bistrita in the western foothills of the Carpathians.
5. From the fifteenth century to 1866, the rulers of Wallachia and Moldavia were called *hospadars*.

the Turks should think that they were preparing to bring in foreign troops, and so hasten the war which was always really at loading point.

Beyond the green swelling hills of the Mittel Land rose mighty slopes of forest up to the lofty steeps of the Carpathians themselves. Right and left of us they towered, with the afternoon sun falling full upon them and bringing out all the glorious colours of this beautiful range, deep blue and purple in the shadows of the peaks, green and brown where grass and rock mingled, and an endless perspective of jagged rock and pointed crags, till these were themselves lost in the distance, where the snowy peaks rose grandly. Here and there seemed mighty rifts in the mountains, through which, as the sun began to sink, we saw now and again the white gleam of falling water. One of my companions touched my arm as we swept round the base of a hill and opened up the lofty, snow-covered peak of a mountain, which seemed, as we wound on our serpentine way, to be right before us:—

'Look! Isten szek!'—'God's seat!'—and he crossed himself reverently. As we wound on our endless way, and the sun sank lower and lower behind us, the shadows of the evening began to creep round us. This was emphasized by the fact that the snowy mountain-top still held the sunset, and seemed to glow out with a delicate cool pink. Here and there we passed Cszeks and Slovaks, all in picturesque attire, but I noticed that goitre[6] was painfully prevalent. By the roadside were many crosses, and as we swept by, my companions all crossed themselves. Here and there was a peasant man or woman kneeling before a shrine, who did not even turn round as we approached, but seemed in the self-surrender of devotion to have neither eyes nor ears for the outer world. There were many things new to me: for instance, hay-ricks in the trees, and here and there very beautiful masses of weeping birch, their white stems shining like silver through the delicate green of the leaves. Now and again we passed a leiter-wagon—the ordinary peasant's cart, with its long, snake-like vertebra, calculated to suit the inequalities of the road. On this were sure to be seated quite a group of home-coming peasants, the Cszeks with their white, and the Slovaks with their coloured, sheepskins, the latter carrying lance-fashion their long staves, with axe at end. As the evening fell it began to get very cold, and the growing twilight seemed to merge into one dark mistiness the gloom of the trees, oak, beech, and pine, though in the valleys which ran deep between the spurs of the hills, as we ascended through the Pass, the dark firs stood out here and there against the background of late-lying snow. Sometimes, as the road was cut through the pine woods that seemed in the darkness to be closing down upon us, great masses of greyness, which here and there bestrewed the trees, produced a peculiarly weird and solemn effect, which carried on the thoughts and grim

---

6. An enlarged thyroid gland resulting in a swollen neck; one symptom of iodine deficiency; particularly common in some mountainous regions; may cause brain damage.

fancies engendered earlier in the evening, when the falling sunset threw into strange relief the ghost-like clouds which amongst the Carpathians seem to wind ceaselessly through the valleys. Sometimes the hills were so steep that, despite our driver's haste, the horses could only go slowly. I wished to get down and walk up them, as we do at home, but the driver would not hear of it. 'No, no,' he said; 'you must not walk here; the dogs are too fierce;' and then he added, with what he evidently meant for grim pleasantry—for he looked round to catch the approving smile of the rest—'and you may have enough of such matters before you go to sleep.' The only stop he would make was a moment's pause to light his lamps.

When it grew dark there seemed to be some excitement amongst the passengers, and they kept speaking to him, one after the other, as though urging him to further speed. He lashed the horses unmercifully with his long whip, and with wild cries of encouragement urged them on to further exertions. Then through the darkness I could see a sort of patch of grey light ahead of us, as though there were a cleft in the hills. The excitement of the passengers grew greater; the crazy coach rocked on its great leather springs, and swayed like a boat tossed on a stormy sea. I had to hold on. The road grew more level, and we appeared to fly along. Then the mountains seemed to come nearer to us on each side and to frown down upon us; we were entering on the Borgo Pass. One by one several of the passengers offered me gifts, which they pressed upon me with an earnestness which would take no denial; these were certainly of an odd and varied kind, but each was given in simple good faith, with a kindly word, and a blessing, and that strange mixture of fear-meaning movements which I had seen outside the hotel at Bistritz—the sign of the cross and the guard against the evil eye. Then, as we flew along, the driver leaned forward, and on each side the passengers, craning over the edge of the coach, peered eagerly into the darkness. It was evident that something very exciting was either happening or expected, but though I asked each passenger, no one would give me the slightest explanation. This state of excitement kept on for some little time; and at last we saw before us the Pass opening out on the eastern side. There were dark, rolling clouds overhead, and in the air the heavy, oppressive sense of thunder. It seemed as though the mountain range had separated two atmospheres, and that now we had got into the thunderous one. I was now myself looking out for the conveyance which was to take me to the Count. Each moment I expected to see the glare of lamps through the blackness; but all was dark. The only light was the flickering rays of our own lamps, in which the steam from our hard-driven horses rose in a white cloud. We could now see the sandy road lying white before us, but there was on it no sign of a vehicle. The passengers drew back with a sigh of gladness, which seemed to mock my own disappointment. I was already thinking what I had best do, when the driver, looking at his watch, said to the others something which I could hardly hear, it was spoken so quietly and in so low a tone; I thought it was 'An hour less than the time.' Then turning to me, he said in German worse than my own:—

'There is no carriage here. The Herr is not expected after all. He will now come on to Bukovina, and return tomorrow or the next day; better the next day.' Whilst he was speaking the horses began to neigh and snort and plunge wildly, so that the driver had to hold them up. Then, amongst a chorus of screams from the peasants and a universal crossing of themselves, a calèche[7] with four horses drove up behind us, overtook us, and drew up beside the coach. I could see from the flash of our lamps, as the rays fell on them, that the horses were coal-black and splendid animals. They were driven by a tall man, with a long brown beard and a great black hat, which seemed to hide his face from us. I could only see the gleam of a pair of very bright eyes, which seemed red in the lamplight, as he turned to us. He said to the driver:—

'You are early tonight, my friend.' The man stammered in reply:—

'The English Herr was in a hurry,' to which the stranger replied:—

'That is why, I suppose, you wished him to go on to Bukovina. You cannot deceive me, my friend; I know too much, and my horses are swift.' As he spoke he smiled, and the lamplight fell on a hard-looking mouth, with very red lips and sharp-looking teeth, as white as ivory. One of my companions whispered to another the line from Burger's 'Lenore:'—[8]

'Denn die Todten reiten schnell'—

('For the dead travel fast.')

The strange driver evidently heard the words, for he looked up with a gleaming smile. The passenger turned his face away, at the same time putting out his two fingers and crossing himself. 'Give me the Herr's luggage,' said the driver; and with exceeding alacrity my bags were handed out and put in the calèche. Then I descended from the side of the coach, as the calèche was close alongside, the driver helping me with a hand which caught my arm in a grip of steel; his strength must have been prodigious. Without a word he shook his reins, the horses turned, and we swept into the darkness of the Pass. As I looked back I saw the steam from the horses of the coach by the light of the lamps, and projected against it the figures of my late companions crossing

7. A light carriage with two or four low wheels and a collapsible top resembling the French bonnet known as a *calèche*.
8. Not an exact quotation from Gottfried August Bürger's 1774 folk ballad, which William Taylor translated into English in 1796. In "Lenore," a soldier returns from the dead to claim his bride. Its refrain is "the dead ride fast."

themselves. Then the driver cracked his whip and called to his horses, and off they swept on their way to Bukovina.

As they sank into the darkness I felt a strange chill, and a lonely feeling came over me; but a cloak was thrown over my shoulders, and a rug across my knees, and the driver said in excellent German:—[9]

'The night is chill, mein Herr, and my master the Count bade me take all care of you. There is a flask of slivovitz [the plum brandy of the country] underneath the seat, if you should require it.' I did not take any, but it was a comfort to know it was there all the same. I felt a little strangely, and not a little frightened. I think had there been any alternative I should have taken it, instead of prosecuting that unknown night journey. The carriage went at a hard pace straight along, then we made a complete turn and went along another straight road. It seemed to me that we were simply going over and over the same ground again; and so I took note of some salient point, and found that this was so. I would have liked to have asked the driver what this all meant, but I really feared to do so, for I thought that, placed as I was, any protest would have had no effect in case there had been an intention to delay. By-and-by, however, as I was curious to know how time was passing, I struck a match, and by its flame looked at my watch; it was within a few minutes of midnight. This gave me a sort of shock, for I suppose the general superstition about midnight was increased by my recent experiences. I waited with a sick feeling of suspense.

Then a dog began to howl somewhere in a farmhouse far down the road—a long, agonized wailing, as if from fear. The sound was taken up by another dog, and then another and another, till, borne on the wind which now sighed softly through the Pass, a wild howling began, which seemed to come from all over the country, as far as the imagination could grasp it through the gloom of the night. At the first howl the horses began to strain and rear, but the driver spoke to them soothingly, and they quieted down, but shivered and sweated as though after a run-away from sudden fright. Then, far off in the distance, from the mountains on each side of us began a louder and a sharper howling— that of wolves—which affected both the horses and myself[1] in the same way—for I was minded to jump from the calèche and run, whilst they reared again and plunged madly, so that the driver had to use all his great strength to keep them from bolting. In a few minutes, however, my own ears got accustomed to the sound, and the horses so far became quiet that the driver was able to descend and to stand before them. He petted and soothed them, and whispered something in their ears, as I have heard of horse-tamers doing, and with extraordinary effect, for

9. The first of many tributes to Dracula's mastery of languages.
1. Throughout the novel, horses are aligned with humans rather than with the wolves, bats, and rats who fall under Dracula's spell. In F. W. Murnau's haunting silent film *Nosferatu* (1922), based loosely on Stoker's novel, horses similarly flee Max Schreck's ratlike Dracula.

under his caresses they became quite manageable again, though they still trembled. The driver again took his seat, and shaking his reins, started off at a great pace. This time, after going to the far side of the Pass, he suddenly turned down a narrow roadway which ran sharply to the right.

Soon we were hemmed in with trees, which in places arched right over the roadway till we passed as through a tunnel; and again great frowning rocks guarded us boldly on either side. Though we were in shelter, we could hear the rising wind, for it moaned and whistled through the rocks, and the branches of the trees crashed together as we swept along. It grew colder and colder still, and fine, powdery snow began to fall, so that soon we and all around us were covered with a white blanket. The keen wind still carried the howling of the dogs, though this grew fainter as we went on our way. The baying of the wolves sounded nearer and nearer, as though they were closing round on us from every side. I grew dreadfully afraid, and the horses shared my fear; but the driver was not in the least disturbed. He kept turning his head to left and right, but I could not see anything through the darkness.

Suddenly, away on our left, I saw a faint flickering blue flame.[2] The driver saw it at the same moment; he at once checked the horses and, jumping to the ground, disappeared into the darkness. I did not know what to do, the less as the howling of the wolves grew closer; but while I wondered the driver suddenly appeared again, and without a word took his seat, and we resumed our journey. I think I must have fallen asleep and kept dreaming of the incident, for it seemed to be repeated endlessly, and now looking back, it is like a sort of awful nightmare. Once the flame appeared so near the road, that even in the darkness around us I could watch the driver's motions. He went rapidly to where the blue flame arose—it must have been very faint, for it did not seem to illumine the place around it at all—and gathering a few stones, formed them into some device. Once there appeared a strange optical effect: when he stood between me and the flame he did not obstruct it, for I could see its ghostly figure all the same. This startled me, but as the effect was only momentary, I took it that my eyes deceived me straining through the darkness. Then for a time there were no blue flames, and we sped onwards through the gloom, with the howling of the wolves around us, as though they were following in a moving circle.

At last there came a time when the driver went further afield than he had yet gone, and during his absence the horses began to tremble worse than ever and to snort and scream with fright. I could not see

2. In medieval folklore, the blue flame rises from the plague dead, but it acquires mystical properties in its association with St. George's Eve, April 23, the commemoration of the Christian knight and dragon-slayer. Frances Ford Coppola's *Bram Stoker's Dracula* (1992) was the first film adaptation to depict the blue flame.

any cause for it, for the howling of the wolves had ceased altogether;
but just then the moon, sailing through the black clouds, appeared
behind the jagged crest of a beetling, pine-clad rock, and by its light I
saw around us a ring of wolves, with white teeth and lolling red tongues,
with long, sinewy limbs and shaggy hair. They were a hundred times
more terrible in the grim silence which held them than ever when they
howled. For myself, I felt a sort of paralysis of fear. It is only when a
man feels himself face to face with such horrors that he can understand
their true import.

All at once the wolves began to howl as though the moonlight had
had some peculiar effect on them. The horses jumped about and
reared, and looked helplessly round with eyes that rolled in a way painful to see; but the living ring of terror encompassed them on every side,
and they had perforce to remain within it. I called to the coachman to
come, for it seemed to me that our only chance was to try to break out
through the ring and to aid his approach. I shouted and beat the side
of the calèche, hoping by the noise to scare the wolves from that side,
so as to give him a chance of reaching the trap. How he came there,
I know not, but I heard his voice raised in a tone of imperious command, and looking towards the sound, saw him stand in the roadway.
As he swept his long arms, as though brushing aside some impalpable
obstacle,[3] the wolves fell back and back further still. Just then a heavy
cloud passed across the face of the moon, so that we were again in
darkness.

When I could see again the driver was climbing into the calèche,
and the wolves had disappeared. This was all so strange and uncanny
that a dreadful fear came upon me, and I was afraid to speak or move.
The time seemed interminable as we swept on our way, now in almost
complete darkness, for the rolling clouds obscured the moon. We kept
on ascending, with occasional periods of quick descent, but in the main
always ascending. Suddenly I became conscious of the fact that the
driver was in the act of pulling up the horses in the courtyard of a vast
ruined castle, from whose tall black windows came no ray of light, and
whose broken battlements showed a jagged line against the moonlit sky.

Chapter II

Jonathan Harker's Journal—(continued)

5 May.—I must have been asleep, for certainly if I had been fully awake
I must have noticed the approach to such a remarkable place. In the

3. Dracula's tone and his sweeping gesture recall the Victorian actor Henry Irving in his heroic
   roles. Characters throughout the novel strike imposing attitudes that recall pictorial nineteenth-century acting styles. Stoker tried, unsuccessfully, to persuade Irving, his longtime employer, to play Dracula on stage.

gloom the courtyard looked of considerable size, and as several dark ways led from it under great round arches it perhaps seemed bigger than it really is. I have not yet been able to see it by daylight.

When the calèche stopped the driver jumped down, and held out his hand to assist me to alight. Again I could not but notice his prodigious strength. His hand actually seemed like a steel vice that could have crushed mine if he had chosen. Then he took out my traps,[1] and placed them on the ground beside me as I stood close to a great door, old and studded with large iron nails, and set in a projecting doorway of massive stone. I could see even in the dim light that the stone was massively carved, but that the carving had been much worn by time and weather. As I stood, the driver jumped again into his seat and shook the reins; the horses started forward, and trap and all disappeared down one of the dark openings.

I stood in silence where I was, for I did not know what to do. Of bell or knocker there was no sign; through these frowning walls and dark window openings it was not likely that my voice could penetrate. The time I waited seemed endless, and I felt doubts and fears crowding upon me. What sort of place had I come to, and among what kind of people? What sort of grim adventure was it on which I had embarked? Was this a customary incident in the life of a solicitor's clerk sent out to explain the purchase of a London estate to a foreigner? Solicitor's clerk! Mina would not like that. Solicitor,—for just before leaving London I got word that my examination was successful; and I am now a full-blown solicitor![2] I began to rub my eyes and pinch myself to see if I were awake. It all seemed like a horrible nightmare to me, and I expected that I should suddenly awake, and find myself at home, with the dawn struggling in through the windows, as I had now and again felt in the morning after a day of overwork. But my flesh answered the pinching test, and my eyes were not to be deceived. I was indeed awake and among the Carpathians. All I could do now was to be patient, and to wait the coming of the morning.

Just as I had come to this conclusion I heard a heavy step approaching behind the great door, and saw through the chinks the gleam of a coming light. Then there was the sound of rattling chains and the clanking of massive bolts drawn back. A key was turned with the loud grating noise of long disuse, and the great door swung back.

Within, stood a tall old man, clean shaven save for a long white moustache, and clad in black from head to foot, without a single speck of colour about him anywhere. He held in his hand an antique silver lamp, in which the flame burned without chimney or globe of any kind, throwing long quivering shadows as it flickered in the draught of

1. Luggage.
2. In British legal practice, solicitors prepare cases for barristers; generally only the latter appear in court. Stoker himself became a barrister in 1890.

the open door. The old man motioned me in with his right hand with a courtly gesture, saying in excellent English, but with a strange into-nation:—

'Welcome to my house! Enter freely and of your own will!'[3] He made no motion of stepping to meet me, but stood like a statue, as though his gesture of welcome had fixed him into stone. The instant, however, that I had stepped over the threshold, he moved impulsively forward, and holding out his hand grasped mine with a strength which made me wince, an effect which was not lessened by the fact that it seemed as cold as ice—more like the hand of a dead than a living man. Again he said:—

'Welcome to my house. Come freely. Go safely; and leave something of the happiness you bring!' The strength of the handshake was so much akin to that which I had noticed in the driver, whose face I had not seen, that for a moment I doubted if it were not the same person to whom I was speaking; so to make sure, I said interrogatively:—

'Count[4] Dracula?' He bowed in a courtly way as he replied:—

'I am Dracula; and I bid you welcome, Mr Harker, to my house. Come in; the night air is chill, and you must need to eat and rest.' As he was speaking he put the lamp on a bracket on the wall, and stepping out, took my luggage; he had carried it in before I could forestall him. I protested but he insisted:—

'Nay, sir, you are my guest. It is late, and my people are not available. Let me see to your comfort myself.' He insisted on carrying my traps along the passage, and then up a great winding stair, and along another great passage, on whose stone floor our steps rang heavily. At the end of this he threw open a heavy door, and I rejoiced to see within a well-lit room in which a table was spread for supper, and on whose mighty hearth a great fire of logs flamed and flared.

The Count halted, putting down my bags, closed the door, and crossing the room, opened another door, which led into a small octa-gonal room lit by a single lamp, and seemingly without a window of any sort. Passing through this, he opened another door, and motioned me to enter. It was a welcome sight; for here was a great bedroom well lighted and warmed with another log fire, which sent a hollow roar up the wide chimney. The Count himself left my luggage inside and with-drew, saying, before he closed the door:—

'You will need, after your journey, to refresh yourself by making your toilet. I trust you will find all you wish. When you are ready come into the other room, where you will find your supper prepared.'

The light and warmth and the Count's courteous welcome seemed

---

3. In folklore, vampires often require complicity from their prey. Just as Jonathan cannot be coerced, but must "enter freely," no vampire can come into a home uninvited.
4. Dracula's Romanian title would be "Prince." Hapsburg emperors created the later rank of "Count," a title Jonathan uses but Dracula eschews.

to have dissipated all my doubts and fears. Having then reached my normal state, I discovered that I was half famished with hunger; so making a hasty toilet, I went into the other room.

I found supper already laid out. My host, who stood on one side of the great fireplace, leaning against the stonework, made a graceful wave of his hand to the table, and said:—

'I pray you, be seated and sup how you please. You will, I trust, excuse me that I do not join you; but I have dined already, and I do not sup.'[5]

I handed to him the sealed letter which Mr Hawkins had entrusted to me. He opened it and read it gravely; then, with a charming smile, he handed it to me to read. One passage of it, at least, gave me a thrill of pleasure:

'I much regret that an attack of gout, from which malady I am a constant sufferer, forbids absolutely any travelling on my part for some time to come; but I am happy to say I can send a sufficient substitute, one in whom I have every possible confidence. He is a young man, full of energy and talent in his own way, and of a very faithful disposition. He is discreet and silent, and has grown into manhood in my service. He shall be ready to attend on you when you will during his stay, and shall take your instructions in all matters.'

The Count himself came forward and took off the cover of a dish, and I fell to at once on an excellent roast chicken. This, with some cheese and a salad and a bottle of old Tokay,[6] of which I had two glasses, was my supper. During the time I was eating it the Count asked me many questions as to my journey, and I told him by degrees all I had experienced.

By this time I had finished my supper, and by my host's desire had drawn up a chair by the fire and begun to smoke a cigar which he offered me, at the same time excusing himself that he did not smoke. I had now an opportunity of observing him, and found him of a very marked physiognomy.

His face was a strong—a very strong—aquiline,[7] with high bridge of the thin nose and peculiarly arched nostrils; with lofty domed forehead, and hair growing scantily round the temples, but profusely elsewhere. His eyebrows were very massive, almost meeting over the nose, and with bushy hair that seemed to curl in its own profusion. The mouth, so far as I could see it under the heavy moustache, was fixed and rather cruel-looking, with peculiarly sharp white teeth; these protruded over the lips, whose remarkable ruddiness showed astonishing vitality in a

5. Nineteenth-century gentlefolk dined lavishly at midday and supped lightly in the evening. Dracula's abstinence may contain a delicate double meaning, but he does not intone the ironic refusal "I never drink—wine," a line made famous by Bela Lugosi's arch reading in Tod Browning's 1931 film.
6. An aromatic wine named for a Hungarian town.
7. That is, a curve like that of an eagle's beak.

man of his years. For the rest, his ears were pale and at the tops
extremely pointed; the chin was broad and strong, and the cheeks
firm though thin. The general effect was one of extraordinary
pallor.

Hitherto I had noticed the backs of his hands as they lay on his knees
in the firelight, and they had seemed rather white and fine; but seeing
them now close to me, I could not but notice that they were rather
coarse—broad, with squat fingers. Strange to say, there were hairs in
the centre of the palm.[8] The nails were long and fine, and cut to a
sharp point. As the Count leaned over me and his hands touched me,
I could not repress a shudder. It may have been that his breath was
rank, but a horrible feeling of nausea came over me, which, do what I
would, I could not conceal. The Count, evidently noticing it, drew
back; and with a grim sort of smile, which showed more than he had
yet done his protuberant teeth, sat himself down again on his own side
of the fireplace. We were both silent for a while; and as I looked towards
the window I saw the first dim streak of the coming dawn. There
seemed a strange stillness over everything; but as I listened I heard as
if from down below in the valley the howling of many wolves. The
Count's eyes gleamed, and he said:—

'Listen to them—the children of the night.[9] What music they
make!' Seeing, I suppose, some expression in my face strange to him,
he added:—

'Ah, sir, you dwellers in the city cannot enter into the feelings of the
hunter.' Then he rose and said:—

'But you must be tired. Your bedroom is all ready, and tomorrow
you shall sleep as late as you will. I have to be away till the afternoon;
so sleep well and dream well!' and, with a courteous bow, he opened
for me himself the door to the octagonal room, and I entered my
bedroom.

I am all in a sea of wonders. I doubt; I fear; I think strange things
which I dare not confess to my own soul. God keep me, if only for the
sake of those dear to me!

7 May.—It is again early morning, but I have rested and enjoyed the
last twenty-four hours. I slept till late in the day, and awoke of my own
accord. When I had dressed myself I went into the room where we had
supped, and found a cold breakfast laid out, with coffee kept hot by

8. Film adaptations avoid Dracula's hairiness; different as they are from each other, most cinematic Draculas are clean-shaven and, in all senses of the word, smooth. These hairy palms
are one of Dracula's few affinities with the werewolf (and, in the opinion of some commentators, with the Victorian masturbator as well).
9. In this line, which Bela Lugosi made famous, Dracula—like a wistful Victorian don—aes-
thetically savors his wolf servants, but he himself is no child of the night: we shall see him
walking about freely in daylight. Not until *Nosferatu* in 1922 did sunlight become lethal to
vampires.

the pot being placed on the hearth. There was a card on the table, on which was written:—

'I have to be absent for a while. Do not wait for me.—D.' So I set to and enjoyed a hearty meal. When I had done, I looked for a bell, so that I might let the servants know I had finished; but I could not find one. There are certainly odd deficiencies in the house, considering the extraordinary evidences of wealth which are round me. The table service is of gold, and so beautifully wrought that it must be of immense value. The curtains and upholstery of the chairs and sofas and the hangings of my bed are of the costliest and most beautiful fabrics, and must have been of fabulous value when they were made, for they are centuries old, though in excellent order. I saw something like them in Hampton Court,[1] but there they were worn and frayed and moth-eaten. But still in none of the rooms is there a mirror. There is not even a toilet glass on my table, and I had to get the little shaving glass from my bag before I could either shave or brush my hair. I have not yet seen a servant anywhere, or heard a sound near the castle except the howling of wolves. When I had finished my meal—I do not know whether to call it breakfast or dinner, for it was between five and six o'clock when I had it—I looked about for something to read, for I did not like to go about the castle until I had asked the Count's permission. There was absolutely nothing in the room, book, newspaper, or even writing materials; so I opened another door in the room and found a sort of library. The door opposite mine I tried, but found it locked.

In the library I found, to my great delight, a vast number of English books, whole shelves full of them, and bound volumes of magazines and newspapers. A table in the centre was littered with English magazines and newspapers, though none of them were of very recent date. The books were of the most varied kind—history, geography, politics, political economy, botany, geology, law—all relating to England and English life and customs and manners. There were even such books of reference as the London Directory, the 'Red' and 'Blue' books, Whitaker's Almanack,[2] the Army and Navy Lists, and—it somehow gladdened my heart to see it—the Law List.

Whilst I was looking at the books, the door opened, and the Count entered. He saluted me in a hearty way, and hoped that I had had a good night's rest. Then he went on:—

'I am glad you found your way in here, for I am sure there is much

1. Hampton Court Palace lies just fifteen miles from London; founded by Cardinal Wolsey in 1515 and appropriated by Henry VIII after Wolsey's fall, it was a royal residence until the eighteenth century.
2. The Red Book enumerated everyone working for the British government or on a government pension. The Blue Book is a British publication, usually Parliamentary, in a blue binder. Whitaker's Almanack gave information on and data (agronomy, population, commerce) concerning the British Empire.

that will interest you. These friends'—and he laid his hand on some of the books—'have been good friends to me, and for some years past, ever since I had the idea of going to London, have given me many, many hours of pleasure. Through them I have come to know your great England; and to know her is to love her. I long to go through the crowded streets of your mighty London, to be in the midst of the whirl and rush of humanity, to share its life, its change, its death, and all that makes it what it is. But alas! as yet I only know your tongue through books. To you, my friend, I look that I know it to speak.'

'But, Count,' I said, 'you know and speak English thoroughly!' He bowed gravely.

'I thank you, my friend, for your all too flattering estimate, but yet I fear that I am but a little way on the road I would travel. True, I know the grammar and the words, but yet I know not how to speak them.'

'Indeed,' I said, 'you speak excellently.'

'Not so,' he answered. 'Well I know that, did I move and speak in your London, none there are who would not know me for a stranger. That is not enough for me. Here I am noble; I am *boyar*;[3] the common people know me, and I am master. But a stranger in a strange land,[4] he is no one; men know him not—and to know not is to care not for. I am content if I am like the rest, so that no man stops if he see me, or pause in his speaking if he hear my words, to say, "Ha, ha! a stranger!" I have been so long master that I would be master still—or at least that none other should be master of me. You come to me not alone as agent of my friend Peter Hawkins, of Exeter, to tell me all about my new estate in London. You shall, I trust, rest here with me a while, so that by our talking I may learn the English intonation; and I would that you tell me when I make error,[5] even of the smallest, in my speaking. I am sorry that I had to be away so long today; but you will, I know, forgive one who has so many important affairs in hand.'

Of course I said all I could about being willing, and asked if I might come into that room when I chose. He answered: 'Yes, certainly,' and added:—

'You may go anywhere you wish in the castle, except where the doors are locked, where of course you will not wish to go. There is reason that all things are as they are, and did you see with my eyes and know with my knowledge, you would perhaps better understand.' I said I was sure of this, and then he went on:—

'We are in Transylvania; and Transylvania is not England. Our ways

---

3. In Russia, a nobleman; in Romania, a member of the privileged classes.
4. Dracula shamelessly takes his self-description from the Old Testament. Having killed an Egyptian, Moses flees Egypt and marries in Midian. He names his son Gershom, "for he said, I have been a stranger in a strange land" (Exodus 2.22). Like Moses, Dracula hopes to return and lead his people to a better country.
5. Dracula has just made a small idiomatic error, which, despite his promise, Jonathan does not correct. Is this a test? Who is testing whom?

are not your ways, and there shall be to you many strange things. Nay, from what you have told me of your experiences already, you know something of what strange things here may be.'

This led to much conversation; and as it was evident that he wanted to talk, if only for talking's sake, I asked him many questions regarding things that had already happened to me or come within my notice. Sometimes he sheered off the subject, or turned the conversation by pretending not to understand; but generally he answered all I asked most frankly. Then as time went on, and I had got somewhat bolder, I asked him of some of the strange things of the preceding night, as, for instance, why the coachman went to the places where we had seen the blue flames. Was it indeed true that they showed where gold was hidden? He then explained to me that it was commonly believed that on a certain night of the year—last night, in fact, when all evil spirits are supposed to have unchecked sway—a blue flame is seen over any place where treasure has been concealed. 'That treasure has been hidden,' he went on, 'in the region through which you came last night, there can be but little doubt; for it was the ground fought over for centuries by the Wallachian, the Saxon, and the Turk. Why, there is hardly a foot of soil in all this region that has not been enriched by the blood of men, patriots or invaders. In old days there were stirring times, when the Austrian and the Hungarian came up in hordes, and the patriots went out to meet them—men and women, the aged and the children too—and waited their coming on the rocks above the passes, that they might sweep destruction on them with their artificial avalanches.[6] When the invader was triumphant he found but little, for whatever there was had been sheltered in the friendly soil.'

'But how,' said I, 'can it have remained so long undiscovered, when there is a sure index to it if men will but take the trouble to look?' The Count smiled, and as his lips ran back over his gums, the long, sharp, canine teeth showed out strangely; he answered:—

'Because your peasant is at heart a coward and a fool! Those flames only appear on one night; and on that night no man of this land will, if he can help it, stir without his doors. And, dear sir, even if he did he would not know what to do. Why, even the peasant that you tell me of who marked the place of the flame would not know where to look in daylight even for his own work. You would not, I dare be sworn, be able to find these places again?'

'There you are right,' I said. 'I know no more than the dead where even to look for them.' Then we drifted into other matters.

'Come,' he said at last, 'tell me of London and of the house which you have procured for me.' With an apology for my remissness, I went

6. In the fourteenth century, Hungary invaded Romania. In November 1330, the king of Hungary advanced through Romania to the pass of Posada, but the armies of Prince Basarab of Wallachia trapped him in the narrow passage by hurling boulders down upon his army.

into my own room to get the papers from my bag. Whilst I was placing them in order I heard a rattling of china and silver in the next room, and as I passed through, noticed that the table had been cleared and the lamp lit, for it was by this time deep into the dark. The lamps were also lit in the study or library, and I found the Count lying on the sofa, reading, of all things in the world, an English Bradshaw's Guide.[7] When I came in he cleared the books and papers from the table; and with him I went into plans and deeds and figures of all sorts. He was interested in everything, and asked me a myriad questions about the place and its surroundings. He clearly had studied beforehand all he could get on the subject of the neighbourhood, for he evidently at the end knew very much more than I did. When I remarked this, he answered:—

'Well, but, my friend, is it not needful that I should? When I go there I shall be all alone, and my friend Harker Jonathan—nay, pardon me, I fall into my country's habit of putting your patronymic first—my friend Jonathan Harker will not be by my side to correct and aid me. He will be in Exeter, miles away, probably working at papers of the law with my other friend, Peter Hawkins. So!'

We went thoroughly into the business of the purchase of the estate at Purfleet.[8] When I had told him the facts and got his signature to the necessary papers, and had written a letter with them ready to post to Mr Hawkins, he began to ask me how I had come across so suitable a place. I read to him the notes which I had made at the time, and which I inscribe here:—

'At Purfleet, on a by-road, I came across just such a place as seemed to be required, and where was displayed a dilapidated notice that the place was for sale. It is surrounded by a high wall, of ancient structure, built of heavy stones, and has not been repaired for a large number of years. The closed gates were of heavy old oak and iron, all eaten with rust.

'The estate is called Carfax,[9] no doubt a corruption of the old *Quatre Face*, as the house is four-sided, agreeing with the cardinal points of the compass. It contains in all some twenty acres, quite surrounded by the solid stone wall above mentioned. There are many trees on it, which make it in places gloomy, and there is a deep, dark-looking pond or small lake, evidently fed by some springs, as the water is clear and flows away in a fair-sized stream. The house is very large and of all

---

7. A book of timetables for the English railway system.
8. A suburb in Essex County about twenty miles east of central London; roughly a thirty-minute train commute to the city. Dracula follows late-nineteenth-century English demographics by making his primary home in the suburbs.
9. Harker's etymology is imprecise: *Carfax* is "a place where four roads meet." Suicides, who, according to some legends, returned to life as vampires, were traditionally buried at a crossroads.

periods back, I should say, to mediaeval times, for one part is of stone immensely thick, with only a few windows high up and heavily barred with iron. It looks like part of a keep,[1] and is close to an old chapel or church. I could not enter it, as I had not the key of the door leading to it from the house, but I have taken with my Kodak[2] views of it from various points. The house has been added to, but in a very straggling way, and I can only guess at the amount of ground it covers, which must be very great. There are but few houses close at hand, one being a very large house only recently added to and formed into a private lunatic asylum. It is not, however, visible from the grounds.'

When I had finished, he said:—

'I am glad that it is old and big. I myself am of an old family, and to live in a new house would kill me. A house cannot be made habitable in a day; and, after all, how few days go to make up a century. I rejoice also that there is a chapel of old times. We Transylvanian nobles love not to think that our bones may be amongst the common dead. I seek not gaiety nor mirth, not the bright voluptuousness of much sunshine and sparkling waters which please the young and gay. I am no longer young; and my heart, through weary years of mourning over the dead, is not attuned to mirth. Moreover, the walls of my castle are broken; the shadows are many, and the wind breathes cold through the broken battlements and casements. I love the shade and the shadow, and would be alone with my thoughts when I may.'

Somehow his words and his look did not seem to accord, or else it was that his cast of face made his smile look malignant and saturnine.

Presently, with an excuse, he left me, asking me to put all my papers together. He was some little time away, and I began to look at some of the books around me. One was an atlas, which I found opened naturally at England, as if that map had been much used. On looking at it I found in certain places little rings marked, and on examining these I noticed that one was near London on the east side, manifestly where his new estate was situated; the other two were Exeter, and Whitby[3] on the Yorkshire coast.

It was the better part of an hour when the Count returned. 'Aha!' he said; 'still at your books? Good! But you must not work always. Come; I am informed that your supper is ready.' He took my arm, and we went into the next room, where I found an excellent supper ready on the table. The Count again excused himself, as he had dined out on his being away from home. But he sat as on the previous night, and

1. The stronghold of a medieval castle.
2. This early camera is one of the many modern gadgets in the novel. Stoker's working notes contain a reference to Dracula registering as a skeleton on photographic film, an effect omitted in the finished novel.
3. London is the vampire's promised land of teeming humanity; Dracula's solicitor Peter Hawkins lives in Exeter; Dracula has already planned to force his ship to dock at Whitby.

chatted[4] whilst I ate. After supper I smoked, as on the last evening, and the Count stayed with me, chatting and asking questions on every conceivable subject, hour after hour. I felt that it was getting very late indeed, but I did not say anything, for I felt under obligation to meet my host's wishes in every way. I was not sleepy, as the long sleep yesterday had fortified me; but I could not help experiencing that chill which comes over one at the coming of the dawn, which is like, in its way, the turn of the tide. They say that people who are near death die generally at the change to the dawn or at the turn of the tide; any one who has when tired, and tied as it were to his post, experienced this change in the atmosphere can well believe it. All at once we heard the crow of a cock coming up with preternatural shrillness through the clear morning air; Count Dracula, jumping to his feet, said:—

'Why, there is the morning again! How remiss I am to let you stay up so long. You must make your conversation regarding my dear new country of England less interesting, so that I may not forget how time flies by us,' and, with a courtly bow, he left me.

I went into my own room and drew the curtains, but there was little to notice; my window opened into the courtyard, all I could see was the warm grey of quickening sky. So I pulled the curtains again, and have written of this day.

8 May.—I began to fear as I wrote in this book that I was getting too diffuse; but now I am glad that I went into detail from the first, for there is something so strange about this place and all in it that I cannot but feel uneasy. I wish I were safe out of it, or that I had never come. It may be that this strange[5] night-existence is telling on me; but would that that were all! If there were any one to talk to I could bear it, but there is no one. I have only the Count to speak with, and he!—I fear I am myself the only living soul within the place. Let me be prosaic so far as facts can be; it will help me to bear up, and imagination must not run riot with me. If it does I am lost. Let me say at once how I stand—or seem to.

I only slept a few hours when I went to bed, and feeling that I could not sleep any more, got up. I had hung my shaving glass by the window, and was just beginning to shave. Suddenly I felt a hand on my shoulder, and heard the Count's voice saying to me, 'Good morning.' I started, for it amazed me that I had not seen him, since the reflection of the glass covered the whole room behind me. In starting I had cut myself slightly, but did not notice it at the moment. Having answered the Count's salutation, I turned to the glass again to see how I had been mistaken. This time there could be no error, for the man was close to

---

4. One wonders in vain what Dracula finds to chat about; though Jonathan fears his account is "too diffuse," it is full of tantalizing omissions.

5. The word *strange* in late Victorian England was often suffused with homoerotic undercurrents.

me, and I could see him over my shoulder. But there was no reflection[6] of him in the mirror! The whole room behind me was displayed; but there was no sign of a man in it, except myself. This was startling, and, coming on the top of so many strange things, was beginning to increase that vague feeling of uneasiness which I always have when the Count is near; but at the instant I saw that the cut had bled a little, and the blood was trickling over my chin. I laid down the razor, turning as I did so half round to look for some sticking plaster. When the Count saw my face, his eyes blazed with a sort of demoniac fury, and he suddenly made a grab at my throat. I drew away, and his hand touched the string of beads which held the crucifix. It made an instant change in him, for the fury passed so quickly that I could hardly believe that it was ever there.

'Take care,' he said, 'take care how you cut yourself. It is more dangerous than you think in this country.' Then seizing the shaving glass, he went on: 'And this is the wretched thing that has done the mischief. It is a foul bauble of man's vanity. Away with it!'[7] and opening the heavy window with one wrench of his terrible hand, he flung out the glass, which was shattered into a thousand pieces on the stones of the courtyard far below. Then he withdrew without a word. It is very annoying, for I do not see how I am to shave, unless in my watch-case or the bottom of the shaving-pot, which is fortunately of metal.

When I went into the dining-room, breakfast was prepared; but I could not find the Count anywhere. So I breakfasted alone. It is strange that as yet I have not seen the Count eat or drink. He must be a very peculiar man! After breakfast I did a little exploring in the castle. I went out on the stairs and found a room looking towards the south. The view was magnificent, and from where I stood there was every opportunity of seeing it. The castle is on the very edge of a terrible precipice. A stone falling from the window would fall a thousand feet without touching anything! As far as the eye can reach is a sea of green tree-tops, with occasionally a deep rift where there is a chasm. Here and there are silver threads where the rivers wind in deep gorges through the forests.

But I am not in heart to describe beauty, for when I had seen the view I explored further; doors, doors, doors everywhere, and all locked

6. Stoker embellishes the folklore tradition that a vampire casts no reflection because he has no soul. His early working notes elaborate on Dracula's lack of a shadow, claiming that "the light in his house must therefore be specially arranged 'to give no shadow,'" an effect more appropriate to the theater than fiction.
7. Dracula does not sup; he does not smoke; he finds mirrors vain baubles. Altogether, he is a Puritanical presence, though he is often written of—and filmed—as a sybaritic liberator. His dark clothes, his obsessive memories, and his rage against human gratification are reminiscent of Henry Irving's famous Hamlet, first staged at the Lyceum in 1874.

and bolted. In no place save from the windows in the castle walls is there an available exit.

The castle is a veritable prison, and I am a prisoner!

Chapter III

Jonathan Harker's Journal (continued)

When I found that I was a prisoner a sort of wild feeling came over me. I rushed up and down the stairs, trying every door and peering out of every window I could find; but after a little the conviction of my helplessness overpowered all other feelings. When I look back after a few hours I think I must have been mad for the time, for I behaved much as a rat does in a trap. When, however, the conviction had come to me that I was helpless I sat down quietly—as quietly as I have ever done anything in my life—and began to think over what was best to be done. I am thinking still, and as yet have come to no definite conclusion. Of one thing only am I certain: that it is no use making my ideas known to the Count. He knows well that I am imprisoned; and as he has done it himself, and has doubtless his own motives for it, he would only deceive me if I trusted him fully with the facts. So far as I can see, my only plan will be to keep my knowledge and my fears to myself, and my eyes open. I am, I know, either being deceived, like a baby, by my own fears, or else I am in desperate straits; and if the latter be so, I need, and shall need, all my brains to get through. I had hardly come to this conclusion when I heard the great door below shut, and knew that the Count had returned. He did not come at once into the library, so I went cautiously to my own room and found him making the bed. This was odd, but only confirmed what I had all along thought—that there were no servants in the house. When later I saw him through the chink of the hinges of the door laying the table in the dining-room, I was assured of it; for if he does himself all these menial offices, surely it is proof that there is no one else to do them.[1] This gave me a fright, for if there is no one else in the castle, it must have been the Count himself who was the driver of the coach that brought me here. This is a terrible thought; for if so, what does it mean that he could control the wolves, as he did, by only holding up his hand in silence? How was it that all the people at Bistritz and on the coach had some terrible fear for me? What meant the giving of the crucifix, of the garlic, of the

---

1. Dracula is his own servant, but a domestic self-sufficiency that charms many readers today may have looked evilly unmasculine, and thus inhuman, to some Victorians.

wild rose, of the mountain ash?[2] Bless that good, good woman who hung the crucifix round my neck! for it is a comfort and a strength to me whenever I touch it. It is odd that a thing which I have been taught to regard with disfavour and as idolatrous should in a time of loneliness and trouble be of help. Is it that there is something in the essence of the thing[3] itself, or that it is a medium, a tangible help, in conveying memories of sympathy and comfort? Some time, if it may be, I must examine this matter and try to make up my mind about it. In the meantime I must find out all I can about Count Dracula, as it may help me to understand. Tonight he may talk of himself, if I turn the conversation that way. I must be very careful, however, not to awake his suspicion.

Midnight.—I have had a long talk with the Count. I asked him a few questions on Transylvanian history, and he warmed up to the subject wonderfully. In his speaking of things and people, and especially of battles, he spoke as if he had been present at them all. This he afterwards explained by saying that to a *boyar* the pride of his house and name is his own pride, that their glory is his glory, that their fate is his fate. Whenever he spoke of his house he always said 'we,' and spoke almost in the plural, like a king speaking. I wish I could put down all he said exactly as he said it, for to me it was most fascinating. It seemed to have in it a whole history of the country. He grew excited as he spoke, and walked about the room pulling his great white moustache and grasping anything on which he laid his hands as though he would crush it by main strength. One thing he said which I shall put down as nearly as I can; for it tells in its way the story of his race:—[4]

'We Szekelys have a right to be proud, for in our veins flows the blood of many brave races who fought as the lion fights, for lordship. Here, in the whirlpool of European races, the Ugric tribe[5] bore down from Iceland the fighting spirit which Thor and Wodin[6] gave them,

2. Jonathan has not mentioned these folk charms against evil spirits before, an editorial lapse on Stoker's part. Garlic is traditionally endowed with magical properties—even the Talmud prescribes it as a remedy for toothache and earache, warning, however, that it will "produce leprosy" if it touches the flesh—but Stoker invented its effectiveness against vampires in particular.

3. Jonathan explains the virtue of the crucifix in terms characteristic of nineteenth-century secularism: it is a medium of healing memories. Jonathan's humanist consolation recalls George Eliot's well-known poem "O May I Join the Choir Invisible" (1865), which finds immortality in human remembrance: "O May I Join the Choir Invisible / Of those immortal dead who live again / In minds made better by their presence." When dealing with crucifixes, Jonathan and his allies must acquire absolute faith in the "essence of the thing."

4. A word with ethnic connotations in the nineteenth century. It is a short step from Dracula's belief in the absolute blood uniqueness of his Szekelys to his identification with a vampire race utterly distinct from the human.

5. A division of Ural-Altaic peoples including Siberians, Finns, and Magyars.

6. Powerful Norse warrior gods. Thor was the son of the patriarchal creator Woden. God of thunder, might, and war, Thor was armed with a magical hammer.

which their Berserkers[7] displayed to such fell intent on the seaboards
of Europe, ay, and of Asia and Africa too, till the peoples thought that
the werewolves themselves had come. Here, too, when they came, they
found the Huns, whose warlike fury had swept the earth like a living
flame, till the dying peoples held that in their veins ran the blood of
those old witches, who, expelled from Scythia[8] had mated with the
devils in the desert. Fools, fools! What devil or what witch was ever so
great as Attila, whose blood is in these veins?' He held up his arms. 'Is
it a wonder that we were a conquering race; that we were proud; that
when the Magyar, the Lombard,[9] the Avar, the Bulgar, or the Turk
poured his thousands on our frontiers, we drove them back? Is it strange
that when Arpad and his legions swept through the Hungarian father-
land he found us here when he reached the frontier; that the Honfoglalas[1] was completed there? And when the Hungarian flood swept
eastward, the Szekelys were claimed as kindred by the victorious Magyars, and to us for centuries was trusted the guarding of the frontier[2] of
Turkey-land; ay and more than that, endless duty of the frontier guard,
for, as the Turks say, "water sleeps, and enemy is sleepless." Who more
gladly than we throughout the Four Nations[3] received the "bloody
sword,"[4] or at its warlike call flocked quicker to the standard of the
King? When was redeemed that great shame of my nation, the shame
of Cassova,[5] when the flags of the Wallach and the Magyar went down
beneath the Crescent, who was it but one of my own race[6] who as
Voivode[7] crossed the Danube and beat the Turk on his own ground?

7. The Viking and Norse warriors wore wolf or bear skins into battle, attempting to frighten
   their opponents into believing they had actually turned into beasts. In Norse mythology these
   warriors actually did became wild beasts in battle. Hence, they were one source of the were-
   wolf legend.
8. Ancient region of southeast Europe and Asia north of the Black and Caspian seas.
9. Inhabitants of Lombardy, a region in northern Italy of which Milan is the capital. From 1815
   until Italian independence in 1861, Lombardy was ruled by Austria. The Avars overran Romania after the Huns. "Bulgar": also called Volga or Kama Bulgars. By the eighth century
   these Turkish-speaking people inhabited eastern Russia. One branch moved into Bulgaria and
   became part of the Slavs.
1. Arpad was the successor to Attila the Hun and a Hungarian national hero. In the Honfoglas,
   or "conquest of the homeland," of A.D. 895, Arpad's descendants led a number of Magyar
   chieftains and their tribes over the Carpathians into the land that is now Hungary.
2. Emily Gerard's *The Land Beyond the Forest* characterizes the Szecklers (or Szekelys) as "frontier guards."
3. Of Transylvania: the Magyars, Szekelys, Germans, and Wallachs.
4. In Hungary, the signal of national emergency.
5. In the first Battle of Kossovso, 1389, the Ottoman Turks defeated Serbia and its allies, placing
   Serbia and Bulgaria under Ottoman rule. In 1448 there was a second Battle of Kossovso—
   presumably the one to which Dracula refers—in which the Turks once again defeated the
   Hungarians and Wallachs.
6. Despite McNally and Florescu's attempt to link this gallant defense to an actual incident in
   the life of Vlad Tepes (1431–1476), whom they see as the historical Dracula (see Selected
   Bibliography, p. 487), this incident remains historically murky. It produced no great results:
   Stoker's working notes admit this lone charge against the Turks brought "only momentarily
   success."
7. Governor or (Romanian) prince.

This was a Dracula indeed! Woe was it that his own unworthy brother,[8] when he had fallen, sold his people to the Turk and brought the shame of slavery on them! Was it not this Dracula, indeed, who inspired that other of his race[9] who in a later age again and again brought his forces over the great river into Turkeyland; who, when he was beaten back, came again, and again, and again, though he had to come alone from the bloody field where his troops were being slaughtered, since he knew that he alone could ultimately triumph? They said that he thought only of himself. Bah! what good are peasants without a leader? Where ends the war without a brain and heart to conduct it? Again, when, after the battle of Mohacs,[1] we threw off the Hungarian yoke, we of the Dracula blood were amongst their leaders, for our spirit would not brook that we were not free. Ah, young sir, the Szekelys—and the Dracula as their heart's blood, their brains, and their swords—can boast a record that mushroom growths like the Hapsburgs and the Romanoffs[2] can never reach. The warlike days are over. Blood is too precious a thing in these days of dishonourable peace; and the glories of the great races are as a tale that is told.'

It was by this time close on morning, and we went to bed. (*Mem.* this diary seems horribly like the beginning of the 'Arabian Nights,'[3] for everything has to break off at cock-crow—or like the ghost of Hamlet's father.)[4]

12 May.—Let me begin with facts—bare, meagre facts, verified by books and figures, and of which there can be no doubt. I must not confuse them with experiences which will have to rest on my own

---

8. In 1444, the Turks captured both Vlad Tepes and his brother Radu. The seductive Radu became politically and sexually entangled in the Ottoman court. As the Turkish candidate to the Wallachian throne, he fought and displaced his patriotic (if sadistic) brother Vlad. From 1462 to 1474, "Radu the handsome" was a shamelessly collaborationist Voivode.

9. Cryptic, to say the least. Leonard Wolf quotes Gabriel Ronay's theory of the other as "Vlad III *Dracul,* who distinguished himself in the battle of Varna in 1444," a guess as plausible as any other. Mina will deduce later on that this solitary warrior was Dracula himself.

1. In 1526, the Turks, under the emperor Süleyman the Magnificent, devastated the Hungarian army. Hungary became a Turkish province; Transylvania gained semi-autonomy until Austria reconquered it.

   Dracula expediently switches sides here: earlier, he had boasted that the Magyars, or Hungarians, claimed his Szekelys "as kindred"; he cast the Turks as villains. Now he celebrates with equal chauvinism the Turkish annihilation of Hungary. Like much patriotic rhetoric of the 1890s, Dracula's speech makes more sound than sense.

2. Dracula is prophetic when he scorns these seemingly omnipotent families as "mushroom growths." The Hapsburgs had ruled Austria (and, after 1867, the Austro-Hungarian Empire) since 1282, but dynasty and empire would end in 1914 with the assassination of the heir apparent, which precipitated World War I. The Romanoffs had ruled Russia since 1613, but they too became extinct when, in 1918, the Bolsheviks executed Czar Nicholas II and his family.

3. Another exotic amalgam of storytelling and murder; enormously popular in Victorian England, especially in Sir Richard Burton's 1885 translation. King Sharyar consummates a series of marriages, then, in the morning, beheads each bride to ensure her fidelity. The clever Shahrazad distracts him with her enthralling and unending nightly stories.

4. In *Hamlet* 1.1, the warrior-king's ghost fades each morning "on the crowing of the cock" to expiate its sins in Purgatory.

observation or my memory of them. Last evening when the Count came from his room he began by asking me questions on legal matters and on the doing of certain kinds of business. I had spent the day wearily over books, and, simply to keep my mind occupied, went over some of the matters I had been examined in at Lincoln's Inn.[5] There was a certain method in the Count's inquiries, so I shall try to put them down in sequence; the knowledge may somehow or some time be useful to me.

First, he asked if a man in England might have two solicitors, or more. I told him he might have a dozen if he wished, but that it would not be wise to have more than one solicitor engaged in one transaction, as only one could act at a time, and that to change would be certain to militate against his interest. He seemed thoroughly to understand, and went on to ask if there would be any practical difficulty in having one man to attend, say, to banking, and another to look after shipping, in case local help were needed in a place far from the home of the banking solicitor. I asked him to explain more fully, so that I might not by any chance mislead him, so he said:—

'I shall illustrate. Your friend and mine, Mr Peter Hawkins, from under the shadow of your beautiful cathedral at Exeter,[6] which is far from London, buys for me through your good self my place at London. Good! Now here let me say frankly, lest you should think it strange that I have sought the services of one so far off from London instead of someone resident there, that my motive was that no local interest might be served save my wish only; and as one of London resident might, perhaps, have some purpose of himself or friend to serve, I went thus afield to seek my agent, whose labours should be only to my interest. Now, suppose I, who have much of affairs, wish to ship goods, say, to Newcastle, or Durham, or Harwich, or Dover, might it not be that it could with more ease be done by consigning to one in these ports?'[7] I answered that certainly it would be most easy, but that we solicitors had a system of agency one for the other, so that local work could be done locally on instruction from any solicitor, so that the client, simply placing himself in the hands of one man, could have his wishes carried out by him without further trouble.

'But,' said he, 'I could be at liberty to direct myself. Is it not so?'

'Of course,' I replied; 'and such is often done by men of business, who do not like the whole of their affairs to be known by any one person.'

'Good!' he said, and then went on to ask about the means of making consignments and the forms to be gone through, and of all sorts of

5. One of London's venerable legal and legal training establishments.
6. A well-known medieval edifice in the Gothic style Victorian architects tried to resurrect. Dracula has studied his guidebooks carefully.
7. After having boasted of his ancestral patriotism and military prowess, Dracula flaunts his up-to-date mercantile and legal sophistication.

difficulties which might arise, but by forethought could be guarded against. I explained all these things to him to the best of my ability, and he certainly left me under the impression that he would have made a wonderful solicitor, for there was nothing that he did not think of or foresee. For a man who was never in the country, and who did not evidently do much in the way of business, his knowledge and acumen were wonderful. When he had satisfied himself on these points of which he had spoken, and I had verified all as well as I could by the books available, he suddenly stood up and said:—

'Have you written since your first letter to our friend Mr Peter Hawkins, or to any other?' It was with some bitterness in my heart that I answered that I had not, that as yet I had not seen any opportunity of sending letters to anybody.

'Then write now, my young friend,' he said, laying a heavy hand on my shoulder; 'write to our friend and to any other; and say, if it will please you, that you shall stay with me until a month from now.'

'Do you wish me to stay so long?' I asked, for my heart grew cold at the thought.

'I desire it much; nay, I will take no refusal. When your master, employer, what you will, engaged that someone should come on his behalf, it was understood that my needs only were to be consulted. I have not stinted. Is it not so?'

What could I do but bow acceptance? It was Mr Hawkins's interest, not mine, and I had to think of him, not myself; and besides, while Count Dracula was speaking, there was that in his eyes and in his bearing which made me remember that I was a prisoner, and that if I wished it I could have no choice. The Count saw his victory in my bow, and his mastery in the trouble of my face, for he began at once to use them, but in his own smooth, resistless way:—

'I pray you, my good young friend, that you will not discourse of things other than business in your letters. It will doubtless please your friends to know that you are well, and that you look forward to getting home to them. Is it not so?' As he spoke he handed me three sheets of note-paper and three envelopes. They were all of the thinnest foreign post, and looking at them, then at him, and noticing his quiet smile, with the sharp, canine teeth lying over the red under-lip, I understood as well as if he had spoken that I should be careful what I wrote, for he would be able to read it. So I determined to write only formal notes now, but to write fully to Mr Hawkins in secret, and also to Mina, for to her I could write in shorthand, which would puzzle the Count, if he did see it. When I had written my two letters I sat quiet, reading a book whilst the Count wrote several notes, referring as he wrote them to some books on his table. Then he took up my two and placed them with his own, and put by his writing materials, after which, the instant the door had closed behind him, I leaned over and looked at the letters, which were face down on the table. I felt no compunction in doing so, for under the circumstances I felt that I should protect myself in every way I could.

One of the letters was directed to Samuel F. Billington, No. 7, The Crescent, Whitby, another to Herr Leutner, Varna; the third was to Coutts & Co., London, and the fourth to Herren Klopstock & Billreuth, bankers, Buda-Pesth. The second and fourth were unsealed. I was just about to look at them when I saw the door-handle move. I sank back in my seat, having just had time to replace the letters as they had been and to resume my book before the Count, holding still another letter in his hand, entered the room. He took up the letters on the table and stamped them carefully, and then turning to me, said:—

'I trust you will forgive me, but I have much work to do in private this evening. You will, I hope, find all things as you wish.' At the door he turned, and after a moment's pause said:—

'Let me advise you, my dear young friend—nay, let me warn you with all seriousness, that should you leave these rooms you will not by any chance go to sleep in any other part of the castle. It is old, and has many memories, and there are bad dreams[8] for those who sleep unwisely. Be warned! Should sleep now or ever overcome you, or be like to do, then haste to your own chamber or to these rooms, for your rest will then be safe. But if you be not careful in this respect, then'—He finished his speech in a gruesome way, for he motioned with his hands as if he were washing them. I quite understood; my only doubt was as to whether any dream could be more terrible than the unnatural, horrible net of gloom and mystery which seemed closing round me.

Later.—I endorse the last words written, but this time there is no doubt in question. I shall not fear to sleep in any place where he is not. I have placed the crucifix over the head of my bed—I imagine that my rest is thus freer from dreams; and there it shall remain.

When he left me I went to my room. After a little while, not hearing any sound, I came out and went up the stone stair to where I could look out towards the south. There was some sense of freedom in the vast expanse, inaccessible though it was to me, as compared with the narrow darkness of the courtyard. Looking out on this, I felt that I was indeed in prison, and I seemed to want a breath of fresh air, though it were of the night. I am beginning to feel this nocturnal existence tell on me. It is destroying my nerve. I start at my own shadow, and am full of all sorts of horrible imaginings. God knows that there is ground

---

8. Beginning with Jonathan, Dracula's victims are inflicted with a terror of sleep and dreaming. Stoker here adapts grand Shakespearean effects from the Lyceum. Jonathan, Lucy, Mina, and Renfield all share Hamlet's and Macbeth's terror of a sleep that may not be sleep bringing dreams that may not be dreams. See *Hamlet* 3.1.63–67 and *Macbeth* 3.2.17–22. Irving had staged a controversial *Macbeth* at the Lyceum in 1888. Stoker was haunted by Ellen Terry's unorthodox Lady Macbeth, as fragile, neurotic, and dreamily feminine a bloody creature as the stricken Lucy Westenra.

for any terrible fear in this accursed place! I looked out over the beautiful expanse, bathed in soft yellow moonlight till it was almost as light as day. In the soft light the distant hills became melted, and the shadows in the valleys and gorges of velvety blackness. The mere beauty seemed to cheer me; there was peace and comfort in every breath I drew. As I leaned from the window my eye was caught by something moving a storey below me, and somewhat to my left, where I imagined, from the lie of the rooms, that the windows of the Count's own room would look out. The window at which I stood was tall and deep, stone-mullioned,[9] and though weather-worn, was still complete; but it was evidently many a day since the case[1] had been there. I drew back behind the stonework, and looked carefully out.

What I saw was the Count's head coming out from the window. I did not see the face, but I knew the man by the neck and the movement of his back and arms. In any case I could not mistake the hands which I had had so many opportunities of studying. I was at first interested and somewhat amused, for it is wonderful how small a matter will interest and amuse a man when he is a prisoner. But my very feelings changed to repulsion and terror when I saw the whole man slowly emerge from the window and begin to crawl down the castle wall over that dreadful abyss, *face down*, with his cloak spreading out around him like great wings. At first I could not believe my eyes. I thought it was some trick of the moonlight, some weird effect of shadow; but I kept looking, and it could be no delusion. I saw the fingers and toes[2] grasp the corners of the stones, worn clear of the mortar by the stress of years, and by thus using every projection and inequality move downwards with considerable speed, just as a lizard[3] moves along a wall.

What manner of man is this, or what manner of creature is it in the semblance of man? I feel the dread of this horrible place overpowering me; I am in fear—in awful fear—and there is no escape for me; I am encompassed about with terrors that I dare not think of . . .

15 *May.*—Once more have I seen the Count go out in his lizard fashion. He moved downwards in a sidelong way, some hundred feet down, and a good deal to the left. He vanished into some hole or window. When his head had disappeared I leaned out to try and see more, but without avail—the distance was too great to allow a proper angle of sight. I knew he had left the castle now, and thought to use the opportunity to explore more than I had dared to do as yet. I went back to the room, and taking a lamp, tried all the doors. They were all

9. That is, the panes are separated by stone dividers.
1. Frame.
2. Modern readers, familiar with an immaculately dressed Dracula shod in opera pumps, may be surprised that Stoker's character leaves home barefoot.
3. Jonathan's repeated association of the crawling Dracula with a lizard aligns the vampire with those monstrous proofs of Darwinian evolution, dinosaurs—which Victorian scientists classified as reptiles—rather than with the mammalian bat.

locked, as I had expected, and the locks were comparatively new; but I went down the stone stairs to the hall where I had entered originally. I found I could pull back the bolts easily enough and unhook the great chains; but the door was locked, and the key was gone! That key must be in the Count's room; I must watch should his door be unlocked, so that I may get it and escape. I went on to make a thorough examination of the various stairs and passages, and to try the doors that opened from them. One or two small rooms near the hall were open, but there was nothing to see in them except old furniture, dusty with age and moth-eaten. At last, however, I found one door at the top of a stairway which, though it seemed to be locked, gave a little under pressure. I tried it harder, and found that it was not really locked, but that the resistance came from the fact that the hinges had fallen somewhat, and the heavy door rested on the floor. Here was an opportunity which I might not have again, so I exerted myself, and with many efforts forced it back so that I could enter. I was now in a wing of the castle further to the right than the rooms I knew and a storey lower down. From the windows I could see that the suite of rooms lay along to the south of the castle, the windows of the end room looking out both west and south. On the latter side, as well as to the former, there was a great precipice. The castle was built on the corner of a great rock, so that on three sides it was quite impregnable, and great windows were placed here where sling, or bow, or culverin[4] could not reach, and consequently light and comfort, impossible to a position which had to be guarded, were secured. To the west was a great valley, and then, rising far away, great jagged mountain fastnesses, rising peak on peak, the sheer rock studded with mountain ash and thorn, whose roots clung in cracks and crevices and crannies of the stone. This was evidently the portion of the castle occupied in bygone days, for the furniture had more air of comfort than any I had seen. The windows were curtainless, and the yellow moonlight, flooding in through the diamond panes, enabled one to see even colours, whilst it softened the wealth of dust which lay over all and disguised in some measure the ravages of time and the moth. My lamp seemed to be of little effect in the brilliant moonlight, but I was glad to have it with me, for there was a dread loneliness in the place which chilled my heart and made my nerves tremble. Still, it was better than living alone in the rooms which I had come to hate from the presence of the Count, and after trying a little to school my nerves, I found a soft quietude come over me. Here I am, sitting at a little oak table where in old times possibly some fair lady sat to pen, with much thought and many blushes, her ill-spelt love-letter, and writing in my diary in shorthand all that has happened since I closed it last. It is nineteenth century up-to-date with a vengeance. And yet, unless my

4. Musket (medieval) or heavy cannon.

senses deceive me, the old centuries had, and have, powers of their own which mere 'modernity' cannot kill.

Later: the Morning of 16 May.—God preserve my sanity, for to this I am reduced. Safety and the assurance of safety are things of the past. Whilst I live on here there is but one thing to hope for: that I may not go mad, if, indeed, I be not mad already. If I be sane, then surely it is maddening to think that of all the foul things that lurk in this hateful place the Count is the least dreadful to me; that to him alone I can look for safety, even though this be only whilst I can serve his purpose. Great God! merciful God! Let me be calm, for out of that way lies madness indeed. I begin to get new lights on certain things which have puzzled me. Up to now I never quite knew what Shakespeare meant when he made Hamlet say:—

> My tablets! quick, my tablets!
> 'Tis meet that I put it down, etc.,[5]

for now, feeling as though my own brain were unhinged or as if the shock had come which must end in its undoing, I turn to my diary for repose. The habit of entering accurately must help to soothe me.

The Count's mysterious warning frightened me at the time; it frightens me more now when I think of it, for in future he has a fearful hold upon me. I shall fear to doubt what he may say!

When I had written in my diary and had fortunately replaced the book and pen in my pocket I felt sleepy. The Count's warning came into my mind, but I took a pleasure in disobeying it. The sense of sleep was upon me, and with it the obstinacy which sleep brings as outrider. The soft moonlight soothed, and the wide expanse without gave a sense of freedom which refreshed me. I determined not to return tonight to the gloom-haunted rooms, but to sleep here, where of old ladies had sat and sung and lived sweet lives whilst their gentle breasts were sad for their menfolk away in the midst of remorseless wars. I drew a great couch out of its place near the corner, so that, as I lay, I could look at the lovely view to east and south, and unthinking of and uncaring for the dust, composed myself for sleep.

I suppose I must have fallen asleep; I hope so, but I fear, for all that followed was startlingly real—so real that now, sitting here in the broad, full sunlight of the morning, I cannot in the least believe that it was all sleep.

I was not alone. The room was the same, unchanged in any way since I came into it; I could see along the floor, in the brilliant moonlight, my own footsteps marked where I had disturbed the long accumulation of dust. In the moonlight opposite me were three young women, ladies by their dress and manner. I thought at the time that I

5. Misquotation of *Hamlet* 1.1.107–08.

must be dreaming when I saw them, for, though the moonlight was behind them, they threw no shadow[6] on the floor. They came close to me and looked at me for some time, and then whispered together. Two were dark, and had high aquiline noses, like the Count,[7] and great dark, piercing eyes, that seemed to be almost red when contrasted with the pale yellow moon. The other was fair, as fair as can be, with great, wavy masses of golden hair and eyes like pale sapphires. I seemed somehow to know her face, and to know it in connection with some dreamy fear, but I could not recollect at the moment how or where.[8] All three had brilliant white teeth, that shone like pearls against the ruby of their voluptuous lips. There was something about them that made me uneasy, some longing and at the same time some deadly fear. I felt in my heart a wicked, burning desire that they would kiss me with those red lips. It is not good to note this down, lest some day it should meet Mina's eyes and cause her pain; but it is the truth. They whispered together, and then they all three laughed—such a silvery, musical laugh, but as hard as though the sound never could have come through the softness of human lips. It was like the intolerable, tingling sweetness of water-glasses when played on by a cunning hand. The fair girl shook her head coquettishly, and the other two urged her on. One said:—

'Go on! You are first, and we shall follow; yours is the right to begin.' The other added:—

'He is young and strong; there are kisses for us all.' I lay quiet, looking out under my eyelashes in an agony of delightful anticipation. The fair girl advanced and bent over me till I could feel the movement of her breath upon me. Sweet it was in one sense, honey-sweet, and sent the same tingling through the nerves as her voice, but with a bitter underlying the sweet, a bitter offensiveness, as one smells in blood.

I was afraid to raise my eyelids, but looked out and saw perfectly under the lashes. The fair girl went on her knees, and bent over me, fairly gloating. There was a deliberate voluptuousness which was both thrilling and repulsive, and as she arched her neck she actually licked her lips like an animal, till I could see in the moonlight the moisture shining on the scarlet lips and on the red tongue as it lapped the white sharp teeth. Lower and lower went her head as the lips went below the range of my mouth and chin and seemed about to fasten on my throat. Then she paused, and I could hear the churning sound of her tongue as it licked her teeth and lips, and could feel the hot breath on my neck. Then the skin of my throat began to tingle as one's flesh does

6. As with Dracula's lack of mirror reflection.
7. Are their noses alike because they are Dracula's sisters, or do they share the racial characteristics of Eastern vampires?
8. Jonathan's puzzling recognition may be an editorial lapse on Stoker's part, referring to the sinister Countess Dolingen in the cancelled chapter (included in this edition, p. 350, below) published in 1914 as "Dracula's Guest," or it may be a subtle equation of the bestial foreigner with virtuous Englishwomen.

when the hand that is to tickle it approaches nearer—nearer. I could feel the soft, shivering touch of the lips on the supersensitive skin of my throat, and the hard dents of two sharp teeth, just touching and pausing there. I closed my eyes in a languorous ecstacy and waited— waited with beating heart.

But at that instant another sensation swept through me as quick as lightning. I was conscious of the presence of the Count, and of his being as if lapped in a storm of fury. As my eyes opened involuntarily I saw his strong hand grasp the slender neck of the fair woman and with giant's power draw it back, the blue eyes transformed with fury, the white teeth champing with rage, and the fair cheeks blazing red with passion. But the Count! Never did I imagine such wrath and fury, even to the demons of the pit. His eyes were positively blazing. The red light in them was lurid, as if the flames of hell-fire blazed behind them. His face was deathly pale, and the lines of it were hard like drawn wires; the thick eyebrows that met over the nose now seemed like a heaving bar of white-hot metal. With a fierce sweep of his arm, he hurled the woman from him, and then motioned to the others, as though he were beating them back; it was the same imperious gesture that I had seen used to the wolves. In a voice which, though low and almost in a whisper, seemed to cut through the air and then ring round the room as he said:—

'How dare you touch him, any of you? How dare you cast eyes on him when I had forbidden it? Back, I tell you all! This man belongs to me![9] Beware how you meddle with him, or you'll have to deal with me.' The fair girl, with a laugh of ribald coquetry, turned to answer him:—

'You yourself never loved; you never love!' On this the other women joined, and such a mirthless, hard, soulless laughter rang through the room that it almost made me faint to hear; it seemed like the pleasure of fiends. Then the Count turned, after looking at my face attentively, and said in a soft whisper:—

'Yes, I too can love; you yourselves can tell it from the past.[1] Is it not so? Well, now I promise you that when I am done with him you shall kiss him at your will. Now go! go! I must awaken him, for there is work to be done.'

'Are we to have nothing tonight?' said one of them, with a low laugh, as she pointed to the bag which he had thrown upon the floor, and which moved as though there were some living thing within it. For answer he nodded his head. One of the women jumped forward and opened it. If my ears did not deceive me there was a gasp and a low

---

9. This proprietary sentence recurs over and over in Stoker's working notes. The phrase *belongs to me* underlies *Dracula*'s vision of love, sexuality, nation, religion, and humanity itself.

1. Touches on a possibility some twentieth-century writers develop: that vampires can have erotic contact only with humans, not with each other.

wail, as of a half-smothered child. The women closed round, whilst I was aghast with horror; but as I looked they disappeared, and with them the dreadful bag. There was no door near them, and they could not have passed me without my noticing. They simply seemed to fade into the rays of the moonlight and pass out through the window, for I could see outside the dim, shadowy forms for a moment before they entirely faded away.

Then the horror overcame me, and I sank down unconscious.

Chapter IV

Jonathan Harker's Journal—(continued)

I awoke in my own bed. If it be that I had not dreamt, the Count must have carried me here. I tried to satisfy myself on the subject, but could not arrive at any unquestionable result. To be sure, there were certain small evidences, such as that my clothes were folded and laid by in a manner which was not my habit. My watch was still unwound, and I am rigorously accustomed to wind it the last thing before going to bed, and many such details. But these things are no proof, for they may have been evidences that my mind was not as usual, and, from some cause or another, I had certainly been much upset. I must watch for proof. Of one thing I am glad: if it was that the Count carried me here and undressed me, he must have been hurried in his task, for my pockets are intact. I am sure this diary would have been a mystery to him which he would not have brooked. He would have taken or destroyed it. As I look round this room, although it has been to me so full of fear, it is now a sort of sanctuary, for nothing can be more dreadful than those awful women, who were—who *are*—waiting to suck my blood.[1]

18 May.—I have been down to look at that room again in daylight, for I *must* know the truth. When I got to the doorway at the top of the stairs I found it closed. It had been so forcibly driven against the jamb that part of the woodwork was splintered. I could see that the bolt of the lock had not been shot, but the door is fastened from the inside. I fear it was no dream, and must act on this surmise.

19 May.—I am surely in the toils.[2] Last night the Count asked me in the suavest tones to write three letters, one saying that my work here was nearly done, and that I should start for home within a few days, another that I was starting on the next morning from the time of the letter, and the third that I had left the castle and arrived at Bistritz. I would fain have rebelled, but felt that in the present state of things it would be madness to quarrel openly with the Count whilst I am so

---

1. Stoker seems to slip here. Harker has not yet seen evidence of blood drinking.
2. Like a trapped animal.

absolutely in his power; and to refuse would be to excite his suspicion and to arouse his anger. He knows that I know too much, and that I must not live, lest I be dangerous to him; my only chance is to prolong my opportunities. Something may occur which will give me a chance to escape. I saw in his eyes something of that gathering wrath which was manifest when he hurled that fair woman from him. He explained to me that posts were few and uncertain, and that my writing now would ensure ease of mind to my friends; and he assured me with so much impressiveness that he would countermand the later letters, which would be held over at Bistritz until due time in case chance would admit of my prolonging my stay, that to oppose him would have been to create new suspicion. I therefore pretended to fall in with his views, and asked him what dates I should put on the letters. He calculated a minute, and then said:—

'The first should be June 12, the second June 19, and the third June 29.'

I know now the span of my life. God help me!

28 *May.*—There is a chance of escape, or at any rate of being able to send word home. A band of Szgany[3] have come to the castle, and are encamped in the courtyard. These Szgany are gipsies; I have notes of them in my book. They are peculiar to this part of the world, though allied to the ordinary gipsies all the world over. There are thousands of them in Hungary and Transylvania, who are almost outside all law. They attach themselves as a rule to some great noble or *boyar*, and call themselves by his name. They are fearless and without religion, save superstition, and they talk only their own varieties of the Romany tongue.

I shall write some letters home, and shall try to get them to have them posted. I have already spoken to them through my window to begin an acquaintanceship. They took their hats off and made obeisance and many signs, which, however, I could not understand any more than I could their spoken language . . .

I have written the letters. Mina's is in shorthand, and I simply ask Mr Hawkins to communicate with her. To her I have explained my situation, but without the horrors which I may only surmise. It would shock and frighten her to death were I to expose my heart to her. Should the letters not carry, then the Count shall not yet know my secret or the extent of my knowledge . . .

I have given the letters; I threw them through the bars of my window with a gold piece, and made what signs I could to have them posted. The man who took them pressed them to his heart and bowed, and then put them in his cap. I could do no more. I stole back to the study,

---

3. Usually *Tsigane*. These Romany gypsies, whose name is etymologically unrelated to the Roman origin of "Romania," are not, in the novel, outside all law: they consistently obey Dracula's.

and began to read. As the Count did not come in, I have written here . . .

The Count has come. He sat down beside me, and said in his smoothest voice as he opened two letters:—

'The Szgany has given me these, of which, though I know not whence they come, I shall, of course, take care. See!'—he must have looked at it—'one is from you, and to my friend Peter Hawkins; the other'—here he caught sight of the strange symbols as he opened the envelope, and the dark look came into his face, and his eyes blazed wickedly—'the other is a vile thing, an outrage upon friendship and hospitality! It is not signed. Well! so it cannot matter to us.' And he calmly held letter and envelope in the flame of the lamp till they were consumed. Then he went on:—

'The letter to Hawkins—that I shall, of course, send on, since it is yours. Your letters are sacred to me. Your pardon, my friend, that unknowingly I did break the seal. Will you not cover it again?' He held out the letter to me, and with a courteous bow handed me a clean envelope. I could only redirect it and hand it to him in silence. When he went out of the room I could hear the key turn softly. A minute later I went over and tried it, and the door was locked.

When, an hour or two after, the Count came quietly into the room; his coming wakened me, for I had gone to sleep on the sofa. He was very courteous and very cheery in his manner, and seeing that I had been sleeping, he said:—

'So, my friend, you are tired? Get to bed. There is the surest rest. I may not have the pleasure to talk tonight, since there are many labours to me; but you will sleep, I pray.' I passed to my room and went to bed, and, strange to say, slept without dreaming. Despair has its own calms.

31 May.—This morning when I woke I thought I would provide myself with some paper and envelopes from my bag and keep them in my pocket, so that I might write in case I should get an opportunity; but again a surprise, again a shock!

Every scrap of paper was gone, and with it all my notes, my memoranda relating to railways and travel, my letter of credit, in fact all that might be useful to me were I once outside the castle. I sat and pondered a while, and then some thought occurred to me, and I made search of my portmanteau and in the wardrobe where I had placed my clothes.

The suit in which I had travelled was gone, and also my overcoat and rug; I could find no trace of them anywhere. This looked like some new scheme of villainy . . .

17 June.[4]—This morning, as I was sitting on the edge of my bed cudgelling my brains, I heard without a cracking of whips and pound-

---

4. Two weeks have lapsed since Jonathan's last journal entry.

ing and scraping of horses' feet up the rocky path beyond the courtyard. With joy I hurried to the window, and saw drive into the yard two great leiter-wagons, each drawn by eight sturdy horses, and at the head of each pair a Slovak, with his wide hat, great, nail-studded belt, dirty sheepskin, and high boots. They had also their long staves in hand. I ran to the door, intending to descend and try and join them through the main hall, as I thought that way might be opened for them. Again a shock: my door was fastened on the outside.

Then I ran to the window and cried to them. They looked up at me stupidly and pointed, but just then the 'hetman'[5] of the Szgany came out, and seeing them pointing to my window, said something, at which they laughed. Henceforth no effort of mine, no piteous cry or agonized entreaty, would make them even look at me. They resolutely turned away. The leiter-wagons contained great, square boxes, with handles of thick rope; these were evidently empty by the ease with which the Slovaks handled them, and by their resonance as they were roughly moved. When they were all unloaded and packed in a great heap in one corner of the yard, the Slovaks were given some money by the Szgany, and spitting on it for luck, lazily went each to his horse's head. Shortly afterwards I heard the cracking of their whips die away in the distance.

24 June, before morning.—Last night the Count left me early, and locked himself into his own room. As soon as I dared I ran up the winding stair, and looked out of the window, which opened south. I thought I would watch for the Count, for there is something going on. The Szgany are quartered somewhere in the castle, and are doing work of some kind. I know it, for now and then I hear a far-away, muffled sound as of mattock[6] and spade, and, whatever it is, it must be to the end of some ruthless villainy.

I had been at the window somewhat less than half an hour, when I saw something coming out of the Count's window. I drew back and watched carefully, and saw the whole man emerge. It was a new shock to me to find that he had on the suit of clothes which I had worn whilst travelling here, and slung over his shoulder the terrible bag which I had seen the women take away. There could be no doubt as to his quest, and in my garb, too! This, then, is his new scheme of evil: that he will allow others to see me, as they think, so that he may both leave evidence that I have been seen in the towns or villages posting my own letters, and that any wickedness which he may do shall by the local people be attributed to me.

It makes me rage to think that this can go on, and whilst I am shut up here, a veritable prisoner, but without that protection of the law which is even a criminal's right and consolation.

5. Polish translation of the German *hauptmann*: leader or commander in chief of the army.
6. Pickaxe.

I thought I would watch for the Count's return, and for a long time sat doggedly at the window. Then I began to notice that there were some quaint little specks floating in the rays of the moonlight. They were like the tiniest grains of dust, and they whirled round and gathered in clusters in a nebulous sort of way. I watched them with a sense of soothing, and a sort of calm stole over me. I leaned back in the embrasure in a more comfortable position, so that I could enjoy more fully the aerial gambolling.

Something made me start up, a low, piteous howling of dogs somewhere far below in the valley, which was hidden from my sight. Louder it seemed to ring in my ears, and the floating motes of dust to take new shapes to the sound as they danced in the moonlight. I felt myself struggling to awake to some call of my instincts; nay, my very soul was struggling, and my half-remembered sensibilities were striving to answer the call. I was becoming hypnotized! Quicker and quicker danced the dust, and the moonbeams seemed to quiver as they went by me into the mass of gloom beyond. More and more they gathered till they seemed to take dim phantom shapes. And then I started, broad awake and in full possession of my senses, and ran screaming from the place. The phantom shapes, which were becoming gradually materialized from the moonbeams, were those of the three ghostly women to whom I was doomed. I fled, and felt somewhat safer in my own room, where there was no moonlight and where the lamp was burning brightly.

When a couple of hours had passed I heard something stirring in the Count's room, something like a sharp wail quickly suppressed; and then there was silence, deep, awful silence, which chilled me. With a beating heart, I tried the door; but I was locked in my prison, and could do nothing. I sat down and simply cried.

As I sat I heard a sound in the courtyard without—the agonized cry of a woman. I rushed to the window, and throwing it up, peered out between the bars. There, indeed, was a woman with dishevelled hair, holding her hands over her heart as one distressed with running. She was leaning against a corner of the gateway. When she saw my face at the window she threw herself forward, and shouted in a voice laden with menace:—

'Monster, give me my child!'

She threw herself on her knees, and raising up her hands, cried the same words in tones which wrung my heart. Then she tore her hair and beat her breast, and abandoned herself to all the violences of extravagant emotion. Finally, she threw herself forward, and, though I could not see her, I could hear the beating of her naked hands against the door.

Somewhere high overhead, probably on the tower, I heard the voice of the Count calling in his harsh, metallic whisper. His call seemed to be answered from far and wide by the howling of wolves. Before many minutes had passed a pack of them poured, like a pent-up dam when liberated, through the wide entrance into the courtyard.

There was no cry from the woman, and the howling of the wolves was but short. Before long they streamed away singly, licking their lips.

I could not pity her, for I knew now what had become of her child, and she was better dead.

What shall I do? what can I do? How can I escape from this dreadful thrall of night and gloom and fear?

25 June, morning.—No man knows till he has suffered from the night how sweet and how dear to his heart and eye the morning can be. When the sun grew so high this morning that it struck the top of the great gateway opposite my window, the high spot which it touched seemed to me as if the dove from the ark had lighted there. My fear fell from me as if it had been a vaporous garment which dissolved in the warmth. I must take action of some sort whilst the courage of the day is upon me. Last night one of my post-dated letters went to post, the first of that fatal series which is to blot out the very traces of my existence from the earth.

Let me not think of it. Action!

It has always been at night-time that I have been molested or threatened, or in some way in danger or in fear. I have not yet seen the Count in the daylight.[7] Can it be that he sleeps when others wake, that he may be awake whilst they sleep? If I could only get into his room! But there is no possible way. The door is always locked, no way for me.

Yes, there is a way, if one dares to take it. Where his body has gone why may not another body go? I have seen him myself crawl from his window; why should not I imitate him, and go in by his window?[8] The chances are desperate, but my need is more desperate still. I shall risk it. At the worst it can only be death; and a man's death is not a calf's, and the dreaded Hereafter may still be open to me. God help me in my task! Goodbye, Mina, if I fail; goodbye, my faithful friend and second father; goodbye, all, and last of all Mina!

Same day, later.—I have made the effort, and, God helping me, have come safely back to this room. I must put down every detail in order. I went whilst my courage was fresh straight to the window on the south side, and at once got outside on the narrow ledge of stone which runs round the building on this side. The stones were big and roughly cut, and the mortar had by process of time been washed away between them. I took off my boots, and ventured out on the desperate way. I looked down once, so as to make sure that a sudden glimpse of the awful depth would not overcome me, but after that kept my eyes away from it. I knew pretty well the direction and distance of the Count's

---

7. In fact, Dracula greeted the shaving Jonathan with "Good morning."
8. No film adaptation has attempted to reproduce Jonathan's mimicry of Dracula's lizardlike slither down the castle walls, a journey whose nonhumanity at first appalled him.

window, and made for it as well as I could, having regard to the opportunities available. I did not feel dizzy—I suppose I was too excited
—and the time seemed ridiculously short till I found myself standing
on the window-sill and trying to raise up the sash. I was filled with
agitation, however, when I bent down and slid feet foremost in through
the window. Then I looked around for the Count, but, with surprise
and gladness, made a discovery. The room was empty! It was barely
furnished with odd things, which seemed to have never been used; the
furniture was something the same style as that in the south rooms, and
was covered with dust. I looked for the key, but it was not in the lock,
and I could not find it anywhere. The only thing I found was a great
heap of gold in one corner—gold of all kinds, Roman, and British, and
Austrian, and Hungarian, and Greek and Turkish money, covered with
a film of dust, as though it had lain long in the ground. None of it that
I noticed was less than three hundred years old. There were also chains
and ornaments, some jewelled, but all of them old and stained.

At one corner of the room was a heavy door. I tried it, for, since I
could not find the key of the room or the key of the outer door, which
was the main object of my search, I must make further examination,
or all my efforts would be in vain. It was open, and led through a stone
passage to a circular stairway, which went steeply down. I descended,
minding carefully where I went, for the stairs were dark, being only lit
by loopholes in the heavy masonry. At the bottom there was a dark,
tunnel-like passage, through which came a deathly, sickly odour, the
odour of old earth newly turned. As I went through the passage the
smell grew closer and heavier. At last I pulled open a heavy door which
stood ajar, and found myself in an old, ruined chapel, which had evidently been used as a graveyard. The roof was broken, and in two places
were steps leading to vaults, but the ground had recently been dug
over, and the earth placed in great wooden boxes, manifestly those
which had been brought by the Slovaks. There was nobody about, and
I made search for any further outlet, but there was none. Then I went
over every inch of the ground, so as not to lose a chance. I went down
even into the vaults, where the dim light struggled, although to do so
was a dread to my very soul. Into two of these I went, but saw nothing
except fragments of old coffins and piles of dust; in the third, however,
I made a discovery.

There, in one of the great boxes, of which there were fifty in all, on
a pile of newly dug earth, lay the Count! He was either dead or asleep,
I could not say which—for the eyes were open and stony, but without
the glassiness of death—and the cheeks had the warmth of life through
all their pallor, and the lips were as red as ever. But there was no sign
of movement, no pulse, no breath, no beating of the heart. I bent over
him, and tried to find any sign of life, but in vain. He could not have
lain there long, for the earthy smell would have passed away in a few

hours. By the side of the box was its cover, pierced with holes here and there. I thought he might have the keys on him, but when I went to search I saw the dead eyes, and in them, dead though they were, such a look of hate, though unconscious of me or my presence, that I fled from the place, and leaving the Count's room by the window, crawled again up the castle wall. Regaining my own chamber, I threw myself panting upon the bed and tried to think . . .

29 *June.*—Today is the date of my last letter, and the Count has taken steps to prove that it was genuine, for again I saw him leave the castle by the same window, and in my clothes. As he went down the wall, lizard fashion, I wished I had a gun or some lethal weapon, that I might destroy him; but I fear that no weapon wrought alone by man's hand would have any effect on him. I dared not wait to see him return, for I feared to see those weird sisters.[9] I came back to the library, and read there till I fell asleep.

I was awakened by the Count, who looked at me as grimly as a man can look as he said:—

'Tomorrow, my friend, we must part. You return to your beautiful England, I to some work which may have such an end that we may never meet. Your letter home has been despatched; tomorrow I shall not be here, but all shall be ready for your journey. In the morning come the Szgany, who have some labours of their own here, and also come some Slovaks. When they have gone, my carriage shall come for you, and shall bear you to the Borgo Pass to meet the diligence from Bukovina to Bistritz. But I am in hopes that I shall see more of you at Castle Dracula.' I suspected him, and determined to test his sincerity. Sincerity! It seems like a profanation of the word to write it in connection with such a monster, so asked him point-blank:—

'Why may I not go tonight?'

'Because, dear sir, my coachman and horses are away on a mission.'

'But I would walk with pleasure. I want to get away at once.' He smiled, such a soft, smooth, diabolical smile that I knew there was some trick behind his smoothness. He said:—

'And your baggage?'

'I do not care about it. I can send for it some other time.'

The Count stood up, and said, with a sweet courtesy which made me rub my eyes, it seemed so real:—

'You English have a saying which is close to my heart, for its spirit is that which rules our *boyars*: "Welcome the coming, speed the parting guest."[1] Come with me, my dear young friend. Not an hour shall you wait in my house against your will, though sad am I at your going, and that you so suddenly desire it. Come!' With a stately gravity, he, with

9. A reference to Shakespeare's *Macbeth*, whose three witches are called the "weird sisters" five times.
1. Paraphrase of a line from Alexander Pope's translation of Homer's *Odyssey*, book 15.

the lamp, preceded me down the stairs and along the hall. Suddenly
he stopped.

'Hark!'

Close at hand came the howling of many wolves. It was almost as if
the sound sprang up at the raising of his hand, just as the music of a
great orchestra seems to leap under the bâton of the conductor. After
a pause of a moment, he proceeded, in his stately way, to the door,
drew back the ponderous bolts, unhooked the heavy chains, and began
to draw it open.

To my intense astonishment I saw that it was unlocked. Suspiciously
I looked all round, but could see no key of any kind.

As the door began to open, the howling of the wolves without grew
louder and angrier; their red jaws, with champing teeth, and their blunt-
clawed feet as they leaped, came in through the opening door. I knew
then that to struggle at the moment against the Count was useless. With
such allies as these at his command, I could do nothing. But still the
door continued slowly to open, and only the Count's body stood in
the gap. Suddenly it struck me that this might be the moment and the
means of my doom; I was to be given to the wolves, and at my own
instigation. There was a diabolical wickedness in the idea great enough
for the Count, and as a last chance I cried out:—

'Shut the door; I shall wait till morning!' and covered my face with
my hands to hide my tears of bitter disappointment. With one sweep
of his powerful arm, the Count threw the door shut, and the great bolts
clanged and echoed through the hall as they shot back into their places.

In silence we returned to the library, and after a minute or two I
went to my own room. The last I saw of Count Dracula was his kissing
his hand to me; with a red light of triumph in his eyes, and with a
smile that Judas in hell might be proud of.

When I was in my room and about to lie down, I thought I heard a
whispering at my door. I went to it softly and listened. Unless my ears
deceived me, I heard the voice of the Count:—

'Back, back, to your own place! Your time is not yet come. Wait.
Have patience. Tomorrow night, tomorrow night, is yours!'[2] There was
a low, sweet ripple of laughter, and in a rage I threw open the door,
and saw without the three terrible women licking their lips. As I appeared they all joined in a horrible laugh, and ran away.

I came back to my room and threw myself on my knees. It is then
so near the end? Tomorrow! tomorrow! Lord, help me, and those to
whom I am dear!

2. In all British editions, Dracula says only: "To-morrow night, to-morrow night is yours," but
in the 1899 American edition, this sentence begins with the line "To-night is mine," stating
baldly that Dracula plans to feed on Jonathan. Stoker's deletion of this sentence was under-
standable, for it leads to a different novel, one probably unpublishable in 1897 England;
Stoker may have imagined that the America that produced his hero Walt Whitman would be
more tolerant of men feeding on men.

30 June, morning.—These may be the last words I ever write in this diary. I slept till just before the dawn, and when I woke threw myself on my knees, for I determined that if Death came he should find me ready.

At last I felt that subtle change in the air, and I knew that the morning had come. Then came the welcome cock-crow, and I felt that I was safe. With a glad heart, I opened my door and ran down to the hall. I had seen that the door was unlocked, and now escape was before me. With hands that trembled with eagerness, I unhooked the chains and drew back the massive bolts.

But the door would not move. Despair seized me. I pulled, and pulled, at the door, and shook it till, massive as it was, it rattled in its casement. I could see the bolt shot. It had been locked after I left the Count.

Then a wild desire took me to obtain that key at any risk, and I determined then and there to scale the wall again and gain the Count's room. He might kill me, but death now seemed the happier choice of evils. Without a pause I rushed up to the east window, and scrambled down the wall, as before, into the Count's room. It was empty, but that was as I expected. I could not see a key anywhere, but the heap of gold remained. I went through the door in the corner and down the winding stair and along the dark passage to the old chapel. I knew now well enough where to find the monster I sought.

The great box was in the same place, close against the wall, but the lid was laid on it, not fastened down, but with the nails ready in their places to be hammered home. I knew I must search the body for the key, so I raised the lid, and laid it back against the wall; and then I saw something which filled my very soul with horror. There lay the Count, but looking as if his youth had been half renewed, for the white hair and moustache were changed to dark iron-grey; the cheeks were fuller, and the white skin seemed ruby-red underneath; the mouth was redder than ever, for on the lips were gouts of fresh blood, which trickled from the corners of the mouth and ran over the chin and neck. Even the deep, burning eyes seemed set amongst swollen flesh, for the lids and pouches underneath were bloated. It seemed as if the whole awful creature were simply gorged with blood; he lay like a filthy leech, exhausted with his repletion. I shuddered as I bent over to touch him, and every sense in me revolted at the contact; but I had to search, or I was lost. The coming night might see my own body a banquet in a similar way to those horrid three. I felt all over the body, but no sign could I find of the key. Then I stopped and looked at the Count. There was a mocking smile on the bloated face which seemed to drive me mad. This was the being I was helping to transfer to London, where, perhaps, for centuries to come he might, amongst its teeming millions, satiate his lust for blood, and create a new and ever-widening circle of semi-demons to batten on the helpless.[3] The very thought drove me mad. A terrible desire came upon me to rid the world of such a monster. There was no lethal weapon at hand, but I seized a shovel which the workmen had been using to fill the cases, and lifting it high struck, with the edge downward, at the hateful face. But as I did so the head turned, and the eyes fell full upon me, with all their blaze of basilisk[4] horror. The sight seemed to paralyse me, and the shovel turned in my hand and glanced from the face, merely making a deep gash above the forehead.[5] The shovel fell from my hand across the box, and as I pulled it away the flange of the blade caught the edge of the lid, which fell over again, and hid the horrid thing from my sight. The last glimpse I had was of the bloated face, bloodstained and fixed with a grin of malice which would have held its own in the nethermost hell.

I thought and thought what should be my next move, but my brain seemed on fire, and I waited with a despairing feeling growing over me. As I waited I heard in the distance a gipsy song sung by merry voices coming closer, and through their song the rolling of heavy wheels and the cracking of whips; the Szgany and the Slovaks of whom the Count had spoken were coming. With a last look around and at the box which contained the vile body, I ran from the place and gained the Count's room, determined to rush out at the moment the door should be opened. With strained ears, I listened, and heard downstairs the grinding of the key in the great lock and the falling back of the heavy door. There must have been some other means of entry, or some one had a key for one of the locked doors. Then there came the sound of many feet tramping and dying away in some passage which sent up a clanging echo. I turned to run down again towards the vault, where I might find the new entrance; but at the moment there seemed to come a violent puff of wind, and the door to the winding stair blew to with a shock that set the dust from the lintels flying. When I ran to push it open, I found that it was hopelessly fast. I was again a prisoner, and the net of doom was closing round me more closely.

As I write there is in the passage below a sound of many tramping feet and the crash of weights being set down heavily, doubtless the boxes, with their freight of earth. There is a sound of hammering; it is the box being nailed down. Now I can hear the heavy feet tramping again along the hall, with many other idle feet coming behind them.

The door is shut, and the chains rattle; there is a grinding of the key in the lock; I can hear the key withdrawn: then another door opens and shuts; I hear the creaking of lock and bolt.

Hark! in the courtyard and down the rocky way the roll of heavy

---

3. Another lapse, for at this point Jonathan has no way of knowing how vampires multiply.
4. Cockatrice. A mythical beast whose stare paralyzes its prey.
5. Oddly, the scar never heals. Have Dracula's other wounds closed spontaneously, or is this gash the only wound Dracula has received during his long Un-death?

wheels, the crack of whips, and the chorus of the Szgany as they pass into the distance.

I am alone in the castle with those awful women. Faugh! Mina is a woman, and there is nought in common. They are devils of the Pit!

I shall not remain alone with them; I shall try to scale the castle wall farther than I have yet attempted. I shall take some of the gold with me, lest I want it later. I may find a way from this dreadful place.

And then away for home! away to the quickest and nearest train! away from this cursed spot, from this cursed land, where the devil and his children still walk with earthly feet!

At least God's mercy is better than that of these monsters, and the precipice is steep and high. At its foot a man may sleep—as a man. Goodbye, all! Mina!

Chapter V

Letter from Miss Mina Murray to Miss Lucy Westenra

9 May.

My dearest Lucy,—

Forgive my long delay in writing, but I have been simply over-whelmed with work. The life of an assistant schoolmistress[1] is some-times trying. I am longing to be with you, and by the sea, where we can talk together freely and build our castles in the air. I have been working very hard lately, because I want to keep up with Jonathan's studies,[2] and I have been practising shorthand very assiduously. When we are married I shall be able to be useful to Jonathan, and if I can stenograph well enough I can take down what he wants to say in this way and write it out for him on the typewriter,[3] at which also I am practising very hard. He and I sometimes write letters in shorthand, and he is keeping a stenographic journal of his travels abroad. When I am with you I shall keep a diary in the same way. I don't mean one of those two-pages-to-the-week-with-Sunday-squeezed-in-a-corner diaries, but a sort of journal which I can write in whenever I feel inclined. I do not suppose there will be much of interest to other people; but it is not intended for them. I may show it to Jonathan some day if there is

1. Mina is a working woman, but not, in the 1890s, an improper one: child-centered work such as governessing or schoolteaching was the traditional occupation of Victorian women who needed to support themselves. Mina is not taking advantage of the careers in medicine, the arts, the theater, the universities, journalism, office work, or school administration available to a new, aspiring generation of women at the end of the century.
2. Mina positions herself as the "helpmate" (or "helpmeet") dear to moderate Victorians: this strong, capable, and independent woman has outgrown women's traditional childlike role, but she is careful to put her strength at the service of her husband.
3. Invented in America in 1867, the typewriter was a new, relatively esoteric mode of technology, one in which Mina possesses an almost preternatural skill. Although Mina does not have an office career, her typing expertise moves her toward subversive—undomestic—ground.

in it anything worth sharing, but it is really an exercise book. I shall try to do what I see lady journalists[4] do: interviewing and writing descriptions and trying to remember conversations. I am told that, with a little practice, one can remember all that goes on or that one hears said during a day. However, we shall see. I shall tell you all my little plans when we meet. I have just had a few hurried lines from Jonathan from Transylvania. He is well, and will be returning in about a week. I am longing to hear all his news. It must be so nice to see strange countries. I wonder if we—I mean Jonathan and I—shall ever see them together. There is the ten o'clock bell ringing. Goodbye.

Your loving
MINA.

Tell me all the news when you write. You have not told me anything for a long time. I hear rumours, and especially of a tall, handsome, curly-haired man???

Letter, Lucy Westenra to Mina Murray

17, Chatham Street,
Wednesday.

My dearest Mina,—

I must say you tax me *very* unfairly with being a bad correspondent. I wrote to you *twice* since we parted, and your last letter was only your *second*.[5] Besides, I have nothing to tell you. There is really nothing to interest you. Town is very pleasant just now, and we go a good deal to picture-galleries and for walks and rides in the park. As to the tall, curly-haired man, I suppose it was the one who was with me at the last Pop.[6] Some one has evidently been telling tales. That was Mr Holmwood.[7] He often comes to see us, and he and mamma get on very well together; they have so many things to talk about in common. We met some time ago a man that would just *do for you,* if you were not already engaged to Jonathan. He is an excellent *parti,*[8] being handsome, well off, and of good birth. He is a doctor and really clever. Just fancy! He is only nine-and-twenty, and he has an immense lunatic asylum all under his own care. Mr Holmwood introduced him to me, and he called here to see us, and often comes now. I think he is one of the most resolute men I ever saw, and yet the most calm. He seems absolutely imper-

---

4. As in her eagerness to master office technology, Mina again flirts with modern professionalism, though she pursues self-discipline, not ambition.
5. Lucy's girlish use of italics and her preoccupation with flirting and marriage announce that, unlike Mina, she is a traditional Victorian lady, cared for and frivolous, not a working woman. Stoker gives this old-fashioned girl an allegorical name, "Light of the West."
6. Popular concert.
7. Possibly an echo of James Malcolm Rymer's popular vampire serial *Varney the Vampyre* (1845–47). Varney's victim, Clara Crofton, whose fate anticipates Lucy's, has a fiancé named Ringwood. Ring is the name of Arthur Holmwood's family home.
8. A marriageable individual; a match.

turbable. I can fancy what a wonderful power he must have over his patients. He has a curious habit of looking one straight in the face, as if trying to read one's thoughts.[9] He tries this on very much with me, but I flatter myself he has got a tough nut to crack. I know that from my glass. Do you ever try to read your own face? *I do*, and I can tell you it is not a bad study, and gives you more trouble than you can well fancy if you have never tried it. He says that I afford him a curious psychological study, and I humbly think I do. I do not, as you know, take sufficient interest in dress to be able to describe the new fashions. Dress is a bore. That is slang again, but never mind; Arthur says that every day. There, it is all out. Mina, we have told all our secrets to each other since we were *children*;[1] we have slept together and eaten together, and laughed and cried together; and now, though I have spoken, I would like to speak more. Oh, Mina, couldn't you guess? I love him. I am blushing as I write, for although I *think* he loves me, he has not told me so in words. But oh, Mina, I love him; I love him; I love him! There, that does me good. I wish I were with you, dear, sitting by the fire undressing, as we used to sit; and I would try to tell you what I feel. I do not know how I am writing this even to you. I am afraid to stop, or I should tear up the letter, and I don't want to stop, for I *do so* want to tell you all. Let me hear from you *at once*, and tell me all that you think about it. Mina, I must stop. Good-night. Bless me in your prayers; and, Mina, pray for my happiness.

LUCY

P.S.—I need not tell you this is a secret. Good-night again.

'L.'

Letter, Lucy Westenra to Mina Murray

24 May.

My dearest Mina,—

Thanks, and thanks, and thanks again for your sweet letter! It was so nice to be able to tell you and to have your sympathy.

My dear, it never rains but it pours. How true the old proverbs are. Here am I, who shall be twenty in September, and yet I never had a proposal till today, not a real proposal, and today I have had three. Just fancy! THREE proposals in one day! Isn't it awful! I feel sorry, really and truly sorry, for two of the poor fellows. Oh, Mina, I am so happy that I don't know what to do with myself. And three proposals! But, for goodness' sake, don't tell any of the girls, or they would be getting all sorts of extravagant ideas and imagining themselves injured and slighted

---

9. Lucy's admiration for Dr. Seward's "power over his patients" and his near clairvoyance indicate the virtually occult power attributed to doctors—particularly the new profession of psychiatry—in the 1890s.
1. *Dracula* gives contradictory histories of Lucy and Mina's friendship. This one implies that, though they began as social equals, Mina has become poorer.

if in their very first day at home they did not get six at least. Some girls are so vain. You and I, Mina dear, who are engaged and are going to settle down soon soberly into old married women, can despise vanity. Well, I must tell you about the three, but you must keep it a secret, dear, from *every one*, except, of course, Jonathan. You will tell him, because I would, if I were in your place, certainly tell Arthur. A woman ought to tell her husband everything—don't you think so, dear?—and I must be fair. Men like women, certainly their wives, to be quite as fair as they are; and women, I am afraid, are not always quite as fair as they should be. Well, my dear, number one came just before lunch. I told you of him, Dr John Seward, the lunatic-asylum man, with the strong jaw and the good forehead. He was very cool outwardly, but was nervous all the same. He had evidently been schooling himself as to all sorts of little things, and remembered them; but he almost managed to sit down on his silk hat, which men don't generally do when they are cool, and then when he wanted to appear at ease he kept playing with a lancet[2] in a way that made me nearly scream. He spoke to me, Mina, very straightforwardly. He told me how dear I was to him, though he had known me so little, and what his life would be with me to help and cheer him. He was going to tell me how unhappy he would be if I did not care for him, but when he saw me cry he said that he was a brute and would not add to my present trouble. Then he broke off and asked if I could love him in time; and when I shook my head his hands trembled, and then with some hesitation he asked me if I cared already for any one else. He put it very nicely, saying that he did not want to wring my confidence from me, but only to know, because if a woman's heart was free a man might have hope. And then, Mina, I felt it a sort of duty to tell him that there was someone. I only told him that much, and then he stood up, and he looked very strong and very grave as he took both my hands in his and said he hoped I would be happy, and that if I ever wanted a friend I must count him one of my best. Oh, Mina dear, I can't help crying; and you must excuse this letter being all blotted. Being proposed to is all very nice and all that sort of thing, but it isn't at all a happy thing when you have to see a poor fellow, whom you know loves you honestly, going away and looking all broken-hearted, and to know that, no matter what he may say at the moment, you are passing quite out of his life. My dear, I must stop here at present, I feel so miserable, though I am so happy.

Evening.

Arthur has just gone, and I feel in better spirits than when I left off, so I can go on telling you about the day. Well, my dear, number two came after lunch. He is such a nice fellow, an American from Texas, and he looks so young and so fresh that it seems almost impossible that

---

2. A two-edged, sharp-pointed surgical instrument.

he has been to so many places and has had such adventures. I sympathize with poor Desdemona when she had such a dangerous stream
poured in her ear, even by a black man.[3] I suppose that we women are
such cowards that we think a man will save us from fears, and we marry
him. I know now what I would do if I were a man and wanted to make
a girl love me. No, I don't, for there was Mr Morris telling us his stories,
and Arthur never told any, and yet—My dear, I am somewhat previous.
Mr Quincey P. Morris[4] found me alone. It seems that a man always
does find a girl alone. No, he doesn't, for Arthur tried twice to *make* a
chance, and I helping him all I could; I am not ashamed to say it now.
I must tell you beforehand that Mr Morris doesn't always speak slang
—that is to say, he never does so to strangers or before them, for he is
really well educated and has exquisite manners—but he found out that
it amused me to hear him talk American slang, and whenever I was
present, and there was no one to be shocked, he said such funny things.
I am afraid, my dear, he has to invent it all, for it fits exactly into
whatever else he has to say. But this is a way slang has. I do not know
myself if I shall ever speak slang; I do not know if Arthur likes it, as I
have never heard him use any as yet. Well, Mr Morris sat down beside
me and looked as happy and jolly as he could, but I could see all the
same that he was very nervous. He took my hand in his, and said ever
so sweetly:—
    'Miss Lucy, I know I ain't good enough to regulate the fixin's of your
little shoes, but I guess if you wait till you find a man that is you will
go join them seven young women with the lamps when you quit. Won't
you just hitch up alongside of me and let us go down the long road
together, driving in double harness?'
    Well, he did look so good-humoured and so jolly that it didn't seem
half so hard to refuse him as it did poor Dr Seward, so I said, as lightly
as I could, that I did not know anything of hitching, and that I wasn't
broken to harness at all yet. Then he said that he had spoken in a light
manner, and he hoped that if he had made a mistake in doing so on
so grave, so momentous, an occasion for him, I would forgive him. He
really did look serious when he was saying it, and I couldn't help feeling
a bit serious too—I know, Mina, you will think me a horrid flirt—
though I couldn't help feeling a sort of exultation that he was number
two in one day. And then, my dear, before I could say a word he began
pouring out a perfect torrent of love-making, laying his very heart and
soul at my feet. He looked so earnest over it that I shall never again
think that a man must be playful always, and never earnest, because
he is merry at times. I suppose he saw something in my face which

---

3. Although the racism may be Stoker's, it may also tell us something about Lucy, who here is
   telling Mina about her conversations with a man from the southern United States.
4. This Texan adventurer, on whom Lucy—and, at a key moment, Mina—bestow the fine old
   English title of *gentleman*, reflects Stoker's hopes for the United States.

checked him, for he suddenly stopped, and said with a sort of manly fervour that I could have loved him for if I had been free:—

'Lucy, you are an honest-hearted girl, I know. I should not be here speaking to you as I am now if I did not believe you clean grit, right through to the very depths of your soul. Tell me, like one good fellow to another, is there any one else that you care for? And if there is I'll never trouble you a hair's breadth again, but will be, if you will let me, a very faithful friend.'

My dear Mina, why are men so noble when we women are so little worthy of them? Here was I almost making fun of this great-hearted, true gentleman. I burst into tears—I am afraid, my dear, you will think this a very sloppy letter in more ways than one—and I really felt very badly. Why can't they let a girl marry three men,[5] or as many as want her, and save all this trouble? But this is heresy, and I must not say it. I am glad to say that, though I was crying, I was able to look into Mr Morris's brave eyes, and I told him out straight:—

'Yes, there is some one I love, though he has not told me yet that he even loves me.' I was right to speak to him so frankly, for quite a light came into his face, and he put out both his hands and took mine—I think I put them into his—and said in a hearty way:—

'That's my brave girl. It's better worth being late for a chance of winning you than being in time for any other girl in the world. Don't cry, my dear. If it's for me, I'm a hard nut to crack; and I take it standing up. If that other fellow doesn't know his happiness, well, he'd better look for it soon, or he'll have to deal with me. Little girl, your honesty and pluck have made me a friend, and that's rarer than a lover; it's more unselfish anyhow. My dear, I'm going to have a pretty lonely walk between this and Kingdom Come. Won't you give me one kiss? It'll be something to keep off the darkness now and then. You can, you know, if you like, for that other good fellow—he must be a good fellow, my dear, and a fine fellow, or you could not love him—hasn't spoken yet.' That quite won me, Mina, for it *was* brave and sweet of him, and noble, too, to a rival—wasn't it?—and he so sad; so I leant over and kissed him. He stood up with my two hands in his, and as he looked down into my face—I am afraid I was blushing very much—he said:—

'Little girl, I hold your hand, and you've kissed me, and if these things don't make us friends nothing ever will. Thank you for your sweet honesty to me, and good-bye.' He wrung my hand, and taking up his hat, went straight out of the room without looking back, without a tear or a quiver or a pause; and I am crying like a baby. Oh, why must a man like that be made unhappy when there are lots of girls about who would worship the very ground he trod on? I know I would if I were

5. *Three* is a significant number to vampires, as it is in fairy tales and Christian iconography: Dracula has three brides and three houses, he forces Jonathan to write three letters, his novel itself is divided into three sections.

free—only I don't want to be free. My dear, this quite upset me, and I feel I cannot write of happiness just at once, after telling you of it; and I don't wish to tell of the number three till it can be all happy.

Ever your loving
LUCY.

P.S.—Oh, about number three—I needn't tell you of number three, need I? Besides, it was all so confused; it seemed only a moment from his coming into the room till both his arms were round me, and he was kissing me. I am very, very happy, and I don't know what I have done to deserve it. I must only try in the future to show that I am not ungrateful for all His goodness to me in sending to me such a lover, such a husband, and such a friend.

Good-bye.

Dr Seward's Diary

(KEPT IN PHONOGRAPH.)[6]

25 April.—Ebb tide in appetite today. Cannot eat, cannot rest, so diary instead. Since my rebuff of yesterday I have a sort of empty feeling; nothing in the world seems of sufficient importance to be worth the doing . . . As I knew that the only cure for this sort of thing was work,[7] I went down amongst the patients. I picked out one who has afforded me a study of much interest. He is so quaint in his ideas, and so unlike the normal lunatic, that I have determined to understand him as well as I can. Today I seemed to get nearer than ever before to the heart of his mystery.

I questioned him more fully than I had ever done, with a view to making myself master of the facts of his hallucination. In my manner of doing it there was, I now see, something of cruelty.[8] I seemed to wish to keep him to the point of his madness—a thing which I avoid with the patients as I would the mouth of hell. (*Mem.*, under what circumstances would I *not* avoid the pit of hell?) *Omnia Romæ venalia sunt.*[9] Hell has its price! *verb. sap.*[1] If there be anything behind this

---

6. Dr. Seward's phonograph diary is even more up-to-date than Jonathan's shorthand or Mina's typewriter: Thomas Edison built the first phonograph in 1877. In *Dracula* it functions as a nineteenth-century tape recorder.

7. Like those tormented Victorian sages Carlyle and Ruskin, Stoker's characters cling to the gospel of work as a distraction from despair and even madness. Their compulsive industry in the face of the abyss shares the urgency of Christ's "I must work the works of him that sent me, while it is day: the night cometh, when no man can work" (John 9.4).

8. Though there is no evidence that Bram Stoker knew of Sigmund Freud or his work, Seward's probing at his patients' buried lives is reminiscent of his pioneering contemporary, whose *Studies on Hysteria* (co-authored with Josef Breuer) appeared in Vienna in 1895. Unlike Freud, however, Seward has no theory and he reaches no conclusions.

9. All Romans are venal (Latin).

1. *Verbum sapienti [est]:* a word to the wise is sufficient (Latin).

instinct it will be valuable to trace it afterwards *accurately*, so I had better commence to do so, therefore—

R. M. Renfield, ætat[2] 59.—Sanguine[3] temperament; great physical strength; morbidly excitable; periods of gloom ending in some fixed idea which I cannot make out. I presume that the sanguine temperament itself and the disturbing influence end in a mentally-accomplished finish; a possibly dangerous man, probably dangerous if unselfish. In selfish men caution is as secure an armour for their foes as for themselves. What I think of on this point is, when self is the fixed point the centripetal force is balanced with the centrifugal; when duty, a cause, etc., is the fixed point, the latter force is paramount, and only accident or a series of accidents can balance it.

Letter, Quincey P. Morris to Hon. Arthur Holmwood

25 May.

My dear Art,—

We've told yarns by the camp-fire in the prairies; and dressed one another's wounds after trying a landing at the Marquesas[4]; and drunk healths on the shore of Titicaca.[5] There are more yarns to be told, and other wounds to be healed, and another health to be drunk. Won't you let this be at my camp-fire tomorrow night? I have no hesitation in asking you, as I know a certain lady is engaged to a certain dinner-party, and that you are free. There will only be one other, our old pal at the Korea,[6] Jack Seward. He's coming, too, and we both want to mingle our weeps over the wine-cup, and to drink a health with all our hearts to the happiest man in all the wide world, who has won the noblest heart that God has made and the best worth winning. We promise you a hearty welcome, and a loving greeting, and a health as true as your own right hand. We shall both swear to leave you at home if you drink too deep to a certain pair of eyes. Come!

Yours, as ever and always,

QUINCEY P. MORRIS.

Telegram from Arthur Holmwood to Quincey P. Morris

26 May.

Count me in every time. I bear messages which will make both your ears tingle.

ART.

2. Age (Latin).
3. Literally, "ruddy," "bloody," "cheerful"; one of the four humors of classical medical theory whose imbalance caused disease.
4. Volcanic islands in the South Pacific, northeast of Tahiti.
5. A large lake in the Andes.
6. An imperialist hot spot in the 1890s, when Europe and the United States tried unsuccessfully to counter Japan's growing commercial control.

Chapter VI

Mina Murray's Journal

24 July. Whitby.[1]—Lucy met me at the station, looking sweeter and
lovelier than ever, and we drove up to the house at the Crescent in
which they have rooms. This is a lovely place. The little river, the Esk,
runs through a deep valley, which broadens out as it comes near the
harbour. A great viaduct runs across, with high piers, through which
the view seems somehow further away than it really is. The valley is
beautifully green, and it is so steep that when you are on the high land
on either side you look right across it, unless you are near enough to
see down. The houses of the old town—the side away from us—are all
red-roofed, and seem piled up one over the other anyhow, like the
pictures we see of Nuremberg. Right over the town is the ruin of
Whitby Abbey, which was sacked by the Danes,[2] and which is the scene
of part of 'Marmion,'[3] where the girl was built up in the wall. It is a
most noble ruin, of immense size, and full of beautiful and romantic
bits; there is a legend that a white lady[4] is seen in one of the windows.
Between it and the town there is another church, the parish one, round
which is a big graveyard, all full of tombstones. This is to my mind the
nicest spot in Whitby, for it lies right over the town, and has a full view
of the harbour and all up the bay to where the headland called Kettleness stretches out into the sea. It descends so steeply[5] over the harbour
that part of the bank has fallen away, and some of the graves have been
destroyed. In one place part of the stonework of the graves stretches out
over the sandy pathway far below. There are walks, with seats beside
them, through the churchyard; and people go and sit there all day long
looking at the beautiful view and enjoying the breeze. I shall come and
sit here very often myself and work. Indeed, I am writing now, with my
book on my knee, and listening to the talk of three old men who are
sitting beside me. They seem to do nothing all day but sit up here and
talk.

1. A port city in Yorkshire, on the North Sea coast of England; in the 1890s, a vacation resort
   where Bram Stoker spent many summers. Whitby's eerie charm is a good setting for the
   ensuing action. It shares the harsh beauty of nearby Brontë country; moreover, in Victorian
   England its best-known product was the black stone worn as part of the mourning costume
   —mourning stone, or jet—a local industry now displaced by Dracula tours.
2. Whitby Abbey was founded in 658 and, along with the surrounding district, destroyed by the
   Danes in 867. Thus, like a domestic reflection of wild Transylvania, Whitby is a vulnerable
   city that bears the scars of invasions.
3. Narrative poem written in 1808 by Walter Scott; its action is a series of betrayals. The nun
   Constance de Beverley abandons her vows to follow the knight Marmion, who betrays her.
   Constance is bricked up alive in the dungeon of Whitby Abbey; Marmion dies of grief.
4. According to one local legend, this is Lady Hilda, daughter of the abbey's founder; another
   identifies her as St. Hilda, the first abbess of Whitby. Neither version explains why she walks.
5. Whitby's precipitous ascents and descents are quaint English reiterations of the landscape of
   Transylvania and the heights and depths of Dracula's castle.

The harbour lies below me, with, on the far side, one long granite wall stretching out into the sea, with a curve outwards at the end of it, in the middle of which is a lighthouse. A heavy sea-wall runs along outside of it. On the near side, the sea-wall makes an elbow crooked inversely, and its end too has a lighthouse. Between the two piers there is a narrow opening into the harbour, which then suddenly widens.

It is nice at high tide; but when the tide is out it shoals away to nothing, and there is merely the stream of the Esk, running between banks of sand, with rocks here and there. Outside the harbour on this side there rises for about half a mile a great reef, the sharp edge of which runs straight out from behind the south lighthouse. At the end of it is a buoy with a bell, which swings in bad weather, and sends in a mournful sound on the wind. They have a legend here that when a ship is lost bells are heard out at sea.[6] I must ask the old man about this; he is coming this way . . .

He is a funny old man. He must be awfully old, for his face is all gnarled and twisted like the bark of a tree. He tells me that he is nearly a hundred, and that he was a sailor in the Greenland fishing fleet when Waterloo[7] was fought. He is, I am afraid, a very sceptical person, for when I asked him about the bells at sea and the White Lady at the Abbey he said very brusquely:—

'I wouldn't fash masel'[8] about them, miss. Them things be all wore out. Mind, I don't say that they never was, but I do say that they wasn't in my time. They be all very well for comers and trippers an' the like, but not for a nice young lady like you. Them feet-folks[9] from York and Leeds[1] that be always eatin' cured herrin's an' drinkin' tea an' lookin' out to buy cheap jet would creed aught.[2] I wonder masel' who'd be bothered tellin' lies to them—even the newspapers, which is full of fool-talk.' I thought he would be a good person to learn interesting things from, so I asked him if he would mind telling me something about the whale-fishing in the old days. He was just settling himself to begin when the clock struck six, whereupon he laboured to get up, and said:—

'I must gang ageeanwards[3] home now, miss. My granddaughter doesn't like to be kept waitin' when the tea is ready, for it takes me

---

6. After the bells at Whitby Abbey were stolen, the thief's ship foundered, but during crises, according to local legend, the sunken bells ring.
7. Wellington defeated Napoleon—an imperial foreign invader like Dracula—at the Battle of Waterloo in 1815.
8. Trouble or worry myself.
9. A native's contemptuous slang for tourists. "Feet-folks" travel on foot, as opposed to the wealthier carriage passengers.
1. Large manufacturing and industrial cities in the north of England.
2. Believe anything.
3. This highly colloquial passage means roughly: "I must return home now, miss. My granddaughter doesn't like to be kept waiting when tea is ready, and it takes me time to hobble down the stairs, for there be many of them; and, miss, the clock tells me I crave nourishment sorely."

time to crammle aboon the grees,[4] for there be a many of 'em; an', miss, I lack belly-timber sairly by the clock.'

He hobbled away, and I could see him hurrying, as well as he could, down the steps. The steps are a great feature of the place. They lead from the town up to the church; there are hundreds of them—I do not know how many—and they wind up in a delicate curve; the slope is so gentle that a horse could easily walk up and down them. I think they must originally have had something to do with the Abbey. I shall go home too. Lucy went out visiting with her mother, and as they were only duty calls, I did not go. They will be home by this.

1 August.—I came up here an hour ago with Lucy, and we had a most interesting talk with my old friend and the two others who always come and join him. He is evidently the Sir Oracle[5] of them, and I should think must have been in his time a most dictatorial person. He will not admit anything, and downfaces everybody. If he can't out-argue them he bullies them, and then takes their silence for agreement with his views. Lucy was looking sweetly pretty in her white lawn[6] frock; she has got a beautiful colour since she has been here. I noticed that the old men did not lose any time in coming up and sitting near her when we sat down. She is so sweet with old people; I think they all fell in love with her on the spot. Even my old man succumbed and did not contradict her, but gave me double share instead. I got him on the subject of the legends, and he went off at once into a sort of sermon. I must try to remember it and put it down:—

'It be all fool-talk, lock, stock, and barrel; that's what it be, an' nowt else. These bans an' wafts an' boh-ghosts an' bar-guests an' bogles an' all anent them is only fit to set bairns an' dizzy women a-belderin'. They be nowt but air-blebs! They, an' all grims an' signs an' warnin's, be all invented by parsons an' illsome beuk-bodies an' railway touters to skeer an' scunner hafflin's, an' to get folks to do somethin' that they don't other incline to. It makes me ireful to think o' them. Why, it's them that, not content with printin' lies on paper an' preachin' them out of pulpits, does want to be cuttin' them on the tombsteans. Look here all around you in what airt ye will; all them steans, holdin' up their heads as well as they can out of their pride, is acant—simply tumblin' down with the weight o' the lies wrote on them, "Here lies the body" or "Sacred to the memory" wrote on all of them, an' yet in nigh half of them there bean't no bodies at all; an' the memories of

---

4. Stairs. Swales is referring to the dramatic stone steps that curve up Whitby's East Cliff from the pier to the churchyard of St. Mary's Church, adjacent to Whitby Abbey. In reality there are 199 steps, not the hundreds that Mina imagines.
5. A self-important authority. Shakespeare makes reference to Sir Oracle in *The Merchant of Venice* 1.1.
6. A light cotton or linen fabric of very fine weave. White lawn is perpetually associated with Lucy.

them bean't cared a pinch of snuff about, much less sacred. Lies all of them, nothin' but lies of one kind or another! My gog, but it'll be a quare scowderment at the Day of Judgment when they come tumblin' up here in their deathsarks, all jouped together an' tryin' to drag their tombsteans with them to prove how good they was; some of them trimmlin' and ditherin', with their hands that dozzened an' slippy from lyin' in the sea that they can't even keep their grup o' them.'[7]

I could see from the old fellow's self-satisfied air and the way in which he looked round for the approval of his cronies that he was 'showing off,' so I put in a word to keep him going:—

'Oh, Mr Swales, you can't be serious. Surely these tombstones are not all wrong?'

'Yabblins![8] There may be a poorish few not wrong, savin' where they make out the people too good; for there be folk that do think a balm-bowl be like the sea, if only it be their own. The whole thing be only lies. Now look you here; you come here a stranger, an' you see this kirk-garth.' I nodded, for I thought it better to assent, though I did not quite understand his dialect. I knew it had something to do with the church. He went on: 'And you consate that all these steans be aboon folk that be happed here, snod an' snog?' I assented again. 'Then that be just where the lie comes in. Why, there be scores of these lay-beds that be toom as old Dun's 'bacca-box on Friday night.' He nudged one of his companions, and they all laughed. 'And my gog! how could they be otherwise? Look at that one, the aftest abaft the bier-bank; read it!' I went over and read:—

'Edward Spencelagh, master mariner, murdered by pirates off the

---

7. Mr. Swales's irreverent, even ghoulish speech deserves full translation: "It's all fool's talk, lock, stock, and barrel, and nothing else. These curses and ghosts and apparitions and bogies and hobgoblins and all such is only fit to set children and dizzy women a-blubbering. They're nothing but air-bubbles! They, and all spooks and signs and warnings, are all invented by parsons and sour pedants and railway touts to scare idiots and to force folks to do things they don't want to. It irritates me to think about them. Why, it's they that, not content with writing lies and preaching them from pulpits, choose to cut them on tombstones. Look here all around you, wherever you like; all these tombstones, holding up their heads as proudly as they can, are tilting—simply tumbling down with the weight of lies written on them, 'Here lies the body' or 'Sacred to the memory' written on all of them, and yet in nearly half there are no bodies at all; and their memories aren't worth a pinch of snuff, much less anything sacred. Lies all of them, nothing but lies of one kind or another! My God, but it'll be a mess at the Day of Judgment when they come tumbling up here in their shrouds, all jumbled together and trying to drag their tombstones with them to prove how good they were; some shaking and trembling, with their hands so withered and slippery from lying in the sea that they can't even hold their grip."

Not only Mr. Swales's preoccupations, but even his name, associate him with living death. *The English Dialect Dictionary* (1898) provides a revealing North Yorkshire definition of the verb "swale": "to consume or waste away; to melt or gutter as a candle in a draught."

8. More loose translations from Mr. Swales: "Blather! There may be a poor few not wrong, except for making people too good; for some think a chamber-pot, if it's their own, is like the sea. It's all lies. Now look here; you come a stranger, and you see this churchyard . . . and you imagine all these stones cover folk who are wrapped up snug and tidy here? . . . That's just where the lie comes in. Why, scores of these graves are as empty as old Dun's tobacco-box on Friday night. . . . And my God! how could they be otherwise? Look at that one, the farthest past the churchyard path; read it!"

coast of Andres, April, 1854, æt. 30.' When I came back Mr Swales went on:—

'Who brought him home, I wonder, to hap him here? Murdered off the coast of Andres! an' you consated his body lay under! Why, I could name ye a dozen whose bones lie in the Greenland seas above'—he pointed northwards—'or where the currents may have drifted them. There be the steans around ye. Ye can, with your young eyes, read the small-print of the lies from here. This Braithwaite Lowrey—I knew his father, lost in the *Lively* off Greenland in '20; or Andrew Woodhouse, drowned in the same seas in 1777; or John Paxton, drowned off Cape Farewell a year later; or old John Rawlings, whose grandfather sailed with me, drowned in the Gulf of Finland in '50. Do ye think that all these men will have to make a rush to Whitby when the trumpet sounds? I have me antherums aboot it![9] I tell ye that when they got here they'd be jommlin'[1] an' jostlin' one another that way that it 'ud be like a fight up on the ice in the old days, when we'd be at one another from daylight to dark, an' tryin' to tie up our cuts by the light of the aurora borealis.' This was evidently local pleasantry, for the old man cackled over it, and his cronies joined in with gusto.

'But,' I said, 'surely you are not quite correct, for you start on the assumption that all the poor people, or their spirits, will have to take their tombstones with them on the Day of Judgment. Do you think that will be really necessary?'

'Well, what else be they tombsteans for? Answer me that, miss!'

'To please their relatives,[2] I suppose.'

'To please their relatives, you suppose!' This he said with intense scorn. 'How will it pleasure their relatives to know that lies is wrote over them, and that everybody in the place knows that they be lies?' He pointed to a stone at our feet which had been laid down as a slab, on which the seat was rested, close to the edge of the cliff. 'Read the lines on that thruff-stean,'[3] he said. The letters were upside down to me from where I sat, but Lucy was more opposite to them, so she leant over and read:—

'Sacred to the memory of George Canon, who died, in the hope of a glorious resurrection, on July 29, 1873, falling from the rocks at Kettleness. This tomb is erected by his sorrowing mother to her dearly beloved son. "He was the only son of his mother, and she was a widow."' 'Really, Mr Swales, I don't see anything very funny in that!' She spoke her comment very gravely and somewhat severely.

'Ye don't see aught funny! Ha! ha! But that's because ye don't gawm[4]

9. I doubt it!
1. Shoving.
2. Like her fiancé, Jonathan, Mina begins with a sensibly secular interpretation of death and burial rituals.
3. A table-shaped tombstone, extending over the length of the grave.
4. Know.

the sorrowin' mother was a hell-cat that hated him because he was acrewk'd[5]—a regular lamiter[6] he was—an' he hated her so that he committed suicide in order that she mightn't get an insurance she put on his life. He blew nigh the top of his head off with an old musket that they had for scarin' the crows with. 'Twarn't for crows then, for it brought the clegs and the dowps[7] to him. That's the way he fell off the rocks. And, as to hopes of a glorious resurrection, I've often heard him say masel' that he hoped he'd go to hell, for his mother was so pious that she'd be sure to go to heaven, an' he didn't wan't to addle[8] where she was. Now isn't that stean at any rate'—he hammered it with his stick as he spoke—'a pack of lies? and won't it make Gabriel keckle[9] when Geordie comes pantin' up the grees with the tombstean balanced on his hump, and asks it to be took as evidence!'

I did not know what to say, but Lucy turned the conversation as she said, rising up:—

'Oh, why did you tell us of this? It is my favourite seat, and I cannot leave it; and now I find I must go on sitting over the grave of a suicide.'[1]

'That won't harm ye, my pretty; an' it may make poor Geordie gladsome to have so trim a lass sittin' on his lap. That won't hurt ye. Why, I've sat here off an' on for nigh twenty years past, an' it hasn't done me no harm. Don't ye fash about them as lies under ye, or that doesn' lie there either! It'll be time for ye to be getting scart when ye see the tombsteans all run away with, and the place as bare as a stubble-field. There's the clock, an' I must gang. My service to ye, ladies!' And off he hobbled.

Lucy and I sat a while, and it was all so beautiful before us that we took hands as we sat; and she told me all over again about Arthur and their coming marriage. That made me just a little heart-sick, for I haven't heard from Jonathan for a whole month.

The same day.—I came up here alone, for I am very sad. There was no letter for me. I hope there cannot be anything the matter with Jonathan. The clock has just struck nine. I see the lights scattered all over the town, sometimes in rows where the streets are, and sometimes singly; they run right up the Esk and die away in the curve of the valley. To my left the view is cut off by a black line of roof of the old house next the Abbey. The sheep and lambs are bleating in the fields away behind me, and there is a clatter of a donkey's hoofs up the paved road below. The band on the pier is playing a harsh waltz in good time, and further along the quay there is a Salvation Army meeting in a back

---

5. Crooked, twisted.
6. Lame one, cripple.
7. Flies and carrion crows.
8. Collect earnings.
9. Chuckle.
1. In some folklore accounts, suicides become vampires. Stoker adapts this legend to make the suicide's grave a convenient home for Dracula when he first lands in England.

street. Neither of the bands hears the other, but up here I hear and see them both. I wonder where Jonathan is and if he is thinking of me! I wish he were here.

Dr Seward's Diary

5 June.—The case of Renfield grows more interesting the more I get to understand the man. He has certain qualities very largely developed: selfishness, secrecy, and purpose. I wish I could get at what is the object of the latter. He seems to have some settled scheme of his own, but what it is I do not yet know. His redeeming quality is a love of animals, though, indeed, he has such curious turns in it that I sometimes imagine he is only abnormally cruel. His pets are of odd sorts. Just now his hobby is catching flies. He has at present such a quantity that I have had myself to expostulate. To my astonishment, he did not break out into a fury, as I expected, but took the matter in simple seriousness. He thought for a moment, and then said: 'May I have three days? I shall clear them away.' Of course, I said that would do. I must watch him.

18 June.—He has turned his mind now to spiders, and has got several very big fellows in a box. He keeps feeding them with his flies, and the number of the latter is becoming sensibly diminished, although he has used half his food in attracting more flies from outside to his room.

1 July.—His spiders are now becoming as great a nuisance as his flies, and today I told him that he must get rid of them. He looked very sad at this, so I said that he must clear out some of them, at all events. He cheerfully acquiesced in this, and I gave him the same time as before for reduction. He disgusted me much while with him, for when a horrid blow-fly, bloated with some carrion food, buzzed into the room, he caught it, held it exultingly for a few moments between his finger and thumb, and, before I knew what he was going to do, put it in his mouth and ate it. I scolded him for it, but he argued quietly that it was very good and very wholesome; that it was life, strong life, and gave life to him. This gave me an idea, or the rudiment of one. I must watch how he gets rid of his spiders. He has evidently some deep problem in his mind, for he keeps a little notebook in which he is always jotting down something. Whole pages of it are filled with masses of figures, generally single numbers added up in batches, and then the totals added in batches again, as though he were 'focussing' some account, as the auditors put it.

8 July.—There is a method in his madness, and the rudimentary idea in my mind is growing. It will be a whole idea soon, and then, oh, unconscious cerebration![2] you will have to give the wall to[3] your con-

---

2. A concept first articulated by Victorian physician-phrenologists in 1842. Like the Freudian unconscious it anticipates, unconscious cerebration valued dreams, myth-making, and irrationality as revelations of the self.
3. Defer to.

scious brother. I kept away from my friend for a few days, so that I might notice if there were any change. Things remain as they were except that he has parted with some of his pets and got a new one. He has managed to get a sparrow, and has already partially tamed it. His means of taming is simple, for already the spiders have diminished. Those that do remain, however, are well fed, for he still brings in the flies by tempting them with his food.

19 July.—We are progressing. My friend has now a whole colony of sparrows, and his flies and spiders are almost obliterated. When I came in he ran to me and said he wanted to ask me a great favour—a very, very great favour; and as he spoke he fawned on me like a dog. I asked him what it was, and he said, with a sort of rapture in his voice and bearing:—

'A kitten, a nice little, sleek, playful kitten, that I can play with, and teach, and feed—and feed—and feed!' I was not unprepared for this request, for I had noticed how his pets went on increasing in size and vivacity, but I did not care that his pretty family of tame sparrows should be wiped out in the same manner as the flies and the spiders; so I said I would see about it, and asked him if he would not rather have a cat than a kitten. His eagerness betrayed him as he answered:—

'Oh yes, I would like a cat! I only asked for a kitten lest you should refuse me a cat. No one would refuse me a kitten, would they?' I shook my head, and said that at present I feared it would not be possible, but that I would see about it. His face fell, and I could see a warning of danger in it, for there was a sudden fierce, sidelong look[4] which meant killing. The man is an undeveloped homicidal maniac. I shall test him with his present craving and see how it will work out; then I shall know more.

10 p.m.—I have visited him again and found him sitting in a corner brooding. When I came in he threw himself on his knees before me and implored me to let him have a cat; that his salvation depended upon it. I was firm, however, and told him that he could not have it, whereupon he went without a word, and sat down, gnawing his fingers, in the corner where I had found him. I shall see him in the morning early.

20 July.—Visited Renfield very early, before the attendant went his rounds. Found him up and humming a tune. He was spreading out his sugar, which he had saved, in the window, and was manifestly beginning his fly-catching again; and beginning it cheerfully and with a good grace. I looked around for his birds, and not seeing them, asked him where they were. He replied, without turning round, that they had all flown away. There were a few feathers about the room and on his

---

4. Renfield expresses his madness in stylized theatrical attitudes.

pillow a drop of blood. I said nothing, but went and told the keeper to report to me if there were anything odd about him during the day.

11 a.m.—The attendant has just been to me to say that Renfield has been very sick and has disgorged a whole lot of feathers. 'My belief is, doctor,' he said, 'that he has eaten his birds, and that he just took and ate them raw!'

11 p.m.—I gave Renfield a strong opiate tonight, enough to make even him sleep, and took away his pocket-book[5] to look at it. The thought that has been buzzing about my brain lately is complete, and the theory proved. My homicidal maniac is of a peculiar kind. I shall have to invent a new classification for him, and call him a zoophagous (life-eating) maniac; what he desires is to absorb as many lives as he can, and he has laid himself out to achieve it in a cumulative way. He gave many flies to one spider and many spiders to one bird, and then wanted a cat to eat the many birds. What would have been his later steps? It would almost be worth while to complete the experiment. It might be done if there were only a sufficient cause. Men sneered at vivisection, and yet look at its results today! Why not advance science in its most difficult and vital aspect—the knowledge of the brain? Had I even the secret of one such mind—did I hold the key to the fancy of even one lunatic—I might advance my own branch of science to a pitch compared with which Burdon-Sanderson's physiology or Ferrier's brain-knowledge[6] would be as nothing. If only there were a sufficient cause! I must not think too much of this, or I may be tempted; a good cause might turn the scale with me, for may not I too be of an exceptional brain, congenitally?

How well the man reasoned; lunatics always do within their own scope. I wonder at how many lives he values a man, or if at only one. He has closed the account most accurately, and today begun a new record. How many of us begin a new record with each day of our lives?

To me it seems only yesterday that my whole life ended with my new hope, and that truly I began a new record. So it will be until the Great Recorder sums me up and closes my ledger account with a balance to profit or loss. Oh, Lucy, Lucy, I cannot be angry with you, nor can I be angry with my friend whose happiness is yours; but I must only wait on hopeless and work. Work! work!

If I only could have as strong a cause as my poor mad friend there, a good, unselfish cause to make me work, that would be indeed happiness.

5. Small notebook.
6. Burdon-Sanderson (1828–1905), an English physician, first measured the electrical impulses that come from the heart. David Ferrier (1843–1928) was a physician who conducted experiments on the brain structure of primates. Antivivisectionists criticized both Burdon-Sanderson and Ferrier; the latter was prosecuted, though eventually acquitted, under the Cruelty to Animals Act of 1876.

Mina Murray's Journal

26 July.—I am anxious, and it soothes me to express myself here; it is like whispering to one's self and listening at the same time. And there is also something about the shorthand symbols that makes it different from writing. I am unhappy about Lucy and about Jonathan. I had not heard from Jonathan for some time, and was very concerned; but yesterday dear Mr Hawkins, who is always so kind, sent me a letter from him. I had written asking him if he had heard, and he said the enclosed had just been received. It is only a line dated from Castle Dracula, and says that he is just starting for home. That is not like Jonathan; I do not understand it, and it makes me uneasy. Then, too, Lucy, although she is so well, has lately taken to her old habit of walking in her sleep. Her mother has spoken to me about it, and we have decided that I am to lock the door of our room every night. Mrs Westenra has got an idea that sleep-walkers always go out on roofs of houses and along the edges of cliffs, and then get suddenly wakened and fall over with a despairing cry that echoes all over the place. Poor dear, she is naturally anxious about Lucy, and she tells me that her husband, Lucy's father, had the same habit; that he would get up in the night and dress himself and go out, if he were not stopped. Lucy is to be married in the autumn, and she is already planning out her dresses and how her house is to be arranged. I sympathize with her, for I do the same, only Jonathan and I will start in life in a very simple way, and shall have to try to make both ends meet. Mr Holmwood—he is the Hon. Arthur Holmwood, only son of Lord Godalming[7]—is coming up here very shortly—as soon as he can leave town, for his father is not very well, and I think dear Lucy is counting the moments till he comes. She wants to take him up to the seat on the churchyard cliff and show him the beauty of Whitby. I daresay it is the waiting which disturbs her; she will be all right when he arrives.

27 July.—No news from Jonathan. I am getting quite uneasy about him, though why I should I do not know; but I *do* wish that he would write, if it were only a single line. Lucy walks more than ever, and each night I am awakened by her moving about the room. Fortunately, the weather is so hot that she cannot get cold; but still the anxiety and the perpetually being wakened is beginning to tell on me, and I am getting nervous and wakeful myself. Thank God, Lucy's health keeps up. Mr Holmwood has been suddenly called to Ring to see his father, who has been taken seriously ill. Lucy frets at the postponement of seeing him, but it does not touch her looks; she is a trifle stouter, and her cheeks are a lovely rose pink. She has lost that anæmic look which she had. I pray it will all last.

---

7. This is the first time we learn that, unlike all the male characters but Dracula, Lucy's fiancé is a titled aristocrat.

3 August.—Another week gone, and no news from Jonathan, not even
to Mr Hawkins, from whom I have heard. Oh, I do hope he is not ill.
He surely would have written. I look at that last letter of his, but somehow it does not satisfy me. It does not read like him, and yet it is his
writing. There is no mistake of that. Lucy has not walked much in her
sleep the last week, but there is an odd concentration about her which
I do not understand; even in her sleep she seems to be watching me.
She tries the door, and finding it locked, goes about the room searching
for the key.

6 August.—Another three days, and no news. This suspense is getting
dreadful. If I only knew where to write to or where to go to, I should
feel easier; but no one has heard a word of Jonathan since that last
letter. I must only pray to God for patience. Lucy is more excitable
than ever, but is otherwise well. Last night was very threatening, and
the fishermen say that we are in for a storm. I must try to watch it and
learn the weather signs.[8] Today is a grey day, and the sun as I write is
hidden in thick clouds, high over Kettleness. Everything is grey—except
the green grass, which seems like emerald amongst it; grey earthy rock;
grey clouds, tinged with the sunburst at the far edge, hang over the
grey sea, into which the sand-points stretch like grey fingers. The sea
is tumbling in over the shallows and the sandy flats with a roar, muffled
in the sea-mists drifting inland. The horizon is lost in a grey mist. All
is vastness; the clouds are piled up like giant rocks, and there is a 'brool'[9]
over the sea that sounds like some presage of doom. Dark figures are
on the beach here and there, sometimes half shrouded in the mist, and
seem 'men like trees walking.'[1] The fishing-boats are racing for home,
and rise and dip in the ground swell as they sweep into the harbour,
bending to the scuppers.[2] Here comes old Mr Swales. He is making
straight for me, and I can see, by the way he lifts his hat, that he wants
to talk . . .

I have been quite touched by the change in the poor old man. When
he sat down beside me, he said in a very gentle way:—

'I want to say something to you, miss.' I could see he was not at ease,
so I took his poor old wrinkled hand in mine and asked him to speak
fully; so he said, leaving his hand in mine:—

'I'm afraid, my deary, that I must have shocked you by all the wicked
things I've been sayin' about the dead, and suchlike, for weeks past; but
I didn't mean them, and I want ye to remember that when I'm gone.

8. Characteristically, Mina turns even her anxiety into an exercise in self-improvement.
9. According to the *OED*, "A low deep humming sound; a murmur"; evidently a variation on
   the English dialect word *bru[le]*, meaning a bellowing, lowing sound.
1. The walking forest echoes the eerie march of Birnam Wood up Dunsinane Hill in Shakespeare's *Macbeth*. See also Mark 8.24, in which a blind man partially healed by Christ looks
   up and says, "I see men as trees, walking." Mina's biblical echo is one of many associations
   of Dracula with a great illuminating divinity.
2. According to the *OED*, "an opening in a ship's side on a level with the deck to allow water
   to run away."

We aud folks that be daffled, and with one foot abaft the krok-hooal, don't altogether like to think of it, and we don't want to feel scart of it;[3] an' that's why I've took to makin' light of it, so that I'd cheer up my own heart a bit. But, Lord love ye, miss, I ain't afraid of dyin', not a bit; only I don't want to die if I can help it. My time must be nigh at hand now, for I be aud, and a hundred years is too much for any man to expect; and I'm so nigh it that the Aud Man is already whettin' his scythe. Ye see, I can't get out o' the habit of caffin'[4] about it all at once; the chafts[5] will wag as they be used to. Some day soon the Angel of Death will sound his trumpet for me. But don't ye dooal an' greet,[6] my deary!'—for he saw that I was crying—'if he should come this very night I'd not refuse to answer his call. For life be, after all, only a waitin' for somethin' else than what we're doin'; and death be all that we can rightly depend on. But I'm content, for it's comin' to me, my deary, and comin' quick. It may be comin' while we be lookin' and wonderin'. Maybe it's in that wind out over the sea that's bringin' with it loss and wreck, and sore distress, and sad hearts. Look! look!' he cried suddenly. 'There's something in that wind and in the hoast beyont that sounds, and looks, and tastes, and smells like death. It's in the air; I feel it comin'. Lord, make me answer cheerful when my call comes!' He held up his arms devoutly, and raised his hat. His mouth moved as though he were praying. After a few minutes' silence, he got up, shook hands with me, and blessed me, and said goodbye, and hobbled off. It all touched me, and upset me very much.

I was glad when the coastguard came along, with his spy-glass under his arm. He stopped to talk with me, as he always does, but all the time kept looking at a strange ship.

'I can't make her out,' he said; 'she's a Russian, by the look of her; but she's knocking about in the queerest way.[7] She doesn't know her mind a bit; she seems to see the storm coming, but can't decide whether to run up north in the open, or to put in here. Look there again! She is steered mighty strangely, for she doesn't mind the hand on the wheel; changes about with every puff of wind. We'll hear more of her before this time tomorrow.'

---

3. "We old folk that are addled, with one foot in the grave, don't much like to think of it, and we don't want to be scared of it."
4. Chafing.
5. Jaws.
6. Mourn and weep.
7. As in Coleridge's *The Rime of the Ancient Mariner* (1798), whose enchanted ship is similarly manned by the dead.

Chapter VII

Cutting[1] from the Dailygraph, 8 August

(PASTED IN MINA MURRAY'S JOURNAL)

From a Correspondent

Whitby.

One of the greatest and suddenest storms on record has just been experienced here, with results both strange and unique. The weather had been somewhat sultry, but not to any degree uncommon in the month of August. Saturday evening was as fine as was ever known, and the great body of holiday-makers laid out yesterday for visits to Mulgrave Woods, Robin Hood's Bay, Rig Mill, Runswick, Staithes,[2] and the various trips in the neighbourhood of Whitby. The steamers *Emma* and *Scarborough* made trips up and down the coast, and there was an unusual amount of 'tripping' both to and from Whitby. The day was unusually fine till the afternoon, when some of the gossips who frequent the East Cliff churchyard, and from that commanding eminence watch the wide sweep of sea visible to the north and east, called attention to a sudden show of 'mares'-tails'[3] high in the sky to the north-west. The wind was then blowing from the south-west in the mild degree which in barometrical language is ranked 'No. 2: light breeze.' The coastguard on duty at once made report, and one old fisherman, who for more than half a century has kept watch on weather signs from the East Cliff, foretold in an emphatic manner the coming of a sudden storm. The approach of sunset was so very beautiful, so grand in its masses of splendidly-coloured clouds, that there was quite an assemblage on the walk along the cliff in the old churchyard to enjoy the beauty. Before the sun dipped below the black mass of Kettleness, standing boldly athwart the western sky, its downward way was marked by myriad clouds of every sunset-colour—flame, purple, pink, green, violet, and all the tints of gold; with here and there masses not large, but of seemingly absolute blackness, in all sorts of shapes, as well outlined as colossal silhouettes. The experience was not lost on the painters, and doubtless some of the sketches of the 'Prelude to the Great Storm' will grace the R.A. and R.I.[4] walls in May next. More than one captain made up his mind then and there that his 'cobble' or his 'mule,' as they term the different classes of boats, would remain in the harbour till the storm

---

1. British idiom for (newspaper) clipping.
2. Picturesque towns and beauty spots in the environs of Whitby.
3. Long straight streaks of clouds, supposed to foreshadow a storm.
4. Royal Academy and Royal Institute. This spectrum of colors and indeterminate shapes may be Stoker's evocation of the acclaimed storm paintings of Joseph M. W. Turner (1775–1851), which the Whitby painters would be likely to copy.

had passed. The wind fell away entirely during the evening, and at midnight there was a dead calm, a sultry heat, and that prevailing intensity which, on the approach of thunder, affects persons of a sensitive nature. There were but few lights in sight at sea, for even the coasting steamers, which usually 'hug' the shore so closely, kept well to seaward, and but few fishing-boats were in sight. The only sail noticeable was a foreign schooner with all sails set, which was seemingly going westwards. The foolhardiness or ignorance of her officers was a prolific theme for comment whilst she remained in sight, and efforts were made to signal her to reduce sail in face of her danger. Before the night shut down she was seen with sails idly flapping as she gently rolled on the undulating swell of the sea,

As idle as a painted ship upon a painted ocean.[5]

Shortly before ten o'clock the stillness of the air grew quite oppressive, and the silence was so marked that the bleating of a sheep inland or the barking of a dog in the town was distinctly heard, and the band on the pier, with its lively French air, was like a discord in the great harmony of nature's silence. A little after midnight came a strange sound from over the sea, and high overhead the air began to carry a strange, faint, hollow booming.

Then without warning the tempest broke. With a rapidity which, at the time, seemed incredible, and even afterwards is impossible to realize, the whole aspect of nature at once became convulsed. The waves rose in growing fury, each overtopping its fellow, till in a very few minutes the lately glassy sea was like a roaring and devouring monster. White-crested waves beat madly on the level sands and rushed up the shelving cliffs; others broke over the piers, and with their spume swept the lanthorns[6] of the lighthouses which rise from the end of either pier of Whitby Harbour. The wind roared like thunder, and blew with such force that it was with difficulty that even strong men kept their feet, or clung with grim clasp to the iron stanchions.[7] It was found necessary to clear the entire piers from the mass of onlookers, or else the fatalities of the night would have been increased manifold. To add to the difficulties and dangers of the time, masses of sea-fog came drifting inland—white, wet clouds, which swept by in ghostly fashion, so dank and damp and cold that it needed but little effort of imagination to think that the spirits of those lost at sea were touching their living brethren with the clammy hands of death, and many a one shuddered as the wreaths of sea-mist swept by. At times the mist cleared, and the

5. *The Rime of the Ancient Mariner,* part II, lines 115–18: "Day after day, day after day, / We stuck, nor breath nor motion; / As idle as a painted ship / Upon a painted ocean." This famous quatrain is ominous for Dracula's ship: in Coleridge's poem, Death and his vampire-like mistress, "the Nightmare Life-in-Death," are about to capture the becalmed vessel.
6. Lanterns.
7. Pillars supporting the decks and other heavy portions of ships.

sea for some distance could be seen in the glare of the lightning, which now came thick and fast, followed by such sudden peals of thunder that the whole sky overhead seemed trembling under the shock of the footsteps of the storm. Some of the scenes thus revealed were of immeasurable grandeur and of absorbing interest—the sea, running mountains high, threw skywards with each wave mighty masses of white foam, which the tempest seemed to snatch at and whirl away into space; here and there a fishing-boat, with a rag of sail, running madly for shelter before the blast; now and again the white wings of a storm-tossed seabird. On the summit of the East Cliff the new searchlight was ready for experiment, but had not yet been tried. The officers in charge of it got it into working order, and in the pauses of the inrushing mist swept with it the surface of the sea. Once or twice its service was most effective, as when a fishing-boat, with gunwale[8] under water, rushed into the harbour, able, by the guidance of the sheltering light, to avoid the danger of dashing against the piers. As each boat achieved the safety of the port there was a shout of joy from the mass of people on shore, a shout which for a moment seemed to cleave the gale and was then swept away in its rush. Before long the searchlight discovered some distance away a schooner with all sails set, apparently the same vessel which had been noticed earlier in the evening. The wind had by this time backed to the east, and there was a shudder amongst the watchers on the cliff as they realized the terrible danger in which she now was. Between her and the port lay the great flat reef on which so many good ships have from time to time suffered, and, with the wind blowing from its present quarter, it would be quite impossible that she should fetch the entrance of the harbour. It was now nearly the hour of high tide,[9] but the waves were so great that in their troughs the shallows of the shore were almost visible, and the schooner, with all sails set, was rushing with such speed that, in the words of one old salt, 'she must fetch up somewhere, if it was only in hell.' Then came another rush of seafog, greater than any hitherto—a mass of dank mist, which seemed to close on all things like a grey pall, and left available to men only the organ of hearing, for the roar of the tempest, and the crash of the thunder, and the booming of the mighty billows came through the damp oblivion even louder than before. The rays of the searchlight were kept fixed on the harbour mouth across the East Pier, where the shock was expected, and men waited breathless. The wind suddenly shifted to the north-east, and the remnant of the sea-fog melted in the blast; and then, *mirabile dictu*,[1] between the piers, leaping from wave to wave as it rushed at headlong speed, swept the strange schooner

8. The upper part of a ship or boat.
9. Since, according to the rules of folklore, Dracula cannot cross running water, he ingeniously creates weather conditions that allow him to land.
1. Wonderful to tell (Latin).

before the blast, with all sail set, and gained the safety of the harbour. The searchlight followed her, and a shudder ran through all who saw her, for lashed to the helm was a corpse, with drooping head, which swung horribly to and fro at each motion of the ship. No other form could be seen on deck at all. A great awe came on all as they realized that the ship, as if by a miracle, had found the harbour, unsteered save by the hand of a dead man! However, all took place more quickly than it takes to write these words. The schooner paused not, but rushing across the harbour, pitched herself on that accumulation of sand and gravel washed by many tides and many storms into the south-east corner of the pier jutting under the East Cliff, known locally as Tate Hill Pier.

There was of course a considerable concussion as the vessel drove up on the sand heap. Every spar, rope, and stay was strained, and some of the 'top-hammer'[2] came crashing down. But, strangest of all, the very instant the shore was touched, an immense dog sprang up on deck from below, as if shot up by the concussion, and running forward, jumped from the bow on the sand. Making straight for the steep cliff, where the churchyard hangs over the laneway to the East Pier so steeply that some of the flat tombstones—'thruff-steans' or 'through-stones,' as they call them in the Whitby vernacular—actually project over where the sustaining cliff has fallen away, it disappeared in the darkness, which seemed intensified just beyond the focus of the searchlight.

It so happened that there was no one at the moment on Tate Hill Pier, as all those whose houses are in close proximity were either in bed or were out on the heights above. Thus the coastguard on duty on the eastern side of the harbour, who at once ran down to the little pier, was the first to climb on board. The men working the searchlight, after scouring the entrance of the harbour without seeing anything, then turned the light on the derelict and kept it there. The coastguard ran aft, and when he came beside the wheel, bent over to examine it, and recoiled at once as though under some sudden emotion. This seemed to pique general curiosity, and quite a number of people began to run. It is a good way round from the West Cliff by the Drawbridge to Tate Hill Pier, but your correspondent is a fairly good runner, and came well ahead of the crowd. When I arrived, however, I found already assembled on the pier a crowd, whom the coastguard and police refused to allow to come on board. By the courtesy of the chief boatman, I was, as your correspondent, permitted to climb on deck, and was one of a small group who saw the dead seaman whilst actually lashed to the wheel.

It was no wonder that the coastguard was surprised, or even awed, for not often can such a sight have been seen. The man was simply fastened by his hands, tied one over the other, to a spoke of the wheel.

2. Weight on the upper portion of the ship, such as the upper masts, sails, and rigging.

Between the inner hand and the wood was a crucifix, the set of beads on which it was fastened being around both wrists and wheel, and all kept fast by the binding cords. The poor fellow may have been seated at one time, but the flapping and buffeting of the sails had worked through the rudder of the wheel and dragged him to and fro, so that the cords with which he was tied had cut the flesh to the bone. Accurate note was made of the state of things, and a doctor—Surgeon J. M. Caffyn, of 33, East Elliot Place—who came immediately after me, declared, after making examination, that the man must have been dead for quite two days. In his pocket was a bottle, carefully corked, empty save for a little roll of paper, which proved to be the addendum to the log. The coastguard said the man must have tied up his own hands, fastening the knots with his teeth. The fact that a coastguard was the first on board may save some complications, later on, in the Admiralty Court; for coastguards cannot claim the salvage which is the right of the first civilian entering on a derelict. Already, however, the legal tongues are wagging, and one young law student is loudly asserting that the rights of the owner are already completely sacrificed, his property being held in contravention of the statutes of mortmain,[3] since the tiller, as emblemship, if not proof, of delegated possession, is held in a *dead hand*. It is needless to say that the dead steersman has been reverently removed from the place where he held his honourable watch and ward till death—a steadfastness as noble as that of the young Casabianca[4]— and placed in the mortuary to await inquest.

Already the sudden storm is passing, and its fierceness is abating; the crowds are scattering homeward, and the sky is beginning to redden over the Yorkshire wolds.[5] I shall send, in time for your next issue, further details of the derelict ship which found her way so miraculously into harbour in the storm.

Whitby.

9 August.—The sequel to the strange arrival of the derelict in the storm last night is almost more startling than the thing itself. It turns out that the schooner is a Russian from Varna, and is called the *Demeter*.[6] She is almost entirely in ballast of silver sand, with only a small amount of cargo—a number of great wooden boxes filled with mould. This cargo was consigned to a Whitby solicitor, Mr S. F. Billington, of 7, The Crescent, who this morning went aboard and formally took possession

3. Literally, "dead hand"; in law, ownership in perpetuity of real estate by institutions like churches that cannot transfer or sell it. Thus, like much of *Dracula*, a ghoulish pun based on a prosaic precept of contemporary life.
4. The stalwart boy who stood on the burning deck in Felicia Hemans's famous poem (1827).
5. Open, elevated stretches of land.
6. Demeter was the Greek goddess of fertility whose daughter, Persephone, was abducted by the lord of the Underworld. Persephone managed to return to her mother for two-thirds of each year, but each time she re-enters Hades, Demeter mourns, nature dies and winter falls.

of the goods consigned to him. The Russian consul,[7] too, acting for the
charter-party, took formal possession of the ship, and paid all harbour
dues, etc. Nothing is talked about here today except the strange coincidence; the officials of the Board of Trade have been most exacting
in seeing that every compliance has been made with existing regula-
tions. As the matter is to be a 'nine days' wonder,' they are evidently
determined that there shall be no cause of after complaint. A good deal
of interest was abroad concerning the dog which landed when the ship
struck, and more than a few of the members of the SPCA, which is
very strong in Whitby, have tried to befriend the animal. To the general
disappointment, however, it was not to be found; it seems to have disappeared entirely from the town. It may be that it was frightened and
made its way on to the moors, where it is still hiding in terror. There
are some who look with dread on such a possibility, lest later on it
should in itself become a danger, for it is evidently a fierce brute. Early
this morning a large dog, a half-bred mastiff belonging to a coal merchant close to Tate Hill Pier, was found dead in the roadway opposite
its master's yard. It had been fighting, and manifestly had had a savage
opponent, for its throat was torn away, and its belly was slit open as if
with a savage claw.

Later.—By the kindness of the Board of Trade inspector, I have been
permitted to look over the log-book of the *Demeter*, which was in order
up to within three days, but contained nothing of special interest except
as to facts of missing men. The greater interest, however, is with regard
to the paper found in the bottle, which was today produced at the
inquest; and a more strange narrative than the two between them unfold it has not been my lot to come across. As there is no motive for
concealment, I am permitted to use them, and accordingly send you a
rescript, simply omitting technical details of seamanship and super-
cargo. It almost seems as though the captain had been seized with some
kind of mania before he had got well into blue water, and that this had
developed persistently throughout the voyage. Of course my statement
must be taken *cum grano*,[8] since I am writing from the dictation of a
clerk of the Russian consul, who kindly translated for me, time being
short.

---

7. The ship is registered as Russian, though the Turks had ceded Varna to independent Bulgaria
   in 1878.
8. With a grain [of salt] (Latin).

Log of the Demeter

On 6 July we finished taking in cargo, silver sand and boxes of earth. At noon set sail. East wind, fresh. Crew, five hands, . . . two mates, cook, and myself (captain).

On 11 July at dawn entered Bosphorus.[9] Boarded by Turkish Customs officers. Backsheesh.[1] All correct. Under way at 4 p.m.

On 12 July through Dardanelles. More Customs officers and flagboat of guarding squadron. Backsheesh again. Work of officers thorough, but quick. Want us off soon. At dark passed into Archipelago.

On 13 July passed Cape Matapan. Crew dissatisfied about something. Seemed scared, but would not speak out.

On 14 July was somewhat anxious about crew. Men all steady fellows, who sailed with me before. Mate could not make out what was wrong; they only told him there was *something*, and crossed themselves. Mate lost temper with one of them that day and struck him. Expected fierce quarrel, but all was quiet.

On 16 July mate reported in the morning that one of crew, Petrofsky, was missing. Could not account for it. Took larboard[2] watch eight bells last night; was relieved by Abramoff, but did not go to bunk. Men more downcast than ever. All said they expected something of the kind, but would not say more than that there was *something* aboard. Mate getting very impatient with them; feared some trouble ahead.

On 17 July, yesterday, one of the men, Olgaren, came to my cabin, and in an awestruck way confided to me that he thought there was a strange man aboard the ship. He said that in his watch he had been sheltering behind the deck-house, as there was a rain-storm, when he saw a tall, thin man, who was not like any of the crew, come up the companion-way, and go along the deck forward, and disappear. He followed cautiously, but when he got to bows found no one, and the hatchways were all closed. He was in a panic of superstitious fear, and I am afraid the panic may spread. To allay it, I shall today search entire ship carefully from stem to stern.

Later in the day I got together the whole crew, and told them, as they evidently thought there was some one in the ship, we would search from stem to stern. First mate angry; said it was folly, and to yield to such foolish ideas would demoralize the men; said he would engage to

---

9. The *Demeter* is traveling south from Turkey through Greece on the Aegean Sea ("Archipelago").
1. Routine bribery.
2. The port (left-hand) side of a ship.

keep them out of trouble with a handspike.[3] I let him take the helm, while the rest began thorough search, all keeping abreast, with lanterns; we left no corner unsearched. As there were only the big wooden boxes, there were no odd corners where a man could hide. Men much relieved when search over, and went back to work cheerfully. First mate scowled, but said nothing.

22 *July.*—Rough weather last three days, and all hands busy with sails—no time to be frightened. Men seem to have forgotten their dread. Mate cheerful again, and all on good terms. Praised men for work in bad weather. Passed Gibraltar and out through Straits.[4] All well.

24 *July.*—There seems some doom over this ship. Already a hand short, and entering on the Bay of Biscay with wild weather ahead, and yet last night another man lost—disappeared. Like the first, he came off his watch and was not seen again. Men all in a panic of fear; sent a round robin,[5] asking to have double watch, as they fear to be alone. Mate violent. Fear there will be some trouble, as either he or the men will do some violence.

28 *July.*—Four days in hell, knocking about in a sort of maelstrom, and the wind a tempest. No sleep for any one. Men all worn out. Hardly know how to set a watch, since no one fit to go on. Second mate volunteered to steer and watch, and let men snatch a few hours' sleep. Wind abating; seas still terrific, but feel them less, as ship is steadier.

29 *July.*—Another tragedy. Had single watch tonight, as crew too tired to double. When morning watch came on deck could find no one except steersman. Raised outcry, and all came on deck. Thorough search, but no one found. Are now without second mate, and crew in a panic. Mate and I agreed to go armed henceforth and wait for any sign of cause.

30 *July.*—Last night. Rejoiced we are nearing England. Weather fine, all sails set. Retired worn out; slept soundly; awaked by mate telling me that both man of watch and steersman missing. Only self and mate and two hands left to work ship.

1 *August.*—Two days of fog, and not a sail sighted. Had hoped when in the English Channel[6] to be able to signal for help or get in somewhere. Not having power to work sails, have to run before wind. Dare not lower, as could not raise them again. We seem to be drifting to some terrible doom. Mate now more demoralized than either of men. His stronger nature seems to have worked inwardly against himself. Men are beyond fear, working stolidly and patiently, with minds made up to worst. They are Russian, he Roumanian.

2 *August, midnight.*—Woke up from few minutes' sleep by hearing

---

3. A bar used as a lever.
4. The ship is traveling through Spain on the western Mediterranean. Since the Rock of Gibraltar is a British base and colony, Dracula has now penetrated the British Empire.
5. A collective petition or protest signed in a circle to mask the initiators.
6. The ship enters England from the east.

a cry, seemingly outside my port. Could see nothing in fog. Rushed on deck, and ran against mate. Tells me heard cry and ran, but no sign of man on watch. One more gone. Lord, help us! Mate says we must be past Straits of Dover, as in a moment of fog lifting he saw North Foreland, just as he heard the man cry out. If so we are now off in the North Sea, and only God can guide us in the fog, which seems to move with us; and God seems to have deserted us.

3 *August.*—At midnight I went to relieve the man at the wheel, but when I got to it found no one there. The wind was steady, and as we ran before it there was no yawing.[7] I dared not leave it, so shouted for the mate. After a few seconds he rushed up on deck in his flannels. He looked wild-eyed and haggard, and I greatly fear his reason has given way. He came close to me and whispered hoarsely, with his mouth to my ear, as though fearing the very air might hear: '*It* is here; I know it, now. On the watch last night I saw It, like a man, tall and thin, and ghastly pale. It was in the bows, and looking out. I crept behind It, and gave It my knife; but the knife went through It, empty as the air.' And as he spoke he took his knife and drove it savagely into space. Then he went on: 'But It is here, and I'll find It. It is in the hold, perhaps, in one of those boxes. I'll unscrew them one by one and see. You work the helm.' And with a warning look and his finger on his lip, he went below. There was springing up a choppy wind, and I could not leave the helm. I saw him come out on deck again with a tool-chest and a lantern, and go down the forward hatchway. He is mad, stark, raving mad, and it's no use my trying to stop him. He can't hurt those big boxes: they are invoiced as 'clay,' and to pull them about is as harmless a thing as he can do. So here I stay, and mind the helm, and write these notes. I can only trust in God and wait till the fog clears. Then, if I can't steer to any harbour with the wind that is, I shall cut down sails and lie by, and signal for help . . .

It is nearly all over now. Just as I was beginning to hope that the mate would come out calmer—for I heard him knocking away at something in the hold, and work is good for him—there came up the hatchway a sudden, startled scream, which made my blood run cold, and up on the deck he came as if shot from a gun—a raging madman, with his eyes rolling and his face convulsed with fear. 'Save me! save me!' he cried, and then looked round on the blanket of fog. His horror turned to despair, and in a steady voice he said: 'You had better come too, captain, before it is too late. *He* is there. I know the secret now. The sea will save me from Him, and it is all that is left!' Before I could say a word, or move forward to seize him, he sprang on the bulwark and deliberately threw himself into the sea. I suppose I know the secret too, now. It was this madman who had got rid of the men one by one,

7. Nautical: to swerve off course momentarily or temporarily.

and now he has followed them himself. God help me! How am I to account for all these horrors when I get to port? *When* I get to port! Will that ever be?

4 *August.*—Still fog, which the sunrise cannot pierce. I know there is sunrise because I am a sailor, why else I know not. I dared not go below, I dared not leave the helm; so here all night I stayed, and in the dimness of the night I saw It—Him! God forgive me, but the mate was right to jump overboard. It is better to die like a man; to die like a sailor in blue water no man can object. But I am captain, and I must not leave my ship. But I shall baffle this fiend or monster, for I shall tie my hands to the wheel when my strength begins to fail, and along with them I shall tie that which He—It!—dare not touch; and then, come good wind or foul, I shall save my soul, and my honour as a captain. I am growing weaker, and the night is coming on. If He can look me in the face again, I may not have time to act . . . If we are wrecked, mayhap this bottle may be found, and those who find it may understand; if not, . . . well, then all men shall know that I have been true to my trust. God and the Blessed Virgin and the saints help a poor ignorant soul trying to do his duty . . .'

Of course the verdict was an open one. There is no evidence to adduce; and whether or not the man himself committed the murders there is now none to say. The folk hold almost universally here that the captain is simply a hero, and he is to be given a public funeral. Already it is arranged that his body is to be taken with a train of boats up the Esk for a piece and then brought back to Tate Hill Pier and up the Abbey steps; for he is to be buried in the churchyard on the cliff. The owners of more than a hundred boats have already given in their names as wishing to follow him to the grave.

No trace has ever been found of the great dog; at which there is much mourning, for, with public opinion in its present state, he would, I believe, be adopted by the town. Tomorrow will see the funeral; and so will end this one more 'mystery of the sea.'

Mina Murray's Journal

8 *August.*—Lucy was very restless all night, and I, too, could not sleep. The storm was fearful, and as it boomed loudly among the chimney-pots, it made me shudder. When a sharp puff came it seemed to be like a distant gun. Strangely enough, Lucy did not wake; but she got up twice and dressed herself. Fortunately, each time I awoke in time, and managed to undress her without waking her, and got her back to bed. It is a very strange thing, this sleep-walking, for as soon as her will is thwarted in any physical way, her intention, if there be any, disappears, and she yields herself almost exactly to the routine of her life.

Early in the morning we both got up and went down to the harbour to see if anything had happened in the night. There were very few people about, and though the sun was bright, and the air clear and fresh, the big, grim-looking waves, that seemed dark themselves because the foam that topped them was like snow, forced themselves in through the narrow mouth of the harbour—like a bullying man going through a crowd. Somehow I felt glad that Jonathan was not on the sea last night, but on land. But, oh, is he on land or sea? Where is he, and how? I am getting fearfully anxious about him. If I only knew what to do, and could do anything!

10 *August.*—The funeral of the poor sea-captain today was most touching. Every boat in the harbour seemed to be there, and the coffin was carried by captains all the way from Tate Hill Pier up to the church-yard. Lucy came with me, and we went early to our old seat, whilst the cortège of boats went up the river to the Viaduct and came down again. We had a lovely view, and saw the procession nearly all the way. The poor fellow was laid to rest quite near our seat, so that we stood on it when the time came and saw everything. Poor Lucy seemed much upset. She was restless and uneasy all the time, and I cannot but think that her dreaming at night is telling on her. She is quite odd in one thing: she will not admit to me that there is any cause for restlessness; or if there be, she does not understand it herself. There is an additional cause in that poor old Mr Swales was found dead this morning on our seat, his neck being broken. He had evidently, as the doctor said, fallen back in the seat in some sort of fright, for there was a look of fear and horror on his face that the men said made them shudder. Poor dear old man! Perhaps he had seen Death with his dying eyes! Lucy is so sweet and sensitive that she feels influences more acutely than other people do. Just now she was quite upset by a little thing which I did not much heed, though I am myself very fond of animals. One of the men who come up here often to look for the boats was followed by his dog. The dog is always with him. They are both quiet persons, and I never saw the man angry, nor heard the dog bark. During the service the dog would not come to its master, who was on the seat with us, but kept a few yards off, barking and howling. Its master spoke to it gently, and then harshly, and then angrily; but it would neither come nor cease to make a noise. It was in a sort of fury, with its eyes savage, and all its hairs bristling out like a cat's tail when puss is on the war-path. Finally the man, too, got angry, and jumped down and kicked the dog, and then took it by the scruff of the neck and half dragged and half threw it on the tombstone on which the seat is fixed. The moment it touched the stone the poor thing became quiet and fell all into a tremble. It did not try to get away, but crouched down, quivering and cowering, and was in such a pitiable state of terror that I tried, though without effect, to comfort it. Lucy was full of pity, too, but she did not attempt to touch the dog, but looked at it in an agonized sort

of way. I greatly fear that she is of too super-sensitive a nature to go through the world without trouble. She will be dreaming of this tonight, I am sure. The whole agglomeration of things—the ship steered into port by a dead man; his attitude, tied to the wheel with a crucifix and beads; the touching funeral; the dog, now furious and now in terror—will all afford material for her dreams.

I think it will be best for her to go to bed tired out physically, so I shall take her for a long walk by the cliffs to Robin Hood's Bay and back. She ought not to have much inclination for sleep-walking then.

Chapter VIII

Mina Murray's Journal

Same day, 11 o'clock p.m.—Oh, but I am tired! If it were not that I have made my diary a duty I should not open it tonight. We had a lovely walk. Lucy, after a while, was in gay spirits, owing, I think, to some dear cows who came nosing towards us in a field close to the lighthouse, and frightened the wits out of us. I believe we forgot everything, except, of course, personal fear, and it seemed to wipe the slate clean and give us a fresh start. We had a capital 'severe tea' at Robin Hood's Bay in a sweet little old-fashioned inn, with a bow-window right over the seaweed-covered rocks of the strand. I believe we should have shocked the 'New Woman'[1] with our appetites. Men are more tolerant, bless them! Then we walked home with some, or rather many, stoppages to rest, and with our hearts full of a constant dread of wild bulls. Lucy was really tired, and we intended to creep off to bed as soon as we could. The young curate came in, however, and Mrs Westenra asked him to stay for supper. Lucy and I had both a fight for it with the dusty miller;[2] I know it was a hard fight on my part, and I am quite heroic. I think that some day the bishops must get together and see about breeding up a new class of curates, who don't take supper, no matter how they may be pressed to, and who will know when girls are tired. Lucy is asleep and breathing softly. She has more colour in her cheeks than usual, and looks, oh, so sweet. If Mr Holmwood fell in love with her seeing her only in the drawing-room, I wonder what he would say if he saw her now. Some of the 'New Women' writers will

1. A popular personification among journalists and novelists in the 1890s. Sarah Grand coined the phrase in her feminist novel *The Heavenly Twins* (1893), but it often took on a derisive edge, connoting a woman given to smoking, working, and sexual aggression. By implication, this personification labeled feminists evolutionary mutations—or aberrations—resembling the alien invading species in *Dracula* and related *fin-de-siècle* fantasies. Some stereotypes of the New Woman fit the anti-appetitive creature Mina ridicules—Thomas Hardy's Sue Brideshead in *Jude the Obscure* (1896) quivers with sensual fastidiousness—but others, such as Ayesha in Rider Haggard's best-selling *She* (1887), rage with intellectual and erotic desire.
2. The sandman.

some day start an idea that men and women should be allowed to see each other asleep before proposing or accepting. But I suppose the New Woman won't condescend in future to accept; she will do the proposing herself. And a nice job she will make of it, too! There's some consolation in that. I am so happy tonight, because dear Lucy seems better. I really believe she has turned the corner, and that we are over her troubles with dreaming. I should be quite happy if I only knew if Jonathan . . . God bless and keep him.

11 August, 3 a.m.—Diary again. No sleep now, so I may as well write. I am too agitated to sleep. We have had such an adventure, such an agonizing experience. I fell asleep as soon as I had closed my diary . . . Suddenly I became broad awake, and sat up, with a horrible sense of fear upon me, and of some feeling of emptiness around me. The room was dark, so I could not see Lucy's bed; I stole across and felt for her. The bed was empty. I lit a match, and found that she was not in the room. The door was shut, but not locked, as I had left it. I feared to wake her mother, who has been more than usually ill lately, so threw on some clothes and got ready to look for her. As I was leaving the room it struck me that the clothes she wore might give me some clue to her dreaming intention. Dressing-gown would mean house; dress, outside. Dressing-gown and dress were both in their places. 'Thank God,' I said to myself, 'she cannot be far, as she is only in her night-dress.' I ran downstairs and looked in the sitting-room. Not there! Then I looked in all the other open rooms of the house, with an ever-growing fear chilling my heart. Finally I came to the hall-door and found it open. It was not wide open, but the catch of the lock had not caught. The people of the house are careful to lock the door every night, so I feared that Lucy must have gone out as she was. There was no time to think of what might happen; a vague, overmastering fear obscured all details. I took a big, heavy shawl and ran out. The clock was striking one as I was in the Crescent, and there was not a soul in sight. I ran along the North Terrace, but could see no sign of the white figure which I expected. At the edge of the West Cliff above the pier I looked across the harbour to the East Cliff, in the hope or fear—I don't know which—of seeing Lucy in our favourite seat. There was a bright full moon, with heavy black, driving clouds, which threw the whole scene into a fleeting diorama[3] of light and shade as they sailed across. For a moment or two I could see nothing, as the shadow of a cloud obscured St Mary's Church and all around it. Then as the cloud passed I could see the ruins of the Abbey coming into view; and as the edge of a narrow band of light as sharp as a sword-cut moved along, the church and the churchyard became gradually visible. Whatever my expectation

---

3. In the nineteenth century, large theaters without human actors, featuring grand natural or artistic spectacles. Seascapes and shipwrecks like those depicted in *Dracula* were staples of Victorian dioramas.

was, it was not disappointed, for there, on our favourite seat, the silver light of the moon struck a half-reclining figure, snowy white. The coming of the cloud was too quick for me to see much, for shadow shut down on light almost immediately; but it seemed to me as though something dark stood behind the seat where the white figure shone, and bent over it. What it was, whether man or beast, I could not tell; I did not wait to catch another glance, but flew down the steep steps to the pier and along by the fish-market to the bridge, which was the only way to reach the East Cliff. The town seemed as dead, for not a soul did I see; I rejoiced that it was so, for I wanted no witness of poor Lucy's condition. The time and distance seemed endless, and my knees trembled and my breath came laboured as I toiled up the endless steps to the Abbey. I must have gone fast, and yet it seemed to me as if my feet were weighted with lead, and as though every joint in my body were rusty. When I got almost to the top I could see the seat and the white figure, for I was now close enough to distinguish it even through the spells of shadow. There was undoubtedly something, long and black, bending over the half-reclining white figure. I called in fright, 'Lucy! Lucy!' and something raised a head, and from where I was I could see a white face and red, gleaming eyes. Lucy did not answer, and I ran on to the entrance of the churchyard. As I entered, the church was between me and the seat, and for a minute or so I lost sight of her. When I came in view again the cloud had passed, and the moonlight struck so brilliantly that I could see Lucy half reclining with her head lying over the back of the seat. She was quite alone, and there was not a sign of any living thing about.

When I bent over her I could see that she was still asleep. Her lips were parted, and she was breathing—not softly, as usual with her, but in long, heavy gasps, as though striving to get her lungs full at every breath. As I came close, she put up her hand in her sleep and pulled the collar of her nightdress close round her throat. Whilst she did so there came a little shudder through her, as though she felt the cold. I flung the warm shawl over her, and drew the edges tight round her neck, for I dreaded lest she should get some deadly chill from the night air, unclad as she was. I feared to wake her all at once, so, in order to have my hands free that I might help her, I fastened the shawl at her throat with a big safety-pin; but I must have been clumsy in my anxiety and pinched or pricked her with it, for by-and-by, when her breathing became quieter, she put her hand to her throat again and moaned. When I had her carefully wrapped up I put my shoes on her feet, and then began very gently to wake her. At first she did not respond; but gradually she became more and more uneasy in her sleep, moaning and sighing occasionally. At last, as time was passing fast, and, for many other reasons, I wished to get her home at once, I shook her more forcibly, till finally she opened her eyes and awoke. She did not seem surprised to see me, as, of course, she did not realize all at once where she was. Lucy always wakes prettily, and even at such a time, when her body must have been chilled with cold, and her mind somewhat appalled at waking unclad in a churchyard at night, she did not lose her grace. She trembled a little, and clung to me; when I told her to come at once with me home she rose without a word, with the obedience of a child. As we passed along, the gravel hurt my feet, and Lucy noticed me wince. She stopped and wanted to insist upon my taking my shoes; but I would not. However, when we got to the pathway outside the churchyard, where there was a puddle of water remaining from the storm, I daubed my feet with mud, using each foot in turn on the other, so that as we went home no one, in case we should meet any one, should notice my bare feet.

Fortune favoured us, and we got home without meeting a soul. Once we saw a man, who seemed not quite sober, passing along a street in front of us; but we hid in a door till he had disappeared up an opening such as there are here, steep little closes, or 'wynds,' as they call them in Scotland. My heart beat so loud all the time that sometimes I thought I should faint. I was filled with anxiety about Lucy, not only for her health, lest she should suffer from the exposure, but for her reputation in case the story should get wind. When we got in, and had washed our feet, and had said a prayer of thankfulness together, I tucked her into bed. Before falling asleep she asked—even implored—me not to say a word to any one, even her mother, about her sleep-walking adventure. I hesitated at first to promise; but on thinking of the state of her mother's health, and how the knowledge of such a thing would fret her, and thinking, too, of how such a story might become distorted—nay, infallibly would—in case it should leak out, I thought it wiser to do so. I hope I did right. I have locked the door, and the key is tied to my wrist, so perhaps I shall not be again disturbed. Lucy is sleeping soundly; the reflex of the dawn is high and far over the sea . . .

Same day, noon.—All goes well. Lucy slept till I woke her, and seemed not to have even changed her side. The adventure of the night does not seem to have harmed her; on the contrary, it has benefited her, for she looks better this morning than she has done for weeks. I was sorry to notice that my clumsiness with the safety-pin hurt her. Indeed, it might have been serious, for the skin of her throat was pierced. I must have pinched up a piece of loose skin and have transfixed it, for there are two little red points[4] like pinpricks, and on the band of her nightdress was a drop of blood. When I apologized and was concerned about it, she laughed and petted me, and said she did not even feel it. Fortunately it cannot leave a scar, as it is so tiny.

Same day, night.—We passed a happy day. The air was clear, and

---

4. Not until *Dracula* were these neck pricks evidence of a vampire visit; earlier vampire writers, such as Coleridge and Sheridan Le Fanu, make the bosom the site of the bite.

the sun bright, and there was a cool breeze. We took our lunch to Mulgrave Woods, Mrs Westenra driving by the road and Lucy and I walking by the cliff-path and joining her at the gate. I felt a little sad myself, for I could not but feel how *absolutely* happy it would have been had Jonathan been with me. But there! I must only be patient. In the evening we strolled in the Casino Terrace, and heard some good music by Spohr and Mackenzie,[5] and went to bed early. Lucy seems more restful than she has been for some time, and fell asleep at once. I shall lock the door and secure the key the same as before, though I do not expect any trouble tonight.

12 August.—My expectations were wrong, for twice during the night I was wakened by Lucy trying to get out. She seemed, even in her sleep, to be a little impatient at finding the door shut, and went back to bed under a sort of protest. I woke with the dawn, and heard the birds chirping outside of the window. Lucy woke, too, and, I was glad to see, was even better than on the previous morning. All her old gaiety of manner seemed to have come back, and she came and snuggled in beside me, and told me all about Arthur; I told her how anxious I was about Jonathan, and then she tried to comfort me. Well, she succeeded somewhat, for, though sympathy can't alter facts, it can help to make them more bearable.

13 August.—Another quiet day, and to bed with the key on my wrist as before. Again I awoke in the night, and found Lucy sitting up in bed, still asleep, pointing to the window. I got up quietly, and pulling aside the blind, looked out. It was brilliant moonlight, and the soft effect of the light over the sea and sky—merged together in one great, silent mystery—was beautiful beyond words. Between me and the moonlight flitted a great bat[6], coming and going in great, whirling circles. Once or twice it came quite close, but was, I suppose, frightened at seeing me, and flitted away across the harbour towards the Abbey. When I came back from the window Lucy had lain down again, and was sleeping peacefully. She did not stir again all night.

14 August.—On the East Cliff, reading and writing all day. Lucy seems to have become as much in love with the spot as I am, and it is hard to get her away from it when it is time to come home for lunch or tea or dinner. This afternoon she made a funny remark. We were coming home for dinner, and had come to the top of the steps up from the West Pier and stopped to look at the view, as we generally do. The setting sun, low down in the sky, was just dropping behind Kettleness; the red light was thrown over on the East Cliff and the old Abbey, and

---

5. German violinist Louis Spohr (1784–1859) was a composer of opera, choral, orchestral, and chamber music pieces. Scottish violinist Sir Alexander Campbell Mackenzie was a renowned composer of vocal music who in 1888 became director of the Royal Academy of Music. He was knighted in 1895.

6. Like the marks on the victim's neck, the now-inevitable association of vampires with bats begins here.

seemed to bathe everything in a beautiful rosy glow. We were silent for
a while, and suddenly Lucy murmured as if to herself:—

'His red eyes again! They are just the same.' It was such an odd
expression, coming *apropos* of nothing, that it quite startled me. I
slewed round a little, so as to see Lucy well without seeming to stare
at her, and saw that she was in a half-dreamy state, with an odd look
on her face that I could not quite make out; so I said nothing, but
followed her eyes. She appeared to be looking over at our own seat,
whereon was a dark figure seated alone. I was a little startled myself,
for it seemed for an instant as if the stranger had great eyes like burning
flames; but a second look dispelled the illusion. The red sunlight was
shining on the windows of St Mary's Church behind our seat, and as
the sun dipped there was just sufficient change in the refraction and
reflection to make it appear as if the light moved. I called Lucy's attention to the peculiar effect, and she became herself with a start, but
she looked sad all the same; it may have been that she was thinking of
that terrible night up there. We never refer to it; so I said nothing, and
we went home to dinner. Lucy had a headache and went early to bed.
I saw her asleep, and went out for a little stroll myself; I walked along
the cliffs to the westward, and was full of sweet sadness, for I was thinking of Jonathan. When coming home—it was then bright moonlight,
so bright that, though the front of our part of the Crescent was in
shadow, everything could be well seen—I threw a glance up at our
window, and saw Lucy's head leaning out. I thought that perhaps she
was looking out for me, so I opened my handkerchief and waved it.
She did not notice or make any movement whatever. Just then, the
moonlight crept round an angle of the building, and the light fell on
the window. There distinctly was Lucy with her head lying up against
the side of the window-sill and her eyes shut. She was fast asleep, and
by her, seated on the window-sill, was something that looked like a
good-sized bird. I was afraid she might get a chill, so I ran upstairs, but
as I came into the room she was moving back to her bed, fast asleep,
and breathing heavily; she was holding her hand to her throat, as
though to protect it from cold.

I did not wake her, but tucked her up warmly; I have taken care that
the door is locked and the window securely fastened.

She looks so sweet as she sleeps; but she is paler than is her wont,
and there is a drawn, haggard look under her eyes which I do not like.
I fear she is fretting about something. I wish I could find out what
it is.

15 August.—Rose later than usual. Lucy was languid and tired, and
slept on after we had been called. We had a happy surprise at breakfast.
Arthur's father is better, and wants the marriage to come off soon. Lucy
is full of quiet joy, and her mother is glad and sorry at once. Later on
in the day she told me the cause. She is grieved to lose Lucy as her

very own, but she is rejoiced that she is soon to have someone to protect her. Poor dear, sweet lady! She confided to me that she has got her death-warrant. She has not told Lucy, and made me promise secrecy; her doctor told her that within a few months, at most, she must die, for her heart is weakening. At any time, even now, a sudden shock would be almost sure to kill her. Ah, we were wise to keep from her the affair of the dreadful night of Lucy's sleep-walking.

17 August.—No diary for two whole days. I have not had the heart to write. Some sort of shadowy pall seems to be coming over our happiness. No news from Jonathan, and Lucy seems to be growing weaker, whilst her mother's hours are numbering to a close. I do not understand Lucy's fading away as she is doing. She eats well and sleeps well, and enjoys the fresh air; but all the time the roses in her cheeks are fading, and she gets weaker and more languid day by day; at night I hear her gasping as if for air. I keep the key of our door always fastened to my wrist at night, but she gets up and walks about the room, and sits at the open window. Last night I found her leaning out when I woke up, and when I tried to wake her I could not; she was in a faint. When I managed to restore her she was as weak as water, and cried silently between long, painful struggles for breath. When I asked her how she came to be at the window she shook her head and turned away. I trust her feeling ill may not be from that unlucky prick of the safety pin. I looked at her throat just now as she lay asleep, and the tiny wounds seem not to have healed. They are still open, and, if anything, larger than before, and the edges of them are faintly white. They are like little white dots with red centres. Unless they heal within a day or two, I shall insist on the doctor seeing about them.

Letter, Samuel F. Billington & Son, Solicitors, Whitby,
to Messrs. Carter, Paterson & Co., London

17 August.

Dear Sirs,—

Herewith please receive invoice of goods sent by Great Northern Railway. Same are to be delivered at Carfax, near Purfleet, immediately on receipt at goods station King's Cross. The house is at present empty, but enclosed please find keys, all of which are labelled.

You will please deposit the boxes, fifty in number, which form the consignment, in the partially ruined building forming part of the house and marked 'A' on rough diagram enclosed. Your agent will easily recognize the locality, as it is the ancient chapel of the mansion. The goods leave by the train at 9.30 tonight, and will be due at King's Cross at 4.30 tomorrow afternoon. As our client wishes the delivery made as soon as possible, we shall be obliged by your having teams ready at King's Cross at the time named and forthwith conveying the goods to destination. In order to obviate any delays possible through any routine requirements as to payment in your departments, we enclose cheque herewith for ten pounds (£10), receipt of which please acknowledge. Should the charge be less than this amount, you can return balance; if greater, we shall at once send cheque for difference on hearing from you. You are to leave the keys on coming away in the main hall of the house, where the proprietor may get them on his entering the house by means of his duplicate key.

Pray do not take us as exceeding the bounds of business courtesy in pressing you in all ways to use the utmost expedition.

> We are, dear Sirs,
> Faithfully yours,
> SAMUEL F. BILLINGTON & SON.

Letter, Messrs. Carter, Paterson & Co., London, to Messrs. Billington & Son, Whitby

21 August.

Dear Sirs,—

We beg to acknowledge £10 received and to return cheque £1 17s.9d., amount of overplus, as shown in receipted account herewith. Goods are delivered in exact accordance with instructions, and keys left in parcel in main hall, as directed.

> We are, dear Sirs,
> Yours respectfully,
> *Pro* CARTER, PATERSON & CO.

Mina Murray's Journal

18 August.—I am happy today, and write sitting on the seat in the churchyard. Lucy is ever so much better. Last night she slept well all night, and did not disturb me once. The roses seem coming back already to her cheeks, though she is still sadly pale and wan-looking. If she were in any way anæmic I could understand it, but she is not. She is in gay spirits and full of life and cheerfulness. All the morbid reticence seems to have passed from her, and she has just reminded me, as if I needed any reminding, of *that* night, and that it was here, on this very seat, I found her asleep. As she told me she tapped playfully with the heel of her boot on the stone slab and said:—

'My poor little feet didn't make much noise then! I daresay poor old Mr Swales would have told me that it was because I didn't want to wake up Geordie.' As she was in such a communicative humour, I asked her if she had dreamed at all that night. Before she answered, that sweet, puckered look came into her forehead, which Arthur—I call him Arthur from her habit—says he loves; and, indeed, I don't wonder that he does. Then she went on in a half-dreaming kind of way, as if trying to recall it to herself:—

'I didn't quite dream; but it all seemed to be real. I only wanted to be here in this spot—I don't know why, for I was afraid of something —I don't know what. I remember, though I suppose I was asleep, passing through the streets and over the bridge. A fish leaped as I went by, and I leaned over to look at it, and I heard a lot of dogs howling—the whole town seemed as if it must be full of dogs all howling at once— as I went up the steps. Then I have a vague memory of something long and dark with red eyes, just as we saw in the sunset, and something very sweet and very bitter all around me at once; and then I seemed sinking into deep green water, and there was a singing in my ears, as I have heard there is to drowning men; and then everything seemed passing away from me; my soul seemed to go out from my body and float about the air. I seem to remember that once the West Lighthouse was right under me, and then there was a sort of agonizing feeling, as if I were in an earthquake, and I came back and found you shaking my body. I saw you do it before I felt you.'

Then she began to laugh. It seemed a little uncanny to me, and I listened to her breathlessly. I did not quite like it, and thought it better not to keep her mind on the subject, so we drifted on to other subjects, and Lucy was like her old self again. When we got home the fresh breeze had braced her up, and her pale cheeks were really more rosy. Her mother rejoiced when she saw her, and we all spent a very happy evening together.

19 *August.*—Joy, joy, joy! although not all joy. At last, news of Jonathan. The dear fellow has been ill; that is why he did not write. I am not afraid to think it or to say it, now that I know. Mr Hawkins sent me on the letter, and wrote himself, oh, so kindly. I am to leave in the morning and to go over to Jonathan, and to help to nurse him if necessary, and to bring him home. Mr Hawkins says it would not be a bad thing if we were to be married out there. I have cried over the good Sister's letter till I can feel it wet against my bosom, where it lies. It is of Jonathan, and must be next my heart, for he is *in* my heart. My journey is all mapped out, and my luggage ready. I am only taking one change of dress; Lucy will bring my trunk to London and keep it till I send for it, for it may be that . . . I must write no more; I must keep it to say to Jonathan, my husband. The letter that he has seen and touched must comfort me till we meet.

*Letter, Sister Agatha, Hospital of St Joseph and
Ste Mary, Buda-Pesth[7], To Miss Wilhelmina Murray*

12 August.

Dear Madam,—

I write by desire of Mr Jonathan Harker, who is himself not strong enough to write, though progressing well, thanks to God and St Joseph and Ste Mary. He has been under our care for nearly six weeks, suffering from a violent brain fever. He wishes me to convey his love, and to say that by this post I write for him to Mr Peter Hawkins, Exeter, to say, with his dutiful respects, that he is sorry for his delay, and that all his work is completed. He will require some few weeks' rest in our sanatorium in the hills, but will then return. He wishes me to say that he has not sufficient money with him, and that he would like to pay for his staying here, so that others who need shall not be wanting for help.

Believe me,

Yours, with sympathy and all blessings,

SISTER AGATHA

P.S.—My patient being asleep, I open this to let you know something more. He has told me all about you, and that you are shortly to be his wife. All blessings to you both! He has had some fearful shock—so says our doctor—and in his delirium his ravings have been dreadful; of wolves and poison and blood; of ghosts and demons; and I fear to say of what. Be careful with him always that there may be nothing to excite him of this kind for a long time to come; the traces of such an illness as his do not lightly die away. We should have written long ago, but we knew nothing of his friends, and there was on him nothing that any one could understand. He came in the train from Klausenburg, and the guard was told by the station-master there that he rushed into the station shouting for a ticket for home. Seeing from his violent demeanour that he was English[8], they gave him a ticket for the furthest station on the way thither that the train reached.

Be assured that he is well cared for. He has won all hearts by his sweetness and gentleness. He is truly getting on well, and I have no doubt will in a few weeks be all himself. But be careful of him for

---

7. A more modern and metropolitan city than any Jonathan visited. Buda and Pest were joined in 1873 by "the most western of splendid bridges" over the Danube, as Jonathan yearningly calls it. The Hapsburgs ruled Budapest from 1686 to 1918; after World War I it became the capital of independent Hungary.
8. Cf. the Gravedigger in *Hamlet* 5.1.149–53:

> *Ham.* Ay, marry; why was he sent into England?
> *First Clo.* Why, because he was mad: he shall recover his wits there; or, if he do not, 't is no great matter there.
> *Ham.* Why?
> *First Clo.* 'T will not be seen in him there; there the men are as mad as he.

safety's sake. There are, I pray God and St Joseph and Ste Mary, many, many happy years for you both.

Dr Seward's Diary

19 August.—Strange and sudden change in Renfield last night. About eight o'clock he began to get excited and to sniff about as a dog does when setting. The attendant was struck by his manner, and knowing my interest in him, encouraged him to talk. He is usually respectful to the attendant, and at times servile; but tonight, the man tells me, he was quite haughty. Would not condescend to talk with him at all. All he would say was:—

'I don't want to talk to you: you don't count now; the Master is at hand.'

The attendant thinks it is some sudden form of religious mania which has seized him. If so, we must look out for squalls, for a strong man with homicidal and religious mania at once might be dangerous. The combination is a dreadful one. At nine o'clock I visited him myself. His attitude to me was the same as that to the attendant; in his sublime self-feeling the difference between myself and attendant seemed to him as nothing. It looks like religious mania, and he will soon think that he himself is God. These infinitesimal distinctions between man and man are too paltry for an Omnipotent Being. How these madmen give themselves away! The real God taketh heed lest a sparrow[9] fall; but the God created from human vanity sees no difference between an eagle and a sparrow. Oh, if men only knew!

For half an hour or more Renfield kept getting excited in greater and greater degree. I did not pretend to be watching him, but I kept strict observation all the same. All at once that shifty look came into his eyes which we always see when a madman has seized an idea, and with it the shifty movement of the head and back which asylum attendants come to know so well. He became quite quiet, and went and sat on the edge of his bed resignedly, and looked into space with lacklustre eyes. I thought I would find out if his apathy were real or only assumed, and tried to lead him to talk of his pets, a theme which had never failed to excite his attention. At first he made no reply, but at length said testily:—

'Bother them all! I don't care a pin about them.'

'What?' I said. 'You don't mean to tell me you don't care about spiders?' (Spiders at present are his hobby, and the notebook is filling up with columns of small figures.) To this he answered enigmatically:—

'The bride-maidens rejoice the eyes that wait the coming of the bride;

9. Matthew 10.29: "Are not two sparrows sold for a farthing? and one of them shall not fall on the ground without your Father."

but when the bride draweth nigh,[1] then the maidens shine not to the eyes that are filled.'

He would not explain himself, but remained obstinately seated on his bed all the time I remained with him.

I am weary tonight and low in spirits. I cannot but think of Lucy, and how different things might have been. If I don't sleep at once, chloral, the modern Morpheus[2]—$C_2HCl_3O \cdot H_2O$! I must be careful not to let it grow into a habit. No, I shall take none tonight! I have thought of Lucy, and I shall not dishonour her by mixing the two. If need be, tonight shall be sleepless . . .

Glad I made the resolution; gladder that I kept to it. I had lain tossing about, and had heard the clock strike only twice, when the night-watchman came to me, sent up from the ward, to say that Renfield had escaped. I threw on my clothes and ran down at once; my patient is too dangerous a person to be roaming about. Those ideas of his might work out dangerously with strangers. The attendant was waiting for me. He said he had seen him not ten minutes before, seemingly asleep in his bed, when he had looked through the observation-trap in the door. His attention was called by the sound of the window being wrenched out. He ran back and saw his feet disappear through the window, and had at once sent up for me. He was only in his night-gear, and cannot be far off. The attendant thought it would be more useful to watch where he should go than to follow him, as he might lose sight of him whilst getting out of the building by the door. He is a bulky man, and couldn't get through the window. I am thin, so, with his aid, I got out, but feet foremost, and, as we were only a few feet above ground, landed unhurt. The attendant told me the patient had gone to the left and had taken a straight line, so I ran as quickly as I could. As I got through the belt of trees I saw a white figure scale the high wall which separates our grounds from those of the deserted house.

I ran back at once, and told the watchman to get three or four men immediately and follow me into the grounds of Carfax, in case our friend might be dangerous. I got a ladder myself, and crossing the wall, dropped down on the other side. I could see Renfield's figure just disappearing behind the angle of the house, so I ran after him. On the far side of the house I found him pressed close against the old iron-bound oak door of the chapel. He was talking, apparently to some one, but I was afraid to go near enough to hear what he was saying, lest I

1. Renfield's biblical-sounding rhapsody equates Dracula's advent with the coming of the Messiah, but its imagery is unorthodox. The New Testament never refers to Jesus as a bride, though he is occasionally a bridegroom. In the Book of Revelation 21.2, however, the new heaven and the new earth generate a bridal city: "And I John saw the holy city, new Jerusalem, coming down from God out of heaven, prepared as a bride adorned for her husband." Renfield exalts not so much the coming of Dracula as the glorious new dispensation Dracula promises.

2. Chloral hydrate is a colorless crystalline compound used medicinally as a sedative and hypnotic. Morpheus is the god of dreams.

might frighten him, and he should run off. Chasing an errant swarm of bees is nothing to following a naked lunatic when the fit of escaping is upon him! After a few minutes, however, I could see that he did not take note of anything around him, and so ventured to draw nearer to him—the more so as my men had now crossed the wall and were closing him in. I heard him say:—

'I am here to do Your bidding, Master. I am Your slave, and You will reward me, for I shall be faithful. I have worshipped You long and afar off. Now that You are near, I await Your commands, and You will not pass me by, will You, dear Master, in Your distribution of good things?'

He *is* a selfish old beggar anyhow. He thinks of the loaves and fishes[3] even when he believes he is in a Real Presence. His manias make a startling combination. When we closed in on him he fought like a tiger. He is immensely strong, and he was more like a wild beast than a man. I never saw a lunatic in such a paroxysm of rage before; and I hope I shall not again. It is a mercy that we have found out his strength and his danger in good time. With strength and determination like his, he might have done wild work before he was caged. He is safe now at any rate. Jack Sheppard[4] himself couldn't get free from the strait-waistcoat that keeps him restrained, and he's chained to the wall in the padded room. His cries are at times awful, but the silences that follow are more deadly still, for he means murder in every turn and movement.

Just now he spoke coherent words for the first time:—

'I shall be patient, Master. It is coming—coming—coming!'

So I took the hint, and came too. I was too excited to sleep, but this diary has quieted me, and I feel I shall get some sleep tonight.

Chapter IX

Letter, Mina Harker to Lucy Westenra

Buda-Pesth, 24 August.

My dearest Lucy,—

I know you will be anxious to hear all that has happened since we parted at the railway station at Whitby. Well, my dear, I got to Hull all right, and caught the boat to Hamburg,[1] and then the train on here. I

---

3. So, of course, did the original disciples. In the New Testament, Jesus, like Dracula, proves his divinity by miraculously feeding his followers. Jesus transformed a handful of loaves and fishes into food for "four thousand men, beside women and children" (Matthew 15.38); Dracula transforms blood into life.

4. A popular eighteenth-century criminal known for spectacular escapes from Newgate before he was hanged in 1724.

1. Hull was, in Stoker's day, the third most important port city in England; in addition to being a major German port, Hamburg was, in the nineteenth century, the major gateway of emigration from the Old to the New Worlds. Mina's journey east has none of the terrifying exoticism of Jonathan's.

feel that I can hardly recall anything of the journey, except that I knew
I was coming to Jonathan, and, that as I should have to do some nursing, I had better get all the sleep I could . . . I found my dear one, oh,
so thin and pale and weak-looking. All the resolution has gone out of
his dear eyes, and that quiet dignity which I told you was in his face
has vanished. He is only a wreck of himself, and he does not remember
anything that has happened to him for a long time past. At least, he
wants me to believe so, and I shall never ask. He has had some terrible
shock, and I fear it might tax his poor brain if he were to try to recall
it. Sister Agatha, who is a good creature and a born nurse, tells me that
he raved of dreadful things whilst he was off his head. I wanted her to
tell me what they were; but she would only cross herself, and say she
would never tell; that the ravings of the sick were the secrets of God,
and that if a nurse through her vocation should hear them, she should
respect her trust. She is a sweet, good soul, and the next day, when she
saw I was troubled, she opened up the subject again, and after saying
that she could never mention what my poor dear raved about, added:
'I can tell you this much, my dear: that it was not about anything which
he has done wrong himself; and you, as his wife to be, have no cause
to be concerned. He has not forgotten you or what he owes to you. His
fear was of great and terrible things, which no mortal can treat of.' I
do believe the dear soul thought I might be jealous lest my poor dear
should have fallen in love with any other girl. The idea of *my* being
jealous about Jonathan! And yet, my dear, let me whisper, I felt a thrill
of joy through me when I *knew* that no other woman was a cause of
trouble. I am now sitting by his bedside, where I can see his face while
he sleeps. He is waking! . . . When he woke he asked me for his coat,
as he wanted to get something from the pocket; I asked Sister Agatha,
and she brought all his things. I saw that amongst them was his notebook, and was going to ask him to let me look at it—for I knew then
that I might find some clue to his trouble—but I suppose he must have
seen my wish in my eyes, for he sent me over to the window, saying
he wanted to be quite alone for a moment. Then he called me back,
and when I came he had his hand over the note-book, and he said to
me very solemnly:—

'Wilhelmina'—I knew then that he was in deadly earnest,[2] for he has
never called me by that name since he asked me to marry him—'you
know, dear, my ideas of the trust between husband and wife: there
should be no secret, no concealment. I have had a great shock, and
when I try to think of what it is I feel my head spin round, and I do
not know if it was all real or the dreaming of a madman. You know I

---

2. Earnestness was the supreme strenuous virtue of the Victorian middle class, a virtue with
which Oscar Wilde mockingly played in his stylish farce *The Importance of Being Earnest*
(1895)—a theatrical triumph that preceded his imprisonment by only a few months. Stoker's
novel allows no space for Wilde's teasing.

have had brain fever,[3] and that is to be mad. The secret is here, and I do not want to know it. I want to take up my life here, with our marriage.' For, my dear, we had decided to be married as soon as the formalities are complete. 'Are you willing, Wilhelmina, to share my ignorance? Here is the book. Take it and keep it, read it if you will, but never let me know; unless, indeed, some solemn duty should come upon me to go back to the bitter hours, asleep or awake, sane or mad, recorded here.' He fell back exhausted, and I put the book under his pillow, and kissed him. I have asked Sister Agatha to beg the Superior to let our wedding be this afternoon, and am waiting her reply . . .

She has come and told me that the chaplain of the English mission church has been sent for. We are to be married in an hour, or as soon after as Jonathan awakes . . .

Lucy, the time has come and gone. I feel very solemn, but very, very happy. Jonathan woke a little after the hour, and all was ready, and he sat up in bed, propped up with pillows. He answered his 'I will' firmly and strongly. I could hardly speak; my heart was so full that even those words seemed to choke me. The dear Sisters were so kind. Please God, I shall never, never forget them, nor the grave and sweet responsibilities I have taken upon me. I must tell you of my wedding present. When the chaplain and the Sisters had left me alone with my husband—oh, Lucy, it is the first time I have written the words 'my husband'—left me alone with my husband, I took the book from under his pillow, and wrapped it up in white paper, and tied it with a little bit of pale blue ribbon which was round my neck, and sealed it over the knot with sealing-wax, and for my seal I used my wedding ring. Then I kissed it and showed it to my husband, and told him that I would keep it so, and then it would be an outward and visible sign[4] for us all our lives that we trusted each other; that I would never open it unless it were for his own dear sake or for the sake of some stern duty. Then he took my hand in his, and oh, Lucy, it was the first time he took *his wife's* hand, and said that it was the dearest thing in all the wide world, and that he would go through all the past again to win it, if need be. The poor dear meant to have said a part of the past; but he cannot think of time yet, and I shall not wonder if at first he mixes up not only the month, but the year.

Well, my dear, what could I say? I could only tell him that I was the happiest woman in all the wide world, and that I had nothing to give

3. This illness regularly afflicts sensitive protagonists of Victorian novels, though twentieth-century physicians find it impossible to diagnose: it is more physical than neurosis, more rooted in psychic torment than physical disease.

4. Mina's words echo the Catholic catechism, according to which "the sacraments are outward (visible) signs instituted by Christ to give grace." As their marriage by a chaplain in a Catholic hospital indicates, Mina and Jonathan are abandoning their secular confidence for the mysteries of an ancient religion, a reversion Van Helsing will reinforce.

him[5] except myself, my life, and my trust, and that with these went my love and duty for all the days of my life. And, my dear, when he kissed me, and drew me to him with his poor weak hands, it was like a very solemn pledge between us . . .

Lucy dear, do you know why I tell you all this? It is not only because it is all sweet to me, but because you have been, and are, very dear to me. It was my privilege to be your friend and guide[6] when you came from the schoolroom to prepare for the world of life. I want you to see now, and with the eyes of a very happy wife, whither duty has led me; so that in your own married life you too may be all happy as I am. My dear, please Almighty God, your life may be all it promises: a long day of sunshine, with no harsh wind, no forgetting duty, no distrust. I must not wish you no pain, for that can never be; but I do hope you will be *always* as happy as I am *now*. Goodbye, my dear. I shall post this at once, and, perhaps, write you very soon again. I must stop, for Jonathan is waking—I must attend to my husband!

Your ever-loving
MINA HARKER.

Letter, Lucy Westenra to Mina Harker

Whitby, 30 August.[7]

My dearest Mina,—

Oceans of love and millions of kisses, and may you soon be in your own home with your husband. I wish you could be coming home soon enough to stay with us here. This strong air would soon restore Jonathan; it has quite restored me. I have an appetite like a cormorant, am full of life, and sleep well. You will be glad to know that I have quite given up walking in my sleep. I think I have not stirred out of my bed for a week, that is when I once got into it at night. Arthur says I am getting fat. By the way, I forgot to tell you that Arthur is here. We have such walks and drives, and rides, and rowing, and tennis, and fishing together; and I love him more than ever. He *tells me* that he loves me more, but I doubt that, for at first he told me that he couldn't love me more than he did then. But this is nonsense. There he is, calling to me. So no more just at present from your loving

LUCY.

P.S.—Mother sends her love. She seems better, poor dear.
P.P.S.—We are to be married on 28 September.

5. No dowry or well-connected family.
6. We initially assumed that Lucy and Mina were privileged schoolgirls together; in most film adaptations they are equally sequestered young ladies. We now learn that Mina was Lucy's teacher. As Mina becomes more enterprising and Lucy more enthralled, their class differences come to the fore.
7. A possible misprint for "August 20," when, according to Mina, Lucy did seem to be improving as Dracula left Whitby for London. By August 24 she is again deteriorating.

Dr Seward's Diary

20 August.—The case of Renfield grows even more interesting. He has now so far quieted that there are spells of cessation from his passion. For the first week after his attack he was perpetually violent. Then one night, just as the moon rose, he grew quiet, and kept murmuring to himself: 'Now I can wait; now I can wait.' The attendant came to tell me, so I ran down at once to have a look at him. He was still in the strait-waistcoat and in the padded room, but the suffused look had gone from his face, and his eyes had something of their old pleading—I might almost say, 'cringing'—softness. I was satisfied with his present condition, and directed him to be relieved. The attendants hesitated, but finally carried out my wishes without protest. It was a strange thing that the patient had humour enough to see their distrust, for, coming close to me, he said in a whisper, all the while looking furtively at them:—

'They think I could hurt you! Fancy *me* hurting *you*! The fools!'

It was soothing, somehow, to the feelings to find myself dissociated even in the mind of this poor madman from the others; but all the same I do not follow his thought. Am I to take it that I have anything in common with him, so that we are, as it were, to stand together; or has he to gain from me some good so stupendous that my well-being is needful to him? I must find out later on. Tonight he will not speak. Even the offer of a kitten or even a full-grown cat will not tempt him. He will only say: 'I don't take any stock in cats. I have more to think of now, and I can wait; I can wait.'

After a while I left him. The attendant tells me that he was quiet until just before dawn, and that then he began to get uneasy, and at length violent, until at last he fell into a paroxysm which exhausted him so that he swooned into a sort of coma.

. . . Three nights has the same thing happened—violent all day, then quiet from moonrise to sunrise. I wish I could get some clue to the cause. It would almost seem as if there was some influence which came and went. Happy thought! We shall tonight play sane wits against mad ones. He escaped before without our help; tonight he shall escape with it. We shall give him a chance, and have the men ready to follow in case they are required . . .

23 August.—'The unexpected always happens.'[8] How well Disraeli knew life. Our bird when he found the cage open would not fly, so all our subtle arrangements went for nought. At any rate, we have proved one thing: that the spells of quietness last a reasonable time. We shall in future be able to ease his bonds for a few hours each day. I have

---

8. From Benjamin Disraeli's 1845 novel *Sybil, or the Two Nations*, an account of the Chartist Movement within the oppressed laboring class.

given orders to the night attendant merely to shut him in the padded room, when once he is quiet, until an hour before sunrise. The poor soul's body will enjoy the relief even if his mind cannot appreciate it. Hark! The unexpected again! I am called; the patient has once more escaped.

Later.— Another night adventure. Renfield artfully waited until the attendant was entering the room to inspect. Then he dashed out past him and flew down the passage. I sent word for the attendants to follow. Again he went into the grounds of the deserted house, and we found him in the same place, pressed against the old chapel door. When he saw me he became furious, and had not the attendants seized him in time, he would have tried to kill me. As we were holding him a strange thing happened. He suddenly redoubled his efforts, and then as suddenly grew calm. I looked round instinctively, but could see nothing. Then I caught the patient's eye and followed it, but could trace nothing as it looked into the moonlit sky except a big bat, which was flapping its silent and ghostly way to the west. Bats usually wheel and flit about, but this one seemed to go straight on, as if it knew where it was bound for or had some intention of its own. The patient grew calmer every instant, and presently said:—

'You needn't tie me; I shall go quietly!' Without trouble we came back to the house. I feel there is something ominous in his calm, and shall not forget this night . . .

Lucy Westenra's Diary

*Hillingham, 24 August.—*I must imitate Mina, and keep writing things down. Then we can have long talks when we do meet. I wonder when it will be. I wish she were with me again, for I feel so unhappy. Last night I seemed to be dreaming again just as I was at Whitby. Perhaps it is the change of air, or getting home again. It is all dark and horrid to me, for I can remember nothing; but I am full of vague fear, and I feel so weak and worn out. When Arthur came to lunch he looked quite grieved when he saw me, and I hadn't the spirit to try to be cheerful. I wonder if I could sleep in mother's room tonight. I shall make an excuse and try.

*25 August.—*Another bad night. Mother did not seem to take to my proposal. She seems not too well herself, and doubtless she fears to worry me. I tried to keep awake, and succeeded for a while; but when the clock struck twelve it waked me from a doze, so I must have been falling asleep. There was a sort of scratching or flapping at the window, but I did not mind it, and as I remember no more, I suppose I must then have fallen asleep. More bad dreams. I wish I could remember them. This morning I am horribly weak. My face is ghastly pale, and my throat pains me. It must be something wrong with my lungs, for I don't seem ever to get air enough. I shall try to cheer up when Arthur comes, or else I know he will be miserable to see me so.

Letter, Arthur Holmwood to Dr Seward

Albemarle Hotel,[9] *31 August.*

My dear Jack,—

I want you to do me a favour. Lucy is ill; that is, she has no special disease, but she looks awful, and is getting worse every day. I have asked her if there is any cause; I do not dare to ask her mother, for to disturb the poor lady's mind about her daughter in her present state of health would be fatal. Mrs Westenra has confided to me that her doom is spoken—disease of the heart—though poor Lucy does not know it yet. I am sure that there is something preying on my dear girl's mind. I am most distracted when I think of her; to look at her gives me a pang. I told her I should ask you to see her, and though she demurred at first—I know why, old fellow—she finally consented. It will be a painful task for you, I know, old friend, but it is for *her* sake, and I must not hesitate to ask, or you to act. You are to come to lunch at Hillingham tomorrow, two o'clock, so as not to arouse any suspicion in Mrs Westenra, and after lunch Lucy will take an opportunity of being alone with you. I shall come in for tea, and we can go away together; I am filled with anxiety, and want to consult with you alone as soon as I can after you have seen her. Do not fail!

ARTHUR.

Telegram, Arthur Holmwood to Dr Seward

1 September.

Am summoned to see my father, who is worse. Am writing. Write me fully by tonight's post to Ring. Wire me if necessary.

Letter from Dr Seward to Arthur Holmwood

2 September.

My dear old fellow,—

With regard to Miss Westenra's health, I hasten to let you know at once that in my opinion there is not any functional disturbance or any malady that I know of. At the same time, I am not by any means satisfied with her appearance; she is woefully different from what she was when I saw her last. Of course you must bear in mind that I did not have full opportunity of examination such as I should wish; our

9. Arthur brings us into another world from Jonathan's coerced and uncomfortable journey and Mina's strenuous self-discipline: the Albemarle was the most fashionable West End hotel of the 1890s.

very friendship makes a little difficulty which not even medical science or custom can bridge over. I had better tell you exactly what happened, leaving you to draw, in a measure, your own conclusions. I shall then say what I have done and propose doing.

I found Miss Westenra in seemingly gay spirits. Her mother was present, and in a few seconds I made up my mind that she was trying all she knew to mislead her mother and prevent her from being anxious. I have no doubt she guesses, if she does not know, what need of caution there is. We lunched alone, and as we all exerted ourselves to be cheerful, we got, as some kind of reward for our labours, some real cheerfulness amongst us. Then Mrs Westenra went to lie down, and Lucy was left with me. We went into her boudoir, and till we got there her gaiety remained, for the servants were coming and going. As soon as the door was closed, however, the mask fell from her face, and she sank down into a chair with a great sigh, and hid her eyes with her hand. When I saw that her high spirits had failed, I at once took advantage of her reaction to make a diagnosis. She said to me very sweetly:—

'I cannot tell you how I loathe talking about myself.' I reminded her that a doctor's confidence was sacred,[1] but that you were grievously anxious about her. She caught on to my meaning at once, and settled that matter in a word. 'Tell Arthur everything you choose. I do not care for myself, but all for him!' So I am quite free.

I could easily see that she is somewhat bloodless, but I could not see the usual anaemic signs, and by a chance I was actually able to test the quality of her blood, for in opening a window which was stiff a cord gave way, and she cut her hand slightly with broken glass. It was a slight matter in itself, but it gave me an evident chance, and I secured a few drops of the blood and have analysed them. The qualitative analysis gives a quite normal condition, and shows, I should infer, in itself a vigorous state of health. In other physical matters I was quite satisfied that there is no need for anxiety; but as there must be a cause somewhere, I have come to the conclusion that it must be something mental. She complains of difficulty in breathing satisfactorily at times, and of heavy, lethargic sleep, with dreams that frighten her, but regarding which she can remember nothing. She says that as a child she used to walk in her sleep, and that when in Whitby the habit came back, and that once she walked out in the night and went to the East Cliff, where Miss Murray found her; but she assures me that of late the habit has not returned. I am in doubt, and so have done the best thing I know of; I have written to my old friend and master, Professor Van Helsing,[2] of Amsterdam, who knows as much about obscure diseases as any one in the world. I have asked him to come over, and as you told me that

1. Seward distributes his medical reports profligately.
2. Seward's initial report presents Van Helsing only in his scientific role: he will acquire more professions as he goes along.

all things were to be at your charge, I have mentioned to him who you are and your relations to Miss Westenra. This, my dear fellow, is only in obedience to your wishes, for I am only too proud and happy to do anything I can for her. Van Helsing would, I know, do anything for me for a personal reason. So, no matter on what ground he comes, we must accept his wishes. He is a seemingly arbitrary man, but this is because he knows what he is talking about better than any one else. He is a philosopher and a metaphysician, and one of the most advanced scientists of his day; and he has, I believe, an absolutely open mind. This, with an iron nerve, a temper of the ice-brook,[3] an indomitable resolution, self-command and toleration exalted from virtues to blessings, and the kindliest and truest heart that beats—these form his equipment for the noble work that he is doing for mankind—work both in theory and practice, for his views are as wide as his all-embracing sympathy. I tell you these facts that you may know why I have such confidence in him. I have asked him to come at once. I shall see Miss Westenra tomorrow again. She is to meet me at the Stores,[4] so that I may not alarm her mother by too early a repetition of my call.

Yours always,
JOHN SEWARD.

Letter, Abraham Van Helsing, M.D., D.PH., D.LIT.,
Etc., Etc., to Dr Seward

2 September.

My good Friend,—

When I have received your letter I am already coming to you. By good fortune I can leave just at once, without wrong to any of those who have trusted me. Were fortune other, then it were bad for those who have trusted, for I come to my friend when he call me to aid those he holds dear. Tell your friend that when that time you suck from my wound[5] so swiftly the poison of the gangrene from that knife that our other friend, too nervous, let slip, you did more for him when he wants my aids and you call for them than all his great fortune could do. But it is pleasure added to do for him, your friend; it is to you that I come. Have then rooms for me at the Great Eastern Hotel,[6] so that I may be near to hand, and please it so arrange that we may see the young lady not too late on tomorrow, for it is likely that I may have to return here

---

3. In describing Van Helsing, Seward misquotes *Othello* 5.2.298–300.
4. Fashionable slang for the elegant department store Harrod's, which was a social meeting place among the wealthy.
5. Van Helsing's startlingly vampiric memory suffuses Stoker's good men with a homoeroticism his vampires shun. It is difficult to picture the respectable Van Helsing and Seward indulging in these adventures; they seem to spring from the romances of Stoker's popular contemporaries, Robert Louis Stevenson and H. Rider Haggard.
6. Convenient to the boat train from Holland, but not as chic as the Albemarle.

that night. But if need be I shall come again in three days, and stay longer if it must. Till then goodbye, my friend John.

VAN HELSING.

Letter, Dr Seward to Hon. Arthur Holmwood

3 September.

My dear Art,—

Van Helsing has come and gone. He came on with me to Hillingham, and found that, by Lucy's discretion, her mother was lunching out, so that we were alone with her. Van Helsing made a very careful examination of the patient. He is to report to me, and I shall advise you, for of course I was not present all the time. He is, I fear, much concerned, but says he must think. When I told him of our friendship and how you trust to me in the matter, he said: 'You must tell him all you think. Tell him what I think, if you can guess it, if you will. Nay, I am not jesting. This is no jest, but life and death, perhaps more.' I asked what he meant by that, for he was very serious. This was when we had come back to town, and he was having a cup of tea before starting on his return to Amsterdam. He would not give me any further clue. You must not be angry with him, Art, because his very reticence means that all his brains are working for her good. He will speak plainly enough when the time comes, be sure. So I told him I would simply write an account of our visit, just as if I were doing a descriptive special article for the *Daily Telegraph*. He seemed not to notice, but remarked that the smuts[7] in London were not quite so bad as they used to be when he was a student here. I am to get his report tomorrow if he can possibly make it. In any case I am to have a letter.

Well, as to the visit. Lucy was more cheerful than on the day I first saw her, and certainly looked better. She had lost something of the ghastly look that so upset you, and her breathing was normal. She was very sweet to the Professor (as she always is), and tried to make him feel at ease; though I could see that the poor girl was making a hard struggle for it. I believe Van Helsing saw it, too, for I saw the quick look under his bushy brows that I knew of old. Then he began to chat of all things, except ourselves and diseases, and with such an infinite geniality that I could see poor Lucy's pretence of animation merge into reality. Then, without any seeming change, he brought the conversation gently round to his visit, and suavely said:—

'My dear young miss, I have the so great pleasure because you are much beloved. That is much, my dear, even were there that which I do not see. They told me you were down in the spirit, and that you were of a ghastly pale. To them I say: "Pouf!" ' And he snapped his fingers at me and went on: 'But you and I shall show them how wrong

7. Smog.

they are. How can he'—and he pointed at me with the same look and gesture as that with which once he pointed me out to his class, on, or rather after, a particular occasion which he never fails to remind me of—'know anything of a young ladies? He has his madmans to play with, and to bring them back to happiness and to those that love them. It is much to do, and, oh, but there are rewards, in that we can bestow such happiness. But the young ladies! He has no wife nor daughter, and the young do not tell themselves to the young, but to the old, like me, who have known so many sorrows and the causes of them. So, my dear, we will send him away to smoke the cigarette in the garden, whiles you and I have little talk all to ourselves.' I took the hint, and strolled about, and presently the Professor came to the window and called me in. He looked grave, but said: 'I have made careful examination, but there is no functional cause. With you I agree that there has been much blood lost; it has been, but is not. But the conditions of her are in no way anaemic. I have asked her to send me her maid, that I may ask just one or two question, that so I may not chance to miss nothing. I know well what she will say. And yet there is cause; there is always cause for everything. I must go back home and think. You must send to me the telegram every day; and if there be cause I shall come again. The disease—for not to be all well is a disease—interest me, and the sweet young dear, she interest me too. She charm me, and for her, if not for you or disease, I come.'

As I tell you, he would not say a word more, even when we were alone. And so now, Art, you know all I know. I shall keep stern watch. I trust your poor father is rallying. It must be a terrible thing to you, my dear old fellow, to be placed in such a position between two people who are both so dear to you. I know your idea of duty to your father, and you are right to stick to it; but, if need be, I shall send you word to come at once to Lucy; so do not be over-anxious unless you hear from me.

Dr Seward's Diary

4 September.—Zoophagous patient still keeps up our interest in him. He had only one outburst, and that was yesterday at an unusual time. Just before the stroke of noon he began to grow restless. The attendant knew the symptoms, and at once summoned aid. Fortunately the men came at a run, and were just in time, for at the stroke of noon he became so violent that it took all their strength to hold him. In about five minutes, however, he began to get more and more quiet, and finally sank into a sort of melancholy, in which state he has remained up to now. The attendant tells me that his screams whilst in the paroxysm were really appalling; I found my hands full when I got in, attending to some of the other patients who were frightened by him. Indeed, I can quite understand the effect, for the sounds disturbed even me, though I was some distance away. It is now after the dinner-hour of the asylum, and as yet my patient sits in a corner brooding, with a dull, sullen, woe-begone look in his face, which seems rather to indicate than to show something directly. I cannot quite understand it.

Later.—Another change in my patient. At five o'clock I looked in on him, and found him seemingly as happy and contented as he used to be. He was catching flies and eating them, and was keeping note of his capture by making nail-marks on the edge of the door between the ridges of padding. When he saw me, he came over and apologized for his bad conduct, and asked me in a very humble, cringing way to be led back to his own room and to have his notebook again. I thought it well to humour him; so he is back in his room, with the window open. He has the sugar of his tea spread out on the window-sill, and is reaping quite a harvest of flies. He is not now eating them, but putting them into a box, as of old, and is already examining the corners of his room to find a spider. I tried to get him to talk about the past few days, for any clue to his thoughts would be of immense help to me; but he would not rise. For a moment or two he looked very sad, and said in a sort of far-away voice, as though saying it rather to himself than to me:—

'All over! all over! He has deserted me. No hope for me now unless I do it for myself!' Then suddenly turning to me in a resolute way, he said: 'Doctor, won't you be very good to me and let me have a little more sugar? I think it would be good for me.'

'And the flies?' I said.

'Yes! The flies like it, too, and I like the flies; therefore I like it.' And there are people who know so little as to think that madmen do not argue. I procured him a double supply, and left him as happy a man as, I suppose, any in the world. I wish I could fathom his mind.

Midnight.—Another change in him. I had been to see Miss Westenra, whom I found much better, and had just returned, and was standing at our own gate looking at the sunset, when once more I heard him yelling. As his room is on this side of the house, I could hear it better than in the morning. It was a shock to me to turn from the wonderful smoky beauty of a sunset over London, with its lurid lights and inky shadows and all the marvelous tints that come on foul clouds even as on foul water, and to realize all the grim sternness of my own cold stone building, with its wealth of breathing misery, and my own desolate heart to endure it all. I reached him just as the sun was going down, and from his window saw the red disc sink. As it sank he became less and less frenzied; and just as it dipped he slid from the hands that held him, an inert mass, on the floor. It is wonderful, however, what intellectual recuperative power lunatics have, for within a few minutes he stood up quite calmly and looked around him. I signalled to the attendants not to hold him, for I was anxious to see what he would do. He went straight over to the window and brushed out the crumbs of sugar; then he took his fly-box and emptied it outside, and threw away the box; then he shut the window, and crossing over, sat down on his bed. All this surprised me, so I asked him: 'Are you not going to keep flies any more?'

'No,' said he; 'I am sick of all that rubbish!' He certainly is a wonderfully interesting study. I wish I could get some glimpse of his mind or of the cause of his sudden passion. Stop; there may be a clue after all, if we can find why today his paroxysms came on at high noon and at sunset. Can it be that there is a malign influence of the sun at periods which affects certain natures—as at times the moon does others? We shall see.

Telegram, Seward, London, to Van Helsing, Amsterdam

4 September.—Patient still better today.

Telegram, Seward, London, to Van Helsing, Amsterdam

5 September.—Patient greatly improved. Good appetite; sleeps naturally; good spirits; colour coming back.

Telegram, Seward, London, to Van Helsing, Amsterdam

6 September.—Terrible change for the worse. Come at once; do not lose an hour. I hold over telegram to Holmwood till have seen you.

Chapter X

Letter, Dr Seward to Hon. Arthur Holmwood

6 September.

My dear Art,—

My news today is not so good. Lucy this morning had gone back a bit. There is, however, one good thing which has arisen from it: Mrs Westenra was naturally anxious concerning Lucy, and has consulted me professionally about her. I took advantage of the opportunity, and told her that my old master, Van Helsing, the great specialist, was coming to stay with me, and that I would put her in his charge conjointly with myself; so now we can come and go without alarming her unduly, for a shock to her would mean sudden death, and this, in Lucy's weak condition, might be disastrous to her. We are hedged in with difficulties, all of us, my poor old fellow; but, please God, we shall come through them all right. If any need I shall write, so that, if you do not hear from me, take it for granted that I am simply waiting for news. In haste,

Yours ever,

JOHN SEWARD.

Dr Seward's Diary

7 September.—The first thing Van Helsing said to me when we met at Liverpool Street was:—

'Have you said anything to our young friend the lover of her?'

'No,' I said. 'I waited till I had seen you, as I said in my telegram. I wrote him a letter simply telling him that you were coming, as Miss Westenra was not so well, and that I should let him know if need be.'

'Right, my friend,' he said, 'quite right! Better he not know as yet; perhaps he shall never know. I pray so; but if it be needed, then he shall know all. And, my good friend John, let me caution you. You deal with the madmen. All men are mad in some way or the other; and inasmuch as you deal discreetly with your madmen, so deal with God's madmen, too—the rest of the world. You tell not your madmen what you do nor why you do it; you tell them not what you think. So you shall keep knowledge in its place, where it may rest—where it may gather its kind around it and breed. You and I shall keep as yet what we know here, and here.' He touched me on the heart and on the forehead, and then touched himself the same way. 'I have for myself thoughts at the present. Later I shall unfold to you.'

'Why not now?' I asked. 'It may do some good; we may arrive at some decision.' He stopped and looked at me, and said:—

'My friend John, when the corn is grown,[1] even before it has ripened—while the milk of its mother-earth is in him, and the sunshine has not yet begun to paint him with his gold, the husbandman he pull the ear and rub him between his rough hands, and blow away the green chaff, and say to you: "Look! he's good corn; he will make good crop when the time comes." ' I did not see the application, and told him so. For reply he reached over and took my ear in his hand and pulled it playfully, as he used long ago to do at lectures, and said: 'The good husbandman tell you so then because he knows, but not till then. But you do not find the good husbandman dig up his planted corn to see if he grow; that is for the children who play at husbandry, and not for

---

1. An ornate bodily and biblical pun in which Van Helsing claims for himself messianic and vampiric powers. In Luke 8.8, Christ tells the parable of the sower and the seed, which he equates with God's word fallen on receptive ears: "And other [seed] fell on good ground, and sprang up, and bare fruit an hundredfold. And when he had said these things, he cried, He that hath ears to hear, let him hear." When he tweaks Dr. Seward's ear, Van Helsing simultaneously plays on ears of corn and compares the good doctor to Christ's disciples and his own words, of course, to God's.

In Luke 8.25, Jesus and his disciples encounter a storm while sailing to Galilee; Jesus controls the wind and water just as Dracula does on the *Demeter.* Dracula and divinity meet in Van Helsing's cryptic, allusive parable.

those who take it as of the work of their life. See you now, friend John? I have sown my corn, and Nature has her work to do in making it sprout; if he sprout at all, there's some promise; and I wait till the ear begins to swell.' He broke off, for he evidently saw that I understood. Then he went on, and very gravely:—

'You were always a careful student, and your casebook was ever more full than the rest. You were only student then; now you are master, and I trust that good habit have not fail. Remember, my friend, that knowledge is stronger than memory, and we should not trust the weaker. Even if you have not kept the good practice, let me tell you that this case of our dear miss is one that may be—mind, I say *may be*—of such interest to us and others that all the rest may not make him kick the beam,[2] as your peoples say. Take then good note of it. Nothing is too small. I counsel you, put down in record even your doubts and surmises. Hereafter it may be of interest to you to see how true you guess. We learn from failure, not from success!'

When I described Lucy's symptoms—the same as before, but infinitely more marked—he looked very grave, but said nothing. He took with him a bag in which were many instruments and drugs, 'the ghastly paraphernalia of our beneficial trade,' as he once called, in one of his lectures, the equipment of a professor of the healing craft. When we were shown in, Mrs Westenra met us. She was alarmed, but not nearly so much as I expected to find her. Nature in one of her beneficent moods has ordained that even death has some antidote to its own terrors. Here, in a case where any shock may prove fatal, matters are so ordered that, from some cause or other, the things not personal—even the terrible change in her daughter to whom she is so attached—do not seem to reach her. It is something like the way Dame Nature gathers round a foreign body an envelope of some insensitive tissue which can protect from evil that which it would otherwise harm by contact. If this be an ordered selfishness, then we should pause before we condemn any one for the vice of egoism, for there may be deeper roots for its causes than we have knowledge of.

I used my knowledge of this phase of spiritual pathology, and laid down a rule that she should not be present with Lucy or think of her illness more than was absolutely required. She assented readily, so readily that I saw again the hand of Nature fighting for life. Van Helsing and I were shown up to Lucy's room. If I was shocked when I saw her yesterday, I was horrified when I saw her today. She was ghastly, chalkily pale; the red seemed to have gone even from her lips and gums, and the bones of her face stood out prominently; her breathing was painful to see or hear. Van Helsing's face grew set as marble, and his eyebrows converged till they almost touched over his nose. Lucy lay motionless

---

2. Presumably, on a balance scale, where the importance of Lucy's case would outweigh all others.

and did not seem to have strength to speak, so for a while we were all silent. Then Van Helsing beckoned to me, and we went gently out of the room. The instant we had closed the door he stepped quickly along the passage to the next door, which was open. Then he pulled me quickly in with him and closed the door. 'My God!' he said; 'this is dreadful. There is no time to be lost. She will die for sheer want of blood to keep the heart's action as it should be. There must be transfusion of blood[3] at once. Is it you or me?'

'I am younger and stronger, Professor. It must be me.'

'Then get ready at once. I will bring up my bag. I am prepared.'

I went downstairs with him, and as we were going there was a knock at the hall door. When we reached the hall the maid had just opened the door, and Arthur was stepping quickly in. He rushed up to me, saying in an eager whisper:—

'Jack, I was so anxious. I read between the lines of your letter, and have been in an agony. The dad was better, so I ran down here to see for myself. Is not that gentleman Dr Van Helsing? I am so thankful to you, sir, for coming.' When first the Professor's eye had lit upon him he had been angry at any interruption at such a time; but now, as he took in his stalwart proportions and recognized the strong young manhood which seemed to emanate from him, his eyes gleamed. Without a pause he said to him gravely as he held out his hand:—

'Sir, you have come in time. You are the lover of our dear miss. She is bad, very, very bad. Nay, my child, do not go like that.' For he suddenly grew pale and sat down in a chair almost fainting. 'You are to help her. You can do more than any that live, and your courage is your best help.'

'What can I do?' asked Arthur hoarsely. 'Tell me, and I shall do it. My life is hers, and I would give the last drop of blood in my body for her.' The Professor has a strongly humorous side, and I could from old knowledge detect a trace of its origin in his answer:—

'My young sir, I do not ask so much as that—not the last!'

'What shall I do?' There was fire in his eyes, and his open nostril quivered with intent. Van Helsing slapped him on the shoulder. 'Come!' he said. 'You are a man, and it is a man we want. You are better than me, better than my friend John.' Arthur looked bewildered, and the Professor went on by explaining in a kindly way:—

'Young miss is bad, very bad. She wants blood,[4] and blood she must have or die. My friend John and I have consulted; and we are about to perform what we call transfusion of blood—to transfer from full veins

---

3. Van Helsing's treatment of Lucy is medically questionable since he transfuses blood into her veins indiscriminately, with no regard for the blood types Karl Landsteiner would discover in the 1920s. We now know that he is more likely to kill his patient than to cure her.

4. This image of Lucy as a natural vampire who, through scientific technology, ingests others' blood and vitality recalls Mary Braddon's medical vampire story "Good Lady Ducayne" (1896).

of one to the empty veins which pine for him. John was to give his blood, as he is the more young and strong than me'—here Arthur took my hand and wrung it hard in silence—'but, now you are here, you are more good than us, old or young, who toil much in the world of thought. Our nerves are not so calm and our blood not so bright than yours!' Arthur turned to him and said:—

'If you only knew how gladly I would die for her you would understand—'

He stopped, with a sort of choke in his voice.

'Good boy!' said Van Helsing. 'In the not-so-far-off you will be happy that you have done all for her you love. Come now and be silent. You shall kiss her once before it is done, but then you must go; and you must leave at my sign. Say no word to Madame; you know how it is with her! There must be no shock; any knowledge of this would be one. Come!'

We all went up to Lucy's room. Arthur by direction remained outside. Lucy turned her head and looked at us, but said nothing. She was not asleep, but she was simply too weak to make the effort. Her eyes spoke to us; that was all. Van Helsing took some things from his bag and laid them on a little table out of sight. Then he mixed a narcotic, and coming over to the bed, said cheerily:—

'Now, little miss, here is your medicine. Drink it off, like a good child. See, I lift you so that to swallow is easy. Yes.' She had made the effort with success.

It astonished me how long the drug took to act. This, in fact, marked the extent of her weakness. The time seemed endless until sleep began to flicker in her eyelids. At last, however, the narcotic began to manifest its potency; and she fell into a deep sleep. When the Professor was satisfied he called Arthur into the room, and bade him strip off his coat. Then he added: 'You may take that one little kiss whiles I bring over the table. Friend John, help to me!' So neither of us looked whilst he bent over her.

Van Helsing turning to me, said:—

'He is so young and strong and of blood so pure that we need not defibrinate[5] it.'

Then with swiftness, but with absolute method, Van Helsing performed the operation. As the transfusion went on something like life seemed to come back to poor Lucy's cheeks, and through Arthur's growing pallor the joy of his face seemed absolutely to shine. After a bit I began to grow anxious, for the loss of blood was telling on Arthur, strong man as he was. It gave me an idea of what terrible strain Lucy's system must have undergone that what weakened Arthur only partially restored her. But the Professor's face was set, and he stood watch in

---

5. Remove fibrin, the clotting material in blood.

hand and with his eyes fixed now on the patient and now on Arthur. I could hear my own heart beat. Presently he said in a soft voice: 'Do not stir an instant. It is enough. You attend him; I will look to her.' When all was over I could see how much Arthur was weakened. I dressed the wound and took his arm to bring him away, when Van Helsing spoke without turning round—the man seems to have eyes in the back of his head:—

'The brave lover, I think deserve another kiss, which he shall have presently.' And as he had now finished his operation, he adjusted the pillow to the patient's head. As he did so the narrow black velvet band which she seems always to wear round her throat, buckled with an old diamond buckle which her lover had given her, was dragged a little up, and showed a red mark on her throat. Arthur did not notice it, but I could hear the deep hiss of indrawn breath which is one of Van Helsing's ways of betraying emotion. He said nothing at the moment, but turned to me, saying: 'Now take down our brave young lover, give him of the port wine, and let him lie down a while. He must then go home and rest, sleep much and eat much, that he may be recruited of what he has so given to his love. He must not stay here. Hold! a moment. I may take it, sir, that you are anxious of result. Then bring it with you that in all ways the operation is successful. You have saved her life this time, and you can go home and rest easy in mind that all that can be is. I shall tell her all when she is well; she shall love you none the less for what you have done. Good-bye.'

When Arthur had gone I went back to the room. Lucy was sleeping gently, but her breathing was stronger; I could see the counterpane move as her breast heaved. By the bedside sat Van Helsing, looking at her intently. The velvet band again covered the red mark. I asked the Professor in a whisper:—

'What do you make of that mark on her throat?'

'What do you make of it?'

'I have not seen it yet,' I answered, and then and there proceeded to loose the band. Just over the external jugular vein there were two punctures, not large, but not wholesome-looking. There was no sign of disease, but the edges were white and worn-looking, as if by some trituration.[6] It at once occurred to me that this wound, or whatever it was, might be the means of that manifest loss of blood; but I abandoned the idea as soon as formed, for such a thing could not be. The whole bed would have been drenched to a scarlet with the blood which the girl must have lost to leave such a pallor as she had before the transfusion.

'Well?' said Van Helsing.

'Well,' said I, 'I can make nothing of it.' The Professor stood up. 'I

6. Bruising, rubbing, or abrasion.

must go back to Amsterdam tonight,' he said. 'There are books and things there which I want. You must remain here all the night, and you must not let your sight pass from her.'

'Shall I have a nurse?' I asked.

'We are the best nurses, you and I. You keep watch all night; see that she is well fed, and that nothing disturbs her. You must not sleep all the night. Later on we can sleep, you and I. I shall be back so soon as possible. And then we may begin.'

'May begin?' I said. 'What on earth do you mean?'

'We shall see!' he answered as he hurried out. He came back a moment later and put his head inside the door, and said, with warning finger held up:—

'Remember, she is your charge. If you leave her, and harm befall, you shall not sleep easy hereafter!'

Dr Seward's Diary (continued)

8 September.—I sat up all night with Lucy. The opiate worked itself off towards dusk, and she waked naturally; she looked a different being from what she had been before the operation. Her spirits even were good, and she was full of a happy vivacity, but I could see evidences of the absolute prostration which she had undergone. When I told Mrs Westenra that Dr Van Helsing had directed that I should sit up with her she almost pooh-poohed the idea, pointing out her daughter's renewed strength and excellent spirits. I was firm, however, and made preparations for my long vigil. When her maid had prepared her for the night I came in, having in the meantime had supper, and took a seat by the bedside. She did not in any way make objection, but looked at me gratefully whenever I caught her eye. After a long spell she seemed sinking off to sleep, but with an effort seemed to pull herself together and shook it off. This was repeated several times, with greater effort and with shorter pauses as the time moved on. It was apparent that she did not want to sleep, so I tackled the subject at once:—

'You do not want to go to sleep?'

'No; I am afraid.'

'Afraid to go to sleep! Why so? It is the boon we all crave for.'

'Ah, not if you were like me—if sleep was to you a presage of horror!'

'A presage of horror! What on earth do you mean?'

'I don't know; oh, I don't know. And that is what is so terrible. All this weakness comes to me in sleep; until I dread the very thought.'

'But, my dear girl, you may sleep tonight. I am here watching you, and I can promise that nothing will happen.'

'Ah, I can trust you!' I seized the opportunity, and said: 'I promise you that if I see any evidence of bad dreams I will wake you at once.'

'You will? Oh, will you really? How good you are to me. Then I will sleep!' And almost at the word she gave a deep sigh of relief, and sank back, asleep.

All night long I watched by her. She never stirred, but slept on and on in a deep, tranquil, life-giving, health-giving sleep. Her lips were slightly parted, and her breast rose and fell with the regularity of a pendulum. There was a smile on her face, and it was evident that no bad dreams had come to disturb her peace of mind.

In the early morning her maid came, and I left her in her care and took myself back home, for I was anxious about many things. I sent a short wire to Van Helsing and to Arthur, telling them of the excellent result of the operation. My own work, with its manifold arrears, took me all day to clear off; it was dark when I was able to inquire about my zoophagous patient. The report was good: he had been quite quiet for the past day and night. A telegram came from Van Helsing at Amsterdam whilst I was at dinner, suggesting that I should be at Hillingham tonight, as it might be well to be at hand, and stating that he was leaving by the night mail and would join me early in the morning.

9 *September.*—I was pretty tired and worn out when I got to Hillingham. For two nights I had hardly had a wink of sleep, and my brain was beginning to feel that numbness which marks cerebral exhaustion. Lucy was up and in cheerful spirits. When she shook hands with me she looked sharply in my face and said:—

'No sitting up tonight for you. You are worn out. I am quite well again; indeed, I am; and if there is to be any sitting up, it is I who will sit up with you.' I would not argue the point, but went and had my supper. Lucy came with me, and, enlivened by her charming presence, I made an excellent meal, and had a couple of glasses of the more than excellent port. Then Lucy took me upstairs, and showed me a room next to her own, where a cosy fire was burning. 'Now,' she said, 'you must stay here. I shall leave this door open and my door too. You can lie on the sofa, for I know that nothing would induce any of you doctors to go to bed whilst there is a patient above the horizon. If I want anything I shall call out, and you can come to me at once.' I could not but acquiesce, for I was 'dog-tired,' and could not have sat up had I tried. So, on her renewing her promise to call me if she should want anything, I lay on the sofa, and forgot all about everything.

Lucy Westenra's Diary

9 *September.*—I feel so happy tonight. I have been so miserably weak, that to be able to think and move about is like feeling sunshine after a long spell of east wind out of a steel sky. Somehow Arthur feels very, very close to me. I seem to feel his presence warm about me. I suppose it is that sickness and weakness are selfish things and turn our inner eyes and sympathy on ourselves, whilst health and strength give Love

rein, and in thought and feeling he can wander where he wills. I know
where my thoughts are. If Arthur only knew! My dear, my dear, your
ears must tingle as you sleep, as mine do waking. Oh, the blissful rest
of last night! How I slept, with that dear, good Dr Seward watching
me. And tonight I shall not fear to sleep, since he is close at hand and
within call. Thank everybody for being so good to me! Thank God!
Good night, Arthur.

Dr Seward's Diary

10 September.—I was conscious of the Professor's hand on my head,
and started awake all in a second. That is one of the things that we
learn in an asylum, at any rate.

'And how is our patient?'

'Well, when I left her, or rather when she left me,' I answered.

'Come, let us see,' he said. And together we went into the room.

The blind was down, and I went over to raise it gently, whilst Van
Helsing stepped, with his soft, cat-like tread, over to the bed.

As I raised the blind, and the morning sunlight flooded the room, I
heard the Professor's low hiss of inspiration, and knowing its rarity, a
deadly fear shot through my heart. As I passed over he moved back,
and his exclamation of horror, 'Gott in Himmel!'[7] needed no enforce-
ment from his agonized face. He raised his hand and pointed to the
bed, and his iron face was drawn and ashen white. I felt my knees
begin to tremble.

There on the bed, seemingly in a swoon, lay poor Lucy, more horribly white and wan-looking than ever. Even the lips were white, and
the gums seemed to have shrunken back from the teeth, as we sometimes see in a corpse after a prolonged illness. Van Helsing raised his
foot to stamp in anger, but the instinct of his life and all the long years
of habit stood to him, and he put it down again softly. 'Quick!' he said.
'Bring the brandy.' I flew to the dining-room, and returned with the
decanter. He wetted the poor white lips with it, and together we rubbed
palm and wrist and heart. He felt her heart, and after a few moments
of agonizing suspense said:—

'It is not too late. It beats, though but feebly. All our work is undone;
we must begin again. There is no young Arthur here now; I have to
call on you yourself this time, friend John.' As he spoke, he was dipping
into his bag and producing the instruments for transfusion; I had taken
off my coat and rolled up my shirt-sleeve. There was no possibility of
an opiate just at present, and no need of one; and so, without a moment's delay, we began the operation. After a time—it did not seem a
short time either, for the draining away of one's blood, no matter how
willingly it be given, is a terrible feeling—Van Helsing held up a warn-

7. "God in heaven!" Van Helsing here cries out in German, not in his native Dutch.

ing finger. 'Do not stir,' he said, 'but I fear that with growing strength she may wake; and that would make danger, oh, so much danger. But I shall precaution take. I shall give hypodermic injection of morphia.' He proceeded then, swiftly and deftly, to carry out his intent. The effect on Lucy was not bad, for the faint seemed to merge subtly into the narcotic sleep. It was with a feeling of personal pride that I could see a faint tinge of colour steal back into the pallid cheeks and lips. No man knows till he experiences it, what it is to feel his own life-blood drawn away into the veins of the woman he loves.

The Professor watched me critically. 'That will do,' he said. 'Already?' I remonstrated. 'You took a great deal more from Art.' To which he smiled a sad sort of smile as he replied:—

'He is her lover, her *fiancé*. You have work, much work, to do for her and for others; and the present will suffice.'

When we stopped the operation, he attended to Lucy, whilst I applied digital pressure to my own incision. I lay down, whilst I waited his leisure to attend to me, for I felt faint and a little sick. By-and-by he bound up my wound, and sent me downstairs to get a glass of wine for myself. As I was leaving the room, he came after me, and half whispered:—

'Mind, nothing must be said of this. If our young lover should turn up unexpected, as before, no word to him. It would at once frighten him and enjealous him, too. There must be none. So!'

When I came back he looked at me carefully, and then said:—

'You are not much the worse. Go into the room, and lie on your sofa, and rest awhile; then have much breakfast, and come here to me.'

I followed out his orders, for I knew how right and wise they were. I had done my part, and now my next duty was to keep up my strength. I felt very weak, and in the weakness lost something of the amazement at what had occurred. I fell asleep on the sofa, however, wondering over and over again how Lucy had made such a retrograde movement, and how she could have been drained of so much blood with no sign anywhere to show for it. I think I must have continued my wonder in my dreams, for, sleeping and waking, my thoughts always came back to the little punctures in her throat and the ragged, exhausted appearance of their edges—tiny though they were.

Lucy slept well into the day; and when she woke she was fairly well and strong, though not nearly so much so as the day before. When Van Helsing had seen her, he went out for a walk, leaving me in charge, with strict injunctions that I was not to leave her for a moment. I could hear his voice in the hall, asking the way to the nearest telegraph office.

Lucy chatted with me freely, and seemed quite unconscious that anything had happened. I tried to keep her amused and interested. When her mother came up to see her, she did not seem to notice any change whatever, but said to me gratefully:—

'We owe you so much, Dr Seward, for all you have done, but you really must now take care not to overwork yourself. You are looking pale yourself. You want a wife to nurse and look after you a bit; that you do!' As she spoke, Lucy turned crimson, though it was only momentarily, for her poor wasted veins could not stand for long such an unwonted drain to the head. The reaction came in excessive pallor as she turned imploring eyes on me. I smiled and nodded, and laid my finger on my lips; with a sigh, she sank back amid her pillows.

Van Helsing returned in a couple of hours, and presently said to me: 'Now you go home, and eat much and drink enough. Make yourself strong. I stay here tonight, and I shall sit up with little miss myself. You and I must watch the case, and we must have none other to know. I have grave reasons. No, do not ask them; think what you will. Do not fear to think even the most not-probable. Good night.'

In the hall two of the maids came to me, and asked if they or either of them might not sit up with Miss Lucy. They implored me to let them; and when I said it was Dr Van Helsing's wish that either he or I should sit up, they asked me quite piteously to intercede with the 'foreign gentleman.' I was much touched by their kindness. Perhaps it is because I am weak at present, and perhaps because it was on Lucy's account, that their devotion was manifested; for over and over again have I seen similar instances of woman's kindness. I got back here in time for a late dinner; went my rounds—all well; and set this down whilst waiting for sleep. It is coming.

11 September.—This afternoon I went over to Hillingham. Found Van Helsing in excellent spirits, and Lucy much better. Shortly after I had arrived, a big parcel from abroad came for the Professor. He opened it with much impressment—assumed, of course—and showed a great bundle of white flowers.

'These are for you, Miss Lucy,' he said.

'For me? Oh, Dr Van Helsing!'

'Yes, my dear, but not for you to play with. These are medicines.' Here Lucy made a wry face. 'Nay, but they are not to take in a decoction[8] or in nauseous form, so you need not snub that so charming nose, or I shall point out to my friend Arthur what woes he may have to endure in seeing so much beauty that he so loves so much distort. Aha, my pretty miss, that bring the so nice nose all straight again. This is medicinal, but you do not know how. I put him in your window, I make pretty wreath, and hang him round your neck, so that you sleep well. Oh yes! they, like the lotus flower,[9] make your trouble forgotten. It smell so like the waters of Lethe,[1] and of that fountain of youth that

8. Extract of a substance, as in medicine.
9. In Homer's *Odyssey*, the mythical lotus eaters eat this plant that causes languor and forgetfulness.
1. In Greek mythology, the dead drink of this river in Hades and thereby forget their lives.

the Conquistadores[2] sought for in the Floridas, and find him all too late.'

Whilst he was speaking, Lucy had been examining the flowers and smelling them. Now she threw them down, saying, with half-laughter and half-disgust:—

'Oh, Professor, I believe you are only putting up a joke on me. Why, these flowers are only common garlic.'

To my surprise, Van Helsing rose up and said with all his sternness, his iron jaw set and his bushy eyebrows meeting:—

'No trifling with me! I never jest! There is grim purpose in all I do; and I warn you that you do not thwart me. Take care, for the sake of others if not for your own.' Then seeing poor Lucy scared, as she might well be, he went on more gently: 'Oh, little miss, my dear, do not fear me. I only do for your good; but there is much virtue to you[3] in those so common flower. See, I place them myself in your room. I make myself the wreath that you are to wear. But hush! no telling to others that make so inquisitive questions. We must obey, and silence is a part of obedience; and obedience is to bring you strong and well into loving arms that wait for you. Now sit still awhile. Come with me, friend John, and you shall help me deck the room with my garlic, which is all the way from Haarlem, where my friend Vanderpool raise herb in his glass-houses all the year. I had to telegraph yesterday, or they would not have been here.'

We went into the room, taking the flowers with us. The Professor's actions were certainly odd and not to be found in any pharmacopoeia that I ever heard of. First he fastened up the windows and latched them securely; next, taking a handful of the flowers, he rubbed them all over the sashes, as though to ensure that every whiff of air that might get in would be laden with the garlic smell. Then with the wisp he rubbed all over the jamb of the door, above, below, and at each side, and round the fireplace in the same way. It all seemed grotesque to me, and presently I said:—

'Well, Professor, I know you always have a reason for what you do, but this certainly puzzles me. It is well we have no sceptic here, or he would say that you were working some spell to keep out an evil spirit.'

'Perhaps I am!' he answered quietly as he began to make the wreath which Lucy was to wear round her neck.

We then waited whilst Lucy made her toilet for the night, and when she was in bed he came and himself fixed the wreath of garlic round her neck. The last words he said to her were:—

2. Spanish adventurers such as Ponce de Leon (1460–1521) searched the New World for a body of water that would restore youth.
3. *Virtue* means not only *goodness*, *chastity* (in women) or *bravery* (in men): Van Helsing uses the word in its archaic sense, "the power or operative influence inherent in a supernatural or divine being" (*OED*).

'Take care you do not disturb it; and even if the room feel close,[4] do not tonight open the window or the door.'

'I promise,' said Lucy, 'and thank you both a thousand times for all your kindness to me! Oh, what have I done to be blessed with such friends?'

As we left the house in my fly,[5] which was waiting, Van Helsing said:—

'Tonight I can sleep in peace, and sleep I want—two nights of travel, much reading in the day between, and much anxiety on the day to follow, and a night to sit up, without to wink. Tomorrow in the morning early you call for me, and we come together to see our pretty miss, so much more strong for my "spell" which I have work. Ho! ho!'

He seemed so confident that I, remembering my own confidence two nights before and with the baneful result, felt awe and vague terror. It must have been my weakness that made me hesitate to tell it to my friend, but I felt it all the more, like unshed tears.

Chapter XI

Lucy Westenra's Diary

12 September.—How good they all are to me. I quite love that dear Dr Van Helsing. I wonder why he was so anxious about these flowers. He positively frightened me, he was so fierce. And yet he must have been right, for I feel comfort from them already. Somehow, I do not dread being alone tonight, and I can go to sleep without fear. I shall not mind any flapping outside the window. Oh, the terrible struggle that I have had against sleep so often of late; the pain of the sleeplessness, or the pain of the fear of sleep,[1] with such unknown horrors as it has for me! How blessed are some people, whose lives have no fears, no dreads; to whom sleep is a blessing that comes nightly, and brings nothing but sweet dreams. Well, here I am tonight, hoping for sleep, and lying like Ophelia in the play, with 'virgin crants and maiden strewments.' I never liked garlic before, but tonight it is delightful! There is peace in its smell; I feel sleep coming already. Good night, everybody.

---

4. With its closed draperies and sealed windows, the typical Victorian sickroom was as airless, even tomblike, as Lucy's chamber.
5. A light one-horse carriage.
1. More Shakespearean echoes and allusions illuminating Lucy's dual condition. In *Macbeth*, fear of sleep torments the guilty king and queen; *Hamlet*'s innocent Ophelia is buried with "virgin crants" and "maiden strewments" (5.1.249–57).

Dr Seward's Diary

13 September.—Called at the Berkeley[2] and found Van Helsing, as usual, up to time. The carriage ordered from the hotel was waiting. The Professor took his bag, which he always brings with him now.

Let all be put down exactly. Van Helsing and I arrived at Hillingham at eight o'clock. It was a lovely morning; the bright sunshine and all the fresh feeling of early autumn seemed like the completion of nature's annual work. The leaves were turning to all kinds of beautiful colours, but had not yet begun to drop from the trees. When we entered we met Mrs Westenra coming out of the morning room. She is always an early riser. She greeted us warmly and said:—

'You will be glad to know that Lucy is better. The dear child is still asleep. I looked into her room and saw her, but did not go in, lest I should disturb her.' The Professor smiled, and looked quite jubilant. He rubbed his hands together, and said:—

'Aha! I thought I had diagnosed the case. My treatment is working,' to which she answered:—

'You must not take all the credit to yourself, doctor. Lucy's state this morning is due in part to me.'

'How do you mean, ma'am?' asked the Professor.

'Well, I was anxious about the dear child in the night, and went into her room. She was sleeping soundly—so soundly that even my coming did not wake her. But the room was awfully stuffy. There were a lot of those horrible, strong-smelling flowers about everywhere, and she had actually a bunch of them round her neck. I feared that the heavy odour would be too much for the dear child in her weak state, so I took them all away and opened a bit of the window to let in a little fresh air. You will be pleased with her, I am sure.'

She moved off into her boudoir, where she usually breakfasted early. As she had spoken, I watched the Professor's face, and saw it turn ashen grey. He had been able to retain his self-command whilst the poor lady was present, for he knew her state and how mischievous a shock would be; he actually smiled on her as he held open the door for her to pass into her room. But the instant she had disappeared he pulled me, suddenly and forcibly, into the dining-room and closed the door.

Then, for the first time in my life, I saw Van Helsing break down. He raised his hands over his head in a sort of mute despair, and then beat his palms together in a helpless way; finally he sat down on a chair, and putting his hands before his face, began to sob, with loud, dry sobs that seemed to come from the very racking of his heart. Then he raised his arms again, as though appealing to the whole universe. 'God! God! God!' he said. 'What have we done, what has this poor thing done, that we are so sore beset? Is there fate amongst us still, sent

2. A comfortable hotel near Piccadilly Circus.

down from the pagan world of old, that such things must be, and in such way? This poor mother, all unknowing, and all for the best as she think, does such thing as lose her daughter body and soul; and we must not tell her, we must not even warn her, or she die, and then both die. Oh, how we are beset! How are all the powers of the devils against us!' Suddenly he jumped to his feet. 'Come,' he said, 'come, we must see and act. Devils or no devils, or all the devils at once, it matters not; we fight him all the same.' He went to the hall-door for his bag, and together we went up to Lucy's room.

Once again I drew up the blind, whilst Van Helsing went towards the bed. This time he did not start as he looked on the poor face with the same awful, waxen pallor as before. He wore a look of stern sadness and infinite pity.

'As I expected,' he murmured, with that hissing inspiration of his which meant so much. Without a word he went and locked the door, and then began to set out on the little table the instruments for yet another operation of transfusion of blood. I had long ago recognized the necessity, and begun to take off my coat, but he stopped me with a warning hand. 'No!' he said. 'Today you must operate. I shall provide. You are weakened already.' As he spoke he took off his coat and rolled up his shirt-sleeve.

Again the operation; again the narcotic; again some return of colour to the ashy cheeks, and the regular breathing of healthy sleep. This time I watched whilst Van Helsing recruited himself and rested.

Presently he took an opportunity of telling Mrs Westenra that she must not remove anything from Lucy's room without consulting him; that the flowers were of medicinal value, and that the breathing of their odour was a part of the system of cure. Then he took over the care of the case himself, saying that he would watch this night and the next and would send me word when to come.

After another hour Lucy waked from her sleep, fresh and bright and seemingly not much the worse for her terrible ordeal.

What does it all mean? I am beginning to wonder if my long habit of life amongst the insane is beginning to tell upon my own brain.

Lucy Westenra's Diary

17 September.—Four days and nights of peace. I am getting so strong again that I hardly know myself. It is as if I had passed through some long nightmare, and had just awakened to see the beautiful sunshine and feel the fresh air of the morning around me. I have a dim half-remembrance of long, anxious times of waiting and fearing; darkness in which there was not even the pain of hope to make present distress more poignant; and then long spells of oblivion, and the rising back to life as a diver coming up through a great press of water. Since, however,

Dr Van Helsing has been with me, all this bad dreaming seems to have passed away; the noises that used to frighten me out of my wits—the flapping against the windows, the distant voices which seemed so close to me, the harsh sounds that came from I know not where and commanded me to do I know not what—have all ceased. I go to bed now without any fear of sleep. I do not even try to keep awake. I have grown quite fond of the garlic, and a boxful arrives for me every day from Haarlem. Tonight Dr Van Helsing is going away, as he has to be for a day in Amsterdam. But I need not be watched; I am well enough to be left alone. Thank God for mother's sake, and dear Arthur's, and for all our friends who have been so kind! I shall not even feel the change, for last night Dr Van Helsing slept in his chair a lot of the time. I found him asleep twice when I awoke; but I did not fear to go to sleep again, although the boughs or bats or something flapped almost angrily against the window-panes.

The Pall Mall Gazette,[3] *18 September*

THE ESCAPED WOLF
PERILOUS ADVENTURE OF OUR INTERVIEWER
Interview with the Keeper in the Zoological Gardens

After many inquiries and almost as many refusals, and perpetually using the words *Pall Mall Gazette* as a sort of talisman, I managed to find the keeper of the section of the Zoological Gardens in which the wolf department is included. Thomas Bilder lives in one of the cottages in the enclosure behind the elephant-house, and was just sitting down to his tea when I found him. Thomas and his wife are hospitable folk, elderly, and without children, and if the specimen I enjoyed of their hospitality be of the average kind, their lives must be pretty comfortable. The keeper would not enter on what he called 'business' until the supper was over, and we were all satisfied. Then when the table was cleared, and he had lit his pipe, he said:—

'Now, sir, you can go on and arsk me what you want. You'll excoose me refoosin' to talk of perfeshunal subjects afore meals. I gives the wolves and the jackals and the hyenas in all our section their tea afore I begins to arsk them questions.'

'How do you mean, ask them questions?' I queried, wishful to get him into a talkative humour.

''Ittin' of them over the 'ead with a pole is one way; scratchin' their hears is another, when gents as is flush wants a bit of a show-orf to their gals. I don't so much mind the fust—the 'ittin' with a pole afore I chucks in their dinner; but I waits till they've 'ad their sherry and kawffee, so to speak, afore I tries on with the ear-scratchin'. Mind you,'

---

he added philosophically, 'there's a deal of the same nature in us as in them theer animiles. Here's you a-comin' and arskin' of me questions about my business, and I that grumpy-like that only for your bloomin' 'arf-quid[4] I'd 'a' seen you blowed fust 'fore I'd answer. Not even when you arsked me sarcastic-like if I'd like you to arsk the Superintendent if you might arsk me questions. Without offence, did I tell yer to go to 'ell?'

'You did.'

'An' when you said you'd report me for usin' of obscene language that was 'ittin' me over the 'ead; but the 'arf-quid made that all right. I weren't a-goin' to fight, so I waited for the food, and did with my 'owl as the wolves, and lions, and tigers does. But, Lor' love yer 'art, now that the old 'ooman has stuck a chunk of her tea-cake in me, an' rinsed me out with her bloomin' old teapot, and I've lit hup, you may scratch my ears for all you're worth, and won't git even a growl out of me. Drive along with your questions. I know what yer a-comin' at, that 'ere escaped wolf.'

'Exactly. I want you to give me your view of it. Just tell me how it happened; and when I know the facts I'll get you to say what you consider was the cause of it, and how you think the whole affair will end.'

'All right, guv'nor. This 'ere is about the 'ole story. That 'ere wolf what we called Bersicker[5] was one of three grey ones that came from Norway to Jamrach's, which we bought off him four year ago. He was a nice well-behaved wolf, that never gave no trouble to talk of. I'm more surprised at 'im for wantin' to get out nor any other animile in the place. But, there, you can't trust wolves no more nor women.'

'Don't you mind him, sir!' broke in Mrs Tom, with a cheery laugh. ''E's got mindin' the animiles so long that blest if he ain't like a old wolf 'isself! But there ain't no 'arm in 'im.'

'Well, sir, it was about two hours after feedin' yesterday when I first hear any disturbance. I was makin' up a litter in the monkey-house for a young puma which is ill; but when I heard the yelpin' and 'owlin' I kem away straight. There was Bersicker a-tearin' like a mad thing at the bars as if he wanted to get out. There wasn't much people about that day, and close at hand was only one man, a tall, thin chap, with a 'ook nose and a pointed beard, with a few white hairs runnin' through it. He had a 'ard, cold look and red eyes, and I took a sort of mislike to him, for it seemed as if it was 'im as they were hirritated at. He 'ad white kid gloves on 'is 'ands, and he pointed out the animiles to me and says: "Keeper, these wolves seem upset at something."

' "Maybe it's you," says I, for I did not like the airs as he give 'isself.

4. Not quite a pound; worth about ten shillings. In 1897, slang for sovereign.
5. Actually, Berserker, recalling Dracula's earlier account of the werewolflike Norse Berserkers, frenzied fighters who wore animal skins in battle.

He didn't git angry, as I 'oped he would, but he smiled a kind of insolent smile, with a mouth full of white, sharp teeth. "Oh no, they wouldn't like me," 'e says.

' "Ow yes, they would," says I, a-imitatin' of him. "They always likes a bone or two to clean their teeth on about tea-time, which you 'as a bagful."

'Well, it was a odd thing, but when the animiles see us a-talking' they lay down, and when I went over to Bersicker he let me stroke his ears same as ever. That there man kem over, and blessed but if he didn't put in his hand and stroke the old wolf's ears too!

' "Tyke care," says I. "Bersicker is quick."

' "Never mind," he says. "I'm used to 'em!"

' "Are you in the business yourself?" I says, tyking off my 'at for a man what trades in wolves, anceterer,[6] is a good friend to keepers.

' "No," says he, "not exactly in the business, but I 'ave made pets of several." And with that he lifts his 'at as perlite as a lord, and walks away. Old Bersicker kep' a-lookin' arter 'im till 'e was out of sight, and then went and lay down in a corner, and wouldn't come hout the 'ole hevening. Well, larst night, so soon as the moon was hup, the wolves here all began a-'owling. There warn't nothing for them to 'owl at. There warn't no one near, except some one that was evidently a-callin' a dog somewheres out back of the gardings in the Park road. Once or twice I went out to see that all was right, and it was, and then the 'owling stopped. Just before twelve o'clock I just took a look round afore turnin' in, an', bust me, but when I kem opposite to old Bersicker's cage, I see the rails broken and twisted about and the cage empty. And that's all I know for certing.'

'Did any one else see anything?'

'One of our gard'ners was a-comin' 'ome about that time from a 'armony,[7] when he sees a big grey dog comin' out through the garding 'edges.[8] At least, so he says; but I don't give much for it myself, for if he did 'e never said a word about it to his missis when 'e got 'ome, and it was only after the escape of the wolf was made known, and we had been up all night a-huntin' of the Park for Bersicker, that he remembered seein' anything. My own belief was that the 'armony 'ad got into his 'ead.'

'Now, Mr Bilder, can you account in any way for the escape of the wolf?'

'Well, sir' he said, with a suspicious sort of modesty, 'I think I can; but I don't know as 'ow you'd be satisfied with the theory.'

'Certainly I shall. If a man like you, who knows the animals from experience, can't hazard a good guess at any rate, who is even to try?'

6. Cockney slang for "etcetera."
7. A glee club.
8. Stoker's Cockney for "garden hedges."

'Well then, sir, I accounts for it this way; it seems to me that 'ere wolf excaped—simply because he wanted to get out.'

From the hearty way that both Thomas and his wife laughed at the joke I could see that it had done service before, and that the whole explanation was simply an elaborate sell. I couldn't cope in badinage with the worthy Thomas, but I thought I knew a surer way to his heart, so I said:—

'Now, Mr Bilder, we'll consider that first half-sovereign worked off, and this brother of his is waiting to be claimed when you've told me what you think will happen.'

'Right y'are, sir,' he said briskly. 'Ye'll excoose me, I know, for a-chaffin' of ye, but the old woman here winked at me, which was as much as telling me to go on.'

'Well, I never!' said the old lady.

'My opinion is this: that 'ere wolf is a-'idin' of, somewheres. The gard'ner wot didn't remember said he was a-gallopin' northward faster than a horse could go; but I don't believe him, for, yer see, sir, wolves don't gallop no more nor dogs does, they not bein' built that way. Wolves is fine things in a storybook, and I dessay when they gets in packs and does be chivyin' somethin' that's more afeared than they is they can make a devel of a noise and chop it up, whatever it is. But, Lor' bless you, in real life a wolf is only a low creature, not half so clever or bold as a good dog; and not half a quarter so much fight in 'im. This one ain't been used to fightin' or even to providin' for hisself, and more like he's somewhere round the Park a-'idin an' a-shiverin' of, and, if he thinks at all, wonderin' where he is to get his breakfast from; or maybe he's got down some area and is in a coal-cellar. My eye, won't some cook get a rum start when she sees his green eyes a-shining at her out of the dark! If he can't get food he's bound to look for it, and mayhap he may chance to light on a butcher's shop in time. If he doesn't, and some nursemaid goes a-walkin' orf with a soldier, leavin' of the hinfant in the perambulator—well then I shouldn't be surprised if the census is one babby the less. That's all.'

I was handing him the half-sovereign, when something came bobbing up against the window, and Mr Bilder's face doubled its natural length with surprise.

'God bless me!' he said. 'If there ain't old Bersicker come back by 'isself!'

He went to the door and opened it; a most unnecessary proceeding it seemed to me. I have always thought that a wild animal never looks so well as when some obstacle of pronounced durability is between us; a personal experience has intensified rather than diminished that idea.

After all, however, there is nothing like custom, for neither Bilder nor his wife thought any more of the wolf than I should of a dog.

The animal itself was as peaceful and well-behaved as that father of all picture-wolves—Red Riding Hood's[9] quondam friend, whilst moving her confidence in masquerade.

The whole scene was an unutterable mixture of comedy and pathos. The wicked wolf that for half a day had paralysed London and set all children in the town shivering in their shoes, was there in a sort of penitent mood, and was received and petted like a sort of vulpine prod-igal son. Old Bilder examined him all over with most tender solicitude, and when he had finished with his penitent said:—

'There, I knew the poor old chap would get into some kind of trou-ble; didn't I say it all along? Here's his head all cut and full of broken glass. 'E's been a-getting over some bloomin' wall or other. It's a shyme that people are allowed to top their walls with broken bottles. This 'ere's what comes of it. Come along. Bersicker.'

He took the wolf and locked him up in a cage, with a piece of meat that satisfied, in quantity at any rate, the elementary conditions of the fatted calf, and went off to report.

I came off, too, to report the only exclusive information that is given today regarding the strange escapade at the Zoo.

Dr Seward's Diary

17 September—I was engaged after dinner in my study posting up[1] my books, which, through press of other work and the many visits to Lucy, had fallen sadly into arrear. Suddenly the door was burst open, and in rushed my patient, with his face distorted with passion. I was thunder-struck, for such a thing as a patient getting of his own accord into the Superintendent's study is almost unknown. Without an instant's pause he made straight at me. He had a dinner-knife in his hand, and, as I saw he was dangerous, I tried to keep the table between us. He was too quick and too strong for me, however; for before I could get my balance he had struck at me and cut my left wrist rather severely. Before he could strike again, however, I got in my right, and he was sprawling on his back on the floor. My wrist bled freely, and quite a little pool trickled on to the carpet. I saw that my friend was not intent on further effort, and occupied myself binding up my wrist, keeping a wary eye on the prostrate figure all the time. When the attendants rushed in, and we turned our attention to him, his employment positively sickened me. He was lying on his belly on the floor licking up, like a dog, the blood which had fallen from my wounded wrist. He was easily secured, and, to my surprise, went with the attendants quite placidly, simply

9. *Grimm's Fairy Tales*, first published in Germany between 1812 and 1815, made this well-known tale of a little girl and the wolf easily available in England. "Quondam": former.
1. Doing accounts.

repeating over and over again: 'The blood is the life! the blood is the life!'[2]

I cannot afford to lose blood just at present: I have lost too much of late for my physical good, and then the prolonged strain of Lucy's illness and its horrible phases is telling on me. I am over-excited and weary, and I need rest, rest, rest. Happily Van Helsing has not summoned me, so I need not forego my sleep; tonight I could not well do without it.

Telegram, Van Helsing, Antwerp, to Seward, Carfax

(SENT TO CARFAX, SUSSEX, AS NO COUNTY GIVEN;
DELIVERED LATE BY TWENTY-TWO HOURS)

17 September. Do not fail to be at Hillingham tonight. If not watching all the time, frequently visit and see that flowers are as placed; very important; do not fail. Shall be with you as soon as possible after arrival.

Dr Seward's Diary

18 September.—Just off for train to London. The arrival of Van Helsing's telegram filled me with dismay. A whole night lost, and I know by bitter experience what may happen in a night. Of course it is possible that all may be well, but what *may* have happened? Surely there is some horrible doom hanging over us that every possible accident should thwart us in all we try to do. I shall take this cylinder with me, and then I can complete my entry on Lucy's phonograph.

Memorandum Left by Lucy Westenra

17 September. Night.—I write this and leave it to be seen, so that no one may by any chance get into any trouble through me. This is an exact record of what took place tonight. I feel I am dying of weakness, and have barely strength to write, but it must be done if I die in the doing.

I went to bed as usual, taking care that the flowers were placed as Dr Van Helsing directed, and soon fell asleep.

I was waked by the flapping at the window, which had begun after that sleep-walking on the cliff at Whitby when Mina saved me, and which now I know so well. I was not afraid, but I did wish that Dr Seward was in the next room—as Dr Van Helsing said he would be—

---

2. Biblical sanction for Renfield's creed is equivocal. The Old Testament is full of prohibitions against blood drinking; see, for instance, Genesis 9.4: "But flesh with the life thereof, which is the blood thereof, shall ye not eat." In the New Testament, however, Jesus famously offers his blood at the Last Supper for sacred consumption: "Then Jesus said unto them, Verily, verily, I say unto you, Except ye eat the flesh of the Son of man, and drink his blood, ye have no life in you" (John 6.53). "Whoso eateth my flesh, and drinketh my blood, hath eternal life; and I will raise him up at the last day" (John 6.54).

so that I might have called him. I tried to go to sleep, but could not. Then there came to me the old fear of sleep, and I determined to keep awake. Perversely sleep would try to come then when I did not want it; so, as I feared to be alone, I opened my door and called out: 'Is there anybody there?' There was no answer. I was afraid to wake mother, and so closed my door again. Then outside in the shrubbery I heard a sort of howl like a dog's, but more fierce and deeper. I went to the window and looked out, but could see nothing, except a big bat, which had evidently been buffeting its wings against the window. So I went back to bed again, but determined not to go to sleep. Presently the door opened, and mother looked in; seeing by my moving that I was not asleep, came in, and sat by me. She said to me even more sweetly and softly than her wont:—

'I was uneasy about you, darling, and came in to see that you were all right.'

I feared she might catch cold sitting there, and asked her to come in and sleep with me, so she came into bed, and lay down beside me; she did not take off her dressing gown, for she said she would only stay a while and then go back to her own bed. As she lay there in my arms, and I in hers, the flapping and buffeting came to the window again. She was startled and a little frightened, and cried out: 'What is that?' I tried to pacify her, and at last succeeded, and she lay quiet; but I could hear her poor dear heart still beating terribly. After a while there was the low howl again out in the shrubbery, and shortly after there was a crash at the window, and a lot of broken glass was hurled on the floor. The window blind blew back with the wind that rushed in, and in the aperture of the broken panes there was the head of a great, gaunt grey wolf. Mother cried out in a fright, and struggled up into a sitting posture, and clutched wildly at anything that would help her. Amongst other things, she clutched the wreath of flowers that Dr Van Helsing insisted on my wearing round my neck, and tore it away from me. For a second or two she sat up, pointing at the wolf, and there was a strange and horrible gurgling in her throat; then she fell over, as if struck with lightning, and her head hit my forehead and made me dizzy for a moment or two. The room and all round seemed to spin round. I kept my eyes fixed on the window, but the wolf drew his head back, and a whole myriad of little specks seemed to come blowing in through the broken window, and wheeling and circling round like the pillar of dust that travellers describe when there is a simoom[3] in the desert. I tried to stir, but there was some spell upon me, and dear mother's poor body, which seemed to grow cold already—for her dear heart had ceased to beat—weighed me down; and I remembered no more for a while.

The time did not seem long, but very, very awful, till I recovered

3. Simoon; a suffocating, sandy wind, common in the Arabian and North African deserts.

consciousness again. Somewhere near, a passing bell was tolling; the dogs all round the neighbourhood were howling; and in our shrubbery, seemingly just outside, a nightingale was singing. I was dazed and stupid with pain and terror and weakness, but the sound of the nightingale seemed like the voice of my dead mother come back to comfort me. The sounds seemed to have awakened the maids, too, for I could hear their bare feet pattering outside my door. I called to them, and they came in, and when they saw what had happened, and what it was that lay over me on the bed, they screamed out. The wind rushed in through the broken window, and the door slammed to. They lifted off the body of my dear mother, and laid her, covered up with a sheet, on the bed after I had got up. They were all so frightened and nervous that I directed them to go to the dining-room and have each a glass of wine. The door flew open for an instant and closed again. The maids shrieked, and then went in a body to the dining-room; and I laid what flowers I had on my dear mother's breast. When they were there I remembered what Dr Van Helsing had told me, but I didn't like to remove them, and, besides, I would have some of the servants to sit up with me now. I was surprised that the maids did not come back. I called them, but got no answer, so I went to the dining-room to look for them.

My heart sank when I saw what had happened. They all four lay helpless on the floor, breathing heavily. The decanter of sherry was on the table half full, but there was a queer, acrid smell about. I was suspicious, and examined the decanter. It smelt of laudanum,[4] and looking on the sideboard, I found that the bottle which mother's doctor uses for her—oh! did use—was empty. What am I to do? what am I to do? I am back in the room with mother. I cannot leave her, and I am alone, save for the sleeping servants, whom someone has drugged. Alone with the dead! I dare not go out, for I can hear the low howl of the wolf through the broken window.

The air seems full of specks, floating and circling in the draught from the window, and the lights burn blue and dim. What am I to do? God shield me from harm this night! I shall hide this paper in my breast, where they shall find it when they come to lay me out. My dear mother gone! It is time that I go too. Goodbye, dear Arthur, if I should not survive this night. God keep you, dear, and God help me!

---

4. A compound of opium and alcohol that was a common Victorian tranquilizer.

Chapter XII

Dr Seward's Diary

18 September.—I drove at once to Hillingham and arrived early. Keeping my cab at the gate, I went up the avenue alone. I knocked gently and rang as quietly as possible, for I feared to disturb Lucy or her mother, and hoped to only bring a servant to the door. After a while, finding no response, I knocked and rang again; still no answer. I cursed the laziness of the servants that they should lie abed at such an hour —for it was now ten o'clock—and so rang and knocked again, but more impatiently, but still without response. Hitherto I had blamed only the servants, but now a terrible fear began to assail me. Was this desolation but another link in the chain of doom which seemed drawing tight around us? Was it indeed a house of death to which I had come, too late? I knew that minutes, even seconds, of delay might mean hours of danger to Lucy, if she had had again one of those frightful relapses; and I went round the house to try if I could find by chance an entry anywhere.

I could find no means of ingress. Every window and door was fastened and locked, and I returned baffled to the porch. As I did so, I heard the rapid pit-pat of a swiftly driven horse's feet. They stopped at the gate, and a few seconds later I met Van Helsing running up the avenue. When he saw me, he gasped out:—

'Then it was you, and just arrived. How is she? Are we too late? Did you not get my telegram?'

I answered as quickly and coherently as I could that I had only got his telegram early in the morning and had not lost a minute in coming here, and that I could not make anyone in the house hear me. He paused and raised his hat as he said solemnly:—

'Then I fear we are too late. God's will be done!' With his usual recuperative energy, he went on: 'Come. If there be no way open to get in, we must make one. Time is all in all to us now.'

We went round to the back of the house, where there was a kitchen window. The Professor took a small surgical saw from his case, and handing it to me, pointed to the iron bars which guarded the window. I attacked them at once and had very soon cut through three of them. Then with a long, thin knife we pushed back the fastening of the sashes and opened the window. I helped the Professor in, and followed him. There was no one in the kitchen or in the servants' rooms, which were close at hand. We tried all the rooms as we went along, and in the dining-room, dimly lit by rays of light through the shutters, found four servant-women lying on the floor. There was no need to think them dead, for their stertorous breathing and the acrid smell of laudanum in the room left no doubt as to their condition. Van Helsing and I looked at each other, and as we moved away he said: 'We can attend to them later.' Then we ascended to Lucy's room. For an instant or two we paused at the door to listen, but there was no sound that we could hear. With white faces and trembling hands, we opened the door gently, and entered the room.

How shall I describe what we saw? On the bed lay two women, Lucy and her mother. The latter lay farthest in, and she was covered with a white sheet, the edge of which had been blown back by the draught through the broken window, showing the drawn, white face, with a look of terror fixed upon it. By her side lay Lucy, with face white and still more drawn. The flowers which had been round her neck we found upon her mother's bosom, and her throat was bare, showing the two little wounds which we had noticed before, but looking horribly white and mangled. Without a word the Professor bent over the bed, his head almost touching poor Lucy's breast; then he gave a quick turn of his head, as of one who listens, and leaping to his feet, he cried out to me:—

'It is not yet too late! Quick! quick! Bring the brandy!'

I flew downstairs and returned with it, taking care to smell and taste it, lest it, too, were drugged like the decanter of sherry which I found on the table. The maids were still breathing, but more restlessly, and I fancied that the narcotic was wearing off. I did not stay to make sure, but returned to Van Helsing. He rubbed the brandy, as on another occasion, on her lips and gums and on her wrists and the palms of her hands. He said to me:—

'I can do this, all that can be at the present. You go wake those maids. Flick them in the face with a wet towel, and flick them hard. Make them get heat and fire and a warm bath. This poor soul is nearly as cold as that beside her. She will need be heated before we can do anything more.'

I went at once, and found little difficulty in waking three of the women. The fourth was only a young girl, and the drug had evidently affected her more strongly, so I lifted her on the sofa and let her sleep. The others were dazed at first, but as remembrance came back to them they cried and sobbed in a hysterical manner. I was stern with them, however, and would not let them talk. I told them that one life was bad enough to lose, and that if they delayed they would sacrifice Miss Lucy. So, sobbing and crying, they went about their way, half clad as they were, and prepared fire and water. Fortunately, the kitchen and boiler fires were still alive, and there was no lack of hot water. We got a bath, and carried Lucy out as she was[1] and placed her in it. Whilst

---

1. That is, still decorously in her nightdress.

we were busy chafing her limbs there was a knock at the hall-door. One of the maids ran off, hurried on some more clothes, and opened it. Then she returned and whispered to us that there was a gentleman who had come with a message from Mr Holmwood. I bade her simply tell him that he must wait, for we could see no one now. She went away with the message, and, engrossed with our work, I clean forgot all about him.

I never saw in all my experience the Professor work in such deadly earnest. I knew—as he knew—that it was a stand-up fight with death, and in a pause told him so. He answered me in a way that I did not understand, but with the sternest look that his face could wear:—

'If that were all, I would stop here where we are now, and let her fade away into peace, for I see no light in life over her horizon.' He went on with his work with, if possible, renewed and more frenzied vigour.

Presently we both began to be conscious that the heat was beginning to be of some effect. Lucy's heart beat a trifle more audibly to the stethoscope, and her lungs had a perceptible movement. Van Helsing's face almost beamed, and as we lifted her from the bath and rolled her in a hot sheet to dry her he said to me:—

'The first gain is ours! Check to the King!'[2]

We took Lucy into another room, which had by now been prepared, and laid her in bed and forced a few drops of brandy down her throat. I noticed that Van Helsing tied a soft silk handkerchief round her throat. She was still unconscious, and was quite as bad as, if not worse than, we had ever seen her.

Van Helsing called in one of the women, and told her to stay with her and not to take her eyes off her till we returned, and then beckoned me out of the room.

'We must consult as to what is to be done,' he said as we descended the stairs. In the hall he opened the dining-room door, and we passed in, he closing the door carefully behind him. The shutters had been opened, but the blinds were already down, with that obedience to the etiquette of death which the British woman of the lower classes always rigidly observes. The room was, therefore, dimly dark. It was, however, light enough for our purposes. Van Helsing's sternness was somewhat relieved by a look of perplexity. He was evidently torturing his mind about something, so I waited for an instant, and he spoke:—

'What are we to do now? Where are we to turn for help? We must have another transfusion of blood, and that soon, or that poor girl's life won't be worth an hour's purchase. You are exhausted already; I am

2. A chess move that places the opponent's most valuable piece in jeopardy. Chess had been popular throughout Europe since the thirteenth century, but in Victorian England it rose to an art: the first international chess tournament was held in London in 1851.

exhausted too. I fear to trust those women, even if they would have courage to submit. What are we to do for some one who will open his veins for her?'

'What's the matter with me, anyhow?'

The voice came from the sofa across the room, and its tones brought relief and joy to my heart, for they were those of Quincey Morris. Van Helsing started angrily at the first sound, but his face softened and a glad look came into his eyes as I cried out: 'Quincey Morris!' and rushed towards him with outstretched hands.

'What brought you here?' I cried as our hands met.

'I guess Art is the cause.'

He handed me a telegram:—

'Have not heard from Seward for three days, and am terribly anxious. Cannot leave. Father still in same condition. Send me word how Lucy is. Do not delay.—HOLMWOOD.'

'I think I came just in the nick of time. You know you have only to tell me what to do.'

Van Helsing strode forward and took his hand, looking him straight in the eyes as he said:—

'A brave man's blood is the best thing on this earth when a woman is in trouble. You're a man, and no mistake. Well, the devil may work against us for all he's worth, but God sends us men when we want them.'

Once again we went through that ghastly operation. I have not the heart to go through with the details. Lucy had got a terrible shock, and it told on her more than before, for though plenty of blood went into her veins, her body did not respond to the treatment as well as on the other occasions. Her struggle back into life was something frightful to see and hear. However, the action of both heart and lungs improved, and Van Helsing made a subcutaneous injection of morphia, as before, and with good effect. Her faint became a profound slumber. The Professor watched whilst I went downstairs with Quincey Morris, and sent one of the maids to pay off one of the cabmen who were waiting. I left Quincey lying down after having a glass of wine, and told the cook to get ready a good breakfast. Then a thought struck me, and I went back to the room where Lucy now was. When I came softly in, I found Van Helsing with a sheet or two of note-paper in his hand. He had evidently read it, and was thinking it over as he sat with his hand to his brow. There was a look of grim satisfaction in his face, as of one who has had a doubt solved. He handed me the paper saying only: 'It dropped from Lucy's breast when we carried her to the bath.'

When I had read it, I stood looking at the Professor, and after a pause asked him: 'In God's name, what does it all mean? Was she, or is she, mad; or what sort of horrible danger is it?' I was so bewildered that I

did not know what to say more. Van Helsing put out his hand and took
the paper, saying:—

'Do not trouble about it now. Forget it for the present. You shall
know and understand it all in good time; but it will be later. And now
what is it that you came to me to say?' This brought me back to fact,
and I was all myself again.

'I came to speak about the certificate of death.[4] If we do not act
properly and wisely, there may be an inquest, and that paper would
have to be produced. I am in hopes that we need have no inquest, for
if we had it would surely kill poor Lucy, if nothing else did. I know,
and you know, and the other doctor who attended her knows, that Mrs
Westenra had disease of the heart, and we can certify that she died of
it. Let us fill up the certificate at once, and I shall take it myself to the
registrar and go on to the undertaker.'

'Good, oh my friend John! Well thought of! Truly Miss Lucy, if she
be sad in the foes that beset her, is at least happy in the friends that
love her. One, two, three, all open their veins for her, besides one old
man. Ah yes, I know, friend John; I am not blind! I love you all the
more for it! Now go.'

In the hall I met Quincey Morris, with a telegram for Arthur telling
him that Mrs Westenra was dead; that Lucy also had been ill, but was
now going on better; and that Van Helsing and I were with her. I told
him where I was going, and he hurried me out, but as I was going
said:—

'When you come back, Jack, may I have two words with you all to
ourselves?' I nodded in reply and went out. I found no difficulty about
the registration, and arranged with the local undertaker to come up in
the evening to measure for the coffin and to make arrangements.

When I got back Quincey was waiting for me. I told him I would
see him as soon as I knew about Lucy, and went up to her room. She
was still sleeping, and the Professor seemingly had not moved from his
seat at her side. From his putting his finger to his lips, I gathered that
he expected her to wake before long and was afraid of forestalling nature. So I went down to Quincey and took him into the breakfast-room,
where the blinds were not drawn down, and which was a little more
cheerful, or rather less cheerless, than the other rooms. When we were
alone, he said to me:—

'Jack Seward, I don't want to shove myself in anywhere where I've
no right to be; but this is no ordinary case. You know I loved that girl
and wanted to marry her; but, although that's all past and gone, I can't
help feeling anxious about her all the same. What is it that's wrong
with her? The Dutchman—and a fine old fellow he is; I can see that—

---

4. Technically, the two doctors are engaging in a coverup of the bizarre and violent circumstances of Mrs. Westenra's death, protecting not only Lucy but themselves.

said, that time you two came into the room, that you must have *another* transfusion of blood, and that both you and he were exhausted. Now I know well that you medical men speak *in camera*[5], and that a man must not expect to know what they consult about in private. But this is no common matter, and whatever it is, I have done my part. Is not that so?'

'That's so,' I said, and he went on:—

'I take it that both you and Van Helsing had done already what I did today. Is not that so?'

'That's so.'

'And I guess Art was in it too. When I saw him four days ago down at his own place he looked queer. I have not seen anything pulled down so quick since I was on the Pampas[6] and had a mare that I was fond of go to grass[7] all in a night. One of those big bats that they call vampires[8] had got at her in the night, and, what with his gorge and the vein left open, there wasn't enough blood in her to let her stand up, and I had to put a bullet through her as she lay. Jack, if you may tell me without betraying confidence, Arthur was the first; is not that so?' As he spoke the poor fellow looked terribly anxious. He was in a torture of suspense regarding the woman he loved, and his utter ignorance of the terrible mystery which seemed to surround her intensified his pain. His very heart was bleeding, and it took all the manhood of him—and there was a royal lot of it, too—to keep him from breaking down. I paused before answering, for I felt that I must not betray anything which the Professor wished kept secret; but already he knew so much, and guessed so much, that there could be no reason for not answering, so I answered in the same phrase: 'That's so.'

'And how long has this been going on?'

'About ten days.'

'Ten days! Then I guess, Jack Seward, that that poor pretty creature that we all love has had put into her veins within that time the blood of four strong men. Man alive, her whole body wouldn't hold it.' Then, coming close to me, he spoke in a fierce half-whisper: 'What took it out?'

I shook my head. 'That,' I said, 'is the crux. Van Helsing is simply frantic about it, and I am at my wits' end. I can't even hazard a guess. There has been a series of little circumstances which have thrown out all our calculations as to Lucy being properly watched. But these shall not occur again. Here we stay until all be well—or ill.' Quincey held

5. Law: "in chambers" or "privately."
6. Grassy plains of temperate southern South America.
7. Decline, die.
8. Quincey gives a plausible-sounding zoological analogy to Dracula's predations: vampire bats do inhabit the Pampas and they do prey on horses, even on humans. No single vampire bat, however, is large enough to drain a horse, much less an adult woman.

out his hand. 'Count me in,' he said. 'You and the Dutchman will tell me what to do, and I'll do it.'

When she woke late in the afternoon, Lucy's first movement was to feel in her breast, and, to my surprise, produced the paper which Van Helsing had given me to read. The careful Professor had replaced it where it had come from, lest on waking she should be alarmed. Her eye then lit on Van Helsing and on me too, and gladdened. Then she looked round the room, and seeing where she was, shuddered; she gave a loud cry, and put her poor thin hands before her pale face. We both understood what that meant—that she had realized to the full her mother's death; so we tried what we could to comfort her. Doubtless sympathy eased her somewhat, but she was very low in thought and spirit, and wept silently and weakly for a long time. We told her that either or both of us would now remain with her all the time, and that seemed to comfort her. Towards dusk she fell into a doze. Here a very odd thing occurred. Whilst still asleep she took the paper from her breast and tore it in two. Van Helsing stepped over and took the pieces from her. All the same, however, she went on with the action of tearing, as though the material were still in her hands; finally she lifted her hands and opened them as though scattering the fragments. Van Helsing seemed surprised, and his brows gathered as if in thought, but he said nothing.

19 September.[9]—All last night she slept fitfully, being always afraid to sleep, and something weaker when she woke from it. The Professor and I took it in turns to watch, and we never left her for a moment unattended. Quincey Morris said nothing about his intention, but I knew that all night long he patrolled round and round the house.

When the day came, its searching light showed the ravages in poor Lucy's strength. She was hardly able to turn her head, and the little nourishment which she could take seemed to do her no good. At times she slept, and both Van Helsing and I noticed the difference in her, between sleeping and waking. Whilst asleep she looked stronger, although more haggard, and her breathing was softer; her open mouth showed the pale gums drawn back from the teeth, which thus looked positively longer and sharper than usual; when she woke the softness of her eyes evidently changed the expression, for she looked her own self, although a dying one. In the afternoon she asked for Arthur, and we telegraphed for him. Quincey went off to meet him at the station.

When he arrived it was nearly six o'clock, and the sun was setting full and warm, and the red light streamed in through the window and gave more colour to the pale cheeks. When he saw her, Arthur was simply choking with emotion, and none of us could speak. In the hours

9. Another slip in Stoker's chronology: the date should read "20 September."

that had passed, the fits of sleep, or the comatose condition that passed for it, had grown more frequent, so that the pauses when conversation was possible were shortened. Arthur's presence, however, seemed to act as a stimulant; she rallied a little, and spoke to him more brightly than she had done since we arrived. He too pulled himself together, and spoke as cheerily as he could, so that the best was made of everything.

It is now nearly one o'clock, and he and Van Helsing are sitting with her. I am to relieve them in a quarter of an hour, and I am entering this on Lucy's phonograph. Until six o'clock they are to try to rest. I fear that tomorrow will end our watching, for the shock has been too great; the poor child cannot rally. God help us all.

Letter, Mina Harker to Lucy Westenra

(UNOPENED BY HER.)

17 September.

My dearest Lucy,—

It seems *an age* since I heard from you, or indeed since I wrote. You will pardon me, I know, for all my faults when you have read all my budget of news. Well, I got my husband back all right; when we arrived at Exeter there was a carriage waiting for us, and in it, though he had an attack of gout, Mr Hawkins. He took us to his own house, where there were rooms for us all nice and comfortable, and we dined together. After dinner Mr Hawkins said:—

'My dears, I want to drink your health and prosperity; and may every blessing attend you both. I know you both from children, and have, with love and pride, seen you grow up. Now I want you to make your home here with me. I have left to me neither chick nor child; all are gone, and in my will I have left you everything.' I cried, Lucy dear, as Jonathan and the old man clasped hands. Our evening was a very, very happy one.

So here we are, installed in this beautiful old house, and from both my bedroom and drawing-room I can see the great elms of the cathedral close, with their great black stems standing out against the old yellow stone of the cathedral; and I can hear the rooks overhead cawing and cawing and chattering and gossiping all day, after the manner of rooks—and humans. I am busy, I need not tell you, arranging things and housekeeping. Jonathan and Mr Hawkins are busy all day; for, now that Jonathan is a partner,[1] Mr Hawkins wants to tell him all about the clients.

How is your dear mother getting on? I wish I could run up to town

---

1. As a barrister himself, Stoker must have known that Jonathan's promotion from clerk to lawyer is wildly unlikely, even under the patronage of a Mr. Hawkins. Perhaps he wanted to elevate his enfeebled hero.

for a day or two to see you, dear, but I dare not go yet, with so much on my shoulders; and Jonathan wants looking after still. He is beginning to put some flesh on his bones again, but he was terribly weakened by the long illness; even now he sometimes starts out of his sleep in a sudden way and awakes all trembling until I can coax him back to his usual placidity. However, thank God, these occasions grow less frequent as the days go on, and they will in time pass away altogether, I trust. And now I have told you my news, let me ask yours. When are you to be married, and where, and who is to perform the ceremony, and what are you to wear, and is it to be a public or a private wedding? Tell me all about it, dear; tell me all about everything, for there is nothing which interests you which will not be dear to me. Jonathan asks me to send his 'respectful duty,' but I do not think that is good enough from the junior partner of the important firm of Hawkins & Harker; and so, as you love me, and he loves me, and I love you with all the moods and tenses of the verb, I send you simply his 'love' instead. Goodbye, my dearest Lucy, and all blessings on you.

Yours,
MINA HARKER.

Report from Patrick Hennessey, M.D., M.R.C.S., L.K.Q.C.P.I.,[2]
Etc., Etc., to John Seward, M.D.

20 September.

My dear Sir,—

In accordance with your wishes, I enclose report of the conditions of everything left in my charge . . . With regard to patient, Renfield, there is more to say. He has had another outbreak which might have had a dreadful ending, but which, as it fortunately happened, was un-attended with any unhappy results. This afternoon a carrier's cart with two men made a call at the empty house whose grounds abut on ours—the house to which, you will remember, the patient twice ran away. The men stopped at our gate to ask the porter their way, as they were strangers. I was myself looking out of the study window, having a smoke after dinner, and saw one of them come up to the house. As he passed the window of Renfield's room, the patient began to rate him from within, and called him all the foul names he could lay his tongue to. The man, who seemed a decent fellow enough, contented himself by telling him to 'shut up for a foul-mouthed beggar,' whereon our man accused him of robbing him and wanting to murder him and said that he would hinder him if he were to swing for it. I opened the window and signed to the man not to notice, so he contented himself after looking the place over and making up his mind as to what kind

2. Doctor of Medicine; Member of the Royal College of Surgeons; Licentiate of the King's and Queen's College of Physicians, Ireland.

of a place he had got to by saying: 'Lor' bless yer, sir, I wouldn't mind what was said to me in a bloomin' madhouse. I pity ye and the guv'nor for havin' to live in the house with a wild beast like that.' Then he asked his way civilly enough, and I told him where the gate of the empty house was; he went away, followed by threats and curses and revilings from our man. I went down to see if I could make out any cause for his anger, since he is usually such a well-behaved man, and except his violent fits nothing of the kind had ever occurred. I found him, to my astonishment, quite composed and most genial in his manner. I tried to get him to talk of the incident, but he blandly asked me questions as to what I meant, and led me to believe that he was completely oblivious of the affair. It was, I am sorry to say, however, only another instance of his cunning, for within half an hour I heard of him again. This time he had broken out through the window of his room, and was running down the avenue. I called to the attendants to follow me, and ran after him, for I feared he was intent on some mischief. My fear was justified when I saw the same cart which had passed before coming down the road, having on it some great wooden boxes. The men were wiping their foreheads, and were flushed in the face, as if with violent exercise. Before I could get up to him the patient rushed at them, and pulling one of them off the cart, began to knock his head against the ground. If I had not seized him just at the moment I believe he would have killed the man there and then. The other fellow jumped down and struck him over the head with the butt-end of his heavy whip. It was a terrible blow; but he did not seem to mind it, but seized him also, and struggled with the three of us, pulling us to and fro as if we were kittens. You know I am no light weight, and the others were both burly men. At first he was silent in his fighting; but as we began to master him, and the attendants were putting a strait-waistcoat on him, he began to shout: 'I'll frustrate them! They shan't rob me! they shan't murder me by inches! I'll fight for my Lord and Master!' and all sorts of similar incoherent ravings. It was with very considerable difficulty that they got him back to the house and put him in the padded room. One of the attendants, Hardy, had a finger broken. However, I set it all right; and he is going on well.

The two carriers were at first loud in their threats of actions for damages, and promised to rain all the penalties of the law on us. Their threats were, however, mingled with some sort of indirect apology for the defeat of the two of them by a feeble madman. They said that if it had not been for the way their strength had been spent in carrying and raising the heavy boxes to the cart they would have made short work of him. They gave as another reason for their defeat the extraordinary state of drouth[3] to which they had been reduced by the dusty nature

3. Thirst (Scots.).

of their occupation and the reprehensible distance from the scene of their labours of any place of public entertainment. I quite understood their drift, and after a stiff glass of grog,[4] or rather more of the same, and with each a sovereign in hand, they made light of the attack, and swore that they would encounter a worse madman any day for the pleasure of meeting so 'bloomin' good a bloke' as your correspondent. I took their names and addresses, in case they might be needed. They are as follows:—Jack Smollet, of Dudding's Rents, King George's Road, Great Walworth, and Thomas Snelling, Peter Parley's Row, Guide Court, Bethnal Green. They are both in the employment of Harris & Sons, Moving and Shipment Company, Orange Master's Yard, Soho.

I shall report to you any matter of interest occurring here, and shall wire you at once if there is anything of importance.

> Believe me, dear Sir,
> Yours faithfully,
>
> PATRICK HENNESSEY.

Letter, Mina Harker to Lucy Westenra

(UNOPENED BY HER.)

18 September.

My dearest Lucy,—

Such a sad blow has befallen us. Mr Hawkins has died very suddenly. Some may not think it so sad for us, but we had both come to so love him that it really seems as though we had lost a father. I never knew either father or mother, so that the dear old man's death is a real blow to me. Jonathan is greatly distressed. It is not only that he feels sorrow, deep sorrow, for the dear, good man who has befriended him all his life, and now at the end has treated him like his own son and left him a fortune which to people of our modest bringing up is wealth beyond the dream of avarice, but Jonathan feels it on another account. He says the amount of responsibility which it puts upon him makes him nervous. He begins to doubt himself. I try to cheer him up, and *my* belief in *him* helps him to have a belief in himself. But it is here that the grave shock that he experienced tells upon him the most. Oh, it is too hard that a sweet, simple, noble, strong nature such as his—a nature which enabled him by our dear, good friend's aid to rise from clerk to master in a few years—should be so injured that the very essence of its strength is gone. Forgive me, dear, if I worry you with my troubles in the midst of your own happiness; but, Lucy dear, I must tell someone, for the strain of keeping up a brave and cheerful appearance to Jonathan tries me, and I have no one here that I can confide in. I dread coming up to London, as we must do the day after tomorrow; for poor

---

4. Rum and water.

Mr Hawkins left in his will that he was to be buried in the grave with his father. As there are no relations at all, Jonathan will have to be chief mourner. I shall try to run over to see you, dearest, if only for a few minutes. Forgive me for troubling you. With all blessings,

Your loving

MINA HARKER.

Dr Seward's Diary

20 September.—Only resolution and habit can let me make an entry tonight. I am too miserable, too low-spirited, too sick of the world and all in it, including life itself, that I would not care if I heard this moment the flapping of the wings of the angel of death. And he has been flapping those grim wings to some purpose of late—Lucy's mother and Arthur's father, and now . . . Let me get on with my work.

I duly relieved Van Helsing in his watch over Lucy. We wanted Arthur to go to rest also, but he refused at first. It was only when I told him that we should want him to help us during the day, and that we must not all break down for want of rest, lest Lucy should suffer, that he agreed to go. Van Helsing was very kind to him. 'Come, my child,' he said; 'come with me. You are sick and weak, and have had much sorrow and much mental pain, as well as that tax on your strength that we know of. You must not be alone; for to be alone is to be full of fears and alarms. Come to the drawing-room, where there is a big fire, and there are two sofas. You shall lie on one, and I on the other, and our sympathy will be comfort to each other, even though we do not speak, and even if we sleep.' Arthur went off with him, casting back a longing look on Lucy's face, which lay on her pillow, almost whiter than the lawn. She lay quite still, and I looked round the room to see that all was as it should be. I could see that the Professor had carried out in this room, as in the other, his purpose of using the garlic; the whole of the window-sashes reeked with it, and round Lucy's neck, over the silk handkerchief which Van Helsing made her keep on, was a rough chaplet[5] of the same odorous flowers. Lucy was breathing somewhat stertorously, and her face was at its worst, for the open mouth showed the pale gums. Her teeth, in the dim, uncertain light, seemed longer and sharper than they had been in the morning. In particular, by some trick of the light, the canine teeth looked longer and sharper than the rest. I sat down by her, and presently she moved uneasily. At the same moment there came a sort of dull flapping or buffeting at the window. I went over to it softly, and peeped out by the corner of the blind. There was a full moonlight, and I could see that the noise was made by a great bat, which wheeled round—doubtless attracted by the

5. Garland.

light, although so dim—and every now and again struck the window with its wings. When I came back to my seat I found that Lucy had moved slightly, and had torn away the garlic flowers from her throat. I replaced them as well as I could, and sat watching her.

Presently she woke, and I gave her food, as Van Helsing had prescribed. She took but a little, and that languidly. There did not seem to be with her now the unconscious struggle for life and strength that had hitherto so marked her illness. It struck me as curious that the moment she became conscious she pressed the garlic flowers close to her. It was certainly odd that whenever she got into that lethargic state, with the stertorous breathing, she put the flowers from her; but that when she waked she clutched them close. There was no possibility of making any mistake about this, for in the long hours that followed, she had many spells of sleeping and waking and repeated both actions many times.

At six o'clock Van Helsing came to relieve me. Arthur had then fallen into a doze, and he mercifully let him sleep on. When he saw Lucy's face I could hear the hissing indraw of his breath, and he said to me in a sharp whisper: 'Draw up the blind; I want light!' Then he bent down, and, with his face almost touching Lucy's, examined her carefully. He removed the flowers and lifted the silk handkerchief from her throat. As he did so he started back, and I could hear his ejaculation, 'Mein Gott!' as it was smothered in his throat. I bent over and looked too, and as I noticed some queer chill came over me.

The wounds on the throat had absolutely disappeared.

For fully five minutes Van Helsing stood looking at her, with his face at its sternest. Then he turned to me and said calmly:—

'She is dying. It will not be long now. It will be much difference, mark me, whether she dies conscious or in her sleep. Wake that poor boy, and let him come and see the last; he trusts us, and we have promised him.'

I went to the dining-room and waked him. He was dazed for a moment, but when he saw the sunlight streaming in through the edges of the shutters he thought he was late, and expressed his fear. I assured him that Lucy was still asleep, but told him as gently as I could that both Van Helsing and I feared that the end was near. He covered his face with his hands, and slid down on his knees by the sofa, where he remained, perhaps a minute, with his head buried, praying, whilst his shoulders shook with grief. I took him by the hand and raised him up. 'Come,' I said, 'my dear old fellow, summon all your fortitude; it will be best and easiest for *her*.'

When we came into Lucy's room I could see that Van Helsing had, with his usual forethought, been putting matters straight and making everything look as pleasing as possible. He had even brushed Lucy's hair, so that it lay on the pillow in its usual sunny ripples.[6] When we came into the room she opened her eyes, and seeing him, whispered softly:—

'Arthur! Oh, my love, I am so glad you have come!' He was stooping to kiss her, when Van Helsing motioned him back. 'No,' he whispered, 'not yet! Hold her hand; it will comfort her more.'

So Arthur took her hand and knelt beside her, and she looked her best, with all the soft lines matching the angelic beauty of her eyes. Then gradually her eyes closed, and she sank to sleep. For a little bit her breast heaved softly, and her breath came and went like a tired child's.

And then insensibly there came the strange change which I had noticed in the night. Her breathing grew stertorous, the mouth opened, and the pale gums, drawn back, made the teeth look longer and sharper than ever. In a sort of sleep-waking, vague, unconscious way she opened her eyes, which were now dull and hard at once, and said in a soft, voluptuous voice, such as I had never heard from her lips:—

'Arthur! Oh, my love, I am so glad you have come! Kiss me!' Arthur bent eagerly over to kiss her; but at that instant Van Helsing, who, like me, had been startled by her voice, swooped upon him, and catching him by the neck with both hands, dragged him back with a fury of strength which I never thought he could have possessed, and actually hurled him almost across the room.

'Not for your life!' he said; 'not for your living soul and hers!' And he stood between them like a lion at bay.

Arthur was so taken aback that he did not for a moment know what to do or say; and before any impulse of violence could seize him he realized the place and the occasion, and stood silent, waiting.

I kept my eyes fixed on Lucy, as did Van Helsing, and we saw a spasm as of rage flit like a shadow over her face; the sharp teeth champed together. Then her eyes closed, and she breathed heavily.

Very shortly after she opened her eyes in all their softness, and putting out her poor pale, thin hand, took Van Helsing's great brown one; drawing it to her, she kissed it. 'My true friend,' she said, in a faint voice, but with untellable pathos, 'My true friend, and his! Oh, guard him, and give me peace!'

'I swear it!' said he solemnly, kneeling beside her and holding up his hand, as one who registers an oath. Then he turned to Arthur, and said to him: 'Come, my child, take her hand in yours, and kiss her on the forehead, and only once.'

Their eyes met instead of their lips; and so they parted.

Lucy's eyes closed; and Van Helsing, who had been watching closely, took Arthur's arm, and drew him away.

6. Lucy's blonde hair is appropriate to her role as innocent young girl, but as we shall see, when her role changes her hair color will change as well.

And then Lucy's breathing became stertorous again, and all at once it ceased.

'It is all over,' said Van Helsing. 'She is dead!'

I took Arthur by the arm, and led him away to the drawing-room, where he sat down, and covered his face with his hands, sobbing in a way that nearly broke me down to see.

I went back to the room, and found Van Helsing looking at poor Lucy, and his face was sterner than ever. Some change had come over her body. Death had given back part of her beauty, for her brow and cheeks had recovered some of their flowing lines; even the lips had lost their deadly pallor. It was as if the blood, no longer needed for the working of the heart, had gone to make the harshness of death as little rude as might be.

> We thought her dying whilst she slept,
> And sleeping when she died.[7]

I stood beside Van Helsing, and said:—

'Ah well, poor girl, there is peace for her at last. It is the end!'

He turned to me, and said with grave solemnity:—

'Not so; alas! not so. It is only the beginning!'

When I asked him what he meant, he only shook his head and answered:—

'We can do nothing as yet. Wait and see.'

Chapter XIII

Dr Seward's Diary (continued)

The funeral was arranged for the next succeeding day, so that Lucy and her mother might be buried together. I attended to all the ghastly formalities, and the urbane undertaker proved that his staff were afflicted—or blessed—with something of his own obsequious suavity. Even the woman who performed the last offices for the dead remarked to me, in a confidential, brother-professional way, when she had come out from the death-chamber:—

'She makes a very beautiful corpse, sir. It's quite a privilege to attend on her. It's not too much to say that she will do credit to our establishment!'

I noticed that Van Helsing never kept far away. This was possible from the disordered state of things in the household. There were no relatives at hand; and as Arthur had to be back the next day to attend at his father's funeral, we were unable to notify anyone who should have been bidden. Under the circumstances, Van Helsing and I took

7. From Thomas Hood's (1799–1845) poem "The Death-Bed."

it upon ourselves to examine papers, etc. He insisted upon looking over Lucy's papers himself. I asked him why, for I feared that he, being a foreigner, might not be quite aware of English legal requirements, and so might in ignorance make some unnecessary trouble. He answered me:—

'I know; I know. You forget that I am a lawyer[1] as well as a doctor. But this is not altogether for the law. You knew that, when you avoided the coroner. I have more than him to avoid. There may be papers more—such as this.'

As he spoke he took from his pocket-book the memorandum which had been in Lucy's breast, and which she had torn in her sleep.

'When you find anything of the solicitor who is for the late Mrs Westenra, seal all her papers, and write him tonight. For me, I watch here in the room and in Miss Lucy's old room all night, and I myself search for what may be. It is not well that her very thoughts go into the hands of strangers.'

I went on with my part of the work, and in another half-hour had found the name and address of Mrs Westenra's solicitor and had written to him. All the poor lady's papers were in order; explicit directions regarding the place of burial were given. I had hardly sealed the letter, when, to my surprise, Van Helsing walked into the room, saying:—

'Can I help you, friend John? I am free, and if I may, my service is to you.'

'Have you got what you looked for?' I asked, to which he replied:—

'I did not look for any specific thing. I only hoped to find, and find I have, all that there was—only some letters and a few memoranda, and a diary new begun. But I have them here, and we shall for the present say nothing of them. I shall see that poor lad tomorrow evening, and, with his sanction, I shall use some.'

When we had finished the work in hand, he said to me:—

'And now, friend John, I think we may to bed. We want sleep, both you and I, and rest to recuperate. Tomorrow we shall have much to do, but for the tonight there is no need of us. Alas!'

Before turning in we went to look at poor Lucy. The undertaker had certainly done his work well, for the room was turned into a small *chapelle ardente*.[2] There was a wilderness of beautiful white flowers, and death was made as little repulsive as might be. The end of the winding-sheet was laid over the face; when the Professor bent over and turned it gently back, we both started at the beauty before us, the tall wax candles showing a sufficient light to note it well. All Lucy's loveliness had come back to her in death, and the hours that had passed,

---

1. This is the first and last we hear of Van Helsing's third career (he is also a physician and a professor). Characteristically, he uses his legal expertise to circumvent the law.
2. An illuminated chamber where a corpse lies ceremonially in state.

instead of leaving traces of 'decay's effacing fingers,'[3] had but restored the beauty of life, till positively I could not believe my eyes that I was looking at a corpse.

The Professor looked sternly grave. He had not loved her as I had, and there was no need for tears in his eyes. He said to me: 'Remain till I return,' and left the room. He came back with a handful of wild garlic from the box waiting in the hall, but which had not been opened, and placed the flowers amongst the others on and around the bed. Then he took from his neck, inside his collar, a little golden crucifix, and placed it over the mouth. He restored the sheet to its place, and we came away.

I was undressing in my own room, when, with a premonitory tap at the door, he entered, and at once began to speak:—

'Tomorrow I want you to bring me, before night, a set of post-mortem knives.'

'Must we make an autopsy?' I asked.

'Yes, and no. I want to operate, but not as you think. Let me tell you now, but not a word to another. I want to cut off her head and take out her heart. Ah! you a surgeon, and so shocked! You, whom I have seen with no tremble of hand or heart, do operations of life and death that make the rest shudder. Oh, but I must not forget, my dear friend John, that you loved her; and I have not forgotten it, for it is I that shall operate, and you must only help. I would like to do it tonight, but for Arthur I must not; he will be free after his father's funeral tomorrow, and he will want to see her—to see *it*. Then, when she is coffined ready for the next day, you and I shall come when all sleep. We shall unscrew the coffin-lid, and shall do our operation; and then replace all, so that none know, save we alone.'

'But why do it at all? The girl is dead. Why mutilate her poor body without need? And if there is no necessity for a post-mortem and nothing to gain by it—no good to her, to us, to science, to human knowledge—why do it? Without such it is monstrous.'

For answer he put his hand on my shoulder, and said, with infinite tenderness:—

'Friend John, I pity your poor bleeding heart; and I love you the more because it does so bleed. If I could, I would take on myself the burden that you do bear. But there are things that you know not, but that you shall know, and bless me for knowing, though they are not pleasant things. John, my child, you have been my friend now many years, and yet did you ever know me to do any without good cause? I may err—I am but man; but I believe in all I do. Was it not for these causes that you send for me when the great trouble came? Yes! Were

---

3. From Byron's poem "The Giaour" (1813), which deals with, among other things, a vengeful vampire.

you not amazed, nay horrified, when I would not let Arthur kiss his love—though she was dying—and snatched him away by all my strength? Yes! And yet you saw how she thanked me, with her so beautiful dying eyes, her voice, too, so weak, and she kiss my rough old hand and bless me? Yes! And did you not hear me swear promise to her, that so she closed her eyes grateful? Yes!

'Well, I have good reason now for all I want to do. You have for many years trust me; you have believe me weeks past, when there be things so strange that you might have well doubt. Believe me yet a little, friend John. If you trust me not, then I must tell what I think; and that is not perhaps well. And if I work—as work I shall, no matter trust or no trust—without my friend trust in me, I work with heavy heart and feel, oh! so lonely when I want all help and courage that may be!' He paused a moment and went on solemnly: 'Friend John, there are strange and terrible days before us. Let us not be two, but one, that so we work to a good end. Will you not have faith in me?'

I took his hand, and promised him. I held my door open as he went away, and watched him go into his room and close the door. As I stood without moving, I saw one of the maids pass silently along the passage—she had her back towards me, so did not see me—and go into the room where Lucy lay. The sight touched me. Devotion is so rare, and we are so grateful to those who show it unasked to those we love. Here was a poor girl putting aside the terrors which she naturally had of death to go watch alone by the bier of the mistress whom she loved, so that the poor clay might not be lonely till laid to eternal rest . . .

I must have slept long and soundly, for it was broad daylight when Van Helsing waked me by coming into my room. He came over to my bedside and said:—

'You need not trouble about the knives; we shall not do it.'

'Why not?' I asked. For his solemnity of the night before had greatly impressed me.

'Because,' he said sternly 'it is too late—or too early. See!' Here he held up the little golden crucifix. 'This was stolen[4] in the night.'

'How, stolen,' I asked in wonder, 'since you have it now?'

'Because I get it back from the worthless wretch who stole it, from the woman who robbed the dead and the living. Her punishment will surely come, but not through me; she knew not altogether what she did, and thus unknowing, she only stole. Now we must wait.'

He went away on the word, leaving me with a new mystery to think of, a new puzzle to grapple with.

The forenoon was a dreary time, but at noon the solicitor came: Mr Marquand, of Wholeman, Sons, Marquand & Lidderdale. He was very genial and very appreciative of what we had done, and took off our

---

4. It is unclear by the logic of Stoker's own rules how the theft of the crucifix affects Lucy's condition.

hands all cares as to details. During lunch he told us that Mrs Westenra had for some time expected sudden death from her heart, and had put her affairs in absolute order; he informed us that, with the exception of a certain entailed property of Lucy's father's which now, in default of direct issue, went back to a distant branch of the family, the whole estate, real and personal, was left absolutely to Arthur Holmwood. When he had told us so much he went on:—

'Frankly we did our best to prevent such a testamentary disposition, and pointed out certain contingencies that might leave her daughter either penniless or not so free as she should be to act regarding a matrimonial alliance. Indeed, we pressed the matter so far that we almost came into collision, for she asked us if we were or were not prepared to carry out her wishes. Of course, we had then no alternative but to accept. We were right in principle, and ninety-nine times out of a hundred we should have proved, by the logic of events, the accuracy of our judgement. Frankly, however, I must admit that in this case any other form of disposition would have rendered impossible the carrying out of her wishes. For by her predeceasing her daughter the latter would have come into possession of the property, and, even had she only survived her mother by five minutes, her property would, in case there were no will—and a will was a practical impossibility in such a case— have been treated at her decease as under intestacy.[5] In which case Lord Godalming, though so dear a friend, would have had no claim in the world; and the inheritors, being remote, would not be likely to abandon their just rights, for sentimental reasons regarding an entire stranger. I assure you, my dear sirs, I am rejoiced at the result, perfectly rejoiced.'

He was a good fellow, but his rejoicing at the one little part—in which he was officially interested—of so great a tragedy, was an object-lesson in the limitations of sympathetic understanding.

He did not remain long, but said he would look in later in the day and see Lord Godalming.[6] His coming, however, had been a certain comfort to us, since it assured us that we should not have to dread hostile criticism as to any of our acts. Arthur was expected at five o'clock, so a little before that time we visited the death-chamber. It was so in very truth, for now both mother and daughter lay in it. The undertaker, true to his craft, had made the best display he could of his goods, and there was a mortuary air about the place that lowered our spirits at once. Van Helsing ordered the former arrangement to be adhered to, explaining that, as Lord Godalming was coming very soon, it would be less harrowing to his feelings to see all that was left of his

5. That is, not having been assigned by a will. Mrs. Westenra's disinheritance of Lucy is unexplained. She may simply be bestowing her property on Lucy's husband-to-be, who, according to Victorian law and convention, would "cover" his wife in all legal matters. On the other hand, her will hints at a prescient awareness of Lucy's death and its consequences.
6. Arthur has inherited not only Lucy's property, but his father's estate and title.

fiancée quite alone. The undertaker seemed shocked at his own stupidity, and exerted himself to restore things to the condition in which we left them the night before, so that when Arthur came such shocks to his feelings as we could avoid were saved.

Poor fellow! He looked desperately sad and broken; even his stalwart manhood seemed to have shrunk somewhat under the strain of his much-tried emotions. He had, I knew, been very genuinely and devotedly attached to his father; and to lose him, and at such a time, was a bitter blow to him. With me he was warm as ever, and to Van Helsing he was sweetly courteous; but I could not help seeing that there was some constraint with him. The Professor noticed it, too, and motioned me to bring him upstairs. I did so, and left him at the door of the room, as I felt he would like to be quite alone with her; but he took my arm and led me in, saying huskily:—

'You loved her too, old fellow; she told me all about it, and there was no friend had a closer place in her heart than you. I don't know how to thank you for all you have done for her. I can't think yet . . .'

Here he suddenly broke down, and threw his arms round my shoulders and laid his head on my breast, crying:—

'Oh, Jack! Jack! What shall I do? The whole of life seems gone from me all at once, and there is nothing in the wide world for me to live for.'

I comforted him as well as I could. In such cases men do not need much expression. A grip of the hand, the tightening of an arm over the shoulder, a sob in unison, are expressions of sympathy dear to a man's heart. I stood still and silent till his sobs died away, and then I said softly to him:—

'Come and look at her.'

Together we moved over to the bed, and I lifted the lawn from her face. God! how beautiful she was. Every hour seemed to be enhancing her loveliness. It frightened and amazed me somewhat; and as for Arthur, he fell a-trembling, and finally was shaken with doubt as with an ague. At last, after a long pause, he said to me in a faint whisper:—

'Jack, is she really dead?'

I assured him sadly that it was so, and went on to suggest—for I felt that such a horrible doubt should not have life for a moment longer than I could help—that it often happened that after death faces became softened and even resolved into their youthful beauty; that this was especially so when death had been preceded by any acute or prolonged suffering. It seemed to quite do away with any doubt, and, after kneeling beside the couch for a while and looking at her lovingly and long he turned aside. I told him that that must be goodbye, as the coffin had to be prepared; so he went back and took her dead hand in his and kissed it, and bent over and kissed her forehead. He came away, fondly looking back over his shoulder at her as he came.

I left him in the drawing-room, and told Van Helsing that he had said goodbye; so the latter went to the kitchen to tell the undertaker's men to proceed with the preparations and to screw up the coffin. When he came out of the room again I told him of Arthur's question, and he replied:—

'I am not surprised. Just now I doubted for a moment myself!'

We all dined together, and I could see that poor Art was trying to make the best of things. Van Helsing had been silent all dinner-time, but when we had lit our cigars he said:—

'Lord—;' but Arthur interrupted him:—

'No, no, not that, for God's sake! not yet at any rate. Forgive me, sir: I did not mean to speak offensively; it is only because my loss is so recent.'

The Professor answered very sweetly:—

'I only used that name because I was in doubt. I must not call you "Mr," and I have grown to love you—yes, my dear boy, to love you—as Arthur.'

Arthur held out his hand, and took the old man's warmly.

'Call me what you will,' he said. 'I hope I may always have the title of a friend. And let me say that I am at a loss for words to thank you for your goodness to my poor dear.' He paused a moment, and went on: 'I know that she understood your goodness even better than I do; and if I was rude or in any way wanting at that time you acted so—you remember'—the Professor nodded—'you must forgive me.'

He answered with a grave kindness:—

'I know it was hard for you to quite trust me then, for to trust such violence needs to understand; and I take it that you do not—that you cannot—trust me now, for you do not yet understand. And there may be more times when I shall want you to trust when you cannot—and may not—and must not yet understand. But the time will come when your trust shall be whole and complete in me, and when you shall understand as though the sunlight himself shone through. Then you shall bless me from first to last for your own sake, and for the sake of others, and for her dear sake to whom I swore to protect.'

'And, indeed, indeed, sir,' said Arthur warmly, 'I shall in all ways trust you. I know and believe you have a very noble heart, and you are Jack's friend, and you were hers. You shall do what you like.'

The Professor cleared his throat a couple of times, as though about to speak, and finally said:—

'May I ask you something now?'

'Certainly.'

'You know that Mrs Westenra left you all her property?'

'No, poor dear; I never thought of it.'

'And as it is all yours, you have a right to deal with it as you will. I want you to give me permission to read all Miss Lucy's papers and letters. Believe me, it is no idle curiosity. I have a motive of which, be sure, she would have approved. I have them all here. I took them before we knew that all was yours, so that no strange hand might touch them—no strange eye look through words into her soul. I shall keep them, if I may; even you may not see them yet, but I shall keep them safe. No word shall be lost; and in the good time I shall give them back to you. It's a hard thing I ask, but you will do it, will you not, for Lucy's sake?'

Arthur spoke out heartily, like his old self:—

'Dr Van Helsing, you may do what you will. I feel that in saying this I am doing what my dear one would have approved. I shall not trouble you with questions till the time comes.'

The old Professor stood up as he said solemnly:—

'And you are right. There will be pain for us all; but it will not be all pain, nor will this pain be the last. We and you too—you most of all, my dear boy—will have to pass through the bitter water before we reach the sweet. But we must be brave of heart and unselfish, and do our duty, and all will be well!'

I slept on a sofa in Arthur's room that night. Van Helsing did not go to bed at all. He went to and fro, as if patrolling the house, and was never out of sight of the room where Lucy lay in her coffin, strewn with the wild garlic flowers, which sent, through the odour of lily and rose, a heavy, overpowering smell into the night.

Mina Harker's Journal

22 September.—In the train to Exeter.[7] Jonathan sleeping. It seems only yesterday that the last entry was made, and yet how much between then, in Whitby and all the world before me, Jonathan away and no news of him; and now, married to Jonathan, Jonathan a solicitor, a partner, rich, master of his business, Mr Hawkins dead and buried, and Jonathan with another attack that may harm him. Some day he may ask me about it. Down it all goes. I am rusty in my shorthand—see what unexpected prosperity does for us—so it may be as well to freshen it up again with an exercise anyhow . . .

The service was very simple and very solemn. There were only ourselves and the servants there, one or two old friends of his from Exeter, his London agent, and a gentleman representing Sir John Paxton, the President of the Incorporated Law Society. Jonathan and I stood hand in hand, and we felt that our best and dearest friend was gone from us . . .

We came back to town quietly, taking a 'bus to Hyde Park Corner. Jonathan thought it would interest me to go into the Row for a while, so we sat down; but there were very few people there, and it was sad-

7. In the 1890s, a six-hour journey from London.

looking and desolate to see so many empty chairs. It made us think of the empty chair at home; so we got up and walked down Piccadilly.[8] Jonathan was holding me by the arm, the way he used to in old days before I went to school. I felt it very improper, for you can't go on for some years teaching etiquette and decorum to other girls without the pedantry of it biting into yourself a bit; but it was Jonathan, and he was my husband, and we didn't know anybody who saw us—and we didn't care if they did—so on we walked. I was looking at a very beautiful girl, in a big cartwheel hat, sitting in a victoria[9] outside Giuliano's, when I felt Jonathan clutch my arm so tight that he hurt me, and he said under his breath: 'My God!' I am always anxious about Jonathan, for I fear that some nervous fit may upset him again; so I turned to him quickly, and asked him what it was that disturbed him.

He was very pale, and his eyes seemed bulging out as, half in terror and half in amazement, he gazed at a tall, thin man, with a beaky nose and black moustache[1] and pointed beard, who was also observing the pretty girl. He was looking at her so hard that he did not see either of us, and so I had a good view of him. His face was not a good face; it was hard, and cruel, and sensual, and his big white teeth, that looked all the whiter because his lips were so red, were pointed like an animal's. Jonathan kept staring at him, till I was afraid he would notice. I feared he might take it ill, he looked so fierce and nasty. I asked Jonathan why he was disturbed, and he answered, evidently thinking that I knew as much about it as he did: 'Do you see who it is?'

'No, dear,' I said; 'I don't know him; who is it?' His answer seemed to shock and thrill me, for it was said as if he did not know that it was to me, Mina, to whom he was speaking:—

'It is the man himself!'

The poor dear was evidently terrified at something—very greatly terrified; I do believe that if he had not had me to lean on and to support him he would have sunk down. He kept staring; a man came out of the shop with a small parcel, and gave it to the lady, who then drove off. The dark man kept his eyes fixed on her, and when the carriage moved up Piccadilly he followed in the same direction, and hailed a hansom. Jonathan kept looking after him, and said, as if to himself:—

'I believe it is the Count, but he has grown young. My God, if this be so! Oh, my God! my God! If I only knew! if I only knew!' He was distressing himself so much that I feared to keep his mind on the sub-

---

8. Like the Regent's Park Zoo, where Dracula released the wolf, these are among the best-known sites of central London ("the Row" is Rotten Row, a one-and-a-half-mile stretch in Hyde Park reserved for horseback riding). From the mountains of Transylvania, Dracula has penetrated the well-regulated center of English civilization.

9. A light horse-driven carriage for two with a seat in front for the driver.

1. Once again, Dracula walks about freely in day, but he is younger here than he has ever been. Has he been feasting on London's "teeming millions" as well as on Lucy and her four blood donors? If so, one wonders about the fate of the "pretty girl" he eyes here.

ject by asking him any questions, so I remained silent. I drew him away quietly, and he, holding my arm, came easily. We walked a little further, and then went in and sat for a while in the Green Park.[2] It was a hot day for autumn, and there was a comfortable seat in a shady place. After a few minutes' staring at nothing, Jonathan's eyes closed, and he went quietly into a sleep, with his head on my shoulder. I thought it was the best thing for him, so did not disturb him. In about twenty minutes he woke up, and said to me, quite cheerfully:—

'Why, Mina, have I been asleep? Oh, do forgive me for being so rude. Come, and we'll have a cup of tea somewhere.' He had evidently forgotten all about the dark stranger, as in his illness he had forgotten all that this episode had reminded him of. I don't like this lapsing into forgetfulness; it may make or continue some injury to the brain. I must not ask him, for fear I shall do more harm than good; but I must somehow learn the facts of his journey abroad. The time is come, I fear, when I must open that parcel and know what is written. Oh, Jonathan, you will, I know, forgive me if I do wrong, but it is for your own dear sake.

Later.—A sad home-coming in every way—the house empty of the dear soul who was so good to us; Jonathan still pale and dizzy under a slight relapse of his malady; and now a telegram from Van Helsing, whoever he may be:—

'You will be grieved to hear that Mrs Westenra died five days ago, and that Lucy died the day before yesterday. They were both buried today.'

Oh, what a wealth of sorrow in a few words! Poor Mrs Westenra! poor Lucy! Gone, gone, never to return to us! And poor, poor Arthur, to have lost such sweetness out of his life! God help us all to bear our troubles.

Dr Seward's Diary

22 September.—It is all over. Arthur has gone back to Ring, and has taken Quincey Morris with him. What a fine fellow is Quincey! I believe in my heart of hearts that he suffered as much about Lucy's death as any of us; but he bore himself through it like a moral Viking. If America can go on breeding men like that, she will be a power in the world indeed. Van Helsing is lying down, having a rest preparatory to his journey. He goes over to Amsterdam tonight, but says he returns tomorrow night; that he only wants to make some arrangements which can only be made personally. He is to stop with me then, if he can; he says he has work to do in London which may take him some time. Poor old fellow! I fear that the strain of the past week has broken down even his iron strength. All the time of the burial he was, I could see,

2. A small secluded park opposite Hyde Park on the east end.

putting some terrible restraint on himself. When it was all over, we were standing beside Arthur, who, poor fellow, was speaking of his part in the operation where his blood had been transfused to his Lucy's veins; I could see Van Helsing's face grow white and purple by turns. Arthur was saying that he felt since then as if they two had been really married, and that she was his wife in the sight of God. None of us said a word of the other operations, and none of us ever shall. Arthur and Quincey went away together to the station, and Van Helsing and I came on here. The moment we were alone in the carriage he gave way to a regular fit of hysterics.[3] He has denied to me since that it was hysterics, and insisted that it was only his sense of humour asserting itself under very terrible conditions. He laughed till he cried, and I had to draw down the blinds lest anyone should see us and misjudge; and then he cried till he laughed again; and laughed and cried together, just as a woman does. I tried to be stern with him, as one is to a woman under the circumstances; but it had no effect. Men and women are so different in manifestations of nervous strength or weakness! Then when his face grew grave and stern again I asked him why his mirth, and why at such a time. His reply was in a way characteristic of him, for it was logical and forceful and mysterious. He said:—

'Ah, you don't comprehend, friend John. Do not think that I am not sad, though I laugh. See, I have cried even when the laugh did choke me. But no more think that I am all sorry when I cry, for the laugh he come just the same. Keep it always with you that laughter who knock at your door and say, "May I come in?" is not the true laughter. No! he is a king, and he come when and how he like. He ask no person; he choose no time of suitability. He say, "I am here." Behold, in example I grieve my heart out for that so sweet young girl; I give my blood for her, though I am old and worn; I give my time, my skill, my sleep; I let my other sufferers want that so she may have all. And yet I can laugh at her very grave—laugh when the clay from the spade of the sexton drop upon her coffin and say, "Thud! thud!" to my heart, till it send back the blood from my cheek. My heart bleed for that poor boy—that dear boy, so of the age of mine own boy had I been so blessed that he live, and with his hair and eyes the same. There, you know now why I love him so. And yet when he say things that touch my husband-heart to the quick, and make my father-heart yearn to him as to no other man—not even to you, friend John, for we are more level in experiences than father and son—yet even at such moment King Laugh he come to me and shout and bellow in my ear, "Here I am! here I am!" till the blood come dance back and bring some of the sunshine

3. *Hysteria* was used throughout the nineteenth century to diagnose a vivid, if vaguely defined, loss of mental control with or without physical symptoms—"a multiplicity of morbid phenomena," as one medical textbook put it. Since the term derives from the Latin word for *uterus*, the condition was naturally associated with women.

that he carry with him to my cheek. Oh, friend John, it is a strange world, a sad world, a world full of miseries, and woes, and troubles; and yet when King Laugh come he make them all dance to the tune he play. Bleeding hearts, and dry bones of the churchyard, and tears that burn as they fall—all dance together to the music that he make with that smileless mouth of him. And believe me, friend John, that he is good to come, and kind. Ah, we men and women are like ropes drawn tight with strain that pull us different ways. Then tears come; and, like the rain on the ropes, they brace us up, until perhaps the strain become too great, and we break. But King Laugh he come like the sunshine, and he ease off the strain again; and we bear to go on with our labour, what it may be.'

I did not like to wound him by pretending not to see his idea; but, as I did not yet understand the cause of his laughter, I asked him. As he answered me his face grew stern, and he said in quite a different tone:—

'Oh, it was the grim irony of it all—this so lovely lady garlanded with flowers, that looked so fair as life, till one by one we wondered if she were truly dead; she laid in that so fine marble house in that lonely churchyard, where rest so many of her kin, laid there with the mother who loved her, and whom she loved; and that sacred bell going "Toll! toll! toll!" so sad and slow; and those holy men, with the white garments of the angel, pretending to read books, and yet all the time their eyes never on the page; and all us with the bowed head. And all for what? She is dead; so! Is it not?'

'Well, for the life of me, Professor,' I said, 'I can't see anything to laugh at in all that. Why, your explanation makes it a harder puzzle than before. But even if the burial service was comic, what about poor Art and his trouble? Why, his heart was simply breaking.'

'Just so. Said he not that the transfusion of his blood to her veins had made her truly his bride?'

'Yes, and it was a sweet and comforting idea for him.'

'Quite so. But there was a difficulty, friend John. If so that, then what about the others? Ho, ho! Then this so sweet maid is a polyandrist,[4] and me, with my poor wife dead to me, but alive by Church's law, though no wits, all gone—even I, who am faithful husband to this now-no-wife, am bigamist.'

'I don't see where the joke comes in there either!' I said; and I did not feel particularly pleased with him for saying such things. He laid his hand on my arm, and said:—

'Friend John, forgive me if I pain. I showed not my feeling to others when it would wound, but only to you, my old friend, whom I can trust. If you could have looked into my very heart that when I want to

---

4. A woman married to more than one husband at the same time.

laugh; if you could have done so when the laugh arrived; if you could do so now, when King Laugh have pack up his crown and all that is to him—for he go far, far away from me, and for a long, long time—maybe you would perhaps pity me the most of all.'

I was touched by the tenderness of his tone, and asked why.

'Because I know!'

And now we are all scattered; and for many a long day loneliness will sit over our roofs with brooding wings. Lucy lies in the tomb of her kin, a lordly death-house in a lonely churchyard, away from teeming London; where the air is fresh, and the sun rises over Hampstead Hill,[5] and where wild flowers grow of their own accord.

So I can finish this diary; and God only knows if I shall ever begin another. If I do, or if I ever open this again, it will be to deal with different people and different themes; for here at the end, where the romance of my life is told, ere I go back to take up the thread of my life-work, I say sadly and without hope,

FINIS.

The Westminster Gazette,[6] *25 September*

A HAMPSTEAD MYSTERY

The neighbourhood of Hampstead is just at present exercised with a series of events which seem to run on lines parallel to those of what was known to the writers of headlines as 'The Kensington Horror,' or 'The Stabbing Woman,' or 'The Woman in Black.' During the past two or three days several cases have occurred of young children straying from home or neglecting to return from their playing on the Heath. In all these cases the children were too young to give any properly intelligible account of themselves, but the consensus of their excuses is that they had been with a 'bloofer[7] lady.' It has always been late in the evening when they have been missed, and on two occasions the children have not been found until early in the following morning. It is generally supposed in the neighbourhood that, as the first child missed gave as his reason for being away that a 'bloofer lady' had asked him to come for a walk, the others had picked up the phrase and used it as occasion served. This is the more natural as the favourite game of the little ones at present is luring each other away by wiles. A correspondent writes us that to see some of the tiny tots pretending to be the 'bloofer

5. Stoker probably refers to Highgate Hill, which leads to Highgate Cemetery. One of England's glamour burial grounds, Highgate houses such Victorian celebrities as Karl Marx, Dante Gabriel Rossetti, and George Eliot. Located in Hampstead Heath, a rural and romantic suburb of London, Highgate is no remote Gothic haunt, but, like all Dracula's favorite spots, one of England's gems.
6. Since the *Gazette*, a tabloidlike newspaper, had been founded as recently as 1893, this is one of Stoker's many up-to-date references.
7. Child-talk for "beautiful."

lady' is supremely funny. Some of our caricaturists might, he says, take a lesson in the irony of grotesque by comparing the reality and the picture. It is only in accordance with general principles of human nature that the 'bloofer lady' should be the popular role at these *al fresco* performances. Our correspondent naïvely says that even Ellen Terry[8] could not be so winningly attractive as some of these grubby-faced little children pretend—and even imagine themselves—to be.

There is, however, possibly a serious side to the question, for some of the children, indeed all who have been missed at night, have been slightly torn or wounded in the throat. The wounds seem such as might be made by a rat or a small dog, and although of not much importance individually, would tend to show that whatever animal inflicts them has a system or method of its own. The police of the division have been instructed to keep a sharp look-out for straying children, especially when very young, in and around Hampstead Heath, and for any stray dog which may be about.

The Westminster Gazette, 25 September

Extra Special
THE HAMPSTEAD HORROR
ANOTHER CHILD INJURED
The 'Bloofer Lady'

We have just received intelligence that another child, missed last night, was only discovered late in the morning under a furze bush at the Shooter's Hill[9] side of Hampstead Heath, which is, perhaps, less frequented than the other parts. It has the same tiny wound in the throat as has been noticed in other cases. It was terribly weak, and looked quite emaciated. It too, when partially restored, had the common story to tell of being lured away by the 'bloofer lady.'

Chapter XIV

Mina Harker's Journal

23 September.—Jonathan is better after a bad night. I am so glad that he has plenty of work to do, for that keeps his mind off the terrible things; and oh, I am rejoiced that he is not now weighed down with the responsibility of his new position. I knew he would be true to himself, and now how proud I am to see my Jonathan rising to the height of his advancement and keeping pace in all ways with the duties that

8. A nod to Henry Irving's Lyceum, where the beloved actress Ellen Terry had presided as Irving's partner since 1878. Like Lucy Westenra, Terry was a giggly, irresistible English rose with an underlying wildness her male governors never subdued.
9. Actually at some distance from Hampstead Heath; near Greenwich, south London.

come upon him. He will be away all day till late, for he said he could not lunch at home. My household work is done, so I shall take his foreign journal, and lock myself up in my room and read it . . .

24 September.—I hadn't the heart to write last night; that terrible record of Jonathan's upset me so. Poor dear! How he must have suffered, whether it be true or only imagination. I wonder if there is any truth in it at all. Did he get his brain fever, and then write all those terrible things; or had he some cause for it all? I suppose I shall never know, for I dare not open the subject to him . . . And yet that man we saw yesterday! He seemed quite certain of him . . . Poor fellow! I suppose it was the funeral upset him and sent his mind back on some train of thought . . . He believes it all himself. I remember how on our wedding-day he said: 'Unless some solemn duty come upon me to go back to the bitter hours, asleep or awake, mad or sane.' There seems to be through it all some thread of continuity . . . That fearful Count was coming to London . . . 'If it should be, and he came to London, with its teeming millions.' . . . There may be a solemn duty; and if it come we must not shrink from it . . . I shall be prepared. I shall get my typewriter this very hour and begin transcribing. Then we shall be ready for other eyes if required. And if it be wanted; then, perhaps, if I am ready, poor Jonathan may not be upset, for I can speak for him and never let him be troubled or worried with it at all. If ever Jonathan quite gets over the nervousness he may want to tell me of it all, and I can ask him questions and find out things, and see how I may comfort him.

Letter, Van Helsing to Mrs Harker

24 September.
(Confidence.)

Dear Madam,—

I pray you to pardon my writing, in that I am so far friend as that I sent to you sad news of Miss Lucy Westenra's death. By the kindness of Lord Godalming, I am empowered to read her letters and papers, for I am deeply concerned about certain matters vitally important. In them I find some letters from you, which show how great friends you were and how you love her. Oh, Madam Mina, by that love, I implore you, help me. It is for others' good that I ask—to redress great wrong, and to lift much and terrible troubles—that may be more great than you can know. May it be that I see you? You can trust me. I am friend of Dr John Seward and of Lord Godalming (that was Arthur of Miss Lucy). I must keep it private for the present from all. I should come to Exeter to see you at once if you tell me I am privilege to come, and where and when. I implore your pardon, madam. I have read your letters to poor Lucy, and know how good you are and how your husband suffer; so I pray you, if it may be, enlighten him not, lest it may harm. Again your pardon, and forgive me.

VAN HELSING.

Telegram, Mrs Harker to Van Helsing

25 September.—Come today by quarter-past ten train if you can catch it. Can see you any time you call.

WILHELMINA HARKER.

Mina Harker's Journal

25 September.—I cannot help feeling terribly excited as the time draws near for the visit of Dr Van Helsing, for somehow I expect that it will throw some light upon Jonathan's sad experience; and as he attended poor dear Lucy in her last illness, he can tell me all about her. That is the reason of his coming; it is concerning Lucy and her sleep-walking, and not about Jonathan. Then I shall never know the real truth now! How silly I am. That awful journal gets hold of my imagination and tinges everything with something of its own colour. Of course it is about Lucy. That habit came back to the poor dear, and that awful night on the cliff must have made her ill. I had almost forgotten in my own affairs how ill she was afterwards. She must have told him of her sleep-walking adventure on the cliff, and that I knew all about it; and now he wants me to tell him about it, so that he may understand. I hope I did right in not saying anything of it to Mrs Westenra; I should never forgive myself if any act of mine, were it even a negative one, brought harm on poor dear Lucy. I hope, too, Dr Van Helsing will not blame me; I have had so much trouble and anxiety of late that I feel I cannot bear more just at present.

I suppose a cry does us all good at times—clears the air as other rain does. Perhaps it was reading the journal yesterday that upset me, and then Jonathan went away this morning to stay away from me a whole day and night, the first time we have been parted since our marriage. I do hope the dear fellow will take care of himself, and that nothing will occur to upset him. It is two o'clock, and the doctor will be here soon now. I shall say nothing of Jonathan's journal unless he asks me. I am so glad I have type-written out my own journal, so that in case he asks about Lucy, I can hand it to him; it will save much questioning.

Later.—He has come and gone. Oh, what a strange meeting, and how it all makes my head whirl round! I feel like one in a dream. Can it be all possible, or even a part of it? If I had not read Jonathan's journal first, I should never have accepted even a possibility. Poor, poor, dear Jonathan! How he must have suffered. Please the good God, all this may not upset him again. I shall try to save him from it; but it may be even a consolation and a help to him—terrible though it be and awful in its consequences—to know for certain that his eyes and ears and brain did not deceive him, and that it is all true. It may be that it is the doubt which haunts him; that when the doubt is removed, no matter which—waking or dreaming—may prove the truth, he will be more satisfied and better able to bear the shock. Dr Van Helsing must be a good man as well as a clever one if he is Arthur's friend and Dr Seward's, and if they brought him all the way from Holland to look after Lucy. I feel from having seen him that he *is* good and kind and of a noble nature. When he comes tomorrow I shall ask him about Jonathan; and then, please God, all this sorrow and anxiety may lead to a good end. I used to think I would like to practise interviewing; Jonathan's friend on the *Exeter News* told him that memory was everything in such work—that you must be able to put down exactly almost every word spoken, even if you had to refine some of it afterwards. Here was a rare interview; I shall try to record it *verbatim*.

It was half-past two o'clock when the knock came. I took my courage *à deux mains*[1] and waited. In a few minutes Mary opened the door, and announced 'Dr Van Helsing.'

I rose and bowed, and he came towards me; a man of medium height, strongly built, with his shoulders set back over a broad, deep chest and a neck well balanced on the trunk as the head is on the neck. The poise of the head strikes one at once as indicative of thought and power; the head is noble, well-sized, broad, and large behind the ears. The face, clean-shaven, shows a hard, square chin, a large, resolute, mobile mouth, a good-sized nose, rather straight, but with quick, sensitive nostrils, that seem to broaden as the big, bushy brows come down and the mouth tightens. The forehead is broad and fine, rising at first almost straight and then sloping back above two bumps or ridges[2] wide apart; such a forehead that the reddish hair cannot possibly tumble over it, but falls naturally back and to the sides. Big, dark blue eyes are set widely apart, and are quick and tender or stern with the man's moods. He said to me:—

'Mrs Harker, is it not?' I bowed assent.

'That was Miss Mina Murray?' Again I assented.

'It is Mina Murray that I came to see that was friend of that poor dear child Lucy Westenra. Madam Mina, it is on account of the dead I come.'

'Sir,' I said, 'you could have no better claim on me than that you were a friend and helper of Lucy Westenra.' And I held out my hand. He took it and said tenderly:—

'Oh, Madam Mina, I knew that the friend of that poor lily girl must

---

1. In both hands (French).
2. Like many advanced Victorians, Mina trusts in phrenology, a science of character reading according to bumps on the head.

be good, but I had yet to learn—' He finished his speech with a courtly bow. I asked him what it was that he wanted to see me about, so he at once began:—

'I have read your letters to Miss Lucy. Forgive me, but I had to begin to inquire somewhere, and there was none to ask. I know that you were with her at Whitby. She sometimes kept a diary—you need not look surprised, Madam Mina; it was begun after you had left, and was made in imitation of you—and in that diary she traces by inference certain things to a sleep-walking in which she puts down that you saved her. In great perplexity then I come to you, and ask you out of your so much kindness to tell me all of it that you remember.'

'I can tell you, I think, Dr Van Helsing, all about it.'

'Ah, then you have good memory for facts, for details? It is not always so with young ladies.'

'No, doctor, but I wrote it all down at the time. I can show it to you if you like.'

'Oh, Madam Mina, I will be grateful; you will do me much favour.' I could not resist the temptation of mystifying him a bit—I suppose it is some of the taste of the original apple that remains still in our mouths—so I handed him the shorthand diary. He took it with a grateful bow, and said:—

'May I read it?'

'If you wish,' I answered as demurely as I could. He opened it, and for an instant his face fell. Then he stood up and bowed.

'Oh, you so clever woman!' he said. 'I long knew that Mr Jonathan was a man of much thankfulness; but see, his wife have all the good things. And will you not so much honour me and so help me as to read it for me? Alas! I know not the shorthand.' By this time my little joke was over, and I was almost ashamed; so I took the typewritten copy from my workbasket and handed it to him.

'Forgive me,' I said: 'I could not help it; but I had been thinking that it was of dear Lucy that you wished to ask, and so that you might not have to wait—not on my account, but because I know your time must be precious—I have written it out on the typewriter for you.'

He took it, and his eyes glistened. 'You are so good,' he said. 'And may I read it now? I may want to ask you some things when I have read.'

'By all means,' I said, 'read it over whilst I order lunch; and then you can ask me questions whilst we eat.' He bowed and settled himself in a chair with his back to the light, and became absorbed in the papers, whilst I went to see after lunch, chiefly in order that he might not be disturbed. When I came back I found him walking hurriedly up and down the room, his face all ablaze with excitement. He rushed up to me and took me by both hands.

'Oh, Madam Mina,' he said, 'how can I say what I owe to you? This paper is as sunshine. It opens the gate to me. I am daze, I am dazzle, with so much light; and yet clouds roll in behind the light every time. But that you do not, cannot, comprehend. Oh, but I am grateful to you, you so clever woman. Madam'—he said this very solemnly—'if ever Abraham Van Helsing can do anything for you or yours, I trust you will let me know. It will be pleasure and delight if I may serve you as a friend; as a friend, but all I have ever learned, all I can ever do, shall be for you and those you love. There are darknesses in life, and there are lights; you are one of the lights. You will have happy life and good life, and your husband will be blessed in you.'

'But, doctor, you praise me too much, and—and you do not know me.'

'Not know you—I, who am old, and who have studied all my life men and women; I, who have made my speciality the brain and all that belongs to him and all that follow from him! And I have read your diary that you have so goodly written to me, and which breathes out truth in every line. I, who have read your so sweet letter to poor Lucy of your marriage and your trust, not know you! Oh, Madam Mina, good women tell all their lives, and by day and by hour and by minute, such things that angels can read; and we men who wish to know have in us something of angels' eyes. Your husband is noble nature, and you are noble too, for you trust, and trust cannot be where there is mean nature. And your husband—tell me of him. Is he quite well? Is all that fever gone, and is he strong and hearty?' I saw here an opening to ask him about Jonathan, so I said:—

'He was almost recovered, but he has been greatly upset by Mr Hawkins's death.' He interrupted:—

'Oh yes, I know, I know. I have read your last two letters.' I went on:—

'I suppose this upset him, for when we were in town on Thursday last he had a sort of shock.'

'A shock, and after brain fever so soon! That was not good. What kind of shock was it?'

'He thought he saw some one who recalled something terrible, something which led to his brain fever.' And here the whole thing seemed to overwhelm me in a rush. The pity of Jonathan, the horror which he experienced, the whole fearful mystery of his diary, and the fear that has been brooding over me ever since, all came in a tumult. I suppose I was hysterical, for I threw myself on my knees and held up my hands to him, and implored him to make my husband well again. He took my hands and raised me up, and made me sit on the sofa, and sat by me; he held my hand in his, and said to me with, oh, such infinite sweetness:—

'My life is a barren and lonely one, and so full of work that I have not had much time for friendships; but since I have been summoned to here by my friend John Seward I have known so many good people and seen such nobility that I feel more than ever—and it has grown with my advancing years—the loneliness of my life. Believe me, then, that I come here full of respect for you, and you have given me hope —hope, not in what I am seeking of, but that there are good women still left to make life happy—good women, whose lives and whose truths may make good lesson for the children that are to be. I am glad, glad, that I may here be of some use to you; for if your husband suffer, he suffer within the range of my study and experience. I promise you that I will gladly do *all* for him that I can—all to make his life strong and manly, and your life a happy one. Now you must eat. You are over-wrought and perhaps over-anxious. Husband Jonathan would not like to see you so pale; and what he like not where he love, is not to his good. Therefore for his sake you must eat and smile. You have told me all about Lucy, and so now we shall not speak of it, lest it distress. I shall stay in Exeter tonight, for I want to think much over what you have told me, and when I have thought I will ask you questions, if I may. And then, too, you will tell me of husband Jonathan's trouble so far as you can, but not yet. You must eat now; afterwards you shall tell me all.'

After lunch, when we went back to the drawing-room, he said to me:—

'And now tell me all about him.' When it came to speaking to this great, learned man, I began to fear that he would think me a weak fool, and Jonathan a madman—that journal is all so strange—and I hesitated to go on. But he was so sweet and kind, and he had promised to help, and I trusted him, so I said:—

'Dr Van Helsing, what I have to tell you is so queer that you must not laugh at me or at my husband. I have been since yesterday in a sort of fever of doubt; you must be kind to me, and not think me foolish that I have even half believed some very strange things.' He reassured me by his manner as well as his words when he said:—

'Oh, my dear, if you only knew how strange is the matter regarding which I am here, it is you who would laugh. I have learned not to think little of any one's belief, no matter how strange it be. I have tried to keep an open mind; and it is not the ordinary things of life that could close it, but the strange things, the extraordinary things, the things that make one doubt if they be mad or sane.'

'Thank you, thank you, a thousand times! You have taken a weight off my mind. If you will let me, I shall give you a paper to read. It is long, but I have typewritten it out. It will tell you my trouble and Jonathan's. It is the copy of his journal when abroad, and all that happened. I dare not say anything of it; you will read for yourself and judge. And then when I see you, perhaps, you will be very kind and tell me what you think.'

'I promise,' he said as I gave him the papers; 'I shall in the morning, so soon as I can, come to see you and your husband, if I may.'

'Jonathan will be here at half-past eleven, and you must come to lunch with us and see him then; you could catch the quick 3.34 train, which will leave you at Paddington[3] before eight.' He was surprised at my knowledge of the trains off-hand, but he does not know that I have made up all the trains to and from Exeter, so that I may help Jonathan in case he is in a hurry.

So he took the papers with him and went away, and I sit here thinking—thinking I don't know what.

Letter (by Hand), Van Helsing to Mrs Harker

25 September, 6 o'clock.

Dear Madam Mina,—

I have read your husband's so wonderful diary. You may sleep without doubt. Strange and terrible as it is, it is *true*! I will pledge my life on it. It may be worse for others; but for him and you there is no dread. He is a noble fellow; and let me tell you from experience of men, that one who would do as he did in going down that wall and to that room—ay, and going a second time—is not one to be injured in permanence by a shock. His brain and his heart are all right; this I swear, before I have even seen him; so be at rest. I shall have much to ask him of other things. I am blessed that today I come to see you, for I have learn all at once so much that again I am dazzle—dazzle more than ever, and I must think.

Yours the most faithful,

ABRAHAM VAN HELSING.

Letter, Mrs Harker to Van Helsing

25 September, 6.30 p.m.

My dear Dr Van Helsing,—

A thousand thanks for your kind letter, which has taken a great weight off my mind. And yet, if it be true, what terrible things there are in the world, and what an awful thing if that man, that monster, be really in London! I fear to think. I have this moment, whilst writing, had a wire from Jonathan, saying that he leaves by the 6.25 tonight from Launceston[4] and will be here at 10.18, so that I shall have no fear tonight. Will you, therefore, instead of lunching with us, please come to breakfast at eight o'clock, if this be not too early for you? You can get away, if you are in a hurry, by the 10.30 train, which will bring you to Pad-

3. Railway terminal in west-central London, near Kensington Gardens.
4. A market city in Cornwall, about fifty miles from Exeter and a hundred miles from London.

dington by 2.35. Do not answer this, as I shall take it that, if I do not hear, you will come to breakfast.

> Believe me,
> Your faithful and grateful friend,
> MINA HARKER.

Jonathan Harker's Journal

26 September.—I thought never to write in this diary again, but the time has come. When I got home last night Mina had supper ready, and when we had supped she told me of Van Helsing's visit, and of her having given him the two diaries copied out, and of how anxious she has been about me. She showed me in the doctor's letter that all I wrote down was true. It seems to have made a new man of me. It was the doubt as to the reality of the whole thing that knocked me over. I felt impotent, and in the dark, and distrustful. But, now that I *know*, I am not afraid, even of the Count. He has succeeded after all, then, in his design in getting to London, and it was he I saw. He has got younger, and how? Van Helsing is the man to unmask him and hunt him out, if he is anything like what Mina says. We sat late, and talked it all over. Mina is dressing, and I shall call at the hotel in a few minutes and bring him over . . .

He was, I think, surprised to see me. When I came into the room where he was, and introduced myself, he took me by the shoulder, and turned my face round to the light, and said, after a sharp scrutiny:—

'But Madam Mina told me you were ill, that you had had a shock.' It was so funny to hear my wife called 'Madam Mina' by this kindly, strong-faced old man. I smiled, and said:—

'I *was* ill, I *have* had a shock; but you have cured me already.'

'And how?'

'By your letter to Mina last night. I was in doubt, and then everything took a hue of unreality, and I did not know what to trust, even the evidence of my own senses. Not knowing what to trust, I did not know what to do; and so had only to keep on working in what had hitherto been the groove of my life. The groove ceased to avail me, and I mistrusted myself. Doctor, you don't know what it is to doubt everything, even yourself. No, you don't; you couldn't with eyebrows like yours.' He seemed pleased, and laughed as he said:—

'So! You are physiognomist. I learn more here with each hour. I am with so much pleasure coming to you to breakfast; and, oh, sir, you will pardon praise from an old man, but you are blessed in your wife.' I would listen to him go on praising Mina for a day, so I simply nodded and stood silent.

'She is one of God's women, fashioned by His own hand to show us men and other women that there is a heaven where we can enter, and that its light can be here on earth. So true, so sweet, so noble, so little an egoist—and that, let me tell you, is much in this age, so sceptical and selfish. And you sir—I have read all the letters to poor Miss Lucy, and some of them speak of you, so I know you since some days from the knowing of others; but I have seen your true self since last night. You will give me your hand, will you not? And let us be friends for all our lives.'

We shook hands, and he was so earnest and so kind that it made me quite choky.

'And now,' he said, 'may I ask you for some more help? I have a great task to do, and at the beginning it is to know. You can help me here. Can you tell me what went before your going to Transylvania? Later on I may ask more help, and of a different kind; but at first this will do.'

'Look here, sir,' I said, 'does what you have to do concern the Count?'

'It does,' he said solemnly.

'Then I am with you heart and soul. As you go by the 10.30 train, you will not have time to read them; but I shall get the bundle of papers. You can take them with you and read them in the train.'

After breakfast I saw him to the station. When we were parting he said:—

'Perhaps you will come to town if I send to you, and take Madam Mina too.'

'We shall both come when you will,' I said.

I had got him the morning papers and the London papers of the previous night, and while we were talking at the carriage window, waiting for the train to start, he was turning them over. His eye suddenly seemed to catch something in one of them, the *Westminster Gazette*—I knew it by the colour—and he grew quite white. He read something intently, groaning to himself: 'Mein Gott! Mein Gott! So soon! so soon!' I do not think he remembered me at the moment. Just then the whistle blew, and the train moved off. This recalled him to himself, and he leaned out of the window and waved his hand, calling out: 'Love to Madam Mina; I shall write so soon as ever I can.'

Dr Seward's Diary

26 September.—Truly there is no such thing as finality. Not a week since I said 'Finis,' and yet here I am starting fresh again, or rather going on with the same record. Until this afternoon I had no cause to think of what is done. Renfield had become, to all intents, as sane as he ever was. He was already well ahead with his fly business; and he had just started in the spider line also; so he had not been of any trouble to me. I had a letter from Arthur, written on Sunday, and from it I gather that he is bearing up wonderfully well. Quincey Morris is with him, and that is much of a help, for he himself is a bubbling well of good spirits. Quincey wrote me a line too, and from him I hear that Arthur is beginning to recover something of his old buoyancy; so as to them all my mind is at rest. As for myself, I was settling down to my work with the enthusiasm which I used to have for it, so that I might fairly have said that the wound which poor Lucy left on me was becoming cicatrized.[5] Everything is, however, now reopened; and what is to be the end God only knows. I have an idea that Van Helsing thinks he knows too, but he will only let out enough at a time to whet curiosity. He went to Exeter yesterday, and stayed there all night. Today he came back, and almost bounded into the room at about half past five o'clock, and thrust last night's *Westminster Gazette* into my hand.

'What do you think of that?' he asked as he stood back and folded his arms.

I looked over the paper, for I really did not know what he meant; but he took it from me and pointed out a paragraph about children being decoyed away at Hampstead. It did not convey much to me, until I reached a passage where it described small punctured wounds on their throats. An idea struck me, and I looked up. 'Well?' he said.

'It is like poor Lucy's.'

'And what do you make of it?'

'Simply that there is some cause in common. Whatever it was that injured her has injured them.' I did not quite understand his answer:—

'That is true indirectly, but not directly.'

'How do you mean, Professor?' I asked. I was a little inclined to take his seriousness lightly—for, after all, four days of rest and freedom from burning, harrowing anxiety does help to restore one's spirits—but when I saw his face, it sobered me. Never, even in the midst of our despair about poor Lucy, had he looked more stern.

'Tell me!' I said. 'I can hazard no opinion. I do not know what to think, and I have no data on which to found a conjecture.'

'Do you mean to tell me, friend John, that you have no suspicion as to what poor Lucy died of; not after all the hints given, not only by events, but by me?'

'Of nervous prostration following on great loss or waste of blood.'

'And how the blood lost or waste?' I shook my head. He stepped over and sat down beside me, and went on:—

'You are clever man, friend John; you reason well, and your wit is bold; but you are too prejudiced. You do not let your eyes see nor your ears hear, and that which is outside your daily life is not of account to you. Do you not think that there are things which you cannot understand, and yet which are; that some people see things that others can-

5. Scar tissue is building up.

not? But there are things old and new which must not be contemplate by men's eyes, because they know—or think they know—some things which other men have told them. Ah, it is the fault of our science that it wants to explain all; and if it explain not, then it says there is nothing to explain. But yet we see around us every day the growth of new beliefs, which think themselves new; and which are yet but the old, which pretend to be young—like the fine ladies at the opera. I suppose now you do not believe in corporeal transference.[6] No? Nor in materialization[7]. No? Nor in astral bodies.[8] No? Nor in the reading of thought. No? Nor in hypnotism—'

'Yes,' I said. 'Charcot[9] has proved that pretty well.' He smiled as he went on: 'Then you are satisfied as to it. Yes? And of course then you understand how it act, and can follow the mind of the great Charcot —alas that he is no more!—into the very soul of the patient that he influence. No? Then, friend John, am I to take it that you simply accept fact, and are satisfied to let from premise to conclusion be a blank? No? Then tell me—for I am student of the brain—how you accept the hypnotism and reject the thought-reading. Let me tell you, my friend, that there are things done today in electrical science which would have been deemed unholy by the very men who discovered electricity—who would themselves not so long before have been burned as wizards. There are always mysteries in life. Why was it that Methuselah lived nine hundred years,[1] and 'Old Parr'[2] one hundred and sixty-nine, and yet that poor Lucy, with four men's blood in her poor veins, could not live even one day? For, had she live one more day, we could have save her.[3] Do you know all the mystery of life and death? Do you know the altogether of comparative anatomy, and can say wherefore the qualities of brutes are in some men, and not in others? Can you tell me why, when other spiders die small and soon, that one great spider lived for centuries in the tower of the old Spanish church and grew and grew, till, on descending, he could drink the oil of all the church lamps? Can you tell me why in the Pampas, ay and elsewhere, there are bats that come at night and open the veins of cattle and horses and suck dry their veins; how in some islands of the Western seas there are bats

6. The movement of objects by thought.
7. A technical term for "ghost" or "apparition," especially at a séance. The Society for Psychical Research, founded in 1882, provided a scientific vocabulary for supernatural phenomena.
8. In occultism, the astral body is an immaterial part of the self that travels while the body remains still.
9. French neurologist (1825–1893) who, through hypnosis, primarily of women, explored the organic causes of hysteria. In the 1860s and 1870s, Charcot's flamboyant exhibitions of hypnotized women at the Salpêtrière Hospital in Paris may have inspired the sleeping Lucy's spectacular transformations before an audience of riveted men. Stoker proudly listed Charcot as a distinguished visitor to the Lyceum in his *Personal Reminiscences of Henry Irving* (1906). Since *Dracula* is set in 1893, Charcot has just died.
1. See Genesis 5.27.
2. Thomas Parr, a legend of longevity, was supposed to have lived from 1483 to 1635, though in all likelihood the legend was perpetuated by a succession of Thomas Parrs and not one person.
3. By the logic of Stoker's own rules, it is unclear how Lucy could have been saved.

which hang on the trees all day, that those who have seen describe as like giant nuts or pods, and that when the sailors sleep on the deck, because that it is hot, flit down on them, and then—and then in the morning are found dead men, white as even Miss Lucy was?'

'Good God, Professor!' I said, starting up. 'Do you mean to tell me that Lucy was bitten by such a bat; and that such a thing is here in London in the nineteenth century?' He waved his hand for silence, and went on:—

'Can you tell me why the tortoise lives more long than generations of men; why the elephant goes on and on till he have seen dynasties; and why the parrot never die only of bite of cat or dog or other complaint? Can you tell me why men believe in all ages and places that there are some few who live on always if they be permit; that there are men and women who cannot die? We all know—because science has vouched for the fact—that there have been toads shut up in rocks for thousands of years, shut in one so small hole that only hold him since the youth of the world. Can you tell me how the Indian fakir can make himself to die and have been buried, and his grave sealed and corn sowed on it, and the corn reaped and be cut and sown and reaped and cut again, and then the men come and take away the unbroken seal, and that there lie the Indian fakir, not dead, but that rise up and walk amongst them as before?' Here I interrupted him. I was getting bewildered; he so crowded on my mind his list of nature's eccentricities and possible impossibilities that my imagination was getting fired. I had a dim idea that he was teaching me some lesson, as long ago he used to do in his study at Amsterdam; but he used then to tell me the thing, so that I could have the object of thought in mind all the time. But now I was without this help, yet I wanted to follow him, so I said:—

'Professor, let me be your pet student again. Tell me the thesis, so that I may apply your knowledge as you go on. At present I am going in my mind from point to point as a mad man, and not a sane one, follows an idea. I feel like a novice blundering through a bog in a mist, jumping from one tussock[4] to another in the mere blind effort to move on without knowing where I am going.'

'That is good image,' he said. 'Well, I shall tell you. My thesis is this: I want you to believe.'

'To believe what?'

'To believe in things that you cannot. Let me illustrate. I heard once of an American[5] who so defined faith: "that which enables us to believe things which we know to be untrue." For one, I follow that man. He meant that we shall have an open mind, and not let a little bit of truth check the rush of a big truth, like a small rock does a railway truck.

4. A clump or tuft, as of growing grass.
5. Presumably Stoker's friend Mark Twain: "Faith is believing what you know ain't so," from *Pudd'nhead Wilson's New Calendar*, which Twain sent Stoker in 1894.

We get the small truth first. Good! We keep him, and we value him; but all the same we must not let him think himself all the truth in the universe.'

'Then you want me not to let some previous conviction injure the receptivity of my mind with regard to some strange matter. Do I read your lesson aright?'

'Ah, you are my favourite pupil still. It is worth to teach you. Now that you are willing to understand, you have taken the first step to understand. You think then that those so small holes in the children's throats were made by the same that made the hole in Miss Lucy?'

'I suppose so.' He stood up and said solemnly:—

'Then you are wrong. Oh, would it were so! but alas! no. It is worse, far, far worse.'

'In God's name, Professor Van Helsing, what do you mean?' I cried.

He threw himself with a despairing gesture into a chair, and placed his elbows on the table, covering his face with his hands as he spoke:—

'They were made by Miss Lucy!'

Chapter XV

Dr Seward's Diary (continued)

For a while sheer anger mastered me; it was as if he had during her life struck Lucy on the face. I smote the table hard and rose up as I said to him:—

'Dr Van Helsing, are you mad?' He raised his head and looked at me, and somehow the tenderness of his face calmed me at once. 'Would I were!' he said. 'Madness were easy to bear compared with truth like this. Oh, my friend, why, think you, did I go so far round, why take so long to tell you so simple a thing? Was it because I hate you and have hated you all my life? Was it because I wished to give you pain? Was it that I wanted, now so late, revenge for that time when you saved my life, and from a fearful death? Ah no!'

'Forgive me,' said I. He went on:—

'My friend, it was because I wished to be gentle in the breaking to you, for I know you have loved that so sweet lady. But even yet I do not expect you to believe. It is so hard to accept at once any abstract truth, that we may doubt such to be possible when we have always believed the "no" of it; it is more hard still to accept so sad a concrete truth, and of such a one as Miss Lucy. Tonight I go to prove it. Dare you come with me?'

This staggered me. A man does not like to prove such a truth; Byron excepted from the category, jealousy.

And prove the very truth he most abhorred.[1]

He saw my hesitation, and spoke:—

'The logic is simple, no madman's logic this time, jumping from tussock to tussock in a misty bog. If it be not true, then proof will be relief; at worst it will not harm. If it be true! Ah, there is the dread; yet very dread should help my cause, for in it is some need of belief. Come, I tell you what I propose: first, that we go off now and see that child in the hospital. Dr Vincent, of the North Hospital, where the papers say the child is, is friend of mine, and I think of yours since you were in class at Amsterdam. He will let two scientists see his case, if he will not let two friends. We shall tell him nothing, but only that we wish to learn. And then—'

'And then?' He took a key from his pocket and held it up. 'And then we spend the night, you and I, in the churchyard where Lucy lies. This is the key that lock the tomb. I had it from the coffin-man to give to Arthur.' My heart sank within me, for I felt that there was some fearful ordeal before us. I could do nothing, however, so I plucked up what heart I could and said that we had better hasten, as the afternoon was passing . . .

We found the child awake. It had had a sleep and taken some food, and altogether was going on well. Dr Vincent took the bandage from its throat, and showed us the punctures. There was no mistaking the similarity to those which had been on Lucy's throat. They were smaller, and the edges looked fresher; that was all. We asked Vincent to what he attributed them, and he replied that it must have been a bite of some animal, perhaps a rat; but, for his own part, he was inclined to think that it was one of the bats which are so numerous on the northern heights of London. 'Out of so many harmless ones,' he said, 'there may be some wild specimen from the South of a more malignant species. Some sailor may have brought one home, and it managed to escape; or even from the Zoological Gardens a young one may have got loose, or one be bred there from a vampire. These things do occur, you know. Only ten days ago a wolf got out, and was, I believe, traced up in this direction. For a week after, the children were playing nothing but Red Riding Hood on the Heath and in every alley in the place until this 'bloofer lady' scare came along, since when it has been quite a gala-time with them. Even this poor little mite, when he woke up today, asked the nurse if he might go away. When she asked him why he wanted to go, he said he wanted to play with the "bloofer lady." '

'I hope,' said Van Helsing, 'that when you are sending the child home you will caution its parents to keep strict watch over it. These fancies to stray are most dangerous; and if the child were to remain out

1. Byron, *Don Juan* 1.139: "To prove himself the thing he most abhorred." In *Don Juan*, the abhorred thing is cuckoldery.

another night, it would probably be fatal. But in any case I suppose you will not let it away for some days?'

'Certainly not, not for a week at least; longer if the wound is not healed.'

Our visit to the hospital took more time than we had reckoned on, and the sun had dipped before we came out. When Van Helsing saw how dark it was, he said:—

'There is no hurry. It is more late than I thought. Come, let us seek somewhere that we may eat, and then we shall go on our way.'

We dined at 'Jack Straw's Castle'[2] along with a little crowd of bicyclists and others who were genially noisy. About ten o'clock we started from the inn. It was then very dark, and the scattered lamps made the darkness greater when we were once outside their individual radius. The Professor had evidently noted the road we were to go, for he went on unhesitatingly; but, as for me, I was in quite a mix-up as to locality.[3] As we went further, we met fewer and fewer people, till at last we were somewhat surprised when we met even the patrol of horse police going their usual suburban round. At last we reached the wall of the churchyard, which we climbed over. With some little difficulty—for it was very dark, and the whole place seemed so strange to us—we found the Westenra tomb. The Professor took the key, opened the creaky door, and standing back, politely, but quite unconsciously, motioned me to precede him. There was a delicious irony in the offer, in the courtliness of giving preference on such a ghastly occasion. My companion followed me quickly, and cautiously drew the door to, after carefully ascertaining that the lock was a falling, and not a spring, one. In the latter case we should have been in a bad plight. Then he fumbled in his bag, and taking out a match-box and a piece of candle, proceeded to make a light. The tomb in the day-time, and when wreathed with fresh flowers, had looked grim and gruesome enough; but now, some days afterwards, when the flowers hung lank and dead, their whites turning to rust and their greens to browns; when the spider and the beetle had resumed their accustomed dominance; when time-discoloured stone, and dust-encrusted mortar, and rusty, dank iron, and tarnished brass, and clouded silver-plating gave back the feeble glimmer of a candle, the effect was more miserable and sordid than could have been imagined. It conveyed irresistibly the idea that life—animal life—was not the only thing which could pass away.

Van Helsing went about his work systematically. Holding his candle so that he could read the coffin plates, and so holding it that the sperm[4] dropped in white patches which congealed as they touched the metal,

---

2. An inn on Hampstead Heath, still open in the 1990s.
3. Understandably, since the isolated setting Seward goes on to describe has no relation to the bustling Highgate Cemetery or to the other adjacent graveyard at St. John's Church.
4. Not only fodder for Freudians, but the wax from a candle made from spermiceti, a waxy solid obtained from the oil of whales, especially sperm whales.

he made assurance of Lucy's coffin. Another search in his bag, and he took out a turnscrew.[5]

'What are you going to do?' I asked.

'To open the coffin. You shall yet be convinced.' Straightway he began taking out the screws, and finally lifted off the lid, showing the casing of lead beneath. The sight was almost too much for me. It seemed to be as much an affront to the dead as it would have been to have stripped off her clothing in her sleep whilst living; I actually took hold of his hand to stop him. He only said: 'You shall see,' and again fumbling in his bag, took out a tiny fret-saw. Striking the turnscrew through the lead with a swift downward stab, which made me wince, he made a small hole, which was, however, big enough to admit the point of the saw. I had expected a rush of gas from the week-old corpse. We doctors, who have had to study our dangers, have to become accustomed to such things, and I drew back towards the door. But the Professor never stopped for a moment; he sawed down a couple of feet along one side of the lead coffin, and then across, and down the other side. Taking the edge of the loose flange,[6] he bent it back towards the foot of the coffin, and holding up the candle into the aperture, motioned to me to look.

I drew near and looked. The coffin was empty.

It was certainly a surprise to me, and gave me a considerable shock, but Van Helsing was unmoved. He was now more sure than ever of his ground, and so emboldened to proceed in his task. 'Are you satisfied now, friend John?' he asked.

I felt all the dogged argumentativeness of my nature awake within me as I answered him:—

'I am satisfied that Lucy's body is not in that coffin; but that only proves one thing.'

'And what is that, friend John?'

'That it is not there.'

'That is good logic,' he said, 'so far as it goes. But how do you—how can you—account for it not being there?'

'Perhaps a body-snatcher,' I suggested. 'Some of the undertaker's people may have stolen it.' I felt that I was speaking folly, and yet it was the only real cause which I could suggest. The Professor sighed. 'Ah well!' he said, 'we must have more proof. Come with me.'

He put on the coffin-lid again, gathered up all his things and placed them in the bag, blew out the light, and placed the candle also in the bag. We opened the door, and went out. Behind us he closed the door and locked it. He handed me the key, saying: 'Will you keep it? You had better be assured.' I laughed—it was not a very cheerful laugh, I

5. Screwdriver.
6. A protruding edge or rib, as on a wheel, used to strengthen an object, hold it in place, or attach it to another object.

am bound to say—as I motioned him to keep it. 'A key is nothing,' I said; 'there may be duplicates; and anyhow it is not difficult to pick a lock of that kind.' He said nothing, but put the key in his pocket. Then he told me to watch at one side of the churchyard whilst he would watch at the other. I took up my place behind a yew-tree, and I saw his dark figure move until the intervening headstones and trees hid it from my sight.

It was a lonely vigil. Just after I had taken my place I heard a distant clock strike twelve, and in time came one and two. I was chilled and unnerved, and angry with the Professor for taking me on such an errand and with myself for coming. I was too cold and too sleepy to be keenly observant, and not sleepy enough to betray my trust; so altogether I had a dreary, miserable time.

Suddenly, as I turned round, I thought I saw something like a white streak, moving between two dark yew-trees at the side of the churchyard farthest from the tomb; at the same time a dark mass moved from the Professor's side of the ground, and hurriedly went towards it. Then I too moved; but I had to go round headstones and railed-off tombs, and I stumbled over graves. The sky was overcast, and somewhere far off an early cock crew. A little way off, beyond a line of scattered juniper-trees, which marked the pathway to the church, a white, dim figure flitted in the direction of the tomb. The tomb itself was hidden by trees, and I could not see where the figure disappeared. I heard the rustle of actual movement where I had first seen the white figure, and coming over, found the professor holding in his arms a tiny child. When he saw me he held it out to me, and said:—

'Are you satisfied now?'

'No,' I said, in a way that I felt was aggressive.

'Do you not see the child?'

'Yes, it is a child, but who brought it here? And is it wounded?' I asked.

'We shall see,' said the Professor, and with one impulse we took our way out of the churchyard, he carrying the sleeping child.

When we had got some little distance away, we went into a clump of trees, and struck a match, and looked at the child's throat. It was without a scratch or scar of any kind.

'Was I right?' I asked triumphantly.

'We were just in time,' said the Professor thankfully.

We had now to decide what we were to do with the child, and so consulted about it. If we were to take it to a police-station we should have to give some account of our movements during the night; at least, we should have had to make some statement as to how we had come to find the child. So finally we decided that we would take it to the Heath, and when we heard a policeman coming, would leave it where he could not fail to find it; we would then seek our way home as quickly as we could. All fell out well. At the edge of Hampstead Heath we heard a policeman's heavy tramp, and laying the child on the pathway, we waited and watched until he saw it as he flashed his lantern to and fro. We heard his exclamation of astonishment, and then we went away silently. By good chance we got a cab near the 'Spaniards,'[7] and drove to town.

I cannot sleep, so I make this entry. But I must try to get a few hours' sleep, as Van Helsing is to call for me at noon. He insists that I shall go with him on another expedition.

27 September.—It was two o'clock before we found a suitable opportunity for our attempt. The funeral held at noon was all completed, and the last stragglers of the mourners had taken themselves lazily away, when, looking carefully from behind a clump of alder-trees, we saw the sexton lock the gate after him. We knew then that we were safe till morning did we desire it; but the Professor told me that we should not want more than an hour at most. Again I felt that horrid sense of the reality of things, in which any effort of imagination seemed out of place; and I realized distinctly the perils of the law which we were incurring in our unhallowed work. Besides, I felt it was all so useless. Outrageous as it was to open a leaden coffin, to see if a woman dead nearly a week were really dead, it now seemed the height of folly to open the tomb again, when we knew, from the evidence of our own eyesight, that the coffin was empty. I shrugged my shoulders, however, and rested silent, for Van Helsing had a way of going on his own road, no matter who remonstrated. He took the key, opened the vault, and again courteously motioned me to precede. The place was not so gruesome as last night, but oh, how unutterably mean-looking when the sunshine streamed in. Van Helsing walked over to Lucy's coffin, and I followed. He bent over and again forced back the leaden flange; and then a shock of surprise and dismay shot through me.

There lay Lucy, seemingly just as we had seen her the night before her funeral. She was, if possible, more radiantly beautiful than ever; and I could not believe that she was dead. The lips were red, nay redder than before; and on the cheeks was a delicate bloom.

'Is this a juggle?' I said to him.

'Are you convinced now?' said the Professor in response, and as he spoke he put over his hand, and in a way that made me shudder, pulled back the dead lips and showed the white teeth.

'See,' he went on, 'see, they are even sharper than before. With this and this'—and he touched one of the canine teeth and that below it— 'the little children can be bitten. Are you of belief now, friend John?' Once more, argumentative hostility woke within me. I *could* not accept

7. The Spaniards Inn, an old pub near Hampstead Heath, still open in the 1990s.

such an overwhelming idea as he suggested; so, with an attempt to argue of which I was even at the moment ashamed, I said:—

'She may have been placed here since last night.'

'Indeed? That is so, and by whom?'

'I do not know. Some one has done it.'

'And yet she had been dead one week. Most peoples in that time would not look so.' I had no answer for this, so was silent. Van Helsing did not seem to notice my silence; at any rate, he showed neither chagrin nor triumph. He was looking intently at the face of the dead woman, raising the eyelids and looking at the eyes, and once more opening the lips and examining the teeth. Then he turned to me and said:—

'Here, there is one thing which is different from all recorded: here is some dual life that is not as the common. She was bitten by the vampire when she was in a trance,[8] sleep-walking—oh, you start; you do not know that, friend John, but you shall know it all later—and in trance could he best come to take more blood. In trance she died, and in trance she is Un-Dead, too. So it is that she differ from all other. Usually when the Un-Dead sleep at home'—as he spoke he made a comprehensive sweep of his arm to designate what to a vampire was 'home'—'their face show what they are, but this so sweet that-was when she not Un-Dead she go back to the nothings of the common dead. There is no malign there, see, and so it make hard that I must kill her in her sleep.' This turned my blood cold, and it began to dawn upon me that I was accepting Van Helsing's theories; but if she were really dead, what was there of terror in the idea of killing her? He looked up at me, and evidently saw the change in my face, for he said almost joyously:—

'Ah, you believe now?'

I answered: 'Do not press me too hard all at once. I am willing to accept. How will you do this bloody work?'

'I shall cut off her head and fill her mouth with garlic, and I shall drive a stake through her body.' It made me shudder to think of so mutilating the body of the woman whom I had loved. And yet the feeling was not so strong as I had expected. I was, in fact, beginning to shudder at the presence of this being, this Un-Dead, as Van Helsing called it, and to loathe it. Is it possible that love is all subjective, or all objective?

I waited a considerable time for Van Helsing to begin, but he stood as if wrapped in thought. Presently he closed the catch of his bag with a snap, and said:—

8. According to Van Helsing, Lucy is a less terrible vampire because she was unconscious during her metamorphosis. Stoker invented this chivalrous piece of hair-splitting; *Dracula*'s adaptors have dropped it, as Stoker himself seems to do in the next tomb scene.

'I have been thinking, and have made up my mind as to what is best. If I did simply follow my inclining I would do now, at this moment, what is to be done; but there are other things to follow, and things that are thousand times more difficult in that them we do not know. This is simple. She have yet no life taken, though that is of time; and to act now would be to take danger from her for ever. But then we may have to want Arthur, and how shall we tell him of this? If you, who saw the wounds on Lucy's throat, and saw the wounds so similar on the child's at the hospital; if you, who saw the coffin empty last night and full today with a woman who have not change only to be more rose and more beautiful in a whole week after she die—if you know of this and know of the white figure last night that brought the child to the church-yard, and yet of your own senses you did not believe, how, then, can I expect Arthur, who know none of those things, to believe? He doubted me when I took him from her kiss when she was dying. I know he has forgiven me because in some mistaken idea I have done things that prevent him say goodbye as he ought; and he may think that in some more mistaken idea this woman was buried alive; and that in most mistake of all we have killed her. He will then argue back that it is we, mistaken ones, that have killed her by our ideas; and so he will be much unhappy always. Yet he never can be sure; and that is the worst of all. And he will sometimes think that she he loved was buried alive, and that will paint his dreams with horrors of what she must have suffered; and, again, he will think that we may be right, and that his so beloved was, after all, an Un-Dead. No! I told him once, and since then I learn much. Now, since I know it is all true, a hundred thousand times more do I know that he must pass through the bitter waters to reach the sweet. He, poor fellow, must have one hour that will make the very face of heaven grow black to him; then we can act for good all round and send him peace. My mind is made up. Let us go. You return home for tonight to your asylum, and see that all be well. As for me, I shall spend the night here in this churchyard in my own way. Tomorrow night you will come to me to the Berkeley Hotel at ten of the clock. I shall send for Arthur to come too, and also that so fine young man of America that gave his blood. Later we shall all have work to do. I come with you so far as Piccadilly and there dine, for I must be back here before the sun set.'

So we locked the tomb and came away, and got over the wall of the churchyard, which was not much of a task, and drove back to Piccadilly.

Note Left by Van Helsing in His Portmanteau, Berkeley Hotel,
Directed to John Seward M.D.

(NOT DELIVERED)

27 September.

Friend John,—

I write this in case anything should happen. I go alone to watch in that churchyard. It pleases me that the Un-Dead, Miss Lucy, shall not leave tonight, that so on the morrow night she may be more eager. Therefore I shall fix some things she like not—garlic and a crucifix— and so seal up the door of the tomb. She is young as Un-Dead, and will heed.[9] Moreover, these are only to prevent her coming out; they may not prevail on her wanting to get in; for then the Un-Dead is desperate, and must find the line of least resistance, whatsoever it may be. I shall be at hand all the night from sunset till after the sunrise, and if there be aught that may be learned I shall learn it. For Miss Lucy, or from her, I have no fear; but that other to whom is there that she is Un-Dead, he have now the power to seek her tomb and find shelter. He is cunning, as I know from Mr Jonathan and from the way that all along he have fooled us when he played with us for Miss Lucy's life, and we lost; and in many ways the Un-Dead are strong. He have always the strength in his hand of twenty men; even we four who gave our strength to Miss Lucy it also is all to him. Besides, he can summon his wolf and I know not what. So if it be that he come thither on this night he shall find me; but none other shall—until it be too late. But it may be that he will not attempt the place. There is no reason why he should; his hunting ground is more full of game than the churchyard where the Un-Dead woman sleep, and one old man watch.

Therefore I write this in case . . . Take the papers that are with this, the diaries of Harker and the rest, and read them, and then find this great Un-Dead, and cut off his head and burn his heart or drive a stake through it, so that the world may rest from him.

If it be so, farewell.

VAN HELSING.

Dr Seward's Diary

28 September.—It is wonderful what a good night's sleep will do for one. Yesterday I was almost willing to accept Van Helsing's monstrous ideas; but now they seem to start out lurid before me as outrages on common sense. I have no doubt that he believes it all. I wonder if his mind can have become in any way unhinged. Surely there must be *some* rational explanation of all these mysterious things. Is it possible

---

9. Stoker implies, provocatively, that seasoned Un-Dead have the freedom to ignore these sup-posedly infallible repellents.

that the Professor can have done it himself? He is so abnormally clever that if he went off his head he would carry out his intent with regard to some fixed idea in a wonderful way. I am loath to think it, and indeed it would be almost as great a marvel as the other to find that Van Helsing was mad; but anyhow I shall watch him carefully. I may get some light on the mystery.

29 September, morning . . . Last night, at a little before ten o'clock, Arthur and Quincey came into Van Helsing's room; he told us all that he wanted us to do, but especially addressing himself to Arthur, as if all our wills were centred in his. He began by saying that he hoped we would all come with him too, 'for,' he said, 'there is a grave duty to be done there. You were doubtless surprised at my letter?' This query was directly addressed to Lord Godalming.

'I was. It rather upset me for a bit. There has been so much trouble around my house of late that I could do without any more. I have been curious, too, as to what you mean. Quincey and I talked it over; but the more we talked, the more puzzled we got, till now I can say for myself that I'm about up a tree as to any meaning about anything.'

'Me, too,' said Quincey Morris laconically.

'Oh,' said the Professor, 'then you are nearer the beginning, both of you, than friend John here, who has to go a long way back before he can even get so far as to begin.'

It was evident that he recognized my return to my old doubting frame of mind without my saying a word. Then, turning to the other two, he said with intense gravity:—

'I want your permission to do what I think good this night. It is, I know, much to ask; and when you know what it is I propose to do you will know, and only then, how much. Therefore may I ask that you promise me in the dark, so that afterwards, though you may be angry with me for a time—I must not disguise from myself the possibility that such may be—you shall not blame yourselves for anything.'

'That's frank anyhow,' broke in Quincey. 'I'll answer for the Professor. I don't quite see his drift, but I swear he's honest; and that's good enough for me.'

'I thank you, sir,' said Van Helsing proudly. 'I have done myself the honour of counting you one trusting friend, and such endorsement is dear to me.' He held out a hand, which Quincey took.

Then Arthur spoke out:—

'Dr Van Helsing, I don't quite like to "buy a pig in a poke," as they say in Scotland, and if it be anything in which my honour as a gentleman or my faith as a Christian is concerned, I cannot make such a promise. If you can assure me that what you intend does not violate either of these two, then I give my consent at once; though, for the life of me, I cannot understand what you are driving at.'

'I accept your limitation,' said Van Helsing, 'and all I ask of you is that if you feel it necessary to condemn any act of mine, you will first consider it well and be satisfied that it does not violate your reservations.'

'Agreed!' said Arthur; 'that is only fair. And now that the *pourparlers*[1] are over, may I ask what it is we are to do?'

'I want you to come with me, and to come in secret, to the churchyard at Kingstead.'[2]

Arthur's face fell as he said in an amazed sort of way:—

'Where poor Lucy is buried?' The Professor bowed. Arthur went on: 'And when there?'

'To enter the tomb!' Arthur stood up.

'Professor, are you in earnest; or is it some monstrous joke? Pardon me, I see that you are in earnest.' He sat down again, but I could see that he sat firmly and proudly, as one who is on his dignity. There was silence until he asked again:—

'And when in the tomb?'

'To open the coffin.'

'This is too much!' he said, angrily rising again. 'I am willing to be patient in all things that are reasonable; but in this—this desecration of the grave—of one who—' He fairly choked with indignation. The Professor looked pityingly at him.

'If I could spare you one pang, my poor friend,' he said, 'God knows I would. But this night our feet must tread in thorny paths; or later, and for ever, the feet you love must walk in paths of flame!'

Arthur looked up with set, white face and said:—

'Take care, sir, take care!'

'Would it not be well to hear what I have to say?' said Van Helsing. 'And then you will at least know the limit of my purpose. Shall I go on?'

'That's fair enough,' broke in Morris.

After a pause Van Helsing went on, evidently with an effort:—

'Miss Lucy is dead; is it not so? Yes! Then there can be no wrong to her. But if she be not dead—'

Arthur jumped to his feet.

'Good God!' he cried. 'What do you mean? Has there been any mistake; has she been buried alive?' He groaned in anguish that not even hope could soften.

'I did not say she was alive, my child; I did not think it. I go no further than to say that she might be Un-Dead.'

'Un-Dead! Not alive! What do you mean? Is this all a nightmare, or what is it?'

'There are mysteries which men can only guess at, which age by age they may solve only in part. Believe me, we are now on the verge of

1. An informal conference preceding a formal encounter (French).
2. There was no such Victorian churchyard; perhaps an alias for "Hampstead."

one. But I have not done. May I cut off the head of dead Miss Lucy?'

'Heavens and earth, no!' cried Arthur in a storm of passion. 'Not for the wide world will I consent to any mutilation of her dead body. Dr Van Helsing, you try me too far. What have I done to you that you should torture me so? What did that poor, sweet girl do that you should want to cast such dishonour on her grave? Are you mad that speak such things, or am I mad that listen to them? Don't dare to think more of such a desecration; I shall not give my consent to anything you do. I have a duty to do in protecting her grave from outrage; and, by God, I shall do it!'

Van Helsing rose up from where he had all the time been seated, and said, gravely and sternly:—

'My Lord Godalming, I, too, have a duty to do, a duty to others, a duty to you, a duty to the dead; and, by God, I shall do it! All I ask you now is that you come with me, that you look and listen; and if when later I make the same request you do not be more eager for its fulfilment even than I am, then—then I shall do my duty, whatever it may seem to me. And then, to follow of your Lordship's wishes, I shall hold myself at your disposal to render an account to you, when and where you will.' His voice broke a little, and he went on with a voice full of pity:—

'But, I beseech you, do not go forth in anger with me. In a long life of acts which were often not pleasant to do, and which sometimes did wring my heart, I have never had so heavy a task as now. Believe me that if the time comes for you to change your mind towards me, one look from you will wipe away all this so sad hour, for I would do what a man can to save you from sorrow. Just think. For why should I give myself so much of labour and so much of sorrow? I have come here from my own land to do what I can of good; at the first to please my friend John, and then to help a sweet young lady, whom, too, I came to love. For her—I am ashamed to say so much, but I say it in kindness—I gave what you gave: the blood of my veins; I gave it, I, who was not, like you, her lover, but only her physician and her friend. I gave to her my nights and days—before death, after death; and if my death can do her good even now, when she is the dead Un-Dead,[3] she shall have it freely.' He said this with a very grave, sweet pride, and Arthur was much affected by it. He took the old man's hand and said in a broken voice:—

'Oh, it is hard to think of it, and I cannot understand; but at least I shall go with you and wait.'

3. *The Dead Un-Dead* was one of Stoker's original titles for *Dracula*. Until a few weeks before publication, the manuscript was titled simply *The Un-Dead*.

Chapter XVI

Dr Seward's Diary (continued)

It was just a quarter before twelve o'clock when we got into the church-yard over the low wall. The night was dark, with occasional gleams of moonlight between the rents of the heavy clouds that scudded across the sky. We all kept somehow close together, with Van Helsing slightly in front as he led the way. When we had come close to the tomb I looked well at Arthur, for I feared that the proximity to a place laden with so sorrowful a memory would upset him; but he bore himself well. I took it that the very mystery of the proceeding was in some way a counteractant to his grief. The Professor unlocked the door, and seeing a natural hesitation amongst us for various reasons, solved the difficulty by entering first himself. The rest of us followed, and he closed the door. He then lit a dark lantern and pointed to the coffin. Arthur stepped forward hesitatingly; Van Helsing said to me:—

'You were with me here yesterday. Was the body of Miss Lucy in that coffin?'

'It was.' The Professor turned to the rest, saying:—

'You hear; and yet there is one who does not believe with me.' He took his screwdriver and again took off the lid of the coffin. Arthur looked on, very pale but silent; when the lid was removed he stepped forward. He evidently did not know that there was a leaden coffin, or, at any rate, had not thought of it. When he saw the rent in the lead, the blood rushed to his face for an instant, but as quickly fell away again, so that he remained of a ghastly whiteness; he was still silent. Van Helsing forced back the leaden flange, and we all looked in and recoiled.

The coffin was empty!

For several minutes no one spoke a word. The silence was broken by Quincey Morris:—

'Professor, I answered for you. Your word is all I want, I wouldn't ask such a thing ordinarily—I wouldn't so dishonour you as to imply a doubt; but this is a mystery that goes beyond any honour or dishonour. Is this your doing?'

'I swear to you by all that I hold sacred that I have not removed nor touched her. What happened was this: Two nights ago my friend Seward and I came here—with good purpose, believe me. I opened that coffin, which was then sealed up, and we found it, as now, empty. We then waited, and saw something white come through the trees. The next day we came here in daytime, and she lay there. Did she not, friend John?'

185

'Yes.'

'That night we were just in time. One more so small child was missing, and we find it, thank God, unharmed amongst the graves. Yesterday I came here before sundown, for at sundown the Un-Dead can move. I waited here all the night till the sun rose, but I saw nothing. It was most probable that it was because I had laid over the clamps of those doors garlic, which the Un-Dead cannot bear, and other things which they shun. Last night there was no exodus, so tonight before the sundown I took away my garlic and other things. And so it is we find this coffin empty. But bear with me. So far there is much that is strange. Wait you with me outside, unseen and unheard, and things much stranger are yet to be. So'—here he shut the dark slide of his lantern— 'now to the outside.' He opened the door, and we filed out, he coming last and locking the door behind him.

Oh! but it seemed fresh and pure in the night air after the terror of that vault. How sweet it was to see the clouds race by, and the passing gleams of the moonlight between the scudding clouds crossing and passing—like the gladness and sorrow of a man's life; how sweet it was to breathe the fresh air, that had no taint of death and decay; how humanizing to see the red lighting of the sky beyond the hill, and to hear far away the muffled roar that marks the life of a great city. Each in his own way was solemn and overcome. Arthur was silent, and was, I could see, striving to grasp the purpose and the inner meaning of the mystery. I was myself tolerably patient, and half inclined again to throw aside doubt and to accept Van Helsing's conclusions. Quincey Morris was phlegmatic in the way of a man who accepts all things, and accepts them in the spirit of cool bravery, with hazard of all he has to stake. Not being able to smoke, he cut himself a good-sized plug of tobacco and began to chew. As to Van Helsing, he was employed in a definite way. First he took from his bag a mass of what looked like thin, wafer-like biscuit, which was carefully rolled up in a white napkin; next he took out a double-handful of some whitish stuff, like dough or putty. He crumbled the wafer up fine and worked it into the mass between his hands. This he then took, and rolling it into thin strips, began to lay them into the crevices between the door and its setting in the tomb. I was somewhat puzzled at this, and being close, asked him what it was that he was doing. Arthur and Quincey drew near also, as they too were curious. He answered:—

'I am closing the tomb, so that the Un-Dead may not enter.'

'And is that stuff you have put there going to do it?' asked Quincey. 'Great Scott! Is this a game?'

'It is.'

'What is that which you are using?' This time the question was by Arthur. Van Helsing reverently lifted his hat as he answered:—

'The Host.[1] I brought it from Amsterdam. I have an Indulgence.'[2] It was an answer that appalled the most sceptical of us, and we felt individually that in the presence of such earnest purpose as the Professor's, a purpose which could thus use the to him most sacred of things, it was impossible to distrust. In respectful silence we took the places assigned to us close round the tomb, but hidden from the sight of any one approaching. I pitied the others, especially Arthur. I had myself been apprenticed by my former visits to this watching horror; and yet I, who had up to an hour ago repudiated the proofs, felt my heart sink within me. Never did tombs look so ghastly white; never did cypress, or yew, or juniper so seem the embodiment of funereal gloom; never did tree or grass wave or rustle so ominously; never did bough creak so mysteriously; and never did the far-away howling of dogs send such a woeful presage through the night.

There was a long spell of silence, a big, aching void, and then from the Professor a keen 'S-s-s-s!' He pointed; and far down the avenue of yews we saw a white figure advance—a dim white figure, which held something dark at its breast. The figure stopped, and at the moment a ray of moonlight fell between the masses of driving clouds and showed in startling prominence a dark-haired woman,[3] dressed in the cerements of the grave. We could not see the face, for it was bent down over what we saw to be a fair-haired child. There was a pause and a sharp little cry, such as a child gives in sleep, or a dog as it lies before the fire and dreams. We were starting forward, but the Professor's warning hand, seen by us as he stood behind a yew-tree, kept us back; and then as we looked the white figure moved forwards again. It was now near enough for us to see clearly, and the moonlight still held. My own heart grew cold as ice, and I could hear the gasp of Arthur, as we recognized the features of Lucy Westenra. Lucy Westenra, but yet how changed. The sweetness was turned to adamantine, heartless cruelty, and the purity to voluptuous wantonness. Van Helsing stepped out, and, obedient to his gesture, we all advanced too; the four of us ranged in a line before the door of the tomb. Van Helsing raised his lantern and drew the slide; by the concentrated light that fell on Lucy's face we could see that the lips were crimson with fresh blood, and that the stream had trickled over her chin and stained the purity of her lawn death-robe.

We shuddered with horror. I could see by the tremulous light that even Van Helsing's iron nerve had failed. Arthur was next to me, and if I had not seized his arm and held him up, he would have fallen.

1. The Catholic communion wafer. If this is a game, Van Helsing has adopted Dracula's rules, pitting the literal body of Christ (the Catholic conception of the Host) against the bodies of the resurrected Un-dead. Despite Van Helsing's reverence, no sane Catholic priest would sanction so blasphemous a use of sacred objects.
2. Stoker errs: in Catholic doctrine, an indulgence cannot be given for a future sin.
3. The hair of this changed Lucy no longer falls in "sunny ripples."

When Lucy—I call the thing that was before us Lucy because it bore her shape—saw us she drew back with an angry snarl, such as a cat gives when taken unawares; then her eyes ranged over us. Lucy's eyes in form and colour; but Lucy's eyes unclean and full of hell-fire, instead of the pure, gentle orbs we knew. At that moment the remnant of my love passed into hate and loathing; had she then to be killed, I could have done it with savage delight. As she looked, her eyes blazed with unholy light, and the face became wreathed with a voluptuous smile. Oh, God, how it made me shudder to see it! With a careless motion, she flung to the ground, callous as a devil, the child that up to now she had clutched strenuously to her breast, growling over it as a dog growls over a bone.[4] The child gave a sharp cry, and lay there moaning. There was a cold-bloodedness in the act which wrung a groan from Arthur; when she advanced to him with outstretched arms and a wanton smile, he fell back and hid his face in his hands.

She still advanced, however, and with a languorous, voluptuous grace, said:—

'Come to me, Arthur. Leave these others and come to me. My arms are hungry for you. Come, and we can rest together. Come, my husband, come!'

There was something diabolically sweet in her tones—something of the tingling of glass when struck—which rang through the brains even of us who heard the words addressed to another. As for Arthur, he seemed under a spell; moving his hands from his face, he opened wide his arms. She was leaping for them, when Van Helsing sprang forward and held between them his little golden crucifix. She recoiled from it, and, with a suddenly distorted face, full of rage, dashed past him as if to enter the tomb.

When within a foot or two of the door, however, she stopped as if arrested by some irresistible force. Then she turned, and her face was shown in the clear burst of moonlight and by the lamp, which had now no quiver from Van Helsing's iron nerves. Never did I see such baffled malice on a face; and never, I trust, shall such ever be seen again by mortal eyes. The beautiful colour became livid, the eyes seemed to throw out sparks of hell-fire, the brows were wrinkled as though the folds of the flesh were the coils of Medusa's snakes,[5] and the lovely, blood-stained mouth grew to an open square, as in the passion masks of the Greeks and Japanese. If ever a face meant death—if looks could kill—we saw it at that moment.

---

4. The vampire Lucy is very much of her decade in this callousness toward children. Lethal anti-mothers were a fixture in 1890s literature, especially in works by conservative polemicists who feared feminism as a threat to woman's maternal mission.

5. In Greek mythology, Medusa was a beautiful woman whom the jealous goddess Athena turned into a hideous Gorgon. Her hair became a nest of serpents; her face turned all who looked at her into stone. She was killed by the hero Perseus, who used her severed head as a weapon against further monsters.

And so for full half a minute, which seemed an eternity, she remained between the lifted crucifix and the sacred closing of her means of entry. Van Helsing broke the silence by asking Arthur:—

'Answer me, oh my friend! Am I to proceed in my work?'

Arthur threw himself on his knees, and hid his face in his hands, as he answered:—

'Do as you will, friend; do as you will. There can be no horror like this ever any more!' and he groaned in spirit. Quincey and I simultaneously moved towards him, and took his arms. We could hear the click of the closing lantern as Van Helsing held it down; coming close to the tomb, he began to remove from the chinks some of the sacred emblem which he had placed there. We all looked on in horrified amazement as we saw, when he stood back, the woman, with a corporeal body as real at the moment as our own, pass in through the interstice where scarce a knife-blade could have gone. We all felt a glad sense of relief when we saw the Professor calmly restoring the strings of putty to the edges of the door.

When this was done, he lifted the child and said:—

'Come now, my friends; we can do no more till tomorrow. There is a funeral at noon, so here we shall all come before long after that. The friends of the dead will all be gone by two, and when the sexton lock the gate we shall remain. Then there is more to do; but not like this of tonight. As for this little one, he is not much harm, and by tomorrow night he shall be well. We shall leave him where the police will find him, as on the other night; and then to home.' Coming close to Arthur, he said:—

'My friend Arthur, you have had sore trial; but after, when you will look back, you will see how it was necessary. You are now in the bitter waters, my child. By this time tomorrow you will, please God, have passed them, and have drunk of the sweet waters; so do not mourn overmuch. Till then I shall not ask you to forgive me.'

Arthur and Quincey came home with me, and we tried to cheer each other on the way. We had left the child in safety, and were tired; so we all slept with more or less reality of sleep.

29 September, night.—A little before twelve o'clock we three—Arthur, Quincey Morris, and myself—called for the Professor. It was odd to notice that by common consent we had all put on black clothes. Of course, Arthur wore black, for he was in deep mourning, but the rest of us wore it by instinct. We got to the churchyard by half-past one, and strolled about, keeping out of official observation, so that when the gravediggers had completed their task and the sexton, under the belief that every one had gone, had locked the gate, we had the place all to ourselves. Van Helsing, instead of his little black bag, had with him a long leather one, something like a cricketing bag; it was manifestly of fair weight.

When we were alone and had heard the last of the footsteps die out up the road, we silently, and as if by ordered intention, followed the Professor to the tomb. He unlocked the door, and we entered, closing it behind us. Then he took from his bag the lantern, which he lit, and also two wax candles, which, when lighted, he stuck, by melting their own ends, on other coffins, so that they might give light sufficient to work by. When he again lifted the lid off Lucy's coffin we all looked —Arthur trembling like an aspen—and saw that the body lay there in all its death-beauty. But there was no love in my own heart, nothing but loathing for the foul Thing which had taken Lucy's shape without her soul. I could see even Arthur's face grow hard as he looked. Presently he said to Van Helsing:—

'Is this really Lucy's body, or only a demon in her shape?'

'It is her body, and yet not it. But wait a while, and you shall see her as she was, and is.'

She seemed like a nightmare of Lucy as she lay there; the pointed teeth, the bloodstained, voluptuous mouth—which it made one shudder to see—the whole carnal and unspiritual appearance, seeming like a devilish mockery of Lucy's sweet purity. Van Helsing, with his usual methodicalness, began taking the various contents from his bag and placing them ready for use. First he took out a soldering iron and some plumbing solder, and then a small oil-lamp, which gave out, when lit in a corner of the tomb, gas which burned at fierce heat with a blue flame; then his operating knives, which he placed to hand; and last a round wooden stake,[6] some two and a half or three inches thick and about three feet long. One end of it was hardened by charring in the fire, and was sharpened to a fine point. With this stake came a heavy hammer, such as in households is used in the coal-cellar for breaking the lumps. To me, a doctor's preparations for work of any kind are stimulating and bracing, but the effect of these things on both Arthur and Quincey was to cause them a sort of consternation. They both, however, kept their courage, and remained silent and quiet.

When all was ready, Van Helsing said:—

'Before we do anything, let me tell you this; it is out of the lore and experience of the ancients and of all those who have studied the powers of the Un-Dead. When they become such, there comes with the change the curse of immortality; they cannot die, but must go on age after age adding new victims and multiplying the evils of the world; for all that die from the preying of the Un-Dead become themselves Un-Dead, and prey on their kind.[7] And so the circle goes on ever widening, like as the ripples from a stone thrown in the water. Friend Arthur, if you

---

6. The function of the stake in folklore is merely to immobilize the living dead, not to destroy them.
7. Stoker does not follow this rule: vampire victims in Transylvania, at sea, and in England seem to be legion, but as far as we know they do not themselves become vampires after death. It was left to twentieth-century horror writers like Stephen King to depict mass vampirism.

had met that kiss which you know of before poor Lucy die; or again, last night when you open your arms to her, you would in time, when you had died, have become *nosferatu*, as they call it in Eastern Europe, and would all time make more of those Un-Deads that so have fill us with horror. The career of this so unhappy dear lady is but just begun. Those children whose blood she suck are not as yet so much the worse; but if she live on, Un-Dead, more and more they lose their blood, and by her power over them they come to her; and so she draw their blood with that so wicked mouth. But if she die in truth, then all cease; the tiny wounds of the throats disappear, and they go back to their plays unknowing ever of what has been. But of the most blessed of all, when this now Un-Dead be made to rest as true dead, then the soul of the poor lady whom we love shall again be free. Instead of working wickedness by night and growing more debased in the assimilation of it by day, she shall take her place with the other Angels. So that, my friend, it will be a blessed hand for her that shall strike the blow that sets her free. To this I am willing; but is there none amongst us who has a better right? Will it be no joy to think of hereafter in the silence of the night when sleep is not: "It was my hand that sent her to the stars; it was the hand of him that loved her best; the hand that of all she would herself have chosen, had it been to her to choose"? Tell me if there be such a one amongst us?'

We all looked at Arthur. He saw, too, what we all did, the infinite kindness which suggested that his should be the hand which would restore Lucy to us as a holy, and not an unholy, memory; he stepped forward and said bravely, though his hand trembled, and his face was as pale as snow:—

'My true friend, from the bottom of my broken heart I thank you. Tell me what I am to do, and I shall not falter!' Van Helsing laid a hand on his shoulder, and said:—

'Brave lad! A moment's courage, and it is done. This stake must be driven through her. It will be a fearful ordeal—be not deceived in that—but it will be only a short time, and you will then rejoice more than your pain was great; from this grim tomb you will emerge as though you tread on air. But you must not falter when once you have begun. Only think that we, your true friends, are round you, and that we pray for you all the time.'

'Go on,' said Arthur hoarsely. 'Tell me what I am to do.'

'Take this stake in your left hand, ready to place the point over the heart, and the hammer in your right. Then when we begin our prayer for the dead—I shall read him, I have here the book, and the others shall follow—strike in God's name, that so all may be well with the dead that we love, and that the Un-Dead pass away.'

Arthur took the stake and the hammer, and when once his mind was set on action his hands never trembled nor even quivered. Van Helsing opened his missal and began to read, and Quincey and I followed as well as we could. Arthur placed the point over the heart, and as I looked I could see its dint in the white flesh. Then he struck with all his might.

The Thing in the coffin writhed; and a hideous, blood-curdling screech came from the opened red lips. The body shook and quivered and twisted in wild contortions; the sharp white teeth champed together till the lips were cut, and the mouth was smeared with a crimson foam. But Arthur never faltered. He looked like a figure of Thor[8] as his un-trembling arm rose and fell, driving deeper and deeper the mercy-bearing stake, whilst the blood from the pierced heart welled and spurted up around it. His face was set, and high duty seemed to shine through it; the sight of it gave us courage, so that our voices seemed to ring through the little vault.

And then the writhing and quivering of the body became less, and the teeth ceased to champ, and the face to quiver. Finally it lay still. The terrible task was over.

The hammer fell from Arthur's hand. He reeled and would have fallen had we not caught him. The great drops of sweat sprang out on his forehead, and his breath came in broken gasps. It had indeed been an awful strain on him; and had he not been forced to his task by more than human considerations he could never have gone through with it. For a few minutes we were so taken up with him that we did not look towards the coffin. When we did, however, a murmur of startled sur-prise ran from one to the other of us. We gazed so eagerly that Arthur rose, for he had been seated on the ground, and came and looked too; and then a glad, strange light broke over his face and dispelled alto-gether the gloom of horror that lay upon it.

There, in the coffin lay no longer the foul Thing that we had so dreaded and grown to hate that the work of her destruction was yielded as a privilege to the one best entitled to it, but Lucy as we had seen her in her life, with her face of unequalled sweetness and purity. True that there were there, as we had seen them in life, the traces of care and pain and waste; but these were all dear to us, for they marked her truth to what we knew. One and all we felt that the holy calm that lay like sunshine over the wasted face and form was only an earthly token and symbol of the calm that was to reign for ever.

Van Helsing came and laid his hand on Arthur's shoulder, and said to him:—

'And now, Arthur, my friend, dear lad, am I not forgiven?'

The reaction of the terrible strain came as he took the old man's hand in his, and raising it to his lips, pressed it, and said:—

'Forgiven! God bless you that you have given my dear one her soul again, and me peace.' He put his hands on the Professor's shoulder,

8. The Norse thunder god whose power Dracula had evoked when boasting to Jonathan of the Szekelys.

and laying his head on his breast, cried for a while silently, whilst we stood unmoving. When he raised his head Van Helsing said to him:—

'And now, my child, you may kiss her. Kiss her dead lips if you will, as she would have you to, if for her to choose. For she is not a grinning devil now—not any more a foul Thing for all eternity. No longer she is the devil's Un-Dead. She is God's true dead, whose soul is with Him!'

Arthur bent and kissed her, and then we sent him and Quincey out of the tomb; the Professor and I sawed the top off the stake, leaving the point of it in the body. Then we cut off the head and filled the mouth with garlic. We soldered up the leaden coffin, screwed on the coffin-lid, and gathering up our belongings, came away. When the Professor locked the door he gave the key to Arthur.

Outside the air was sweet, the sun shone, and the birds sang, and it seemed as if all nature were tuned to a different pitch. There was gladness and mirth and peace everywhere, for we were at rest ourselves on one account, and we were glad, though it was with a tempered joy.

Before we moved away Van Helsing said:—

'Now, my friends, one step of our work is done, one the most harrowing to ourselves. But there remains a greater task: to find out the author of all this our sorrow and to stamp him out. I have clues which we can follow; but it is a long task, and a difficult, and there is danger in it, and pain. Shall you not all help me? We have learned to believe, all of us—is it not so? And since so, do we not see our duty? Yes! And do we not promise to go on to the bitter end?'

Each in turn, we took his hand, and the promise was made. Then said the Professor as we moved off:—

'Two nights hence you shall meet with me and dine together at seven of the clock with friend John. I shall entreat two others, two that you know not as yet; and I shall be ready to all our work and our plans unfold. Friend John, you come with me home, for I have much to consult about, and you can help me. Tonight I leave for Amsterdam, but shall return tomorrow night. And then begins our great quest. But first I shall have much to say, so that you may know what is to do and to dread. Then our promise shall be made to each other anew; for there is a terrible task before us, and once our feet are on the ploughshare,[9] we must not draw back.'

9. Van Helsing's absurd version of Luke 9.62: "And Jesus said unto him, No man, having put his hand to the plough, and looking back, is fit for the kingdom of God." Van Helsing turns Jesus' condemnation into a heroic exhortation.

Chapter XVII

Dr Seward's Diary (continued)

When we arrived at the Berkeley Hotel, Van Helsing found a telegram waiting for him:—

'Am coming up by train. Jonathan at Whitby. Important news.—MINA HARKER.'

The Professor was delighted. 'Ah, that wonderful Madam Mina,' he said, 'pearl among women! She arrive, but I cannot stay. She must go to your house, friend John. You must meet her at the station. Telegraph her *en route*, so that she may be prepared.'

When the wire was despatched he had a cup of tea; over it he told me of a diary kept by Jonathan Harker when abroad, and gave me a typewritten copy of it, as also of Mrs Harker's diary at Whitby. 'Take these,' he said, 'and study them well. When I have returned you will be master of all the facts, and we can then better enter on our inquisition. Keep them safe, for there is in them much of treasure. You will need all your faith, even you who have had such an experience as that of today. What is here told,' he laid his hand heavily and gravely on the packet of papers as he spoke, 'may be the beginning of the end to you and me and many another; or it may sound the knell of the Un-Dead who walk the earth. Read all, I pray you, with the open mind; and if you can add in any way to the story here told do so, for it is all-important. You have kept diary of all these so strange things; is it not so? Yes! Then we shall go through all these together when that we meet.' He then made ready for his departure, and shortly after drove off to Liverpool Street.[1] I took my way to Paddington, where I arrived about fifteen minutes before the train came in.

The crowd melted away, after the bustling fashion common to arrival platforms; and I was beginning to feel uneasy, lest I might miss my guest, when a sweet-faced, dainty-looking girl stepped up to me, and, after a quick glance, said: 'Dr Seward, is it not?'

'And you are Mrs Harker!' I answered at once; whereupon she held out her hand.

'I knew you from the description of poor dear Lucy; but—' She stopped suddenly, a quick blush overspread her face.

The blush that rose to my own cheeks somehow set us both at ease, for it was a tacit answer to her own. I got her luggage, which included a typewriter, and we took the Underground to Fenchurch Street,[2] after

---

1. A large railroad terminal in central London.
2. A smaller London terminal. The first electric underground railway, or subway, opened in 1890.

I had sent a wire to my housekeeper to have a sitting-room and bedroom prepared at once for Mrs Harker.

In due time we arrived. She knew, of course, that the place was a lunatic asylum, but I could see that she was unable to repress a slight shudder when we entered.

She told me that, if she might, she would come presently to my study, as she had much to say. So here I am finishing my entry in my phonograph diary whilst I await her. As yet I have not had the chance of looking at the papers which Van Helsing left with me, though they lie open before me. I must get her interested in something, so that I may have an opportunity of reading them. She does not know how precious time is, or what a task we have in hand. I must be careful not to frighten her. Here she is!

Mina Harker's Journal

29 September.—After I had tidied myself, I went down to Dr Seward's study. At the door I paused a moment, for I thought I heard him talking with someone. As, however, he had pressed me to be quick, I knocked at the door, and on his calling out, 'Come in,' I entered.

To my intense surprise, there was no one with him. He was quite alone, and on the table opposite him was what I knew at once from the description to be a phonograph. I had never seen one, and was much interested.

'I hope I did not keep you waiting,' I said; 'but I stayed at the door as I heard you talking, and thought there was some one with you.'

'Oh,' he replied, with a smile, 'I was only entering my diary.'

'Your diary?' I asked him in surprise.

'Yes,' he answered. 'I keep it in this.' As he spoke he laid his hand on the phonograph. I felt quite excited over it, and blurted out:—

'Why, this beats even shorthand! May I hear it say something?'

'Certainly,' he replied with alacrity, and stood up to put it in train for speaking. Then he paused, and a troubled look overspread his face.

'The fact is,' he began awkwardly, 'I only keep my diary in it; and it is entirely—almost entirely—about my cases, it may be awkward—that is, I mean'—He stopped, and I tried to help him out of his embarrassment:—

'You helped to attend dear Lucy at the end. Let me hear how she died; for all that I can know of her, I shall be very grateful. She was very, very dear to me.'

To my surprise, he answered, with a horrorstruck look in his face:—

'Tell you of her death? Not for the wide world!'

'Why not?' I asked, for some grave, terrible feeling was coming over me. Again he paused, and I could see that he was trying to invent an excuse. At length he stammered out:—

'You see, I do not know how to pick out any particular part of the diary.' Even while he was speaking an idea dawned upon him, and he said with unconscious simplicity, in a different voice, and with the naïvety of a child: 'That's quite true, upon my honour. Honest Indian!' I could not but smile, at which he grimaced. 'I gave myself away that time!' he said. 'But do you know that, although I have kept the diary for months past, it never once struck me how I was going to find any particular part of it in case I wanted to look it up?' By this time my mind was made up that the diary of a doctor who attended Lucy might have something to add to the sum of our knowledge of that terrible Being, and I said boldly:—

'Then, Dr Seward, you had better let me copy it out for you on my typewriter.' He grew to a positively deathly pallor as he said:—

'No! no! no! For all the world, I wouldn't let you know that terrible story!'

Then it was terrible; my intuition was right! For a moment I thought, and as my eyes ranged the room, unconsciously looking for something or some opportunity to aid me, they lit on the great batch of typewriting on the table. His eyes caught the look in mine, and, without his thinking, followed their direction. As they saw the parcel he realized my meaning.

'You do not know me,' I said. 'When you have read those papers— my own diary and my husband's also, which I have typed—you will know me better. I have not faltered in giving every thought of my own heart in this cause; but, of course, you do not know me—yet; and I must not expect you to trust me so far.'

He is certainly a man of noble nature; poor dear Lucy was right about him. He stood up and opened a large drawer, in which were arranged in order a number of hollow cylinders of metal covered with dark wax, and said:—

'You are quite right. I did not trust you because I did not know you. But I know you now; and let me say that I should have known you long ago. I know that Lucy told you of me; she told me of you too. May I make the only atonement in my power? Take the cylinders and hear them—the first half-dozen of them are personal to me, and they will not horrify you; then you will know me better. Dinner will by then be ready. In the meantime I shall read over some of these documents, and shall be better able to understand certain things.' He carried the phonograph himself up to my sitting-room and adjusted it for me. Now I shall learn something pleasant, I am sure; for it will tell me the other side of a true love episode of which I know one side already . . .

Dr Seward's Diary

29 September.—I was so absorbed in that wonderful diary of Jonathan Harker and that other of his wife that I let the time run on without thinking. Mrs Harker was not down when the maid came to announce dinner, so I said: 'She is possibly tired; let dinner wait an hour;' and I went on with my work. I had just finished Mrs Harker's diary, when she came in. She looked sweetly pretty, but very sad, and her eyes were flushed with crying. This somehow moved me much. Of late I have had cause for tears, God knows! but the relief of them was denied me; and now the sight of those sweet eyes, brightened with recent tears, went straight to my heart. So I said as gently as I could:—

'I greatly fear I have distressed you.'

'Oh no, not distressed me,' she replied, 'but I have been more touched than I can say by your grief. That is a wonderful machine, but it is cruelly true. It told me, in its very tones, the anguish of your heart. It was like a soul crying out to almighty God. No one must hear them spoken ever again! See, I have tried to be useful. I have copied out the words on my typewriter, and none other need now hear your heart beat, as I did.'

'No one need ever know, shall ever know,' I said in a low voice. She laid her hand on mine and said very gravely:—

'Ah, but they must!'

'Must! But why?' I asked.

'Because it is a part of the terrible story, a part of poor dear Lucy's death and all that led to it; because in the struggle which we have before us to rid the earth of this terrible monster we must have all the knowledge and all the help which we can get. I think that the cylinders which you gave me contained more than you intended me to know; but I can see that there are in your record many lights to this dark mystery. You will let me help, will you not? I know all up to a certain point; and I see already, though your diary only took me to 7 September, how poor Lucy was beset, and how her terrible doom was being wrought out. Jonathan and I have been working day and night since Professor Van Helsing saw us. He is gone to Whitby to get more information, and he will be here tomorrow to help us. We need have no secrets amongst us; working together and with absolute trust, we can surely be stronger than if some of us were in the dark.' She looked at me so appealingly, and at the same time manifested such courage and resolution in her bearing, that I gave in at once to her wishes. 'You shall,' I said, 'do as you like in the matter. God forgive me if I do wrong! There are terrible things yet to learn of; but if you have so far travelled on the road to poor Lucy's death, you will not be content, I know, to remain in the dark. Nay, the end—the very end—may give you a gleam of peace. Come, there is dinner. We must keep one another strong for what is before us; we have a cruel and dreadful task. When you have eaten you shall learn the rest, and I shall answer any questions you ask—if there be anything which you do not understand, though it was apparent to us who were present.'

Mina Harker's Journal

29 September.—After dinner I came with Dr Seward to his study. He brought back the phonograph from my room, and I took my typewriter. He placed me in a comfortable chair, and arranged the phonograph so that I could touch it without getting up, and showed me how to stop it in case I should want to pause. Then he very thoughtfully took a chair, with his back to me, so that I might be as free as possible, and began to read. I put the forked metal to my ears and listened.

When the terrible story of Lucy's death, and—and all that followed, was done, I lay back in my chair powerless. Fortunately I am not of a fainting disposition. When Dr Seward saw me he jumped up with a horrified exclamation, and hurriedly taking a case-bottle[3] from a cupboard, gave me some brandy, which in a few minutes somewhat restored me. My brain was all in a whirl, and only that there came through all the multitude of horrors, the holy ray of light that my dear, dear Lucy was at last at peace, I do not think I could have borne it without making a scene. It is all so wild, and mysterious, and strange that if I had not known Jonathan's experience in Transylvania I could not have believed. As it was, I didn't know what to believe, and so got out of my difficulty by attending to something else. I took the cover off my typewriter, and said to Dr Seward:—

'Let me write this all out now. We must be ready for Dr Van Helsing when he comes. I have sent a telegram to Jonathan to come on here when he arrives in London from Whitby. In this matter dates are everything, and I think that if we get all our material ready, and have every item put in chronological order, we shall have done much. You tell me that Lord Godalming and Mr Morris are coming too. Let us be able to tell them when they come.' He accordingly set the phonograph at a slow pace, and I began to typewrite from the beginning of the seventh cylinder. I used manifold,[4] and so took three copies of the diary, just as I had done with all the rest. It was late when I got through, but Dr Seward went about his work of going his round of the patients; when he had finished he came back and sat near me, reading, so that I did not feel too lonely whilst I worked. How good and thoughtful he is; the world seems full of good men—even if there *are* monsters in it. Before I left him I remembered what Jonathan put in his diary of the

---

3. A bottle designed to fit in a suitcase.
4. Like carbon paper, which came later, manifold was designed to produce one or several copies of a typed page.

Professor's perturbation at reading something in an evening paper at the station at Exeter; so, seeing that Dr Seward keeps his newspapers, I borrowed the files of the *Westminster Gazette* and the *Pall Mall Gazette* and took them to my room. I remember how much the *Daily-graph* and the *Whitby Gazette*, of which I had made cuttings, helped us to understand the terrible events at Whitby when Count Dracula landed, so I shall look through the evening papers since then, and perhaps I shall get some new light. I am not sleepy, and the work will help to keep me quiet.

Dr Seward's Diary

30 September. —Mr Harker arrived at nine o'clock. He had got his wife's wire just before starting. He is uncommonly clever, if one can judge from his face, and full of energy. If his journal be true—and judging by one's own wonderful experiences, it must be—he is also a man of great nerve. That going down to the vault a second time was a remarkable piece of daring. After reading his account of it I was prepared to meet a good specimen of manhood, but hardly the quiet, business-like gentleman who came here today.

Later. —After lunch Harker and his wife went back to their own room, and as I passed a while ago I heard the click of the typewriter. They are hard at it. Mrs Harker says that they are knitting together in chronological order every scrap of evidence they have. Harker has got the letters between the consignee of the boxes at Whitby and the carriers in London who took charge of them. He is now reading his wife's typescript of my diary. I wonder what they make out of it. Here he is . . .

Strange that it never struck me that the very next house might be the Count's hiding-place! Goodness knows that we had enough clues from the conduct of the patient Renfield! The bundle of letters relating to the purchase of the house were with the typescript. Oh, if we had only had them earlier we might have saved poor Lucy! Stop; that way madness lies! Harker has gone back, and is again collating his material. He says that by dinner-time they will be able to show a whole connected narrative. He thinks that in the meantime I should see Renfield, as hitherto he has been a sort of index to the coming and going of the Count. I hardly see this yet, but when I get at the dates I suppose I shall. What a good thing that Mrs Harker put my cylinders into type! We never could have found the dates otherwise . . .

I found Renfield sitting placidly in his room with his hands folded, smiling benignly. At the moment he seemed as sane as any one I ever saw. I sat down and talked with him on a lot of subjects, all of which he treated naturally. He then, of his own accord, spoke of going home, a subject he has never mentioned to my knowledge during his sojourn here. In fact, he spoke quite confidently of getting his discharge at once. I believe that, had I not had the chat with Harker and read the letters and the dates of his outbursts, I should have been prepared to sign for him after a brief time of observation. As it is, I am darkly suspicious. All those outbreaks were in some way linked with the proximity of the Count. What then does this absolute content mean? Can it be that his instinct is satisfied as to the vampire's ultimate triumph? Stay; he is himself zoophagous, and in his wild ravings outside the chapel door of the deserted house he always spoke of 'master'. This all seems confirmation of our idea. However, after a while I came away; my friend is just a little too sane at present to make it safe to probe him too deep with questions. He might begin to think, and then—! So I came away. I mistrust these quiet moods of his; so I have given the attendant a hint to look closely after him, and to have a strait-waistcoat ready in case of need.

Jonathan Harker's Journal

29 September, in train to London.—When I received Mr Billington's courteous message that he would give me any information in his power, I thought it best to go down to Whitby and make, on the spot, such inquiries as I wanted. It was now my object to trace that horrid cargo of the Count's to its place in London. Later, we may be able to deal with it. Billington junior, a nice lad, met me at the station, and brought me to his father's house, where they had decided that I must stay the night. They are hospitable, with true Yorkshire hospitality: give a guest everything, and leave him free to do as he likes. They all knew that I was busy, and that my stay was short, and Mr Billington had ready in his office all the papers concerning the consignment of boxes. It gave me almost a turn to see again one of the letters which I had seen on the Count's table before I knew of his diabolical plans. Everything had been carefully thought out, and done systematically and with precision. He seemed to have been prepared for every obstacle which might be placed by accident in the way of his intentions being carried out. To use an Americanism, he had 'taken no chances,' and the absolute accuracy with which his instructions were fulfilled, was simply the logical result of his care. I saw the invoice, and took note of it: 'Fifty cases of common earth, to be used for experimental purposes.' Also the copy of the letter to Carter Paterson, and their reply; of both of these I got copies. This was all the information Mr Billington could give me, so I went down to the port and saw the coastguards, the Customs officers and the harbour-master. They had all something to say of the strange entry of the ship, which is already taking its place in local tradition; but no one could add to the simple description 'Fifty cases of common earth.' I then saw the station-master, who kindly put me in communication with the men who had actually received the boxes. Their tally was exact with the list, and they had nothing to add except that the boxes were 'main and mortal heavy,' and that shifting them was dry work. One of them added that it was hard lines that there wasn't any gentleman 'such-like as yourself, squire,' to show some sort of appreciation of their efforts in a liquid form; another put in a rider that the thirst then generated was such that even the time which had elapsed had not completely allayed it. Needless to add, I took care before leaving to lift, for ever and adequately, this source of reproach.

30 *September.*—The station-master was good enough to give me a line to his old companion the station-master at King's Cross, so that when I arrived there in the morning I was able to ask him about the arrival of the boxes. He, too, put me at once in communication with the proper officials, and I saw that their tally was correct with the original invoice. The opportunities of acquiring an abnormal thirst had been here limited; a noble use of them had, however, been made, and again I was compelled to deal with the result in an *ex post facto*[5] manner.

From thence I went on to Carter Paterson's central office, where I met with the utmost courtesy. They looked up the transaction in their day-book and letter-book, and at once telephoned to their King's Cross office for more details. By good fortune, the men who did the teaming[6] were waiting for work, and the official at once sent them over, sending also by one of them the waybill and all the papers connected with the delivery of the boxes at Carfax. Here again I found the tally agreeing exactly; the carriers' men were able to supplement the paucity of the written words with a few details. These were, I shortly found, connected almost solely with the dusty nature of the job, and of the consequent thirst engendered in the operators. On my affording an opportunity, through the medium of the currency of the realm, of the allaying, at a later period, this beneficent evil, one of the men remarked:—

'That 'ere 'ouse, guv'nor, is the rummiest I ever was in. Blyme! but it ain't been touched sence a hundred years. There was dust that thick in the place that you might have slep' on it without 'urtin' of yer bones' an' the place was that neglected that yer might 'ave smelled ole Jerusalem in it. But the ole chapel—that took the cike, that did! Me and my mate, we thort we wouldn't never git out quick enough. Lor', I wouldn't take less nor a quid a moment to stay there arter dark.'

Having been in the house, I could well believe him; but if he knew what I know, he would, I think, have raised his terms.

Of one thing I am now satisfied; that *all* the boxes which arrived at

5. After the fact (Latin).
6. Teamsters.

Whitby from Varna in the *Demeter* were safely deposited in the old chapel of Carfax. There should be fifty of them there, unless any have since been removed—as from Dr Seward's diary I fear.

I shall try to see the carter who took away the boxes from Carfax when Renfield attacked them. By following up this clue we may learn a good deal.

Later.—Mina and I have worked all day, and we have put all the papers into order.

Mina Harker's Journal

30 September.—I am so glad that I hardly know how to contain myself. It is, I suppose, the reaction from the haunting fear which I have had: that this terrible affair and the reopening of his old wound might act detrimentally on Jonathan. I saw him leave for Whitby with as brave a face as I could, but I was sick with apprehension. The effort has, however, done him good. He was never so resolute, never so strong, never so full of volcanic energy, as at present. It is just as that dear, good Professor Van Helsing said: he is true grit, and he improves under strain that would kill a weaker nature. He came back full of life and hope and determination; we have got everything in order for tonight. I feel myself quite wild with excitement. I suppose one ought to pity any thing so hunted as is the Count. That is just it: this Thing is not human—not even beast. To read Dr Seward's account of poor Lucy's death, and what followed, is enough to dry up the springs of pity in one's heart.

Later.—Lord Godalming and Mr Morris arrived earlier than we expected. Dr Seward was out on business, and had taken Jonathan with him, so I had to see them. It was to me a painful meeting, for it brought back all poor dear Lucy's hopes of only a few months ago. Of course they had heard Lucy speak of me, and it seemed that Dr Van Helsing, too, has been quite 'blowing my trumpet,' as Mr Morris expressed it. Poor fellows, neither of them is aware that I know all about the proposals they made to Lucy. They did not quite know what to say or do, as they were ignorant of the amount of my knowledge; so they had to keep on neutral subjects. However, I thought the matter over, and came to the conclusion that the best thing I could do would be to post them in affairs right up to date. I knew from Dr Seward's diary that they had been at Lucy's death—her real death—and that I need not fear to betray any secret before the time. So I told them, as well as I could, that I had read all the papers and diaries, and that my husband and I, having typewritten them, had just finished putting them in order. I gave them each a copy to read in the library. When Lord Godalming got his and turned it over—it does make a pretty good pile—he said:—

'Did you write all this, Mrs Harker?'

I nodded, and he went on:—

'I don't quite see the drift of it; but you people are all so good and kind, and have been working so earnestly and so energetically, that all I can do is to accept your ideas blindfold and try to help you. I have had one lesson already in accepting facts that should make a man humble to the last hour of his life. Besides, I know you loved my poor Lucy—' Here he turned away and covered his face with his hands. I could hear the tears in his voice. Mr Morris, with instinctive delicacy, just laid a hand for a moment on his shoulder, and then walked quietly out of the room. I suppose there is something in woman's nature[7] that makes a man free to break down before her and express his feelings on the tender or emotional side without feeling it derogatory to his manhood; for when Lord Godalming found himself alone with me he sat down on the sofa and gave way utterly and openly. I sat down beside him and took his hand. I hope he didn't think it forward of me, and that if he ever thinks of it afterwards he never will have such a thought. There I wrong him: I *know* he never will—he is too true a gentleman. I said to him, for I could see that his heart was breaking:—

'I loved dear Lucy, and I know what she was to you, and what you were to her. She and I were like sisters; and now she is gone, will you not let me be like a sister to you in your trouble? I know what sorrows you have had, though I cannot measure the depth of them. If sympathy and pity can help in your affliction, won't you let me be of some little service—for Lucy's sake?'

In an instant the poor dear fellow was overwhelmed with grief. It seemed to me that all that he had of late been suffering in silence found a vent at once. He grew quite hysterical, and raising his open hands, beat his palms together in a perfect agony of grief. He stood up and then sat down again, and the tears rained down his cheeks. I felt an infinite pity for him, and opened my arms unthinkingly. With a sob he laid his head on my shoulder, and cried like a wearied child, whilst he shook with emotion.

We women have something of the mother in us that makes us rise above smaller matters when the mother-spirit is invoked; I felt this big, sorrowing man's head resting on me, as though it were that of the baby that some day may lie on my bosom, and I stroked his hair as though he were my own child. I never thought at the time how strange it all was.

After a little bit his sobs ceased, and he raised himself with an apology, though he made no disguise of his emotion. He told me that for days and nights past—weary days and sleepless nights—he had been unable to speak with anyone, as a man must speak in his time of sorrow. There was no woman whose sympathy could be given to him, or with

7. Though Mina has many of the skills associated with the New Woman, she explains herself in reassuringly mid-Victorian separatist idioms.

whom, owing to the terrible circumstance with which his sorrow was surrounded, he could speak freely. 'I know now how I suffered,' he said, as he dried his eyes, 'but I do not know even yet—and none other can ever know—how much your sweet sympathy has been to me today. I shall know better in time; and believe me that, though I am not un-grateful now, my gratitude will grow with my understanding. You will let me be like a brother, will you not, for all our lives—for dear Lucy's sake?'

'For dear Lucy's sake,' I said as we clasped hands. 'Ay, and for your own sake,' he added, 'for if a man's esteem and gratitude are ever worth the winning, you have won mine today. If ever the future should bring to you a time when you need a man's help, believe me, you will not call in vain. God grant that no such time may ever come to you to break the sunshine of your life; but if it should ever come, promise me that you will let me know.' He was so earnest, and his sorrow was so fresh, that I felt it would comfort him, so I said:—

'I promise.'

As I came along the corridor I saw Mr Morris looking out of a win-dow. He turned as he heard my footsteps. 'How is Art?' he said. Then noticing my red eyes, he went on: 'Ah, I see you have been comforting him. Poor old fellow! he needs it. No one but a woman can help a man when he is in trouble of the heart; and he had no one to comfort him.'

He bore his own trouble so bravely that my heart bled for him. I saw the manuscript in his hand, and I knew that when he read it he would realize how much I knew; so I said to him:—

'I wish I could comfort all who suffer from the heart. Will you let me be your friend, and will you come to me for comfort if you need it? You will know, later on, why I speak.' He saw that I was in earnest, and stooping, took my hand, and raising it to his lips, kissed it. It seemed but poor comfort to so brave and unselfish a soul, and impulsively I bent over and kissed him. The tears rose in his eyes, and there was a momentary choking in his throat; he said quite calmly:—

'Little girl, you will never regret that true-hearted kindness, so long as ever you live!' Then he went into the study to his friend.

'Little girl!'—the very words he had used to Lucy, and oh, but he proved himself a friend!

Chapter XVIII

Dr Seward's Diary

30 September.—I got home at five o'clock, and found that Godalming and Morris had not only arrived, but had already studied the transcript of the various diaries and letters which Harker and his wonderful wife had made and arranged. Harker had not yet returned from his visit to the carriers' men, of whom Dr Hennessey had written to me. Mrs Harker gave us a cup of tea, and I can honestly say that, for the first time since I have lived in it, this old house seemed like *home*. When we had finished, Mrs Harker said:—

'Dr Seward, may I ask a favour? I want to see your patient, Mr Renfield. Do let me see him. What you have said of him in your diary interests me so much!' She looked so appealing and so pretty that I could not refuse her, and there was no possible reason why I should; so I took her with me. When I went into the room, I told the man that a lady would like to see him; to which he simply answered: 'Why?'

'She is going through the house, and wants to see everyone in it,' I answered. 'Oh, very well,' he said; 'let her come in, by all means; but just wait a minute till I tidy up the place.' His method of tidying was peculiar: he simply swallowed all the flies and spiders in the boxes before I could stop him. It was quite evident that he feared, or was jealous of, some interference. When he had got through his disgusting task, he said cheerfully: 'Let the lady come in,' and sat down on the edge of his bed with his head down, but with his eyelids raised so that he could see her as she entered. For a moment I thought that he might have some homicidal intent; I remembered how quiet he had been just before he attacked me in my own study, and I took care to stand where I could seize him at once if he attempted to make a spring at her. She came into the room with an easy gracefulness which would at once command the respect of any lunatic—for easiness is one of the qualities mad people most respect. She walked over to him, smiling pleasantly, and held out her hand.

'Good evening, Mr Renfield,' said she. 'You see, I know you, for Dr Seward has told me of you.' He made no immediate reply, but eyed her all over intently with a set frown on his face. This look gave way to one of wonder, which merged in doubt; then, to my intense astonishment, he said:—

'You're not the girl the doctor wanted to marry, are you? You can't be, you know, for she's dead.' Mrs Harker smiled sweetly as she replied:—

'Oh no! I have a husband of my own, to whom I was married before I ever saw Dr Seward, or he me. I am Mrs Harker.'

'Then what are you doing here?'

'My husband and I are staying on a visit with Dr Seward.'

'Then don't stay.'

'But why not?' I thought that this style of conversation might not be pleasant to Mrs Harker, any more than it was to me, so I joined in:—

'How did you know I wanted to marry any one?' His reply was simply contemptuous, given in a pause in which he turned his eyes from Mrs Harker to me, instantly turning them back again:—

'What an asinine question!'

'I don't see that at all, Mr Renfield,' said Mrs Harker, at once championing me. He replied to her with as much courtesy and respect as he had shown contempt to me:—

'You will, of course, understand, Mrs Harker, that when a man is so loved and honoured as our host is, everything regarding him is of interest in our little community. Dr Seward is loved not only by his household and his friends, but even by his patients, who, being some of them hardly in mental equilibrium, are apt to distort causes and effects. Since I myself have been an inmate of a lunatic asylum, I cannot but notice that the sophistic[1] tendencies of some of its inmates lean towards the errors of *non causæ* and *ignoratio elenchi*.'[2] I positively opened my eyes at this new development. Here was my own pet lunatic—the most pronounced of his type that I had ever met with—talking elemental philosophy, and with the manner of a polished gentleman[3]. I wonder if it was Mrs Harker's presence which had touched some chord in his memory. If this new phase was spontaneous, or in any way due to her unconscious influence[4], she must have some rare gift or power.

We continued to talk for some time; and, seeing that he was seemingly quite reasonable, she ventured, looking at me questioningly as she begun, to lead him to his favourite topic. I was again astonished, for he addressed himself to the question with the impartiality of the completest sanity; he even took himself as an example when he mentioned certain things.

'Why, I myself am an instance of a man who had a strange belief. Indeed, it was no wonder that my friends were alarmed, and insisted on my being put under control. I used to fancy that life was a positive and perpetual entity, and that by consuming a multitude of live things, no matter how low in the scale of creation, one might indefinitely prolong life. At times I held the belief so strongly that I actually tried to take human life. The doctor here will bear me out that on one occasion I tried to kill him for the purpose of strengthening my vital powers by the assimilation with my own body of his life through the medium of his blood—relying, of course, upon the Scriptural phrase, "For the blood is the life." Though, indeed, the vendor of a certain

---

1. Apparently sound but really fallacious; specious.
2. Legal Latin for *no reason* and *ignorance of the charge*.
3. Renfield demonstrates his sanity by adopting genteel idioms, suggesting, in his doctor's mind at least, an association between sanity and class.
4. Mid-Victorian domestic rhetoric justified the exclusion of women from social power—indeed, from civil rights—by lauding their indirect "influence" over men.

nostrum[5] has vulgarized the truism to the very point of contempt. Isn't that true, doctor?' I nodded assent, for I was so amazed that I hardly knew what to either think or say; it was hard to imagine that I had seen him eat up his spiders and flies not five minutes before. Looking at my watch, I saw that I should go to the station to meet Van Helsing, so I told Mrs Harker that it was time to leave. She came at once, after saying pleasantly to Mr Renfield: 'Good-bye, and I hope I may see you often, under auspices pleasanter to yourself,' to which, to my astonishment, he replied:—

'Goodbye, my dear. I pray God I may never see your sweet face again. May He bless and keep you!'

When I went to the station to meet Van Helsing I left the boys behind me. Poor Art seemed more cheerful than he has been since Lucy first took ill, and Quincey is more like his own bright self than he has been for many a long day.

Van Helsing stepped from the carriage with the eager nimbleness of a boy. He saw me at once, and rushed up to me, saying:—

'Ah, friend John, how goes all? Well? So! I have been busy, for I come here to stay if need be. All affairs are settled with me, and I have much to tell. Madam Mina is with you? Yes. And her so fine husband? And Arthur and my friend Quincey, they are with you, too? Good!'

As I drove to the house I told him of what had passed, and of how my own diary had come to be of some use through Mrs Harker's suggestion; at which the Professor interrupted me:—

'Ah, that wonderful Madam Mina! She has man's brain—a brain that a man should have were he much gifted—and woman's heart.[6] The good God fashioned her for a purpose, believe me, when He made that so good combination. Friend John, up to now fortune has made that woman of help to us; after tonight she must not have to do with this so terrible affair. It is not good that she run a risk so great.' We men are determined—nay, are we not pledged?—to destroy this monster; but it is no part for a woman. Even if she be not harmed, her heart may fail her in so much and so many horrors; and hereafter she may suffer—both in waking, from her nerves, and in sleep, from her dreams. And, besides, she is young woman and not so long married; there may be other things to think of some time, if not now. You tell me she has wrote all, then she must consult with us; but tomorrow she say goodbye to this work, and we go alone.' I agreed heartily with him, and then I told him what we had found in his absence: that the house which Dracula had bought was the very next one to my own. He was amazed,

---

5. Various late Victorian tonics used the advertising slogan "The Blood is the Life." Renfield might be referring to Hughe's Blood Pills or Clarke's World-Famed Blood Mixture. Both claimed to vitalize the body by purifying the blood.

6. An extreme extension of the conservative Victorian doctrine of separate spheres, in which men and women were assigned different, mutually exclusive attributes.

and a great concern seemed to come on him. 'Oh that we had known it before!' he said, 'for then we might have reached him in time to save poor Lucy. However, "the milk that is spilt cries not out afterwards," as you say. We shall not think of that, but go on our way to the end.' Then he fell into a silence that lasted till we entered my own gateway. Before we went to prepare for dinner he said to Mrs Harker:—

'I am told, Madam Mina, by my friend John that you and your husband have put up in exact order all things that have been, up to this moment.'

'Not up to this moment, Professor,' she said impulsively, 'but up to this morning.'

'But why not up to now? We have seen hitherto how good light all the little things have made. We have told our secrets, and yet no one who has told is the worse for it.'

Mrs Harker began to blush, and taking a paper from her pocket, she said:—

'Dr Van Helsing, will you read this, and tell me if it must go in. It is my record of today. I too have seen the need of putting down at present everything, however trivial; but there is little in this except what is personal. Must it go in?' The Professor read it over gravely, and handed it back, saying:—

'It need not go in if you do not wish it; but I pray that it may. It can but make your husband love you the more, and all us, your friends, more honour you—as well as more esteem and love.' She took it back with another blush and a bright smile.

And so now, up to this very hour, all the records we have are complete and in order. The Professor took away one copy to study after dinner, and before our meeting, which is fixed for nine o'clock. The rest of us have already read everything; so when we meet in the study we shall all be informed as to facts, and can arrange our plan of battle with this terrible and mysterious enemy.

Mina Harker's Journal

30 September.—When we met in Dr Seward's study two hours after dinner, which had been at six o'clock, we unconsciously formed a sort of board or committee. Professor Van Helsing took the head of the table, to which Dr Seward motioned him as he came into the room. He made me sit next to him on his right, and asked me to act as secretary;[7] Jonathan sat next to me. Opposite us were Lord Godalming, Dr Seward, and Mr Morris—Lord Godalming being next to the Professor, and Dr Seward in the centre. The Professor said:—

'I may, I suppose, take it that we are all acquainted with the facts

---

7. Stoker notes shrewdly the characteristic behavior of all-male committees toward their sole female member.

that are in these papers.' We all expressed assent, and he went on:—

'Then it were, I think good that I tell you something of the kind of enemy with which we have to deal. I shall then make known to you something of the history of this man, which has been ascertained for me. So we then can discuss how we shall act, and can take our measure according.

'There are such beings as vampires; some of us have evidence that they exist. Even had we not the proof of our own unhappy experience, the teachings and the records of the past give proof enough for sane peoples. I admit that at the first I was sceptic. Were it not that through long years I have train myself to keep an open mind, I could not have believe until such time as that fact thunder on my ear. "See! see! I prove; I prove." Alas! Had I known at the first what now I know—nay, had I even guess at him—one so precious life had been spared to many of us who did love her. But that is gone; and we must so work, that other poor souls perish not, whilst we can save. The *nosferatu* do not die like the bee when he sting once. He is only stronger; and being stronger, have yet more power to work evil. This vampire which is amongst us is of himself so strong in person as twenty men; he is of cunning more than mortal, for his cunning be the growth of ages; he have still the aids of necromancy, which is, as his etymology imply, the divination by the dead, and all the dead that he can come nigh to are for him at command; he is brute, and more than brute: he is devil in callous, and the heart of him is not; he can, within limitations, appear at will when, and where, and in any of the forms that are to him; he can, within his range, direct the elements: the storm, the fog, the thunder; he can command all the meaner things: the rat, and the owl, and the bat—the moth, and the fox, and the wolf; he can grow and become small; and he can at times vanish and come unknown. How then are we to begin our strife to destroy him? How shall we find his where; and having found it, how can we destroy? My friends, this is much; it is a terrible task that we undertake, and there may be consequence to make the brave shudder. For if we fail in this our fight he must surely win; and then where end we? Life is nothings; I heed him not. But to fail here, is not mere life or death. It is that we become as him; that we henceforward become foul things of the night like him—without heart or conscience, preying on the bodies and the souls of those we love best. To us for ever are the gates of heaven shut; for who shall open them to us again? We go on for all time abhorred by all; a blot on the face of God's sunshine; an arrow in the side of Him who died for man. But we are face to face with duty; and in such case must we shrink? For me, I say, no; but then I am old, and life, with his sunshine, his fair places, his song of birds, his music, and his love, lie far behind. You others are young. Some have seen sorrow; but there are fair days yet in store. What say you?'

Whilst he was speaking Jonathan had taken my hand. I feared, oh so much, that the appalling nature of our danger was overcoming him when I saw his hand stretch out; but it was life to me to feel its touch—so strong, so self-reliant, so resolute. A brave man's hand can speak for itself; it does not even need a woman's love to hear its music.

When the Professor had done speaking my husband looked in my eyes, and I in his; there was no need for speaking between us.

'I answer for Mina and myself,' he said.

'Count me in, Professor,' said Mr Quincey Morris, laconically as usual.

'I am with you,' said Lord Godalming, 'for Lucy's sake, if for no other reason.'

Dr Seward simply nodded. The Professor stood up and, after laying his golden crucifix on the table, held out his hand on either side. I took his right hand, and Lord Godalming his left; Jonathan held my right with his left and stretched across to Mr Morris. So as we all took hands our solemn compact was made. I felt my heart icy cold, but it did not even occur to me to draw back. We resumed our places, and Dr Van Helsing went on with a sort of cheerfulness which showed that the serious work had begun. It was to be taken as gravely, and in as businesslike a way, as any other transaction of life:—

'Well, you know what we have to contend against; but we, too, are not without strength. We have on our side power of combination—a power denied to the vampire kind;[8] we have resources of science; we are free to act and think; and the hours of the day and the night are ours equally. In fact, so far as our powers extend, they are unfettered, and we are free to use them. We have self-devotion in a cause, and an end to achieve which is not a selfish one. These things are much.

'Now let us see how far the general powers arrayed against us are restrict, and how the individual cannot. In fine, let us consider the limitations of the vampire in general, and of this one in particular.

'All we have to go upon are traditions and superstitions. These do not at the first appear much, when the matter is one of life and death—nay of more than either life or death. Yet must we be satisfied; in the first place because we have to be—no other means is at our control—and secondly, because, after all, these things—tradition and superstition—are everything. Does not the belief in vampires rest for others—though not, alas! for us—on them? A year ago which of us would have received such a possibility, in the midst of our scientific, matter-of-fact nineteenth century? We even scouted a belief that we saw justified under our very eyes. Take it, then, that the vampire, and the belief in his limitations and his cure, rest for the moment on the same

---

8. Van Helsing's insistence that Dracula is isolated by definition is inconsistent with the vampire's power to command animals and the elements and to reproduce himself—a power scarcely evident in Stoker's novel.

base. For, let me tell you, he is known everywhere that men have been. In old Greece, in old Rome; he flourish in Germany all over, in France, in India, even in the Chersonese;[9] and in China, so far from us in all ways, there even is he, and the people fear him at this day. He have follow the wake of the berserker Icelander, the devil-begotten Hun, the Slav, the Saxon, the Magyar. So far, then, we have all we may act upon; and let me tell you that very much of the beliefs are justified by what we have seen in our own so unhappy experience. The vampire live on, and cannot die by mere passing of the time; he can flourish when that he can fatten on the blood of the living. Even more, we have seen amongst us that he can even grow younger; that his vital faculties grow strenuous, and seem as though they refresh themselves when his special pabulum[1] is plenty. But he cannot flourish without this diet; he eat not as others. Even friend Jonathan, who lived with him for weeks, did never see him to eat, never! He throws no shadow; he make in the mirror no reflect, as again Jonathan observe. He has the strength of many in his hand—witness again Jonathan when he shut the door against the wolfs, and when he help him from the diligence too. He can transform himself to wolf, as we gather from the ship arrival in Whitby, when he tear open the dog; he can be as bat, as Madam Mina saw him on the window at Whitby, and as friend John saw him fly from this so near house, and as my friend Quincey saw him at the window of Miss Lucy. He can come in mist which he create—that noble ship's captain proved him of this; but, from what we know, the distance he can make this mist is limited, and it can only be round himself. He come on moonlight rays as elemental dust—as again Jonathan saw those sisters in the castle of Dracula. He become so small— we ourselves saw Miss Lucy, ere she was at peace, slip through a hairbreadth space at the tomb door. He can, when once he find his way, come out from anything or into anything, no matter how close it be bound or even fused up with fire—solder you call it. He can see in the dark—no small power this, in a world which is one half shut from the light. Ah, but hear me through. He can do all these things, yet he is not free. Nay; he is even more prisoner than the slave of the galley, than the madman in his cell. He cannot go where he lists; he who is not of nature has yet to obey some of nature's laws—why we know not. He may not enter anywhere at the first, unless there be some one of the household who bid him to come; though afterwards he can come as he please. His power ceases, as does that of all evil things, at the coming of the day. Only at certain times can he have limited freedom. If he be not at the place whither he is bound, he can only change himself at noon or at exact sunrise or sunset. These things are we told, and in this record of ours we have proof by inference. Thus, whereas

9. An ancient Thracian peninsula, west of the Greek Hellespont.
1. Food, diet.

he can do as he will within his limit, when he have his earth-home, his coffin-home, his hell-home, the place unhallowed, as we saw when he went to the grave of the suicide as Whitby; still at other time he can only change when the time come. It is said, too, that he can only pass running water at the slack or the flood of the tide. Then there are things which so afflict him that he has no power, as the garlic that we know of; and as for things sacred, as this symbol, my crucifix, that was amongst us even now when we resolve, to them he is nothing, but in their presence he take his place far off and silent with respect. There are others, too, which I shall tell you of, lest in our seeking we may need them. The branch of wild rose on his coffin keep him that he move not from it; a sacred bullet fired into the coffin kill him so that he be true dead; and as for the stake through him, we know already of its peace; or the cut-off head that giveth rest. We have seen it with our eyes.[2]

'Thus when we find the habitation of this man-that-was, we can confine him to his coffin and destroy him, if we obey what we know. But he is clever. I have asked my friend Arminius,[3] of Buda-Pesth University, to make his record; and, from all the means that are, he tell me of what he has been. He must, indeed, have been that Voivode Dracula who won his name against the Turk, over the great river on the very frontier of Turkey-land. If it be so, then was he no common man; for in that time, and for centuries after, he was spoken of as the cleverest and the most cunning, as well as the bravest of the sons of the "land beyond the forest."[4] That mighty brain and that iron resolution went with him to his grave, and are even now arrayed against us. The Draculas were, says Arminius, a great and noble race, though now and again were scions who were held by their coevals to have had dealings with the Evil One. They learned his secrets in the Scholomance, amongst the mountains over Lake Hermanstadt,[5] where the devil claims the tenth scholar as his due. In the records are such words as "stregoica"—witch, "ordog", and "pokol"—Satan and hell; and in one manuscript this very Dracula is spoken of as "wampyr", which we all understand too well. There have been from the loins of this very one

---

2. Van Helsing's systematic rules are a melange of research and invention on Stoker's part. Dracula's inability to cross running water and his susceptibility to the wild rose and sacred bullet were available in such folklore sources as Emily Gerard's *The Land Beyond the Forest*. But Dracula's malleability of being—his ability to shapeshift, to transform his victims into his likeness—is Stoker's contribution to the legend.

3. A compliment to Arminius Vambéry (1832–1913), Professor of Oriental Languages at Budapest. Stoker met Vambéry in 1890, at one of Irving's stylish dinners in the Lyceum's Beefsteak Room; presumably Vambéry introduced him to Transylvanian history and legend.

4. The literal English translation of "Transylvania."

5. According to Gerard's *The Land Beyond the Forest*, the Scholomance is a school where "the secrets of nature, the language of animals, and all magic spells are taught by the devil in person." Lake Hermanstadt, "immeasurably deep," is the repository for the thunder and a sleeping dragon. The descendants of the children lured away by the Pied Piper live on its banks.

great men and good women, and their graves make sacred the earth where alone this foulness can dwell. For it is not the least of its terrors that this evil thing is rooted deep in all good; in soil barren of holy memories it cannot rest.'[6]

Whilst they were talking Mr Morris was looking steadily at the window, and he now got up quietly, and went out of the room. There was a little pause, and then the Professor went on:—

'And now we must settle what we do. We have here much data, and we must proceed to lay out our campaign. We know from the inquiry of Jonathan that from the castle to Whitby came fifty boxes of earth, all of which were delivered at Carfax; we also know that at least some of these boxes have been removed. It seems to me, that our first step should be to ascertain whether all the rest remain in the house beyond that wall where we look today; or whether any more have been removed. If the latter, we must trace—'

Here we were interrupted in a very startling way. Outside the house came the sound of a pistol-shot; the glass of the window was shattered with a bullet, which, ricochetting from the top of the embrasure, struck the far wall of the room. I am afraid I am at heart a coward, for I shrieked out. The men all jumped to their feet; Lord Godalming flew over to the window and threw up the sash. As he did so we heard Mr Morris's voice without:—

'Sorry! I fear I have alarmed you. I shall come in and tell you about it.' A minute later he came in and said:—

'It was an idiotic thing of me to do, and I ask your pardon, Mrs Harker, most sincerely; I fear I must have frightened you terribly. But the fact is that whilst the Professor was talking there came a big bat and sat on the window-sill. I have got such a horror of the damned brutes from recent events that I cannot stand them, and I went out to have a shot, as I have been doing of late of evenings whenever I have seen one. You used to laugh at me for it then, Art.'

'Did you hit it?' asked Dr Van Helsing.

'I don't know; I fancy not, for it flew away into the wood.' Without saying any more he took his seat, and the Professor began to resume his statement:—

'We must trace each of these boxes; and when we are ready, we must either capture or kill this monster in his lair; or we must, so to speak, sterilize the earth, so that no more he can seek safety in it. Thus in the end we may find him in his form of man between the hours of noon and sunset, and so engage with him when he is at his most weak.

'And now for you, Madam Mina, this night is the end until all be well. You are too precious to us to have such risk. When we part to-

6. This is the first time we hear that Dracula's boxes hold not simply his native earth, but soil consecrated according to traditional Christian procedures—a rule Stoker apparently invented, leaving us wondering why already-sacred soil must be "cleansed" once more with the Host.

night, you no more must question. We shall tell you all in good time. We are men, and are able to bear; but you must be our star and our hope, and we shall act all the more free that you are not in the danger, such as we are.'

All the men, even Jonathan, seemed relieved; but it did not seem to me good that they should brave danger and, perhaps, lessen their safety—strength being the best safety—through care of me; but their minds were made up, and, though it was a bitter pill for me to swallow, I could say nothing, save to accept their chivalrous care of me.

Mr Morris resumed the discussion:—

'As there is no time to lose, I vote we have a look at his house right now. Time is everything with him; and swift action on our part may save another victim.'

I own that my heart began to fail me when the time for action came so close, but I did not say anything, for I had a greater fear that if I appeared as a drag or a hindrance to their work, they might even leave me out of their counsels altogether. They have now gone off to Carfax, with means to get into the house.

Manlike, they have told me to go to bed and sleep; as if a woman can sleep when those she loves are in danger! I shall lie down and pretend to sleep, lest Jonathan have added anxiety about me when he returns.

Dr Seward's Diary

1 October, 4 a.m.—Just as we were about to leave the house, an urgent message was brought to me from Renfield to know if I would see him at once, as he had something of the utmost importance to say to me. I told the messenger to say that I would attend to his wishes in the morning; I was busy just at the moment. The attendant added:—

'He seems very importunate, sir. I have never seen him so eager. I don't know but what, if you don't see him soon, he will have one of his violent fits.' I knew the man would not have said this without some cause, so I said: 'All right; I'll go now;' and I asked the others to wait a few minutes for me, as I had to go and see my 'patient.'

'Take me with you, friend John,' said the Professor. 'His case in your diary interested me much, and it had bearing, too, now and again on *our* case. I should much like to see him, and especial when his mind is disturbed.'

'May I come also?' asked Lord Godalming.

'Me too?' said Quincey Morris. I nodded, and we all went down the passage together.

We found him in a state of considerable excitement, but far more rational in his speech and manner than I had ever seen him. There was an unusual understanding of himself, which was unlike anything I had ever met with in a lunatic; and he took it for granted that his reasons would prevail with others entirely sane. We all four went into the room, but none of the others at first said anything. His request was that I would at once release him from the asylum and send him home. This he backed up with arguments regarding his complete recovery, and adduced his own existing sanity. 'I appeal to your friends,' he said; 'they will, perhaps, not mind sitting in judgment on my case. By the way, you have not introduced me.' I was so much astonished that the oddness of introducing a madman in an asylum did not strike me at the moment; and, besides, there was a certain dignity in the man's manner, so much of the habit of equality, that I at once made the introduction: 'Lord Godalming; Professor Van Helsing; Mr Quincey Morris, of Texas; Mr Renfield.' He shook hands with each of them, saying in turn:—

'Lord Godalming, I had the honour of seconding your father at the Windham;[7] I grieve to know, by your holding the title, that he is no more. He was a man loved and honoured by all who knew him; and in his youth was, I have heard, the inventor of a burnt rum punch, much patronized on Derby night.[8] Mr Morris, you should be proud of your great state. Its reception into the Union[9] was a precedent which may have far-reaching effects hereafter, when the Pole and the Tropics[1] may hold allegiance to the Stars and Stripes. The power of Treaty may yet prove a vast engine of enlargement, when the Monroe doctrine[2] takes its true place as a political fable. What shall any man say of his pleasure at meeting Van Helsing? Sir, I make no apology for dropping all forms of conventional prefix. When an individual has revolutionized therapeutics by his discovery of the continuous evolution of brain-matter,[3] conventional forms are unfitting, since they would seem to limit him to one of a class. You, gentlemen, who by nationality, by heredity, or by the possession of natural gifts, are fitted to hold your respective places in the moving world, I take to witness that I am as sane as at least the majority of men who are in full possession of their liberties. And I am sure that you, Dr Seward, humanitarian and medico-jurist[4] as well as scientist, will deem it a moral duty to deal with me as

7. An exclusive gentlemen's club with a literary ambience.
8. The Derby is England's famous and elegant annual horse race, founded by the twelfth earl of Derby.
9. Texas became a state in 1845.
1. Alaska and Hawaii. Renfield, or Stoker, is prescient here: Alaska and Hawaii were admitted into the Union in the mid-twentieth century.
2. In 1823, President James Monroe declared the Spanish-American states in the Western Hemisphere under the jurisdiction of the United States, and thus closed to colonial invasion from Europe.
3. This grandiose tribute is as close as we come to learning the nature of Van Helsing's work.
4. This establishes Dr. Seward as a practitioner of forensic medicine, linking him, as well as his teacher, Van Helsing, to the field of law.

one to be considered as under exceptional circumstances.' He made this last appeal with a courtly air of conviction which was not without its own charm.

I think we were all staggered. For my own part, I was under the conviction, despite my knowledge of the man's character and history, that his reason had been restored; and I felt under a strong impulse to tell him that I was satisfied as to his sanity, and would see about the necessary formalities for his release in the morning. I thought it better to wait, however, before making so grave a statement, for of old I knew the sudden changes to which this particular patient was liable. So I contented myself with making a general statement that he appeared to be improving very rapidly; that I would have a longer chat with him in the morning, and would then see what I could do in the direction of meeting his wishes. This did not at all satisfy him, for he said quickly:—

'But I fear, Dr Seward, that you hardly apprehend my wish. I desire to go at once—here—now—this very hour—this very moment, if I may. Time presses, and in our implied agreement with the old scytheman it is of the essence of the contract. I am sure it is only necessary to put before so admirable a practitioner as Dr Seward so simple, yet so momentous a wish, to ensure its fulfilment.' He looked at me keenly, and seeing the negative in my face, turned to the others, and scrutinized them closely. Not meeting any sufficient response, he went on:—

'Is it possible that I have erred in my supposition?'

'You have,' I said frankly, but at the same time, as I felt, brutally. There was a considerable pause, and then he said slowly:—

'Then I suppose I must only shift my ground of request. Let me ask for this concession—boon, privilege, what you will. I am content to implore in such a case, not on personal grounds, but for the sake of others. I am not at liberty to give you the whole of my reasons; but you may, I assure you, take it from me that they are good ones, sound and unselfish, and springing from the highest sense of duty. Could you look, sir, into my heart, you would approve to the full the sentiments which animate me. Nay, more, you would count me amongst the best and truest of your friends.' Again he looked at us all keenly. I had a growing conviction that this sudden change of his entire intellectual method was but yet another form or phase of his madness, and so determined to let him go on a little longer, knowing from experience that he would, like all lunatics, give himself away in the end. Van Helsing was gazing at him with a look of the utmost intensity, his bushy eyebrows almost meeting with the fixed concentration of his look. He said to Renfield in a tone which did not surprise me at the time, but only when I thought of it afterwards—for it was as of one addressing an equal:—

'Can you not tell frankly your real reason for wishing to be free tonight? I will undertake that if you will satisfy even me—a stranger, without prejudice, and with the habit of keeping an open mind—Dr Seward will give you, at his own risk and on his own responsibility, the privilege you seek.' He shook his head sadly, and with a look of poignant regret on his face. The Professor went on:—

'Come, sir, bethink yourself. You claim the privilege of reason in the highest degree, since you seek to impress us with your complete reasonableness. You do this, whose sanity we have reason to doubt, since you are not yet released from medical treatment for this very defect. If you will not help us in our effort to choose the wisest course, how can we perform the duty which you yourself put upon us? Be wise, and help us; and if we can we shall aid you to achieve your wish.' He still shook his head as he said:—

'Dr Van Helsing, I have nothing to say. Your argument is complete, and if I were free to speak I should not hesitate a moment; but I am not my own master in the matter. I can only ask you to trust me. If I am refused, the responsibility does not rest with me.' I thought it was now time to end the scene, which was becoming too comically grave, so I went towards the door, simply saying:—

'Come, my friends, we have work to do. Good night.'

As, however, I got near the door, a new change came over the patient. He moved towards me so quickly that for the moment I feared that he was about to make another homicidal attack. My fears, however, were groundless, for he held up his two hands imploringly, and made his petition in a moving manner. As he saw that the very excess of his emotion was militating against him, by restoring us more to our old relations, he became still more demonstrative. I glanced at Van Helsing, and saw my conviction reflected in his eyes; so I became a little more fixed in my manner, if not more stern, and motioned to him that his efforts were unavailing. I had previously seen something of the same constantly growing excitement in him when he had to make some request of which at the time he had thought much, such, for instance, as when he wanted a cat; and I was prepared to see the collapse into the same sullen acquiescence on this occasion. My expectation was not realized, for, when he found that his appeal would not be successful, he got into quite a frantic condition. He threw himself on his knees, and held up his hands, wringing them in plaintive supplication, and poured forth a torrent of entreaty, with the tears rolling down his cheeks and his whole face and form expressive of the deepest emotion—

'Let me entreat you, Dr Seward, oh, let me implore you, to let me out of this house at once. Send me away how you will and where you will; send keepers with me with whips and chains; let them take me in a strait-waistcoat, manacled and leg-ironed, even to a gaol; but let me go out of this. You don't know what you do by keeping me here. I am speaking from the depths of my heart—of my very soul. You don't know whom you wrong, or how; and I may not tell. Woe is me! I may not tell. By all you hold sacred—by all you hold dear—by your love that is lost—by your hope that lives—for the sake of the Almighty, take me out of this and save my soul from guilt! Can't you hear me, man? Can't you understand? Will you never learn? Don't you know that I am sane and earnest now; that I am no lunatic in a mad fit, but a sane man fighting for his soul? Oh, hear me! hear me! Let me go! let me go! let me go!'

I thought that the longer this went on the wilder he would get, and so would bring on a fit; so I took him by the hand and raised him up.

'Come,' I said sternly, 'no more of this; we have had quite enough already. Get to your bed and try to behave more discreetly.'

He suddenly stopped and looked at me intently for several moments. Then, without a word, he rose and moving over, sat down on the side of the bed. The collapse had come, as on former occasions, just as I had expected.

When I was leaving the room, last of our party, he said to me in a quiet, well-bred voice:—

'You will, I trust, Dr Seward, do me the justice to bear in mind, later on, that I did what I could to convince you tonight.'

Chapter XIX

Jonathan Harker's Journal

1 October, 5 a.m.—I went with the party to the search with an easy mind, for I think I never saw Mina so absolutely strong and well. I am so glad that she consented to hold back and let us men do the work. Somehow, it was a dread to me that she was in this fearful business at all; but now that her work is done, and that it is due to her energy and brains and foresight that the whole story is put together in such a way that every point tells, she may well feel that her part is finished, and that she can henceforth leave the rest to us. We were, I think, all a little upset by the scene with Mr Renfield. When we came away from his room we were silent till we got back to the study. Then Mr Morris said to Dr Seward:—

'Say, Jack, if that man wasn't attempting a bluff, he is about the sanest lunatic I ever saw. I'm not sure, but I believe that he had some serious purpose, and if he had, it was pretty rough on him not to get a chance.' Lord Godalming and I were silent, but Dr Van Helsing added:—

'Friend John, you know more of lunatics that I do, and I'm glad of it, for I fear that if it had been to me to decide I would before that last hysterical outburst have given him free. But we live and learn, and in our present task we must take no chance, as my friend Quincey would say. All is best as they are.' Dr Seward seemed to answer them both in a dreamy kind of way:—

'I don't know but that I agree with you. If that man had been an ordinary lunatic I would have taken my chance of trusting him; but he seems so mixed up with the Count in an indexy[1] kind of way that I am afraid of doing anything wrong by helping his fads. I can't forget how he prayed with almost equal fervour for a cat, and then tried to tear my throat out with his teeth. Besides, he called the Count "lord and master", and he may want to get out to help him in some diabolical way. That horrid thing has the wolves and the rats and his own kind to help him, so I suppose he isn't above trying to use a respectable lunatic. He certainly did seem earnest, though. I only hope we have done what is best. These things, in conjunction with the wild work we have in hand, help to unnerve a man.' The Professor stepped over, and laying his hand on his shoulder, said in his grave, kindly way:—

'Friend John, have no fear. We are trying to do our duty in a very sad and terrible case; we can only do as we deem best. What else have we to hope for, except the pity of the good God?' Lord Godalming had slipped away for a few minutes, but he now returned. He held up a little silver whistle as he remarked:—

'That old place may be full of rats, and if so, I've got an antidote on call.' Having passed the wall, we took our way to the house, taking care to keep in the shadows of the trees on the lawn when the moonlight shone out. When we got to the porch the Professor opened his bag and took out a lot of things, which he laid on the step, sorting them into four little groups, evidently one for each. Then he spoke:—

'My friends, we are going into a terrible danger, and we need arms of many kinds. Our enemy is not merely spiritual. Remember that he has the strength of twenty men, and that, though our necks or our windpipes are of the common kind—and therefore breakable or crushable—his are not amenable to mere strength. A stronger man, or a body of men more strong in all than him, can at certain times hold him; but yet they cannot hurt him as we can be hurt by him. We must, therefore, guard ourselves from his touch. Keep this near your heart'— as he spoke he lifted a little silver crucifix and held it out to me, I being nearest to him—'put these flowers round your neck'—here he handed to me a wreath of withered garlic blossoms—'for other enemies more mundane, this revolver and this knife; and for aid in all, these so small electric lamps[2], which you can fasten to your breast; and for all, and above all at the last, this, which we must not desecrate needless.' This

---

1. An obsolete meaning of index is "informer" (who may point an index finger at important persons or information).
2. Stoker steals an effect from his master: in Henry Irving's lavish production of W. G. Wills's *Faust*, which opened in 1885, Irving's Mephistopheles illuminated his face by wearing tiny electric lights in his cap.

was a portion of sacred wafer, which he put in an envelope and handed to me. Each of the others was similarly equipped. 'Now,' he said, 'friend John, where are the skeleton keys? If so that we can open the door, we need not break house by the window, as before at Miss Lucy's.'

Dr Seward tried one or two skeleton keys, his mechanical dexterity as a surgeon standing him in good stead. Presently he got one to suit; after a little play back and forward the bolt yielded, and, with a rusty clang, shot back. We pressed on the door, the rusty hinges creaked, and it slowly opened. It was startlingly like the image conveyed to me in Dr Seward's diary of the opening of Miss Westenra's tomb; I fancy that the same idea seemed to strike the others, for with one accord they shrank back. The Professor was the first to move forward, and stepped into the open door.

'*In manus tuas, Domine!*'[3] he said, crossing himself as he passed over the threshold. We closed the door behind us, lest when we should have lit our lamps we should possibly attract attention from the road. The Professor carefully tried the lock, lest we might not be able to open it from within should we be in a hurry making our exit. Then we all lit our lamps and proceeded on our search.

The light from the tiny lamps fell in all sorts of odd forms, as the rays crossed each other, or the opacity of our bodies threw great shadows. I could not for my life get away from the feeling that there was someone else amongst us. I suppose it was the recollection, so powerfully brought home to me by the grim surroundings, of that terrible experience in Transylvania. I think the feeling was common to us all, for I noticed that the others kept looking over their shoulders at every sound and every new shadow, just as I felt myself doing.

The whole place was thick with dust.[4] The floor was seemingly inches deep, except where there were recent footsteps, in which on holding down my lamp I could see marks of hobnails[5] where the dust was caked. The walls were fluffy and heavy with dust, and in the corners were masses of spiders' webs, whereon the dust had gathered till they looked like old tattered rags as the weight had torn them partly down. On a table in the hall was a great bunch of keys, with a time-yellowed label on each. They had been used several times, for on the table were several similar rents in the blanket of dust, similar to that exposed when the Professor lifted them. He turned to me and said:—

'You know this place, Jonathan. You have copied maps of it, and you

---

3. With characteristic piety, Van Helsing quotes Jesus' last words: "And when Jesus had cried with a loud voice, he said, Father, into thy hands I commend my spirit: and having said thus, he gave up the ghost" (Luke 23.46). He is also quoting Irving in his saintly guise: his famous last words in the title role of Tennyson's *Becket* were "Into Thy hands, O Lord! Into thy hands."

4. This foul British crypt, rather than the relatively well-kept Castle Dracula, inspired the grotesque Transylvanian sets of Tod Browning's 1931 film *Dracula*.

5. Short nails with thick heads.

know at least more than we do. Which is the way to the chapel?' I had
an idea of its direction, though on my former visit I had not been able
to get admission to it; so I led the way, and after a few wrong turnings
found myself opposite a low, arched oaken door, ribbed with iron
bands. 'This is the spot,' said the Professor as he turned his lamp on a
small map of the house, copied from the file of my original correspondence regarding the purchase. With a little trouble we found the key
on the bunch and opened the door. We were prepared for some un-
pleasantness, for as we were opening the door a faint, malodorous air
seemed to exhale through the gaps, but none of us ever expected such
an odour as we encountered. None of the others had met the Count
at all at close quarters, and when I had seen him he was either in the
fasting stage of his existence in his rooms or, when he was gloated with
fresh blood, in a ruined building open to the air; but here the place
was small and close, and the long disuse had made the air stagnant and
foul. There was an earthy smell, as of some dry miasma, which came
through the fouler air. But as to the odour itself, how shall I describe
it? It was not alone that it was composed of all the ills of mortality and
with the pungent, acrid smell of blood, but it seemed as though corruption had become itself corrupt. Faugh! it sickens me to think of it.
Every breath exhaled by that monster seemed to have clung to the place
and intensified its loathsomeness.

Under ordinary circumstances such a stench would have brought our
enterprise to an end; but this was no ordinary case, and the high and
terrible purpose in which we were involved gave us a strength which
rose above merely physical considerations. After the involuntary shrink-
ing consequent on the first nauseous whiff, we one and all set about
our work as though that loathsome place were a garden of roses.

We made an accurate examination of the place, the Professor saying
as we began:—

'The first thing is to see how many of the boxes are left; we must
then examine every hole and corner and cranny, and see if we cannot
get some clue as to what has become of the rest.' A glance was sufficient
to show how many remained, for the great earth chests were bulky, and
there was no mistaking them.

There were only twenty-nine left out of fifty! Once I got a fright, for,
seeing Lord Godalming suddenly turn and look out of the vaulted door
into the dark passage beyond, I looked too, and for an instant my heart
stood still. Somewhere, looking out from the shadow, I seemed to see
the high lights of the Count's evil face, the ridge of the nose, the red
eyes, the red lips, the awful pallor. It was only for a moment, for, as
Lord Godalming said, 'I thought I saw a face, but it was only the
shadows,' and resumed his inquiry, I turned my lamp in the direction,
and stepped into the passage. There was no sign of any one; and as
there were no corners, no doors, no aperture of any kind, but only the

solid walls of the passage, there could be no hiding-place even for *him*. I took it that fear had helped imagination, and said nothing.

A few minutes later I saw Morris step suddenly back from a corner, which he was examining. We all followed his movements with our eyes, for undoubtedly some nervousness was growing on us, and we saw a whole mass of phosphorescence, which twinkled like stars. We all instinctively drew back. The whole place was becoming alive with rats.[6]

For a moment or two we stood appalled, all save Lord Godalming, who was seemingly prepared for such an emergency. Rushing over to the great iron-bound oaken door, which Dr Seward had described from the outside, and which I had seen myself, he turned the key in the lock, drew the huge bolts, and swung the door open. Then, taking his little silver whistle from his pocket, he blew a low, shrill call. It was answered from behind Dr Seward's house by the yelping of dogs, and after about a minute three terriers came dashing round the corner of the house. Unconsciously we had all moved towards the door, and as we moved I noticed that the dust had been much disturbed: the boxes which had been taken out had been brought this way. But even in the minute that had elapsed the number of the rats had vastly increased. They seemed to swarm over the place all at once, till the lamplight, shining on their moving dark bodies and glittering, baleful eyes, made the place look like a bank of earth set with fireflies. The dogs dashed on, but at the threshold suddenly stopped and snarled, and then, simultaneously lifting their noses, began to howl in most lugubrious fashion. The rats were multiplying in thousands, and we moved out.

Lord Godalming lifted one of the dogs and carrying him in, placed him on the floor. The instant his feet touched the ground he seemed to recover his courage, and rushed at his natural enemies. They fled before him so fast that before he had shaken the life out of a score, the other dogs, who had by now been lifted in in the same manner, had but small prey ere the whole mass had vanished.

With their going it seemed as if some evil presence had departed, for the dogs frisked about and barked merrily as they made sudden darts at their prostrate foes, and turned them over and over and tossed them in the air with vicious shakes. We all seemed to find our spirits rise. Whether it was the purifying of the deadly atmosphere by the opening of the chapel door, or the relief which we experienced by finding ourselves in the open I know not; but most certainly the shadow of dread seemed to slip from us like a robe, and the occasion of our coming lost something of its grim significance, though we did not slacken a whit in our resolution. We closed the outer door and barred and locked it, and bringing the dogs with us, began our search of the house. We found

---

6. These rats are clearly the inspiration for the plague carriers that accompany the vampire in F. W. Murnau's film *Nosferatu* (1922), though those rats, like the vampire, were foreign invaders; these rats are British.

nothing throughout except dust in extraordinary proportions, and all untouched save for my own footsteps when I had made my first visit. Never once did the dogs exhibit any symptom of uneasiness, and even when we returned to the chapel they frisked about as though they had been rabbit-hunting in a summer wood.

The morning was quickening in the east when we emerged from the front. Dr Van Helsing had taken the key of the halldoor from the bunch, and locked the door in orthodox fashion, putting the key into his pocket when he had done.

'So far,' he said, 'our night has been eminently successful. No harm has come to us such as I feared might be, and yet we have ascertained how many boxes are missing. More than all do I rejoice that this, our first—and perhaps our most difficult and dangerous—step has been accomplished without the bringing thereinto our most sweet Madam Mina or troubling her waking or sleeping thoughts with sights and sounds and smells of horror which she might never forget. One lesson, too, we have learned, if it be allowable to argue *a particulari*: that the brute beasts which are to the Count's command are yet themselves not amenable to his spiritual power; for look, these rats that would come to his call, just as from his castle top he summon the wolves to your going and to that poor mother's cry, though they come to him, they run pell-mell from the so little dogs of my friend Arthur. We have other matters before us, other dangers, other fears; and that monster—he has not used his power over the brute world for the only or the last time tonight. So be it that he has gone elsewhere. Good! It has given us opportunity to cry "check" in some ways in this chess game, which we play for the stake of human souls. And now let us go home. The dawn is close at hand, and we have reason to be content with our first night's work. It may be ordained that we have many nights and days to follow, if full of peril; but we must go on, and from no danger shall we shrink.'

The house was silent when we got back, save for some poor creature who was screaming away in one of the distant wards, and a low, moaning sound from Renfield's room. The poor wretch was doubtless torturing himself, after the manner of the insane, with needless thoughts of pain.

I came tiptoe into our own room, and found Mina asleep, breathing so softly that I had to put my ear down to hear it. She looks paler than usual. I hope the meeting tonight has not upset her. I am truly thankful that she is to be left out of our future work, and even of our deliberations. It is too great a strain for a woman to bear. I did not think so at first, but I know better now. Therefore I am glad that it is settled. There may be things which would frighten her to hear; and yet to conceal them from her might be worse than to tell her if once she suspected that there was any concealment. Henceforth our work is to be a sealed book to her, till at least such time as we can tell her that all is finished, and the earth free from a monster of the nether world. I daresay it will be difficult to begin to keep silence after such confidence as ours; but I must be resolute, and tomorrow I shall keep dark over tonight's doings, and shall refuse to speak of anything that has happened. I rest on the sofa, so as not to disturb her.

1 October, later.—I suppose it was natural that we should have all overslept ourselves, for the day was a busy one, and the night had no rest at all. Even Mina must have felt its exhaustion, for though I slept till the sun was high, I was awake before her, and had to call two or three times before she awoke. Indeed, she was so sound asleep that for a few seconds she did not recognize me, but looked at me with a sort of blank terror, as one looks who has been waked out of a bad dream. She complained a little of being tired, and I let her rest till later in the day. We now know of twenty-one boxes having been removed, and if it be that several were taken in any of these removals we may be able to trace them all. Such will, of course, immensely simplify our labour, and the sooner the matter is attended to the better. I shall look up Thomas Snelling today.

Dr Seward's Diary

1 October.—It was towards noon when I was awakened by the Professor walking into my room. He was more jolly and cheerful than usual, and it is quite evident that last night's work has helped to take some of the brooding weight off his mind. After going over the adventure of the night he suddenly said:—

'Your patient interests me much. May it be that with you I visit him this morning? Or if that you are too occupy, I can go alone if it may be. It is a new experience to me to find a lunatic who talk philosophy, and reason so sound.' I had some work to do which pressed, so I told him that if he would go alone I would be glad, as then I should not have to keep him waiting; so I called an attendant and gave him the necessary instructions. Before the Professor left the room I cautioned him against getting any false impression from my patient. 'But,' he answered, 'I want him to talk of himself and of his delusion as to consuming live things. He said to Madam Mina, as I see in your diary of yesterday, that he had once had such a belief. Why do you smile, friend John?'

'Excuse me,' I said, 'but the answer is here.' I laid my hand on the type-written matter. 'When our sane and learned lunatic made that very statement of how he *used* to consume life, his mouth was actually nauseous with the flies and spiders which he had eaten just before Mrs Harker entered the room.' Van Helsing smiled in turn. 'Good!' he said. 'Your memory is true, friend John. I should have remembered. And yet it is this very obliquity of thought and memory which makes mental disease such a fascinating study. Perhaps I may gain more knowledge out of the folly of this madman than I shall from the teaching of the most wise. Who knows?' I went on with my work, and before long was through that in hand. It seemed that the time had been very short indeed, but there was Van Helsing back in the study. 'Do I interrupt?' he asked politely as he stood at the door.

'Not at all,' I answered. 'Come in. My work is finished, and I am free. I can go with you now, if you like.'

'It is needless; I have seen him!'

'Well?'

'I fear that he does not appraise me at much. Our interview was short. When I entered his room he was sitting on a stool in the centre, with his elbows on his knees, and his face was the picture of sullen discontent. I spoke to him as cheerfully as I could, and with such a measure of respect as I could assume. He made no reply whatever. "Don't you know me?" I asked. His answer was not reassuring; "I know you well enough; you are the old fool Van Helsing. I wish you would take yourself and your idiotic brain theories somewhere else. Damn all thick-headed Dutchmen!" Not a word more would he say, but sat in his implacable sullenness as indifferent to me as though I had not been in the room at all. Thus departed for this time my chance of much learning from this so clever lunatic; so I shall go, if I may, and cheer myself with a few happy words with that sweet soul Madam Mina. Friend John, it does rejoice me unspeakable that she is no more to be pained, no more to be worried, with our terrible things. Though we shall much miss her help, it is better so.'

'I agree with you with all my heart,' I answered earnestly, for I did not want him to weaken in this matter. 'Mrs Harker is better out of it. Things are quite bad enough to us, all men of the world, and who have been in many tight places in our time; but it is no place for a woman, and if she had remained in touch with the affair, it would in time infallibly have wrecked her.'

So Van Helsing has gone to confer with Mrs Harker and Harker; Quincey and Art are all out following up the clues as to the earth-boxes. I shall finish my round of work, and we shall meet tonight.

Mina Harker's Journal

1 October.—It is strange to me to be kept in the dark as I am today; after Jonathan's full confidence for so many years, to see him manifestly avoid certain matters, and those the most vital of all. This morning I slept late after the fatigues of yesterday, and though Jonathan was late too, he was the earlier. He spoke to me before he went out, never more sweetly or tenderly, but he never mentioned a word of what had happened in the visit to the Count's house. And yet he must have known

how terribly anxious I was. Poor dear fellow! I suppose it must have
distressed him even more than it did me. They all agreed that it was
best that I should not be drawn further into this awful work, and I
acquiesced. But to think that he keeps anything from me! And now
I am crying like a silly fool, when I *know* it comes from my husband's great love and from the good, good wishes of those other strong
men . . .

That has done me good. Well, some day Jonathan will tell me all;
and lest it should ever be that he should think for a moment that I
kept anything from him, I still keep my journal as usual. Then if he
has feared of my trust I shall show it to him, with every thought of my
heart put down for his dear eyes to read. I feel strangely sad and low-
spirited today. I suppose it is the reaction from the terrible excitement.

Last night I went to bed when the men had gone, simply because
they told me to. I didn't feel sleepy, and I did feel full of devouring
anxiety. I kept thinking over everything that has been ever since Jonathan came to see me in London, and it all seems like a horrible tragedy,
with fate pressing on relentlessly to some destined end. Everything that
one does seems, no matter how right it may be, to bring on the very
thing which is most to be deplored. If I hadn't gone to Whitby, perhaps
poor dear Lucy would be with us now. She hadn't taken to visiting the
churchyard till I came, and if she hadn't come there in the daytime
with me she wouldn't have walked there in her sleep; and if she hadn't
gone there at night and asleep, that monster couldn't have destroyed
her as he did. Oh, why did I ever go to Whitby? There now, crying
again! I wonder what has come over me today. I must hide it from
Jonathan, for if he knew that I had been crying twice in one morning
—I, who never cried on my own account, and whom he has never
caused to shed a tear—the dear fellow would fret his heart out. I shall
put a bold face on, and if I do feel weepy, he shall never see it. I
suppose it is one of the lessons that we poor women have to learn . . .

I can't quite remember how I fell asleep last night. I remember
hearing the sudden barking of the dogs and a lot of queer sounds, like
praying on a very tumultuous scale, from Mr Renfield's room, which
is somewhere under this. And then there was silence over everything,
silence so profound that it startled me, and I got up and looked out of
the window. All was dark and silent, the black shadows thrown by the
moonlight seeming full of a silent mystery of their own. Not a thing
seemed to be stirring, but all to be grim and fixed as death or fate; so
that a thin streak of white mist, that crept with almost imperceptible
slowness across the grass towards the house, seemed to have a sentience
and a vitality of its own. I think that the digression of my thoughts must
have done me good, for when I got back to bed I found a lethargy
creeping over me. I lay a while, but could not quite sleep, so I got out
and looked out of the window again. The mist was spreading, and was

now close up to the house, so that I could see it lying thick against the wall, as though it were stealing up to the windows. The poor man was more loud than ever, and though I could not distinguish a word he said, I could in some way recognize in his tones some passionate entreaty on his part. Then there was the sound of a struggle, and I knew that the attendants were dealing with him. I was so frightened that I crept into bed, and pulled the clothes over my head, putting my fingers in my ears. I was not then a bit sleepy, at least so I thought; but I must have fallen asleep, for, except dreams, I do not remember anything until the morning when Jonathan woke me. I think that it took me an effort and a little time to realize where I was, and that it was Jonathan who was bending over me. My dream was very peculiar, and was almost typical of the way that waking thoughts become merged in, or continued in, dreams.

I thought that I was asleep, and waiting for Jonathan to come back. I was very anxious about him, and I was powerless to act; my feet, and my hands, and my brain were weighted, so that nothing could proceed at the usual pace. And so I slept uneasily and thought. Then it began to dawn upon me that the air was heavy, and dank, and cold. I put back the clothes from my face, and found, to my surprise, that all was dim around me. The gas-light which I had left lit for Jonathan, but turned down, came only like a tiny red spark through the fog, which had evidently grown thicker and poured into the room. Then it occurred to me that I had shut the window before I had come to bed. I would have got out to make certain on the point, but some leaden lethargy seemed to chain my limbs and even my will. I lay still and endured; that was all. I closed my eyes, but could still see through my eyelids. (It is wonderful what tricks our dreams play us, and how conveniently we can imagine.) The mist grew thicker and thicker, and I could see now how it came in, for I could see it like smoke—or with the white energy of boiling water—pouring in, not through the window, but through the joinings of the door. It got thicker and thicker, till it seemed as if it became concentrated into a sort of pillar of cloud[7] in the room, through the top of which I could see the light of the gas shining like a red eye. Things began to whirl through my brain just as the cloudy column was now whirling in the room, and through it all came the scriptual words 'a pillar of cloud by day and of fire by night.' Was it indeed some such spiritual guidance that was coming to me in my sleep? But the pillar was composed of both the day and the night-guiding, for the fire was in the red eye, which at the thought got a new fascination for me; till, as I looked, the fire divided, and seemed to

7. "And the LORD went before them by day in a pillar of a cloud, to lead them the way; and by night in a pillar of fire, to give them light; to go by day and night: He took not away the pillar of the cloud by day, nor the pillar of fire by night, from before the people" (Exodus 13.21–22). Like Renfield, Mina perceives Dracula in the imagery of biblical revelation.

shine on me through the fog like two red eyes, such as Lucy told me of in her momentary mental wandering when, on the cliff, the dying sunlight struck the windows of St Mary's Church. Suddenly the horror burst upon me that it was thus that Jonathan had seen those awful women growing into reality through the whirling mist in the moonlight, and in my dream I must have fainted, for all became black darkness. The last conscious effort which imagination made was to show me a livid white face bending over me out of the mist. I must be careful of such dreams, for they would unseat one's reason if there were too much of them. I would get Dr Van Helsing or Dr Seward to prescribe something for me which would make me sleep, only that I fear to alarm them. Such a dream at the present time would become woven into their fears for me. Tonight I shall strive hard to sleep naturally. If I do not, I shall tomorrow night get them to give me a dose of chloral; that cannot hurt me for once, and it will give me a good night's sleep. Last night tired me more than if I had not slept at all.

2 *October*, 10 *p.m.*—Last night I slept, but did not dream. I must have slept soundly, for I was not waked by Jonathan coming to bed; but the sleep has not refreshed me, for today I feel terribly weak and spiritless. I spent all yesterday trying to read, or lying down dozing. In the afternoon Mr Renfield asked if he might see me. Poor man, he was very gentle, and when I came away he kissed my hand and bade God bless me. Some way it affected me much; I am crying when I think of him. This is a new weakness, of which I must be careful. Jonathan would be miserable if he knew I had been crying. He and the others were out until dinner-time, and they all came in tired. I did what I could to brighten them up, and I suppose that the effort did me good, for I forgot how tired I was. After dinner they sent me to bed, and all went off to smoke together, as they said, but I knew that they wanted to tell each other of what had occurred to each during the day; I could see from Jonathan's manner that he had something important to communicate. I was not so sleepy as I should have been; so before they went I asked Dr Seward to give me a little opiate of some kind, as I had not slept well the night before. He very kindly made me up a sleeping draught, which he gave to me, telling me that it would do me no harm, as it was very mild . . . I have taken it, and am waiting for sleep, which still keeps aloof. I hope I have not done wrong, for as sleep begins to flirt with me, a new fear comes: that I may have been foolish in thus depriving myself of the power of waking. I might want it. Here comes sleep. Good night.

Chapter XX

Jonathan Harker's Journal

1 October, evening.—I found Thomas Snelling in his house at Bethnal Green,[1] but unhappily he was not in a condition to remember anything. The very prospect of beer which my expected coming had opened to him had proved too much, and he had begun too early on his expected debauch. I learned, however, from his wife, who seemed a decent, poor soul, that he was only the assistant to Smollet, who of the two mates was the responsible person. So off I drove to Walworth, and found Mr Joseph Smollet at home and in his shirtsleeves, taking a late tea out of a saucer. He is a decent, intelligent fellow, distinctly a good, reliable type of workman, and with a headpiece of his own. He remembered all about the incident of the boxes, and from a wonderful dog's-eared notebook, which he produced from some mysterious receptacle about the seat of his trousers, and which had hieroglyphical entries in thick, half-obliterated pencil, he gave me the destinations of the boxes. There were, he said, six in the cartload which he took from Carfax and left at 197, Chicksand Street, Mile End New Town, and another six which he deposited at Jamaica Lane, Bermondsey.[2] If then the Count meant to scatter these ghastly refuges of his over London, these places were chosen as the first of delivery, so that later he might distribute more fully. The systematic manner in which this was done made me think that he could not mean to confine himself to two sides of London. He was now fixed on the far east of the northern shore, on the east of the southern shore, and on the south. The north and west were surely never meant to be left out of his diabolical scheme—let alone the City[3] itself and the very heart of fashionable London in the south-west and west. I went back to Smollet, and asked him if he could tell us if any other boxes had been taken from Carfax.

He replied:—

'Well, guv'nor, you've treated me very 'an'some'—I had given him half a sovereign—'an' I'll tell yer all I know. I heeard a man by the name of Bloxam say four nights ago in the 'Are an' 'Ounds, in Pincher's Alley, as 'ow he an' his mate 'ad 'ad a rare dusty job in old 'ouse at Purfleet. There ain't a-many such jobs as this 'ere, an' I'm thinkin' that maybe Sam Bloxam could tell ye summut.' I asked if he could tell me where to find him. I told him that if he could get me the address it would be worth another half-sovereign to him. So he gulped down the

---

1. Manufacturing district north of London on the left bank of the Thames.
2. Neighborhoods on London's east and southeast. Mile End New Town is a continuation of London's Whitechapel district, where the Jack the Ripper murders had taken place in 1888.
3. The self-governing district of central London.

rest of his tea and stood up, saying that he was going to begin the search then and there. At the door he stopped, and said:—

'Look 'ere, guv'nor, there ain't no sense in me a-keepin' you 'ere. I may find Sam soon, or I mayn't; but anyhow he ain't like to be in a way to tell ye much tonight. Sam is a rare one when he starts on the booze. If you can give me a envelope with a stamp on it, and put yer address on it, I'll find out where Sam is to be found and post it ye tonight. But ye'd better be up arter 'im soon in the mornin', or maybe ye won't ketch 'im; for Sam gets off main early, never mind the booze the night afore.'

This was all practical, so one of the children went off with a penny to buy an envelope and a sheet of paper, and to keep the change. When she came back, I addressed the envelope and stamped it, and when Smollet had again faithfully promised to post the address when found, I took my way to home. We're on the track anyhow. I am tired tonight, and want sleep. Mina is fast asleep, and looks a little too pale; her eyes look as though she had been crying. Poor dear, I've no doubt it frets her to be kept in the dark, and it may make her doubly anxious about me and the others. But it is best as it is. It is better to be disappointed and worried in such a way now than to have her nerve broken. The doctors were quite right to insist on her being kept out of this dreadful business. I must be firm, for on me this particular burden of silence must rest. I shall not ever enter on the subject with her under any circumstances. Indeed, it may not be a hard task, after all, for she herself has become reticent on the subject, and has not spoken of the Count or his doings ever since we told her of our decision.

2 October, evening.—A long and trying and exciting day. By the first post I got my directed envelope with a dirty scrap of paper enclosed, on which was written with a carpenter's pencil in a sprawling hand:—

'Sam Bloxam, Korkrans, 4, Poters Cort, Bartel Street, Walworth. Arsk for the depite.'

I got the letter in bed, and rose without waking Mina. She looked heavy and sleepy and pale, and far from well. I determined not to wake her, but that, when I should return from this new search, I would arrange for her going back to Exeter. I think she would be happier in our own home, with her daily tasks to interest her, than in being here amongst us and in ignorance. I only saw Dr Seward for a moment, and told him where I was off to, promising to come back and tell the rest so soon as I should have found out anything. I drove to Walworth and found, with some difficulty, Potter's Court. Mr Smollet's spelling misled me, as I asked for Poter's Court instead of Potter's Court. However, when I had found the court, I had no difficulty in discovering Corcoran's lodging-house. When I asked the man who came to the door for the 'depite', he shook his head, and said: 'I dunno 'im. There ain't no such a person 'ere; I never 'eard of 'im in all my bloomin' days. Don't believe there ain't nobody of that kind livin' 'ere or anywheres.' I took out Smollet's letter, and as I read it it seemed to me that the lesson of the spelling of the name of the court might guide me. 'What are you?' I asked.

'I'm the depity,' he answered. I saw at once that I was on the right track; phonetic spelling[4] had again misled me. A half-crown tip put the deputy's knowledge at my disposal, and I learned that Mr Bloxam, who had slept off the remains of his beer on the previous night at Corcoran's, had left for his work at Poplar[5] at five o'clock that morning. He could not tell me where the place or work was situated, but he had a vague idea that it was some kind of a 'new-fangled ware'us;' and with this slender clue I had to start for Poplar. It was twelve o'clock before I got any satisfactory hint of such a building, and this I got at a coffee-shop, where some workmen were having their dinner. One of these suggested that there was being erected at Cross Angel Street a new 'cold storage' building; and as this suited the condition of a 'new-fangled ware'us', I at once drove to it. An interview with a surly gatekeeper and a surlier foreman, both of whom were appeased with coin of the realm, put me on the track of Bloxam; he was sent for on my suggesting that I was willing to pay his day's wages to his foreman for the privilege of asking him a few questions on a private matter. He was a smart enough fellow, though rough of speech and bearing. When I had promised to pay for his information and given him an earnest, he told me that he had made two journeys between Carfax and a house in Piccadilly, and had taken from this house to the latter nine great boxes—'main heavy ones'—with a horse and cart hired by him for this purpose. I asked him if he could tell me the number of the house in Piccadilly, to which he replied:—

'Well, guv'nor, I forgits the number, but it was only a few doors from a big white church or somethink of the kind, not long built. It was a dusty old 'ouse, too, though nothin' to the dustiness of the 'ouse we tooked the bloomin' boxes from.'

'How did you get into the houses if they were both empty?'

'There was the old party what engaged me a-waitin' in the 'ouse at Purfleet. He 'elped me to lift the boxes and put them in the dray. Curse me, but he was the strongest chap I ever struck, an' him a old feller, with a white moustache,[6] one that thin you would think he couldn't throw a shadder.'

How this phrase thrilled through me!

'Why, 'e took up 'is end o' the boxes like they was pounds of tea, and me a-puffin' an' a-blowin' afore I could up-end mine anyhow—an' I'm no chicken, neither.'

4. Again, the British characters have more difficulty communicating with each other than with the Romanian vampire.
5. An industrial and shipping neighborhood in east London.
6. Dracula is presumably between feedings and thus older than when Mina saw him in Hyde Park.

'How did you get into the house in Piccadilly?' I asked.

'He was there too. He must 'a' started off and got there afore me, for when I rung of the bell he kem an' opened the door 'isself an' 'elped me to carry the boxes into the 'all.'

'The whole nine?' I asked.

'Yus; there was five in the first load an' four in the second. It was main dry work, an' I don't so well remember 'ow I got 'ome.' I interrupted him:—

'Were the boxes left in the hall?'

'Yus; it was a big 'all, an' there was nothin' else in it.' I made one more attempt to further matters:—

'You didn't have any key?'

'Never used no key nor nothink. The old gent, he opened the door 'isself an' shut it again when I druv off. I don't remember the last time—but that was the beer.'

'And you can't remember the number of the house?'

'No, sir. But ye needn't have no difficulty about that. It's a 'igh 'un with a stone front with a bow on it, an' 'igh steps up to the door. I know them steps, 'avin 'ad to carry the boxes up with three loafers what come round to earn a copper. The old gent give them shillin's, an' they seein' they got so much, they wanted more; but 'e took one of them by the shoulder and was like to throw 'im down the steps, till the lot of them went away cussin'.' I thought that with this description I could find the house, so, having paid my friend for his information, I started off for Piccadilly. I had gained a new painful experience: the Count could, it was evident, handle the earth-boxes himself. If so, time was precious; for, now that he had achieved a certain amount of distribution, he could, by choosing his own time, complete the task unobserved. At Piccadilly Circus[7] I discharged my cab, and walked westward; beyond the Junior Constitutional[8] I came across the house described, and was satisfied that this was the next of the lairs arranged by Dracula. The house looked as though it had been long untenanted. The windows were encrusted with dust, and the shutters were up. All the framework was black with time, and from the iron the paint had mostly scaled away. It was evident that up to lately there had been a large notice-board in front of the balcony; it had, however, been roughly torn away, the uprights which had supported it still remaining. Behind the rails of the balcony I saw there were some loose boards, whose raw edges looked white. I would have given a good deal to have been able to see the notice-board intact, as it would, perhaps, have given some clue to the ownership of the house. I remembered my experience of the investigation and purchase of Carfax, and I could not but feel that if I

---

7. In the 1890s, the center of London's theater, hotel, club, and shopping districts, where Regent Street, Shaftesbury Avenue, Haymarket, Coventry Street, and Piccadilly come together.
8. A conservative club.

could find the former owner there might be some means discovered of gaining access to the house.

There was at present nothing to be learned from the Piccadilly side, and nothing could be done; so I went round to the back to see if anything could be gathered from this quarter. The mews[9] were active, the Piccadilly houses being mostly in occupation. I asked one or two of the grooms and helpers whom I saw round if they could tell me anything about the empty house. One of them said that he heard it had lately been taken, but he couldn't say from whom. He told me, however, that up to very lately there had been a notice-board of 'For sale' up, and that perhaps Mitchell, Sons, & Candy, the house agents, could tell me something, as he thought he remembered seeing the name of that firm on the board. I did not wish to seem too eager, or to let my informant know or guess too much, so, thanking him in the usual manner, I strolled away. It was now growing dusk, and the autumn night was closing in, so I did not lose any time. Having learned the address of Mitchell, Sons, & Candy from a directory at the Berkeley, I was soon at their office in Sackville Street.[1]

The gentleman who saw me was particularly suave in manner, but uncommunicative in equal proportion. Having once told me that the Piccadilly house—which throughout our interview he called a 'mansion'—was sold, he considered my business as concluded. When I asked who had purchased it, he opened his eyes a thought wider, and paused a few seconds before replying:—

'It is sold, sir.'

'Pardon me,' I said, with equal politeness, 'but I have a special reason for wishing to know who purchased it.'

Again he paused longer, and raised his eyebrows still more. 'It is sold, sir,' was again his laconic reply.

'Surely,' I said, 'you do not mind letting me know so much.'

'But I do mind,' he answered. 'The affairs of their clients are absolutely safe in the hands of Mitchell, Sons, & Candy.' This was manifestly a prig of the first water, and there was no use arguing with him. I thought I had best meet him on his own ground, so I said:—

'Your clients, sir, are happy in having so resolute a guardian of their confidence. I am myself a professional man.' Here I handed him my card. 'In this instance I am not prompted by curiosity; I act on the part of Lord Godalming,[2] who wishes to know something of the property which was, he understood, lately for sale.' These words put a different complexion on affairs. He said:—

'I would like to oblige you if I could, Mr Harker, and especially would I like to oblige his lordship. We once carried out a small matter

9. An alley or open yard to accommodate horses and carriages.
1. Just west of Piccadilly Circus.
2. Arthur's inherited title is far more influential than Jonathan's professional achievements.

of renting some chambers for him when he was the Honourable Arthur Holmwood. If you will let me have his lordship's address I will consult the House on the subject, and will, in any case, communicate with his lordship by tonight's post. It will be a pleasure if we can so far deviate from our rules as to give the required information to his lordship.'

I wanted to secure a friend, and not to make an enemy, so I thanked him, gave the address at Dr Seward's, and came away. It was now dark, and I was tired and hungry. I got a cup of tea at the Aërated Bread Company[3] and came down to Purfleet by the next train.

I found all the others at home. Mina was looking tired and pale, but she made a gallant effort to be bright and cheerful; it wrung my heart to think that I had had to keep anything from her and so caused her inquietude. Thank God, this will be the last night of her looking on at our conferences, and feeling the sting of our not showing our confidence. It took all my courage to hold to the wise resolution of keeping her out of our grim task. She seems somehow more reconciled; or else the very subject seems to have become repugnant to her, for when any accidental allusion is made she actually shudders. I am glad we made our resolution in time, as with such a feeling as this, our growing knowledge would be torture to her.

I could not tell the others of the day's discovery till we were alone; so after dinner—followed by a little music to save appearances even amongst ourselves—I took Mina to her room and left her to go to bed. The dear girl was more affectionate with me than ever, and clung to me as though she would detain me; but there was much to be talked of and I came away. Thank God, the ceasing of telling things had made no difference between us.

When I came down again I found the others all gathered round the fire in the study. In the train I had written my diary so far, and simply read it off to them as the best means of letting them get abreast of my own information; when I had finished Van Helsing said:—

'This has been a great day's work, friend Jonathan. Doubtless we are on the track of the missing boxes. If we find them all in that house, then our work is near the end. But if there be some missing, we must search until we find them. Then shall we make our final *coup,* and hunt the wretch to his real death.' We all sat silent awhile and all at once Mr Morris spoke:—

'Say! how are we going to get into that house?'

'We got into the other' answered Lord Godalming quickly.

'But, Art, this is different. We broke house at Carfax, but we had night and a walled park to protect us. It will be a mighty different thing to commit burglary in Piccadilly, either by day or night. I confess I don't see how we are going to get in unless that agency duck can find

3. This chain of tea shops is still serving in the 1990s.

us a key of some sort; perhaps we shall know when you get his letter in the morning.' Lord Godalming's brows contracted, and he stood up and walked about the room. By-and-by he stopped and said, turning from one to another of us:—

'Quincey's head is level. This burglary business is getting serious; we got off once all right; but we have now a rare job on hand—unless we can find the Count's key basket.'

As nothing could well be done before morning, and as it would be at least advisable to wait till Lord Godalming should hear from Mitchell's, we decided not to take any active step before breakfast time. For a good while we sat and smoked, discussing the matter in its various lights and bearings; I took the opportunity of bringing this diary right up to the moment. I am very sleepy and shall go to bed . . .

Just a line. Mina sleeps soundly and her breathing is regular. Her forehead is puckered up into little wrinkles, as though she thinks even in her sleep. She is still too pale, but does not look so haggard as she did this morning. Tomorrow will, I hope, mend all this; she will be herself at home in Exeter. Oh, but I am sleepy!

Dr Seward's Diary

1 October.—I am puzzled about Renfield. His moods change so rapidly that I find it difficult to keep touch of them, and as they always mean something more than his own well-being, they form a more than interesting study. This morning, when I went to see him after his repulse of Van Helsing, his manner was that of a man commanding destiny. He was, in fact, commanding destiny—subjectively. He did not really care for any of the things of mere earth; he was in the clouds and looked down on all the weaknesses and wants of us poor mortals. I thought I would improve the occasion and learn something, so I asked him:—

'What about the flies these times?' He smiled on me in quite a superior sort of way—such a smile as would have become the face of Malvolio[4]—as he answered me:—

'The fly, my dear sir, has one striking feature: its wings are typical of the aerial powers of the psychic faculties. The ancients did well when they typified the soul as a butterfly!'[5]

I thought I would push his analogy to its utmost logically, so I said quickly:—

'Oh, it is a soul you are after now, is it?' His madness foiled his reason, and a puzzled look spread over his face as, shaking his head with a decision which I had but seldom seen in him, he said:—

---

4. In Shakespeare's *Twelfth Night*, Olivia's pompous and presumptuous steward. Victimized by a practical joke, Malvolio woos Olivia by grinning fatuously at her. The Lyceum performed *Twelfth Night* in 1884.

5. The word *psyche* means, in its original Greek, both *spirit* or *soul* and *butterfly*.

'Oh no, oh no! I want no souls. Life is all I want.' Here he brightened up; 'I am pretty indifferent about it at present. Life is all right; I have all I want. You must get a new patient, doctor, if you wish to study zoophagy!'

This puzzled me a little, so I drew him on:—

'Then you command life; you are a god I suppose?' He smiled with an ineffably benign superiority.

'Oh no! Far be it from me to arrogate to myself the attributes of the Deity. I am not even concerned in His especially spiritual doings. If I may state my intellectual position I am, so far as concerns things purely terrestrial, somewhat in the position which Enoch[6] occupied spiritually!' This was a poser to me. I could not at the moment recall Enoch's appositeness; so I had to ask a simple question, though I felt that by so doing I was lowering myself in the eyes of the lunatic:—

'And why with Enoch?'

'Because he walked with God.' I could not see the analogy, but did not like to admit it; so I harked back to what he had denied:—

'So you don't care about life and you don't want souls. Why not?' I put my question quickly and somewhat sternly, on purpose to disconcert him. The effort succeeded; for an instant he unconsciously relapsed into his old servile manner, bent low before me, and actually fawned upon me as he replied:—

'I don't want any souls, indeed, indeed! I don't. I couldn't use them if I had them; they would be no manner of use to me. I couldn't eat them or—' he suddenly stopped and the old cunning look spread over his face, like a wind-sweep on the surface of the water. 'And doctor, as to life, what is it after all? When you've got all you require, and you know that you will never want, that is all. I have friends—good friends—like you Dr Seward;' this was said with a leer of inexpressible cunning, 'I know that I shall never lack the means of life!'

I think that through the cloudiness of his insanity he saw some antagonism in me, for he at once fell back on the last refuge of such as he—a dogged silence. After a short time I saw that for the present it was useless to speak to him. He was sulky, and so I came away.

Later in the day he sent for me. Ordinarily I would not have come without special reason, but just at present I am so interested in him that I would gladly make an effort. Besides, I am glad to have anything to help to pass the time. Harker is out, following up clues; and so are Lord Godalming and Quincey. Van Helsing sits in my study poring over the record prepared by the Harkers; he seems to think that by accurate knowledge of all details he will light upon some clue. He does

---

6. "And Enoch walked with God after he begat Methuselah three hundred years, and begat sons and daughters" (Genesis 5.22). Enoch is of a long-lived line according to Genesis: though he himself lived only 365 years, his father, Jared, lived 962 years and his son Methuselah, 969 years. Renfield similarly hopes for "more life" from his god Dracula.

not wish to be disturbed in the work, without cause. I would have taken him with me to see the patient, only I thought that after his last repulse he might not care to go again. There was also another reason: Renfield might not speak so freely before a third person as when he and I were alone.

I found him sitting out in the middle of the floor on his stool, a pose which is generally indicative of some mental energy on his part. When I came in, he said at once, as though the question had been waiting on his lips:—

'What about souls?' It was evident then that my surmise had been correct. Unconscious cerebration was doing its work, even with the lunatic. I determined to have the matter out. 'What about them yourself?' I asked. He did not reply for a moment but looked all round him, and up and down, as though he expected to find some inspiration for an answer.

'I don't want any souls!' he said in a feeble, apologetic way. The matter seemed preying on his mind, and so I determined to use it—to 'be cruel only to be kind.'[7] So I said:—

'You like life, and you want life?'

'Oh yes! but that is all right; you needn't worry about that!'

'But,' I asked, 'how are we to get the life without getting the soul[8] also?' This seemed to puzzle him, so I followed it up:—

'A nice time you'll have some time when you're flying out there, with the souls of thousands of flies and spiders and birds and cats buzzing and twittering and miaowing all round you. You've got their lives, you know, and you must put up with their souls!' Something seemed to affect his imagination, for he put his fingers to his ears and shut his eyes, screwing them up tightly just as a small boy does when his face is being soaped. There was something pathetic in it that touched me; it also gave me a lesson, for it seemed that before me was a child— only a child, though the features were worn, and the stubble on the jaws was white. It was evident that he was undergoing some process of mental disturbance, and, knowing how his past moods had interpreted things seemingly foreign to himself, I thought I would enter into his mind as well as I could and go with him. The first step was to restore confidence, so I asked him, speaking pretty loud so that he would hear me through his closed ears:—

'Would you like some sugar to get your flies round again!' He seemed to wake up all at once, and shook his head. With a laugh he replied:—

'Not much! flies are poor things, after all!' After a pause he added. 'But I don't want their souls buzzing round me, all the same.'

'Or spiders,' I went on.

'Blow spiders! What's the use of spiders? There isn't anything in them

7. *Hamlet* 3.4.178.
8. The boundary between life and soul is a problem for all players in Stoker's materialist tale.

to eat or'—he stopped suddenly, as though reminded of a forbidden topic.

'So, so!' I thought to myself, 'this is the second time he has suddenly stopped at the word "drink"; what does it mean?' Renfield seemed himself aware of having made a lapse, for he hurried on, as though to distract my attention from it:—

'I don't take any stock at all in such matters. "Rats and mice and such small deer"[9] as Shakespeare has it "chicken-feed of the larder" they might be called. I'm past all that sort of nonsense. You might as well ask a man to eat molecules with a pair of chop-sticks, as to try to interest me about the lesser carnivora, when I know of what is before me.'

'I see,' I said. 'You want big things that you can make your teeth meet in? How would you like to breakfast on elephant?'

'What ridiculous nonsense you are talking!' He was getting too wide awake, so I thought I would press him hard. 'I wonder,' I said reflectively, 'what an elephant's soul is like!'

The effect I desired was obtained, for he at once fell from his high-horse and became a child again.

'I don't want an elephant's soul, or, any soul at all!' he said. For a few moments he sat despondently. Suddenly he jumped to his feet, with his eyes blazing and all the signs of intense cerebral excitement. 'To hell with you and your souls!' he shouted. 'Why do you plague me about souls. Haven't I got enough to worry, and pain, and distract me already, without thinking of souls!' He looked so hostile that I thought he was in for another homicidal fit, so I blew my whistle. The instant, however, that I did so he became calm, and said apologetically:—

'Forgive me, Doctor; I forgot myself. You do not need any help. I am so worried in my mind that I am apt to be irritable. If you only knew the problem I have to face, and that I am working out, you would pity, and tolerate, and pardon me. Pray do not put me in a strait-waistcoat. I want to think and I cannot think freely when my body is confined. I am sure you will understand!' He had evidently self-control; so when the attendants came I told them not to mind, and they withdrew. Renfield watched them go; when the door was closed he said, with considerable dignity and sweetness:—

'Dr Seward, you have been very considerate towards me. Believe me that I am very very grateful to you!' I thought it well to leave him in this mood, and so I came away. There is certainly something to ponder over in this man's state. Several points seem to make what the American interviewer calls 'a story', if one could only get them in proper order. Here they are:—

Will not mention 'drinking.'

---

9. Slight misquotation of *King Lear* 3.4.142. The Lyceum staged *King Lear* in 1892.

Fears the thought of being burdened with the 'soul' of anything.

Has no dread of wanting 'life' in the future.

Despises the meaner forms of life altogether, though he dreads being haunted by their souls.

Logically all these things point one way! he has assurance of some kind that he will acquire some higher life. He dreads the conse-quence—the burden of a soul. Then it is a human life he looks to!

And the assurance—?

Merciful God! the Count has been to him, and there is some new scheme of terror afoot!

Later.—I went after my round to Van Helsing and told him my suspicion. He grew very grave; and, after thinking the matter over for a while asked me to take him to Renfield. I did so. As we came to the door we heard the lunatic within singing gaily, as he used to do in the time which now seems so long ago. When we entered we saw with amazement that he had spread out his sugar as of old; the flies, lethargic with the autumn, were beginning to buzz into the room. We tried to make him talk of the subject of our previous conversation, but he would not attend. He went on with his singing, just as though we had not been present. He had got a scrap of paper and was folding it into a note-book. We had to come away as ignorant as we went in.

His is a curious case indeed; we must watch him tonight.

Letter, Mitchell, Sons and Candy to Lord Godalming

1 October.

My Lord,

We are at all times only too happy to meet your wishes. We beg, with regard to the desire of your Lordship, expressed by Mr Harker on your behalf, to supply the following information concerning the sale and purchase of No. 347, Piccadilly. The original vendors are the ex-ecutors of the late Mr Archibald Winter-Suffield. The purchaser is a foreign nobleman, Count De Ville, who effected the purchase himself paying the purchase money in notes 'over the counter,' if your Lordship will pardon us using so vulgar an expression. Beyond this we know nothing whatever of him.

We are, my Lord,

Your Lordship's humble servants,

MITCHELL, SONS & CANDY

Dr Seward's Diary

2 October.—I placed a man in the corridor last night, and told him to make an accurate note of any sound he might hear from Renfield's room, and gave him instructions that if there should be anything strange he was to call me. After dinner, when we had all gathered round the fire in the study—Mrs Harker having gone to bed—we discussed the attempts and discoveries of the day. Harker was the only one who had any result, and we are in great hopes that his clue may be an important one.

Before going to bed I went round to the patient's room and looked in through the observation trap. He was sleeping soundly, and his heart rose and fell with regular respiration.

This morning the man on duty reported to me that a little after midnight he was restless and kept saying his prayers somewhat loudly. I asked him if that was all; he replied that it was all he heard. There was something about his manner so suspicious that I asked him point blank if he had been asleep. He denied sleep, but admitted to having 'dozed' for a while. It is too bad that men cannot be trusted unless they are watched.

Today Harker is out following up his clue, and Art and Quincey are looking after horses. Godalming thinks that it will be well to have horses always in readiness, for when we get the information which we seek there will be no time to lose. We must sterilize all the imported earth between sunrise and sunset; we shall thus catch the Count at his weakest, and without a refuge to fly to. Van Helsing is off to the British Museum looking up some authorities on ancient medicine. The old physicians took account of things which their followers do not accept, and the Professor is searching for witch and demon cures which may be useful to us later.

I sometimes think we must be all mad and that we shall wake to sanity in strait-waistcoats.

Later.—We have met again. We seem at last to be on the track, and our work of tomorrow may be the beginning of the end. I wonder if Renfield's quiet has anything to do with this. His moods have so followed the doings of the Count, that the coming destruction of the monster may be carried to him in some subtle way. If we could only get some hint as to what passed in his mind, between the time of my argument with him today and his resumption of fly-catching, it might afford us a valuable clue. He is now seemingly quiet for a spell . . . Is he?—that wild yell seemed to come from his room . . .

The attendant came bursting into my room and told me that Renfield had somehow met with some accident. He had heard him yell; and when he went to him found him lying on his face on the floor, all covered with blood. I must go at once . . .

Chapter XXI

Dr Seward's Diary

3 October.—Let me put down with exactness all that happened, as well as I can remember it, since last I made an entry. Not a detail that I can recall must be forgotten; in all calmness I must proceed.

When I came to Renfield's room I found him lying on the floor on his left side in a glittering pool of blood. When I went to move him, it became at once apparent that he had received some terrible injuries; there seemed none of that unity of purpose between the parts of the body which marks even lethargic sanity. As the face was exposed I could see that it was horribly bruised, as though it had been beaten against the floor—indeed it was from the face wounds that the pool of blood originated. The attendant who was kneeling beside the body said to me as we turned him over:—

'I think, sir, his back is broken. See, both his right arm and leg and the whole side of his face are paralysed.' How such a thing could have happened puzzled the attendant beyond measure. He seemed quite bewildered, and his brows were gathered in as he said:—

'I can't understand the two things. He could mark his face like that by beating his own head on the ground. I saw a young woman do it once at the Eversfield Asylum before anyone could lay hands on her. And I suppose he might have broke his back by falling out of bed, if he got in an awkward kink. But for the life of me I can't imagine how the two things occurred. If his back was broke, he couldn't beat his head; and if his face was like that before the fall out of bed, there would be marks of it.' I said to him:—

'Go to Dr Van Helsing, and ask him to kindly come here at once. I want him without an instant's delay.' The man ran off, and within a very few minutes the Professor, in his dressing gown and slippers, appeared. When he saw Renfield on the ground, he looked keenly at him a moment and then turned to me. I think he recognized my thought in my eyes, for he said very quietly, manifestly for the ears of the attendant:—

'Ah, a sad accident! He will need very careful watching, and much attention. I shall stay with you myself; but I shall first dress myself. If you will remain I shall in a few minutes join you.'

The patient was now breathing stertorously, and it was easy to see that he had suffered some terrible injury. Van Helsing returned with extraordinary celerity, bearing with him a surgical case. He had evidently been thinking and had his mind made up; for, almost before he looked at the patient, he whispered to me:—

241

'Send the attendant away. We must be alone with him when he becomes conscious, after the operation.' So I said:—

'I think that will do now, Simmons. We have done all that we can at present. You had better go your round, and Dr Van Helsing will operate. Let me know instantly if there be anything unusual anywhere.'

The man withdrew, and we went into a strict examination of the patient. The wounds of the face were superficial; the real injury was a depressed fracture of the skull, extending right up through the motor area. The Professor thought a moment and said:—

'We must reduce the pressure and get back to normal conditions, as far as can be; the rapidity of the suffusion shows the terrible nature of his injury. The whole motor area seems affected. The suffusion of the brain will increase quickly, so we must trephine[1] at once or it may be too late.' As he was speaking there was a soft tapping at the door. I went over and opened it and found in the corridor without, Arthur and Quincey in pyjamas and slippers: the former spoke:—

'I heard your man call up Dr Van Helsing and tell him of an accident. So I woke Quincey, or rather called for him as he was not asleep. Things are moving too quickly and too strangely for sound sleep for any of us these times. I've been thinking that tomorrow night will not see things as they have been. We'll have to look back—and forward a little more than we have done. May we come in?' I nodded, and held the door open till they had entered; then I closed it again. When Quincey saw the attitude and state of the patient, and noted the horrible pool on the floor, he said softly:—

'My God! what has happened to him? Poor, poor devil!' I told him briefly, and added that we expected he would recover consciousness after the operation—for a short time at all events. He went at once and sat down on the edge of the bed, with Godalming beside him; we all watched in patience.

'We shall wait,' said Van Helsing, 'just long enough to fix the best spot for trephining, so that we may most quickly and perfectly remove the blood clot; for it is evident that the haemorrhage is increasing.'

The minutes during which we waited passed with fearful slowness. I had a horrible sinking in my heart, and from Van Helsing's face I gathered that he felt some fear or apprehension as to what was to come. I dreaded the words that Renfield might speak. I was positively afraid to think; but the conviction of what was coming was on me, as I have read of men who have heard the death-watch.[2] The poor man's breathing came in uncertain gasps. Each instant he seemed as though he would open his eyes and speak; but then would follow a prolonged

---

1. That is, perform an ancient operation in which a circular piece of bone is cut out of the skull to relieve pressure on the brain.
2. In times of plague, the death-watch came through the streets crying "Bring out your dead!"

stertorous breath, and he would relapse into a more fixed insensibility. Inured as I was to sick beds and death, this suspense grew, and grew upon me. I could almost hear the beating of my own heart; and the blood surging through my temples sounded like blows from a hammer. The silence finally became agonizing. I looked at my companions, one after another, and saw from their flushed faces and damp brows that they were enduring equal torture. There was a nervous suspense over us all, as though overhead some dread bell would peal out powerfully when we should least expect it.

At last there came a time when it was evident that the patient was sinking fast; he might die at any moment. I looked up at the Professor and caught his eyes fixed on mine. His face was sternly set as he spoke:—

'There is no time to lose. His words may be worth many lives; I have been thinking so, as I stood here. It may be there is a soul at stake! We shall operate just above the ear.'

Without another word he made the operation. For a few moments the breathing continued to be stertorous. Then there came a breath so prolonged that it seemed as though it would tear open his chest. Suddenly his eyes opened, and became fixed in a wild, helpless stare. This was continued for a few moments; then it softened into a glad surprise, and from the lips came a sigh of relief. He moved convulsively, and as he did so, said:—

'I'll be quiet, Doctor. Tell them to take off the strait-waistcoat. I have had a terrible dream, and it has left me so weak that I cannot move. What's wrong with my face? It feels all swollen, and it smarts dreadfully.' He tried to turn his head; but even with the effort his eyes seemed to grow glassy again, so I gently put it back. Then Van Helsing said in a quiet grave tone:—

'Tell us your dream, Mr Renfield.' As he heard the voice his face brightened through its mutilation, and he said:—

'That is Dr Van Helsing. How good it is of you to be here. Give me some water, my lips are dry; and I shall try to tell you. I dreamed'— he stopped and seemed fainting, I called quietly to Quincey—'The brandy—it is in my study—quick!' He flew and returned with a glass, the decanter of brandy and a carafe of water. We moistened the parched lips, and the patient quickly revived. It seemed however that his poor injured brain had been working in the interval, for, when he was quite conscious, he looked at me piercingly with an agonized confusion which I shall never forget, and said:—

'I must not deceive myself; it was no dream, but all a grim reality.' Then his eyes roved round the room; as they caught sight of the two figures sitting patiently on the edge of the bed he went on:—

'If I were not sure already, I would know from them.' For an instant his eyes closed—not with pain or sleep but voluntarily, as though he were bringing all his faculties to bear; when he opened them he said, hurriedly, and with more energy than he had yet displayed:—

'Quick, Doctor, quick. I am dying! I feel that I have but a few minutes; and then I must go back to death—or worse! Wet my lips with brandy again. I have something that I must say before I die; or before my poor crushed brain dies anyhow. Thank you! It was that night after you left me, when I implored you to let me go away. I couldn't speak then, for I felt my tongue was tied; but I was as sane then, except in that way, as I am now. I was in an agony of despair for a long time after you left me; it seemed hours. Then there came a sudden peace to me. My brain seemed to become cool again, and I realized where I was. I heard the dogs bark behind our house, but not where He was!' As he spoke Van Helsing's eyes never blinked, but his hand came out and met mine and gripped it hard. He did not, however, betray himself; he nodded slightly, and said: 'Go on,' in a low voice. Renfield proceeded:—

'He came up to the window in the mist, as I had seen him often before; but he was solid then—not a ghost, and his eyes were fierce like a man's when angry. He was laughing with his red mouth; the sharp white teeth glinted in the moonlight when he turned to look back over the belt of trees, to where the dogs were barking. I wouldn't ask him to come in at first, though I knew he wanted to—just as he had wanted all along.[3] Then he began promising me things—not in words but by doing them.' He was interrupted by a word from the Professor:—

'How?'

'By making them happen; just as he used to send in the flies when the sun was shining. Great big fat ones with steel and sapphire on their wings; and big moths, in the night, with skull and cross-bones on their backs.' Van Helsing nodded to him as he whispered to me unconsciously:—

'The *Acherontia atropos of the Sphinges*—what you call the "Death's-head moth!"' The patient went on without stopping.

'Then he began to whisper: "Rats, rats, rats! Hundreds, thousands, millions of them, and every one a life; and dogs to eat them, and cats too. All lives! all red blood, with years of life in it; and not merely buzzing flies!" I laughed at him, for I wanted to see what he could do. Then the dogs howled, away beyond the dark trees in His house. He beckoned me to the window. I got up and looked out, and He raised his hands, and seemed to call out without using any words. A dark mass spread over the grass, coming on like the shape of a flame of fire; and then He moved the mist to the right and left, and I could see that there

---

3. Presumably to attack Mina. Dracula cannot enter a house for the first time unless one of its inhabitants invites him.

were thousands of rats with their eyes blazing red—like His, only smaller. He held up his hand, and they all stopped; and I thought He seemed to be saying: "All these lives will I give you, ay, and many more and greater, through countless ages, if you will fall down and worship me!" And then a red cloud, like the colour of blood, seemed to close over my eyes; and before I knew what I was doing, I found myself opening the sash and saying to Him: "Come in, Lord and Master!" The rats were all gone, but He slid into the room through the sash, though it was only open an inch wide—just as the Moon herself has often come in through the tiniest crack, and has stood before me in all her size and splendour.'

His voice was weaker, so I moistened his lips with the brandy again, and he continued; but it seemed as though his memory had gone on working in the interval for his story was further advanced. I was about to call him back to the point, but Van Helsing whispered to me: 'Let him go on. Do not interrupt him; he cannot go back, and maybe could not proceed at all if once he lost the thread of his thought.' He proceeded:—

'All day I waited to hear from him, but he did not send me anything, not even a blow-fly, and when the moon got up I was pretty angry with him. When he slid in through the window, though it was shut, and did not even knock, I got mad with him. He sneered at me, and his white face looked out of the mist with his red eyes gleaming, and he went on as though he owned the whole place, and I was no one. He didn't even smell the same as he went by me. I couldn't hold him. I thought that, somehow, Mrs Harker had come into the room.'

The two men sitting on the bed stood up and came over standing behind him so that he could not see them, but where they could hear better. They were both silent, but the Professor started and quivered; his face, however, grew grimmer and sterner still. Renfield went on without noticing:—

'When Mrs Harker came in to see me this afternoon she wasn't the same; it was like tea after the teapot had been watered.' Here we all moved, but no one said a word; he went on:—

'I didn't know that she was here till she spoke; and she didn't look the same. I don't care for the pale people; I like them with lots of blood in them, and hers had all seemed to have run out. I didn't think of it at the time; but when she went away I began to think, and it made me mad to know that He had been taking the life out of her.' I could feel that the rest quivered, as I did; but we remained otherwise still. 'So when He came tonight I was ready for Him. I saw the mist stealing in, and I grabbed it tight. I had heard that madmen have unnatural strength; and as I knew I was a madman—at times anyhow—I resolved to use my power. Ay, and He felt it too, for He had to come out of the mist to struggle with me. I held tight;[4] and I thought I was going to win, for I didn't mean Him to take any more of her life, till I saw His eyes. They burned into me, and my strength became like water. He slipped through it, and when I tried to cling to Him, He raised me up and flung me down. There was a red cloud before me, and a noise like thunder, and the mist seemed to steal away under the door.' His voice was becoming fainter and his breath more stertorous. Van Helsing stood up instinctively.

'We know the worst now,' he said. 'He is here, and we know his purpose. It may not be too late. Let us be armed—the same as we were the other night, but lose no time; there is not an instant to spare.' There was no need to put our fear, nay our conviction, into words—we shared them in common. We all hurried[5] and took from our rooms the same things that we had when we entered the Count's house. The Professor had his ready, and as we met in the corridor he pointed to them significantly as he said:—

'They never leave me; and they shall not till this unhappy business is over. Be wise also, my friends. It is no common enemy that we deal with. Alas! alas! that that dear Madam Mina should suffer.' He stopped; his voice was breaking, and I do not know if rage or terror predominated in my own heart.

Outside the Harkers' door we paused. Art and Quincey held back, and the latter said:—

'Should we disturb her?'

'We must,' said Van Helsing grimly. 'If the door be locked, I shall break it in.'

'May it not frighten her terribly? It is unusual to break into a lady's room!' Van Helsing said solemnly—

'You are always right; but this is life and death. All chambers are alike to the doctor; and even were they not they are all as one to me tonight. Friend John, when I turn the handle, if the door does not open, do you put your shoulder down and shove; and you too, my friends. Now!'

He turned the handle as he spoke, but the door did not yield. We threw ourselves against it; with a crash it burst open, and we almost fell headlong into the room. The Professor did actually fall, and I saw across him as he gathered himself up from hands and knees. What I saw appalled me. I felt my hair rise like bristles on the back of my neck, and my heart seemed to stand still.

The moonlight was so bright that through the thick yellow blind the room was light enough to see. On the bed beside the window lay Jonathan Harker, his face flushed and breathing heavily as though in a stupor. Kneeling on the near edge of the bed facing outwards was the

4. In Genesis 32, Jacob similarly wrestles with his god.
5. They leave the dying Renfield alone, just as Dracula had done.

white-clad figure of his wife. By her side stood a tall, thin man, clad in black. His face was turned from us, but the instant we saw we all recognized the Count—in every way, even to the scar on his forehead. With his left hand he held both Mrs Harker's hands, keeping them away with her arms at full tension; his right hand gripped her by the back of the neck, forcing her face down on his bosom. Her white nightdress was smeared with blood, and a thin stream trickled down the man's bare breast which was shown by his torn-open dress. The attitude of the two had a terrible resemblance to a child forcing a kitten's nose into a saucer of milk to compel it to drink. As we burst into the room, the Count turned his face, and the hellish look that I had heard described seemed to leap into it. His eyes flamed red with devilish passion; the great nostrils of the white aquiline nose opened wide and quivered at the edge; and the white sharp teeth, behind the full lips of the blood-dripping mouth, champed together like those of a wild beast. With a wrench, which threw his victim back upon the bed as though hurled from a height, he turned and sprang at us. But by this time the Professor had gained his feet, and was holding towards him the envelope which contained the Sacred Wafer. The Count suddenly stopped, just as poor Lucy had done outside the tomb, and cowered back. Further and further back he cowered, as we, lifting our crucifixes, advanced. The moonlight suddenly failed, as a great black cloud sailed across the sky; and when the gaslight sprang up under Quincey's match, we saw nothing but a faint vapour. This, as we looked, trailed under the door, which with the recoil from its bursting open, had swung back to its old position. Van Helsing, Art, and I moved forward to Mrs Harker, who by this time had drawn her breath and with it had given a scream so wild, so ear-piercing, so despairing that it seems to me now that it will ring in my ears till my dying day. For a few seconds she lay in her helpless attitude and disarray. Her face was ghastly, with a pallor which was accentuated by the blood which smeared her lips and cheeks and chin; from her throat trickled a thin stream of blood. Her eyes were mad with terror. Then she put before her face her poor crushed hands, which bore on their whiteness the red mark of the Count's terrible grip, and from behind them came a low desolate wail which made the terrible scream seem only the quick expression of an endless grief. Van Helsing stepped forward and drew the coverlet gently over her body, whilst Art, after looking at her face for an instant despairingly, ran out of the room. Van Helsing whispered to me:—

'Jonathan is in a stupor such as we know the Vampire can produce. We can do nothing with poor Madam Mina for a few moments till she recovers herself; I must wake him!' He dipped the end of a towel in cold water and with it began to flick him on the face, his wife all the while holding her face between her hands and sobbing in a way that was heart-breaking to hear. I raised the blind, and looked out of the window. There was much moonshine; and as I looked I could see Quincey Morris run across the lawn and hide himself in the shadow of a great yew tree. It puzzled me to think why he was doing this; but at the instant I heard Harker's quick exclamation as he woke to partial consciousness, and turned to the bed. On his face, as there might well be, was a look of wild amazement. He seemed dazed for a few seconds, and then full consciousness seemed to burst upon him all at once, and he started up. His wife was aroused by the quick movement, and turned to him with her arms stretched out, as though to embrace him; instantly, however, she drew them in again, and putting her elbows together, held her hands before her face, and shuddered till the bed beneath her shook.

'In God's name what does this mean?' Harker cried out, 'Dr Seward, Dr Van Helsing, what is it? What has happened? What is wrong? Mina, dear, what is it? What does that blood mean? My God, my God! has it come to this!' and, raising himself to his knees, he beat his hands wildly together. 'Good God help us! help her! oh, help her!' With a quick movement he jumped from bed, and began to pull on his clothes,—all the man in him awake at the need for instant exertion. 'What has happened? Tell me all about it?' he cried without pausing. 'Dr Van Helsing, you love Mina, I know. Oh, do something to save her. It cannot have gone too far yet. Guard her while I look for *him!*' His wife, through her terror and horror and distress, saw some sure danger to him; instantly forgetting her own grief, she seized hold of him and cried out:—

'No! no! Jonathan, you must not leave me. I have suffered enough tonight, God knows, without the dread of his harming you. You must stay with me. Stay with these friends who will watch over you!' Her expression became frantic as she spoke; and, he yielding to her, she pulled him down sitting on the bed side, and clung to him fiercely.

Van Helsing and I tried to calm them both. The Professor held up his little golden crucifix, and said with wonderful calmness:—

'Do not fear, my dear. We are here; and whilst this is close to you no foul thing can approach. You are safe for tonight; and we must be calm and take counsel together.' She shuddered and was silent, holding down her head on her husband's breast. When she raised it, his white night-robe was stained with blood where her lips had touched, and where the thin open wound in her neck had sent forth drops. The instant she saw it she drew back, with a low wail, and whispered, amidst choking sobs:—

'Unclean, unclean![6] I must touch him or kiss him no more. Oh, that

6. "And the leper in whom the plague is, his clothes shall be rent, and his head bare, and he shall put a covering upon his upper lip, and shall cry, Unclean, unclean" (Leviticus 13.45).

it should be that it is I who am now his worst enemy, and whom he may have most cause to fear.' To this he spoke out resolutely:—

'Nonsense, Mina. It is a shame to me to hear such a word. I would not hear it of you; and I shall not hear it from you. May God judge me by my deserts, and punish me with more bitter suffering than even this hour, if by any act or will of mine anything ever come between us!' He put out his arms and folded her to his breast; and for a while she lay there sobbing. He looked at us over her bowed head, with eyes that blinked damply above his quivering nostrils; his mouth was set as steel. After a while her sobs became less frequent and more faint, and then he said to me, speaking with a studied calmness which I felt tried his nervous power to the utmost:—

'And now, Dr Seward, tell me all about it. Too well I know the broad fact; tell me all that has been.' I told him exactly what had happened, and he listened with seeming impassiveness; but his nostrils twitched and his eyes blazed as I told how the ruthless hands of the Count had held his wife in that terrible and horrid position, with her mouth to the open wound in his breast. It interested me, even at that moment, to see, that, whilst the face of white set passion worked convulsively over the bowed head, the hands tenderly and lovingly stroked the ruffled hair. Just as I had finished, Quincey and Godalming knocked at the door. They entered in obedience to our summons. Van Helsing looked at me questioningly. I understood him to mean if we were to take advantage of their coming to divert if possible the thoughts of the unhappy husband and wife from each other and from themselves; so on nodding acquiescence to him he asked them what they had seen or done. To which Lord Godalming answered:—

'I could not see him anywhere in the passage, or in any of our rooms. I looked in the study but, though he had been there, he had gone. He had however—' He stopped suddenly looking at the poor drooping figure on the bed. Van Helsing said gravely:—

'Go on friend Arthur. We want here no more concealments. Our hope now is in knowing all. Tell freely!' So Art went on:—

'He had been there, and though it could only have been for a few seconds, he made rare hay of the place. All the manuscript had been burned, and the blue flames were flickering amongst the white ashes; the cylinders of your phonograph too were thrown on the fire, and the wax had helped the flames.'[7] Here I interrupted. 'Thank God there is the other copy in the safe!' His face lit for a moment, but fell again as he went on: 'I ran down stairs then, but could see no sign of him. I looked into Renfield's room; but there was no trace there except—!' Again he paused. 'Go on,' said Harker hoarsely; so he bowed his head

---

7. Despite the transcript copies, the destruction of the primary documents is a severe blow, for there is now no proof of Dracula's nature and no justification for hunting him.

and moistening his lips with his tongue, added: 'except that the poor fellow is dead.' Mrs Harker raised her head, looking from one to the other of us as she said solemnly:—

'God's will be done!' I could not but feel that Art was keeping back something; but, as I took it that it was with a purpose, I said nothing. Van Helsing turned to Morris and asked:—

'And you, friend Quincey, have you any to tell?'

'A little,' he answered. 'It may be much eventually, but at present I can't say. I thought it well to know if possible where the Count would go when he left the house. I did not see him; but I saw a bat rise from Renfield's window, and flap westward. I expected to see him in some shape go back to Carfax; but he evidently sought some other lair. He will not be back tonight; for the sky is reddening in the east, and the dawn is close. We must work tomorrow!'

He said the latter words through his shut teeth. For a space of perhaps a couple of minutes there was silence, and I could fancy that I could hear the sound of our hearts beating; then Van Helsing said, placing his hand very tenderly on Mrs Harker's head:—

'And now, Madam Mina—poor, dear, dear Madam Mina—tell us exactly what happened. God knows that I do not want that you be pained; but it is need that we know all. For now more than ever has all work to be done quick and sharp, and in deadly earnest. The day is close to us that must end all, if it may so be; and now is the chance that we may live and learn.'

The poor, dear lady shivered, and I could see the tension of her nerves as she clasped her husband closer to her and bent her head lower and lower still on his breast. Then she raised her head proudly, and held out one hand to Van Helsing who took it in his, and, after stooping and kissing it reverently, held it fast. The other hand was locked in that of her husband, who held his other arm thrown round her protectingly. After a pause in which she was evidently ordering her thoughts, she began:—

'I took the sleeping draught which you had so kindly given me, but for a long time it did not act. I seemed to become more wakeful, and myriads of horrible fancies began to crowd in upon my mind—all of them connected with death, and vampires; with blood, and pain, and trouble.' Her husband involuntarily groaned as she turned to him and said lovingly: 'Do not fret, dear. You must be brave and strong, and help me through the horrible task. If you only knew what an effort it is to me to tell of this fearful thing at all, you would understand how much I need your help. Well, I saw I must try to help the medicine to its work with my will, if it was to do me any good, so I resolutely set myself to sleep. Sure enough sleep must soon have come to me, for I remember no more. Jonathan coming in had not waked me, for he lay by my side when next I remember. There was in the room the same thin white mist that I had before noticed. But I forget now if you know of this; you will find it in my diary which I shall show you later. I felt the same vague terror which had come to me before, and the same sense of some presence. I turned to wake Jonathan, but found that he slept so soundly that it seemed as if it was he who had taken the sleeping draught, and not I. I tried, but I could not wake him. This caused me a great fear, and I looked around terrified. Then indeed, my heart sank within me: beside the bed, as if he had stepped out of the mist—or rather as if the mist had turned into his figure, for it had entirely disappeared—stood a tall, thin man, all in black. I knew him at once from the description of the others.[8] The waxen face; the high aquiline nose, on which the light fell in a thin white line; the parted red lips, with the sharp white teeth showing between; and the red eyes that I had seemed to see in the sunset on the windows of St Mary's Church at Whitby. I knew, too, the red scar on his forehead where Jonathan had struck him. For an instant my heart stood still, and I would have screamed out, only that I was paralysed. In the pause he spoke in a sort of keen, cutting, whisper, pointing as he spoke to Jonathan:—

' "Silence! If you make a sound I shall take him and dash his brains out before your very eyes." I was appalled and was too bewildered to do or say anything. With a mocking smile, he placed one hand upon my shoulder and, holding me tight, bared my throat with the other, saying as he did so: "First, a little refreshment to reward my exertions. You may as well be quiet; it is not the first time, or the second, that your veins have appeased my thirst!" I was bewildered, and, strangely enough, I did not want to hinder him. I suppose it is a part of the horrible curse that such is, when his touch is on his victim. And oh, my God, my God, pity me! He placed his reeking lips upon my throat!' Her husband groaned again. She clasped his hand harder, and looked at him pityingly, as if he were the injured one, and went on:—

'I felt my strength fading away, and I was in a half swoon. How long this horrible thing lasted I know not; but it seemed that a long time must have passed before he took his foul, awful, sneering mouth away. I saw it drip with the fresh blood!' The remembrance seemed for a while to overpower her, and she drooped and would have sunk down but for her husband's sustaining arm. With a great effort she recovered herself and went on:—

'Then he spoke to me mockingly, "And so you, like the others, would play your brains against mine. You would help these men to hunt me and frustrate me in my designs! You know now, and they know in part already, and will know in full before long, what it is to cross my path. They should have kept their energies for use closer to home. Whilst they played wits against me—against me who commanded nations, and

---

8. Does Mina forget that she has seen Dracula in Hyde Park, or has he changed radically since then?

intrigued for them, and fought for them, hundreds of years before they were born—I was countermining them. And you, their best beloved one, are now to me, flesh of my flesh;[9] blood of my blood; kin of my kin; my bountiful wine-press for a while; and shall be later on my companion and my helper.[1] You shall be avenged in turn; for not one of them but shall minister to your needs. But as yet you are to be punished for what you have done. You have aided in thwarting me; now you shall come to my call. When my brain says 'Come!' to you, you shall cross land or sea to do my bidding; and to that end this!" With that he pulled open his shirt, and with his long sharp nails opened a vein in his breast. When the blood began to spurt out, he took my hands in one of his, holding them tight, and with the other seized my neck and pressed my mouth to the wound, so that I must either suffocate or swallow some of the—Oh my God! my God! what have I done? What have I done to deserve such a fate, I who have tried to walk in meekness and righteousness all my days. God pity me! Look down on a poor soul in worse than mortal peril; and in mercy pity those to whom she is dear!' Then she began to rub her lips as though to cleanse them from pollution.

As she was telling her terrible story, the eastern sky began to quicken, and everything became more and more clear. Harker was still and quiet; but over his face, as the awful narrative went on, came a grey look which deepened and deepened in the morning light, till when the first red streak of the coming dawn shot up, the flesh stood darkly out against the whitening hair.

We have arranged that one of us is to stay within call of the unhappy pair till we can meet together and arrange about taking action.

Of this I am sure: the sun rises today on no more miserable house in all the great round of its daily course.

Chapter XXII

Jonathan Harker's Journal

3 *October.*—As I must do something or go mad, I write this diary. It is now six o'clock, and we are to meet in the study in half an hour and take something to eat; for Dr Van Helsing and Dr Seward are agreed that if we do not eat we cannot work our best. Our best will be, God

---

9. Cf. the biblical creation of woman: "And Adam said, This is now bone of my bones, and flesh of my flesh: she shall be called Woman, because she was taken out of Man" (Genesis 2.23).

1. Dracula's speech is the inspiration for romantic vows of immortal love in such films as John Badham's and Francis Ford Coppola's adaptations of *Dracula*, as well as in Anne Rice's series of novels, *The Vampire Chronicles*. Stoker's Victorian novel is far more brutal.

knows, required today. I must keep writing at every chance, for I dare not stop to think. All, big and little, must go down; perhaps at the end the little things may teach us most. The teaching, big or little, could not have landed Mina or me anywhere worse than we are today. However, we must trust and hope. Poor Mina told me just now, with the tears running down her dear cheeks, that it is in trouble and trial that our faith is tested—that we must keep on trusting; and that God will aid us up to the end. The end! oh my God! what end? . . . To work! To work!

When Dr Van Helsing and Dr Seward had come back from seeing poor Renfield, we went gravely into what was to be done. First, Dr Seward told us that when he and Dr Van Helsing had gone down to the room below they had found Renfield lying on the floor, all in a heap. His face was all bruised and crushed in, and the bones of the neck were broken.

Dr Seward asked the attendant who was on duty in the passage if he had heard anything. He said that he had been sitting down—he confessed to half dozing—when he heard loud voices in the room, and then Renfield had called out loudly several times, 'God! God! God!' After that there was a sound of falling, and when he entered the room he found him lying on the floor, face down, just as the doctors had seen him. Van Helsing asked if he had heard 'voices' or 'a voice', and he said he could not say; that at first it had seemed to him as if there were two, but as there was no one in the room it could have been only one. He could swear to it, if required, that the word 'God' was spoken by the patient. Dr Seward said to us, when we were alone, that he did not wish to go into the matter; the question of an inquest had to be considered, and it would never do to put forward the truth, as no one would believe it. As it was, he thought that on the attendant's evidence he could give a certificate of death by misadventure in falling from bed. In case the coroner should demand it, there would be a formal inquest, necessarily to the same result.

When the question began to be discussed as to what should be our next step, the very first thing we decided was that Mina should be in full confidence; that nothing of any sort—no matter how painful—should be kept from her. She herself agreed as to its wisdom, and it was pitiful to see her so brave and yet so sorrowful, and in such a depth of despair. 'There must be no more concealment,' she said, 'Alas! we have had too much already. And besides there is nothing in all the world that can give me more pain that I have already endured—than I suffer now! Whatever may happen, it must be of new hope or of new courage to me!' Van Helsing was, looking at her fixedly as she spoke, and said, suddenly but quietly:—

'But dear Madam Mina are you not afraid; not for yourself, but for others from yourself, after what has happened?' Her face grew set in its lines, but her eyes shone with the devotion of a martyr as she answered:—

'Ah no! for my mind is made up!'

'To what?' he asked gently, whilst we were all very still; for each in our own way we had a sort of vague idea of what she meant. Her answer came with direct simplicity, as though she were simply stating a fact:—

'Because if I find in myself—and I shall watch keenly for it—a sign of harm to any that I love, I shall die!'

'You would not kill yourself?' he asked, hoarsely.

'I would; if there were no friend who loved me, who would save me such a pain, and so desperate an effort!' She looked at him meaningly as she spoke. He was sitting down; but now he rose and came close to her and put his hand on her head as he said solemnly:

'My child, there is such an one if it were for your good. For myself I could hold it in my account with God to find such an euthanasia for you, even at this moment if it were best. Nay, were it safe! But my child—' for a moment he seemed choked, and a great sob rose in his throat; he gulped it down and went on:—

'There are here some who would stand between you and death. You must not die. You must not die by any hand; but least of all by your own. Until the other, who has fouled your sweet life, is true dead you must not die; for if he is still with the quick Un-dead, your death would make you even as he is. No, you must live! You must struggle and strive to live, though death would seem a boon unspeakable. You must fight Death himself, though he come to you in pain or in joy; by the day, or the night; in safety or in peril! On your living soul I charge you that you do not die—nay nor think of death—till this great evil be past.' The poor dear grew white as death, and shook and shivered, as I have seen a quicksand shake and shiver at the incoming of the tide. We were all silent; we could not nothing. At length she grew more calm and turning to him said, sweetly, but oh! so sorrowfully, as she held out her hand:—

'I promise you, my dear friend, that if God will let me live, I shall strive to do so; till, if it may be in His good time, this horror may have passed away from me.' She was so good and brave that we all felt that our hearts were strengthened to work and endure for her, and we began to discuss what we were to do. I told her that she was to have all the papers in the safe, and all the papers or diaries and phonographs we might hereafter use; and was to keep the record as she had done before. She was pleased with the prospect of anything to do—if 'pleased' could be used in connection with so grim an interest.

As usual Van Helsing had thought ahead of everyone else, and was prepared with an exact ordering of our work.

'It is perhaps well,' he said 'that at our meeting after our visit to Carfax we decided not to do anything with the earthboxes that lay there. Had we done so, the Count must have guessed our purpose, and would doubtless have taken measures in advance to frustrate such an effort with regard to the others; but now he does not know our intentions. Nay more, in all probability, he does not know that such a power exists to us as can sterilize his lairs, so that he cannot use them as of old. We are now so much further advanced in our knowledge as to their disposition, that, when we have examined the house in Piccadilly, we may track the very last of them. Today, then, is ours; and in it rests our hope. The sun that rose on our sorrow this morning guards us in its course. Until it sets tonight, that monster must retain whatever form he now has. He is confined within the limitations of his earthly envelope. He cannot melt into thin air nor disappear through cracks or chinks or crannies. If he go through a doorway, he must open the door like a mortal. And so we have this day to hunt out all his lairs and sterilize them. So we shall, if we have not yet catch him and destroy him, drive him to bay in some place where the catching and the destroying shall be, in time, sure.' Here I started up for I could not contain myself at the thought that the minutes and seconds so preciously laden with Mina's life and happiness were flying from us, since whilst we talked action was possible. But Van Helsing held up his hand warningly. 'Nay, friend Jonathan,' he said, 'in this, the quickest way home is the longest way, so your proverb say. We shall all act, and act with desperate quick, when the time has come. But think, in all probable the key of the situation is in that house in Piccadilly. The Count may have many houses which he has bought. Of them he will have deeds of purchase, keys and other things. He will have paper that he write on; he will have his book of cheques. There are many belongings that he must have somewhere; why not in this place so central, so quiet, where he come and go by the front or the back at all hour, when in the very vast of the traffic there is none to notice. We shall go there and search that house; and when we learn what it holds, then we do what our friend Arthur call, in his phrases of hunt "stop the earths"[1] and so we run down our old fox—so? is it not?'

'Then let us come at once,' I cried, 'we are wasting the precious, precious time!' The Professor did not move, but simply said:—

'And how are we to get into that house in Piccadilly?'

'Any way!' I cried. 'We shall break in if need be.'

'And your police; where will they be, and what will they say?'

I was staggered; but I knew that if he wished to delay he had a good reason for it. So I said, as quietly as I could:—

---

1. Van Helsing here uses metaphors from the aristocratic sport of fox hunting. To "stop the earths" is to close up burrows in which the pursued fox might take refuge.

'Don't wait more than need be; you know, I am sure, what torture I am in.'

'Ah, my child, that I do; and indeed there is no wish of me to add to your anguish. But just think, what can we do, until all the world be at movement. Then will come our time. I have thought and thought, and it seems to me that the simplest way is the best of all. Now we wish to get into the house, but we have no key; is it not so?' I nodded.

'Now suppose that you were, in truth, the owner of that house, and could not still get it; and think there was to you no conscience of the housebreaker, what would you do?'

'I should get a respectable locksmith, and set him to work to pick the lock for me.'

'And your police, they would interfere, would they not?'

'Oh, no! not if they knew the man was properly employed.'

'Then,' he looked at me keenly as he spoke, 'all that is in doubt is the conscience of the employer, and the belief of your policemen as to whether or no that employer has a good conscience or a bad one. Your police must indeed be zealous men and clever—oh so clever!— in reading the heart, that they trouble themselves in such matter. No, no, my friend Jonathan, you go take the lock off a hundred empty house in this your London, or of any city in the world; and if you do it as such things are rightly done, and at the time such things are rightly done, no one will interfere. I have read of a gentleman who owned a so fine house in your London, and when he went for months of summer to Switzerland and lock up his house, some burglar came and broke window at back and got in. Then he went and made open the shutters in front and walk out and in through the door, before the very eyes of the police. Then he have an auction in that house, and advertise it, and put up big notice; and when the day come he sell off by a great auctioneer all the goods of that other man who own them. Then he go to a builder, and he sell him that house, making an agreement that he pull it down and take all away within a certain time. And your police and other authority help him all they can. And when that owner come back from his holiday in Switzerland he find only an empty hole where his house had been. This was all done *en règle*;[2] and in our work we shall be *en règle* too. We shall not go so early that the policeman who have then little to think of, shall deem it strange; but we shall go after ten o'clock when there are many about, and when such things would be done were we indeed owners of the house.'

I could not but see how right he was, and the terrible despair of Mina's face became relaxed a thought; there was hope in such good counsel. Van Helsing went on:—

'When once within that house we may find more clues; at any rate

2. By the rules (French).

some of us can remain there whilst the rest find the other places where there be more earth-boxes—at Bermondsey and Mile End.'

Lord Godalming stood up. 'I can be of some use here,' he said. 'I shall wire to my people to have horses and carriages where they will be most convenient.'

'Look here, old fellow,' said Morris, 'it is a capital idea to have all ready in case we want to go horsebacking; but don't you think that one of your snappy carriages with its heraldic adornments in a byeway of Walworth or Mile End would attract too much attention for our purposes? It seems to me that we ought to take cabs when we go south or east; and even leave them somewhere near the neighbourhood we are going to.'

'Friend Quincey is right!' said the Professor. 'His head is what you call in plane with the horizon. It is a difficult thing that we go to do, and we do not want no peoples to watch us if so it may.'

Mina took a growing interest in everything, and I was rejoiced to see that the exigency of affairs was helping her to forget for a time the terrible experience of the night. She was very, very pale—almost ghastly, and so thin that her lips were drawn away, showing her teeth in somewhat of prominence. I did not mention this last, lest it should give her needless pain; but it made my blood run cold in my veins to think of what had occurred with poor Lucy when the Count had sucked her blood. As yet there was no sign of the teeth growing sharper; but the time as yet was short, and there was time for fear.

When we came to the discussion of the sequence of our efforts and of the disposition of our forces, there were new sources of doubt. It was finally agreed that before starting for Piccadilly we should destroy the Count's lair close at hand. In case he should find it out too soon, we should thus be still ahead of him in our work of destruction; and his presence in his purely material shape, and at his weakest, might give us some new clue.

As to the disposal of forces, it was suggested by the Professor that, after our visit to Carfax, we should all enter the house in Piccadilly; that the two doctors and I should remain there whilst Lord Godalming and Quincey found the lairs at Walworth and Mile End and destroyed them. It was possible, if not likely, the Professor urged, that the Count might appear in Piccadilly during the day, and that if so we might be able to cope with him then and there. At any rate we might be able to follow him in force. To this plan I strenuously objected, in so far as my going was concerned, for I said that I intended to stay and protect Mina. I thought that my mind was made up on the subject; but Mina would not listen to my objection. She said that there might be some law matter in which I could be useful; that amongst the Count's papers might be some clue which I could understand out of my experience in Transylvania; and that, as it was, all the strength we could muster was required to cope with the Count's extraordinary power. I had to give in, for Mina's resolution was fixed; she said that it was the last hope for *her* that we should all work together. 'As for me,' she said, 'I have no fear. Things have been as bad as they can be; and whatever may happen must have in it some element of hope or comfort. Go my husband! God can, if He wishes it, guard me as well alone as with any one present.' So I started up crying out: 'Then in God's name let us come at once, for we are losing time. The Count may come to Piccadilly earlier than we think.'

'Not so!' said Van Helsing holding up his hand.

'But why?' I asked.

'Do you forget,' he said, with actually a smile, 'that last night he banqueted heavily, and will sleep late?'

Did I forget! shall I ever—can I ever! Can any of us ever forget that terrible scene! Mina struggled hard to keep her brave countenance; but the pain overmastered her and she put her hands before her face, and shuddered whilst she moaned. Van Helsing had not intended to recall her frightful experience. He had simply lost sight of her and her part in the affair in his intellectual effort. When it struck him what he had said, he was horrified at his thoughtlessness and tried to comfort her. 'Oh Madam Mina,' he said, 'dear, dear Madam Mina, alas! that I of all who so reverence you, should have said anything so forgetful. These stupid old lips of mine and this stupid old head do not deserve so; but you will forget it, will you not?' He bent low beside her as he spoke; she took his hand, and looking at him through her tears, said hoarsely:—

'No, I shall not forget, for it is well that I remember; and with it I have so much in memory of you that is sweet, that I take it all together. Now, you must all be going soon. Breakfast is ready, and we must all eat that we may be strong.'

Breakfast was a strange meal to us all. We tried to be cheerful and encourage each other, and Mina was the brightest and most cheerful of us. When it was over, Van Helsing stood up and said:—

'Now, my dear friends, we go forth to our terrible enterprise. Are we all armed, as we were on that night when first we visited our enemy's lair; armed against ghostly as well as carnal attack?' We all assured him. 'Then it is well. Now Madam Mina, you are in any case *quite* safe here until the sunset; and before then we shall return—if—We shall return! But before we go let me see you armed against personal attack. I have myself, since you came down, prepared your chamber by the placing of the things of which we know, so that He may not enter. Now let me guard yourself. On your forehead I touch this piece of Sacred Wafer in the name of the Father, the Son, and—'

There was a fearful scream which almost froze our hearts to hear. As he had placed the Wafer on Mina's forehead, it had seared it—had burned into the flesh[3] as though it had been a piece of white-hot metal. My poor darling's brain told her the significance of the fact as quickly as her nerves received the pain of it; and the two so overwhelmed her that her overwrought nature had its voice in that dreadful scream. But the words to her thought came quickly; the echo of the scream had not ceased to ring on the air when there came the reaction, and she sank on her knees on the floor in an agony of abasement. Pulling her beautiful hair over her face, as the leper of old his mantle, she wailed out:—

'Unclean! Unclean! Even the Almighty shuns my polluted flesh! I must bear this mark of shame upon my forehead until the Judgment Day.' They all paused. I had thrown myself beside her in an agony of helpless grief, and putting my arms around held her tight. For a few minutes our sorrowful hearts beat together, whilst the friends around us turned away their eyes that ran tears silently. Then Van Helsing turned and said gravely; so gravely that I could not help feeling that he was in some way inspired, and was stating things outside himself:—

'It may be that you may have to bear that mark till God himself see fit, as He most surely shall on the Judgment Day to redress all wrongs of the earth and of His children that He has placed thereon. And oh, Madam Mina, my dear, my dear, may we who love you be there to see, when that red scar, the sign of God's knowledge of what has been, shall pass away and leave your forehead as pure as the heart we know. For so surely as we live, that scar shall pass away when God sees right to lift the burden that is hard upon us. Till then we bear our Cross, as His Son did in obedience to His will. It may be that we are chosen instruments of His good pleasure, and that we ascend to His bidding as that other through stripes and shame; through tears and blood; through doubts and fears, and all that makes the difference between God and man.'

There was hope in his words, and comfort; and they made for resignation. Mina and I both felt so, and simultaneously we each took one of the old man's hands and bent over and kissed it. Then without a word we all knelt down together, and, all holding hands, swore to be true to each other. We men pledged ourselves to raise the veil of sorrow from the head of her whom, each in his own way, we loved; and we prayed for help and guidance in the terrible task which lay before us.

It was then time to start. So I said farewell to Mina, a parting which neither of us shall forget to our dying day; and we set out.

To one thing I have made up my mind; if we find out that Mina must be a vampire in the end, then she shall not go into that unknown and terrible land alone. I suppose it is thus that in old times one vampire meant many; just as their hideous bodies could only rest in sacred

---

3. Recalling the scar Jonathan's shovel had made on Dracula's forehead.

earth, so the holiest love[4] was the recruiting sergeant for their ghastly ranks.

We entered Carfax without trouble and found all things the same as on the first occasion. It was hard to believe that amongst so prosaic surroundings of neglect and dust and decay there was any ground for such fear as already we knew. Had not our minds been made up, and had there not been terrible memories to spur us on, we could hardly have proceeded with our task. We found no papers, or any sign of use in the house; and in the old chapel the great boxes looked just as we had seen them last. Dr Van Helsing said to us solemnly as we stood before them:—

'And now, my friends, we have a duty here to do. We must sterilize this earth, so sacred of holy memories, that he has brought from a far distant land for such fell use. He has chosen this earth because it has been holy. Thus we defeat him with his own weapon, for we make it more holy still. It was sanctified to such use of man, now we sanctify it to God.' As he spoke he took from his bag a screw-driver and a wrench, and very soon the top of one of the cases was thrown open. The earth smelled musty and close; but we did not somehow seem to mind, for our attention was concentrated on the Professor. Taking from his box a piece of the Sacred Wafer he laid it reverently on the earth, and then shutting down the lid began to screw it home, we aiding him as he worked.

One by one we treated in the same way each of the great boxes, and left them as we had found them to all appearance; but in each was a portion of the Host.

When we closed the door behind us, the Professor said solemnly:—

'So much is already done. If it may be that with all the others we can be so successful, then the sunset of this evening may shine on Madam Mina's forehead all white as ivory and with no stain!'

As we passed across the lawn on our way to the station to catch our train we could see the front of the asylum. I looked eagerly, and in the window of my own room saw Mina. I waved my hand to her, and nodded to tell that our work there was successfully accomplished. She nodded in reply to show that she understood. The last I saw, she was waving her hand in farewell. It was with a heavy heart that we sought the station and just caught the train, which was steaming in as we reached the platform.

I have written this in the train.

Piccadilly, 12:30 o'clock.—Just before we reached Fenchurch Street Lord Godalming said to me:

'Quincey and I will find a locksmith. You had better not come with

4. In folklore, revenants, or those who return from the dead, prey only on their families, but we never see Dracula feed on intimates: all his victims are strangers.

us in case there should be any difficulty; for under the circumstances it wouldn't seem so bad for us to break into an empty house. But you are a solicitor and the Incorporated Law Society might tell you that you should have known better.' I demurred as to my not sharing any danger even of odium, but he went on: 'Besides, it will attract less attention if there are not too many of us. My title will make it all right with the locksmith, and with any policeman that may come along. You had better go with Jack and the Professor and stay in the Green Park, somewhere in sight of the house; and when you see the door opened and the smith has gone away, do you all come across. We shall be on the look out for you, and shall let you in.'

'The advice is good!' said Van Helsing, so we said no more. Godalming and Morris hurried off in a cab, we following in another. At the corner of Arlington Street our contingent got out and strolled into the Green Park. My heart beat as I saw the house on which so much of our hope was centred, looming up grim and silent in its deserted condition amongst its more lively and spruce-looking neighbours. We sat down on a bench within good view, and began to smoke cigars so as to attract as little attention as possible. The minutes seemed to pass with leaden feet as we waited for the coming of the others.

At length we saw a four-wheeler drive up. Out of it, in leisurely fashion, got Lord Godalming and Morris; and down from the box descended a thick-set working man with his rush-woven basket of tools. Morris paid the cabman, who touched his hat and drove away. Together the two ascended the steps and Lord Godalming pointed out what he wanted done. The workman took off his coat leisurely and hung it on one of the spikes of the rail, saying something to a policeman who just then sauntered along. The policeman nodded acquiescence, and the man kneeling down placed his bag beside him. After searching through it, he took out a selection of tools which he proceeded to lay beside him in orderly fashion. Then he stood up, looked into the keyhole, blew into it, and, turning to his employers, made some remark. Lord Godalming smiled, and the man lifted a good sized bunch of keys; selecting one of them, he began to probe the lock, as if feeling his way with it. After fumbling about for a bit he tried a second, and then a third. All at once the door opened under a slight push from him, and he and the two others entered the hall. We sat still; my own cigar burnt furiously, but Van Helsing's went cold altogether. We waited patiently as we saw the workman come out and bring in his bag. Then he held the door partly open, steadying it with his knees, whilst he fitted a key to the lock. This he finally handed to Lord Godalming, who took out his purse and gave him something. The man touched his hat, took his bag, put on his coat and departed; not a soul took the slightest notice of the whole transaction.

When the man had fairly gone, we three crossed the street and knocked at the door. It was immediately opened by Quincey Morris, beside whom stood Lord Godalming lighting a cigar.

'The place smells so vilely,' said the latter as we came in. It did indeed smell vilely—like the old chapel at Carfax—and with our previous experience it was plain to us that the Count had been using the place pretty freely. We moved to explore the house, all keeping together in case of attack; for we knew we had a strong and wily enemy to deal with, and as yet we did not know whether the Count might not be in the house. In the dining-room, which lay at the back of the hall, we found eight boxes of earth. Eight boxes only out of the nine which were sought! Our work was not over, and would never be until we should have found the missing box. First we opened the shutters of the window which looked out across a narrow stone-flagged yard at the blank face of a stable, pointed to look like the front of a miniature house. There were no windows in it, so we were not afraid of being overlooked. We did not lose any time in examining the chests. With the tools which we had brought with us we opened them, one by one, and treated them as we had treated those others in the old chapel. It was evident to us that the Count was not at present in the house, and we proceeded to search for any of his effects.

After a cursory glance at the rest of the rooms, from basement to attic, we came to the conclusion that the dining-room contained any effects which might belong to the Count; and so we proceeded to minutely examine them. They lay in a sort of orderly disorder on the great dining-room table. There were title deeds of the Piccadilly house in a great bundle; deeds of the purchase of the houses at Mile End and Bermondsey; notepaper, envelopes, and pens and ink. All were covered up in thin wrapping paper to keep them from the dust. There were also a clothes brush, a brush and comb, and a jug and basin— the latter containing dirty water which was reddened as if with blood. Last of all was a little heap of keys of all sorts and sizes, probably those belonging to the other houses. When we had examined this last find, Lord Godalming and Quincey Morris taking accurate notes of the various addresses of the houses in the East and the South, took with them the keys in a great bunch, and set out to destroy the boxes in these places. The rest of us are, with what patience we can, waiting their return—or the coming of the Count.

Chapter XXIII

Dr Seward's Diary

3 October.—The time seemed terribly long whilst we were waiting for the coming of Godalming and Quincey Morris. The Professor tried to keep our minds active by using them all the time. I could see his beneficent purpose, by the side glances which he threw from time to time at Harker. The poor fellow is overwhelmed in a misery that is appalling to see. Last night he was a frank, happy-looking man, with strong youthful face, full of energy, and with dark brown hair. Today he is a drawn, haggard old man, whose white hair matches well with the hollow burning eyes and grief-written lines of his face. His energy is still intact; in fact he is like a living flame. This may yet be his salvation, for, if all go well, it will tide him over the despairing period; he will then, in a kind of way, wake again to the realities of life. Poor fellow, I thought my own trouble was bad enough, but his—! The Professor knows this well enough, and is doing his best to keep his mind active. What he has been saying was, under the circumstances, of absorbing interest. So well as I can remember, here it is:—

'I have studied, over and over again since they came into my hands, all the papers relating to this monster; and the more I have studied, the greater seems the necessity to utterly stamp him out. All through there are signs of his advance; not only of his power, but of his knowledge of it. As I learned from the researches of my friend Arminius of Buda-Pesth, he was in life a most wonderful man. Soldier, statesman, and alchemist—which latter was the highest development of the science-knowledge of his time. He had a mighty brain, a learning beyond compare, and a heart that knew no fear and no remorse. He dared even to attend the Scholomance, and there was no branch of knowledge of his time that he did not essay. Well, in him the brain powers survived the physical death; though it would seem that memory was not all complete. In some faculties of mind he has been, and is, only a child; but he is growing, and some things that were childish at the first are now of man's stature. He is experimenting, and doing it well; and if it had not been that we have crossed his path he would be yet—he may be yet if we fail—the father or furtherer of a new order of beings,[1] whose road must lead through Death, not Life.'

Harker groaned and said, 'And this is all arrayed against my darling! But how is he experimenting? The knowledge may help us to defeat him!'

---

1. Here, as throughout, Van Helsing gives opposed interpretations of Dracula: the vampire is simultaneously a primitive throwback and a Nietzschian harbinger of an advanced, inhuman race.

'He has all along, since his coming, been trying his power, slowly but surely; that big child-brain of his is working. Well for us, it is, as yet, a child-brain; for had he dared, at the first, to attempt certain things he would long ago have been beyond our power. However, he means to succeed, and a man who has centuries before him can afford to wait and to go slow. *Festina lente*[2] may well be his motto.'

'I fail to understand,' said Harker wearily. 'Oh, do be more plain to me! Perhaps grief and trouble are dulling my brain.' The Professor laid his hand tenderly on his shoulder as he spoke:—

'Ah, my child, I will be plain. Do you not see how, of late, this monster has been creeping into knowledge experimentally. How he has been making use of the zoophagous patient to effect his entry into friend John's home; for your Vampire, though in all afterwards he can come when and how he will, must at the first make entry only when asked thereto by an inmate. But these are not his most important ex-periments. Do we not see how at first all these so great boxes were moved by others. He knew not then but that must be so. But all the time that so great child-brain of his was growing, and he began to consider whether he might not himself move the box. So he begin to help; and then, when he found that this be all right, he try to move them all alone. And so he progress, and he scatter these graves of him; and none but he know where they are hidden. He may have intend to bury them deep in the ground. So that he only use them in the night, or at such time as he can change his form, they do him equal well; and none may know these are his hiding place! But, my child, do not despair; this knowledge come to him just too late! Already all of his lairs but one be sterilize as for him; and before the sunset this shall be so. Then he have no place where he can move and hide. I delayed this morning that so we might be sure. Is there not more at stake for us than him? Then why we not be even more careful than him? By my clock it is one hour, and already, if all be well, friend Arthur and Quincey are on their way to us. Today is our day, and we must go sure, if slow, and lose no chance. See! there are five of us when those absent ones return.'

Whilst he was speaking we were startled by a knock at the hall door, the double postman's knock of the telegraph boy. We all moved out to the hall with one impulse, and Van Helsing, holding up his hand to us to keep silence, stepped to the door and opened it. The boy handed in a despatch. The Professor closed the door again and, after looking at the direction, opened it and read it aloud.

'Look out for D. He has just now, 12.45, come from Carfax hurriedly and hastened towards the south. He seems to be going the round and may want to see you: Mina.'

2. Make haste slowly (Latin).

There was a pause, broken by Jonathan Harker's voice:—

'Now, God be thanked, we shall soon meet!' Van Helsing turned to him quickly and said:—

'God will act in His own way and time. Do not fear, and do not rejoice as yet; for what we wish for at the moment may be our undoings.'

'I care for nothing now,' he answered hotly, 'except to wipe out this brute from the face of creation. I would sell my soul to do it!'

'Oh hush, hush, my child!' said Van Helsing, 'God does not purchase souls in this wise; and the Devil, though he may purchase, does not keep faith. But God is merciful and just, and knows your pain and your devotion to that dear Madam Mina. Think you, how her pain would be doubled, did she but hear your wild words. Do not fear any of us; we are all devoted to this cause, and today shall see the end. The time is coming for action; today this Vampire is limit to the powers of man, and till sunset he may not change. It will take him time to arrive here—see it is twenty minutes past one—and there are yet some times before he can hither come, be he never so quick. What we must hope for is that my Lord Arthur and Quincey arrive first.'

About half an hour after we had received Mrs Harker's telegram, there came a quiet resolute knock at the hall door. It was just an ordinary knock, such as is given hourly by thousands of gentlemen, but it made the Professor's heart and mine beat loudly. We looked at each other, and together moved out into the hall; we each held ready to use our various armaments—the spiritual in the left hand, the mortal in the right. Van Helsing pulled back the latch, and, holding the door half open, stood back, having both hands ready for action. The gladness of our hearts must have shown upon our faces when on the step, close to the door, we saw Lord Godalming and Quincey Morris. They came quickly in and closed the door behind them, the former saying, as they moved along the hall:—

'It is all right. We found both places; six boxes in each, and we destroyed them all!'

'Destroyed?' asked the Professor.

'For him!' We were silent for a minute, and then Quincey said:—

'There's nothing to do but to wait here. If, however, he doesn't turn up by five o'clock, we must start off; for it won't do to leave Mrs Harker alone after sunset.'

'He will be here before long now,' said Van Helsing, who had been consulting his pocket-book. 'Nota bene,[3] in Madam's telegram he went south from Carfax, that means he went to cross the river, and he could only do so at slack of tide, which should be something before one o'clock. That he went south has a meaning for us. He is as yet only

3. Note well (Latin).

suspicious; and he went from Carfax first to the place where he would suspect interference least. You must have been at Bermondsey only a short time before him. That he is not here already shows that he went to Mile End next. This took him some time; for he would then have to be carried over the river in some way. Believe me, my friends, we shall not have long to wait now. We should have ready some plan of attack, so that we may throw away no chance. Hush, there is no time now. Have all your arms! Be ready!' He held up a warning hand as he spoke, for we all could hear a key softly inserted in the lock of the hall door.

I could not but admire, even at such a moment, the way in which a dominant spirit asserted itself. In all our hunting parties and adventures in different parts of the world, Quincey Morris had always been the one to arrange the plan of action, and Arthur and I had been accustomed to obey him implicitly. Now, the old habit seemed to be renewed instinctively. With a swift glance round the room, he at once laid out our plan of attack, and, without speaking a word, with a gesture, placed us each in position. Van Helsing, Harker, and I were just behind the door so that when it was opened the Professor could guard it whilst we two stepped between the incomer and the door. Godalming behind and Quincey in front stood just out of sight ready to move in front of the window. We waited in a suspense that made the seconds pass with nightmare slowness. The slow, careful steps came along the hall; the Count was evidently prepared for some surprise—at least he feared it.

Suddenly with a single bound he leaped into the room, winning a way past us before any of us could raise a hand to stay him. There was something so panther-like in the movement—something so unhuman, that it seemed to sober us all from the shock of his coming. The first to act was Harker, who with a quick movement, threw himself before the door leading into the room in the front of the house. As the Count saw us, a horrible sort of snarl passed over his face, showing the eye-teeth long and pointed; but the evil smile as quickly passed into a cold stare of lion-like disdain. His expression again changed, as, with a single impulse, we all advanced upon him. It was a pity that we had not some better organized plan of attack, for even at the moment I wondered what we were to do. I did not myself know whether our lethal weapon would avail us anything. Harker evidently meant to try the matter, for he had ready his great Kukri knife,[4] and made a fierce and sudden cut at him. The blow was a powerful one; only the diabolical quickness of the Count's leap back saved him. A second less and the trenchant blade had shorne through his heart. As it was, the point just cut the cloth of his coat, making a wide gap whence a bundle of bank-notes and a stream of gold fell out. The expression of the Count's face was so hell-

---

4. Used by the fierce Gurkhas of Nepal, who fought alongside the imperial British army in India.

ish, that for a moment I feared for Harker, though I saw him throw the terrible knife aloft again for another stroke. Instinctively I moved forward with a protective impulse, holding the crucifix and wafer in my left hand. I felt a mighty power fly along my arm; and it was without surprise I saw that the monster cower back before a similar movement made spontaneously by each one of us. It would be impossible to describe the expression of hate and baffled malignity—of anger and hellish rage—which came over the Count's face. His waxen hue became greenish-yellow by the contrast of his burning eyes, and the red scar on the forehead showed on the pallid skin like a palpitating wound. The next instant, with a sinuous dive he swept under Harker's arm, ere his blow could fall, and, grasping a handful of the money from the floor, dashed across the room, threw himself at the window. Amid the crash and glitter of the falling glass, he tumbled into the flagged area below. Through the sound of the shivering glass I could hear the 'ting' of the gold, as some of the sovereigns fell on the flagging.

We ran over and saw him spring unhurt from the ground. He, rushing up the steps, crossed the flagged yard, and pushed open the stable door. There he turned and spoke to us:—

'You think to baffle me, you—with your pale faces all in a row, like sheep in a butcher's. You shall be sorry yet, each one of you! You think you have left me without a place to rest; but I have more. My revenge is just begun! I spread it over centuries, and time is on my side. Your girls that you all love are mine already; and through them you and others shall yet be mine—my creatures, to do my bidding and to be my jackals when I want to feed. Bah!' With a contemptuous sneer, he passed quickly through the door, and we heard the rusty bolt creak as he fastened it behind him. A door beyond opened and shut. The first of us to speak was the Professor, as, realizing the difficulty of following him through the stable, we moved towards the hall.

'We have learnt something—much! Notwithstanding his brave words, he fears us; he fear time, he fear want! For if not, why he hurry so? His very tone betray him, or my ears deceive. Why take that money? You follow quick. You are hunters of wild beast, and understand it so. For me, I make sure that nothing here may be of use to him, if so that he return.' As he spoke he put the money remaining into his pocket; took the title-deeds in the bundle as Harker had left them; and swept the remaining things into the open fireplace where he set fire to them with a match.

Godalming and Morris had rushed out into the yard and Harker had lowered himself from the window to follow the Count. He had, however, bolted the stable door; and by the time they had forced it open there was no sign of him. Van Helsing and I tried to make inquiry at the back of the house; but the mews was deserted and no one had seen him depart.

It was now late in the afternoon, and sunset was not far off. We had to recognize that our game was up; with heavy hearts we agreed with the Professor when he said:—

'Let us go back to Madam Mina—poor, poor, dear Madam Mina. All we can do just now is done; and we can there, at least, protect her. But we need not despair. There is but one more earth-box, and we must try to find it; when that is done all may yet be well.' I could see that he spoke as bravely as he could to comfort Harker. The poor fellow was quite broken down; now and again he gave a low groan which he could not suppress—he was thinking of his wife.

With sad hearts we came back to my house, where we found Mrs Harker waiting us, with an appearance of cheerfulness which did honour to her bravery and unselfishness. When she saw our faces, her own became as pale as death; for a second or two her eyes were closed as if she were in secret prayer; and then she said cheerfully:—

'I can never thank you all enough. Oh, my poor darling!' as she spoke, she took her husband's grey head in her hands and kissed it— 'Lay your poor head here and rest it. All will yet be well, dear! God will protect us if He so will it in His good intent.' The poor fellow only groaned. There was no place for words in his sublime misery.

We had a sort of perfunctory supper together, and I think it cheered us all up somewhat. It was, perhaps, the mere animal heat of food to hungry people—for none of us had eaten anything since breakfast—or the sense of companionship may have helped us; but anyhow we were all less miserable, and saw the morrow as not altogether without hope. True to our promise, we told Mrs Harker everything which had passed; and although she grew snowy white at times when danger had seemed to threaten her husband, and red at others when his devotion to her was manifested, she listened bravely and with calmness. When we came to the part where Harker had rushed at the Count so recklessly, she clung to her husband's arm, and held it tight as though her clinging could protect him from any harm that might come. She said nothing, however, till the narration was all done, and matters had been brought right up to the present time. Then without letting go her husband's hand she stood up amongst us and spoke. Oh that I could give any idea of the scene; of that sweet, sweet, good, good woman in all the radiant beauty of her youth and animation, with the red scar on her forehead of which she was conscious, and which we saw with grinding of our teeth—remembering whence and how it came; her loving kindness against our grim hate; her tender faith against all our fears and doubting; and we, knowing that so far as symbols went, she with all her goodness and purity and faith, was outcast from God.

'Jonathan,' she said, and the word sounded like music on her lips it was so full of love and tenderness, 'Jonathan dear, and you all my true, true friends, I want you to bear something in mind through all this dreadful time. I know that you must fight—that you must destroy even as you destroyed the false Lucy so that the true Lucy might live here-after; but it is not a work of hate. That poor soul who has wrought all this misery is the saddest case of all. Just think what will be his joy when he too is destroyed in his worser part that his better part may have spiritual immortality. You must be pitiful to him too, though it may not hold your hands from his destruction.'

As she spoke I could see her husband's face darken and draw to-gether, as though the passion in him were shrivelling his being to its core. Instinctively the clasp on his wife's hand grew closer, till his knuckles looked white. She did not flinch from the pain which I knew she must have suffered, but looked at him with eyes that were more appealing than ever. As she stopped speaking he leaped to his feet, almost tearing his hand from hers as he spoke:—

'May God give him into my hand just for long enough to destroy that earthly life of him which we are aiming at. If beyond it I could send his soul for ever and ever to burning hell I would do it!'

'Oh, hush! oh, hush! in the name of the good God. Don't say such things, Jonathan, my husband; or you will crush me with fear and horror. Just think, my dear—I have been thinking all this long, long day of it—that . . . perhaps . . . some day . . . I too may need such pity; and that some other like you—and with equal cause for anger—may deny it to me! Oh my husband! my husband, indeed I would have spared you such a thought had there been another way; but I pray that God may not have treasured your wild words, except as the heart-broken wail of a very loving and sorely stricken man. Oh God, let these poor white hairs go in evidence of what he has suffered, who all his life has done no wrong, and on whom so many sorrows have come.'

We men were all in tears now. There was no resisting them, and we wept openly. She wept too, to see that her sweeter counsels had pre-vailed. Her husband flung himself on his knees beside her, and putting his arms round her, hid his face in the folds of her dress. Van Helsing beckoned to us and we stole out of the room, leaving the two loving hearts alone with their God.

Before they retired the Professor fixed up the room against any com-ing of the Vampire, and assured Mrs Harker that she might rest in peace. She tried to school herself to the belief, and, manifestly for her husband's sake, tried to seem content. It was a brave struggle; and was, I think and believe, not without its reward. Van Helsing had placed at hand a bell which either of them was to sound in case of any emer-gency. When they had retired, Quincey, Godalming, and I arranged that we should sit up, dividing the night between us, and watch over the safety of the poor stricken lady. The first watch falls to Quincey, so the rest of us shall be off to bed as soon as we can. Godalming has already turned in, for his is the second watch. Now that my work is done I, too, shall go to bed.

Jonathan Harker's Journal

3–4 October, close to midnight.—I thought yesterday would never end. There was over me a yearning for sleep, in some sort of blind belief that to wake would be to find things changed, and that any change must now be for the better. Before we parted, we discussed what our next step was to be, but we could arrive at no result. All we knew was that one earth-box remained, and that the Count alone knew where it was. If he chooses to lie hidden, he may baffle us for years; and in the meantime!—the thought is too horrible, I dare not think of it even now. This I know: that if ever there was a woman who was all perfection, that one is my poor wronged darling. I love her a thousand times more for her sweet pity of last night, a pity that made my own hate of the monster seem despicable. Surely God will not permit the world to be the poorer by the loss of such a creature. This is hope to me. We are all drifting reefwards now, and faith is our only anchor. Thank God! Mina is sleeping, and sleeping without dreams. I fear what her dreams might be like, with such terrible memories to ground them in. She has not been so calm, within my seeing, since the sunset. Then, for a while, there came over her face a repose which was like spring after the blasts of March. I thought at the time that it was the softness of the red sunset on her face, but somehow now I think it has a deeper meaning. I am not sleepy myself, though I am weary—weary to death. However, I must try to sleep; for there is tomorrow to think of, and there is no rest for me until . . .

Later.—I must have fallen asleep, for I was awaked by Mina, who was sitting up in bed, with a startled look on her face. I could see easily, for we did not leave the room in darkness; she had placed a warning hand over my mouth, and now she whispered in my ear:—

'Hush! there is someone in the corridor!' I got up softly, and, crossing the room, gently opened the door.

Just outside, stretched on a mattress lay Mr Morris, wide awake. He raised a warning hand for silence as he whispered to me:—

'Hush! go back to bed; it is all right. One of us will be here all night. We don't mean to take any chances!'

His look and gesture forbade discussion, so I came back and told Mina. She sighed, and positively a shadow of a smile stole over her poor, pale face as she put her arms round me and said softly:—

'Oh, thank God for good brave men!' With a sigh she sank back again to sleep. I write this now as I am not sleepy, though I must try again.

4 October, morning.—Once again during the night I was wakened by Mina. This time we had all had a good sleep, for the grey of the coming dawn was making the windows into sharp oblongs, and the gas flame was like a speck rather than a disc of light. She said to me hurriedly:—

'Go, call the Professor. I want to see him at once.'

'Why?' I asked.

'I have an idea. I suppose it must have come in the night, and matured without my knowing it. He must hypnotize me before the dawn, and then I shall be able to speak. Go quick, dearest; the time is getting close.' I went to the door. Dr Seward was resting on the mattress, and, seeing me, he sprang to his feet.

'Is anything wrong?' he asked, in alarm.

'No,' I replied; 'but Mina wants to see Dr Van Helsing at once.'

'I will go,' he said, and hurried into the Professor's room.

In two or three minutes later Van Helsing was in the room in his dressing-gown, and Mr Morris and Lord Godalming were with Dr Seward at the door asking questions. When the Professor saw Mina a smile—a positive smile ousted the anxiety of his face; he rubbed his hands as he said:—

'Oh, my dear Madam Mina, this is indeed a change. See! friend Jonathan, we have got our dear Madam Mina, as of old, back to us today!' Then turning to her, he said, cheerfully: 'And what am I do for you? For at this hour you do not want me for nothings.'

'I want you to hypnotize me!' she said. 'Do it before the dawn, for I feel that then I can speak, and speak freely. Be quick, for the time is short!' Without a word he motioned her to sit up in bed.

Looking fixedly at her, he commenced to make passes in front of her, from over the top of her head downward, with each hand in turn. Mina gazed at him fixedly for a few minutes, during which my own heart beat like a trip hammer, for I felt that some crisis was at hand. Gradually her eyes closed, and she sat, stock still; only by the gentle heaving of her bosom could one know that she was alive. The Professor made a few more passes and then stopped, and I could see that his forehead was covered with great beads of perspiration. Mina opened her eyes; but she did not seem the same woman.[5] There was a far-away look in her eyes, and her voice had a sad dreaminess which was new to me. Raising his hand to impose silence, the Professor motioned to me to bring the others in. They came on tip-toe, closing the door behind them, and stood at the foot of the bed, looking on. Mina appeared not to see them. The stillness was broken by Van Helsing's voice speaking in a low level tone which would not break the current of her thoughts:—

5. The heroine of George du Maurier's *Trilby* (1894), a huge best-seller, was similarly hypnotized by Svengali, an evil-smelling refugee from Eastern Europe who is simultaneously demon and artist. Like Trilby, Mina becomes mysteriously enlarged under hypnosis.

'Where are you?' The answer came in a neutral way:—

'I do not know. Sleep has no place it can call its own.' For several minutes there was silence. Mina sat rigid, and the Professor stood staring at her fixedly; the rest of us hardly dared to breathe. The room was growing lighter; without taking his eyes from Mina's face, Dr Van Helsing motioned me to pull up the blind. I did so, and the day seemed just upon us. A red streak shot up, and a rosy light seemed to diffuse itself through the room. On the instant the Professor spoke again:—

'Where are you now?' The answer came dreamily, but with intention; it were as though she were interpreting something. I have heard her use the same tone when reading her shorthand notes.

'I do not know. It is all strange to me!'

'What do you see?'

'I can see nothing; it is all dark.'

'What do you hear?' I could detect the strain in the Professor's patient voice.

'The lapping of water. It is gurgling by, and little waves leap. I can hear them on the outside.'

'Then you are on a ship?' We all looked at each other, trying to glean something each from the other. We were afraid to think. The answer came quick:—

'Oh, yes!'

'What else do you hear?'

'The sound of men stamping overhead as they run about. There is the creaking of a chain, and the loud tinkle as the check of the capstan falls into the rachet.'[6]

'What are you doing?'

'I am still—oh, so still. It is like death!' The voice faded away into a deep breath as of one sleeping, and the open eyes closed again.

By this time the sun had risen, and we were all in the full light of day. Dr Van Helsing placed his hands on Mina's shoulders, and laid her head down softly on her pillow. She lay like a sleeping child for a few moments, and then, with a long sigh, awoke and stared in wonder to see us all around her. 'Have I been talking in my sleep?' was all she said. She seemed, however, to know the situation without telling; though she was eager to know what she had told. The Professor repeated the conversation, and she said:—

'Then there is not a moment to lose; it may not be yet too late!' Mr Morris and Lord Godalming started for the door but the Professor's calm voice called them back:—

'Stay, my friends. That ship wherever it was, was weighing anchor whilst she spoke. There are many ships weighing anchor at the moment

---

6. Nautical terms. A capstan is an apparatus used for hoisting weights, in which a cable is wound about a vertical spool-shaped cylinder; a rachet, or ratchet, is a bar or wheel with inclined teeth, moved by a pivoted tongue or sliding bolt called a pawl.

in your so great Port of London. Which of them is it that you seek? God be thanked that we have once again a clue, though whither it may lead us we know not. We have been blind somewhat; blind after the manner of men, since when we can look back we see what we might have seen looking forward if we had been able to see what we might have seen! Alas! but that sentence is a puddle; is it not? We can know now what was in the Count's mind when he seize that money, though Jonathan's so fierce knife put him in the danger that even he dread. He meant escape. Hear me, ESCAPE! He saw that with but one earth-box left, and a pack of men following like dogs after a fox, this London was no place for him. He have take his last earth-box on board a ship, and he leave the land. He think to escape, but no! we follow him. Tally Ho! as friend Arthur would say when he put on his red frock! Our old fox is wily; oh! so wily and we must follow with wile. I too am wily and I think his mind in a little while. In meantime we may rest and in peace, for there are waters between us which he do not want to pass, and which he could not if he would—unless the ship were to touch the land, and then only at full or slack tide. See, and the sun is just rose, and all day to sunset is to us. Let us take bath, and dress, and have breakfast which we all need, and which we can eat comfortable since he be not in the same land with us.' Mina looked at him appealingly as she asked:—

'But why need we seek him further, when he is gone away from us?' He took her hand and patted it as he replied:—

'Ask me nothings as yet. When we have breakfast, then I answer all questions.' He would say no more, and we separated to dress.

After breakfast Mina repeated her question. He looked at her gravely for a minute and then said sorrowfully:—

'Because my dear, dear Madam Mina, now more than ever must we find him even if we have to follow him to the jaws of Hell!' She grew paler as she asked faintly:—

'Why?'

'Because,' he answered solemnly, 'he can live for centuries, and you are but mortal woman. Time is now to be dreaded—since once he put that mark upon your throat.'

I was just in time to catch her as she fell forward in a faint.

Chapter XXIV

Dr Seward's Phonograph Diary, Spoken by Van Helsing

This to Jonathan Harker.

You are to stay with your dear Madam Mina. We shall go to make our search—if I can call it so, for it is not search but knowing, and we seek confirmation only. But do you stay and take care of her today. This is your best and most holiest office. This day nothing can find him here. Let me tell you that so you will know what we four know already, for I have tell them. He, our enemy, have gone away; he have gone back to his Castle in Transylvania. I know it so well, as if a great hand of fire wrote it on the wall. He have prepare for this in some way, and that last earth-box was ready to ship somewheres. For this he took the money; for this he hurry at the last, lest we catch him before the sun go down. It was his last hope, save that he might hide in the tomb that he think poor Miss Lucy, being as he thought like him, keep open to him. But there was not of time. When that fail he make straight for his last resource—his last earthwork I might say did I wish *double entente*.[1] He is clever, oh so clever! he know that his game here was finish; and so he decide he go back home. He find ship going by the route he came, and he go in it. We go off now to find what ship, and whither bound; when we have discover that, we come back and tell you all. Then we will comfort you and poor dear Madam Mina with new hope. For it will be hope when you think it over: that all is not lost. This very creature that we pursue, he take hundreds of years to get so far as London; and yet in one day, when we know of the disposal of him we drive him out. He is finite, though he is powerful to do much harm and suffers not as we do. But we are strong, each in our purpose; and we are all more strong together. Take heart afresh dear husband of Madam Mina. This battle is but begun, and in the end we shall win —so sure as that God sits on high to watch over His children. Therefore be of much comfort till we return.

VAN HELSING.

Jonathan Harker's Journal

4 October.—When I read to Mina, Van Helsing's message in the phonograph, the poor girl brightened up considerably. Already the certainty that the Count is out of the country has given her comfort; and comfort is strength to her. For my own part, now that this horrible danger is not face to face with us, it seems almost impossible to believe in it. Even my own terrible experiences in Castle Dracula seem like a long-forgotten dream. Here in the crisp autumn air in the bright sunlight—

Alas! how can I disbelieve! In the midst of my thought my eye fell on the red scar on my poor darling's white forehead. Whilst that lasts, there can be no disbelief. And afterwards the very memory of it will keep faith crystal clear. Mina and I fear to be idle, so we have been over all the diaries again and again. Somehow, although the reality seems greater each time, the pain and the fear seem less. There is something of a guiding purpose manifest throughout, which is com-

---

1. Perhaps a malapropism for *double entendre*.

forting. Mina says that perhaps we are the instruments of ultimate good. It may be! I shall try to think as she does. We have never spoken to each other yet of the future. It is better to wait till we see the Professor and the others after their investigations.

The day is running by more quickly than I ever thought a day could run for me again. It is now three o'clock.

Mina Harker's Journal

5 October, 5 p.m.—Our meeting for report. Present: Professor Van Helsing, Lord Godalming, Dr Seward, Mr Quincey Morris, Jonathan Harker, Mina Harker.

Dr Van Helsing described what steps were taken during the day to discover on what boat and whither bound Count Dracula made his escape:—

'As I knew that he wanted to get back to Transylvania, I felt sure that he must go by the Danube mouth; or by somewhere in the Black Sea, since by that way he come. It was a dreary blank that was before us. *Omne ignotum pro magnifico*;[2] and so with heavy hearts we start to find what ships leave for the Black Sea last night. He was in sailing ship, since Madam Mina tell of sails being set. These not so important as to go in your list of the shipping in the *Times*, and so we go, by suggestion of my Lord Godalming, to your Lloyd's, where are note of all ships that sail, however so small. There we find that only one Black-Sea-bound ship go out with the tide. She is the *Czarina Catherine*,[3] and she sail from Doolittle's Wharf for Varna,[4] and thence on to other parts and up the Danube. "Soh!" said I, "this is the ship whereon is the Count." So off we go to Doolittle's Wharf, and there we find a man in an office of wood so small that the man look bigger than the office. From him we inquire of the goings of the *Czarina Catherine*. He swear much, and he red face and loud of voice, but he good fellow all the same; and when Quincey give him something from his pocket which crackle as he roll it up, and put it in a so small bag which he have hid deep in his clothing, he still better fellow and humble servant to us. He come with us, and ask many men who are rough and hot; these be better fellows too when they have been no more thirsty. They say much of blood and bloom and of others which I comprehend not, though I

---

2. Tacitus: The unknown is enchanting (Latin).
3. Named after Catherine II or Catherine the Great, empress of Russia between 1762 and 1796. An uncommonly powerful empress, Catherine extended Russia's imperial power into the Balkans, the Ukraine, Alaska, the Crimea, Poland, and southwest Asia. She was reputed to be sexually omnivorous as well. We recall that Dracula arrived in England on the *Demeter*. He not only depends on women for nourishment; he chooses ships named after powerful female rulers.
4. A major port city on the Black Sea. The Turks ruled it between 1391 and 1878, when it was ceded to an independent Bulgaria.

guess what they mean; but nevertheless they tell us all things which we want to know.

'They make known to us among them, how last afternoon[5] at about five o'clock comes a man so hurry. A tall man, thin and pale, with high nose and teeth so white, and eyes that seem to be burning. That he be all in black, except that he have a hat of straw which suit not him or the time. That he scatter his money in making quick inquiry as to what ship sails for the Black Sea and for where. Some took him to the office and then to the ship, where he will not go aboard[6] but halt at shore end of gang-plank, and ask that the captain come to him. The captain come, when told that he will be pay well; and though he swear much at the first he agree to term. Then the thin man go and some one tell him where horse and cart can be hired. He go there, and soon he come again, himself driving cart on which is a great box; this he himself lift down, though it take several to put it on truck for the ship. He give much talk to captain as to how and where his box is to be place; but the captain like it not and swear at him in many tongues, and tell him that if he like he can come and see where it shall be. But he say "no"; that he come not yet, for that he have much to do. Whereupon the captain tell him that he had better be quick—with blood—for that his ship will leave the place—of blood—before the turn of the tide—with blood. Then the thin man smile, and say that of course he must go when he think fit; but he will be surprise if he go quite so soon. The captain swear again, polyglot, and the thin man make him bow, and thank him, and say that he will so far intrude on his kindness as to come aboard before the sailing. Final the captain, more red than ever, and in more tongues, tell him that he doesn't want no Frenchmen— with bloom upon them and also with blood—in his ship—with blood on her also. And so, after asking where there might be close at hand a shop where he might purchase ship forms, he departed.

'No one knew where he went "or bloomin' well cared", as they said, for they had something else to think of—well with blood again; for it soon became apparent to all that the Czarina Catherine would not sail as was expected. A thin mist began to creep up from the river, and it grew, and grew; till soon a dense fog enveloped the ship and all around her. The captain swore polyglot—very polyglot—polyglot with bloom and blood; but he could do nothing. The water rose and rose; and he began to fear that he would lose the tide altogether. He was in no friendly mood, when just at full tide, the thin man came up the gang-plank again and asked to see where his box had been stowed. Then the captain replied that he wished that he and his box—old and with much bloom and blood—were in hell. But the thin man did not be offend,

---

5. By the logic of internal chronology, Dracula would have located his ship on October 3, not on October 4 as it says here.
6. Because he must wait for the tide to turn before crossing running water.

and went down with the mate and saw where it was place, and came up and stood awhile on deck in fog. He must have come off by himself, for none notice him. Indeed they thought not of him; for soon the fog begin to melt away, and all was clear again. My friends of the thirst and the language that was of bloom and blood laughed, as they told how the captain's swears exceeded even his usual polyglot, and was more than ever full of picturesque, when on questioning other mariners who were on movement up and down on the river that hour, he found that few of them had seen any of fog at all, except where it lay round the wharf. However the ship went out on the ebb tide; and was doubt-less by morning far down the river mouth. She was by then, when they told us, well out to sea.

'And so my dear Madam Mina, it is that we have to rest for a time, for our enemy is on the sea, with the fog at his command, on his way to the Danube mouth. To sail a ship takes time, go she never so quick; and when we start we go on land more quick, and we meet him there. Our best hope is to come on him when in the box between sunrise and sunset; for then he can make no struggle, and we may deal with him as we should. There are days for us, in which we can make ready our plan. We know all about where he go; for we have seen the owner of the ship, who have shown us invoices and all papers that can be. The box we seek is to be landed in Varna, and to be given to an agent, one Ristics, who will there present his credentials; and so our merchant friend will have done his part. When he ask if there be any wrong, for that so, he can telegraph and have inquiry made at Varna, we say "no"; for what is to be done is not for police or of the customs. It must be done by us alone and in our own way.'

When Dr Van Helsing had done speaking, I asked him if it were certain the the Count had remained on board the ship. He replied: 'We have the best proof of that; your own evidence, when in the hyp-notic trance this morning.' I asked him again if it were really necessary that they should pursue the Count, for oh! I dread Jonathan leaving me, and I know that he would surely go if the others went. He answered in growing passion, at first quietly. As he went on, however, he grew more angry and more forceful, till in the end we could not but see wherein was at least some of that personal dominance which made him so long a master amongst men:—

'Yes it is necessary—necessary—necessary! For your sake in the first, and then for the sake of humanity. This monster has done much harm already, in the narrow scope where he find himself, and in the short time when as yet he was only as a body groping his so small measure in darkness and not knowing. All this have I told these others; you, my dear Madam Mina, will learn it in the phonograph of my friend John, or in that of your husband. I have told them how the measure of leaving his own barren land—barren of peoples—and coming to a new land

where life of man teems till they are like the multitude of standing
corn,[7] was the work of centuries. Were another of the Un-Dead, like
him, to try to do what he has done, perhaps not all the centuries of
the world that have been, or that will be, could aid him. With this one,
all the forces of nature that are occult and deep and strong must have
worked together in some wondrous way. The very place, where he have
been alive, Un-dead for all these centuries, is full of strangeness of the
geologic and chemical world. There are deep caverns and fissures that
reach none know whither. There have been volcanoes, some of whose
openings still send out waters of strange properties, and gases that kill
or make to vivify. Doubtless, there is something magnetic or electric in
some of these combinations of occult forces[8] which work for physical
life in strange way; and in himself were from the first some great qualities. In a hard and warlike time he was celebrate that he have more
iron nerve, more subtle brain, more braver heart, than any man. In
him some vital principle have in strange way found their utmost; and
as his body keep strong and grow and thrive, so his brain grow too. All
this without that diabolic aid which is surely to him; for it have to yield
to the powers that come from, and are, symbolic of good. And now this
is what he is to us. He have infect you—oh forgive me, my dear, that
I must say such; but it is for good of you that I speak. He infect you in
such wise, that even if he do no more, you have only to live—to live
in your own old, sweet way; and so in time, death, which is of man's
common lot and with God's sanction, shall make you like to him. This
must not be! We have sworn together that it must not. Thus are we
ministers of God's own wish: that the world, and men for whom His
Son die, will not be given over to monsters, whose very existence would
defame Him. He have allowed us to redeem one soul already, and we
go out as the old knights of the Cross to redeem more. Like them we
shall travel towards the sunrise; and like them, if we fall, we fall in
good cause.'

He paused and I said:—

'But will not the Count take his rebuff wisely? Since he has been
driven from England, will he not avoid it, as a tiger does the village
from which he has been hunted?'

'Aha!' he said, 'your simile of the tiger good, for me, and I shall adopt
him. Your man-eater, as they of India call the tiger who has once taste
blood of the human, care no more for other prey, but prowl unceasing
till he get him. This that we hunt from our village is a tiger, too, a
man-eater, and he never cease to prowl. Nay in himself he is not one
to retire and stay afar. In his life, his living life, he go over the Turkey

---

7. May echo the biblical injunction "When thou comest into the standing corn of thy neighbor,
    then thou mayest pluck the ears with thine hand; but thou shalt not move a sickle unto thy
    neighbor's standing corn" (Deuteronomy 23.25).
8. One of Stoker's periodic attempts to identify vampires with the landscape of Transylvania,
    ignoring the ease with which they adapt to England.

frontier and attack his enemy on his own ground; he be beaten back, but did he stay? No! He come again, and again, and again. Look at his persistence and endurance. With the child-brain that was to him he have long since conceive the idea of coming to a great city. What does he do? He find out the place of all the world most of promise for him. Then he deliberately set himself down to prepare for the task. He find in patience just how is his strength, and what are his powers. He study new tongues. He learn new social life; new environment of old ways, the politic, the law, the finance, the science, the habit of a new land and a new people who have come to be since he was. His glimpse that he have had, whet his appetite only and enkeen his desire. Nay, it help him to grow as to his brain; for it all prove to him how right he was at the first in his surmises. He have done this alone; all alone! from a ruin tomb in a forgotten land. What more may he not do when the greater world of thought is open to him. He that can smile at death, as we know him; who can flourish in the midst of diseases that kill off whole peoples. Oh! if such an one was to come from God, and not the Devil, what a force for good might he not be in this old world of ours. But we are pledged to set the world free. Our toil must be in silence, and our efforts all in secret; for in this enlightened age, when men believe not even what they see, the doubting of wise men would be his greatest strength. It would be at once his sheath and his armour, and his weapons to destroy us, his enemies, who are willing to peril even our own souls for the safety of one we love—for the good of mankind, and for the honour and glory of God.'

After a general discussion it was determined that for tonight nothing be definitely settled; that we should all sleep on the facts, and try to think out the proper conclusions. Tomorrow at breakfast we are to meet again, and, after making our conclusions known to one another, we shall decide on some definite cause of action.

I feel a wonderful peace and rest tonight. It is as if some haunting presence were removed from me. Perhaps . . .

My surmise was not finished, could not be; for I caught sight in the mirror of the red mark upon my forehead; and I knew that I was still unclean.

Dr Seward's Diary

5 October.—We all rose early, and I think that sleep did much for each and all of us. When we met at early breakfast there was more general cheerfulness than any of us had ever expected to experience again.

It is really wonderful how much resilience there is in human nature. Let any obstructing cause, no matter what, be removed in any way— even by death—and we fly back to first principles of hope and enjoyment. More than once as we sat around the table, my eyes opened in wonder whether the whole of the past days had not been a dream. It was only when I caught sight of the red blotch on Mrs Harker's forehead that I was brought back to reality. Even now, when I am gravely revolving the matter, it is almost impossible to realize that the cause of all our trouble is still existent. Even Mrs Harker seems to lose sight of her trouble for whole spells; it is only now and again, when something recalls it to her mind, that she thinks of her terrible scar. We are to meet here in my study in half an hour and decide on our course of action. I see only one immediate difficulty, I know it by instinct rather than reason: we shall all have to speak frankly; and yet I fear that in some mysterious way poor Mrs Harker's tongue is tied. I *know* that she forms conclusions of her own, and from all that has been I can guess how brilliant and how true they must be; but she will not, or cannot, give them utterance. I have mentioned this to Van Helsing, and he and I are to talk it over when we are alone. I suppose it is some of that horrid poison which has got into her veins beginning to work. The Count had his own purposes when he gave her what Van Helsing called 'the Vampire's baptism of blood.' Well, there may be a poison that distils itself out of good things; in an age when the existence of ptomaines[9] is a mystery we should not wonder at anything! One thing I know: that if my instinct be true regarding poor Mrs Harker's silences, then there is a terrible difficulty—an unknown danger—in the work before us. The same power that compels her silence may compel her speech. I dare not think further; for so I should in my thoughts dishonour a noble woman!

Van Helsing is coming to my study a little before the others. I shall try to open the subject with him.

Later.—When the Professor came in, we talked over the state of things. I could see that he had something on his mind which he wanted to say, but felt some hesitancy about broaching the subject. After beating about the bush a little, he said suddenly:—

'Friend John, there is something that you and I must talk of alone, just at the first at any rate. Later, we may have to take the others into our confidence;' then he stopped, so I waited; he went on:—

'Madam Mina, our poor, dear Madam Mina is changing.' A cold shiver ran through me to find my worst fears thus endorsed. Van Helsing continued:—

'With the sad experience of Miss Lucy, we must this time be warned before things go too far. Our task is now in reality more difficult than ever, and this new trouble makes every hour of the direst importance. I can see the characteristics of the vampire coming in her face. It is now but very, very slight; but it is to be seen if we have eyes to notice

9. Poisonous alkaloid substances found in decaying animal or vegetable bodies.

without to prejudge. Her teeth are some sharper, and at times her eyes are more hard. But these are not all, there is to her the silence now often; as so it was with Miss Lucy. She did not speak, even when she wrote that which she wished to be known later. Now my fear is this. If it be that she can, by our hypnotic trance, tell what the Count see and hear, is it not more true that he who have hypnotize her first, and who have drink of her very blood and make her drink of his, should, if he will, compel her mind to disclose to him that which she know?' I nodded acquiescence; he went on:—

'Then, what we must do is to prevent this; we must keep her ignorant[1] of our intent, and so she cannot tell what she know not. This is a painful task! Oh! so painful that it heartbreak me to think of; but it must be. When today we meet, I must tell her that for reason which we will not to speak she must not more be of our council, but be simply guarded by us.' He wiped his forehead, which had broken out in profuse perspiration at the thought of the pain which he might have to inflict upon the poor soul already so tortured. I knew that it would be some sort of comfort to him if I told him that I also had come to the same conclusion; for at any rate it would take away the pain of doubt. I told him, and the effect was as I expected.

It is now close to the time of our general gathering. Van Helsing has gone away to prepare for the meeting, and his painful part of it. I really believe his purpose is to be able to pray alone.

Later.—At the very outset of our meeting a great personal relief was experienced by both Van Helsing and myself. Mrs Harker had sent a message by her husband to say that she would not join us at present, as she thought it better that we should be free to discuss our movements without her presence to embarrass us. The Professor and I looked at each other for an instant, and somehow we both seemed relieved. For my own part, I thought that if Mrs Harker realized the danger herself, it was much pain as well as much danger averted. Under the circumstances we agreed, by a questioning look and answer, with finger on lip, to preserve silence of our suspicions, until we should have been able to confer alone again. We went at once into our plan of campaign. Van Helsing roughly put the facts before us first:—

'The *Czarina Catherine* left the Thames yesterday morning. It will take her at the quickest speed she has ever made at least three weeks to reach Varna; but we can travel overland to the same place in three days. Now, if we allow for two days less for the ship's voyage, owing to such weather influences as we know that the Count can bring to bear; and if we allow a whole day and night for any delays which may occur to us, then we have a margin of nearly two weeks. Thus, in order to

1. These men cannot make up their minds whether or not to include Mina in their work. In their peculiar circumstances, both inclusion and exclusion of a woman are likely to lead to disaster, but their vacillation also mirrors that of all Victorian men.

be quite safe, we must leave here on 17th at latest. Then we shall at any rate be in Varna a day before the ship arrives, and able to make such preparations as may be necessary. Of course we shall all go armed—armed against evil things, spiritual as well as physical.' Here Quincey Morris added:—

'I understand that the Count comes from a wolf country, and it may be that he shall get there before us. I propose that we add Winchesters[2] to our armament. I have a kind of belief in a Winchester when there is any trouble of that sort around. Do you remember Art, when we had the pack after us at Tobolsk?[3] What wouldn't we have given then for a repeater apiece.'

'Good!' said Van Helsing. 'Winchesters it shall be. Quincey's head is level at all times, but most so when there is to hunt, though my metaphor be more dishonour to science than wolves be of danger to man. In the meantime we can do nothing here; and as I think that Varna is not familiar to any of us, why not go there more soon? It is as long to wait here as there. Tonight and tomorrow we can get ready, and then, if all be well, we four can set out on our journey.'

'We four?' said Harker interrogatively, looking from one to another of us.

'Of course!' answered the Professor quickly, 'You must remain to take care of your so sweet wife!' Harker was silent for awhile and then said in a hollow voice:—

'Let us talk of that part of it in the morning. I want to consult with Mina.' I thought that now was the time for Van Helsing to warn him not to disclose our plans to her; but he took no notice. I looked at him significantly and coughed. For answer he put his finger on his lip and turned away.

Jonathan Harker's Journal

5 October, afternoon.—For some time after our meeting this morning I could not think. The new phases of things leave my mind in a state of wonder which allows not room for active thought. Mina's determination not to take any part in the discussion set me thinking; and as I could not argue the matter with her, I could only guess. I am as far as ever from a solution now. The way the others received it, too, puzzled me; the last time we talked of the subject we agreed that there was to be no more concealment of anything amongst us. Mina is sleeping now, calmly and sweetly like a little child. Her lips are curved and her face beams with happiness. Thank God there are such moments still for her.

Later.—How strange it all is. I sat watching Mina's happy sleep, and

2. Winchester rifles, introduced in the northern United States and Canada in 1866.
3. A city in western Siberia.

came as near to being happy myself as I suppose I shall ever be. As the evening drew on, and the earth took its shadows from the sun sinking lower, the silence of the room grew more and more solemn to me. All at once Mina opened her eyes, and looking at me tenderly, said:—

'Jonathan, I want you to promise me something on your word of honour. A promise made to me, but made holily on God's hearing, and not to be broken though I should go down on my knees and implore you with bitter tears. Quick, you must make it to me at once.'

'Mina,' I said, 'a promise like that, I cannot make at once. I may have no right to make it.'

'But, dear one,' she said, with such spiritual intensity that her eyes were like pole stars, 'it is I who wish it; and it is not for myself. You can ask Dr Van Helsing if I am not right; if he disagrees you may do as you will. Nay more, if you all agree, later, you are absolved from the promise.'

'I promise!' I said, and for a moment she looked supremely happy; though to me all happiness for her was denied by the red scar on her forehead. She said:—

'Promise me that you will not tell me anything of the plans formed for the campaign against the Count. Not by word, or inference, or implication; not at any time whilst this remains to me!' and she solemnly pointed to the scar. I saw that she was in earnest, and said solemnly:—

'I promise!' and as I said it I felt that from that instant a door had been shut between us.

Later, midnight.—Mina has been bright and cheerful all the evening. So much so that all the rest seemed to take courage, as if infected somewhat with her gaiety; as a result even I myself felt as if the pall of gloom which weighs us down were somewhat lifted. We all retired early. Mina is now sleeping like a little child; it is a wonderful thing that her faculty of sleep remains to her in the midst of her terrible trouble. Thank God for it, for then at least she can forget her care. Perhaps her example may affect me as her gaiety did tonight. I shall try it. Oh! for a dreamless sleep.

6 October, morning.—Another surprise. Mina woke me early, about the same time as yesterday,[4] and asked me to bring Dr Van Helsing. I thought that it was another occasion for hypnotism, and without question went for the Professor. He had evidently expected some such call, for I found him dressed in his room. His door was ajar, so that he could hear the opening of the door of our room. He came at once; as he passed into the room, he asked Mina if the others might come too.

'No,' she said quite simply, 'it will not be necessary. You can tell them just as well. I must go with you on your journey.'

4. Another inconsistency of dates: the first hypnotic session took place on October 4.

Dr Van Helsing was as startled as I was. After a moment's pause he asked:—

'But why?'

'You must take me with you. I am safer with you, and you shall be safer too.'

'But why, dear Madam Mina? You know that your safety is our solemnest duty. We go into danger, to which you are, or may be, more liable than any of us from—from circumstances—things that have been.' He paused embarrassed.

As she replied, she raised her finger and pointed to her forehead:—

'I know. That is why I must go. I can tell you now, whilst the sun is coming up; I may not be able again. I know that when the Count wills me I must go. I know that if he tells me to come in secret, I must come by wile; by any device to hoodwink—even Jonathan.' God saw the look that she turned on me as she spoke, and if there be indeed a Recording Angel that look is noted to her everlasting honour. I could only clasp her hand. I could not speak; my emotion was too great for even the relief of tears. She went on:—

'You men are brave and strong. You are strong in your numbers, for you can defy that which would break down the human endurance of one who had to guard alone. Besides, I may be of service, since you can hypnotize me and so learn that which even I myself do not know.' Dr Van Helsing said very gravely:—

'Madam Mina, you are, as always, most wise. You shall with us come; and together we shall do that which we go forth to achieve.' When he had spoken, Mina's long spell of silence made me look at her. She had fallen back on her pillow asleep; she did not even wake when I had pulled up the blind and let in the sunlight which flooded the room. Van Helsing motioned to me to come with him quietly. We went to his room, and within a minute Lord Godalming, Dr Seward, and Mr Morris were with us also. He told them what Mina had said, and went on:—

'In the morning we shall leave for Varna. We have now to deal with a new factor: Madam Mina. Oh, but her soul is true. It is to her an agony to tell us so much as she has done; but it is most right, and we are warned in time. There must be no chance lost, and in Varna we must be ready to act the instant when that ship arrives.'

'What shall we do exactly?' asked Mr Morris laconically. The Professor paused before replying:—

'We shall at the first board that ship; then, when we have identified the box, we shall place a branch of the wild rose on it. This we shall fasten, for when it is there none can emerge; so at least says the superstition. And to superstition must we trust at the first; it was man's faith in the early, and it have its root in faith still. Then, when we get the opportunity that we seek, when none are near to see, we shall open the box, and—and all will be well.'

'I shall not wait for any opportunity,' said Morris. 'When I see the box I shall open it and destroy the monster, though there were a thousand men looking on, and if I am to be wiped out for it the next moment!' I grasped his hand instinctively and found it as firm as a piece of steel. I think he understood my look; I hope he did.

'Good boy,' said Dr Van Helsing. 'Brave boy. Quincey is all man, God bless him for it. My child, believe me none of us shall lag behind or pause from any fear. I do but say what we may do—what we must do. But, indeed, indeed we cannot say what we shall do. There are so many things which may happen and their ways and their ends are so various that until the moment we may not say. We shall all be armed, in all ways; and when the time for the end has come, our effort shall not be lack. Now let us today put all our affairs in order. Let all things which touch on others dear to us, and who on us depend, be complete; for none of us can tell what, or when, or how, the end may be. As for me, my own affairs are regulate; and as I have nothing else to do, I shall go make arrangement for the travel. I shall have all tickets and so forth for our journey.'

There was nothing further to be said, and we parted. I shall now settle up all my affairs of earth, and be ready for whatever may come . . .

Later.—It is all done; my will is made, and all complete. Mina if she survive is my sole heir. If it should not be so, then the others who have been so good to us shall have remainder.

It is now drawing towards the sunset; Mina's uneasiness calls my attention to it. I am sure that there is something on her mind which the time of exact sunset will reveal. These occasions are becoming harrowing times for us all, for each sunrise and sunset opens up some new danger—some new pain, which however, may in God's will be means to a good end. I write all these things in the diary since my darling must not hear them now; but if it may be that she can see them again, they shall be ready.

She is calling to me.

Chapter XXV

Dr Seward's Diary

11 October, Evening.—Jonathan Harker has asked me to note this, as he says he is hardly equal to the task, and he wants an exact record kept.

I think that none of us were surprised when we were asked to see Mrs Harker a little before the time of sunset. We have of late come to understand that sunrise and sunset are to her times of peculiar freedom; when her old self can be manifest without any controlling force subduing or restraining her, or inciting her to action. This mood or condition begins some half hour or more before actual sunrise or sunset, and lasts till either the sun is high, or whilst the clouds are still aglow with the rays streaming above the horizon. At first there is a sort of negative condition, as if some tie were loosened, and then the absolute freedom quickly follows; when however the freedom ceases the change-back or relapse comes quickly preceded only by a spell of warning silence.

Tonight, when we met she was somewhat constrained, and bore all the signs of an internal struggle. I put it down myself to her making a violent effort at the earliest instant she could do so. A very few minutes, however, gave her complete control of herself; then, motioning her husband to sit beside her on the sofa where she was half reclining, she made the rest of us bring chairs up close. Taking her husband's hand in hers she began:—

'We are all here together in freedom, for perhaps the last time! I know, dear; I know that you will always be with me to the end.' This was to her husband whose hand had, as we could see, tightened upon hers. 'In the morning we go out upon our task, and God alone knows what may be in store for any of us. You are going to be so good to me as to take me with you. I know that all that brave earnest men can do for a poor weak woman, whose soul perhaps is lost—no, no, not yet, but is at any rate at stake—you will do. But you must remember that I am not as you are. There is a poison in my blood, in my soul, which may destroy me; which must destroy me, unless some relief comes to us. Oh, my friends, you know as well as I do, that my soul is at stake; and though I know there is one way out for me, you must not and I must not take it!' She looked appealingly to us all in turn, beginning and ending with her husband.

'What is that way?' asked Van Helsing in a hoarse voice. 'What is that way, which we must not—may not—take?'

'That I may die now, either by my own hand or that of another, before the greater evil is entirely wrought. I know and you know, that were I once dead you could and would set free my immortal spirit, even as you did my poor Lucy's. Were death, or the fear of death, the only thing that stood in the way I would not shrink to die here, now, amidst the friends who love me. But death is not all. I cannot believe that to die in such a case, when there is hope before us and a bitter task to be done, is God's will. Therefore, I on my part, give up here the certainty of eternal rest, and go out into the dark where may be the blackest things that the world or the nether world holds!' We were all silent, for we knew instinctively that this was only a prelude. The faces of the others were set, and Harker's grew ashen grey; perhaps he guessed better than any of us what was coming. She continued:—

'This is what I can give into the hotch-pot.'[1] I could not but note the quaint legal phrase which she used in such a place, and with all seriousness. 'What will each of you give? Your lives I know,' she went on quickly, 'that is easy for brave men. Your lives are God's, and you can give them back to Him; but what will you give to me?' She looked again questioningly, but this time avoided her husband's face. Quincey seemed to understand; he nodded, and her face lit up. 'Then I shall tell you plainly what I want, for there must be no doubtful matter in this connection between us now. You must promise me, one and all— even you my beloved husband—that, should the time come, you will kill me.'

'What is that time?' The voice was Quincey's, but it was low and strained.

'When you shall be convinced that I am so changed that it is better that I die that I may live. When I am thus dead in the flesh, then you will, without a moment's delay, drive a stake through me and cut off my head; or do whatever else may be wanting to give me rest!'

Quincey was the first to rise after the pause. He knelt down before her and taking her hand in his said solemnly:—

'I'm only a rough fellow, who hasn't, perhaps, lived as a man should to win such distinction, but I swear to you by all that I hold sacred and dear that, should the time ever come, I shall not flinch from the duty that you have set us. And I promise you, too, that I shall make all certain, for if I am only doubtful I shall take it that the time has come!'

'My true friend!' was all she could say amid her fast-falling tears, as, bending over, she kissed his hand.

'I swear the same, my dear Madam Mina!' said Van Helsing.

'And I!' said Lord Godalming, each of them in turn kneeling to her to take the oath.[2] I followed, myself. Then her husband turned to her, wan-eyed and with a greenish pallor which subdued the snowy whiteness of his hair, and asked:—

'And must I, too, make such a promise, oh, my wife?'

'You too, my dearest,' she said, with infinite yearning of pity in her voice and eyes. 'You must not shrink. You are nearest and dearest and all the world to me; our souls are knit into one, for all life and all time. Think dear, that there have been times when brave men have killed their wives and their womenkind, to keep them from falling into the hands of the enemy. Their hands did not falter any the more because

1. Legal slang, usually referring to the property of a deceased person that is to be divided.
2. The ritual oaths and stately tableaux so frequent in the last third of the novel reflect the contemporary popularity of Arthurian legend in poetry, plays, and paintings. In 1895 the Lyceum staged Comyns-Carr's *King Arthur*, a picturesque adaptation of Tennyson's *Idylls of the King*.

those that they loved implored them to slay them. It is men's duty towards those whom they love, in such times of sore trial! And oh, my dear, if it is to be that I must meet death at any hand, let it be at the hand of him that loves me best. Dr Van Helsing, I have not forgotten your mercy in poor Lucy's case to him who loved'—she stopped with a flying blush, and changed her phrase—'to him who had best right to give her peace. If that time shall come again, I look to you to make it a happy memory of my husband's life that it was his loving hand which set me free from the awful thrall upon me.'

'Again I swear!' came the Professor's resonant voice. Mrs Harker smiled, positively smiled, as with a sigh of relief she leaned back and said:—

'And now one word of warning, a warning which you must never forget: this time, if it ever come, may come quickly and unexpectedly, and in such case you must lose no time in using your opportunity. At such a time I myself might be—nay! if the time ever comes, *shall* be —leagued with your enemy against you.'

'One more request;' she became very solemn as she said this, 'it is not vital and necessary like the other, but I want you to do one thing for me, if you will.' We all acquiesced, but no one spoke; there was no need to speak:—

'I want you to read the Burial Service.' She was interrupted by a deep groan from her husband; taking his hand in hers, she held it over her heart, and continued. 'You must read it over me some day. Whatever may be the issue of all this fearful state of things, it will be a sweet thought to all or some of us. You, my dearest, will I hope read it, for then it will be in your voice in my memory for ever—come what may!'

'But oh, my dear one,' he pleaded, 'death is afar off from you.'

'Nay,' she said holding up a warning hand. 'I am deeper in death at this moment than if the weight of an earthly grave lay heavy upon me!'

'Oh, my wife, must I read it?' he said, before he began.

'It would comfort me, my husband!' was all she said; and he began to read when she had got the book ready.

How can I—how could anyone—tell of that strange scene, its solemnity, its gloom, its sadness, its horror; and, withal, its sweetness. Even a sceptic, who can see nothing but a travesty of bitter truth in anything holy or emotional, would have been melted to the heart had he seen that little group of loving and devoted friends kneeling round that stricken and sorrowing lady; or heard the tender passion of her husband's voice, as in tones so broken with emotion that often he had to pause, he read the simple and beautiful service for the Burial of the Dead. I—I cannot go on—words—and—v-voice—f-fail m-me! . . .

She was right in her instinct. Strange as it all was, bizarre as it may hereafter seem even to us who felt its potent influence at the time, it comforted us much; and the silence, which showed Mrs Harker's coming relapse from her freedom of soul, did not seem so full of despair to any of us as we had dreaded.

Jonathan Harker's Journal

15 October. Varna.—We left Charing Cross[3] on the morning of the 12th, got to Paris the same night, and took the places secured for us in the Orient Express.[4] We travelled night and day, arriving here at about five o'clock. Lord Godalming went to the Consulate to see if any telegram had arrived for him, whilst the rest of us came on to this hotel —the Odessus. The journey may have had incidents; I was, however, too eager to get on, to care for them. Until the *Czarina Catherine* comes into port there will be no interest for me in anything in the wide world. Thank God! Mina is well, and looks to be getting stronger; her colour is coming back. She sleeps a great deal; throughout the journey she slept nearly all the time. Before sunrise and sunset, however, she is very wakeful and alert; and it has become a habit for Van Helsing to hypnotize her at such times. At first, some effort was needed, and he had to make many passes; but now, she seems to yield at once, as if by habit, and scarcely any action is needed. He seems to have power at these particular moments to simply will, and her thoughts obey him. He always asks her what she can see and hear. She answers to the first:—

'Nothing; all is dark.' And to the second:—

'I can hear the waves lapping against the ship, and the water rushing by. Canvas and cordage strain and masts and yards creak. The wind is high—I can hear it in the shrouds, and the bow throws back the foam.'

It is evident that the *Czarina Catherine* is still at sea, hastening on her way to Varna. Lord Godalming has just returned. He had four telegrams, one each day since we started, and all to the same effect: that the *Czarina Catherine* had not been reported to Lloyd's[5] from anywhere. He had arranged before leaving London that his agent should send him every day a telegram saying if the ship had been reported. He was to have a message even if she were not reported, so that he might be sure that there was a watch being kept at the other end of the wire.

We had dinner and went to bed early. Tomorrow we are to see the Vice-Consul, and to arrange, if we can, about getting on board the ship as soon as she arrives. Van Helsing says that our chance will be to get on board between sunrise and sunset. The Count, even if he takes the form of a bat, cannot cross the running water of his own volition, and

3. One of London's largest railroad terminals, near Trafalgar Square.
4. A luxurious express train from Paris to Istanbul. Jonathan is traveling in high style compared to his difficult journey in the beginning of the book. It is unlikely, though, that even the best accommodations could get our heroes from London to Varna in three days.
5. Lloyd's of London, a magisterial insurance company.

so cannot leave the ship. As he dare not change to man's form without suspicion—which he evidently wishes to avoid—he must remain in the box. If, then, we can come on board after sunrise, he is at our mercy; for we can open the box and make sure of him, as we did of poor Lucy, before he wakes. What mercy he shall get from us will not count for much. We think that we shall not have much trouble with officials or the seamen. Thank God! this is the country where bribery can do anything, and we are well supplied with money. We have only to make sure that the ship cannot come into port between sunset and sunrise without our being warned, and we shall be safe. Judge Moneybag will settle this case, I think!

16 October.—Mina's report still the same: lapping waves and rushing water, darkness and favouring winds. We are evidently in good time, and when we hear of the *Czarina Catherine* we shall be ready. As she must pass the Dardanelles[6] we are sure to have some report.

17 October.—Everything is pretty well fixed now, I think, to welcome the Count on his return from his tour. Godalming told the shippers that he fancied that the box sent aboard might contain something stolen from a friend of his, and got a half consent that he might open it at his own risk. The owner gave him a paper telling the Captain to give him every facility in doing whatever he chose on board the ship, and also a similar authorization to his agent at Varna. We have seen the agent, who was much impressed with Godalming's kindly manner to him, and we are all satisfied that whatever he can do to aid our wishes will be done. We have already arranged what to do in case we get the box open. If the Count is there, Van Helsing and Seward will cut off his head at once and drive a stake through his heart. Morris and Godalming and I shall prevent interference, even if we have to use the arms which we shall have ready. The Professor says that if we can so treat the Count's body, it will soon after fall into dust. In such case there would be no evidence against us, in case any suspicion of murder were aroused. But even if it were not, we should stand or fall by our act, and perhaps some day this very script may be evidence to come between some of us and a rope. For myself, I should take the chance only too thankfully if it were to come. We mean to leave no stone unturned to carry out our intent. We have arranged with certain officials that the instant the *Czarina Catherine* is seen, we are to be informed by a special messenger.

24 October.—A whole week of waiting. Daily telegrams to Godalming, but only the same story: 'Not yet reported.' Mina's morning and evening hypnotic answer is unvaried: lapping waves, rushing water, and creaking masts.

6. A narrow strait, formerly called the Hellespont, separating European from Asian Turkey. Along with the Bosporous and the Sea of Marmara, it is the only outlet of the Black Sea.

Rufus Smith, Lloyd's, London, to Lord Godalming, Care of H.B.M.[7]
Vice-Consul, Varna

Telegram, October 24th.
Czarina Catherine reported this morning from Dardanelles.

Dr Seward's Diary

25 October.—How I miss my phonograph! To write diary with a pen is irksome to me; but Van Helsing says I must. We were all wild with excitement yesterday when Godalming got his telegram from Lloyd's. I know now what men feel in battle when the call to action is heard. Mrs Harker, alone of our party, did not show any signs of emotion. After all, it is not strange that she did not; for we took special care not to let her know anything about it, and we all tried not to show any excitement when we were in her presence. In old days she would, I am sure, have noticed, no matter how we might have tried to conceal it; but in this way she is greatly changed during the past three weeks. The lethargy grows upon her, and though she seems strong and well, and is getting back some of her colour, Van Helsing and I are not satisfied. We talk of her often; we have not, however, said a word to the others. It would break poor Harker's heart—certainly his nerve—if he knew that we had even a suspicion on the subject. Van Helsing examines, he tells me, her teeth very carefully, whilst she is in the hypnotic condition, for he says that so long as they do not begin to sharpen there is no active danger of a change in her. If this change should come, it would be necessary to take steps! . . . We both know what those steps would have to be, though we do not mention our thoughts to each other. We should neither of us shrink from the task —awful though it be to contemplate. 'Euthanasia' is an excellent and a comforting word! I am grateful to whoever invented it.

It is only about 24 hours' sail from the Dardanelles to here, at the rate the *Czarina Catherine* has come from London. She should therefore arrive some time in the morning; but as she cannot possibly get in before then, we are all about to retire early. We shall get up at one o'clock, so as to be ready.

25 October, Noon.—No news yet of the ship's arrival. Mrs Harker's hypnotic report this morning was the same as usual, so it is possible that we may get news at any moment. We men are all in a fever of excitement, except Harker, who is calm; his hands are as cold as ice, and an hour ago I found him whetting the edge of the great Ghurka knife which he now always carries with him. It will be a bad look out

7. Her Britannic Majesty.

for the Count if the edge of that 'Kúkri' ever touches his throat, driven by that stern, ice-cold hand!

Van Helsing and I were a little alarmed about Mrs Harker today. About noon she got into a sort of lethargy which we did not like; although we kept silence to the others, we were neither of us happy about it. She had been restless all the morning, so that we were at first glad to know that she was sleeping. When, however, her husband mentioned casually that she was sleeping so soundly that he could not wake her, we went to her room to see for ourselves. She was breathing naturally and looked so well and peaceful that we agreed that the sleep was better for her than anything else. Poor girl, she has so much to forget that it is no wonder that sleep, if it brings oblivion to her, does her good.

Later.—Our opinion was justified, for when after a refreshing sleep of some hours she woke up, she seemed brighter and better than she has been for days. At sunset she made the usual hypnotic report. Wherever he may be in the Black Sea, the Count is hurrying to his destination. To his doom I trust!

26 October.—Another day and no tidings of the *Czarina Catherine*. She ought to be here by now. That she is still journeying *somewhere* is apparent, for Mrs Harker's hypnotic report at sunrise was still the same. It is possible that the vessel may be lying by, at times, for fog; some of the steamers which came in last evening reported patches of fog both to north and south of the port. We must continue our watching, as the ship may now be signalled any moment.

27 October, Noon.—Most strange; no news yet of the ship we wait for. Mrs Harker reported last night and this morning as usual: 'lapping waves and rushing water,' though she added that 'the waves were very faint.' The telegrams from London have been the same: 'no further report.' Van Helsing is terribly anxious, and told me just now that he fears the Count is escaping us. He added significantly:—

'I did not like that lethargy of Madam Mina's. Souls and memories can do strange things during trance.' I was about to ask him more, but Harker just then came in, and he held up a warning hand. We must try tonight, at sunset, to make her speak more fully when in her hypnotic state.

28 October—Telegram, Rufus Smith, London, to Lord Godalming, Care of H.B.M. Vice-Consul, Varna

Czarina Catherine reported entering Galatz[8] at one o'clock today.

8. A Romanian port on the Black Sea, built-up and cosmopolitan in the 1890s.

Dr Seward's Diary

28 October.—When the telegram came announcing the arrival in Galatz I do not think it was such a shock to any of us as might have been expected. True, we did not know whence, or how, or when, the bolt would come; but I think we all expected that something strange would happen. The delay of arrival at Varna made us individually satisfied that things would not be just as we had expected; we only waited to learn where the change would occur. None the less, however, was it a surprise. I suppose that nature works on such a hopeful basis that we believe against ourselves that things will be as they ought to be, not as we should know that they will be. Transcendentalism[9] is a beacon to the angels, even if it be a will-o'-the-wisp to man. It was an odd experience, and we all took it differently. Van Helsing raised his hands over his head for a moment, as though in remonstrance with the Almighty; but he said not a word, and in a few seconds stood up with his face sternly set. Lord Godalming grew very pale, and sat breathing heavily. I was myself half stunned and looked in wonder at one after another. Quincey Morris tightened his belt with that quick movement which I knew so well; in our old wandering days it meant 'action.' Mrs Harker grew ghastly white, so that the scar on her forehead seemed to burn, but she folded her hands meekly and looked up in prayer. Harker smiled—actually smiled—the dark bitter smile of one who is without hope; but at the same time his action belied his words, for his hands instinctively sought the hilt of the great Kukri knife and rested there. 'When does the next train start for Galatz?' said Van Helsing to us generally.

'At 6.30 tomorrow morning!' We all stared, for the answer came from Mrs Harker.

'How on earth do you know?' said Art.

'You forget—or perhaps you do not know, though Jonathan does and so does Dr Van Helsing—that I am the train fiend. At home in Exeter I always used to make up the timetables, so as to be helpful to my husband. I found it so useful sometimes, that I always make a study of the timetables now. I knew that if anything were to take us to Castle Dracula we should go by Galatz, or at any rate through Bucharest, so I learned the times very carefully. Unhappily there are not many to learn, as the only train tomorrow leaves as I say.'

'Wonderful woman!' murmured the Professor.

'Can't we get a special?' asked Lord Godalming. Van Helsing shook his head: 'I fear not. This land is very different from yours or mine; even if we did have a special, it would probably not arrive as soon as

9. A nineteenth-century system of secular mysticism, relying not on religious dogma but on each individual's affinity with immanent cosmic forces in the universe. Transcendentalism reached its height of influence in New England between 1830 and 1850, but it went on to influence future generations of American writers, including Bram Stoker's hero Walt Whitman.

our regular train. Moreover we have something to prepare. We must think. Now let us organize. You, friend Arthur, go to the train and get the tickets and arrange that all be ready for us to go in the morning. Do you, friend Jonathan, go to the agent of the ship and get from him letters to the agent in Galatz, with authority to make search the ship just as it was here. Morris Quincey, you see the Vice-Consul, and get his aid with his fellow in Galatz and all he can do to make our way smooth, so that no times be lost when over the Danube. John will stay with Madam Mina and me, and we shall consult. For so if time be long you may be delayed; and it will not matter when the sun set, since I am here with Madam to make report.'

'And I,' said Mrs Harker brightly, and more like her old self than she had been for many a long day, 'shall try to be of use in all ways, and shall think and write for you as I used to do. Something is shifting from me in some strange way, and I feel freer than I have been of late!' The three younger men looked happier at the moment as they seemed to realize the significance of her words; but Van Helsing and I, turning to each other, met each a grave and troubled glance. We said nothing at the time however.

When the three men had gone out to their tasks Van Helsing asked Mrs Harker to look up the copy of the diaries and find him the part of Harker's journal at the Castle. She went away to get it; when the door was shut upon her he said to me:—

'We mean the same! speak out!'

'There is some change. It is a hope that makes me sick, for it may deceive us.'

'Quite so. Do you know why I asked her to get the manuscript?'

'No!' said I, 'unless it was to get an opportunity of seeing me alone.'

'You are in part right, friend John, but only in part. I want to tell you something. And oh, my friend, I am taking a great—a terrible—risk; but I believe it is right. In the moment when Madam Mina said those words that arrest both our understanding, an inspiration come to me. In the trance of three days ago the Count sent her his spirit to read her mind; or more like he took her to see him in his earth-box in the ship with water rushing, just as it go free at rise and set of sun. He learn then that we are here; for she have more to tell in her open life with eyes to see and ears to hear than he, shut, as he is, in his coffin-box. Now he make his most effort to escape us. At present he want her not. He is sure with his so great knowledge that she will come at his call; but he cut her off—take her, as he can do, out of his own power, that so she come not to him. Ah! there I have hope that our man-brains that have been of man so long and that have not lost the grace of God, will come higher than his child-brain that lie in his tomb for centuries, that grow not yet to our stature, and that do only work selfish and therefore small. Here comes Madam Mina; not a word to her of her trance! She know it not; and it would overwhelm her and make despair just when we want all her hope, all her courage; when most we want all her great brain which is trained like man's brain, but is of sweet woman and have a special power which the Count give her, and which he may not take away altogether—though he think not so. Hush! let me speak, and you shall learn. Oh John, my friend, we are in awful straits. I fear, as I never feared before. We can only trust the good God. Silence! here she comes!'

I thought that the Professor was going to break down and have hysterics, just as he had when Lucy died, but with a great effort he controlled himself and was at perfect nervous poise when Mrs Harker tripped into the room, bright and happy-looking and, in the doing of work, seemingly forgetful of her misery. As she came in, she handed a number of sheets of typewriting to Van Helsing. He looked over them gravely, his face brightening up as he read. Then holding the pages between his finger and thumb he said:—

'Friend John, to you with so much of experience already—and you too, dear Madam Mina, that are young,—here is a lesson: do not fear ever to think. A half-thought has been buzzing often in my brain, but I fear to let him loose his wings. Here now, with more knowledge, I go back to where that half-thought come from, and I find that he be no half-thought at all; that be a whole thought, though so young that he is not yet strong to use his little wings. Nay, like the 'Ugly Duck' of my friend Hans Andersen,[1] he be no duck-thought at all, but a big swan-thought that sail nobly on big wings, when the time come for him to try them. See I read here what Jonathan have written:—

'That other of his race who, in a later age, again and again, brought his forces over the Great River into Turkey Land; who, when he was beaten back, came again, and again, and again, though he had to come alone from the bloody field where his troops were being slaughtered, since he knew that he alone could ultimately triumph.'

What does this tell us? Not much? no! The Count's child-thought see nothing; therefore he speak so free. Your man-thought see nothing; my man-thought see nothing, till just now. No! But there comes another word from someone who speak without thought because she too know not what it mean—what it *might* mean. Just as there are elements which rest, yet when in nature's course they move on their way and they touch—then pouf! and there comes a flash of light, heaven's wide, that blind and kill and destroy some; but that show up all earth below for leagues and leagues. Is it not so? Well, I shall explain. To begin, have you ever study the philosophy of crime? 'Yes' and 'No.' You, John, yes; for it is a study of insanity. You, no, Madam Mina; for crime touch

---

1. The Danish writer Hans Christian Andersen (1805–1875) invented many fantasies that have passed into legend. His "Ugly Duckling," like many of his other tales and like *Dracula* itself, features surprising physical transformations.

you not—not but once. Still, your mind works true, and argues not *a particulari ad universale*.[2] There is this peculiarity in criminals. It is so constant, in all countries and at all times, that even police, who know not much from philosophy, come to know it empirically, that *it is*. That is to be empiric. The criminal always work at one crime—that is the true criminal who seems predestinate to crime, and who will of none other. This criminal has not full man-brain. He is clever and cunning and resourceful; but he be not of man-stature as to brain. He be of child-brain in much. Now this criminal of ours is predestinate to crime also; he too have child-brain, and it is of the child to do what he have done. The little bird, the little fish, the little animal learn not by principle, but empirically; and when he learn to do, then there is to him the ground to start from to do more. 'Dos *pou sto*,' said Archimedes. 'Give me a fulcrum, and I shall move the world!' To do once, is the fulcrum whereby child-brain become man-brain; and until he have the purpose to do more, he continue to do the same again every time, just as he have done before! Oh, my dear. I see that your eyes are opened, and that to you the lightning flash show all the leagues,' for Mrs Harker began to clap her hands, and her eyes sparkled. He went on:—

'Now you shall speak. Tell us two dry men of science what you see with those so bright eyes.' He took her hand and held it whilst she spoke. His finger and thumb closed on her pulse, as I thought instinctively and unconsciously, as she spoke:—

'The Count is a criminal and of criminal type. Nordau[3] and Lombroso[4] would so classify him, and *qua* criminal he is of imperfectly formed mind. Thus, in a difficulty he has to seek resource in habit. His past is a clue, and the one page of it that we know—and that from his own lips—tells that once before, when in what Mr Morris would call a 'tight place,' he went back to his own country from the land he had tried to invade, and thence, without losing purpose, prepared himself for a new effort. He came again, better equipped for his work; and won. So he came to London to invade a new land. He was beaten, and when all hope of success was lost, and his existence in danger, he fled back over the sea to his home; just as formerly he had fled back over the Danube from Turkey land.'

'Good, good! oh, you so clever lady!' said Van Helsing, enthusiastically, as he stooped and kissed her hand. A moment later he said to me, as calmly as though we had been having a sick room consultation:—

2. From the particular to the general (Latin).
3. Max Nordau's *Degeneration* (1893) argued that the human race, especially the Anglo-Saxons, was deteriorating and was thus fated to endure cultural decay. Nordau's prophecy of doom had a great influence on *fin-de-siècle* Victorian assumptions.
4. Cesare Lombroso's *L'uomo Delinqente*, or *Criminal Man* (1875), was an influential anatomy of deviance in criminals, who, Lombroso claimed, could be identified by their facial and racial characteristics.

'Seventy-two only; and in all this excitement. I have hope.' Turning to her again, he said with keen expectation:—

'But go on. Go on! there is more to tell if you will. Be not afraid; John and I know. I do in any case, and shall tell you if you are right. Speak, without fear!'

'I will try to; but you will forgive me if I seem egotistical.'

'Nay! fear not, you must be egotist, for it is of you that we think.'

'Then, as he is criminal he is selfish; and as his intellect is small and his action is based on selfishness, he confines himself to one purpose. That purpose is remorseless. As he fled back over the Danube, leaving his forces to be cut to pieces, so now he is intent on being safe, careless of all. So, his own selfishness frees my soul somewhat of the terrible power which he acquired over me on that dreadful night. I felt it, Oh! I felt it. Thank God, for His great mercy! My soul is freer than it has been since that awful hour; and all that haunts me is a fear lest in some trance or dream he may have used my knowledge for his ends.' The Professor stood up:—

'He has so used your mind; and by it he has left us here in Varna, whilst the ship that carried him rushed through enveloping fog up to Galatz, where, doubtless, he had made preparation for escaping from us. But his child-mind only saw so far; and it may be that, as ever is in God's Providence, the very thing that the evil doer most reckoned on for his selfish good, turns out to be his chiefest harm. The hunter is taken in his own snare, as the great Psalmist says.[5] For now that he think he is free from every trace of us all, and that he has escaped us with so many hours to him, then his selfish child-brain will whisper him to sleep. He think, too, that as he cut himself off from knowing your mind, there can be no knowledge of him to you; there is where he fail! That terrible baptism of blood which he give you makes you free to go to him in spirit, as you have as yet done in your times of freedom, when the sun rise and set. At such times you go by my volition and not by his; and this power to good of you and others, you have won from your suffering at his hands. This is now all more precious that he know it not, and to guard himself have even cut himself off from his knowledge of our where. We, however, are not all selfish, and we believe that God is with us through all this blackness, and these many dark hours. We shall follow him; and we shall not flinch; even if we peril ourselves that we become like him. Friend John, this has been a great hour; and it have done much to advance us on our way. You must be scribe and write him all down, so that when the others return from their work you can give it to them; then they shall know as we do.'

5. See, for instance, Psalm 57.6: "They have prepared a net for my steps; my soul is bowed down: they have digged a pit before me, into the midst whereof they are fallen themselves."

And so I have written it whilst we wait their return, and Mrs Harker has written with her typewriter all since she brought the MS to us.

Chapter XXVI

Dr Seward's Diary

29 October.—This is written in the train from Varna to Galatz. Last night we all assembled a little before the time of sunset. Each of us had done his work as well as he could; so far as thought, and endeavour, and opportunity go, we are prepared for the whole of our journey, and for our work when we get to Galatz. When the usual time came round Mrs Harker prepared herself for her hypnotic effort; and after a longer and more strenuous effort on the part of Van Helsing than has been usually necessary, she sank into the trance. Usually she speaks on a hint; but this time the Professor had to ask her questions, and to ask them pretty resolutely, before we could learn anything; at last her answer came:—

'I can see nothing; we are still; there are no waves lapping, but only a steady swirl of water softly running against the hawser.[1] I can hear men's voices calling, near and far, and the roll and creak of oars in the rowlocks. A gun is fired somewhere; the echo of it seems far away. There is tramping of feet overhead, and ropes and chains are dragged along. What is this? There is a gleam of light; I can feel the air blowing upon me.'

Here she stopped. She had risen, as if impulsively, from where she lay on the sofa, and raised both her hands, palms upwards, as if lifting a weight. Van Helsing and I looked at each other with understanding. Quincey raised his eyebrows slightly and looked at her intently, whilst Harker's hand instinctively closed round the hilt of his kúkri. There was a long pause. We all knew that the time when she could speak was passing; but we felt that it was useless to say anything. Suddenly she sat up, and, as she opened her eyes, said sweetly:—

'Would none of you like a cup of tea? You must all be so tired!' We would only make her happy, and so acquiesced. She bustled off to get tea; when she had gone Van Helsing said:—

'You see, my friends. *He* is close to land: he has left his earth-chest. But he has yet to get on shore. In the night he may lie hidden somewhere; but if he be not carried on shore, or if the ship do not touch it, he cannot achieve the land. In such case he can, if it be in the night, change his form and can jump or fly on shore, as he did at Whitby. But if the day come before he get on shore, then, unless he

1. Ship's rope or cable.

be carried he cannot escape. And if he be carried, then the customs may discover what the box contains. Thus, in fine, if he escape not on shore tonight, or before dawn, there will be the whole day lost to him. We may then arrive in time; for if he escape not at night we shall come on him in daytime, boxed up and at our mercy; for he dare not be his true self, awake and visible, lest he be discovered.'

There was no more to be said, so we waited in patience until the dawn; at which time we might learn more from Mrs Harker.

Early this morning we listened, with breathless anxiety, for her response in her trance. The hypnotic stage was even longer in coming than before; and when it came the time remaining until full sunrise was so short that we began to despair. Van Helsing seemed to throw his whole soul into the effort; at last, in obedience to his will she made reply:—

'All is dark. I hear lapping water, level with me, and some creaking as of wood on wood.' She paused, and the red sun shot up. We must wait till tonight.

And so it is that we are travelling towards Galatz in an agony of expectation. We are due to arrive between two and three in the morning; but already, at Bucharest,[2] we are three hours late, so we cannot possibly get in till well after sun-up. Thus we shall have two more hypnotic messages from Mrs Harker; either or both may possibly throw more light on what is happening.

Later.—Sunset has come and gone. Fortunately it came at a time when there was no distraction; for had it occurred whilst we were at a station, we might not have secured the necessary calm and isolation. Mrs Harker yielded to the hypnotic influence even less readily than this morning. I am in fear that her power of reading the Count's sensations may die away, just when we want it most. It seems to me that her imagination is beginning to work. Whilst she has been in the trance hitherto she has confined herself to the simplest of facts. If this goes on it may ultimately mislead us. If I thought that the Count's power over her would die away equally with her power of knowledge it would be a happy thought; but I am afraid that it may not be so. When she did speak, her words were enigmatical:—

'Something is going out; I can feel it pass me like a cold wind. I can hear, far off, confused sounds—as of men talking in strange tongues, fierce-falling water, and the howling of wolves.' She stopped and a shudder ran through her, increasing in intensity for a few seconds, till, at the end, she shook as though in a palsy. She said no more, even in answer to the Professor's imperative questioning. When she woke from the trance, she was cold, and exhausted, and languid; but her mind

2. The capital of Romania; a large and lively city. Like most of this return journey, it is a modernized contrast to Jonathan's eerie introduction to Romania at the beginning.

was all alert. She could not remember anything, but asked what she had said; when she was told, she pondered over it deeply, for a long time and in silence.

30 October, 7 a.m.—We are near Galatz now, and I may not have time to write later. Sunrise this morning was anxiously looked for by us all. Knowing of the increasing difficulty of procuring the hypnotic trance Van Helsing began his passes earlier than usual. They produced no effect, however, until the regular time when she yielded with a still greater difficulty, only a minute before the sun rose. The Professor lost no time in his questioning; her answer came with equal quickness:—

'All is dark. I hear water swirling by, level with my ears, and the creaking of wood on wood. Cattle low far off. There is another sound, a queer one like—' she stopped and grew white, and whiter still.

'Go on; Go on! Speak, I command you!' said Van Helsing in an agonized voice. At the same time there was despair in his eyes, for the risen sun was reddening even Mrs Harker's pale face. She opened her eyes, and we all started as she said, sweetly and seemingly with the utmost unconcern:—

'Oh Professor why ask me to do what you know I can't? I don't remember anything.' Then, seeing the look of amazement on our faces, she said, turning from one to the other with a troubled look:—

'What have I said? What have I done? I know nothing, only that I was lying here, half asleep, and I heard you say "go on! speak, I command you!" It seemed so funny to hear you order me about, as if I were a bad child!'[3]

'Oh, Madam Mina' he said, sadly, 'it is proof, if proof be needed, of how I love and honour you, when a word for your good, spoken more earnest than ever, can seem so strange because it is to order her whom I am proud to obey!'

The whistles are sounding; we are nearing Galatz. We are on fire with anxiety and eagerness.

Mina Harker's Journal

30 October.—Mr Morris took me to the hotel where our rooms had been ordered by telegraph, he being the one who could best be spared, since he does not speak any foreign language. The forces were distributed much as they had been at Varna, except that Lord Godalming went to the Vice-Consul as his rank might serve as an immediate guarantee of some sort to the official, we being in extreme hurry. Jonathan and the two doctors went to the shipping agent to learn particulars of the arrival of the *Czarina Catherine.*

Later.—Lord Godalming has returned. The Consul is away, and the

---

3. Mina has, until now, embraced male control; her faint complaint here echoes many late Victorian feminists' resistance to infantilization.

Vice-Consul sick; so the routine work has been attended to by a clerk. He was very obliging, and offered to do anything in his power.

Jonathan Harker's Journal

30 October.—At nine o'clock Dr Van Helsing, Dr Seward, and I called on Messrs Mackenzie & Steinkoff, the agents of the London firm of Hapgood. They had received a wire from London, in answer to Lord Godalming's telegraphed request, asking them to show us any civility in their power. They were more than kind and courteous, and took us at once on board the *Czarina Catherine* which lay at anchor out in the river harbour. There were sat the Captain, Donelson[4] by name, who told us of his voyage. He said that in all his life he had never had so favourable a run.

'Man!' he said, 'but it made us afeard, for we expeckit that we should have to pay for it wi' some rare piece o'ill luck, so as to keep up the average. It's no canny[5] to run frae London to the Black Sea wi' a wind ahint[6] ye, as though the Deil himself were blawin' on yer sail for his ain purpose. An' a' the time we could no speer[7] a thing. Gin[8] we were nigh a ship, or a port, or a headland, a fog fell on us and travelled wi' us, till when after it had lifted and we looked out, the deil a thing could we see. We ran by Gibralter wi'oot bein' able to signal; an' till we came to the Dardanelles and had to wait to get our permit to pass, we never were within hail o'aught. At first I inclined to slack off sail and beat about till the fog was lifted; but whiles,[9] I thocht that if the Deil was minded to get us into the Black Sea quick, he was like to do it whether we would or no. If we had a quick voyage it would be no to our miscredit wi' the owners, or no hurt to our traffic' an' the Old Mon[1] who had served his ain purpose wad be decently grateful to us for no hinderin' him.' This mixture of simplicity and cunning of superstition and commercial reasoning, aroused Van Helsing, who said:—

'Mine friend, that Devil is more clever than he is thought by some; and he know when he meet his match!' The skipper was not displeased with the compliment, and went on:—

'When we got past the Bosphorus the men began to grumble; some o' them, the Roumanians, came and asked me to heave overboard a big box which had been put on board by a queer lookin' old man just before we had started frae London. I had seen them speer at the fellow, and put out their twa fingers when they saw him, to guard against the

4. Donelson's thick Scottish dialect is the last obfuscating language we will hear. Like Mr. Swales's impenetrable Yorkshire speech, it is ostensibly British.
5. Not natural.
6. Behind.
7. See.
8. When.
9. But then.
1. The old man: the devil.

evil eye. Man! But the supersteetion of foreigners is pairfectly ridee-culous! I sent them aboot their business pretty quick; but as just after a fog closed in on us, I felt a wee bit as they did anent[2] something, though I wouldn't say it was agin[3] the bit box. Well, on we went, and as the fog didn't let up for five days I joost let the wind carry us; for if the Deil wanted to get somewheres—well, he would fetch it up a'reet. An' if he didn't, well we'd keep a sharp look out anyhow. Sure enuch, we had a fair way and deep water all the time; and two days ago, when the mornin' sun came through the fog, we found ourselves just in the river opposite Galatz. The Roumanians were wild, and wanted me right or wrong to take out the box and flint it in the river. I had to argy wi' them aboot it wi' a handspike; an' when the last o' them rose off the deck, wi' his head in his hand, I had convinced them that, evil eye or no evil eye, the property and the trust of my owners were better in my hands than in the river Danube. They had, mind ye, taken the box on the deck ready to fling in, and as it was marked Galatz *viâ* Varna, I thocht I'd let it lie till we discharged in the port an' get rid o't athe-gither. We didn't do much clearin' that day, an' had to remain the nicht at anchor; but in the mornin', braw[4] an' airly, an hour before sun-up, a man came aboard wi' an order, written to him from England, to receive a box marked for one Count Dracula. Sure enuch the matter was one ready to his hand. He had his papers a' reet, an' glad I was to be rid o' the dam thing, for I was beginnin' masel' to feel uneasy at it. If the Deil did have any luggage aboord the ship, I'm thinkin' it was nane ither than that same!'

'What was the name of the man who took it?' asked Dr Van Helsing with restrained eagerness.

'I'll be tellin' ye quick!' he answered, and, stepping down to his cabin, produced a receipt signed 'Immanuel Hildesheim.' Burgen-strasse 16 was the address. We found out that this was all the Captain knew; so with thanks we came away.

We found Hildesheim in his office, a Hebrew of rather the Adelphi Theatre type, with a nose like a sheep,[5] and a fez. His arguments were pointed with specie[6]—we doing the punctuation—and with a little bar-gaining he told us what he knew. This turned out to be simple but important. He had received a letter from Mr de Ville of London, telling him to receive, if possible before sunrise so as to avoid customs, a box which would arrive at Galatz in the *Czarina Catherine*. This he was to

2. About.
3. Against.
4. Brave; here, good, fine.
5. Jonathan's cavalier anti-Semitism may accompany his rise in the social scale: throughout the Victorian age, a casual contempt for Jews was part of a gentleman's idiom. In the 1890s, as Jewish emigration swelled, so did pseudoscientific racial theories, and anti-Semitism became increasingly virulent in England. The Adelphi Theater specialized in farces and melodramas.
6. Coins.

give in charge to a certain Petrof Skinsky, who dealt with the Slovaks who traded down the river to the port. He had been paid for his work by an English bank note, which had been duly cashed for gold at the Danube International Bank. When Skinsky had come to him, he had taken him to the ship and handed over the box, so as to save porterage. That was all he knew.

We then sought for Skinsky, but were unable to find him. One of his neighbours, who did not seem to bear him any affection, said that he had gone away two days before, no one knew whither. This was corroborated by his landlord who had received by messenger the key of the house together with the rent due, in English money. This had been between ten and eleven o'clock last night. We were at a standstill again.

Whilst we were talking one came running and breathlessly gasped out that the body of Skinsky had been found inside the wall of the churchyard of St Peter, and that the throat had been torn open as if by some wild animal. Those we had been speaking with ran off to see the horror, the women crying out 'This is the work of a Slovak!' We hurried away lest we should have been in some way drawn into the affair, and so detained.

As we came home we could arrive at no definite conclusion. We were all convinced that the box was on its way, by water, to somewhere; but where that might be we would have to discover. With heavy hearts we came home to the hotel to Mina.

When we met together, the first thing was to consult as to taking Mina again into our confidence. Things are getting desperate, and it is at least a chance, though a hazardous one. As a preliminary step, I was released from my promise to her.

Mina Harker's Journal

30 October, evening.—They were so tired and worn out and dispirited that there was nothing to be done till they had some rest; so I asked them all to lie down for half an hour whilst I should enter everything up to the moment. I feel so grateful to the man who invented the 'Traveller's' typewriter, and to Mr Morris for getting this one for me. I should have felt quite astray doing the work if I had to write with a pen . . .

It is all done; poor dear, dear Jonathan, what he must have suffered, what must he be suffering now. He lies on the sofa hardly seeming to breathe, and his whole body appears in collapse. His brows are knit; his face is drawn with pain. Poor fellow, maybe he is thinking, and I can see his face all wrinkled up with the concentration of his thoughts. Oh! if I could only help at all . . . I shall do what I can . . .

I have asked Dr Van Helsing, and he has got me all the papers that

I have not yet seen . . . Whilst they are resting, I shall go over all carefully, and perhaps I may arrive at some conclusion. I shall try to follow the Professor's example, and think without prejudice on the facts before me . . .

I do believe that under God's providence I have made a discovery. I shall get the maps and look over them . . .

I am more than ever sure that I am right. My new conclusion is ready, so I shall get our party together and read it. They can judge it; it is well to be accurate, and every minute is precious.

Mina Harker's Memorandum

(ENTERED IN HER JOURNAL)

Ground of inquiry.—Count Dracula's problem is to get back to his own place.

(*a*) He must be *brought back* by someone. This is evident; for had he power to move himself as he wished he could go either as man, or wolf, or bat, or in some other way. He evidently fears discovery or interference, in the state of helplessness in which he must be—confined as he is between dawn and sunset in his wooden box.

(*b*) *How is he to be taken?*—Here a process of exclusions may help us. By road, by rail, by water?

1. *By Road.*—There are endless difficulties, especially in leaving a city.

(*x*) There are people; and people are curious, and investigate. A hint, a surmise, a doubt as to what might be in the box, would destroy him.

(*y*) There are, or there might be, customs and octroi[7] officers to pass.

(*z*) His pursuers might follow. This is his greatest fear; and in order to prevent his being betrayed he has repelled, so far as he can, even his victim—me!

2. *By Rail.*—There is no one in charge of the box. It would have to take its chance of being delayed; and delay would be fatal, with enemies on the track. True, he might escape at night; but what would he be, if left in a strange place with no refuge that he could fly to? This is not what he intends; and he does not mean to risk it.

3. *By Water.*—Here is the safest way, in one respect, but with most danger in another. On the water he is powerless except at night; even then he can only summon fog and storm and snow and his wolves. But were he wrecked, the living water would engulf him, helpless; and he would indeed be lost. He could have the vessel drive to land; but if it were unfriendly land, wherein he was not free to move, his position would still be desperate.

7. Tax collectors on imported goods.

We know from the record that he was on the water; so what we have to do is to ascertain *what* water.

The first thing is to realize exactly what he has done as yet; we may, then, get a light on what his later task is to be.

Firstly.—We must differentiate between what he did in London as part of his general plan of action, when he was pressed for moments and had to arrange as best he could.

Secondly we must see, as well as we can surmise it from the facts we know of, what he has done here.

As to the first, he evidently intended to arrive at Galatz, and sent invoice to Varna to deceive us lest we should ascertain his means of exit from England; his immediate and sole purpose then was to escape. The proof of this is the letter of instructions sent to Immanuel Hildesheim to clear and take away the box *before sunrise*. There is also the instruction to Petrof Skinsky. There we must only guess at; but there must have been some letter or message, since Skinsky came to Hildesheim.

That, so far, his plans were successful we know. The *Czarina Catherine* made a phenomenally quick journey—so much so that Captain Donelson's suspicions were aroused; but his superstition united with his canniness played the Count's game for him, and he ran with his favouring wind through fogs and all till he brought up blindfold at Galatz. That the Count's arrangements were well made has been proved. Hildesheim cleared the box, took it off, and gave it to Skinsky. Skinsky took it—and here we lose the trail. We only know that the box is somewhere on the water, moving along. The customs and the octroi, if there be any, have been avoided.

Now we come to what the Count must have done after his arrival—*on land*, at Galatz.

The box was given to Skinsky before sunrise. At sunrise the Count could appear in his own form. Here, we ask why Skinsky was chosen at all to aid in the work? In my husband's diary, Skinsky is mentioned as dealing with the Slovaks who trade down the river to the port; and the man's remark,[8] that the murder was the work of a Slovak, showed the general feeling against his class. The Count wanted isolation.

My surmise is, this: that in London the Count decided to get back to his Castle by water, as the most safe and secret way. He was brought from the Castle by Szgany, and probably they delivered their cargo to Slovaks who took the boxes to Varna, for there they were shipped for London. Thus the Count had knowledge of the persons who could arrange this service. When the box was on land, before sunrise or after sunset, he came out from his box, met Skinsky and instructed him what to do as to arranging the carriage of the box up some river. When this

---

8. Actually it was women who cried out, "This is the work of a Slovak!" (p. 303).

was done, and he knew that all was in train, he blotted out his traces, as he thought, by murdering his agent.

I have examined the map and find that the river most suitable for the Slovaks to have ascended is either the Pruth or the Sereth.[9] I read in the typescript that in my trance I heard cows low and water swirling level with my ears and the creaking of wood. The Count in his box, then, was on a river in an open boat—propelled probably either by oars or poles, for the banks are near and it is working against stream. There would be no such sound if floating down stream.

Of course it may not be either the Sereth or the Pruth, but we may possibly investigate further. Now of these two, the Pruth is the more easily navigated, but the Sereth is, at Fundu,[1] joined by the Bistritza which runs up round the Borgo pass. The loop it makes is manifestly as close to Dracula's Castle as can be got by water.

Mina Harker's Journal (continued)

When I had done reading, Jonathan took me in his arms and kissed me. The others kept shaking me by both hands, and Dr Van Helsing said:—

'Our dear Madam Mina is once more our teacher. Her eyes have seen where we were blinded. Now we are on the track once again, and this time we may succeed. Our enemy is at his most helpless; and if we can come on him by day, on the water, our task will be over. He has a start, but he is powerless to hasten, as he may not leave his box lest those who carry him may suspect; for them to suspect would be to prompt them to throw him in the stream where he perish. This he knows, and will not. Now men, to our Council of War; for, here and now, we must plan what each and all shall do.'

'I shall get a steam launch and follow him,' said Lord Godalming.

'And I, horses to follow on the bank lest by chance he land,' said Mr Morris.

'Good!' said the Professor, 'both good. But neither must go alone. There must be force to overcome force if need be; the Slovak is strong and rough, and he carries rude arms.' All the men smiled, for amongst them they carried a small arsenal. Said Mr Morris:—

'I have brought some Winchesters; they are pretty handy in a crowd, and there may be wolves. The Count, if you remember, took some other precautions; he made some requisitions on others that Mrs Harker could not quite hear or understand. We must be ready at all points.' Dr Seward said:—

'I think I had better go with Quincey. We have been accustomed to

9. Both rivers flow into the Danube from the Carpathians. The Pruth (Russian *Prut*) joins the Danube above Reni, the Sereth above Galati.
1. There is some debate about the accuracy of Stoker's geography here.

hunt together, and we two, well armed, will be a match for whatever may come along. You must not be alone, Art. It may be necessary to fight the Slovaks, and a chance thrust—for I don't suppose these fellows carry guns—would undo all our plans. There must be no chances, this time; we shall not rest until the Count's head and body have been separated, and we are sure that he cannot reincarnate.' He looked at Jonathan as he spoke, and Jonathan looked at me. I could see that the poor dear was torn about in his mind. Of course he wanted to be with me; but then the boat service would, most likely, be the one which would destroy the . . . the . . . the . . . Vampire. (Why did I hesitate to write the word?) He was silent awhile, and during his silence Dr Van Helsing spoke:—

'Friend Jonathan, this is to you for twice reasons. First, because you are young and brave and can fight, and all energies may be needed at the last; and again that it is your right to destroy him—that—which has wrought such woe to you and yours. Be not afraid for Madam Mina; she will be my care, if I may. I am old. My legs are not so quick to run as once; and I am not used to ride so long or to pursue as need be, or to fight with lethal weapons. But I can be of other service; I can fight in other way. And I can die, if need be, as well as younger men. Now let me say that what I would is this: while you, my Lord Godalming, and friend Jonathan go in your so swift little steamboat up the river, and whilst John and Quincey guard the bank where perchance he might be landed, I will take Madam Mina right into the heart of the enemy's country. Whilst the old fox is tied in his box, floating on the running stream whence he cannot escape to land—where he dares not raise the lid of his coffin-box lest his Slovak carriers should in fear leave him to perish—we shall go in the track where Jonathan went,— from Bistritz over the Borgo, and find our way to the Castle of Dracula. Here, Madam Mina's hypnotic power will surely help, and we shall find our way—all dark and unknown otherwise—after the first sunrise when we are near that fateful place. There is much to be done, and other places to be made sanctify, so that that nest of vipers be obliterated.' Here Jonathan interrupted him hotly:—

'Do you mean to say, Professor Van Helsing, that you would bring Mina, in her sad case and tainted as she is with that devil's illness, right into the jaws of his death-trap? Not for the world! Not for Heaven or Hell!' He became almost speechless for a minute, and then went on:—

'Do you know what the place is? Have you seen that awful den of hellish infamy—with the very moonlight alive with grisly shapes, and every speck of dust that whirls in the wind a devouring monster in embryo? Have you felt the Vampire's lips upon your throat?' Here he turned to me, and as his eyes lit on my forehead, he threw up his arms with a cry: 'Oh, my God, what have we done to have this terror upon us!' and he sank down on the sofa in a collapse of misery. The Professor's voice, as he spoke in clear, sweet tones, which seemed to vibrate in the air, calmed us all:—

'Oh my friend, it is because I would save Madam Mina from that awful place that I would go. God forbid that I should take her into that place. There is work—wild work—to be done there, that her eyes may not see. We men here, all save Jonathan, have seen with their own eyes what is to be done before that place can be purify. Remember that we are in terrible straits. If the Count escape us this time—and he is strong and subtle and cunning—he may choose to sleep him for a century; and then in time our dear one'—he took my hand—'would come to him to keep him company, and would be as those others that you, Jonathan, saw. You have told us of their gloating lips; you heard their ribald laugh as they clutched the moving bag that the Count threw to them. You shudder; and well may it be. Forgive me that I make you so much pain, but it is necessary. My friend, is it not a dire need for the which I am giving, if need me, my life? If it were that anyone went into that place to stay, it is I who would have to go, to keep them company.'

'Do as you will,' said Jonathan, with a sob that shook him all over, 'We are in the hands of God!'

Later.—Oh, it did me good to see the way that these brave men worked. How can women help loving men when they are so earnest, and so true, and so brave! And, too, it made me think of the wonderful power of money! What can it not do when it is properly applied; and what might it do when basely used. I felt so thankful that Lord Godalming is rich, and that both he and Mr Morris, who also has plenty of money, are willing to spend it so freely. For if they did not, our little expedition could not start, either so promptly or so well equipped, as it will within another hour. It is not three hours since it was arranged what part each of us was to do; and now Lord Godalming and Jonathan have a lovely steam launch,[2] with steam up ready to start at a moment's notice. Dr Seward and Mr Morris have half a dozen beautiful horses, well appointed. We have all the maps and appliances of various kinds that can be had. Professor Van Helsing and I are to leave by the 11.40 train tonight to Veresti,[3] where we are to get a carriage to drive to the Borgo Pass. We are bringing a good deal of ready money, as we are to buy a carriage and horses. We shall drive ourselves, for we have no one whom we can trust in the matter. The Professor knows something of a great many languages, so we shall get on all right. We have all got arms, even for me a large-bore revolver; Jonathan would not be happy

---

2. Neither the Bistrita nor the Sireth rivers accommodated steam. The launch nevertheless personifies the triumph of Western capitalist technology over the forbidding landscapes of the East.

3. About ninety rugged miles from the Borgo Pass.

unless I was armed like the rest. Alas! I cannot carry one arm that the rest do; the scar on my forehead forbids that. Dear Dr Van Helsing comforts me by telling me that I am fully armed as there may be wolves; the weather is getting colder every hour, and there are snow-flurries which come and go as warnings.

Later.—It took all my courage to say goodbye to my darling. We may never meet again. Courage, Mina! the Professor is looking at you keenly; his look is a warning. There must be no tears now—unless it may be that God will let them fall in gladness.

Jonathan Harker's Journal

October 30, Night.—I am writing this in the light from the furnace door of the steam launch; Lord Godalming is firing up. He is an experienced hand at the work, as he has had for years a launch of his own on the Thames, and another on the Norfolk Broads.[4] Regarding our plans, we finally decided that Mina's guess was correct, and that if any waterway was chosen for the Count's escape back to his Castle, the Sereth and then the Bistritza at its junction, would be the one. We took it, that somewhere about the 47th degree, north latitude, would be the place chosen for crossing the country between the river and the Carpathians. We have no fear in running at good speed up the river at night; there is plenty of water, and the banks are wide enough apart to make steaming, even in the dark, easy enough. Lord Godalming tells me to sleep for a while, as it is enough for the present for one to be on watch. But I cannot sleep—how can I with the terrible danger hanging over my darling, and her going out into that awful place . . . My only comfort is that we are in the hands of God. Only for that faith it would be easier to die than to live, and so be quit of all the trouble. Mr Morris and Dr Seward were off on their long ride before we started; they are to keep up the right bank, far enough off to get on higher lands where they can see a good stretch of river and avoid the following of its curves. They have, for the first stages, two men to ride and lead their spare horses—four in all, so as not to excite curiosity. When they dismiss the men, which shall be shortly, they shall themselves look after the horses. It may be necessary for us to join forces; if so they can mount our whole party. One of the saddles had a movable horn,[5] and can be easily adapted for Mina, if required.

It is a wild adventure we are on. Here, as we are rushing along through the darkness, with the cold from the river seeming to rise up and strike us; with all the mysterious voices of the night around us, it all comes home. We seem to be drifting into unknown places and

4. On England's southeast coast.
5. So that Mina can ride sidesaddle, in ladylike fashion.

unknown ways; into a whole world of dark and dreadful things. God-alming is shutting the furnace door . . .

31 October.—Still hurrying along. The day has come, and Godalm-ing is sleeping. I am on watch. The morning is bitterly cold; the furnace heat is grateful, though we have heavy fur coats. As yet we have passed only a few open boats, but none of them had on board any box or package of anything like the size of the one we seek. The men were scared every time we turned our electric lamp on them, and fell on their knees and prayed.

1 November, evening.—No news all day; we have found nothing of the kind we seek. We have now passed into the Bistritza; and if we are wrong in our surmise our chance is gone. We have overhauled every boat, big and little. Early this morning, one crew took us for a Govern-ment boat, and treated us accordingly. We saw in this a way of smooth-ing matters, so at Fundu, where the Bistritza runs into the Sereth, we got a Roumanian flag which we now fly conspicuously. With every boat which we have overhauled since then this trick has succeeded; we have had every deference shown to us, and not once any objection to what-ever we chose to ask or do. Some of the Slovaks tell us that a big boat passed them, going at more than usual speed as she had a double crew on board. This was before they came to Fundu, so they could not tell us whether the boat turned into the Bistritza or continued on up the Sereth. At Fundu we could not hear of any such boat, so she must have passed there in the night. I am feeling very sleepy;[6] the cold is perhaps beginning to tell upon me, and nature must have rest some time. Godalming insists that he shall keep the first watch. God bless him for all his goodness to poor dear Mina and me.

2 November, morning.—It is broad daylight. That good fellow would not wake me. He says it would have been a sin to, for I slept so peace-fully and was forgetting my trouble. It seems brutally selfish of me to have slept so long, and let him watch all night; but he was quite right. I am a new man this morning; and, as I sit here and watch him sleep-ing, I can do all that is necessary both as to minding the engine, steer-ing, and keeping watch. I can feel that my strength and energy are coming back to me. I wonder where Mina is now, and Van Helsing. They should have got to Veresti about noon on Wednesday. It would take them some time to get the carriage and horses; so if they had started and travelled hard, they would be about now at the Borgo Pass. God guide and help them! I am afraid to think what may happen. If we could only go faster! but we cannot; the engines are throbbing and doing their utmost. I wonder how Dr Seward and Mr Morris are getting on. There seem to be endless streams running down from the moun-

6. As he approaches Dracula's castle, Jonathan shares this overwhelming sleepiness with Mina, who, Van Helsing says uneasily, "sleeps, and sleeps, and sleeps!" The parallel is suggestive but unexplained.

tains into this river, but as none of them are very large—at present, at all events, though they are terrible doubtless in winter and when the snow melts—the horsemen may not have met much obstruction. I hope that before we get to Strasba[7] we may see them; for if by that time we have not overtaken the Count, it may be necessary to take counsel together what to do next.

Dr Seward's Diary

2 November.—Three days on the road. No news, and no time to write it if there had been, for every moment is precious. We have had only the rest needful for the horses; but we are both bearing it wonderfully. Those adventurous days of ours are turning up useful. We must push on; we shall never feel happy till we get the launch in sight again.

3 November.—We heard at Fundu that the launch had gone up the Bistritza. I wish it wasn't so cold. There are signs of snow coming; and if it falls heavy it will stop us. In such case we must get a sledge and go on, Russian fashion.

4 November.—Today we heard of the launch having been detained by an accident when trying to force a way up the rapid. The Slovak boats get up all right, by aid of a rope, and steering with knowledge. Some went up only a few hours before. Godalming is an amateur fitter[8] himself, and evidently it was he who put the launch in trim again. Finally, they got up the Rapids all right, with local help, and are off on the chase afresh. I fear that the boat is not any better for the accident; the peasantry tell us that after she got upon the smooth water again, she kept stopping every now and again so long as she was in sight. We must push on harder than ever; our help may be wanted soon.

Mina Harker's Journal

31 October.—Arrived at Veresti at noon. The Professor tells me that this morning at dawn he could hardly hypnotize me at all, and that all I could say was: 'dark and quiet.' He is off now buying a carriage and horses. He says that he will later on try to buy additional horses, so that we may be able to change them on the way. We have something more than 70 miles before us. The country is lovely, and most interesting; if only we were under different conditions, how delightful it would be to see it all. If Jonathan and I were driving through it alone what a pleasure it would be. To stop and see people, and learn something of their life, and to fill our minds and memories with all the colour and picturesqueness of the whole wild, beautiful country and the quaint people! But alas!—

---

7. Possibly Straja, where the Sireth and Bistrita rivers join.
8. Steamfitter, one able to install or repair steam-driven equipment.

Later.—Dr Van Helsing has returned. He has got the carriage and horses; we are to have some dinner, and to start in an hour. The landlady is putting us up a huge basket of provisions; it seems enough for a company of soldiers. The Professor encourages her, and whispers to me that it may be a week before we can get any good food again. He has been shopping too, and has sent home such a wonderful lot of fur coats and wraps, and all sorts of warm things. There will not be any chance of our being cold.

We shall soon be off. I am afraid to think what may happen to us. We are truly in the hands of God. He alone knows what may be, and I pray Him, with all the strength of my sad and humble soul, that He will watch over my beloved husband; that whatever may happen, Jonathan may know that I loved him and honoured him more than I can say, and that my latest and truest thought will be always for him.

Chapter XXVII

Mina Harker's Journal

1 November.—All day long we have travelled, and at a good speed. The horses seem to know that they are being kindly treated, for they go willingly their full stage at best speed. We have now had so many changes and find the same thing so constantly that we are encouraged to think that the journey will be an easy one. Dr Van Helsing is laconic; he tells the farmers that he is hurrying to Bistritz, and pays them well to make the exchange of horses. We get hot soup, or coffee, or tea; and off we go. It is a lovely country; full of beauties of all imaginable kinds, and the people are brave, and strong, and simple, and seem full of nice qualities. They are *very, very* superstitious. In the first house where we stopped, when the woman who served us saw the scar on my forehead, she crossed herself and put out two fingers towards me, to keep off the evil eye. I believe they went to the trouble of putting an extra amount of garlic into our food; and I can't abide garlic. Ever since then I have taken care not to take off my hat or veil, and so have escaped their suspicions. We are travelling fast, and as we have no driver with us to carry tales, we go ahead of scandal; but I daresay that fear of the evil eye will follow hard behind us all the way. The Professor seems tireless; all day he would not take any rest, though he made me sleep for a long spell. At sunset time he hypnotized me, and he says that I answered as usual 'darkness, lapping water and creaking wood;' so our enemy is still on the river. I am afraid to think of Jonathan, but somehow I have now no fear for him, or for myself. I write this whilst we wait in a farmhouse for the horses to be got ready. Dr Van Helsing is sleeping. Poor dear, he looks very tired and old and grey, but his mouth is set as firmly as a conqueror's; even in his sleep he is instinct with resolution. When we have well started I must make him rest whilst I drive. I shall tell him that we have days before us, and he must not break down when most of all his strength will be needed . . . All is ready; we are off shortly.

2 *November, morning.*—I was successful, and we took turns driving all night; now the day is on us, bright though cold. There is a strange heaviness in the air—I say heaviness for want of a better word; I mean that it oppresses us both. It is very cold, and only our warm furs keep us comfortable. At dawn Van Helsing hypnotized me; he says I answered 'darkness, creaking wood and roaring water,' so the river is changing as they ascend. I do hope that my darling will not run any chance of danger—more than need be; but we are in God's hands.

2 *November, night.*—All day long driving. The country gets wilder as we go, and the great spurs of the Carpathians, which at Veresti seemed so far from us and so low on the horizon, now seem to gather round us and tower in front. We both seem in good spirits; I think we make an effort each to cheer the other; in the doing so we cheer ourselves. Dr Van Helsing says that by morning we shall reach the Borgo Pass. The houses are very few here now, and the Professor says that the last horses we got will have to go on with us, as we may not be able to change. He got two in addition to the two we changed, so that now we have a rude four-in-hand. The dear horses are patient and good, and they give us no trouble. We are not worried with other travellers, and so even I can drive. We shall get to the Pass in daylight; we do not want to arrive before. So we take it easy, and have each a long rest in turn. Oh, what will tomorrow bring to us? We go to seek the place where my poor darling suffered so much. God grant that we may be guided aright, and that He will deign to watch over my husband and those dear to us both, and who are in such deadly peril. As for me, I am not worthy in His sight. Alas! I am unclean to His eyes, and shall be until He may deign to let me stand forth in His sight as one of those who have not incurred His wrath.

Memorandum by Abraham Van Helsing

4 *November.*—This to my old and true friend John Seward, MD, of Purfleet, London, in case I may not see him. It may explain. It is morning, and I write by a fire which all the night I have kept alive—Madam Mina aiding me. It is cold, cold; so cold that the grey heavy sky is full of snow, which when it falls will settle for all winter as the ground is hardening to receive it. It seems to have affected Madam Mina; she has been so heavy of head all day that she was not like herself. She sleeps, and sleeps, and sleeps! She, who is usual so alert,

have done literally nothing all the day; she even have lost her appetite. She make no entry into her little diary, she who write so faithful at every pause. Something whisper to me that all is not well. However, tonight she is more *vif*.[1] Her long sleep all day have refresh and restore her, for now she is all sweet and bright as ever. At sunset I try to hypnotize her, but alas! with no effect; the power has grown less and less with each day, and tonight it fail me altogether. Well, God's will be done—whatever it may be, and whithersoever it may lead!

Now to the historical, for as Madam Mina write not in her stenography, I must, in my cumbrous old fashion, that so each day of us may not go unrecorded.

We got to the Borgo Pass just after sunrise yesterday morning. When I saw the signs of the dawn I got ready for the hypnotism. We stopped our carriage, and got down so that there might be no disturbance. I made a couch with furs, and Madam Mina, lying down, yield herself as usual, but more slow and more short time than ever, to the hypnotic sleep. As before, came the answer: 'darkness and the swirling of water.' Then she woke, bright and radiant, and we go on our way and soon reach the Pass. At this time and place she become all on fire with zeal; some new guiding power be in her manifested, for she point to a road and say:—

'This is the way.'

'How know you it?' I ask.

'Of course I know it,' she answer, and with a pause, add: 'Have not my Jonathan travel and wrote of his travel?'

At first I think somewhat strange, but soon I see that there be only one such by-road. It is used but little, and very different from the coach road from Bukovina to Bistritz, which is more wide and hard, and more of use.

So we came down this road; when we meet other ways—not always were we sure that they were roads at all, for they be neglect and light snow have fallen—the horses know and they only. I give rein to them, and they go on so patient. By-and-by we find all the things which Jonathan have note in that wonderful diary of him. Then we go on for long, long hours and hours. At the first, I tell Madam Mina to sleep; she try, and she succeed. She sleep all the time; till at the last, I feel myself to suspicious grow, and attempt to wake her. But she sleep on, and I may not wake her though I try. I do not wish to try too hard lest I harm her; for I know that she have suffer much, and sleep at times be all-in-all to her. I think I drowse myself, for all of sudden I feel guilt, as though I have done something; I find myself bolt up, with the reins in my hand, and the good horses go along jog, jog, just as ever. I look down and find Madam Mina still sleep. It is now not far off sunset

---

1. Keen, animated (French). Van Helsing incorrectly uses the masculine form of the word.

time, and over the snow the light of the sun flow in big yellow flood, so that we throw great long shadow on where the mountain rise so steep. For we are going up, and up; and all is oh! so wild and rocky, as though it were the end of the world.

Then I arouse Madam Mina. This time she wake with not much trouble, and then I try to put her to hypnotic sleep. But she sleep not, being as though I were not. Still I try and try, till all at once I find her and myself in dark; so I look round, and find that the sun have gone down. Madam Mina laugh, and I turn and look at her. She is now quite awake, and look so well as I never saw her since that night at Carfax when we first enter the Count's house. I am amaze, and not at ease then; but she is so bright and tender and thoughtful for me that I forget all fear. I light a fire, for we have brought supply of wood with us, and she prepare food while I undo the horses and set them, tethered in shelter, to feed. Then when I return to the fire she have my supper ready. I go to help her; but she smile, and tell me that she have eat already—that she was so hungry that she would not wait. I like it not, and I have grave doubts; but I fear to affright her, and so I am silent of it. She help me and I eat alone; and then we wrap in fur and lie beside the fire, and I tell her to sleep while I watch. But presently I forget all of watching; and when I sudden remember that I watch, I find her lying quiet, but awake, and looking at me with so bright eyes. Once, twice more the same occur, and I get much sleep till before morning. When I wake I try to hypnotize her; but alas! though she shut her eyes obedient, she may not sleep. The sun rise up, and up, and up; and then sleep come to her too late, but so heavy that she will not wake. I have to lift her up, and place her sleeping in the carriage when I have harnessed the horses and made all ready. Madam still sleep, and sleep; and she look in her sleep more healthy and more redder than before. And I like it not. And I am afraid, afraid, afraid!—I am afraid of all things—even to think; but I must go on my way. The stake we play for is life and death, or more than these, and we must not flinch.

5 November, morning.—Let me be accurate in everything, for though you and I have seen some strange things together, you may at the first think that I, Van Helsing, am mad—that the many horrors and the so long strain on nerves has at the last turn my brain.

All yesterday we travel, ever getting closer to the mountains, and moving into a more and more wild and desert land. There are great, frowning precipices and much falling water, and Nature seem to have held sometime her carnival. Madam Mina still sleep and sleep; and though I did have hunger and appeased it, I could not waken her— even for food. I began to fear that the fatal spell of the place was upon her, tainted as she is with that Vampire baptism. 'Well,' said I to myself, 'if it be that she sleep all the day, it shall also be that I do not sleep at night.' As we travel on the rough road, for a road of an ancient and

imperfect kind there was, I held down my head and slept. Again I waked
with a sense of guilt and of time passed, and found Madam Mina still
sleeping, and the sun low down. But all was indeed changed; the frowning mountains seemed further away, and we were near the top of a
steep-rising hill, on summit of which was such a castle as Jonathan tell
of in his diary. At once I exulted and feared; for now, for good or ill,
the end was near. I woke Madam Mina, and again tried to hypnotize
her; but alas! unavailing till too late. Then, ere the great dark came
upon us—for even after down-sun the heavens reflected the gone sun
on the snow, and all was for a time in a great twilight—I took out the
horses and fed them in what shelter I could. Then I make a fire; and
near it I make Madam Mina, now awake and more charming than
ever, sit comfortable amid her rugs. I got ready food: but she would not
eat, simply saying that she had not hunger. I did not press her, knowing
her unavailingness. But I myself eat, for I must needs now be strong
for all. Then, with the fear on me of what might be, I drew a ring so
big for her comfort, round where Madam Mina sat; and over the ring
I passed some of the wafer, and I broke it fine so that all was well
guarded. She sat still all the time—so still as one dead; and she grew
whiter and ever whiter till the snow was not more pale; and no word
she said. But when I drew near, she clung to me, and I could know
that the poor soul shook her from head to feet with a tremor that
was pain to feel. I said to her presently, when she had grown more
quiet:—

'Will you not come over to the fire?' for I wished to make a test of
what she could. She rose obedient, but when she then made a step she
stopped, and stood as one stricken.

'Why not go on?' I asked. She shook her head, and, coming back,
sat down in her place. Then, looking at me with open eyes, as of one
waked from sleep, she said simply:—

'I cannot!' and remained silent. I rejoiced, for I knew that what she
could not, none of those that we dreaded could. Though there might
be danger to her body, yet her soul was safe!

Presently the horses began to scream, and tore at their tethers till I
came to them and quieted them. When they did feel my hands on
them, they whinnied low as in joy, and licked at my hands and were
quiet for a time. Many times through the night did I come to them,
till it arrive to the cold hour when all nature is at lowest; and every
time my coming was with quiet of them. In the cold hour the fire
began to die, and I was about stepping forth to replenish it, for now
the snow came in flying sweeps and with it a chill mist. Even in the
dark there was a light of some kind, as there ever is over snow; and it
seemed as though the snow-flurries and the wreaths of mist took shape
as of women with trailing garments. All was in dead, grim silence only
that the horses whinnied and cowered, as if in terror of the worst. I

began to fear—horrible fears; but then came to me the sense of safety in that ring wherein I stood. I began, too, to think that my imaginings were of the night, and the gloom, and the unrest that I have gone through, and all the terrible anxiety. It was as though my memories of all Jonathan's horrid experience were befooling me; for the snow flakes and the mist began to wheel and circle round, till I could get as though a shadowy glimpse of those women that would have kissed him. And then the horses cowered lower and lower, and moaned in terror as men do in pain. Even the madness of fright was not to them, so that they could break away. I feared for my dear Madam Mina when these weird figures drew near and circled round. I looked at her, but she sat calm, and smiled at me; when I would have stepped to the fire to replenish it, she caught me and held me back, and whispered, like a voice that one hears in a dream, so low it was:—

'No! No! Do not go without. Here you are safe!' I turned to her, and looking in her eyes, said:—

'But you? It is for you that I fear!' whereat she laughed—a laugh, low and unreal, and said:—

'Fear for *me*! Why fear for me? None safer in all the world from them than I am,' and as I wondered at the meaning of her words, a puff of wind made the flame leap up, and I see the red scar on her forehead. Then, alas! I knew. Did I not, I would soon have learned, for the wheeling figures of mist and snow came closer, but keeping ever without the Holy circle. Then they began to materialize, till—if God have not take away my reason, for I saw it through my eyes—there were before me in actual flesh the same three women that Jonathan saw in the room, when they would have kissed his throat. I knew the swaying round forms, the bright hard eyes, the white teeth, the ruddy colour, the voluptuous lips. They smiled ever at poor dear Madam Mina; and as their laugh came through the silence of the night, they twined their arms and pointed to her, and said in those so sweet tingling tones that Jonathan said were of the intolerable sweetness of the water-glasses:—

'Come, sister. Come to us. Come! Come!' In fear I turned to my poor Madam Mina, and my heart with gladness leapt like flame; for oh! the terror in her sweet eyes, the repulsion, the horror, told a story to my heart that was all of hope. God be thanked she was not, yet, of them. I seized some of the firewood which was by me, and holding out some of the Wafer, advanced on them towards the fire. They drew back before me, and laughed their low horrid laugh. I fed the fire, and feared them not; for I knew that we were safe within our protections. They could not approach me, whilst so armed, nor Madam Mina whilst she remained within the ring, which she could not leave no more than they could enter. The horses had ceased to moan, and lay still on the ground; the snow fell on them softly, and they grew whiter. I knew that there was for the poor beasts no more of terror.

And so we remained till the red of the dawn began to fall through the snow-gloom. I was desolate and afraid, and full of woe and terror; but when that beautiful sun began to climb the horizon life was to me again. At the first coming of the dawn the horrid figures melted in the whirling mist and snow; the wreaths of transparent gloom moved away towards the castle, and were lost.

Instinctively, with the dawn coming, I turned to Madam Mina, intending to hypnotize her; but she lay in a deep and sudden sleep, from which I could not wake her. I tried to hypnotize through her sleep, but she made no response, none at all; and the day broke. I fear yet to stir. I have made my fire and have seen the horses, they are all dead. Today I have much to do here, and I keep waiting till the sun is up high; for there may be places where I must go, where that sunlight, though snow and mist obscure it, will be to me a safety.

I will strengthen me with breakfast, and then I will to my terrible work. Madam Mina still sleeps; and, God be thanked! she is calm in her sleep . . .

Jonathan Harker's Journal

4 November, evening.—The accident to the launch has been a terrible thing for us. Only for it we should have overtaken the boat long ago; and by now my dear Mina would have been free. I fear to think of her, off on the wolds near that horrid place. We have got horses, and we follow on the track. I note this whilst Godalming is getting ready. We have our arms. The Szgany must look out if they mean fight. Oh, if only Morris and Seward were with us. We must only hope! If I write no more Goodbye, Mina! God bless and keep you.

Dr Seward's Diary

5 November.—With the dawn we saw the body of Szgany before us dashing away from the river with their leiter-waggon. They surrounded it in a cluster, and hurried along as though beset. The snow is falling lightly and there is a strange excitement in the air. It may be our own excited feelings, but the depression is strange. Far off I hear the howling of wolves; the snow brings them down from the mountains, and there are dangers to all of us, and from all sides. The horses are nearly ready, and we are soon off. We ride to death of some one. God alone knows who, or where, or what, or when, or how it may be . . .

Dr Van Helsing's Memorandum

5 November, afternoon.—I am at least sane. Thank God for that mercy at all events, though the proving it has been dreadful. When I left Madam Mina sleeping within the Holy circle, I took my way to the

castle. The blacksmith hammer which I took in the carriage from Veresti was useful; though the doors were all open I broke them off the
rusty hinges, lest some ill-intent or ill-chance should close them, so that
being entered I might not get out. Jonathan's bitter experience served
me here. By memory of his diary I found my way to the old chapel,
for I knew that here my work lay. The air was oppressive; it seemed as
if there was some sulphurous fume, which at times made me dizzy.
Either there was a roaring in my ears or I heard afar off the howl of
wolves. Then I bethought me of my dear Madam Mina, and I was in
terrible plight. The dilemma had me between his horns. Her, I had
not dare to take into this place, but left safe from the Vampire in that
Holy circle; and yet even there would be the wolf! I resolve me that
my work lay here, and that as to the wolves we must submit, if it were
God's Will. At any rate it was only death and freedom beyond. So did
I choose for her. Had it but been for myself the choice had been easy;
the maw of the wolf were better to rest in than the grave of the Vampire!
So I make my choice to go on with my work.

I knew that there were at least three graves to find—graves that are
inhabit; so I search, and search, and I find one of them. She lay in her
Vampire sleep, so full of life and voluptuous beauty that I shudder as
though I have come to do murder. Ah, I doubt not that in old time,
when such things were, many a man who set forth to do such a task
as mine, found at the last his heart fail him, and then his nerve. So he
delay, and delay, and delay, till the mere beauty and the fascination of
the wanton Un-dead have hypnotize him; and he remain on, and on,
till sunset come, and the Vampire sleep be over. Then the beautiful
eyes of the fair woman open and look love, and the voluptuous mouth
present to a kiss—and man is weak. And there remain one more victim
in the Vampire fold; one more to swell the grim and grisly ranks of the
Un-dead! . . .

There is some fascination, surely, when I am moved by the mere
presence of such an one, even lying as she lay in a tomb fretted with
age and heavy with the dust of centuries, though there be that horrid
odour such as the lairs of the Count have had. Yes, I was moved—I,
Van Helsing, with all my purpose and with my motive for hate—I was
moved to a yearning for delay which seemed to paralyse my faculties
and to clog my very soul. It may have been that the need of natural
sleep, and the strange oppression of the air were beginning to overcome
me. Certain it was that I was lapsing into sleep, the open-eyed sleep of
one who yields to a sweet fascination, when there came through the
snow-stilled air a long, low wail, so full of woe and pity that it woke
me like the sound of a clarion. For it was the voice of my dear Madam
Mina that I heard.

Then I braced myself again to my horrid task, and found by wrench-
ing away tomb-tops one other of the sisters, the other dark one. I dared

not pause to look on her as I had on her sister, lest once more I should begin to be enthrall; but I go on searching until, presently, I find in a high great tomb as if made to one much beloved that other fair sister which, like Jonathan I had seen to gather herself out of the atoms of the mist. She was so fair to look on, so radiantly beautiful, so exquisitely voluptuous, that the very instinct of man in me, which calls some of my sex to love and to protect one of hers, made my head whirl with new emotion. But God be thanked, that soul-wail of my dear Madam Mina had not died out of my ears; and, before the spell could be wrought further upon me, I had nerved myself to my wild work. By this time I had searched all the tombs in the chapel, so far as I could tell; and as there had been only three of these Un-Dead phantoms around us in the night, I took it that there were no more of active Un-Dead existent.[2] There was one great tomb more lordly than all the rest; huge it was, and nobly proportioned. On it was but one word

DRACULA

This then was the Un-Dead home of the King-Vampire, to whom so many more were due. Its emptiness spoke eloquent to make certain what I knew. Before I began to restore these women to their dead selves through my awful work, I laid in Dracula's tomb some of the Wafer, and so banished him from it, Un-Dead, for ever.

Then began my terrible task, and, I dreaded it. Had it been but one, it had been easy, comparative. But three! To begin twice more after I had been through a deed of horror; for if it was terrible with the sweet Miss Lucy, what would it not be with these strange ones who had survived through centuries, and who had been strengthened by the passing of the years; who would, if they could, have fought for their foul lives . . .

Oh, my friend John, but it was butcher work; had I not been nerved by thoughts of other dead, and of the living over whom hung such a pall of fear, I could not have gone on. I tremble and tremble even yet, though till all was over, God be thanked, my nerve did stand. Had I not seen the repose in the first face, and the gladness that stole over it just ere the final dissolution came, as realization that the soul had been won, I could not have gone further with my butchery. I could not have endured the horrid screeching as the stake drove home; the plunging of writhing form, and lips of bloody foam. I should have fled in terror and left my work undone. But it is over! And the poor souls, I can pity them now and weep, as I think of them placid each in her full sleep of death, for a short moment ere fading. For, friend John, hardly had my knife severed the head of each, before the whole body began to

---

2. Perplexing, since Dracula and his three women have been prowling there for centuries.

melt away and crumble into its native dust, as though the death that should have come centuries agone had at last assert himself and say at once and loud 'I am here!'

Before I left the castle I so fixed its entrances that never more can the Count enter there Un-Dead.

When I stepped into the circle where Madam Mina slept, she woke from her sleep, and, seeing me, cried out in pain that I had endured too much.

'Come!' she said, 'Come away from this awful place! Let us go to meet my husband who is, I know, coming towards us.' She was looking thin and pale and weak; but her eyes were pure and glowed with fervour. I was glad to see her paleness and her illness, for my mind was full of the fresh horror of that ruddy vampire sleep.

And so with trust and hope, and yet full of fear, we go eastward to meet our friends—and *him*—whom Madam Mina tell me that she *know* are coming to meet us.

Mina Harker's Journal

6 November.—It was late in the afternoon when the Professor and I took our way towards the east whence I knew Jonathan was coming. We did not go fast, though the way was steeply downhill, for we had to take heavy rugs and wraps with us; we dared not face the possibility of being left without warmth in the cold and the snow. We had to take some of our provisions too, for we were in a perfect desolation, and, so far as we could see through the snow-fall, there was not even the sign of a habitation. When we had gone about a mile, I was tired with the heavy walking and sat down to rest. Then we looked back and saw where the clear line of Dracula's castle cut the sky; for we were so deep under the hill whereon it was set that the angle of perspective of the Carpathian mountains was far below it. We saw it in all its grandeur, perched a thousand feet on the summit of a sheer precipice, and with seemingly a great gap between it and the steep of the adjacent mountain on any side. There was something wild and uncanny about the place. We could hear the distant howling of wolves. They were far off, but the sound, even though coming muffled through the deadening snowfall, was full of terror. I knew from the way Dr Van Helsing was searching about that he was trying to seek some strategic point, where we would be less exposed in case of attack. The rough roadway still led downwards; we could trace it through the drifted snow.

In a little while the Professor signalled to me, so I got up and joined him. He had found a wonderful spot, a sort of natural hollow in a rock, with an entrance like a doorway between two boulders. He took me by the hand and drew me in: 'See!' he said, 'here you will be in shelter; and if the wolves do come I can meet them one by one.' He brought in our furs, and made a snug nest for me, and got out some provisions and forced them upon me. But I could not eat; to even try to do so was repulsive to me, and, much as I would have liked to please him, I could not bring myself to the attempt. He looked very sad, but did not reproach me. Taking his field-glasses from the case, he stood on the top of the rock, and began to search the horizon. Suddenly he called out:—

'Look! Madam Mina, look! look!' I sprang up and stood beside him on the rock; he handed me his glasses and pointed. The snow was now falling more heavily, and swirled about fiercely, for a high wind was beginning to blow. However there were times when there were pauses between the snow flurries and I could see a long way round. From the height where we were it was possible to see a great distance; and far off, beyond the white waste of snow, I could see the river lying like a black ribbon in kinks and curls as it wound its way. Straight in front of us and not far off—in fact so near that I wondered we had not noticed before—came a group of mounted men hurrying along. In the midst of them was a cart, a long leiter-wagon which swept from side to side, like a dog's tail wagging, with each stern inequality of the road. Outlined against the snow as they were, I could see from the men's clothes that they were peasants or gypsies of some kind.

On the cart was a great square chest. My heart leaped as I saw it, for I felt that the end was coming. The evening was now drawing close, and well I knew that at sunset the Thing, which was till then imprisoned there, would take new freedom and could in any of many forms elude all pursuit. In fear I turned to the Professor; to my consternation, however, he was not there. An instant later, I saw him below me. Round the rock he had drawn a circle, such as we had found shelter in last night. When he had completed it he stood beside me again, saying:—

'At least you shall be safe here from *him*!' He took the glasses from me, and at the next lull of the snow swept the whole space below us. 'See,' he said, 'they come quickly; they are flogging the horses, and galloping as hard as they can.' He paused and went on in a hollow voice:—

'They are racing for the sunset. We may be too late. God's will be done!' Down came another blinding rush of driving snow, and the whole landscape was blotted out. It soon passed, however, and once more his glasses were fixed on the plain. Then came a sudden cry:—

'Look! Look! Look! See, two horsemen follow fast, coming up from the south. It must be Quincey and John. Take the glass. Look, before the snow blots it all out!' I took it and looked. The two men might be Dr Seward and Mr Morris. I knew at all events that neither of them was Jonathan. At the same time I *knew* that Jonathan was not far off; looking around I saw on the north side of the coming party two other men, riding at break-neck speed. One of them I knew was Jonathan, and the other I took, of course, to be Lord Godalming. They, too, were pursuing the party with the cart. When I told the Professor he shouted in glee like a schoolboy, and, after looking intently till a snowfall made sight impossible, he laid his Winchester rifle ready for use against the boulder at the opening of our shelter. 'They are all converging,' he said. 'When the time comes we shall have the gypsies on all sides.' I got out my revolver ready to hand, for whilst we were speaking the howling of wolves came louder and closer. When the snowstorm abated a moment we looked again. It was strange to see the snow falling in such heavy flakes close to us, and beyond, the sun shining more and more brightly as it sank down towards the far mountain tops. Sweeping the glass all around us I could see here and there dots moving singly and in twos and threes and larger numbers—the wolves were gathering for their prey.

Every instant seemed an age whilst we waited. The wind came now in fierce bursts, and the snow was driven with fury as it swept upon us in circling eddies. At times we could not see an arm's length before us; but at others as the hollow-sounding wind swept by us, it seemed to clear the air-space around us so that we could see afar off. We had of late been so accustomed to watch for sunrise and sunset, that we knew with fair accuracy when it would be; and we knew that before long the sun would set.

It was hard to believe that by our watches it was less than an hour that we waited in that rocky shelter before the various bodies began to converge close upon us. The wind came now with fiercer and more bitter sweeps, and more steadily from the north. It seemingly had driven the snow clouds from us, for, with only occasional bursts, the snow fell. We could distinguish clearly the individuals of each party, the pursued and the pursuers. Strangely enough those pursued did not seem to realize, or at least to care, that they were pursued; they seemed, however, to hasten with redoubled speed as the sun dropped lower and lower on the mountain tops.

Closer and closer they drew. The Professor and I crouched down behind our rock, and held our weapons ready; I could see that he was determined that they should not pass. One and all were quite unaware of our presence.

All at once two voices shouted out to: 'Halt!' One was my Jonathan's, raised in a high key of passion; the other Mr Morris's strong resolute tone of quiet command. The gypsies may not have known the language, but there was no mistaking the tone, in whatever tongue the words were spoken. Instinctively they reined in, and at the instant Lord Godalming and Jonathan dashed up at one side and Dr Seward and Mr Morris on the other. The leader of the gypsies, a splendid looking fellow who sat his horse like a centaur, waved them back, and in a fierce voice gave to his companions some word to proceed. They lashed the horses which sprang forward; but the four men raised their Winchester rifles, and in an unmistakeable way commanded them to stop. At the same moment Dr Van Helsing and I rose behind the rock and pointed our weapons at them. Seeing that they were surrounded the men tightened their reins and drew up. The leader turned to them and gave a word at which every man of the gipsy party drew what weapon he carried, knife or pistol, and held himself in readiness to attack. Issue was joined in an instant.

The leader, with a quick movement of his rein, threw his horse out in front, and pointing first to the sun—now close down on the hill tops—and then to the castle, said something which I did not understand. For answer, all four men of our party threw themselves from their horses and dashed towards the cart. I should have felt terrible fear at seeing Jonathan in such danger, but that the ardour of battle must have been upon me as well as the rest of them; I felt no fear, but only a wild, surging desire to do something. Seeing the quick movement of our parties, the leader of the gypsies gave a command; his men instantly formed round the cart in a sort of undisciplined endeavour, each one shouldering and pushing the other in his eagerness to carry out the order.

In the midst of this I could see[3] that Jonathan on one side of the ring of men, and Quincey on the other, were forcing a way to the cart; it was evident that they were bent on finishing their task before the sun should set. Nothing seemed to stop or even to hinder them. Neither the levelled weapons or the flashing knives of the gypsies in front, or the howling of the wolves behind, appeared to even attract their attention. Jonathan's impetuosity, and the manifest singleness of his purpose, seemed to overawe those in front of him; instinctively they cowered aside and let him pass. In an instant he had jumped upon the cart, and, with a strength which seemed incredible, raised the great box, and flung it over the wheel to the ground. In the meantime, Mr Morris had had to use force to pass through his side of the ring of Szgany. All the time I had been breathlessly watching Jonathan I had, with the tail of my eye, seen him pressing desperately forward, and had seen the knives of the gypsies flash as he won a way through them, and they cut at him. He had parried with his great bowie knife, and at first I thought that he too had come through in safety; but as he sprang beside Jonathan, who had by now jumped from the cart, I could see that with his left hand he was clutching at his side, and that the blood was spurting through his fingers. He did not delay notwithstanding this, for as Jonathan, with desperate energy, attacked one end of the chest, attempting to prize off the lid with his great kukri knife, he attacked the other

3. Since Mina is looking down from a height, her sudden detailed vision makes her the lens of
    a movie camera rather than a plausible human observer.

frantically with his bowie. Under the efforts of both men the lid began to yield; the nails drew with a quick screeching sound, and the top of the box was thrown back.

By this time the gypsies, seeing themselves covered by the Winchesters, and at the mercy of Lord Godalming and Dr Seward, had given in and made no further resistance. The sun was almost down on the mountain tops, and the shadows of the whole group fell long upon the snow. I saw the Count lying within the box upon the earth, some of which the rude falling from the cart had scattered over him. He was deathly pale, just like a waxen image, and the red eyes glared with the horrible vindictive look which I knew too well.

As I looked, the eyes saw the sinking sun, and the look of hate in them turned to triumph.

But, on the instant, came the sweep and flash of Jonathan's great knife. I shrieked as I saw it shear through the throat; whilst at the same moment Mr Morris's bowie knife plunged into the heart.[4]

It was like a miracle; but before our very eyes, and almost in the drawing of a breath, the whole body crumbled into dust and passed from our sight.

I shall be glad as long as I live that even in that moment of final dissolution, there was in the face a look of peace, such as I never could have imagined might have rested there.

The Castle of Dracula now stood out against the red sky, and every stone of its broken battlements was articulated against the light of the setting sun.[5]

The gypsies, taking us as in some way the cause of the extraordinary disappearance of the dead man, turned, without a word, and rode away as if for their lives. Those who were unmounted jumped upon the leiter-wagon and shouted to the horsemen not to desert them. The wolves, which had withdrawn to a safe distance, followed in their wake, leaving us alone.

---

4. This is not the ritual communal killing the vampire hunters had planned. Dracula's supposed death is riddled with ambiguity.
5. In a canceled paragraph of Stoker's original manuscript, Dracula's death is more final than in the published novel, for his castle explodes in response: "As we looked there came a terrible convulsion of the earth so that we seemed to rock to and fro and fell to our knees. At the same moment, with a roar which seemed to shake the very heavens, the whole castle and the rock and even the hill on which it stood seemed to rise into the air and scatter in fragments while a mighty cloud of black and yellow smoke volume on volume in rolling grandeur was shot upwards with inconceivable rapidity. Then there was a stillness in nature as the echoes of that thunderous report seemed to come as with the hollow boom of a thunder clap—the long reverberating roll which seems as though the floors of heaven shook. Then down in a mighty ruin falling whence they rose [shot?] the fragments that had been tossed skywards in the cataclysm.
    "From where we stood it seemed as though the one fierce volcano burst had satisfied the need of nature and that the castle and the structure of the hill had sank again into the void. We were so appalled with the suddenness and the grandeur that we forgot to think of ourselves."

Mr Morris, who had sunk to the ground, leaned on his elbow, holding his hand pressed to his side; the blood still gushed through his fingers. I flew to him, for the Holy circle did not now keep me back; so did the two doctors. Jonathan knelt behind him and the wounded man laid back his head on his shoulder. With a sigh he took, with a feeble effort, my hand in that of his own which was unstained. He must have seen the anguish of my heart in my face, for he smiled at me and said:—

'I am only too happy to have been of any service! Oh, God!' he cried suddenly, struggling up to a sitting posture and pointing to me, 'It was worth this to die! Look! look!'

The sun was now right down upon the mountain top, and the red gleams fell upon my face, so that it was bathed in rosy light. With one impulse the men sank on their knees and a deep and earnest 'Amen' broke from all as their eyes followed the pointing of his finger as the dying man spoke:—

'Now God be thanked that all has not been in vain! See! the snow is not more stainless than her forehead! The curse has passed away!'

And, to our bitter grief, with a smile and in silence, he died, a gallant gentleman.

Note

Seven years ago we all went through the flames; and the happiness of some of us since then is, we think, well worth the pain we endured. It is an added joy to Mina and to me that our boy's birthday is the same day as that on which Quincey Morris died. His mother holds, I know, the secret belief that some of our brave friend's spirit has passed into him. His bundle of names links all our little band of men together; but we call him Quincey.

In the summer of this year we made a journey to Transylvania, and went over the old ground which was, and is, to us so full of vivid and terrible memories. It was almost impossible to believe that the things which we had seen with our own eyes and heard with our own ears were living truths. Every trace of all that had been was blotted out. The castle stood as before, reared high above a waste of desolation.

When we got home we got to talking of the old time—which we could all look back on without despair, for Godalming and Seward are both happily married. I took the papers from the safe where they have been ever since our return so long ago. We were struck with the fact, that in all the mass of material of which the record is composed, there is hardly one authentic document; nothing but a mass of type-writing, except the later notebooks of Mina and Seward and myself, and Van Helsing's memorandum. We could hardly ask anyone, even did we wish to, to accept these as proofs of so wild a story. Van Helsing summed it all up as he said, with our boy on his knee:—

'We want no proofs; we ask none to believe us! This boy will some day know what a brave and gallant woman his mother is. Already he knows her sweetness and loving care; later on he will understand how some men so loved her, that they did dare much for her sake.'

JONATHAN HARKER

CONTEXTS

Bram Stoker didn't invent the vampire in literature; the motif had a distinguished pedigree decades before his birth, beginning with Dr. John Polidori's "The Vampyre: A Tale" (1820), originally attributed to Lord Byron. Polidori was Byron's physician and travel companion; "The Vampyre" was the result of a writing contest proposed by Byron at a literary house party on Lake Geneva in 1816; the most famous product of the challenge was Mary Wollstonecraft Shelley's *Frankenstein* (1818). Polidori's story was first adapted to the stage in 1820 and became an opera in 1828. Actor Dion Boucicault produced his own theatrical elaboration on Polidori, called *The Vampyre: A Phantasm* (1852), which was revived in America as *The Phantom* (1856). Stoker was also influenced by James Malcom Rymer's melodramatic, nine-hundred-page "penny dreadful" *Varney the Vampyre: Or, the Feast of Blood,* originally published in installments between 1845 and 1847, as well as J. Sheridan Le Fanu's elegant vampire novella *Carmilla* (1872), which evidently gave him the initial idea of setting his novel in the district of Austria known as Styria, later changed to Transylvania. Much has been made, in recent years, of the fictional Dracula's relationship to his historical namesake, Vlad "the Impaler" Tepes, warlord of Wallachia (1431–1476). "Dracul" means devil or dragon, and "Dracula" refers to such a creature's offspring. But Stoker himself never visited Transylvania and seems to have limited his library research on Tepes to a single volume by William Wilkinson, *An Account of the Principalities of Wallachia and Moldavia: with Various Political Observations Related to Them* (1820), which briefly mentions Vlad's exploits. It is entirely possible that Stoker never knew of Vlad's sobriquet "the Impaler" and intended no specific connection between the ruler's favorite method of dispatching enemies via the wooden stake and the traditional method of destroying, or at least immobilizing, vampires. Though Vlad was indeed bloodthirsty, there is no evidence connecting him to any folklore tradition of vampirism. Therefore, the following selection of contextual pieces will focus on literary rather than historical antecedents and on Stoker's methods of devising his plot. Also included is the short story "Dracula's Guest" (1914), an abandoned opening chapter to *Dracula* published posthumously by Stoker's widow.

EMILY GERARD

From Transylvanian Superstitions†

(1885)

[Stoker gleaned his primary information on Transylvania folklore from Emily de Laszowska Gerard's 1885 essay "Transylvanian Superstitions," later incorporated into her two-volume book *The Land Beyond the Forest* (1888). Gerard, also a novelist, was married to a Hungarian cavalry commander and lived for two years in Transylvania, giving her research a first-hand immediacy.]

† From *The Nineteenth Century,* July 1885, pp. 128–44.

*   *   *

Transylvania might well be termed the land of superstition, for nowhere else does this curious crooked plant of delusion flourish as persistently and in such bewildering variety. It would almost seem as though the whole species of demons, pixies, witches, and hobgoblins, driven from the rest of Europe by the wand of science, had taken refuge within this mountain rampart, well aware that here they would find secure lurking-places, whence they might defy their persecutors yet awhile.

There are many reasons why these fabulous beings should retain an abnormally firm hold on the soil of these parts; and looking at the matter closely we find here no less than three separate sources of superstition.

First, there is what may be called the indigenous superstition of the country, the scenery of which is peculiarly adapted to serve as background to all sorts of supernatural beings and monsters. There are innumerable caverns, whose mysterious depths seem made to harbour whole legions of evil spirits: forest glades fit only for fairy folk on moonlight nights, solitary lakes which instinctively call up visions of water sprites; golden treasures lying hidden in mountain chasms, all of which have gradually insinuated themselves into the minds of the oldest inhabitants, the Roumenians, and influenced their way of thinking, so that these people, by nature imaginative and poetically inclined, have built up for themselves out of the surrounding materials a whole code of fanciful superstition, to which they adhere as closely as to their religion itself.

Secondly, there is here the imported superstition! that is to say, the old German customs and beliefs brought hither seven hundred years ago by the Saxon colonists from their native land, and like many other things, preserved here in greater perfection than in the original country.

Thirdly, there is the wandering superstition of the gypsy tribes, themselves a race of fortune-tellers and witches, whose ambulating caravans cover the country as with a network, and whose less vagrant members fill up the suburbs of towns and villages.

Of course all these various sorts of superstition have twined and intermingled, acted and reacted upon each other, until in many cases it is a difficult matter to determine the exact parentage of some particular belief or custom; but in a general way the three sources I have named may be admitted as a rough sort of classification in dealing with the principal superstitions afloat in Transylvania.

There is on this subject no truer saying than that of Grimm, to the effect that 'superstition in all its manifold varieties constitutes a sort of religion, applicable to the common household necessities of daily life,'[1] and as such, particular forms of superstition may very well serve as guide to the characters and habits of the particular nation in which they are prevalent.

The spirit of evil (or, not to put too fine a point upon it, the devil) plays a conspicuous part in the Roumenian code of superstition, and such designations as the Gregynia Drakuluj (devil's garden), the Gania Drakuluj (devil's mountain), Yadu Drakuluj (devil's hell or abyss), & c, & c, which we frequently find attached to rocks, caverns, or heights, attest the fact that these people believe themselves to be surrounded on all sides by a whole legion of evil spirits.

The devils are furthermore assisted by witches and dragons, and to all of these dangerous beings are ascribed peculiar powers on particular days and at certain places.

Perhaps the most important day in the year is St George's, the 23rd of April (corresponds to our 5th of May), the eve of which is still frequently kept by occult meetings taking place at night in lonely caverns or within ruined walls, and where all the ceremonies usual to the celebration of a witches' Sabbath are put into practice.

The feast itself is the great day to beware of witches, to counteract whose influence square-cut blocks of green turf are placed in front of each door and window.[2] This is supposed effectually to bar their entrance to the house or stables, but for still greater safety it is usual here for the peasants to keep watch all night by the sleeping cattle.

This same night is the best for finding treasures, and many people spend it in wandering about the hills trying to probe the earth for the gold it contains. Vain and futile as such researches usually are, yet they have in this country a somewhat greater semblance of reason than in most other parts, for perhaps nowhere else have so many successive nations been forced to secrete their riches in flying from an enemy, to say nothing of the numerous veins of undiscovered gold and silver which must be seaming the country in all directions. Not a year passes without bringing to light some earthern jar containing old Dacian coins, or golden ornaments of Roman origin, and all such discoveries serve to feed and keep up the national superstition.

In the night of St George's Day (so say the legends) all these treasures begin to burn, or, to speak in mystic language, to 'bloom' in the bosom of the earth, and the light they give forth, described as a bluish flame resembling the colour of lighted spirits of wine, serves to guide favoured mortals to their place of concealment. The conditions to the successful

1. 'Der Aberglaube in seiner Mannigfaltigkeit bildet gewissermassen eine Religion fur den ganzen niederen Hausbedarf.' [Jakob Ludwig Karl Grimm (1785–1863) and Wilhelm Karl Grimm (1786–1859), German folklorists—*Editors.*]
2. This is also usual in Poland, Moldavia and the Bukowina.

raising of such a treasure are manifold, and difficult of accomplishment. In the first place, it is by no means easy for a common mortal who has not been born on a Sunday nor at midday when the bells are ringing, to hit upon a treasure at all. If he does, however, catch sight of a flame such as I have described, he must quickly stick a knife through the swaddling rags of his right foot,[3] and then throw the knife in the direction of the flame he has seen. If two people are together during this discovery they must not on any account break silence till the treasure is removed, neither is it allowed to fill up the hole from which anything has been taken, for that would induce a speedy death. Another important feature to be noted is that the lights seen before midnight on St George's Day, denote treasures kept by benevolent spirits, while those which appear at a later hour are unquestionably of a pernicious nature.

*   *   *

There are two sorts of vampires—living and dead. The living vampire is in general the illegitimate offspring of two illegitimate persons, but even a flawless pedigree will not ensure anyone against the intrusion of a vampire into his family vault, since every person killed by a *nosferatu*[4] becomes likewise a vampire after death, and will continue to suck the blood of other innocent people till the spirit has been exorcised, either by opening the grave of the person suspected and driving a stake through the corpse, or firing a pistol shot into the coffin. In very obstinate cases it is further recommended to cut off the head and replace it in the coffin with the mouth filled with garlic, or to extract the heart and burn it, strewing the ashes over the grave.

That such remedies are often resorted to, even in our enlightened days, is a well-attested fact, and there are probably few Roumenian villages where such has not taken place within the memory of the inhabitants.

First cousin to the vampire, the long exploded were-wolf of the Germans is here to be found, lingering yet under the name of the *Prikolitsch*. Sometimes it is a dog instead of a wolf, whose form a man has taken either voluntarily or as penance for his sins. In one of the villages a story is still told (and believed) of such a man, who driving home from church on Sunday with his wife, suddenly felt that the time for his transformation had come. He therefore gave over the reins to her, and stepped aside into the bushes, where, murmuring the mystic formula, he turned three somersaults over a ditch. Soon after this the woman, waiting in vain for her husband, was attacked by a furious dog, which rushed, barking, out of the bushes and succeeded in biting her

---

3. The Roumenian peasant does not wear shoes or stockings, but has his feet swaddled up in linen rags, which are kept in their place by a rough sandal made of a flat piece of leather.
4. The word *nosferatu* appears in no Romanian or Hungarian dictionary, nor in any standard text on Eastern European folklore available to Gerard. It is possible she mistook a usage of the Romanian adjective *nesuferit* ("plaguesome") in connection with vampires and inadvertantly coined the now familiar term [*Editors*].

severely, as well as tearing her dress. When, an hour later, this woman reached home alone she was met by her husband, who advanced smiling to meet her, but between his teeth she caught sight of the shreds of her dress which had been bitten out by the dog, and the horror of the discovery caused her to faint away.

Another man used gravely to assert that for more than five years he had gone about in the form of a wolf, leading on a troop of these animals, until a hunter, in striking off his head, restored him to his natural shape.

A French traveller relates an instance of a harmless botanist who, while collecting herbs on a hillside in a crouching attitude, was observed by some peasants at a distance and taken for a wolf. Before they had time to reach him, however, he had risen to his feet and disclosed himself in the form of a man; but this, in the minds of the Roumenians, who now regarded him as an aggravated case of wolf, was but additional motive for attacking him. They were quite sure that he must be a Prikolitsch, for only such could change his shape in such an unaccountable manner, and in another minute they were all in full cry after the wretched victim of science, who might have fared badly indeed, had he not happened to gain a carriage on the high road before his pursuers came up.

We do not require to go far for the explanation of the extraordinary tenacity of life of the were-wolf legend in a country like Transylvania, where real wolves still abound. Every winter here brings fresh proof of the boldness and cunning of these terrible animals, whose attacks on flocks and farms are often conducted with a skill which would do honour to a human intellect. Sometimes a whole village is kept in trepidation for weeks together by some particularly audacious leader of a flock of wolves, to whom the peasants not unnaturally attribute a more than animal nature, and one may safely prophesy that so long as the real wolf continues to haunt the Transylvanian forests, so long will his spectre brother survive in the minds of the inhabitants.

* * *

JAMES MALCOLM RYMER

From Varney the Vampyre: Or, The Feast of Blood†

(1845–47)

[First published in book form the year of Bram Stoker's birth, Rymer's "penny-dreadful" serial (so-called because individual installments were typ-

† From *Varney the Vampyre: Or, The Feast of Blood* (London: E. Lloyd, 1847) 842–43. Published anonymously, *Varney* was originally believed to be the work of the Victorian popular writer Thomas Peskett Prest, though recent scholarship accepts Rymer as the more likely author.

ically sold for a penny) was an immensely popular Victorian horror soap opera, vulgarizing and attenuating the theme of Polidori's "The Vampyre" in its literary and theatrical incarnations. Its story of a mysterious continental nobleman, Lord Francis Varney, who arrives in England by way of a shipwreck in a storm to vampirize young maidens, gave Stoker ample inspiration. The following excerpt clearly anticipates the melodramatic destruction of Lucy Westenra in *Dracula*.]

* * *

The blacksmith laid his hand upon Clara's coffin.

"Here it is," he said, "I know the very pattern of the cloth, and the fashion of the nails, I saw it at Grigson's the undertaker's before it was taken to the Grange."

"Is she there—is she there," cried half a dozen voices at once.

Even the blacksmith hesitated a moment ere he removed the lid from the receptacle of death, but when he did so, and his eyes fell upon the face of the presumed vampyre, he seemed rejoiced to find in the appearances then exhibited some sort of justification for the act of violence of which already he had been the instigator.

"Here you are," he said, "look at the bloom upon her lips, why her cheeks are fresher and rosier than ever they were while she was alive, a vampyre my mates, this is a vampyre, or may I never break bread again; and now what's to be done."

"Burn her, burn her," cried several.

"Well," said the blacksmith, "mind its as you like. I've brought you here, and shown you what it is, and now you can do what you like, and of course I'll lend you a hand to do it."

Any one who had been very speculative in this affair, might have detected in these last words of the blacksmith, something like an inclination to creep out of the future consequences of what might next be done, while at the same time shame deterred him from exactly leaving his companions in the lurch.

After some suggestions then, and some argumentation as to the probability or possibility of interruption—the coffin itself, was with its sad and wretched occupant, lifted from the niche where it should have remained until that awful day when the dead shall rise for judgment, and carried up the steps into the church, from thence they passed into the graveyard, but scarcely had they done so, when the surcharged clouds burst over their heads, and the rain came down in perfect torrents.

The deluge was of so frightful, and continuous a character, that they shrank back again beneath the shelter of the church porch, and there waited until its first fury had passed away.

Such an even down storm seldom lasts long in our climate, and the consequence was that in about ten minutes the shower had so far subsided that although a continuous rain was falling it bore but a very distant comparison to what had taken place.

"How are we to burn the body on such a night as this?"

"Aye, how indeed," said another; "you could not so much as kindle a fire, and if you did, it would not live many minutes."

"I'll tell you what to do at once," said one who had as yet borne but a quiet part in the proceedings; I'll tell you what to do at once, for I saw it done myself; a vampyre is quite as secure buried in a cross-road with a stake through its body, as if you burned it in all the fires in the world; come on, the rain won't hinder you doing that."

This was a suggestion highly approved of, and the more so as there was a cross road close at hand, so that the deed could be done quick, and the parties dispersed to their respective homes, for already the exertion they had taken, and the rain that had fallen, had had a great effect in sobering them.

And even now the perilous and disgusting operation of destroying the body, by fire or any other way, might have been abandoned, had any one of the party suggested such a course—but the dread of a future imputation of cowardice kept all silent.

Once more the coffin was raised by four of the throng, and carried through the church-yard, which was now running in many little rivulets, in consequence of the rain. The cross-road was not above a quarter of a mile from the spot, and while those who were disengaged from carrying the body, were hurrying away to get spades and mattocks, the others walked through the rain, and finally paused at the place they thought suitable for that ancient superstitious rite, which it was thought would make the vampyre rest in peace.

It is hard to suppose that Sir George Crofton, his sons, and Mr. Bevan were all deceived concerning these symptoms of vitality which they had observed in the corpse of Clara; but certainly now, there was no appearance of anything of the kind, and the only suspicious circumstances appeared to be the blood upon the lips, and the very fresh-like appearance of the face.

If it were really a fact that the attack of Varney the Vampyre upon this fair young girl had converted her into one of those frightful existences, and that she had been about to leave her tomb for the purpose of seeking a repast of blood, it would appear that the intention had been checked and frustrated by the presence of Sir George and his party in the vault.

At last a dozen men now arrived well armed with spades and picks, and they commenced the work of digging a deep, rather than a capacious grave, in silence.

A gloomy and apprehensive spirit seemed to come over the whole assemblage, and the probability is that this was chiefly owing to the fact that they now encountered no opposition, and that they were permitted unimpeded to accomplish a purpose which had never yet been attempted within the memory of any of the inhabitants of the place.

The grave was dug, and about two feet depth of soil was thrown in a huge mound upon the surface; the coffin was lowered, and there lay the corpse within that receptacle of poor humanity, unimprisoned by any lid for that had been left in the vault, and awaiting the doom which they had decreed upon it, but which they now with a shuddering horror shrunk from performing.

A hedge stake with a sharp point had been procured, and those who held it looked around them with terrified countenances, while the few links that had not been extinguished by the rain, shed a strange and lurid glare upon all objects.

"It must be done," said the blacksmith, "don't let it be said that we got thus far and then were afraid."

"Do it then yourself," said the man that held the stake, "I dare not."

"Aye, do," cried several voices; "you brought us here, why don't you do it—are you afraid after all your boasting."

"Afraid—afraid of the dead; I'm not afraid of any of you that are alive, and it's not likely I'm going to be afraid of a dead body; you're a pretty set of cowards. I've no animosity against the girl, but I want that we shall all sleep in peace, and that our wives and children should not be disturbed nocturnally in their blessed repose. I'll do it if none of you'll do it, and then you may thank me afterwards for the act, although I suppose if I get into trouble I shall have you all turn tail upon me."

"No, we won't—no, we won't."

"Well, well, here goes, whether you do or not. I—I'll do it directly."

"He shrinks," cried one.

"No," said another; "he'll do it—now for it, stand aside."

"Stand aside yourself—do you want to fall into the grave."

The blacksmith shuddered as he held the stake in an attitude to pierce the body, and even up to that moment it seemed to be a doubtful case, whether he would be able to accomplish his purpose or not; at length, when they all thought he was upon the point of abandoning his design, and casting the stake away, he thrust it with tremendous force through the body and the back of the coffin.

The eyes of the corpse opened wide—the hands were clenched, and a shrill, piercing shriek came from the lips—a shriek that was answered by as many as there were persons present, and then with pallid fear upon their countenances they rushed headlong from the spot.

CHRISTOPHER FRAYLING

Bram Stoker's Working Papers for *Dracula*†

* * *

The first notes are dated '8/3/90' and consist of a brief outline of the opening section of the novel. At that early stage, the novel was to begin with a letter from 'Count Wampyr' to the President of the Law Society, followed by much legal correspondence involving the President, a solicitor named Abraham Aaronson, and another letter from the Count, in Styria, asking Aaronson to come in person or send a trustworthy agent who, he stipulates, is not able to speak the German language.

[Abraham Aaronson was to become Peter Hawkins, solicitor of Exeter, and the published novel dealt with the Count's business transaction—the purchase of the estate at Purfleet—in flashback, during Chapter II of Harker's journal (entries for 5 and 7 May). The only legal document to survive the transition from notes to finished text was a nine-line extract from Peter Hawkins's sealed letter, which the Count hands to Harker. Otherwise, the details all emerge from two conversations between Dracula and his guest. In these notes of March 1890, the Count evidently lives in Styria (where Le Fanu's *Carmilla* was set). Since Styria was largely German-speaking, the stipulation that the agent does not speak German was presumably to protect the Count from gossiping peasants. As historian Clive Leatherdale has pointed out, in Stoker's short story *Dracula's Guest* Jonathan Harker cannot speak German—'it was difficult to argue with a man', writes Harker, 'when I did not know his language'—whereas in the final version of *Dracula* we are told on the first page that he has a 'smattering of German . . . indeed, I don't know how I should be able to get on without it'.]

Then there were to be letters from the trustworthy agent to his Principal, and to his girlfriend, describing the journey to the castle in Styria, including a visit to the Munich Dead House,[1] followed by a train journey to Styria, where he is met by a coachman (who is really the Count) at the station.

[This Munich incident is developed by Stoker in subsequent notes. It involves Harker catching his first glimpse of the Count near a mortuary; only when Harker is safely back in England, and the Count has come to look exactly as he did in Munich, does the young solicitor realize

---

† From *Vampyres: Lord Byron to Count Dracula* (London: Faber and Faber, 1992) 303–16. Reprinted by permission of the Peters Fraser & Dunlop Group LTD.
1. Presumably, a mausoleum or mortuary [*Editors*].

the connection. The incident survived the change of locale from Styria to Transylvania.]

The letters would then describe the arrival at an ancient castle, the first appearance of the Count (as himself), with his devil-dark eyes, and the atmosphere in the castle where the old Count *seems* alone but clearly is not. There followed the incident with the girls who try to kiss him not on the lips but on the throat, culminating in the Count saying, 'This man belongs to me I want him.' After that, the young lawyer describes becoming a prisoner in the castle and, to pass the time, consulting his law directory for the Sortes Virgilianae:[2] he has been instructed to buy a large property for the Count, with a consecrated church in the grounds, situated near a river.

[This is the earliest example of Bram Stoker extending the 'rules' of the vampire genre: the Count, it seems, has to rest in consecrated earth. There will be many more such extensions.]

The next notes are, in effect, an early cast list for the novel. The cast (in spring 1890) includes Abraham Aaronson; the lawyer's clerk who goes to Styria; a mad doctor; a mad patient who has 'a theory of perpetual life'; a 'Philosophic Historian'; a German professor of history; a detective inspector; an undertaker; a girl who dies; another girl who is the young lawyer's bright and sceptical sister; and the Count's two servants in London (a silent man and a dumb woman), who are said to be controlled by the evil powers of the Count.

[In this cast list the character who was to become the Dutch Professor Abraham Van Helsing was no less than *three* separate characters: historian, German professor of history and detective inspector. In the event, Van Helsing was to become historian, philosopher, priest, detective and scientist. The detective-story element of the story was evidently to be stronger during the early stages: there are references in subsequent notes to 'tracing the criminal' and to the conundrum caused to the Count's trackers because they are 'in want of a clue to whereabouts'. Also in this list the Count has two strange servants in London, whereas in *Dracula* one of Stoker's more atmospheric touches was to have the Count a shabby genteel aristocrat, without servants—he does all the domestic chores himself. Although the Count apologizes to Harker, 'My people are not available', the young solicitor realizes that the Count has no 'people' in his employ when he discovers his host making the

2. A process of divination in which the querent selects a random passage from a classical text— e.g., the works of Virgil—for insight or guidance. In a pinch, Harker substitutes a law directory. *Sortes* is Latin for "chances" or "lots" [*Editors*].

bed and laying the dinner table. The Mina Harker character was at this stage to be the young lawyer's 'shrewd, sceptical sister.']

Then comes a full chapter outline, written on Lyceum Theatre note-paper and dated '14/3/90'. The outline consists of four 'Books', headed *Styria to London, Tragedy, Discovery* and *Punishment*, each broken up into seven chapters. It reads like the synopsis page of a theatre programme.

Book I begins with the lawyer's correspondence, and the clerk's visit to Styria, via Munich (where he encounters 'wolves' and 'blue flame and c'). After arriving at the castle, he experiences 'Loneliness, the Kiss "this man belongs to me"'. Then Dr Seward's diary takes over, with details of the old chapel and the Sortes Virgilianae ('notes in letter'), and of someone called the fly patient who, the notes add, is in love with death.

[The name 'Styria' was written first by Stoker and then, at a later date, deleted to make way for 'Transylvania'. The names Seward, Lucy, Mina and Harker were all written first time round. This may mean that be-tween 8 March and 14 March 1890 Bram Stoker settled on these proper names. The Van Helsing character (or characters) does not appear at all in this outline.]

Book II begins at Whitby, Yorkshire, with arguments concerning un-canny happenings, a storm, the arrival of a ship and Lucy walking in her sleep. Then Mina's wedding takes place in London, followed by a night of terror ('wolf missing') and Count Dracula's visit to the lunatic asylum. It ends with the death of Lucy (the 'tragedy' of the Book's title), the opening of the vault and a vow.

[The phrase 'Count Dracula' was evidently added later, between Chap-ters 5 and 6 of Book II, as must have been another reference to 'Dra-cula' in Book III, Chapter 3. In March 1890, he was still 'Count Wampyr'.]

Book III opens with Harker's diary, various suspicions and inquiries, and 'The Dinner'. Mina begins to suspect the Count, and the Texan goes on a visit to Transylvania, where he finds himself 'on the track'. The Count's house is searched for clues, and a 'blood-red room' is discovered. The Count disappears, but at the end of the Book he is sighted by Harker.

[Bram Stoker originally had the idea of including a dinner-party scene (at Dr Seward's), in Book III, where each of the thirteen diners would be given a number and would be asked to tell something strange, the 'order of numbers' making the story complete. The punch-line would be that the Count would enter the room. This strange variation on Lord Byron's 'we will each write a ghost story' (at the end of which, in a sense, *The Vampyre* walked in) also, perhaps, relates to one of Stoker's odder performances, which was serialized on 30 January 1892 in the *Gentlewoman* magazine. It was Chapter 10 of *The Fate of Fenella*, the other nine chapters being written by 'well-known writer(s) of Fiction, without consulting his or her collaborateurs, the result being a . . . literary curiosity'; they included Arthur Conan Doyle and F. Anstey. *The Fate of Fenella* was published, complete, later in the year. Stoker eventually junked the idea of the 'dinner of thirteen'. Later in Book III, the (as yet unnamed) Texan was to visit Transylvania on his own, and possibly be killed by a were-wolf. In the final version of *Dracula*, Quincey P. Morris falls victim to the 'knives of the gypsies', but he has such a tangential relationship to the rest of the plot that some commentators have even suggested he is secretly in league with the Count himself (in a kind of American-Transylvanian unholy alliance). Morris (at first named 'Brutus') was also originally, to have been 'an . . . inventor from Texas', a 'Tourist' and a walking example of Yankee know-how who arms himself with the latest Maxim Gun for the final assault on the Castle. Stoker's reference to 'a vigilante committee' and 'a necktie party' suggest that the novel had more Western connections in the author's mind at one stage, in common with his novel *The Shoulder of Shasta*, published in October 1895.]

Book IV opens on another dinner party and a vigilante committee. The net closes on the Count ('remaining earth') and the scene shifts back to Styria. The last chapter, entitled 'A Tourist's Tale', includes 'one killed by a wolf (wehr?)', and finishes on the *aide-mémoire* 'Bring in the Texan'.

There follows another cast list, this time headed *Historiae Personae*, which includes some characters who were to appear in the finished novel: Dr Seward, the 'Girl engaged to him', Lucy Westenra, the lawyer Peter Hawkins from Exeter, his clerk Jonathan Harker, Harker's fianceé, the pupil teacher Wilhelmina Murray, known as Mina, and a Texan named 'Brutus Morris'. It includes even more characters who were *not* to survive the drafting process: two lawyers called William Abbott and A. M. Young, a friend and schoolfellow of Mina called Kate Reed, the Count's two English servants, a detective named Cotford, a psychical research agent named Alfred Singleton, an American inventor from Texas (unnamed), a German professor named Max Windshoeffel and a painter named Francis Aytown. At this early stage, the Count was still to be called 'Count Wampyr'.

[In this cast list the Van Helsing character was still to be divided into three—only this time it was a detective, a psychical research agent and a German professor, and each of these characters had been given a name: Cotford, Alfred Singleton and Max Windshoeffel. Perhaps Professor Windshoeffel was based upon the other German professor called Max in Bram Stoker's life at the time—Professor Max Muller of Oxford. The appearance of the fine artist 'Francis Aytown' may relate to the next two documents. Wilhelmina gets her full name for the first time, as does Lucy, and Mina's friend and confidante Kate Reed (later to be jettisoned) makes her first appearance. The phrase 'Count Wampyr' was changed by Stoker to 'Count Dracula' at a later date.]

The next document, again written on Lyceum Theatre notepaper, consists of three short checklists of the 'characteristics of Count Wampyr'. According to Stoker's notes, the Count:

> goes through life entirely by instinct;
> must cross running water at the exact flood or slack of the tide;
> has an influence over rats, and over the animals in the zoological gardens ('rage of lion, eagle and c . . . wolves, hyenas cowed');
> absolutely despises death and the dead;
> loves creating evil thoughts in others, and banishing good ones— thus destroying their will;
> can see in the dark, and can even get through the thickest of London fogs by instinct;
> is insensible to the beauties of music;
> has 'white teeth and c', and the magic power of making himself large or small;
> must be carried, led, helped, or in some way welcomed over the threshold;
> is enormously strong, even though he never—apparently—eats or drinks;
> has an ambivalent attitude towards the icons of religion: he can be moved only by relics older than his own *real* date or century (that is, when he actually lived)—more recent relics leave him unmoved;
> always uses for money his stores of old gold, which are eventually 'traced to Salzburg banking house';
> 'Immortality—Gladstone' . . .

Where the Count's image is concerned:

painters can't make a likeness of him—however hard the artist tries, the subject always ends up looking like someone else;

equally, it is impossible to photograph (or 'Codak') him—the resulting print always makes him appear 'black or like skeleton corpse';

and there are no looking glasses in the Count's house—because he has no reflection and casts no shadow; the lights in his house must therefore be specially arranged 'to give no shadow'.

As to the Count's folkloric background:

a long branch of a wild rose must be placed in his coffin, to prevent him leaving it;

a swallow—or 'galinele lui Dieu'—is considered lucky, as the fowl of the Lord;

so is a crow, notably when it flies over a person's head;

St George's Day is on 24 April ('our May 6th'), and the night before is, by tradition, a Witches' Sabbat.

[These three check-lists of Count Wampyr's 'characteristics' (rather than those of vampires in general) include some predictable entries as well as some surprises. In addition to the 'characteristics' of the folkloric vampire, they incorporate some plot elements (the Count at London zoo; the influence over rats and 'lower' life forms; the London fog, the Count's favoured currency of old gold) which relate only to the story of *Dracula*. Other 'characteristics', which Stoker did not in the end use, seem to belong to the world of *The Yellow Book*[3] and have more to do with Oscar Wilde than folklore: the *fin-de-siècle* vampire is insensible to the beauties of music, he *loves* to create evil thoughts and 'painters cannot paint him—their likenesses [are] always like someone else'. This latter 'characteristic' suggests a close family resemblance to Wilde's *The Picture of Dorian Gray*[4] (which, in 1891, had just been published) and may also connect with the character 'A Painter—Francis Aytown' in the previous cast list. Stoker was, of course, an acquaintance of Wilde, and a close friend of his neighbour in Cheyne Walk, Chelsea, James McNeill Whistler.[5] Wilde's play *Salomé* was written in Paris in 1891. He decided to cast Sarah Bernhardt[6] in the title role during a party at Henry Irving's (with Stoker probably present), and when *Salomé*, was published in February 1893, Wilde immediately sent a signed copy of it to Florence Stoker (this Salomé, especially in Beardsley's famous illustration, is a seductive little vampire, part-vampire and part vamp). The idea that vampires could be moved only by relics older than their

---

3. A Victorian literary magazine, notorious for its "decadent" contributors [*Editors*].
4. An allegorical novel, which, like *Dracula*, features a malignant title character who remains supernaturally young while corrupting and destroying those around him [*Editors*].
5. American painter (1834–1903), resident of France and England after 1855 [*Editors*].
6. Legendary French actress (1845–1923) [*Editors*].

own *real* date sounds ancient and folkloric, but appears to have been invented by Stoker. The more up-to-date idea that you cannot photograph (or 'Codak') a vampire because he will come out looking like a corpse is logical—if that is the correct word in the circumstances—but also new. In *Dracula* Harker does use his 'Kodak' to photograph the house at Purfleet (or rather 'views of it from various points') but sadly, he never tries this relatively new process out on the Count himself. The references to the swallow as the fowl of the Lord, the crow as unlucky and the dates of St George's Day are all taken verbatim from Gerard's *Transylvanian Superstitions*. The 'Salzburg banking house' reference would suggest that these lists date from the time when the book was still to be set in Austrian Styria—that is, before February 1892; in the finished text Dracula's bankers are Herren Klopstock and Billreuth of Buda-Pesth. The bizarre line, 'Immortality—Gladstone', unless it refers to the bag of that name, remains a puzzle, whatever the date. There is no mention of the fact that vampires are nocturnal creatures. That may be because Stoker chose to ignore this particular 'rule'; Dracula can function in the daytime, although he is not at his best. When Stoker notes that the Count never eats or drinks, he must presumably be referring to solid food and vintage wine; in the novel itself, the Count does have a preferred beverage, but it has to be served at body temperature. After noting that he has never *seen* the Count eat or drink, Harker sensibly observes, 'He must be a very peculiar man.']

Also appended to the document is a series of short notes concerning the visit of the lawyer's clerk to Munich, en route for the Castle. As he is walking past the Dead House in Munich, the young man is to see a waxen face among the funeral flowers. At first he thinks it is a corpse, but it turns out to be the face of a living man. Long afterwards, when the Count is in London—and when his 'white moustache' has grown —Harker will recognize the Count's face as the one he saw among the flowers in Munich. Evidently, the face presented by the Count when he is in his castle is appreciably different—perhaps younger.

[In the published novel the Count has a 'great white moustache', or a 'heavy moustache'—as befits a retired military commander—when Harker first meets him at the Castle. There is the suggestion that Dracula gets *younger* (rather than more ancient) as the story progresses.]

There follows a brief memo, dated '29/2/92', outlining the structure of the beginning of the novel. Harker's diary, with its Munich interlude, still forms Chapter 2. Chapter 1 consists of correspondence about 'Purchase of Estate'. Chapter 3 continues the Munich story (so it remains an extensive section of the narrative) and Chapter 4 takes us to

'Bistritz—Borgo Pass—Castle'. What happens there, as Stoker crypti-cally adds, is 'Sortes Virgil. Belongs to Me'.

[This revised structure is particularly significant for its references to 'Bistritz—Borgo Pass'. By the end of February 1892 Stoker had evidently decided to shift the location from Styria to Bistrita in Transylvania. Since his knowledge of the Borgo Pass (and of how to spell Romanian place-names) came from Charles Boner's *Transylvania*, and of local folklore from Gerard, it appears that he had read these two books by this date. He may also have known about the name 'Dracula' as early as Summer 1890. So by 1892 all the key pieces of the jigsaw were already in place—*five years* before publication.]

Another memo represents a slight refinement of the outline structure of February 1892. It still opens on lawyers' letters about 'Purchase of Estate' but is more explicit about 'Harker's diary—Munich—Wolf' and 'Harker's diary—Munich—Death House', and cross-cuts between Har-ker's journey from 'Bistritz to Castle Dracula' and Dr Seward's diary entries concerning the 'Fly man', so that the 'Fly man' (who was later to become Renfield) heralds Harker's arrival at the Castle rather than, as in the published version, the Count's arrival at his English residence. Also, the 'Belongs to Me' incident appears to be cross-cut with events in Whitby. The most significant aspect of this memo is that it explicitly mentions 'Castle Dracula' for the very first time.

The next document is a fully worked-out structure, letter by letter, of Book I. It begins with a letter from Sir Robert Parton, President of the Law Society, to Peter Hawkins of Cathedral Place, Exeter, stating that he has been contacted by one 'Count Wampyr'. Peter Hawkins, we learn from another letter, has gout and decides to let Harker handle the conveyancing of an estate to the Count (which he finds at Purfleet). Letter 6 is from Kate Reed to Lucy Westenra, telling Lucy about Har-ker's visit to a school to see pupil-teacher Mina Murray; there is a postscript in which Kate tells of 'how she thought after waiting it would be well to ask Mina's permission before telling her story'. Letter 7 con-tinues this theme: 'she knows it's all dead long ago, and that she goes to stay with her' on her summer holidays at Whitby. Letter 8 is a tel-egram from 'Dracula to Hawkins', asking that Harker set out for Munich.

[Strangely, although the name 'Count Wampyr' appears in Letters 1–5, later crossed out by Bram Stoker and superseded by the new name 'Count Dracula', from Letter 8 onwards the name 'Dracula' was written first time round—and continues that way throughout Stoker's summary. Perhaps the early chapters were being copied from a previous (but post-

'Abraham Aaronson') version. Peter Hawkins's attack of gout, mentioned here for the first time, is still there in the finished novel. 'An attack of gout,' he writes in Chapter II, 'from which malady I am a constant sufferer, forbids absolutely any travelling on my part.'

The two letters from confidante Kate Reed seem to imply, first, that she has some 'story' which is of interest to Mina and, second, that it is 'all dead long ago', so they can remain friends. Could it possibly have been a romance with Jonathan? In the published version, he is *very* correct on such matters.]

The structure then changes from the letter form to 'journal in shorthand of Jonathan Harker on his first journey abroad'. Since this journal is being written especially to show Mina on Harker's return, all business matters have been deliberately omitted. Chapter 2 begins with the directions which have been sent by the Count, to go by the direct service to Munich and then to 'stop at (Hotel Marienbad) Quatre Saisons and await instructions'. On his first day, Harker visits the Pinakothek Museum 'and c', and also the Dead House. There he catches sight of 'old man on bier'—among some flowers—who seems at first to be a corpse but in fact isn't. He goes back to the Quatre Saisons hotel. The following morning he receives a wire from 'Transylvania. Bistritz', giving him details of the next leg of his journey. Chapter 3 (still in journal form) describes the journey to Bistritz, where Harker checks into his hotel. The Count's name is well known there, for it was the hoteliers who sent on the telegram; but when they hear of the young man's destination, they become 'all very sad and mysterious'. There are some strange gifts for him ('see xix century'). [These 'gifts' are an explicit reference to Gerard's article in the *Nineteenth Century* magazine.] Harker is deposited at the Borgo Pass by the Diligence, where he is met by a 'driver man muffled' on a carriage. The journey from the Borgo Pass to the Castle is eventful: some wolves surround the carriage, some blue flames are sighted, until, amid the howlings of wolves and dogs, thunder and other 'weird sounds'—they eventually arrive at the Castle at midnight. At this juncture, 'enter Count-supper-to bed-describe room, &c'. [Stoker's shorthand 'enter Count' reads like a stage direction for Henry Irving!]

Chapter 4 continues Harker's account in his journal of his stay in the Castle. Although Harker is left all alone in the daytime, he feels he is a prisoner: 'the books—Sortes Virgilianae—and the visitors—is it a dream—women stoop to kiss him. terror of death. Suddenly Count turns her away—"this man belongs to me".' [Later in this structure, at Book III, Chapter 7, Jonathan Harker 'sees the Count—met him going into the Munich Death-House': clearly, for some reason, by then the

Count's appearance has become the same as in Book I, Chapter 2. The 'dinner of revenge' is also still there.]

Bram Stoker's final outline of the early part of the novel—the next document—is evidently an attempt to sort out the timescale of his story. It is written on a printed, all-purpose diary with no dates on it—just the headings *189—Mon—Sat, Morn Eve* and *Remarks*.

The outline begins on 16 March with Count Dracula's letter to Peter Hawkins (dated, Stoker adds, 4 March old style), then continues on 21 March with Sir Robert Parton's letter to Hawkins—the President of the Law Society to a senior solicitor. Hawkins's letter to the Count is written on Thursday, 23 March and the reply a week later (18 March old style). Jonathan Harker visits Purfleet on 12 April and starts his house-deeds search on Thursday, 13 April—the same day as Count Dracula writes to the *maître d'hôtel* of the Quatre Saisons in Munich. Two days later, Harker writes to Hawkins, and on Sunday, 16 April, he visits Mina at the school where she teaches.

[Either Stoker wan't concentrating, or Mina taught at a boarding-school. Otherwise, why should she be visited at school on a Sunday?]

The following day, Katie writes to Lucy, and on Wednesday, 19 April, Hawkins writes to Dracula.

Following a telegram from Dracula dispatched on Monday, 24 April, Harker leaves London on the night of the 25th, arrives in Paris early the following morning, leaves Paris at 8.25 a.m. and arrives in Munich at 8.35 p.m. Having checked into the Quatre Saisons late on Wednesday, 26 April, Harker has his adventure with 'snowstorm and wolf' on the following day, gets back to the Hotel early on the morning of the 28th and spends all 29 April recovering. On the evening of Sunday, 30 April, he goes to the opera to see Wagner's *Flying Dutchman*. Monday, 1 May, is the day of the Dead House incident, and is also the day after Walpurgis Night. Harker leaves Munich by train at 8.35 that evening. His destination is Vienna, via Salzburg.

[This Wagnerian curtain-raiser to the events in Transylvania provides a nice link with the world of Henry Irving (who performed W. G. Wills's version of the legend of the Flying Dutchman, *Vanderdecken*, from June 1878 onwards) and with Bram Stoker's personal interests. *Vanderdecken* was reviewed by Stoker: 'the chief actor is not quick but dead . . . and in the last act . . . answers the question "where are we?": "Between the living and the dead".' After the opening night, Stoker helped Irving to 'cut and alter the play', and in 1891–2 was involved in discussions with Irving and Hall Caine about a new version of the story—which were to come to nothing. He was a great fan of Wagner's operatic music, and especially of Hans Richter's interpretations. In the 1890s, according to the *Personal Reminiscences*, 'with my wife I attended the Wagner Cycle at Bayreuth . . . and heard Wagner's *Meistersinger* in all its magnificent perfection'. Stoker was also to discuss the lighting effects in *The Flying Dutchman*, with Richter, over lunch on 24 October 1900. The events in Munich, according to this late timescale by Stoker, occur in an unexpected order. First, the adventure of the 'snowstorm and wolf', then the visit to the opera, then Walpurgis Nacht, then the Dead House incident. On the first line of *Dracula* as published, all of this is reduced to 'Left Munich at 8.35 p.m.'; only the time of departure survives from the drafting stage.]

Tuesday, 2 May, is spent travelling: a change of trains at Vienna in the morning (arrive 6.45 a.m., depart 8.25 a.m.), another at Buda-Pesth over lunchtime (arrive 1.30 p.m., depart 2.00 p.m.), followed by arrival at Klausenburg at 10.34 p.m. After an overnight stay at Klausenburg (2–3 May), Harker leaves by the 8 a.m. train and arrives in Bistritz twelve hours later. After another overnight stay, he leaves Bistritz at 2 p.m.—by coach—and reaches the Borgo Pass seven hours later at 9.00 p.m. (or one hour earlier than the scheduled eight hours). Harker finally reaches the Castle, driven by the muffled and disguised coachman, in the early hours of Friday, 5 May. It takes him two days to realize that the Castle is in fact a prison, and on Tuesday, 9 May, he tries to write home about his experiences so far. On the Wednesday, he sees the Count crawling out of his window and down the wall of the Castle, and on Thursday, 11 May, he sees 'the women kissing'. Friday is spent in bed, writing letters. To judge by the crossings-out, Bram Stoker then changed his mind about the dating of the incidents in the Castle. He substituted the night of Saturday, 13 May, for the window incident, and Monday, 15 May, for 'women kissing'.

[On the manuscript of this timescale, Stoker wrote—just before the entry for Thursday, 11 May—'Jonathan Diary' as a heading. This would suggest that all the previous incidents were to be communicated in the form of a collection of documents: the legal letters, Katie's letter, Dracula's telegram, then letters home from the Castle. Stoker also wrote 'Seward's Diary' against the dates Wednesday, 3 May, and Saturday, 6 May, so at one stage the account of the journey from Vienna to Transylvania *may* have been compiled from Harker's reminiscences to Dr Seward; or he may still have intended to cross-cut between the journey and Seward's simultaneous experiences. If 'Jonathan Diary' *was* to begin on Thursday, 11 May, then its first page would have described 'the women kissing' incident, which would, of course, have given it even more prominence in the story. The date he finally settled on for this incident, Monday, 15 May, was the same as in the published novel.

The whole of this detailed breakdown of the story outline into dates and times was evidently written *after* Stoker had made up his mind about the details of the story itself. It suggests that the initial legal correspondence was present until the final stages of drafting the novel, as was Katie Reed's correspondence with Lucy. Also Jonathan Harker's five-day stopover in Munich (why five days?) survived until a very late stage. As McNally and Florescu have pointed out,[7] these dates and days correspond with the year 1893. It is quite possible that Stoker was already sorting out the timescale of *Dracula* in that same year, for we know that he wanted the events to seem 'exactly contemporary'.]

Appended to the timescale was a detailed timetable of train arrivals and departures from London to Paris, Paris to Munich, Munich to Vienna via Salzburg, Vienna to Budapest, Budapest to Klausenburg, Klausenburg to Bistritz and of the coach journey from Bistritz to the Borgo Pass. Stoker simply transposed this timetable (from Baedeker's) into his own order of events.

[He was evidently keen to establish an aura of 'authenticity' around his story, by getting all the dates and timetables right, so that, as he put it in his opening words to *Dracula*, his history 'may stand forth as simple fact'. It was a passion shared by Count Dracula himself, who owns 'such books of reference as the London Directory, the "Red" and "Blue" books, Whitaker's Almanack, the Army and Navy Lists, and . . . the Law List'. Later, Jonathan Harker discovers the Count 'lying on the sofa, reading, of all things in the world, an English Bradshaw's Guide'. As Henry Irving's manager, Stoker would have had to look after the complex logistics of his national and international tours, involving constant reference to Bradshaw's and, for overseas, Baedeker's guides.]

BRAM STOKER

Dracula's Guest†

(1914)

When we started for our drive the sun was shining brightly on Munich, and the air was full of the joyousness of early summer. Just as we were about to depart, Herr Delbrück (the maître d'hôtel of the Quatre Saisons, where I was staying) came down, bareheaded, to the carriage and,

---

7. Raymond T. McNally and Radu Florescu, authors of *In Search of Dracula*; see Selected Bibliography, below [*Editors*].
† From *Dracula's Guest—And Other Weird Stories* (London: Routledge, 1914).

after wishing me a pleasant drive, said to the coachman, still holding
his hand on the handle of the carriage door:

'Remember you are back by nightfall. The sky looks bright but there
is a shiver in the north wind that says there may be a sudden storm.
But I am sure you will not be late.' Here he smiled, and added, 'for
you know what night it is.'

Johann answered with an emphatic, 'Ja, mein Herr,' and, touching
his hat, drove off quickly. When we had cleared the town, I said, after
signalling to him to stop:

'Tell me, Johann, what is tonight?'

He crossed himself, as he answered laconically: 'Walpurgis Nacht.'
Then he took out his watch, a great, old-fashioned German silver thing
as big as a turnip, and looked at it, with his eyebrows gathered together
and a little impatient shrug of his shoulders. I realised that this was his
way of respectfully protesting against the unnecessary delay, and sank
back in the carriage, merely motioning him to proceed. He started off
rapidly, as if to make up for lost time. Every now and then the horses
seemed to throw up their heads and sniffed the air suspiciously. On
such occasions I often looked round in alarm. The road was pretty
bleak, for we were traversing a sort of high, wind-swept plateau. As we
drove, I saw a road that looked but little used, and which seemed to
dip through a little, winding valley. It looked so inviting that, even at
the risk of offending him, I called Johann to stop—and when he had
pulled up, I told him I would like to drive down that road. He made
all sorts of excuses, and frequently crossed himself as he spoke. This
somewhat piqued my curiosity, so I asked him various questions. He
answered fencingly, and repeatedly looked at his watch in protest. Finally I said:

'Well, Johann, I want to go down this road. I shall not ask you to
come unless you like; but tell me why you do not like to go, that is all
I ask.' For answer he seemed to throw himself off the box, so quickly
did he reach the ground. Then he stretched out his hands appealingly
to me, and implored me not to go. There was just enough of English
mixed with the German for me to understand the drift of his talk. He
seemed always just about to tell me something—the very idea of which
evidently frightened him; but each time he pulled himself up, saying,
as he crossed himself: 'Walpurgis Nacht!'

I tried to argue with him, but it was difficult to argue with a man
who did not know one's language. The advantage certainly rested with
him, for although he began to speak in English, of a very crude and
broken kind, he always got excited and broke into his native tongue—
and every time he did so, he looked at his watch. Then the horses
became restless and sniffed the air. At this he grew very pale, and,
looking around in a frightened way, he suddenly jumped forward, took
them by the bridles and led them on some twenty feet. I followed, and

asked why he had done this. For answer he crossed himself, pointed to the spot we had left and drew his carriage in the direction of the other road, indicating a cross, and said, first in German, then in English: 'Buried him—him what killed themselves.'

I remembered the old custom of burying suicides at cross-roads: 'Ah! I see, a suicide. How interesting!' But for the life of me I could not make out why the horses were frightened.

Whilst we were talking, we heard a sort of sound between a yelp and a bark. It was far away; but the horses got very restless, and it took Johann all his time to quiet them. He was pale, and said, 'It sounds like a wolf—but yet there are no wolves here now.'

'No?' I said, questioning him; 'isn't it long since the wolves were so near the city?'

'Long, long', he answered, 'in the spring and summer; but with the snow the wolves have been here not so long.'

Whilst he was petting the horses and trying to quiet them, dark clouds drifted rapidly across the sky. The sunshine passed away, and a breath of cold wind seemed to drift past us. It was only a breath, however, and more in the nature of a warning than a fact, for the sun came out brightly again. Johann looked under his lifted hand at the horizon and said:

'The storm of snow he comes before long time.' Then he looked at his watch again, and, straightway holding his reins firmly—for the horses were still pawing the ground restlessly and shaking their heads —he climbed to his box as though the time had come for proceeding on our journey.

I felt a little obstinate and did not at once get into the carriage.

'Tell me,' I said, 'about this place where the road leads,' and I pointed down.

Again he crossed himself and mumbled a prayer, before he answered, 'It is unholy.'

'What is unholy?' I enquired.

'The village.'

'Then there is a village?'

'No, no. No one lives there hundreds of years.' My curiosity was piqued, 'But you said there was a village.'

'There was.'

'Where is it now?'

Whereupon he burst out into a long story in German and English, so mixed up that I could not quite understand exactly what he said, but roughly I gathered that long ago, hundreds of years, men had died there and been buried in their graves; and sounds were heard under the clay, and when the graves were opened, men and women were found rosy with life, and their mouths red with blood. And so, in haste to save their lives (aye, and their souls!—and here he crossed himself)

those who were left fled away to other places, where the living lived,
and the dead were dead and not—not something. He was evidently
afraid to speak the last words. As he proceeded with his narration, he
grew more and more excited. It seemed as if his imagination had got
hold of him, and he ended in a perfect paroxysm of fear—white-faced,
perspiring, trembling and looking round him, as if expecting that some
dreadful presence would manifest itself there in the bright sunshine on
the open plain. Finally, in an agony of desperation, he cried:

'Walpurgis Nacht!' and pointed to the carriage for me to get in. All
my English blood rose at this, and, standing back, I said:

'You are afraid, Johann—you are afraid. Go home; I shall return
alone; the walk will do me good.' The carriage door was open. I took
from the seat my oak walking-stick—which I always carry on my holiday
excursions—and closed the door, pointing back to Munich, and said,
'Go home, Johann—Walpurgis Nacht doesn't concern Englishmen.'

The horses were now more restive than ever, and Johann was trying
to hold them in, while excitedly imploring me not to do anything so
foolish. I pitied the poor fellow, he was deeply in earnest; but all the
same I could not help laughing. His English was quite gone now. In
his anxiety he had forgotten that his only means of making me understand was to talk my language, so he jabbered away in his native
German. It began to be a little tedious. After giving the direction,
'Home!' I turned to go down the cross-road into the valley.

With a despairing gesture, Johann turned his horses towards Munich.
I leaned on my stick and looked after him. He went slowly along the
road for a while: then there came over the crest of the hill a man tall
and thin. I could see so much in the distance. When he drew near the
horses, they began to jump and kick about, then to scream with terror.
Johann could not hold them in; they bolted down the road, running
away madly. I watched them out of sight, then looked for the stranger,
but I found that he, too, was gone.

With a light heart I turned down the side road through the deepening
valley to which Johann had objected. There was not the slightest reason,
that I could see, for his objection; and I daresay I tramped for a couple
of hours without thinking of time or distance, and certainly without
seeing a person or a house. So far as the place was concerned, it was
desolation itself. But I did not notice this particularly till, on turning a
bend in the road, I came upon a scattered fringe of wood; then I recognised that I had been impressed unconsciously by the desolation of
the region through which I had passed.

I sat down to rest myself, and began to look around. It struck me
that it was considerably colder than it had been at the commencement
of my walk—a sort of sighing sound seemed to be around me, with,
now and then, high overhead, a sort of muffled roar. Looking upwards
I noticed that great thick clouds were drifting rapidly across the sky

from North to South at a great height. There were signs of coming storm in some lofty stratum of the air. I was a little chilly, and, thinking that it was the sitting still after the exercise of walking, I resumed my journey.

The ground I passed over was now much more picturesque. There were no striking objects that the eye might single out; but in all there was a charm of beauty. I took little heed of time and it was only when the deepening twilight forced itself upon me that I began to think of how I should find my way home. The brightness of the day had gone. The air was cold, and the drifting of clouds high overhead was more marked. They were accompanied by a sort of far-away rushing sound, through which seemed to come at intervals that mysterious cry which the driver had said came from a wolf. For a while I hesitated. I had said I would see the deserted village, so on I went, and presently came on a wide stretch of open country, shut in by hills all around. Their sides were covered with trees which spread down to the plain, dotting, in clumps, the gentler slopes and hollows which showed here and there. I followed with my eye the winding of the road, and saw that it curved close to one of the densest of these clumps and was lost behind it.

As I looked there came a cold shiver in the air, and the snow began to fall. I thought of the miles and miles of bleak country I had passed, and then hurried on to seek the shelter of the wood in front. Darker and darker grew the sky, and faster and heavier fell the snow, till the earth before and around me was a glistening white carpet the further edge of which was lost in misty vagueness. The road was here but crude, and when on the level its boundaries were not so marked as when it passed through the cuttings; and in a little while I found that I must have strayed from it, for I missed underfoot the hard surface, and my feet sank deeper in the grass and moss. Then the wind grew stronger and blew with ever increasing force, till I was fain to run before it. The air became icy-cold, and in spite of my exercise I began to suffer. The snow was now falling so thickly and whirling around me in such rapid eddies that I could hardly keep my eyes open. Every now and then the heavens were torn asunder by vivid lightning, and in the flashes I could see ahead of me a great mass of trees, chiefly yew and cypress all heavily coated with snow.

I was soon amongst the shelter of the trees, and there, in comparative silence, I could hear the rush of the wind high overhead. Presently the blackness of the storm had become merged in the darkness of the night. By-and-by the storm seemed to be passing away: it now only came in fierce puffs or blasts. At such moments the weird sound of the wolf appeared to be echoed by many similar sounds around me.

Now and again, through the black mass of drifting cloud, came a straggling ray of moonlight, which lit up the expanse, and showed me that I was at the edge of a dense mass of cypress and yew trees. As the

snow had ceased to fall, I walked out from the shelter and began to
investigate more closely. It appeared to me that, amongst so many old
foundations as I had passed, there might be still standing a house in
which, though in ruins, I could find some sort of shelter for a while.
As I skirted the edge of the copse, I found that a low wall encircled it,
and following this I presently found an opening. Here the cypresses
formed an alley leading up to a square mass of some kind of building.
Just as I caught sight of this, however, the drifting clouds obscured the
moon, and I passed up the path in darkness. The wind must have grown
colder, for I felt myself shiver as I walked; but there was hope of shelter,
and I groped my way blindly on.

I stopped, for there was a sudden stillness. The storm had passed;
and, perhaps in sympathy with nature's silence, my heart seemed to
cease to beat. But this was only momentarily; for suddenly the moonlight broke through the clouds, showing me that I was in a graveyard,
and that the square object before me was a great massive tomb of
marble, as white as the snow that lay on and all around it. With the
moonlight there came a fierce sigh of the storm, which appeared to
resume its course with a long, low howl, as of many dogs or wolves. I
was awed and shocked, and felt the cold perceptibly grow upon me till
it seemed to grip me by the heart. Then while the flood of moonlight
still fell on the marble tomb, the storm gave further evidence of renewing, as though it was returning on its track. Impelled by some sort of
fascination, I approached the sepulchre to see what it was, and why
such a thing stood alone in such a place. I walked around it, and read,
over the Doric door, in German:

COUNTESS DOLINGEN OF GRATZ

IN STYRIA

SOUGHT AND FOUND DEATH

1801

On the top of the tomb, seemingly driven through the solid marble
—for the structure was composed of a few vast blocks of stone—was a
great iron spike or stake. On going to the back I saw, graven in Great
Russian letters:

'The dead travel fast.'

There was something so weird and uncanny about the whole thing
that it gave me a turn and made me feel quite faint. I began to wish,
for the first time, that I had taken Johann's advice. Here a thought
struck me, which came under almost mysterious circumstances and
with a terrible shock. This was Walpurgis Night!

Walpurgis Night, when, according to the belief of millions of people,
the devil was abroad—when the graves were opened and the dead came
forth and walked. When all evil things of earth and air and water held

revel. This very place the driver had specially shunned. This was the depopulated village of centuries ago. This was where the suicide lay; and this was the place where I was alone—unmanned, shivering with cold in a shroud of snow with a wild storm gathering again upon me! It took all my philosophy, all the religion I had been taught, all my courage, not to collapse in a paroxysm of fright.

And now a perfect tornado burst upon me. The ground shook as though thousands of horses thundered across it; and this time the storm bore on its icy wings, not snow, but great hailstones which drove with such violence that they might have come from the throngs of Balearic slingers[1]—hailstones that beat down leaf and branch and made the shelter of the cypresses of no more avail than though their stems were standing-corn. At the first I had rushed to the nearest tree; but I was soon fain to leave it and seek the only spot that seemed to afford refuge, the deep Doric doorway of the marble tomb. There, crouching against the massive bronze door, I gained a certain amount of protection from the beating of the hailstones, for now they only drove against me as they ricocheted from the ground and the side of the marble.

As I leaned against the door, it moved slightly and opened inwards. The shelter of even a tomb was welcome in that pitiless tempest, and I was about to enter it when there came a flash of forked-lightning that lit up the whole expanse of the heavens. In the instant, as I am a living man, I saw, as my eyes were turned into the darkness of the tomb, a beautiful woman, with rounded cheeks and red lips, seemingly sleeping on a bier. As the thunder broke overhead, I was grasped as by the hand of a giant and hurled out into the storm. The whole thing was so sudden that, before I could realise the shock, moral as well as physical, I found the hailstones beating me down. At the same time I had a strange, dominating feeling that I was not alone. I looked towards the tomb. Just then there came another blinding flash, which seemed to strike the iron stake that surmounted the tomb and to pour through to the earth, blasting and crumbling the marble, as in a burst of flame. The dead woman rose for a moment of agony, while she was lapped in the flame, and her bitter scream of pain was drowned in the thunder-crash. The last thing I heard was this mingling of dreadful sound, as again I was seized in the giant-grasp and dragged away, while the hail-stones beat on me, and the air around seemed reverberant with the howling of wolves. The last sight that I remembered was a vague, white, moving mass, as if all the graves around me had sent out the phantoms of their sheeted-dead, and that they were closing in on me through the white cloudiness of the driving hail.

* * *

1. Warriors in Hannibal's army, trained from an early age to hurl leaden pellets with legendary force and accuracy. "Balearic" refers to a Spanish province of islands in the western Mediterranean Sea (including Ibiza, Mallorca, and Minorca) [Editors].

Gradually there came a sort of vague beginning of consciousness; then a sense of weariness that was dreadful. For a time I remembered nothing; but slowly my senses returned. My feet seemed positively racked with pain, yet I could not move them. They seemed to be numbed. There was an icy feeling at the back of my neck and all down my spine, and my ears, like my feet, were dead, yet in torment; but there was in my breast a sense of warmth which was, by comparison, delicious. It was as a nightmare—a physical nightmare, if one may use such an expression; for some heavy weight on my chest made it difficult for me to breathe.

This period of semi-lethargy seemed to remain a long time, and as it faded away I must have slept or swooned. Then came a sort of loathing, like the first stage of sea-sickness, and a wild desire to be free from something—I knew not what. A vast stillness enveloped me, as though all the world were asleep or dead—only broken by the low panting as of some animal close to me. I felt a warm rasping at my throat, then came a consciousness of the awful truth, which chilled me to the heart and sent the blood surging up through my brain. Some great animal was lying on me and now licking my throat. I feared to stir, for some instinct of prudence bade me lie still; but the brute seemed to realise that there was now some change in me, for it raised its head. Through my eye-lashes I saw above me the two great flaming eyes of a gigantic wolf. Its sharp white teeth gleamed in the gaping red mouth, and I could feel its hot breath fierce and acrid upon me.

For another spell of time I remembered no more. Then I became conscious of a low growl, followed by a yelp, renewed again and again. Then, seemingly very far away, I heard a 'Holloa! holloa!' as of many voices calling in unison. Cautiously I raised my head and looked in the direction whence the sound came; but the cemetery blocked my view. The wolf still continued to yelp in a strange way, and a red glare began to move round the grove of cypresses, as though following the sound. As the voices drew closer, the wolf yelped faster and louder, I feared to make either sound or motion. Nearer came the red glow, over the white pall which stretched into the darkness around me. Then all at once from beyond the trees there came at a trot a troop of horsemen bearing torches. The wolf rose from my breast and made for the cemetery. I saw one of the horsemen (soldiers by their caps and their military cloaks) raise his carbine and take aim. A companion knocked up his arm, and I heard the ball whizz over my head. He had evidently taken my body for that of the wolf. Another sighted the animal as it slunk away, and a shot followed. Then, at a gallop, the troop rode forward—some towards me, others following the wolf as it disappeared amongst the snow-clad cypresses.

As they drew nearer I tried to move, but was powerless, although I could see and hear all that went on around me. Two or three of the soldiers jumped from their horses and knelt beside me. One of them raised my head, and placed his hand over my heart.

'Good news, comrades!' he cried. 'His heart still beats!'

Then some brandy was poured down my throat; it put vigour into me, and I was able to open my eyes fully and look around. Lights and shadows were moving among the trees, and I heard men call to one another. They drew together, uttering frightening exclamations; and the lights flashed as the others came pouring out of the cemetery pell-mell, like men possessed. When the further ones came close to us, those who were around me asked them eagerly:

'Well, have you found him?'

The reply rang out hurriedly:

'No! no! Come away quick—quick! This is no place to stay, and on this of all nights!'

'What was it?' was the question, asked in all manner of keys. The answer came variously and all indefinitely as though the men were moved by some common impulse to speak, yet were restrained by some common fear from giving their thoughts.

'It—it—indeed!' gibbered one, whose wits had plainly given out for the moment.

'A wolf—and yet not a wolf!' another put in shudderingly.

'No use trying for him without the sacred bullet,' a third remarked in a more ordinary manner.

'Serve us right for coming out on this night! Truly we have earned our thousand marks!' were the ejaculations of a fourth.

'There was blood on the broken marble,' another said after a pause —'the lightning never brought that there. And for him—is he safe? Look at his throat! See, comrades, the wolf has been lying on him and keeping his blood warm.'

The officer looked at my throat and replied:

'He is all right; the skin is not pierced. What does it all mean? We should never have found him but for the yelping of the wolf.'

'What became of it?' asked the man who was holding up my head, and who seemed the least panic-stricken of the party, for his hands were steady and without tremor. On his sleeve was the chevron of a petty officer.

'It went to its home,' answered the man, whose long face was pallid, and who actually shook with terror as he glanced around fearfully. 'There are graves enough there in which it may lie. Come, comrades —come quickly! Let us leave this cursed spot.'

The officer raised me to a sitting posture, as he uttered a word of command; then several men placed me upon a horse. He sprang to the saddle behind me, took me in his arms, gave the word to advance; and, turning our faces away from the cypresses, we rode away in swift, military order.

As yet my tongue refused its office, and I was perforce silent. I must have fallen asleep; for the next thing I remembered was finding myself standing up, supported by a soldier on each side of me. It was almost broad daylight, and to the north a red streak of sunlight was reflected, like a path of blood, over the waste of snow. The officer was telling the men to say nothing of what they had seen, except that they found an English stranger, guarded by a large dog.

'Dog! that was no dog,' cut in the man who had exhibited such fear. 'I think I know a wolf when I see one.'

The young officer answered calmly: 'I said a dog.'

'Dog!' reiterated the other ironically. It was evident that his courage was rising with the sun; and, pointing to me, he said, 'Look at his throat. Is that the work of a dog, master?'

Instinctively I raised my hand to my throat, and as I touched it I cried out in pain. The men crowded round to look, some stooping down from their saddles; and again there came the calm voice of the young officer.

'A dog, as I said. If aught else were said we should only be laughed at.'

I was then mounted behind a trooper, and we rode on into the suburbs of Munich. Here we came across a stray carriage, into which I was lifted, and it was driven off to the Quatre Saisons—the young officer accompanying me, whilst a trooper followed with his horse, and the others rode off to their barracks.

When we arrived, Herr Delbrück rushed so quickly down the steps to meet me, that it was apparent he had been watching within. Taking me by both hands he solicitously led me in. The officer saluted me and was turning to withdraw, when I recognised his purpose, and insisted that he should come to my rooms. Over a glass of wine I warmly thanked him and his brave comrades for saving me. He replied simply that he was more than glad, and that Herr Delbrück had at the first taken steps to make all the searching party pleased; at which ambiguous utterance the maître d'hôtel smiled, while the officer pleaded duty and withdrew.

'But Herr Delbrück,' I enquired, 'how and why was it that the soldiers searched for me?'

He shrugged his shoulders, as if in depreciation of his own deed, as he replied:

'I was so fortunate as to obtain leave from the commander of the regiment in which I served, to ask for volunteers.

'But how did you know that I was lost?' I asked.

'The driver came hither with the remains of his carriage, which had been upset when the horses ran away.'

'But surely you would not send a search-party of soldiers merely on this account.

'Oh, no!' he answered; 'but even before the coachman arrived, I had this telegram from the Boyar whose guest you are,' and he took from his pocket a telegram which he handed to me, and I read:

Bistritz.

Be careful of my guest—his safety is most precious to me. Should aught happen to him, or if he be missed, spare nothing to find him and ensure his safety. He is English and therefore adventurous. There are often dangers from snow and wolves and night. Lose not a moment if you suspect harm to him. I answer your zeal with my fortune. —*Dracula.*

As I held the telegram in my hand, the room seemed to whirl around me; and, if the attentive maître d'hôtel had not caught me, I think I should have fallen. There was something so strange in all this, something so weird and impossible to imagine, that there grew on me a sense of my being in some way the sport of opposite forces—the mere vague idea of which seemed in a way to paralyse me. I was certainly under some form of mysterious protection. From a distant country had come, in the very nick of time, a message that took me out of the danger of the snow-sleep and the jaws of the wolf.

REVIEWS AND
REACTIONS

While modern readers and critics of *Dracula* are transfixed by both the story's primal narrative power and its extraordinary psychosexual, sociopolitical subtexts, the novel was initially treated by reviewers as a harmless, if thrill-producing, entertainment. This seems somewhat puzzling today; Stoker, after all, published his book within a year of H. G. Wells's *The Island of Doctor Moreau* (1896), which created a firestorm of controversy with its anxious Darwinian images of human beings blurring into animals—also a major thematic preoccupation of *Dracula*. And not a single reviewer of the time related Dracula's story of "degenerate" sexuality and blood contamination to the syphilis epidemic which cut a wide swath through 1890s London, possibly killing Stoker himself. Despite the correspondences, Victorian critics reserved their brickbats for works such as Ibsen's *Ghosts* (1882), a realistic play which dared to deal openly with the subject of venereal disease. In supernatural disguise, however, almost any "unwholesome" topic might walk freely through Victorian London, much like Dracula himself.

THE DAILY MAIL

Review

(June 1, 1897)

It is said of Mrs. Radcliffe[1] that when writing her now almost forgotten romances she shut herself up in absolute seclusion, and fed upon raw beef, in order to give her work the desired atmosphere of gloom, tragedy and terror. If one had no assurance to the contrary one might well suppose that a similar method and regimen had been adopted by Mr. Bram Stoker while writing his new novel "Dracula." In seeking for a parallel to this weird, powerful, and horrorful story our mind reverts to such tales as "The Mysteries of Udolpho," "Frankenstein," "Wuthering Heights," "The Fall of the House of Usher," and "Marjery [sic] of Quether."[1] But "Dracula" is even more appalling in its gloomy fascination than any one of these.

We started reading it early in the evening, and followed Jonathan Harker on his mission to the Carpathians with no definite conjecture as to what waited us in the castle of Dracula. When we came to the night journey over the mountain road and were chased by the wolves, which the driver, with apparently miraculous power, repelled by a mere gesture, we began to scent mystery, but were not perturbed. The first

---

1. Ann Radcliffe, English novelist.
2. *The Mysteries of Udolpho* (1794), novel by Ann Radcliffe; *Frankenstein, or the Modern Prometheus* (1818), novel by Mary Wollstonecraft Shelley; *Wuthering Heights* (1850), novel by Emily Brontë; "The Fall of the House of Usher" (1839), short story by Edgar Allan Poe; "Margery of Quether" (1892), short story by Sabine Baring-Gould (1834–1924), a prolific authority on religion, folklore, mythology, and the occult [*Editors*].

thrill of horrible sensation came with the discovery that the driver and the Count Dracula were one and the same person, that the count was the only human inhabitant of the castle, and that the rats, the bats, the ghosts, and the howling wolves were his familiars.

By ten o'clock the story had so fastened itself upon our attention that we could not pause even to light our pipe. At midnight the narrative had fairly got upon our nerves; a creepy terror had seized upon us, and when at length, in the early hours of the morning, we went upstairs to bed it was with the anticipation of nightmare. We listened anxiously for the sound of bats' wings against the window; we even felt at our throat in dread lest an actual vampire should have left there the two ghastly punctures which in Mr. Stoker's book attested to the hellish operations of Dracula.

The recollection of this weird and ghostly tale will doubtless haunt us for some time to come. It would be unfair to the author to divulge the plot. We therefore restrict ourselves to the statement that the eerie chapters are written and strung together with very considerable art and cunning, and also with unmistakable literary power. Tribute must also be paid to the rich imagination of which Mr. Bram Stoker here gives liberal evidence. Persons of small courage and weak nerves should confine their reading of these gruesome pages strictly to the hours between dawn and sunset.

ATHENAEUM

Review

(June 26, 1897)

Stories and novels appear just now in plenty stamped with a more or less genuine air of belief in the visibility of supernatural agency. The strengthening of a bygone faith in the fantastic and magical view of things in lieu of the purely material is a feature of the hour, a reaction—artificial, perhaps, rather than natural—against late tendencies in thought. Mr. Stoker is a purveyor of so many strange wares that 'Dracula' reads like a determined effort to go, as it were, "one better" than others in the same field. How far the author is himself a believer in the phenomena described is not for the reviewer to say. He can but attempt to gauge how far the general faith in witches, warlocks and vampires—supposing it to exist in any general and appreciable measure—is likely to be stimulated by this story. The vampire idea is very ancient indeed, and there are in nature, no doubt, mysterious powers to account for the vague belief in such beings. Mr. Stoker's way of presenting his matter, and still more the matter itself, are of too direct and uncompromising a kind. They lack the essential note of awful remoteness and at the same time subtle affinity that separates while it links our humanity with unknown beings and possibilities hovering on the confines of the known world. 'Dracula' is highly sensational, but it is wanting in the constructive art as well as in the higher literary sense. It reads at times like a mere series of grotesquely incredible events; but there are better moments that show more power, though even these are never productive of the tremor such subjects evoke under the hand of a master. An immense amount of energy, a certain degree of imaginative faculty, and many ingenious and gruesome details are there. At times Mr. Stoker almost succeeds in creating the sense of possibility in impossibility; at others he merely commands an array of crude statements of incredible actions. The early part goes best, for it promises to unfold the roots of mystery and fear lying deep in human nature; but the want of skill and fancy grows more and more conspicuous. The people who band themselves together to run the vampire to earth have no real individuality or being. The German [sic] man of science is particularly poor, and indulges, like a German, in much weak sentiment. Still, Mr. Stoker has got together a number of "horrid details," and his object, assuming it to be ghastliness, is fairly well fulfilled. Isolated scenes and touches are probably quite uncanny enough to please those for whom they are designed.

SPECTATOR

Review

(July 31, 1897)

Mr. Bram Stoker gives us the impression—we may be doing him an injustice—of having deliberately laid himself out in *Dracula* to eclipse all previous efforts in the domain of the horrible,—to "go one better" than Wilkie Collins[1] (whose method of narration he has closely followed), Sheridan Le Fanu, and all the other professors of the flesh-creeping school. * * * Its strength lies in the invention of incident, for the sentimental element is decidedly mawkish. Mr. Stoker has shown considerable ability in the use that he has made in all the available traditions of vampirology, but we think his story would have been all the more effective if he had chosen an earlier period. The up-to-dateness of the book—the phonograph diaries, typewriters, and so on—hardly fits in with the mediaeval methods which ultimately secure the victory for Count Dracula's foes.

1. Author of *The Woman in White* (1860), a mystery similarly constructed from letters, diaries, and the like [*Editors*].

BOOKMAN

Review

(August 1897)

Since Wilkie Collins left us we have had no tale of mystery so liberal in manner and so closely woven. But with the intricate plot, and the methods of the narrative, the resemblance to the stories of the author of "The Woman in White" ceases; for the audacity and horror of "Dracula" are Mr. Stoker's own. A summary of the book would shock and disgust; but we must own that, though here and there in the course of the tale we hurried over things with repulsion, we read nearly the whole thing with rapt attention. It is something of a triumph for the writer that neither the improbability, nor the unnecessary number of hideous incidents recounted of the man-vampire, are long foremost on the reader's mind, but that the interest of the danger, of the complications, of the pursuit of the villain, of human skill and courage pitted against inhuman wrong and superhuman strength, rises always to the top. Keep "Dracula" out of the way of nervous children, certainly; but a grown reader, unless he be of unserviceably delicate stuff, will both shudder and enjoy from p. 35 [39], when Harker sees the Count "emerge from the window and begin to crawl down the castle wall over that dreadful abyss, *face down*, with his cloak spreading out around him like great wings."

SAN FRANCISCO CHRONICLE

New Novels and Holiday Books

(December 17, 1899)†

One of the most powerful novels of the day, and one set apart by its originality of plot and treatment is "Dracula," by Bram Stoker. The author is well known in the dramatic world for his long connection with Sir Henry Irving as manager. Several years ago he wrote a weird story of Irish life, but this is his first long romance. It is a somber study of a human vampire, the Count Dracula, who uses beautiful women as his agents and compasses the death of many innocent people. Theo-

---

† *Dracula* was not published in America until November 1899, when Doubleday McClure published a slightly revised version of the text following the book's newspaper serialization.

phile Gautier[1] essayed the same subject, but his vampire, who was a priest by day and ravening wolf by night, was not half so terrible as this malignant Count with the three beautiful female devils who do his bidding. Nothing in fiction is more powerful than the scene at the killing of the vampire in Lucy's tomb or that other fearful scene at the extinction of the malign power of the Count. The story is told in such a realistic way that one actually accepts its wildest flights of fancy as real facts. It is a superb tour de force which stamps itself on the memory.

1. Influential poet and novelist of the French Romantic movement. The story referred to is "La mort amoureuse" (1836), the tale of a vampire courtesan, Clarimonda, who haunts a young priest [Editors].

DRAMATIC AND FILM
VARIATIONS

DAVID J. SKAL

"His Hour Upon the Stage": Theatrical
Adaptations of *Dracula*†

Yet who would have thought the old man to have had so much blood
in him?

Macbeth 5.1

Although Dracula is best-known to the public as a quintessential
Hollywood icon, and only secondarily as the fictional creation of Bram
Stoker, our modern image of the king of vampires is largely a creation
of the legitimate theatre. Stoker himself had a strong sense of the book's
theatrical possibilities. By the time of *Dracula's* publication he had
served as the acting manager of the Lyceum Theatre for seventeen
years, the right-hand man and confidante of its impresario, the great
Victorian actor Sir Henry Irving.

Stoker, born in Clontarf, Dublin, in 1847 and educated at Trinity
College, had long been drawn to the exaggerated reality of the debating
team and the theatre, and to literature and individuals who embodied
dramatic, archteypal qualities. He positively idolized Walt Whitman,
defending the poet at the height of the controversy over *Leaves of Grass*,
writing the poet long, emotionally revealing letters.[1] Whitman re-
sponded, and they eventually met.

But the most significant adoration of Stoker's life—indeed, most commentators agree that the relationship eclipsed even his marriage—was
Henry Irving. In 1876 Stoker was working as a civil servant in Dublin,
but also contributing unpaid theatre reviews to the *Dublin Mail*. His
glowing appraisals of Irving's Shakespearean performances attracted the
attention of the thespian himself, who felt underappreciated in Ireland,
and requested an introduction. After their second dinner together, Irving recited a grisly dramatic monologue, Thomas Hood's "The Dream
of Eugene Aram," in which a murderer is overcome by guilt and the
fear of God. Stoker himself was overcome by the force of Irving's acting,
and "burst into something like hysterics."[2]

† Portions of this essay originally appeared in *Hollywood Gothic: The Tangled Web of Dracula
from Novel to Stage to Screen* (New York: Norton, 1990), and *Dracula: The Ultimate Illustrated
Edition of the World-Famous Vampire Play* (New York: St. Martin's Press, 1993) and are
reprinted by permission of the author. Excerpts from Stoker's 1897 dramatic adaptation are
taken from the forthcoming Transylvania Press edition of the playscript. The editors gratefully
acknowledge the cooperation of Robert Eighteen-Bisang and Sylvia Starshine in making a
transcription of Stoker's manuscript available.

1. Stoker's letters to Whitman are included in Horace Traubel, *With Walt Whitman in Camden*,
   vol. 4 (Philadelphia: U of Pennsylvania P, 1953) 181–85.
2. Bram Stoker, *Personal Reminiscences of Henry Irving*, 2 vols. (New York: Macmillan, 1906),
   vol. 1, p. 31.

Irving was impressed ("Soul had looked into soul!" wrote Stoker. "From that hour began a friendship as profound, as close, as lasting as can be between two men"[3]) and a few seasons later claimed the young man as his own, at least professionally. Stoker assumed the acting managership of Irving's new venture, London's Lyceum Theatre, in December 1878. Irving was both commanding as a performer and demanding as an employer; Stoker's own language in describing their crucial encounter evokes a sense of the demonic, using phrases like "commanding force," "the magnetism of his genius," "so profound was the sense of his dominance that I set spellbound. . . ."[4] By the time Stoker began to work on the novel that would become *Dracula*, Irving had been playing the role of Mephistopheles in *Faust* for five years. Both Stoker and the public had become accustomed to Irving in the role of a showy devil, and, at some point during *Dracula*'s composition, Stoker decided his vampire might have the potential to be a signature Irving characterization.

According to veteran Chicago drama critic Frederick Donaghey, who made the writer's acquaintance during one of the Lyceum's American tours around the turn of the century, "When the late Bram Stoker told me that he had put endless hours in trying to persuade Henry Irving to have a play made from *Dracula* and to act in it, he added that he had nothing in mind save the box office. 'If,' he explained, 'I am able to afford to have my name on the book, the Governor certainly can afford, with business bad, to have his name on the play. But he laughs at me whenever I talk about it; and then we have to go out and raise money to put on something in which the public has no interest.' "

Stoker went on to tell Donaghey his conception of Irving in the role of king vampire: "The Governor as Dracula would be the Governor in a composite of so many of the parts in which he has been liked— Matthias in 'The Bells,' Shylock, Mephistopheles, Peter the Great, the Bad Fellow in 'The Lyons Mail,' Louis XI, and ever so many others, including Iachimo in 'Cymbeline.' But he just laughs at me!" In Donaghey's recollection, Stoker's grandiose theatrical ambitions were countervailed by a literary humility. "He knew he had written, in 'Dracula,'' a shilling shocker, however successful a one, and was frank about it," Donaghey wrote in 1929.[5]

Assuming that the Chicago critic is quoting Stoker accurately, it seems immediately apparent that issues of power, control, and Stoker's ambivalence about his own creative abilities are more important issues than box-office receipts. While there is no documentation that Stoker

3. Ibid. 33.
4. Ibid. 29–30.
5. Frederick Donaghey, review of Deane and Balderston's *Dracula; Chicago Daily Tribune*, April 3, 1929, p. 37.

may have grown to resent Irving, virtually all of Stoker's chroniclers find in *Dracula* an allegory of an unequal, draining relationship between the two men; Stoker locked up in the Lyceum castle, as it were, serving a master's wishes while having his own attempts at written expression inhibited. Harker's letters are confiscated; Stoker's direct dramatic collaboration with Irving is never realized.

Dracula is filled with overreaching allusions to Shakespeare; in addition to the roles mentioned by Stoker in his conversation with Donaghey, there are ample references to *Macbeth* (Irving's favorite role): a cursed warrior-king in a desolate castle, three weird sisters, somnabulism, and blood imagery. The shipwreck in a storm and Dracula's ability to drive the elements seem dark reflections of *The Tempest*; Dracula's funereal puritanism—his black clothing, his rejection of ordinary human pleasures like food, his inveighing against mirrors and human vanity—all darkly conjure the character of Hamlet, metamorphosed into a ghost like his father. There are passing quotations from and references to *King Lear, Twelfth Night,* and *The Merchant of Venice* (see in this edition notes on pp. 65, 235, and 238). And Stoker's admission that he had Irving's Shylock in mind underscores the tacit anti-Semitism in Dracula's physical appearance, a Transylvanian variation on villainous literary Jews like Svengali and Fagin.

Stoker prepared a dramatic adbridgement of his book entitled *Dracula: Or the Un-Dead*, which was given a staged reading at the Lyceum on May 18, 1897. Ostensibly for purposes of protecting the novel's dramatic copyright, the marathon event may have also been something of an exercise in vanity—or simply a vain, last attempt to favorably impress Henry Irving. The Lyceum briefly became Stoker's macabre toy theatre, though brevity may have seemed an eternity; the reading was stupefyingly long—a prologue followed by five acts in forty-seven scenes, lasting over five hours. A formal programme was printed, showing that the reading was elaborately cast with fifteen actors, drawn primarily from the second tier of Lyceum actors. Dracula was portrayed by a "Mr. Jones," whose precise identity remains obscure. But the most reasonable candidate for the part is Whitworth Jones, who the same year portrayed Fortinbras in Johnston Forbes-Robertson's celebrated Lyceum production of *Hamlet*. (Jones, who also acted under the name Robert Whitworth, was sufficiently Henry Irving-like to be cast as Mephistopheles in America some years later. He frequently portrayed wizards, kings, and demons.) Jonathan Harker was played by an actor named Herbert Passmore, and Van Helsing by Tom Reynolds, a popular character actor in Irving's employ. Edith Craig, the daughter of Ellen Terry, Irving's leading lady, took the role of Mina. The programme credits the Lyceum's musical director, Meredith Ball, suggesting at least an overture or entr'acte accompaniment. The script

indicates twenty separate scenes. The standing sets at the Lyceum the
day of Stoker's reading were those of the comedy *Madame Sans-Gêne*
by Victorien Sardou and Emile Moreau.

The "script" Stoker later submitted to the Lord Chamberlain's Office
on May 31, 1897, is a cut-and-paste of printer's proofs of the book, with
numerous handwritten additions and emendations. Presumably, this is
the only copy that ever existed, and it is reasonable to assume that the
actors read from it at a lectern; it cannot be determined whether the
stage directions were read aloud or indicated, but it can probably be
safely assumed: certain scenes, such as Dracula's crawling down the
wall of his castle, would make no sense unless the action was somehow
described, if not actually staged.

Stoker's abridgement is only fitfully theatrical, and he seems to have
been hampered by the same difficulties with which later adaptors would
also wrestle. The book's vast geographical sweep and outdoor scenes,
with breakneck carriage chases, shipwrecks, and gypsies on horseback,
are obviously unsuited to the stage. Stoker is forced to provide Jonathan
Harker with a breathless opening speech that is almost a parody of
Victorian melodramatic exposition:

> *Enter Jonathan Harker followed by driver of Calèche carrying his
> hand portmanteau and bag. Latter leaves luggage close to door (c)
> and Exit[s] hurriedly.*

> HARKER   Hi! Hi! Where are you off to! Gone already! *(knocks
> at door)* Well this is a pretty nice state of things! After a drive
> through solid darkness with an unknown man whose face I have
> not seen and who has in his hand the strength of twenty men and
> who can drive back a pack of wolves by holding up his hand; who
> visits mysterious blue flames and who wouldn't speak a word that
> he could help, to be left here in the dark before a—a ruin. Upon
> my life I'm beginning my professional experience in a romantic
> way! Only passed my exam at Lincoln's Inn before I left London,
> and here I am conducting my business—or rather my employer
> Mr. Hawkins's business with an accompaniment of wolves and
> mystery. *(knocks)* If this Count Dracula were a little more attentive
> to a guest when he *does* arrive he needn't have been so effusive
> in his letters to Mr. Hawkins regarding my having the best of
> everything on the journey. *(Knocks)* I wondered why the people
> in the Hotel at Bistritz were so frightened and why the old lady
> hung the Crucifix round my neck and why the people on the
> coach made signs against the evil eye! By Jove, if any of them had
> this kind of experience, no wonder at anything they did—or
> thought. *(knocks)* This is becoming more than a joke. If it were
> my own affair I should go straight back to Exeter; but as I act for
> another and have the papers of the Count's purchase of [a] Lon-

don estate I suppose I must go on and do my duty—thank God
there is a light, someone is coming.

Overall, Stoker's treatment of the scenes in Transylvania are the most
successful from a dramatic standpoint, though most of the speeches are
still far too long to be stageworthy. Nonetheless, some effects are striking; following Dracula's confrontation with the vampire women about
to attack Harker, the Count picks up the fainted solicitor like another
bride and carries him off into darkness (an action that underscores the
homoerotic aspects of the novel that have recently been the subject of
several critical studies). One of Lucy's encounters with the vampire in
the Whitby cemetery is indicated with remarkable theatrical economy
and impact: *Enter Lucy sleepwalking in nightdress, and reclines on seat.
Moonlight and shadow alternate. When a shadow moves Count Dracula
is seen bending over her and with his face on her throat.* And when
Mina interrupts his feast: *Shadow. Dracula raises his head, sees her, and
sinks down through tombstone.* Stoker was evidently quite familiar with
"the vampire trap," a sprung opening in the stage so-named for its
original use in James Robinson Planché's 1820 melodrama *The Vampire, or, The Bride of the Isles.* The vampire trap effected dramatic entries and exits of supernatural characters and was first employed at the
Lyceum (then the English Opera House) for Planché's thrilling play.

In the end, any hopes Stoker may have had about impressing Henry
Irving with his dramaturgical skills came to naught in a possibly apoc-
ryphal scene recounted by Stoker's biographer and great-nephew Daniel
Farson: "Legend has it that Sir Henry entered the theatre during the
reading and listened for a few moments with a warning glint of amuse-
ment. 'What do you think of it?' someone asked him unwisely, as he
left for his dressing room. '*Dreadful!*' came the devastating reply, projected with such resonance that it filled the theatre."[6]

Stoker, of course, was correct in his intuition that *Dracula* deserved
a dramatic afterlife, though it would not come to pass in his own lifetime. He staged another "copyright reading" of his 1898 novel *Miss
Betty*, once more using members of the Lyceum company. Following
the death of Henry Irving in 1905, and his own recovery from a debil-
itating stroke, Stoker seems to have at least considered donning an
Irving-like mantle in the American theatre. On April 1, 1906, a
columnist for the *San Francisco Chronicle* revealed some of the details.
Referring to an account published in a New York newspaper, the item
noted that "Stoker, for many years, directed the business end of Irving's
tours. There has never been word of Stoker's taking more than casual
interest in the actual staging of plays, yet it is said, and apparently in
good faith, that he has been invited to become the stage manager of
one of the 'artistic' theatres which 'society', in the whirligig of its jeal-

6. Daniel Farson, *The Man Who Wrote "Dracula"* (New York: St. Martin's Press, 1975) 164.

ousies, plans to build in this city." The unsigned piece went on, a bit cynically, concerning the current state of theatre in San Francisco, where Irving, and Stoker, had toured. "Before Stoker is pressed for a contract it might be profitable to come here and report on conditions as they exist. . . . But Mr. Stoker has a weakness for a joke that may lead him to accept the offer. This is as much to be desired as the other. In either pole his geniality would add to the diversion which the public already is finding in these proposed temples of high art."[7] A few weeks later the question was rendered moot as San Francisco was destroyed by one of the most theatrical natural disasters in history.

Whatever theatrical ambitions Stoker may have harbored went unrealized in his remaining years, which were difficult, physically and financially. Despite three decades of loyal service, Stoker was not included Irving's will. In *Personal Reminiscences of Henry Irving*, published in two volumes in 1906, Stoker did manage to achieve a final "collaboration" with his dead employer, if only by superimposing his own biography over that of Irving, fusing their lives forever in print.

Stoker died on April 20, 1912. His widow, Florence (née Balcombe, a Victorian beauty in the Pre-Raphaelite mode and a youthful infatuation of Oscar Wilde), was left with few tangible assets, save her husband's copyrights, and the only one that continued to generate income was *Dracula*. Forced into genteel poverty, she clung to the demon jealously. Dracula became Florence Stoker's guardian angel, of a kind, providing a steady if meager sustenance. She was determined to make money from stage and motion picture rights, but interlopers vexed her. A now-obscure 1920 film called *Drakula*, a Hungarian production filmed in Berlin by Károly Lajthay, apparently escaped her notice. But when *Dracula* was pirated by German filmmakers in 1921, the widow Stoker launched a protracted legal war against F. W. Murnau's now-classic *Nosferatu: Eine Symphonie des Grauens* (*Nosferatu: A Symphony of Horror*). With the aid of the British Society of Authors, she won a judgment from the German courts ordering the destruction of all copies. Fortunately, the film and its negative survived in scattered fragments; reconstituted, it was eventually recognized as a masterpiece of German expressionism.

Tired and infuriated by unauthorized encroachments, Mrs. Stoker granted the first license for a stage adaptation of *Dracula* to a touring actor-manager named Hamilton Deane, whose family had known Stoker's in Dublin. Deane had quite a following in the provinces, but almost no reputation in London; his barnstorming style was decidedly at odds with prevailing taste in the West End. Deane's *Dracula*, first produced in 1924, was conceived as a touring vehicle for less sophisticated regional audiences.

7. "Things Theatrical," *San Francisco Chronicle Sunday Supplement*, April 1, 1906, p. 9.

Stoker's novel, however theatrical its intentions, had built-in problems for would-be stage adaptors. For reasons of physical and economic practicality, the play needed to be reduced to the dimensions of a drawing-room mystery melodrama with minimal scenery and stage effects. (Deane originally included a Transylvanian prologue in which Dracula emerged from a castle window in half-human form, but never produced it because of cost.) Dracula himself presented difficulties: for most of the novel, Stoker's monster is an offstage presence who never interacts with the main characters in anything resembling a normal fashion. To work as a drawing-room mystery, Dracula would have to be reconfigured as the kind of character who might be reasonably invited into a drawing room to begin with. And thus began an essential dichotomy in the evolution of *Dracula*, which served practical, dramatic, and commercial considerations while working against Stoker's original vision.

Deane conceived the now-familiar appearance of Dracula as a kind of devilish vaudeville magician in evening dress and an opera cloak, who insinuates himself into the lives of the human characters by feigning neighborly interest in Mina's mysterious anemia. The associations with stage magic were especially appropriate given the variety-show effects Deane employed: flash boxes; demonstrations of hypnotism; and a trick coffin for Dracula's ultimate destruction, built along the lines of a standard conjurer's cabinet.

Deane originally wanted to play Dracula himself, but eventually realized that Van Helsing was the meatier role. An actor named Edmund Blake inaugurated the part and was succeeded by Raymond Huntley, who took the role to London's West End in 1927, where it was a surprise hit. As Deane feared, the critics did their best to drive a stake through *Dracula*, but audiences flocked to the Little Theatre, Adelphi, despite a decidedly second-class production. In 1989, not long before his death, Huntley told this writer that the production was so threadbare that he was required to provide his own evening clothes. When the production was forced to move to the larger Duke of York's, the London *Evening News* noticed, with some amazement, "while glittering productions costing thousands of pounds have wilted and died after a week or so in the West End, 'Dracula' has gone on drinking blood nightly."[8]

The flamboyant American publisher and producer Horace Liveright, ever on the prowl for properties with sensational possibilities, liked the premise of *Dracula* but disliked the stiff dialogue of Deane's original script. He enlisted the American journalist and dramatist John L. Balderston, who had recently scored a success as coauthor (with J. C. Squire) of the supernatural romance *Berkeley Square*, to rewrite the dialogue completely and improve the structure for Broadway.

8. Harry Ludlam, *A Biography of Dracula: The Life Story of Bram Stoker* (London: Fireside Press/W. Foulsham, 1962) 161.

Thereafter, and until World War II, *Dracula* was performed in two distinctly different versions, one for British audiences and one for Americans (in strict point of fact there were three existing versions—Florence Stoker commissioned yet another adaptation from a playwright named Charles Morrell; this version she owned outright; she resented paying adaptor's royalties. But the Morrell play was static and talky, retaining long speeches taken verbatim from the novel as Stoker did in his 1897 dramatic abridgement, and was only performed briefly). Hamilton Deane's version is notable for introducing most of the standard trappings we now associate with *Dracula*: the enveloping, crimson-lined cape; French doors; fog machines; secret panels; and, perhaps most memorably, easily hypnotized maids who can be relied upon to remove a range of annoyances ranging from crucifixes to garlic flowers to noxious necklaces of vampire-repelling wolfbane. One familiar costume detail, the exaggerated stand-up collar on Dracula's cape, had a particular stage function: to hide the back of the actor's head while he slipped through a trap door or panel, leaving the other company members holding the empty cloak. Though the collar had no function in motion pictures, where camera tricks replaced trap doors, it has nonetheless become a signature feature of vampire costuming in all media.

Liveright wanted the British actor Raymond Huntley to reprise his West End role on Broadway, but the actor refused the skimpy salary offered—$150 a week. Rebuffed, Liveright offered even less money to a hungry expatriate actor from Lugos, Hungary, who was in no position to turn down work. And so Béla Ferenc Dezsö Blasko—known professionally as Bela Lugosi—became the strangest matinee idol the New York theatre had ever seen, and soon was one of the most instantly identifiable presences in theatrical history. Liveright understood the implied Freudian aspects of the story and their potential Jazz Age appeal; terms such as "libido" and "death wish" were bandied about routinely in smart Manhattan conversation, and Lugosi's weird characterization —patent-leather hair, patent-leather shoes, a continental accent, and bilious green makeup—was the perfect amalgam of Rudolph Valentino and the grave.

Dracula enjoyed a two-week tryout in New Haven, Hartford, and other nearby venues in late September 1927 before opening on Broadway on October 5. The sheer audacity of the production guaranteed a large box office. Here was a new kind of mystery play, which, contrary to prevailing stage conventions, did not attempt to "explain away" its terrors as the result of nefarious human agency. *Dracula*, the press releases warned, "deals frankly with the supernatural." Liveright's theatrical manager Louis Cline, a wizard at publicity stunts, had a field day with outrageous and attention-getting promotions. As in London, lobby nurses and fainting patrons were both provided by the management—a conflict of interest, perhaps, but one which drew no serious complaint.

Dracula ran for thirty-three weeks in New York, followed by two simultaneous tours, one on the West Coast with Bela Lugosi, the other covering the rest of the country, with Raymond Huntley. The success of the stage play (which earned over $2 million in America alone) brought *Dracula* to the attention of Hollywood, which had shied away from the novel because its sensational horrors had always been considered unfilmable. But a film based on the much tamer thrills of the play would be another matter entirely. Following two years of tempestuous negotiations among Florence Stoker, Hamilton Deane, John L. Balderston, their agents, and the studios of Universal, Metro-Goldwyn-Mayer, Columbia, and Fox Films, Universal purchased the film rights to the novel and all three stage versions for $40,000 in the summer of 1930. The studio planned a "superproduction" starring the silent screen's "Man of a Thousand Faces," Lon Chaney, in one of his first talking roles. Chaney, however, was stricken with terminal cancer and Universal's plans went into a tailspin. The mounting economic realities of the deepening Depression forced the financially strapped studio to develop a script based almost exclusively on the stage play and to turn to Bela Lugosi for a part they originally intended for an established film star. Lugosi was paid a total of $3,500 for seven weeks of work on the film and never received additional payment related directly to Universal's 1931 film, despite his lifelong identification with the part.[9]

Dracula, directed by Tod Browning, was a major moneymaker for Universal and has been credited with rescuing the studio from the jaws of bankruptcy. The film's success sparked a renewed interest in the stage play; released to stock in 1930, Deane and Balderston's *Dracula* has been in almost continuous performance somewhere in the world ever since, a permanent fixture of the regional, college, and community theatre circuits.

To understand the popularity and persistence of *Dracula*, it is necessary to appreciate the novel's essential theatricality, beginning with its origins in Bram Stoker's problematic relationship with a major theatrical figure of the nineteenth century, and continuing with crucial twentieth-century embellishments, which first and foremost served the purposes of the theatre. While popularizing *Dracula*, the theatre has also, ironically, created a powerful secondary set of images and expectations which have made a definitive dramatic adaptation on stage or screen virtually impossible from a commercial standpoint. Even the most careful dramatic reproduction of the book, the 1977 BBC television miniseries, refrained from depicting Dracula as the repulsive mon-

---

9. Lugosi's identification with the Dracula persona was so complete that the role followed him even after death: he was buried in full vampire regalia in August 1956.

ster Stoker described, instead casting actor Louis Jourdan as an update on Bela Lugosi's ambiguously attractive aristocrat. Francis Ford Coppola's misleadingly titled film *Bram Stoker's Dracula* (1992) also refused to face the primal horror of Stoker's count in favor of a romantic/ Byronic image of the vampire popularized in the early-nineteenth-century theatre, but unequivocally rejected by Stoker at the fin-de-siècle.

Dramatic Adaptations: A Checklist

The following list includes significant theatrical adaptations owing a true debt to Stoker, omitting casual spoofs, versions intended for amateurs, children's groups, and so on.

1897
Stoker, Bram. *Dracula or the Un-Dead.* Lyceum Theatre, London, May 18, 1897. A lengthy reading of Stoker's novel to secure theatrical copyright protection, this cumbersome manuscript (held by the Lord Chamberlain's Collection, British Library Department of Manuscripts) anticipates the difficulties later adaptors would encounter while attempting to translate the complex story to other media.

1924–27
Deane, Hamilton. *Dracula.* The first licensed adaptation of Stoker's novel toured the English provinces successfully for three years before opening in a slightly revised form at London's Little Theatre in February 1927.

Morrell, Charles. *Dracula.* An alternate stage adaptation, commissioned by Stoker's widow, evidently to preserve "literary" qualities of her husband's book not included in Hamilton Deane's version. Produced briefly in September 1927, the script proved unstageworthy, but Universal Pictures purchased motion picture rights to this adaptation, as well as the Deane/Balderston play and the novel itself; a few lines from Morrell were, in fact, used in the 1931 film, directed by Tod Browning.

Deane, Hamilton, and John L. Balderston. *Dracula [The Vampire Play].* Plymouth Theatre, New York, October 1927. American journalist and playwright Balderston adapted Deane's British script for Broadway, retaining the dramatic structure but almost completely rewriting the dialogue. The 1977 Broadway stage revival starring Frank Langella added new lines for Dracula, including borrowings from the 1931 film version ("I never drink . . . wine.")

1970

Katz, Leon. *Dracula: Sabbat.* A ritualistic performance piece, attracting highly laudatory reviews from the national press during its run at the Judson Poet's Theatre in New York City.

1972

Tiller, Ted. *Count Dracula.* Tiller's adaptation is similar in many respects to Deane and Balderston's, but includes considerably more comic relief and was quite successful on the regional and amateur theatre circuits in the 1970s. Arguably more influenced by the earlier play than by Stoker.

1977

Hall, Bob, and David Richmond. *The Passion of Dracula.* Commercially successful in New York and London, this version retains the stagebound drawing-room conventions as established by Hamilton Deane.

1978

Johnson, Douglas, and John Aschenbrenner. *Dracula: A Musical Nightmare.* The best of many attempts at setting *Dracula* to music. A "concept" production combining the story of a third-rate English touring company and its production of *Dracula* with music-hall song-and-dance numbers. Johnson (book and lyrics) and Aschenbrenner (music) received excellent notices.

1983

Sharp, Richard. *Dracula: The Story You Thought You Knew.* A critically acclaimed production, in repertory for two seasons at the Oregon Shakespeare Festival, Sharp's adaptation—which included elaborate stage effects—received additional praise when it was restaged as a commercial production in a San Francisco church in 1985.

1985

Lochhead, Liz. *Dracula.* One of the most critically praised adaptations, written by a noted Scottish poet/playwright, largely jettisoning the traditional drawing-room settings for a more fluid and theatrically evocative physical production. To date, produced only in Scotland.

1994

Wellman, Mac. *Mac Wellman's Dracula.* Produced by New York's SoHo Rep, a densely postmodernist interpretation of Stoker, with the action taking the form of a Victorian peepshow surrounding the audience on all sides.

GREGORY A. WALLER

[Tod Browning's *Dracula*]†

Dracula, 1927, 1931, 1979

* * *

The introductory credits of Tod Browning's *Dracula* (1931)—probably the single most well-known version of Count Dracula's story—announce the film as "*Dracula* by Bram Stoker. From the play adapted by Hamilton Deane and John L. Balderston." Based to some degree on a Broadway play and starring the two actors who were featured in the stage production (Bela Lugosi as Dracula and Edward Van Sloan as Van Helsing), Browning's film has often been criticized for what Roy Huss calls its "static staginess" and its failure to exploit certain "cinematic" possibilities, such as varying camera set-ups, "montage" editing, and "suggestive" lighting effects.[1] Even though such criticisms are generally based upon simplistic, prescriptive assumptions about the nature of the "cinematic" and the "theatrical,"[2] they do begin to suggest the extent to which Browning and screenwriter Garrett Fort borrow from *Dracula: The Vampire Play*, particularly for the characterization and the alignment of the major figures and for the mise-en-scène of the scenes set in Seward's home.

Yet for all of its use of static tableaus and theatrical entrances and exits, Browning's *Dracula* is obviously not merely a filmed version of Deane and Balderston's play. For example, Browning's reliance on readily identifiable sound effects to create the sense of off-screen space and his use of dissolves to provide spatial and temporal transitions (rather than to create metaphoric juxtapositions) are typical of American movies during the early 1930s. So, too, is his dependence on intrusive close-ups and medium shots, particularly of the vampire, for dramatic emphasis. And like almost all Hollywood adaptors of Broadway productions, Browning and Fort attempt to open up the theatrical text—filming what is only discussed in the play, greatly expanding the number and the magnitude of the sets (interior as well as exterior, natural settings), and reinstating sequences from Stoker's novel that

---

† From *The Living and the Undead*; © 1986 by the Board of Trustees of the University of Illinois. Used with the permission of the author and of the University of Illinois Press.
1. Roy Huss, "Vampire's Progress: *Dracula* from Novel to Film via Broadway," in *Focus on the Horror Film*, ed. Roy Huss and T. J. Ross (Englewood Cliffs, N.J.: Prentice-Hall, 1972), pp. 51–53. See also, for example, John Brosnan, *The Horror People* (New York: New American Library, 1977), p. 30.
2. I discuss this prescriptive aesthetic in more detail in *The Stage/Screen Debate: A Study in Popular Aesthetics* (New York: Garland Press, 1983).

Deane and Balderston had omitted.[3] Thus Browning's *Dracula*, unlike *Dracula: The Vampire Play*, begins with a journey to Castle Dracula in Transylvania and includes the Count's sea voyage to England, as well as images of London, Seward's sanitarium, Carfax Abbey, Renfield's cell, and even Van Helsing's study.

Such images do not situate this horror film within the context of identifiable, quotidian reality (as Murnau's on-location images often do in *Nosferatu* [1922]). But they do expand the highly circumscribed boundaries of Deane and Balderston's three-act, three-set play and provide us with additional information about the principal characters and about the values involved when the living confront the undead. None of the sets or locations in Browning's *Dracula* is merely background, merely a place; all tell us a great deal about the characters who visit or inhabit or own them. (We should never cease to marvel at the enormous amount of information the cinematic image can convey—casually, indirectly, without the narrative pause that literary description so often requires.)

Transylvania, with its rocky, inhospitable countryside, isolated peasant village, and ancient, impregnable castle, is the obvious example of the significance of the locations in Browning's film, for this strange land is rarely mentioned, much less shown, in *Dracula: The Vampire Play*. Unlike in Stoker's novel, in *Dracula* (1931), it is Renfield who journeys to Transylvania. With this young traveler we encounter a land in which the terrified, pious, superstitious human beings live in a state of constant watchfulness. Language here is only used for issuing warnings, repeating local legends about the vampire, and reciting prayers. Armed with religious talismans, this rural civilization expends all its energy in protecting itself. It cannot hope to conquer and exploit its environment, and so it seems less picturesque than pitifully anachronistic in contrast to Western societies, which measure progress in terms of industrialization and imperialism. With its luxurious music hall, freely traveled paved streets, and landscaped sanitarium, England could almost be on another planet than Transylvania, though the vampire proves to us that his wild and primitive homeland is within easy striking distance of the modern world.

The heart of Transylvania is Castle Dracula, which exerts an influence greater than any feudal estate. The very magnitude of this fortress

---

3. See Barrie Pattison, *The Seal of Dracula* (New York: Bounty Books, 1975), pp. 15–18. For background on the production of the film and on Lugosi's performance in *Dracula: The Vampire Play*, see Arthur Lennig, *The Count: The Life and Times of Bela 'Dracula' Lugosi* (New York: G. P. Putnam's Sons, 1974), pp. 66–109. The visual style of *Dracula* (1931) no doubt owes a great deal to the film's cinematographer, Karl Freund, who had filmed several noteworthy German silent films (including *The Golem* [1920], *Metropolis* [1927], and a number of films directed by F. W. Murnau) and who would direct *The Mummy* (1932) and *Mad Love* (1935). David Pirie goes so far as to argue that in *Dracula* (1931), "Freund's brilliance is continually undercut by Browning" (*The Vampire Cinema* [London: Hamlyn, 1977], p. 53).

is a mark of its dominance. Unlike the peasants' homes, the castle's rooms are huge, with no ceilings in sight, as the walls rise thirty feet or more. Before Renfield enters the vampire's domain, Browning carries us with a series of dissolves into the seemingly endless, mist-filled, cavernous crypt area of Castle Dracula. Then, after several brief detail shots of, for example, the vampire's wives emerging from their coffins, the Count appears, standing motionless while the camera moves toward him like a supplicant. (It will be similarly drawn toward the vampiric Mina later in the film.) No scene in *Dracula: The Vampire Play* even approximates Browning's emphasis here on the commanding power of the Count and on the utter barrenness of his undead existence. Furthermore, the presence of Dracula's three white-robed wives—who do not appear in the play—directly links vampirism with voracious, "perverse," destructive sexuality. Browning's Dracula does not simply desire to carry off two pretty Englishwomen, he seeks to create more wives who sleep in coffins and rise to satisfy unnatural desires. And the Count in *Dracula* (1931) takes Renfield as his victim/paramour as well, kneeling to embrace/feed off the defenseless young man in an act that prefigures Dracula's seduction of the young women in England.

Because we see and therefore know Count Dracula better even than do the Transylvanian peasants and the informed Van Helsing, the real horror in *Dracula* (1931) is the ease with which this monster can enter and move through British society (in contrast to Renfield, who fails so abysmally in his business trip to Transylvania). In scenes that, again, have no source in *Dracula: The Vampire Play*, the vampire seems not at all out of place at night on the streets of London. Just prior to his first encounter with Lucy and Mina, Dracula murders a lower-class young woman who sells flowers on a foggy street, and this brief, seemingly digressive episode pointedly suggests how successfully the formally dressed vampire can thrive in the open, unprotected modern world. Thus before Browning finally takes us to Seward's asylum for a series of interior scenes that are derived to a great extent from Deane and Balderston's play, *Dracula* (1931) has allowed us to gauge both the nature of the vampire and the type of threat this foreign aristocrat poses to a secular society that does not arm itself with religious talismans and traditional beliefs.

By showing us images of London, Browning is also able to draw clear distinctions between the two major female victims of the vampire: Mina Seward (called Lucy Seward in the play, Mina Harker in Stoker's novel) and Lucy Western (called Mina Weston in the play, Lucy Westenra in the novel), a character who serves in Deane and Balderston's play only as an offstage validation of Van Helsing's theories and as a lesson about what might befall Miss Seward. Once again, the story of the living and the undead provides an occasion for assessing what makes women both uniquely valuable and particularly vulnerable.

Regardless of the policeman who strolls next to Dracula below the window of her London home, Lucy of Browning's film is easy prey for the vampire, not only because she recites somber poetry and is immediately fascinated by the Count's melancholia and Old World mien, but also because she is to some degree independent, with no father or lover to protect her. Mina, on the contrary, is first seen at a concert in the company of both her father and John Harker, her fiancé. Fully (and falsely) confident of her own role as daughter and wife-to-be in an upper-middle-class, male-dominated environment, Mina mockingly chides her friend's deviations from the normal: the Count is "fascinating," Lucy declares as she sits before her mirror and vanity table. Mina laughs and tells her friend that "you need someone a little more normal . . . like John." The film bears out Mina's criticism, even though we will later see this young woman leave her father's home to embrace the vampire. After Dracula's attack, the undead Lucy appears on screen only once. Closely resembling Dracula's white-gowned wives in Transylvania, Lucy glides past a cemetery like a mannequin on wheels while a child cries in the distance. Although Van Helsing vows to release Lucy's soul, this redemptive act is neither shown as in Stoker's *Dracula* nor reported as in *Dracula: The Vampire Play*. Lucy is, in effect, an expendable victim (with her admittedly romantic sensibility and her slight degree of independence, she is perhaps even more dangerous alive than undead), while Mina—who lacks the intelligence, faith, and the all-important spiritual significance of Stoker's heroine—must be saved if the world is to be returned to normal.

Unlike Stoker's orphaned women, Mina in Browning's *Dracula* has a father, but the elderly Dr. Seward plays no part in the salvation of his daughter. At first, in the name of "modern medical science," Seward unconvincingly counters Van Helsing's strange speculations. Soon, however, as both the pastoral calm of his sanitarium and the security of his home break down, Seward cedes his authority to Van Helsing. Whereas in the play Seward participates in the final confrontation with the vampire and shares in the triumph of the living, he disappears from the film just when the danger to his daughter is greatest and when the active pursuit of Dracula begins. We could say that once the vampire gains access to Mina's bedroom, any protection her father might provide is completely negated—thus indirectly Dr. Seward is also a victim of Dracula, who causes the destruction of an already incomplete family.

If Mina's father seems easily taken in by the Count's formal attire and aristocratic manners, John Harker quickly sizes up Dracula as a potential rival or at least as a bad influence. The complete fiancé, John lives only for Mina (he has no home of his own, no family, no vocation) and is, needless to say, prepared to do anything to protect her. Yet his concern, born of worshipful love, only renders Mina more susceptible to the vampire, and John alone can no more protect his fiancée than he can drive away the large bat that hovers over the terrace next to Mina's bedroom. Unlike his counterpart in *Dracula: The Vampire Play*, who instinctively and immediately accepts Van Helsing's guidance, Browning's young man wants to "call the police" and take Mina away with him so that she can be "safe." Even more naively, John suggests that she merely "forget" her dreams of Dracula's embrace, and later he accepts with relief Mina's suspiciously rapid "cure," which is in fact only the devious ploy of a dissembling vampire. Much more than Lucy's suitors in Stoker's novel or Jonathan in *Dracula: The Vampire Play*, Browning's John Harker is the young man as vain fool, untutored and almost untutorable, and therefore a danger to the welfare of the living.

Faced with Seward and John Harker, it is no wonder that Browning's Van Helsing declares: "I must be master here or I can do nothing." This line is derived from Deane and Balderston, as is much of the characterization of Van Helsing in *Dracula* (1931). Van Helsing is master from his first appearance in the film, when he—dressed in a white labcoat—examines Lucy's body in a large operating room (while other doctors watch from a gallery of seats) and then views Renfield's blood under a microscope. Costume and decor in these two scenes (which have no analogue in the novel or the play) immediately establish Van Helsing as an authoritative man of science. Later he reveals that he has devoted a "lifetime to the study of many strange things, little known facts which the world is perhaps better off for not knowing."[4] As the stern, unemotional master, Van Helsing issues orders and provides explanations (although he is not our sole source of information about vampires in the film, as he is in *Dracula: The Vampire Play*). Yet his knowledge and strength of will are not tempered by the sentiment and Christian wisdom of Stoker's paternal guide. The crucifix, for Browning's hero, is only a weapon—more effective than wolfsbane, but less effective than a stake. Set apart from the vulnerable women and ineffectual men of England through his personal attributes and often through Browning's staging, Van Helsing is the sole human being capable of defeating the vampire. Thus when these two foreigners first confront each other in the parlor of Seward's home, the other characters stand apart, unaware that the parlor—another embodiment of the normal—has become the setting for a struggle that will determine their fate. And when Dracula and Van Helsing match wills in the parlor for the second time, none of the Englishmen is even present in the room.

4. Van Helsing in Browning's *Dracula* bears a very marked resemblance to Dr. Waldman in James Whale's *Frankenstein*, a film also released by Universal in 1931. Waldman, also played by Edward Van Sloan, is the representative of and spokesperson for institutionalized, socially accepted science in *Frankenstein*. With absolute certainty, Waldman and his colleagues at the Goldstadt Medical College are able to distinguish between the normal and the abnormal. R. H. W. Dillard, "Even a Man Who Is Pure in Heart: Poetry and Danger in the Horror Film," in *Man and the Movies*, ed. W. R. Robinson (Baltimore: Penguin, 1969), pp. 60–96, offers an excellent examination of the role of the Van Helsing/Waldman figure in the "morality play" structure of Hollywood horror films of the 1930s.

These two confrontations are based on similar scenes in the play, but Browning omits Deane and Balderston's climactic showdown in Act III, when Dracula is able to escape from Van Helsing, Seward, and Jonathan, who have used crucifixes to corner the vampire in the library. Instead, the Count in *Dracula* (1931) enters Mina's bedroom with the assistance of a maid he has hypnotized; then, as Dracula reaches for his victim, Browning cuts to Carfax Abbey just as the vampire and his new bride are about to enter the massive, old building. After Dracula has abducted Mina, Van Helsing and John pursue the vampire back to his English estate, a home in the modern world that very clearly calls to mind Castle Dracula. But no communal action is required, much less celebrated in Browning's *Dracula*. While John futilely searches for Mina, Van Helsing discovers and opens the two coffins, breaks apart a coffin lid to fashion a stake, and hammers the stake into the vampire's body. He accomplishes what the frightened Transylvanian peasants never dared to attempt. John comes upon Mina only after Van Helsing has freed her from Dracula's control—she awakens as if from a trance. Van Helsing then places John's arm protectively around Mina's shoulder. The couple leaves the Professor behind as they slowly climb a steep stairway, ascending toward the light in an image that clearly evokes a wedding march and that contrasts with Count Dracula's solitary ascent out of the underground crypt of Castle Dracula early in the film.[5] No prayers of thanksgiving are offered, and the young lovers, it appears, have not changed because of their ordeal. By slaying the seducer who comes in dreams, the aged foreign master has made England once again safe for marriage. And Browning, even more than Deane and Balderston, has brought center stage what R. H. W. Dillard calls the "heroic man"—the utterly unique, wise elder who guards and rescues the living.[6] Unlike the final affirmation of the family and the birth of new life in Stoker's novel or the restoration that marks the end of *Dracula: The Vampire Play*, in Browning's version of *Dracula* the final image associates the return to normality with the reunion and marriage of John and Mina, a legitimate heterosexual relationship that answers and narratively supersedes Dracula's relationship with his wives and with Renfield. Like Dracula, Lucy and Dr. Seward are excluded from this image, as is Van Helsing, who remains in the shadowy subterranean vaults with death and the vampire and all those "strange things . . . which the world is perhaps better off for not knowing."

Since Browning's *Dracula* does not include the vampire hunters' holy crusade to Transylvania, Carfax Abbey—Count Dracula's Gothic

5. Again, the parallels with Whale's *Frankenstein* are illuminating. In both films normality is associated with marriage, but *Frankenstein* ends with the foolish, elderly Baron Frankenstein firmly in control of the situation, offering a toast to the future as a continuation of the past ("An heir to the House of Frankenstein!"), while his once-rebellious son has been reduced to an invalid who is cared for by his new wife.

6. Dillard, "Poetry and Danger," p. 69.

lair in England—becomes a sort of repository for all that most threatens the normal world. Whereas Deane and Balderston only take us into the Abbey's dark vaults for the play's concluding scene, Browning repeatedly uses cross-cutting to contrast the vampire's English domain with the Sewards' brightly lit, well-furnished home, which is not intended to be a fortress and so can provide no true safety. Thus not only Dracula and Van Helsing but also Renfield, who has been strangled by Dracula, his false master, are left behind in the vaults as John and Mina move away from death, seductive dreams, and violence and literally rise toward the light—civilization triumphing over the apparent causes of its discontents.

It is appropriate that Renfield is included in the final sequence of the film, because this English "madman" figures much more prominently in *Dracula* (1931) than in any of the other cinematic versions of Stoker's novel or in *Dracula: The Vampire Play*, even though Browning borrows extensively from the play in his characterization of Renfield. As I noted earlier, it is Renfield and not John Harker who first journeys to Castle Dracula, thereby contributing to the vampire's invasion of England. And in Browning's film, unlike *Dracula: The Vampire Play*, Renfield as well as Dracula must die, thereby severing all links between Transylvania and England. Perhaps most important, however, Renfield embodies Browning's conception of madness, a disease directly caused by the vampire. In the novel Renfield has been committed to Seward's asylum long before Dracula leaves Transylvania, and thus Stoker implies that England harbors insanity that can be manipulated by the vampire. In Browning's film Renfield begins as a rather effete, fashionably dressed, modern Westerner—naive and blind to all but business concerns, to be sure, but not insane. Yet after Dracula's bite, Renfield is transformed into a glazed-eyed fanatic, grovelling to fulfill the wishes of his new master. When the ship bearing Dracula arrives in England, Renfield stares up from the dark hold, and an off-screen voice declares: "He's mad. Look at his eyes. Why the man's crazy!" Like the rats that accompany Nosferatu in Murnau's film, madness in Browning's *Dracula* is a plague that the vampire introduces into a "healthy" society.

Hence Seward's sanitarium is first seen—in direct contrast to Castle Dracula and Carfax Abbey—as a spacious, sunlit resthome, with carefully attended, well-behaved patients recuperating in manicured gardens. This establishing shot ends, however, with the camera moving from a view of the grounds to reveal Renfield, screaming in his barred cell. The bars cannot prevent this madman, the only obvious mentally ill patient in the asylum, from entering the domain of the normal. Like Dracula, Renfield repeatedly invades the parlor, alternately taunting the men and trying to save Mina, in a series of scenes adapted almost verbatim from *Dracula: The Vampire Play*. While the Count transforms his wives into somnambulistic puppets, he transforms Renfield into a schizophrenic, who instantaneously shifts from one extreme mood to its opposite, torn between his allegiance to his master and his moral concern for Mina, avatar of the normal. Seward, the promoter of mental health, has no cure for this foreign-bred insanity; the Doctor can only attempt—unsuccessfully in every case—to keep Renfield locked up.

Browning's most interesting suggestion in *Dracula* is that those who struggle against the vampire and his abnormal creations could also be considered insane. (Deane and Balderston lay the groundwork for such an interpretation with their presentation of Renfield, and in the novel Van Helsing at one point tells Seward that "all men are mad in some way or the other" [D, 128][7].) Thus John, still trusting in the power of love and in his own ability to protect Mina, accuses Van Helsing of "driving her crazy." And Renfield, after overhearing Van Helsing's plans for destroying Dracula, ironically declares: "Isn't this a strange conversation for men who aren't crazy?" Once Van Helsing has finally convinced the others to face the "incredible" facts and to follow his course of action, an attendant at the sanitarium tells a nurse that "they're all crazy except you and me, and sometimes I have my doubts about you." Browning's implication, though never fully explored or directly faced in *Dracula* (1931), is that to believe in Van Helsing, and hence to accept the existence of "strange things," to trust in the power of wolfsbane and crucifix, and to acknowledge the necessity for purgative violence, is to be "crazy"—only insanity can restore normality. Once the normal world is restored in the film, however, all vestiges of madness can and must be left behind. Perhaps that is why Van Helsing must ultimately remain in the cavernous vaults with the corpses of Dracula and Renfield, while John and Mina climb toward the light, never glancing back.

*   *   *

NINA AUERBACH

Vampires in the Light[†]

When he first appeared in 1897, Dracula seduced Victorians by exuding the glamor of the night; his twentieth-century descendants shocked audiences by bringing light. One could almost see the '60s dawning in *Horror of Dracula* (1958; dir. Terence Fisher), the first and most startling of the Christopher Lee *Dracula*s that swarmed out of England's Hammer Studios between 1958 and 1970. As the series pro-

7. See above, p. 111.
† Excerpted from *Our Vampires, Ourselves* (Chicago: U of Chicago P, 1995) 119–47. Reprinted by permission of the author and the University of Chicago Press.

gressed, Lee was reduced to snarls and stares, but in this inaugural appearance he is brisk and entrepreneurial, more up-to-date than the little men who scurry around to protect their strapping, sexy women.

Even before the story begins, the post-credit sequence announces a brave new world for vampires, one that dispels the gloom of Tod Browning's 1931 adaptation. In that famous film, Bela Lugosi made his first entrance in a crypt furnished with rats, coffins, cobwebs, and other inhospitable props. His hand creeps out of his battered coffin, but we never see his body move: in the next shot he stands cloaked and still "while the camera moves toward him like a supplicant."[1] He never climbs out of his coffin: he is prone and then he is erect; his power is his immobility. His formal attire makes him a statuesque and rather sad discord in his ghastly home.

By contrast, Christopher Lee's coffin, on which DRACULA is elegantly carved on a gleaming surface, is, like his castle, immaculate. The credits roll as we admire his taste and care in maintaining a coffin so handsome. Suddenly, bright red blood, the Hammer trademark, splashes on his white name from some indeterminate source, making a pattern as stylishly vivid as a painting by Jackson Pollock. Is Christopher Lee splashing his own coffin as he comes home from a kill? Or does his presence *inside* his coffin magically attract any blood around? Logic is nonexistent. It doesn't finally matter whose blood we are watching, since it looks so good. Christopher Lee's taste does not desert him on his travels: when he goes off to prey on Lucy and Mina, he brings a white portable traveling coffin that will be an important prop in the story. These tasteful accouterments define a vampire who spurns decay and cobwebs. His element is modernity, speed, and above all, color.

The bright colors of Hammer movies were their exhilarating innovation. Hammer vampires and other monsters are not segregated in the black-and-white gloom of 1930s America. In vibrant color, they are substance, not shadows. They are not primarily costumes and make-up, like Lugosi and Karloff: they are bodies. Technically they remain children of the night—though Christopher Lee wastes no time with this or any lugubrious self-definition in *Horror of Dracula*—but the vampires we see are children of the light.

In these vivid spectacles, blood is beautiful, but it is no longer the life. Appropriately for movies shockingly bathed in light, the sun becomes for the first time the primary vampire-killer: stronger than Catholic ritual, modern technology, or even Van Helsing, the sun displaces all these as Dracula's pre-eminent adversary and double. Stoker's Dracula could not shape-shift in daylight, but he walked around in it freely.

1. This happy phrase is Gregory A. Waller's in *The Living and the Undead: From Stoker's Dracula to Romero's Dawn of the Dead* (Urbana and Chicago: U of Illinois P, 1986) 87. Future references to this edition will appear in the text.

Max Schreck in F. W. Murnau's beautiful silent film *Nosferatu* (1922) is technically the first vampire destroyed by the sun: when Nina detains him past dawn, he dissolves.[2] Tod Browning's Mina claims Dracula failed to kill her because "the daylight stopped him," but Lugosi must be staked before even nominally dying. He and Max Schreck fade in sunlight, but they never burn. Neither endures the scorching inflicted on Christopher Lee when Van Helsing pulls down his draperies—a scorching that has become our primary image of vampire destruction.

The closing sequence of *Horror of Dracula* is as innovative as its beginning, helping us forget the florid incoherence that dominates the middle. Confronted by dawn, Dracula retreats to the library of his gorgeous castle. He is pursued by Peter Cushing's athletic Van Helsing, who is less an occultist or sonorous patriarch than a shrewd fighter who, like his double Dracula, exists above all as a body.[3] Outmatched after a bravura fight, Cushing throws down the lush draperies and floods the room with sunlight, sending the vampire into balletic paroxysms of anguish.

Cushing does pay lip service to the supernatural by making a cross out of Dracula's elegant candlesticks and advancing on the vampire with this unconsecrated artifact, a strategy more ingenious than reverent, but this pseudo-cross only reinforces the potency of the sun that quickly reduces Dracula to a pile of ashes—at least until he rises in the next Lee movie, *Dracula, Prince of Darkness* (1966), whose pre-credit sequence replays this ravishing burning.

This "death" frees Dracula from the old metaphysics, steeping him in a physical empiricism that will define him throughout the century. Stoker's Van Helsing needed carefully consecrated weapons: presumably nothing without clerical sanction would work against the vampire. For the Hammer Dracula, symbol becomes body; he recoils from the mere shape of a cross. Hammer's rules insist on this loss of metaphysical signification. Van Helsing, solitary rule-giver, listens solemnly to his own recorded voice reminding himself that Dracula is *allergic* to light—not repelled by its goodness.

Stoker's Dracula was vulnerable to time, not light: no matter where he was, sunrise enervated him and sunset invigorated him. The Ham-

---

2. Lane Roth notes acutely, p. 246, that with *Nosferatu* the ritual hour for vampire-killing changes from dusk to dawn. Stoker's Dracula, who dies (if he does) just as he is coming to life, shows a vitality absent in Max Schreck and his sun-scorched progeny, who die at the same time they would normally fall into a deathlike trance. Here and often, Stoker's rituals commemorate the life in his Undead, while those of his successors dwell on somnolence. See Lane Roth, "Film, Society and Ideas: *Nosferatu* and *Horror of Dracula*," *Planks of Reason: Essays on the Horror Film*, ed. Barry Keith Grant (Metuchen, N.J., and London: Scarecrow Press, 1984).

3. In the next Hammer film, *Brides of Dracula* (1960), Peter Cushing has his finest moment when he cauterizes his vampire bite with a red-hot poker and holy water—a treatment he might have learned from his contemporary, Emily Brontë, who cauterized in the same way the bite of a rabid dog, though she omitted the holy water.

mer Dracula is disconnected from time. Indoors in day, he is as strong as ever, but his body is vulnerable to a stronger body, the sun's.[4] Like twentieth-century mortals, this Dracula has severed his tie to the universe. He is bounded by senses and flesh.

For better or worse, the vampires that follow Christopher Lee are shorn of their occult identities. They may yearn for them, as do Anne Rice's spirit-haunted seducers, but they live in their own sensations, not in the cosmos. Vibrant and lethal at once, the Hammer sun struck a new kind of vampire. This creature was invented in the late 1950s, but anatomists of horror exalted him as mythic and timeless: "A single beam of the sun falling upon [the vampire's] body will bring instant, complete and absolute disintegration," Drake Douglas' compendium of horror assured readers.[5] Decades after Christopher Lee, the sun can destroy even such refined, self-healing predators as Frank Langella's Dracula, Chelsea Quinn Yarbro's Count Saint-Germain, Fred Saberhagen's Vlad, Anne Rice's Lestat, Jewelle Gomez' Gilda, and Patrick Whale's Braille (in *Night Thirst*, 1991). In novels like George R. Martin's *Fevre Dream* (1982) and movies like Kathryn Bigelow's *Near Dark* (1987), the primary sensory experience is neither biting nor bloodsucking, but the sun's rending of tender vampire flesh. The lethal Hammer sun inspired as extensive a vampire paradigm-shift in 1958 as Planché's moon had done in 1820, when Polidori's elliptical tale became Planché's spectacular melodrama, *The Vampire*.[6]

But what the early-nineteenth-century moon bestowed, the mid-twentieth-century sun destroys. Planché's Ruthven quivers to life under the full moon; the Hammer Dracula writhes and twitches into dissolution when the sun strikes him. Until Stoker changed the rules, Planché's moon had spiritualized nineteenth-century vampires; it diluted their dependence on blood and obscured their addiction to human intercourse, refining them into clean and pure communion. Hammer's sun, and the great welts it caused for decades after *Horror of Dracula*, throws vampires into the pain of physical existence. But at the same time as the sun aligns vampires with mortals, it limits their access to mortal society. For all their style and charm, photophobic vampires are too weak to belong to the devil, too delicate to live in human company.

"Listen to them—the children of the night. What music they make!" Child of nobody, Stoker's vampire listened from his castle, but because of their tender skin, Christopher Lee and his progeny became the mid-

---

4. In 1979, Frank Langella's Dracula gives a highly sophisticated explanation of his ability to function around the clock: "It is always daylight somewhere on earth, Professor. After my rest my need is only to stay in darkness." Stoker's xenophobic characters were aware only of the sun rising and setting *in their homelands*. Langella's Dracula has acquired a global perspective.
5. Drake Douglas, *Horror!* (New York: Macmillan, 1966) 35. Future references to this edition will appear in the text.
6. *The Rime of the Ancient Mariner*, Coleridge's vampire-tinged epic, may be the source of both the Planché moon and the Hammer sun. In *The Ancient Mariner*, "the moving Moon" is generally a fulfilling presence, while the sun is huge, static, and assaultive.

twentieth-century's children of the night. We now gaze at vampires with the admiration Stoker's Dracula reserved for wolves. For as twentieth-century vampires became more material and thus more human, they acquired an allergy that forbade them to live human lives. They exchanged crypts for stylish homes, but they could not leave those homes at will. Planché's moon and Hammer's sun elevate vampires but isolate them from mortal life. The moon revives and the sun kills, but neither quarantines the vampire completely.

The changing influence of heavenly bodies is an index of restlessness on earth. For the British working-class audiences and American students who devoured Hammer films in the 1960s, even sun-struck vampires carried subliminal messages about their own societies.[7] The early Christopher Lee is a freeing alternative to Lugosi. There is nothing foreign in his line readings: he rattles through the familiar speeches with brisk, British efficiency, making them as suitable for a London corporation as a Transylvanian fortress. Lee's castle is spacious and modern, full of expensive furniture, abounding in sinuous columns and candelabras. Its colorful rooms have just been painted; even its crypt is sparkling. Anyone in the Hammer target audience would covet this art deco home, a pointed contrast to Lugosi's unlivable mausoleum. Lee's decor announces his allegiance to a sleek future, not a dusty past; his Castle Dracula is a streamlined respite from the suffocating clutter of the virtuous family's Victorian home. Before Van Helsing throws his curtains open, Lee himself has let the light in on a timid, claustrophobic domesticity.

One of the more enticing incoherences in *Horror of Dracula* is its bizarre handling of space. There is no dislocating journey from London to Transylvania and back. Jonathan, a disguised vampire hunter in this one, does have to take some sort of trip to Dracula's castle, but in the course of the movie, the characters scurry back and forth so easily that Dracula's castle seems to creep next door to the cluttered Victorian home. The distance between vampire and family is so inconstant that Dracula manages to hide his sparkling coffin in Arthur Holmwood's own cellar: while protective men are waiting for him to invade the house, he rises from within it. Some sort of Van Helsing-like logic has evaporated from this *Dracula*, leaving a presence who is the emanation, not the enemy, of the family.

7. Roth, p. 252, defines the probable working-class audience of Hammer films in England. I suspect that British students would have found them trite; I know only their curiously powerful impact in America. When they were imported to the United States, they became a wicked addiction for middle-class '60s students like myself. Conventional and sexist as they ostensibly were, their fatuous patriarchs, ravenous women, and modish Dracula flooded viewers like me with ineffable feelings of rebellion. *The Rocky Horror Picture Show* (1975) institutionalized this rebellion for the next generation, but in the inchoate early '60s, Hammer provided no costumes, songs, or mass rituals that told us even before the movie began that we were there to transgress.

This family is itself a scrambled version of Stoker's clearly differentiated international community of vampire hunters. *Horror of Dracula* shuffles Stoker's good characters around for no discernible reason, thereby draining integrity from the vampire hunters more effectively than Dracula does: in a world where Lucy and Mina, Arthur and Jonathan, change places with impunity, the only constant is Dracula himself. In *Horror of Dracula*, the Western alliance shrinks to a household in which everyone is related to everyone else: screenwriter Jimmy Sangster replaces Stoker's elite, carefully selected vigilante community, the cream of Western civilization, with a series of ingrown relations. This Lucy is the fiancée of the dead Jonathan and the sister of Arthur, who is married to Mina. A little girl, Tania, floats around with no clear antecedents: a vampire she calls "*Aunt* Lucy" abducts her, though she is not Arthur and Mina's child, but the daughter of the housekeeper. All human relationships in this movie are literally or essentially familial, with the exception of Van Helsing, who hovers alone, austere and above the circle, and Dracula, its devouring potential.

The heart and the horror of *Horror of Dracula* is the family, and in its family-bounded environment, women rise. Lucy and Mina are under the control of a slew of interchangeable paternalistic men—until Dracula comes. But as Fisher directs these scenes, Dracula is scarcely there. This vampire is too elusive to be another overbearing male; he is an emanation of the anger, pride, and sexuality that lie dormant in the women themselves. Stoker's nightmare of violation becomes a dream of female self-possession.

A docile Lucy is bustled over in bed, childish in braids and demure blue nightgown. Once let alone, she undergoes an inward change with no vampire catalyst. Deliberately, she rises and listens at the door, then opens the window; we see a woman's body within the suddenly sheer little-girl nightgown. She removes her crucifix, lies down, and, in a tender rhythm of autoeroticism, fondles the vampire bites on her neck. We never see Christopher Lee enter her room; the sequence fades out on the open window. The scene suggests vampirism, but we see, instead, a woman alone, claiming herself. This sequence is all the more suggestive because, unlike Stoker's novel, the screenplay gives us no "normal," pre-bitten Lucy: we see only an infantilized girl shutting out her keepers and opening the window to her adult self.

The bitten Mina repeats this gleeful autoeroticism. Throughout the movie, Mina has been a leaden, matronly presence, sitting dully while the men plan futile attacks on Dracula. When the vampire lures her into his power, we never see him touch her. She simply returns home sparkling, clutching the fur collar around her neck. In a witty close-up, she smiles deliciously and snuggles into the fur, seeming to caress her animal self. The close-up is not only postcoital; like Lucy fondling her bites, Mina's grin is, as far as we see, an infusion of self-delight, not delight in Dracula.

Of course, Lucy is staked and Mina is purified. These glimpses of exhilarated women, aroused by neither husband nor vampire, are only interludes in a traditional script, but though Terence Fisher's men always kill their vampire and reappropriate their women, *Horror of Dracula* exposes women, teenagers, and other restless spectators to a future more colorful than the restrictive 1950s. Postwar America had celebrated its victory over fascism by targeting enemies within. Self-canonized authorities—medical, moral, and patriotic—proliferated, all preaching the health of domesticity (national and familial) and the horror of the world beyond. With a ferocity alien even to most Victorians, they implanted in women family values and no others. Popular psychiatry insisted that not only women's lives but our dreams and desires were limited to endless reiterations of the patriarchal family plot. *Horror of Dracula* provided an image of disobedience, showing us two women opening windows beyond the family and, in the guise of vampire victims, surging into themselves.

Stoker's Lucy is the only character who crosses the borders from human to vampire: she accomplishes the metamorphosis that threatens Jonathan, Renfield, Mina, and, by extension, England. The long middle of Stoker's novel is a voyeuristic account of Lucy's protracted transformation. Until Hammer's *Dracula* series, this transforming woman was relegated to the margins of the story. *Horror of Dracula* places her at its heart: the next thirty years would play sophisticated ideological variations on her unstable form. In the 1970s, women would write new vampire conventions, but the Hammer series provided tantalizing images of transformation that later, flagrantly unorthodox films would develop into structural principles.[8]

8. Fisher's claustrophobic Holmwood family harboring vampires it doesn't recognize anticipates a dreadful family in a quite different vampire movie: George Romero's *Night of the Living Dead* (1968). Superficially these films could not be farther apart. The hordes of reanimated corpses who rise to eat the living in Romero's America have none of the dashing individuality of Hammer vampires: they are disposable and indistinguishable. Hammer's opulent colors look garishly old-fashioned next to Romero's grainy, cinema verité black-and-white; Hammer's beautiful predators pale before Romero's slovenly ghouls; and the opulent Hammer Victorian England looks like Disneyland next to Romero's grainy Pittsburgh.

Nevertheless, Romero's awful Cooper family springs from the Hammer Holmwoods. Mr. Cooper, a bullying idiot, takes refuge in an abandoned house. Unlike the more enterprising refugees, Cooper boards his family in a sealed cellar. Mrs. Cooper's complaint—"there's a radio upstairs and you boarded us in down here?"—translates into the language of modern America the unexpressed complaint of Fisher's boarded-in Lucy and Mina. This later wife is at least free to grumble, "We may not enjoy living together, but dying together isn't going to solve anything."

The vampire they harbor as they bicker is not Christopher Lee in a clean white coffin, but their own wounded daughter, who, transformed into a ghoul, rises and eats her parents. The other ghouls are automata; this child alone shows relish for the kill, grinning with her bloody mouth as adorably as a child in a TV commercial, then grabbing a trowel to stab her mother enthusiastically. In 1968 America, a year whose political idiom was violent denunciation, George Romero was free to make explicit the monsters bred in the ordinary cloistered family, but these monsters rose first, if more demurely, in the stylized and remote Hammer ambience.

For most of the young women who, like me, loved Hammer films in the 1960s and weren't sure why, these grins of aroused discovery were subliminal surprises in a waste of staked bimbos. Hammer films never explicitly challenged the status quo, becoming more authoritarian as they became more popular.[9] As the films became increasingly pious, on the surface at least, Hammer women grew more swollen and soporific: tiny crucifixes swung enticingly in the crevasse between their mountainous breasts, but their faces had little energy. The *Dracula* series hinted only intermittently at the delights of awakening; its primary effect was an almost hypnotic insistence on the eroticism of repression. The brightly colored Victorian decor was a plush evocation of barely contained sexiness. For young people in the 1960s, who, as Walter Kendrick shrewdly notes, were "the first generation . . . that had probably never met a Victorian," Victorian England oozed out of Hammer movies as a psychedelic goofy glow—though the ostensible setting was Switzerland![1]

Children of a tasteless American suburbia that was invaded in the 1950s only by the Blob, the Thing, giant ants, and other preconscious monsters with whom it was impossible to identify loved the ripe, somewhat sickly innocence of Hammer England. Like the Beatles, those similarly seductive Edwardian revenants, Hammer films led Americans on a mythic return to their glamorous British origin. The lyrical Hammer wood, where in movie after movie someone falls out of a coach and is attacked; those enormous Hammer beds, with their puffy comforters and infinite pillows, where women writhe delicately as they wait for the vampire; those cluttered Hammer drawing rooms, whose inhabitants are so languid that we can't tell whether they've been bitten or not—all created a picture of Victorian England as a sadistic fairyland, a respite from too knowing times. In Stoker's *Dracula*, 1897 is the model of sophisticated technology on which vampires intrude from prehistoric antiquity; Hammer films generated nostalgia for a magically remote Victorian past where vampires were at home. The 1960s was a decade whose young Americans were haunted by Utopias of sweet, pseudochildish sexuality. The Hammer Victorian England was one of the silliest and the sweetest.

For young women, though, its violence was strangely contemporary,

---

9. Waller, p. 142, emphasizes Hammer films' stabilizing endorsement of the couple, "an exceedingly safe image that underlies and perpetuates bourgeois society's all-important reliance on the discrimination between sexual roles and on monogamous, heterosexual relationships." In my opinion, he makes too little of the resonant images of potent transformation that erode all bourgeois couples.
1. Walter Kendrick, *The Thrill of Fear: 250 Years of Scary Entertainment* (New York: Grove Wiedenfeld, 1991) 229. Of course, as Kendrick goes on to remark, Victorian England was greyer and grimmer than its Oz-like Hammer image. The most famous Victorian literature features the dreary contours of England blurred in rain and fog. For Victorians themselves, Italy was the land of color and arousal.

or, as we used to say, "relevant." Hammer films courted the youth market, but not with wars and political protests. *Taste the Blood of Dracula* (1970; dir. Peter Sasdy) does show a group of giggling teenage girls killing their debauched, hypocritical fathers under Dracula's influence, but a fatherly fiancé quickly places Alice, their leader, under his solemn control. For the most part, the violence of Hammer films involved the staking of female vampires, an activity so overtly sexual that, in those days when politics was associated only with war, it did not seem political.

Vampirism threatens to spread among women in Hammer films. Perhaps for that reason, only female vampires are staked; their male leaders generally earn more ingenious deaths. In *Horror of Dracula*, "Aunt" Lucy, smiling and fanged, leads little Tania through that wonderful Hammer wood. The sequence bristles with suggestions of witchcraft, with forbidden knowledge passed down through generations of women, suggestions more potent because Tania is a new character: Stoker's Lucy abducted a little Cockney *boy* who learned nothing from her, but only burbled about her beauty as the men did. The Hammer Lucy is not an antimaternal seductress of men, but a subverter of women. Tania returns intact—but what did they talk about in the forest?—and Lucy is staked, but in *Dracula, Prince of Darkness* (1966; dir. Terence Fisher), there is a still more explicit interchange between a female vampire and a mortal woman.

Helen (Barbara Shelley) is the starchiest of two British couples sightseeing in Carlsbad (the Hammer substitute for Transylvania). They ignore warnings and visit Castle Dracula, which in this movie is so spiffy that it does duty as a luxury hotel. Clove, the sinister servant of the supposedly dead Dracula, serves them a scrumptious meal. Only Helen is afraid, and Helen is right, for Clove murders her silly prowling husband in the night and hangs him by his feet. The blood that drips from his throat resuscitates the ashes of Dracula, who promptly vampirizes Helen as she prowls after her husband.

The vampire Helen is as intelligent as the mortal, but she is no longer prim and fearful. As a sign of her condition, she wears a new, low-cut nightgown when Diana, the other Englishwoman, comes upon her while searching for her husband. "Come sister," Helen replies, baring her fangs and opening her arms. *"You don't need Charles."* This resonant sentence has none of the insinuating intimacy of Le Fanu's Carmilla and the loving lesbian vampires she inspired: Helen infiltrates Diana's social conditioning, not her dreams. Helen's wicked remark is as true as her earlier insistence that they get out of the castle and back to England, but it brings down the fury of humans and vampires alike: Dracula enters, snarling, blocking her access to Diana; Charles runs in and flings her to the floor, then escapes with Diana. Helen tries to

embrace Dracula, who flings her back to the floor. The forces of darkness and light converge against the vampire who told the woman that
she didn't need her man.

Helen's staking by a coven of faceless, chanting monks is the most
authentically frightening sequence in the Hammer series. There is no
masterful Van Helsing, no sobbing Arthur, no other familiar men who
throb sympathetically as they kill for eternity the woman they claim to
love, but only a faintly sadistic priest named Father Sandor directing
his efficient, anonymous monks.

This Helen is not encased in her coffin as Stoker's Lucy was: the
monks heft her up, twisting in terror, onto a raised slab that looks like
an operating table. Moreover, we do not *watch* Helen as Stoker's Van
Helsing and his crew watched the writhing Lucy, filtering her agony
through their own convictions. The point of view in the sequence is
that of the terrified woman. As her powerful body is held down, arranged, and finally staked, we experience through her eyes the imper-
sonality of her destruction. Barbara Shelley is large and strong. The
central image of the scene is not her fangs or even the blood that wells
from her, but the strapping arm the little monks hold down as they
prepare to stake her.

For many of us, the scene was close to home. Only a fanatic could
believe that Helen, the film's central authority, is saved for Heaven.
The sequence is closer to gang rape, or to gynecological surgery, or to
any of the collective violations women were and are prone to, than to
the sacred marriage Stoker's reverent narrators made readers accept.
Stripped of the sensibility of loving, maiming men, seen instead from
her own point of view, the staking of the female vampire is less a rite
of purification than the licensed torture of a woman who knew women
didn't need men.[2]

Frank Langella's Byronic savior in John Badham's ambitious *Dracula*
(1979) realizes Christopher Lee's promise as a rescuer of oppressed
women. In this breathtaking if confusing movie, Stoker's good men are
villains; Stoker's vampire is a hero; the women, victims no more, embrace vampirism with rapture as the sole available escape from patriarchy. W. D. Richter's screenplay never bothers to tell the familiar story;
it retells it for its age. Badham's unapologetic revisionism assumes that
Stoker's novel has passed into folklore, becoming a gauge of the present,
not an anchor to the past.

2. Ira Levin's obstetrical thriller, *Rosemary's Baby*, become a best-seller in America in 1967, only
   a year after *Dracula, Prince of Darkness*. Images of women violated by husbands, doctors,
   churches, and other institutionally sanctioned bodies of men entered the American consciousness through horror literature before they became part of the feminist political platform in
   the 1970s. David J. Skal's *The Monster Show* (New York: Norton, 1993) 287–305, has a
   fascinating chapter on gynecological violations and 1960s horror conventions.

Badham's *Dracula* makes radical claims, turning the old story into a vehicle for twentieth-century social critiques, especially feminist critiques. Stoker's brave and good men become overbearing fathers and paternalistic doctors whose sole mission is to control women: Seward is now Lucy's father and Van Helsing is Mina's. Both are monuments of medical malpractice. When Jonathan, Lucy's grumpy and sleazy fiancé, is not destroying the landscape with his car,[3] he sours every scene in which he appears. For Lucy and Mina, the transfiguring embrace of the vampire is a glorious evasion of patriarchal control. The movie's lush emphasis on transfiguration converges with the feminist vampire plots of novelists like Tanith Lee, Jody Scott, Suzy McKee Charnas, and especially Chelsea Quinn Yarbro, whose sartorially splendid and sadly wise Count Saint-Germain is scarcely distinguishable from Frank Langella.

But the heart of this radicalism is restoration. Badham does not expel past vampires as Stoker tried to do; he restores the suppressed significance of forgotten stories. Like the so-called minority studies that burgeoned in universities in the 1970s, Badham's *Dracula* aims to reclaim a past arrogant power had debased.

Not only does Badham restore the old play; he transforms it. When Langella starred in the Balderston-Deane *Dracula* on Broadway, it was the same confined drawing-room melodrama it had been in 1927. Badham opens it out, not only to sweeping shots of the English landscape, but to unstable depths of sea and sky. The movie is full of overhead shots and rapid, destabilizing pans; it begins and ends on a turbulent sea. Motion and space demolish the play's four walls, its monotonous interior set. In the same spirit, the immobility of Bela Lugosi, star of the original play and film, dissolves in the incessant motion of Frank Langella, who is always touching, moving, dancing, climbing, or riding horses. Langella's graceful hands replace Lugosi's transfixing eyes. Lugosi was anomalous and unmateable; the sympathetic Langella flows into mortal women. He and Lucy first explore their attraction by dancing together, a communion unimaginable in 1931. Langella's hands, like those of Yarbro's Count Saint-Germain, free the vampire to absorb everyone and everything he touches. Lugosi was an estranged and estranging Dracula; Langella is a Dracula of fusion.

Badham also restores the ingrown Hammer family, an impeccably virtuous unit that houses its own vampires. In the 1979 *Dracula*, however, there are no paternal husbands, only obstructive, incompetent fathers; the target is no longer bourgeois marriage, but patriarchy itself. Thus, unlike the cluttered respectability of the Hammer household,

---

3. Like its ostensible source, Balderston and Deane's 1927 play, this *Dracula* is set not in Victorian England, but in the 1920s. In Badham's 1920s, the romantic, tactile nineteenth century Langella represents is being overrun by gramophones, cars, and common little men.

Badham's family inhabits the brutal chaos of Dr. Seward's madhouse.[4] The movie opens in incoherence: the chaos of the shipwreck that brings Dracula to England is cross-cut with Seward's screaming lunatics. Authorities are not only ineffectual, but inaudible: the sailors shouting incomprehensible orders are the equivalent of Dr. Seward (Donald Pleasence, fresh from playing an ineffectual psychiatrist in *Halloween*) drifting helplessly through his asylum. Nature, madhouse, and family are part of a single upheaval. The movie's first audible line belongs to its women: Lucy and Mina, shut away from the noise in their bedroom, chant in giggling unison, "We are not chattel." Authority is overwhelmed from the beginning; only the women's voices are clear.

The madhouse/family brings Renfield back to the story. Renfield was excluded from the Hammer series, whose vampires themselves were touchstones of civilized madness. Renfield is usually a bridge from supernatural to clinical cannibalism, embodying a hunger society can label and contain, but society existed only by implication in the confined stories of the '60s and early '70s. By 1979, vampire stories have become political barometers, and Renfield returns to catalyze inept abuses of power.

This Renfield is a whistle-blower, silenced (as Lucy will be before Dracula saves her) by incarceration in Seward's asylum. He opens the movie by exposing Jonathan as a crooked lawyer who cheated not only Renfield himself, but Dracula, whom he duped into buying the dilapidated Carfax Abbey. When he insists later on that Dracula is a vampire, Jonathan hands him over to Seward, who ignores his warnings as an inmate's ravings. This Renfield is the truth-telling victim of authority's apparent sanity, not an embodiment of its potential madness: he has moved from id to commentator. Like other post-1960s culture heroes who vanished after giving fragmentary warnings—the Black Panthers, Karen Silkwood—Renfield becomes a silenced seer.

Like Renfield, Mina (who plays the role of Stoker's Lucy) is authority's scapegoat; she dies to illuminate the necessity of escape. As in *Horror of Dracula*, the names of Stoker's familiar characters are scrambled: the old death-haunted Lucy becomes Mina, "frail all her life," while Stoker's mighty Mina, supreme mother and stenographer, becomes the Lucy, powerfully played by Kate Nelligan, whom Dracula singles out with a praise peculiar to the 1970s: "She is stronger than most women, isn't she?" This seemingly wanton reversal of the old names unmoors those of us who think we know the story. It may also

---

4. This too is a restoration, one that goes back to Stoker's novel: Badham's adaptation is the first to highlight the residence of Stoker's Dr. Seward in his own madhouse, though Stoker's doctor was no patriarch, but a wistful family man manqué.

remind us that the weak woman who dies and the strong woman who escapes are part of each other. The women's movement of the 1970s insisted that there were no "strong" exceptions to general subordination; women are part of a cohesive social category whereby each of us is implicated in the fate of all. This activist premise infiltrates a politically sophisticated *Dracula* that aims to destabilize the rigid categories of the old story.

There is nothing pretty about Mina's death or undeath. Badham makes her corpse a horrible sight, as if to suggest that even when their killer is a sexy vampire, murdered women are dreadful spectacles. Mina doesn't fade into robust new life: she chokes graphically to a death made more painful by the laudanum Dr. Seward idiotically gives her, afterwards muttering apologetically, "it's been so long since I've practiced real medicine." Paternalistic psychiatry mangles her death, as it mangles the lives of the asylum inmates. The collaboration of medicine, especially psychiatry, with patriarchy, a frequent concern of feminism in the 1970s and beyond, makes Dr. Seward, not the vampire, the murderer the movie indicts.

There is nothing seductive about the Mina who rises: she is no swollen Hammer sexpot, but a decomposing corpse with broken, bloody teeth. This Mina is contrary to literary vampire mythology, where undead corpses, like saints, remain in a state of perpetual preservation, but she is true to the vampires of folklore, who are not transfigurations, but actual corpses who leave their graves to devour their families.[5] Like these folklore vampires, Mina advances on the man closest to her: her terrified father, Van Helsing (Laurence Olivier, in a performance so flustered and overwrought that it seems designed to strip both character and actor of all the authority the years had given). She offers no ripe conjugal embrace. Instead, she croons disgustingly and repeatedly, "Papa, come." Since the movie's world is run by incompetent fathers, it is appropriate that the "frail" Mina become a folklore vampire, licensed by definition to kill her family. The clumsy, keening Van Helsing stakes her not ritually, but by accident.[6]

Lucy has no folklore rot about her; she is everything a feminist vam-

---

5. See Paul Barber, *Vampires, Burial, and Death: Folklore and Reality* (New Haven and London: Yale UP, 1988). In many movies, folklore vampires were replacing glamorized Hammer corpses; Romero's *Night of the Living Dead* (1968) is overrun with these awkward, festering, feasting revenants. Graphic footage of the war in Viet Nam and the assassinations and rumblings of civil war at home had made corpses revert to the rot and dread they had embodied before the so-called enlightenment of the eighteenth century, when they gained the potential to become uplifting icons.

6. In all the prints I have seen, Mina seems, confusingly, to die twice: sometime after the scene I have just described, Lucy watches in horror as the men cut the heart out of a ruddy, unstaked and undecomposed Mina. Moreover, this Mina does not reflect in a mirror, while the decomposing Mina revealed herself to her father by her reflection in water. Is this a glitch in editing, a bit of Wonderland logic to dislodge our expectations, or a Cubist attempt to juxtapose a folkloric with a literary vampire?

pire should be. Her romance with Frank Langella could be one of the swoonier inserts of *Ms. Magazine*. He loves her strength and self-assertion: she asks him to dance, she declares himself to him, while he responds to her unfemininity with delight. Most wonderful of all, in the 1970s at least, he invites her to dinner at Carfax Abbey.

Stoker's dinner scene, where the vampire plays servant to an unknowing Jonathan in order to become his master, undergoes its most baroque movie mutation in this meal. In the Lugosi *Dracula*, the never-served dinner was an ineffably decadent homoerotic tease between the stiffly amused vampire and the effete Renfield. In 1979, a dangerous flirtation modulates into enlightened heterosexual romance. Lucy goes eagerly to a Carfax that is nothing like Lugosi's barren castle. Though Jonathan bilked him into buying it, Dracula has decorated it in a striking candle-and-cobweb motif: Carfax is no longer dark and gloomy, but a heaven of refracted light. Like a perfect '70s man, Dracula does not sit back to be served; he entertains Lucy in his lovely home, and, presumably, cooks her a gourmet dinner—though alas, when they commune affectionately over the long table, the camera never shows us Lucy's plate.

Like a good assertive feminist, Lucy declares herself passionately, while Dracula, open and honest, tries to discourage her by telling her the loneliness of vampire life. As the ardent heterosexual replacement for the Jonathan who, in Stoker's novel, "belonged" to Dracula, Lucy is a sympathetic repository of his confidences, which are no longer boastful, but openly vulnerable. Listening to the wolves, he adds a resonant word to Stoker's famous line: "what *sad* music they make," he ruminates softly. But Lucy is supportive: "Do you think it's sad? I think it's a wonderful sound. I really love the night; it's so exciting." After she persuades a reluctant Dracula that he is not a rapist—she came of her own accord—Lucy's transformation into vampirism takes place in a languorous red-tinted sex scene. Vampirism here is all erotic tenderness. There are no fangs, no blood, no penetration or violence, simply a merging of bodies. When Lucy drinks from the vein in his chest, this Dracula is not coercive, but tender and enfeebled-looking, an ideal nonphallic man who relishes his passive role.

After many disappointing years, this vampire romance of the 1970s may seem merely, in that deadening phrase, "politically correct." Frank Langella may be as laughable a love object now as Bela Lugosi was when I was growing up. But the rapidity with which our Draculas date tells us only that every age embraces the vampire it needs. In 1979, one image of a magical leader was Frank Langella, sad and wise and far-seeing, erotically easy in his animal self (for the most part Badham avoids artificial transformations; instead, at intervals, Langella *plays* himself as bat and wolf). Positioned constantly on heights, looking down at the scurrying little mortals—as opposed to Lugosi, who was always rising from depths—Langella was an enticing image of gentle power in a postwar decade that seemed to have evaded political revolution. Many progressives believed, in 1979, that power could be transformed or surmounted; feminists wrote of gender polarities reconciled in an androgynous union of opposites. Probably, though, such a consummation is possible only for an angel or a vampire.

Dracula's origins are vague; he has only a history long enough to make him sad. Lucy, a defiant woman of the present, is on the verge of rejuvenating him when littler people trap them. Langella neither weeps nor looks back, but he is an aristocrat in a reduced world. He may win Lucy, but we know that Jonathan's car will supersede his gorgeous horses. Though this Dracula is not nostalgic himself, he is a symptom of the nostalgia for a chosen elite that suffused (and still suffuses) ostensibly radical works. This Dracula is not the tyrant Lugosi was; he is an elect being. As such, in a democratic age, he will always be hunted.

In approved Hammer fashion, Langella's Dracula is scorched to death, thus institutionalizing the sun as weapon of choice against vampires, but he dies exalted. Cornered with Lucy on a ship to Romania, he stakes Van Helsing, thus completing their role reversal; the dying Van Helsing, ever an inadvertent killer, accidentally impales the vampire on a great hook that sends him soaring skyward. From Dracula's stricken perspective, we see an assaultive sun so powerful that it could never rise on England: it would be more at home in *The Rime of the Ancient Mariner* or in such celestial science fiction films as *2001: A Space Odyssey* or *Star Wars*. The camera moves through the colors of the spectrum as the vampire's dying vision transfigures the object that is killing it.

The final sequence is less an opening for a sequel than a paean to resurrection. Dracula's cloak flies off and soars through the sky; as a wolf howls, the cloak assumes the shape of a great bat. Lucy watches rapturously, enduring sullen Jonathan because she knows Dracula lives and will return for her. The crypt that had enclosed Lugosi opens out to space and sky.

This heroic conclusion is far from Lugosi's ignominious offscreen staking. The entrance of the sun in *Horror of Dracula* seemed originally to isolate the vampire from the dominant rhythms of sleeping and waking life, but in the 1970s, when ordinariness shrinks into perfidy, the sun becomes a medium of romantic consecration. It no longer shrivels Dracula, but shares with him its celestial dominance. Like the burning boy in Blake's *Glad Day* who steps joyfully out of an encompassing sun, the vampire vulnerable to solar death becomes a kind of sun-king. Frank Langella never shrivels to dust, as Christopher Lee did; instead, he dies into his own heroic image, soaring straight upward, like Shelley's skylark, beyond common sights and sounds.

Evolving from the self-imprisoned Bela Lugosi to the spiffily modern Christopher Lee to the Promethean Frank Langella, Dracula progresses from death-bringing foreigner to witty liberator to angelic harbinger of better times. But as he casts off crypt and coffin for erotic enlightenment, Langella's savior looks to the past, not the future, for a society beyond taboos. This adaptation that so wantonly defies its source moves backward, away from the 1970s as well as forward to them, returning the viewer to an age when vampires were not scum, but authentic aristocrats. These blazing Draculas strive to restore the stories Stoker's rules and taboos forbade.

Film Adaptations: A Checklist

As one of the most mediagenic cultural icons of the twentieth century, Dracula has made hundreds of appearances on the screen, usually in transmutations having nothing whatsoever to do with the original novel. The following checklist includes only those films having a significant connection to Stoker's book.

Drakula (Hungary, 1920). Director: Károly Lajthay. Cast: Margit Lux, Paul Askonas. Presumed to be the first, unauthorized adaptation of Stoker's novel, Lajthay's *Drakula* is now a lost film, about which even written documentation is scanty. Lead actor Askonas (spelled Askenas in some sources) had a small part as a cadaverous butler in the eerie German film *Orlacs Hände* (*The Hands of Orlac*, 1924), a characterization strongly suggesting that his role in *Drakula* was indeed that of Stoker's vampire.

Nosferatu: Eine Symphonie des Grauens (Germany, 1922). Director: F. W. Murnau. Screenplay: Henrick Galeen. Cast: Max Schreck (as Orlock/Dracula), Gustav von Wangenheim, Greta Schroeder. Murnau's interpretation of Stoker as a German expressionist fairy tale was an unauthorized adaptation; Stoker's widow successfully sued for plagiarism and won a German court's order that the negative and all prints be destroyed. Fortunately, sufficient material remained in circulation to earn the film a reputation as one of the best *Dracula* adaptations, unique in its depiction of Dracula as the repellent creature Stoker originally described.

Dracula (U.S.A., 1931). Director: Tod Browning. Screenplay: Garrett Fort. Cast: Bela Lugosi (Dracula), Helen Chandler, David Manners,

Dwight Frye, Edward Van Sloan. The most famous *Dracula* film of all time is an odd blend of Stoker's novel and the Deane/Balderston play, which transformed the book's ancient satyr into a suave Mephisto in evening clothes. Following an atmospheric opening in Transylvania, the largely stagebound film is most notable for Lugosi's indelible performance.

Dracula (U.S.A., 1931). Spanish-language version. Director: George Melford. Screenplay: Garrett Fort, translated by B. Fernandez Cue. Cast: Carlos Villarias (Dracula), Lupita Tovar, Barry Norton, Eduardo Arozamena, Pablo Alvarez Rubio, Carmen Guerrero. Filmed at night on the same sets as Tod Browning's film, the Spanish *Dracula* is the more technically polished of the two, of special interest for its more fluid camerawork, visual effects, and eroticism.

Dracula (U.S.A., 1957). There appear to be no surviving copies of this live television production (based on Stoker's book rather than the play), presented as part of NBC's *Matinee Theater* series. John Carradine starred as Dracula.

Horror of Dracula (U.K., 1958). Director: Terence Fisher. Screenplay: Jimmy Sangster. Cast: Peter Cushing, Michael Gough, Melissa Stribling, Christopher Lee (Dracula). Known simply as *Dracula* in England, this film was said to have the most profitable cost-to-revenue ratio in British film history. The streamlined plot eliminates the character of Renfield, introduces bright red technicolor blood, and showcases Christopher Lee in a role he would repeat eight times on screen.

Dracula (Television, U.K., 1969). Director: Patrick Dromgoole. Teleplay: Charles Graham. Cast: Corin Redgrave, Denholm Elliot (Dracula), Suzanne Neve, Susan George. A modestly budgeted but inventive television adaptation in which the Renfieldlike madman in the asylum (Redgrave) is discovered to be Jonathan Harker, driven insane by his experiences in Transylvania.

Count Dracula (Spain/West Germany/Italy, 1970). Director: Jesus Franco. Screenplay: Franco and Augusto Finochi. Cast: Christopher Lee (Dracula), Herbert Lom, Klaus Kinski, Frederick Williams, Maria Rohm. First large-screen attempt to faithfully adapt Stoker's novel, but hampered by a low budget (despite complicated multinational financing). Christopher Lee bears a strong resemblance to the monster as Stoker described him, a white-haired old man who grows younger as he drinks blood.

*   *   *

Dracula (Television, Canada, 1973). Director: Jack Nixon Browne. Teleplay: Rod Coneybeare. Cast: Norman Walsh (Dracula), Blair Brown, Nehemiah Persoff. A television production, part of the *Purple Playhouse* series, which reportedly adhered closely to Stoker's original plot.

Dracula (Television, U.S.A., 1974). Director: Dan Curtis. Teleplay: Richard Matheson. Cast: Jack Palance (Dracula), Nigel Davenport, Simon Ward, Fiona Lewis, Penelope Horner, Murray Brown. The first adaptation to romanticize the character of Dracula, presenting him as a lovesick vampire seeking the reincarnation of his lost, fifteenth-century love. The theme was repeated in Coppola's 1992 *Bram Stoker's Dracula*.

Count Dracula (Television, U.K., 1977). Director: Phillip Saville. Teleplay: Gerald Savory. Cast: Louis Jourdan (Dracula), Frank Finlay, Jack Shepard, Bosco Hogan, Susan Penhaligon, Judi Bowker, Mark Burns. Probably the most ambitious attempt to date to faithfully adapt Stoker, retaining all major plot elements. Upon its second broadcast on American public television, censors deleted the scene in which Dracula's wives prepare to feast on a baby.

Nosferatu the Vampyre (Germany, 1979). Director and Screenplay: Werner Herzog. Cast: Klaus Kinski (Nosferatu/Dracula), Isabelle Adjani, Bruno Ganz, Jacques Dufilho, Roland Topor, Walter Laderigast. Filmed in two separate versions, one in English and one in German, Herzog's moody, uneven homage to F. W. Murnau and Stoker is most successful in presenting Dracula as simultaneously repellent and oddly pathetic.

Dracula (U.S.A., 1979). Director: John Badham. Screenplay: W. D. Richter. Cast: Frank Langella (Dracula), Laurence Olivier, Donald Pleasance, Kate Nelligan, Jan Francis, Trevor Eve. An elaborate remake of the Deane/Balderston stage play, this *Dracula* was not a commercial success when first released, but is nonetheless of interest for Langella's velvety, understated performance, imported from the 1977 Broadway revival.

Bram Stoker's Dracula (U.S.A., 1992). Director: Frances Ford Coppola. Screenplay: James V. Hart. Cast: Gary Oldman (Dracula), Winona Ryder, Anthony Hopkins, Keanu Reeves, Richard E. Grant, Cary Elwes, Sadie Frost, Tom Waits. At a reported cost of $50 million, this, the most expensive horror film ever produced, disingenuously claimed to be a completely faithful adaptation of the book. While it did lavishly realize surface details of the novel, it completely subverted Stoker's conception of the vampire, adding a "Beauty and the Beast"-style re-incarnation romance between Oldman and Ryder, presumably for commercial purposes.

CRITICISM

PHYLLIS A. ROTH

Suddenly Sexual Women in Bram Stoker's *Dracula*†

Criticism of Bram Stoker's *Dracula*, though not extensive, yet not insubstantial, points primarily in a single direction: the few articles published perceive *Dracula* as the consistent success it has been because, in the words of Royce MacGillwray, "Such a myth lives not merely because it has been skillfully marketed by entrepreneurs [primarily the movie industry] but because it expresses something that large numbers of readers feel to be true about their own lives."[1] In other words, *Dracula* successfully manages a fantasy which is congruent with a fundamental fantasy shared by many others. Several of the interpretations of *Dracula* either explicitly or implicitly indicate that this "core fantasy"[2] derives from the Oedipus complex—indeed, Maurice Richardson calls *Dracula* "a quite blatant demonstration of the Oedipus complex . . . a kind of incestuous, necrophilous, oral-anal-sadistic all-in-wrestling match"[3] and this reading would seem to be valid.

Nevertheless, the Oedipus complex and the critics' use of it does not go far enough in explaining the novel: in explaining what I see to be the primary focus of the fantasy content and in explaining what allows Stoker and, vicariously, his readers, to act out what are essentially threatening, even horrifying wishes which must engage the most polarized of ambivalences. I propose, in the following, to summarize the interpretations to date, to indicate the pre-Oedipal focus of the fantasies, specifically the child's relation with and hostility toward the mother, and to indicate how the novel's fantasies are managed in such a way as to transform horror into pleasure. Moreover, I would emphasize that for both the Victorians and twentieth century readers, much of the novel's great appeal derives from its hostility toward female sexuality. In "Fictional Convention and Sex in *Dracula*," Carrol Fry observes that the female vampires are equivalent to the fallen women of eighteenth and nineteenth century fiction.[4]

The facile and stereotypical dichtomy between the dark woman and the fair, the fallen and the idealized, is obvious in *Dracula*. Indeed, among the more gratuitous passages in the novel are those in which

† First appeared in *Literature* and *Psychology* 27 (1977) 113–21. © 1977 by *Literature and Psychology*. Reprinted by premission.
1. Royce MacGillwray, "*Dracula*: Bram Stoker's Spoiled Masterpiece," *Queen's Quarterly*, LXXIX, 518.
2. See Norman N. Holland, *The Dynamics of Literary Response* (New York: W. W. Norton & Co., 1975).
3. Maurice Richardson, "The Psychoanalysis of Ghost Stories," *Twentieth Century*, CLXVI (December 1959), 427.
4. *Victorian Newsletter*, XLII.

the "New Woman" who is sexually aggressive is verbally assaulted. Mina Harker remarks that such a woman, whom she holds in contempt, "will do the proposing herself."[5] Additionally, we must compare Van Helsing's hope "that there are good women still left to make life happy" (207) [166] with Mina's assertion that "the world seems full of good men—even if there *are* monsters in it" (250) [198]. A remarkable contrast![6]

Perhaps nowhere is the dichotomy of sensual and sexless woman more dramatic than it is in *Dracula* and nowhere is the suddenly sexual woman more violently and self-righteously persecuted than in Stoker's "thriller."

The equation of vampirism with sexuality is well established in the criticism. Richardson refers to Freud's observation that "morbid dread always signifies repressed sexual wishes."[7] We must agree that *Dracula* is permeated by "morbid dread." However, another tone interrupts the dread of impending doom throughout the novel; that note is one of lustful anticipation, certainly anticipation of catching and destroying forever the master vampire, Count Dracula, but additionally, lustful anticipation of a consummation one can only describe as sexual. One thinks, for example, of the candle's "sperm which "dropped in white patches" on Lucy's coffin as Van Helsing opens it for the first time (220) [175]. Together the critics have enumerated the most striking instances of this tone and its attendant imagery, but to recall: first, the scene in which Jonathan Harker searches the Castle Dracula, in a state of fascinated and morbid dread, for proof of his host's nature. Harker meets with three vampire women (whose relation to Dracula is incestuous[8]) whose appeal is described almost pornographically:

> All three had brilliant white teeth that shone like pearls against the ruby of their voluptuous lips. There was something about them

5. Bram Stoker, *Dracula* (New York: Dell, 1974), 103–104. All subsequent references will be to this edition and will appear parenthetically. Bracketed page numbers refer to this Norton Critical Edition.
6. While it is not my concern in this paper to deal biographically with *Dracula*, the Harry Ludlam biography (a book which is admittedly anti-psychological in orientation despite its provocative title, *A Biography of Dracula: The Life Story of Bram Stoker*) includes some suggestive comments about Bram Stoker's relationship with his mother. Ludlam remarks an ambivalence toward women on the part of Charlotte Stoker, who, on the one hand, decried the situation of poor Irish girls in the workhouse which was "the very hot-bed of vice" and advocated respectability through emigration for the girls and, on the other, "declared often that she 'did not care tuppence' for her daughters." Too, Charlotte told her son Irish folk tales of banshee horrors and a true story of "the horrors she had suffered as a child in Sligo during the great cholera outbreak that claimed many thousands of victims in Ireland alone, and which provoked the most dreadful cruelties" (New York: The Fireside Press, 1962, p. 14). I cannot help but wonder how old Stoker was when his mother discussed these matters with him. Certainly, they made a vivid impression, for later, Charlotte wrote her story down and Bram based his own "The Invisible Giant" on his mother's tale of the cholera epidemic in Sligo.
7. Richardson, p. 419.
8. C. F. Bentley, "The Monster in the Bedroom: Sexual Symbolism in Bram Stoker's *Dracula*," *Literature and Psychology*, XXII, 1 (1972), 29.

that made me uneasy, some longing and at the same time deadly fear. I felt in my heart a wicked, burning desire that they would kiss me with those red lips. [42]

The three debate who has the right to feast on Jonathan first, but they conclude, "He is young and strong; there are kisses for us all" (47) [42]. While this discussion takes place, Jonathan is "in an agony of delightful anticipation" (48) [42]. At the very end of the novel, Van Helsing falls prey to the same attempted seduction by, and the same ambivalence toward, the three vampires.

Two more scenes of relatively explicit and uninhibited sexuality mark the novel about one-half, then two-thirds, through. First the scene in which Lucy Westenra is laid to her final rest by her fiance, Arthur Holmwood, later Lord Godalming, which is worth quoting from at length:

> Arthur placed the point [of the stake] over the heart, and as I looked I could see its dint in the white flesh. Then he struck with all his might.
>
> The thing in the coffin writhed; and a hideous, blood-curdling screech came from the opened red lips. The body shook and quivered and twisted in wild contortions; the sharp white teeth champed together till the lips were cut, and the mouth was smeared with a crimson foam. But Arthur never faltered. He looked like a figure of Thor as his untrembling arm rose and fell, driving deeper and deeper the mercy-bearing stake, whilst the blood from the pierced heart welled and spurted up around it (241). [192]

Such a description needs no comment here, though we will return to it in another context. Finally, the scene which Joseph Bierman has described quite correctly as a "primal scene in oral terms,"[9] the scene in which Dracula slits open his breast and forces Mina Harker to drink his blood:

> With his left hand he held both Mrs. Harker's hands, keeping them away with her arms at full tension; his right hand gripped her by the back of the neck, forcing her face down on his bosom. Her white nightdress was smeared with blood, and a thin stream trickled down the man's bare chest which was shown by his torn-open dress. The attitude of the two had a terrible resemblance to a child forcing a kitten's nose into a saucer of milk to compel it to drink (313). [247]

Two major points are to be made here, in addition to marking the clearly erotic nature of the descriptions. These are, in the main, the

9. Joseph S. Bierman, "*Dracula*: Prolonged Childhood Illness and the Oral Triad," *American Image*, XXIX, 194.

only sexual scenes and descriptions in the novel; and, not only are the scenes heterosexual,[1] they are incestuous, especially when taken together, as we shall see.

To consider the first point, only relations with vampires are sexualized in this novel; indeed, a deliberate attempt is made to make sexuality seem unthinkable in "normal relations" between the sexes. All the close relationships, including those between Lucy and her three suitors and Mina and her husband, are spiritualized beyond credibility. Only when Lucy becomes a vampire is she allowed to be "voluptuous," yet she must have been so long before, judging from her effect on men and from Mina's descriptions of her. (Mina, herself, never suffers the fate of voluptuousness before or after being bitten, for reasons which will become apparent later.) Clearly, then, vampirism is associated not only with death, immortality and orality; it is equivalent to sexuality.[2]

Moreover, in psychoanalytic terms, the vampirism is a disguise for greatly desired and equally strongly feared fantasies. These fantasies, as stated, have encouraged critics to point to the Oedipus complex at the center of the novel. Dracula, for example, is seen, as the "father-figure of huge potency."[3] Royce MacGillwray remarks that:

> Dracula even aspires to be, in a sense, the father of the band that is pursuing him. Because he intends, as he tells them, to turn them all into vampires, he will be their creator and therefore "father."[4]

The major focus of the novel, in this analysis, is the battle of the sons against the father to release the desired woman, the mother, she whom it is felt originally belonged to the son till the father seduced her away. Richardson comments:

> the set-up reminds one rather of the primal horde as pictured somewhat fantastically perhaps by Freud in *Totem and Taboo*, with the brothers banding together against the father who has tried to keep all the females to himself.[5]

The Oedipal rivalry is not, however, merely a matter of the Van Helsing group, in which, as Richardson says, "Van Helsing represents the good father figure,"[6] pitted against the Big Daddy, Dracula. Rather, from the novel's beginning, a marked rivalry among the men is evident. This rivalry is defended against by the constant, almost obsessive, assertion of the value of friendship and *agape* among members of the Van Hels-

1. Bentley, p. 27,
2. See Tsvetan Todorov, *The Fantastic*, trans, Richard Howard (Cleveland: Case Western Reserve, 1973), pp. 136–39.
3. Richardson, p. 427.
4. MacGillwray, p. 522.
5. Richardson, p. 428. The Oedipal fantasy of the destruction of the father is reinforced by a number of additional, and actually gratuitous, paternal deaths in the novel. See also MacGillwray, p. 523.
6. Richardson, p. 428.

ing group. Specifically, the defense of overcompensation is employed, most often by Van Helsing in his assertions of esteem for Dr. Seward and his friends. The others, too, repeat expressions of mutual affection *ad* nauseam: they clearly protest too much. Perhaps this is most obviously symbolized, and unintentionally exposed, by the blood transfusions from Arthur, Seward, Quincey Morris, and Van Helsing to Lucy Westenra. The great friendship among rivals for Lucy's hand lacks credibility and is especially strained when Van Helsing makes it clear that the transfusions (merely the reverse of the vampire's blood-letting) are in their nature sexual; others have recognized, too, that Van Helsing's warning to Seward not to tell Arthur that anyone else has given Lucy blood, indicates the sexual nature of the operation.[7] Furthermore, Arthur himself feels that, as a result of having given Lucy his blood, they are in effect married. Thus, the friendships of the novel mask a deep-seated rivalry and hostility.

Dracula does then appear to enact the Oedipal rivalry among sons and between the son and the father for the affections of the mother. The fantasy of parricide and its acting out is obviously satisfying. According to Holland, such a threatening wish-fulfillment can be rewarding when properly defended against or associated with other pleasurable fantasies. Among the other fantasies are those of life after death, the triumph of "good over evil," mere man over super-human forces, and the rational West over the mysterious East.[8] Most likely not frightening and certainly intellectualized, these simplistic abstractions provide a diversion from more threatening material and assure the fantast that God's in his heaven; all's right with the world. On the surface, this is the moral of the end of the novel: Dracula is safely reduced to ashes, Mina is cleansed, the "boys" are triumphant. Were this all the theme of interest the novel presented, however, it would be neither so popular with Victorians and their successors nor worthy of scholarly concern.

Up to now my discussion has been taken from the point of view of reader identification with those who are doing battle against the evil in this world, against Count Dracula. On the surface of it, this is where one's sympathies lie in reading the novel and it is this level of analysis which has been explored by previous critics. However, what is far more significant in the interrelation of fantasy and defense is the duplication of characters and structure which betrays an identification with Dracula and a fantasy of matricide underlying the more obvious parricidal wishes.

As observed, the split between the sexual vampire family and the asexual Van Helsing group is not at all clear-cut: Jonathan, Van Helsing, Seward and Holmwood are all overwhelmingly attracted to the vampires, to sexuality. Fearing this, they employ two defenses, projec-

---

7. See, for instance, Richardson, p. 427.
8. Richard Wasson, "The Politics of *Dracula*," *English Literature in Translation*, IX, pp. 24–27.

tion[9] and denial: it is not we who want the vampires, it is they who want us (to eat us, to seduce us, to kill us). Despite the projections, we should recall that almost all the on-stage killing is done by the "good guys": that of Lucy, the vampire women, and Dracula. The projection of the wish to kill onto the vampires wears thinnest perhaps when Dr. Seward, contemplating the condition of Lucy, asserts that "had she then to be killed I could have done it with savage delight" (236) [188]. Even earlier, when Dr. Seward is rejected by Lucy, he longs for a cause with which to distract himself from the pain of rejection: "Oh, Lucy, Lucy, I cannot be angry with you. . . . If I only could have as strong a cause as my poor mad friend there [significantly, he refers to Renfield]—a good, unselfish cause to make me work—that would be indeed happiness" (84) [71]. Seward's wish is immediately fulfilled by Lucy's vampirism and the subsequent need to destroy her. Obviously, the acting out of such murderous impulses is threatening: in addition to the defenses mentioned above, the use of religion not only to exorcise the evil but to justify the murders is striking. In other words, Christianity is on our side, *we must* be right. In this connection, it is helpful to mention Wasson's observation[1] of the significance of the name "Lord Godalming" (the point is repeated). Additional justification is provided by the murdered themselves: the peace into which they subside is to be read as a thank you note. Correlated with the religious defense is one described by Freud in *Totem and Taboo* in which the violator of the taboo can avert disaster by Lady MacBeth-like compulsive rituals and renunciations.[2] The repeated use of the Host, the complicated ritual of the slaying of the vampires, and the ostensible, though not necessarily conscious, renunciation of sexuality are the penance paid by those in *Dracula* who violate the taboos against incest and the murder of parents.

Since we now see that Dracula acts out the repressed fantasies of the others, since those others wish to do what he can do, we have no difficulty in recognizing an identification with the aggressor on the part of characters and reader alike. It is important, then, to see what it is that Dracula is after.

The novel tells of two major episodes, the seduction of Lucy and of Mina, to which the experience of Harker at Castle Dracula provides a preface, a hero, one whose narrative encloses the others and with whom, therefore, one might readily identify. This, however, is a defense against the central identification of the novel with Dracula and his attacks on the women. It is relevant in this context to observe how spontaneous and ultimately trivial Dracula's interest in Harker is. When

9. Freud, *Totem and Taboo*, trans. James Strachey in *The Standard Edition of the Complete Psychological Works of Sigmund Freud*, Vol. XIII (1913–1914) (London: Hogarth press, 1962), 60–63.
1. Wasson, p. 26.
2. Freud, pp. 37ff.

Harker arrives at Castle Dracula, his host makes a lunge for him, but only after Harker has cut his finger and is bleeding. Dracula manages to control himself and we hear no more about his interest in Harker's blood until the scene with the vampire women when he says, "This man belongs to me!" (49) [43] and, again a little later, "have patience. Tonight is mine. To-morrow night is yours!" (61) [52] After this we hear no more of Dracula's interest in Jonathan; indeed, when Dracula arrives in England, he never again goes after Jonathan. For his part, Jonathan appears far more concerned about the vampire women than about Dracula—they are more horrible and fascinating to him. Indeed, Harker is relieved to be saved from the women by Dracula. Moreover, the novel focusses on the Lucy and Mina episodes from which, at first, the Jonathan episodes may seem disconnected; actually, they are not, but we can only see why after we understand what is going on in the rest of the novel.

In accepting the notion of identification with the aggressor in *Dracula*, as I believe we must, what we accept is an understanding of the reader's identification with the aggressor's victimization of women. Dracula's desire is for the destruction of Lucy and Mina and what this means is obvious when we recall that his attacks on these two closest of friends seem incredibly coincidental on the narrative level. Only on a deeper level is there no coincidence at all: the level on which one recognizes that Lucy and Mina are essentially the same figure: the mother. Dracula is, in fact, the same story told twice with different outcomes. In the former, the mother is more desirable, more sexual, more threatening and must be destroyed. And the physical descriptions of Lucy reflect this greater ambivalence: early in the story, when Lucy is not yet completely vampirized, Dr. Seward describes her hair "in its usual sunny ripples"; (180) [146]; later, when the men watch her return to her tomb, Lucy is described as "a dark-haired woman" (235) [187]. The conventional fair/dark split, symbolic of respective moral casts, seems to be unconscious here, reflecting the ambivalence aroused by the sexualized female. Not only is Lucy the more sexualized figure, she is the more rejecting figure, rejecting two of the three "sons" in the novel. This section of the book ends with her destruction, not by Dracula but by the man whom she was to marry. The novel could not end here, though; the story had to be told again to assuage the anxiety occasioned by matricide. This time, the mother is much less sexually threatening and is ultimately saved. Moreover, Mina is never described physically and is the opposite of rejecting: all the men become her sons, symbolized by the naming of her actual son after them all. What remains constant is the attempt to destroy the mother. What changes is the way the fantasies are managed. To speak of the novel in terms of the child's ambivalence toward the mother is not just to speak psychoanalytically. We need only recall that Lucy, as "bloofer lady," as well as the other vampire women, prey on children. In the case of Lucy, the children are as attracted to her as threatened by her.

I have already described the evidence that the Van Helsing men themselves desire to do away with Lucy. Perhaps the story needed to be retold because the desire was too close to the surface to be satisfying; certainly, the reader would not be satisfied had the novel ended with Arthur's murder of Lucy. What is perhaps not so clear is that the desire to destroy Mina is equally strong. Let us look first at the defenses against this desire. I have already mentioned the great professions of affection for Mina made by most of the male characters. Mina indeed acts and is treated as both the saint and the mother (ironically, this is particularly clear when she comforts Arthur for the loss of Lucy). She is all good, all pure, all true. When, however, she is seduced away from the straight and narrow by Dracula, she is "unclean," tainted and stained with a mark on her forehead immediately occasioned by Van Helsing's touching her forehead with the Host. Van Helsing's hostility toward Mina is further revealed when he cruelly reminds her of her "intercourse" with Dracula: " 'Do you forget,' he said, with actually a smile, 'that last night he banqueted heavily and will sleep late?' " (328) [258] This hostility is so obvious that the other men are shocked. Nevertheless, the "sons," moreover, and the reader as well, identify with Dracula's attack on Mina; indeed, the men cause it, as indicated by the events which transpire when all the characters are at Seward's hopsital-asylum. The members of the brotherhood go out at night to seek out Dracula's lairs, and they leave Mina undefended at the hospital. They claim that this insures her safety; in fact, it insures the reverse. Furthermore, this is the real purpose in leaving Mina out of the plans and in the hospital. They have clear indications in Renfield's warnings of what is to happen to her and they all, especially her husband, observe that she is not well and seems to be getting weaker. That they could rationalize these signs away while looking for and finding them everywhere else further indicates that they are avoiding seeing what they want to ignore; in other words, they want Dracula to get her. This is not to deny that they also want to save Mina; it is simply to claim that the ambivalence toward the mother is fully realized in the novel.

We can now return to that ambivalence and, I believe, with the understanding of the significance of the mother figure, comprehend the precise perspective of the novel. Several critics have correctly emphasized the regression to both orality and anality[3] in *Dracula*. Certainly, the sexuality is perceived in oral terms. The primal scene already discussed makes abundantly clear that intercourse is perceived in terms of nursing. As C. F. Bentley sees it:

3. Bentley, pp. 29–30; MacGillwray, p. 522.

> Stoker is describing a symbolic act of enforced fellation, where
> blood is again a substitute for semen, and where a chaste female
> suffers a violation that is essentially sexual. Of particular interest
> in the . . . passage is the striking image of "a child forcing a kitten's
> nose into a saucer of milk to compel it to drink," suggesting an
> element of regressive infantilism in the vampire superstition.[4]

The scene referred to is, in several senses, the climax of the novel; it
is the most explicit view of the act of vampirism and is, therefore, all
the more significant as an expression of the nature of sexual intercourse
as the novel depicts it. In it, the woman is doing the sucking. Bierman
comments that "The reader by this point in the novel has become used
to Dracula doing the sucking, but not to Dracula being sucked and
specifically at the breast."[5] While it is true that the reader may most
often think of Dracula as the active partner, the fact is that the scenes
of vampire sexuality are described from the male perspective, with the
females as the active assailants.[6] Only the acts of phallic aggression,
the killings, involve the males in active roles. *Dracula*, then, dramatizes
the child's view of intercourse insofar as it is seen as a wounding and
a killing. But the primary preoccupation, as attested to by the primal
scene, is with the role of the female in the act. Thus, it is not surprising
that the central anxiety of the novel is the fear of the devouring woman
and, in documenting this, we will find that all the pieces of the novel
fall into place, most especially the Jonathan Harker prologue.

As mentioned, Harker's desire and primary anxiety is not with Dracula but with the female vampires. In his initial and aborted seduction
by them, he describes his ambivalence. Interestingly, Harker seeks out
this episode by violating the Count's (father's) injunction to remain in
his room; "let me warn you with all seriousness, that should you leave
these rooms you will not by any chance go to sleep in any other part
of the castle" (42) [38]. This, of course, is what Harker promptly does.
When Dracula breaks in and discovers Harker with the vampire
women, he acts like both a jealous husband and an irate father: "His
eyes were positively blazing. The red light in them was lurid. . . . 'How
dare you touch him, any of you?' " (48–49) [43]. Jonathan's role as
child here is reinforced by the fact that, when Dracula takes him away
from the women, he gives them a child as substitute. But most interesting is Jonathan's perspective as he awaits, in a state of erotic arousal,

4. Bentley, p. 30.
5. Bierman, p. 194. Bierman's analysis is concerned to demonstrate that "*Dracula* mirrors Stoker's early childhood . . . ," and is a highly speculative but fascinating study. The emphasis
is on Stoker's rivalry with his brothers but it provides, albeit indirectly, further evidence of
hostility toward the rejecting mother.
6. Ludlam cites one of the actors in the original stage production of *Dracula* as indicating that
the adaptation was so successful that "Disturbances in the circle or stalls as people felt faint
and had to be taken out were not uncommon—and they were perfectly genuine, not a publicity stunt. Strangely enough, they were generally men'. " (Ludlam, 1.165).

the embraces of the vampire women, especially the fair one: "The other was fair as fair can be, with great wavy masses of golden hair and eyes like pale sapphires. I seemed somehow to know her face and to know it in connection with some dreamy fear, but I could not recollect at the moment how or where" (47) [42]. As far as we know, Jonathan never recollects, but we should be able to understand that the face is that of the mother (almost archetypally presented), she whom he desires yet fears, the temptress-seductress, Medusa. Moreover, this golden girl reappears in the early description of Lucy.

At the end of the following chapter, Jonathan exclaims, "I am alone in the castle with those awful women. Faugh! Mina is a woman, and there is nought in common." Clearly, however, there is. Mina at the breast of Count Dracula is identical to the vampire women whose desire is to draw out of the male the fluid necessary for life. That this is viewed as an act of castration is clear from Jonathan's conclusion: "At least God's mercy is better than that of these monsters, and the precipice is steep and high. At its foot a man may sleep—*as a man*. Goodbye, all! Mina!" (4; emphasis mine) [55].

The threatening Oedipal fantasy, the regression to a primary oral obsession, the attraction and destruction of the vampires of *Dracula* are, then, interrelated and interdependent. What they spell out is a fusion of the memory of nursing at the mother's breast with a primal scene fantasy which results in the conviction that the sexually desirable woman will annihilate if she is not first destroyed. The fantasy of incest and matricide evokes the mythic image of the *vagina dentata* evident in so many folk tales[7] in which the mouth and the vagina are identified with one another by the primitive mind and pose the threat of castration to all men until the teeth are extracted by the hero. The conclusion of *Dracula*, the "salvation" of Mina, is equivalent to such an "extraction": Mina will not remain the *vagina dentata* to threaten them all.

Central to the structure and unconscious theme of *Dracula* is, then, primarily the desire to destroy the threatening mother, she who threatens by being desirable. Otto Rank best explains why it is Dracula whom the novel seems to portray as the threat when he says, in a study which is pertinent to ours:

> through the displacement of anxiety on to the father, the renunciation of the mother, necessary for the sake of life is assured. For this feared father prevents the return to the mother and thereby the releasing of the much more painful primary anxiety, which is related to the mother's genitals as the place of birth and later transferred to objects taking the place of the genitals [such as the mouth].[8]

7. See, for instance, Wolfgang Lederer, M.D., *The Fear of Women* (New York: Harcourt Brace Jovanovich, Inc., 1968), especially the chapter entitled, "A Snapping of Teeth."
8. Otto Rank, *The Trauma of Birth* (New York: Harper & Row, 1973), p. 73.

Finally, the novel has it both ways: Dracula is destroyed[9] and Van Helsing saved; Lucy is destroyed and Mina saved. The novel ends on a rather ironic note, given our understanding here, as Harker concludes with a quote from the good father, Van Helsing:

> "We want no proofs; we ask none to believe us! This boy will some day know what a brave and gallant woman his mother is. Already he knows her sweetness and loving care; later on he will understand how some men so loved her, that they did dare so much for her sake" (416). [327]

CAROL A. SENF

Dracula: The Unseen Face in the Mirror†

The fault, dear Brutus, is not in our stars,
But in ourselves, that we are underlings.
Julius Caesar, I, ii, 134–35

Published in 1897, *Dracula* is an immensely popular novel which has never been out of print, has been translated into at least a dozen languages, and has been the subject of more films than any other novel. Only recently, however, have students of literature begun to take it seriously, partially because of the burgeoning interest in popular culture and partially because *Dracula* is a work which raises a number of troubling questions about ourselves and our society.[1] Despite this growing interest in Bram Stoker's best-known novel, the majority of literary critics read *Dracula* as a popular myth about the opposition of Good and Evil without bothering to address more specifically literary matters such as style, characterization, and method of narration. This article, on the other hand, focuses on Stoker's narrative technique in general and specifically on his choice of unreliable narrators. As a result, my reading of *Dracula* is a departure from most standard interpretations in that it revolves, not around the conquest of Evil by Good, but on the similarities between the two.

---

9. When discussing this paper with a class, two of my students argued that Dracula is not, in fact, destroyed at the novel's conclusion. They maintained that his last look is one of triumph and that his heart is not staked but pierced by a mere bowie knife. Their suggestion that, at least, the men do not follow the elaborate procedures to insure the destruction of Dracula that they religiously observe with regard to that of the women, is certainly of value here, whether one agrees that Dracula still stalks the land. My thanks to Lucinda Donnelly and Barbara Kotacka for these observations.

† Reprinted by permission from *The Journal of Narrative Technique* 9 (1979): 160–70.

1. Recent full-length studies of *Dracula* include the following books: Radu Florescu and Raymond T. McNally, *In Search of Dracula* (New York: New York Graphic Society, 1972); Gabriel Ronay, *The Truth About Dracula* (New York: Stein and Day, 1972); and Leonard Wolf, *A Dream of Dracula: In Search of the Living Dead* (Boston: Little, Brown and Company, 1972).

More familiar with the numerous film interpretations than with
Stoker's novel, most modern readers are likely to be surprised by *Dracula* and its intensely topical themes; and both the setting and the
method of narration which Stoker chose contribute to this sense of
immediacy. Instead of taking place in a remote Transylvanian castle or
a timeless and dreamlike "anywhere," most of the action occurs in
nineteenth-century London. Furthermore, Stoker de-emphasizes the
novel's mythic qualities by telling the story through a series of journal
extracts, personal letters, and newspaper clippings—the very written record of everyday life. The narrative technique resembles a vast jigsaw
puzzle of isolated and frequently trivial facts; and it is only when the
novel is more than half over that the central characters piece these
fragments together and, having concluded the Dracula is a threat to
themselves and their society, band together to destroy him.

On the surface, the novel appears to be a mythic re-enactment of
the opposition between Good and Evil because the narrators attribute
their pursuit and ultimate defeat of Dracula to a high moral purpose.
However, although his method of narration doesn't enable him to comment directly on his characters' failures in judgment or lack of self-
knowledge, Stoker provides several clues to their unreliability and
encourages the reader to see the frequent discrepancies between their
professed beliefs and their actions. The first clue is an anonymous preface (unfortunately omitted in many modern editions) which gives the
reader a distinct warning:

> How these papers have been placed in sequence will be made
> manifest in the reading of them. All needless matters have been
> eliminated, so that a history almost at variance with the possibilities
> of later-day belief may stand forth as simple fact. There is through-
> out no statement of past things wherein memory may err, for all
> the records chosen are exactly contemporary, *given from the stand-
> points and within the range of knowledge of those who made them.*[2]

Writers of Victorian popular fiction frequently rely on the convention
of the anonymous editor to introduce their tales and to provide additional comments throughout the text; and Stoker uses this convention
to stress the subjective nature of the story which his narrators relate.
The narrators themselves occasionally question the validity of their per-
ceptions, but Stoker provides numerous additional clues to their unreliability. For example, at the conclusion, Jonathan Harker questions
their interpretation of the events:

> We were stuck with the fact, that in all the mass of material of
> which the record is composed, there is hardly one authentic doc-
> ument; nothing but a mass of typewriting, except the later note-

---

2. Leonard Wolf, *The Annotated Dracula* (New York: Clarkson N. Potter, Inc., 1975), my italics.

books of Mina and Seward and myself, and Van Helsing's
memorandum. We could hardly ask any one, even did we wish
to, to accept these as proofs of so wild a story.[3] [326–27]

The conclusion reinforces the subjective nature of their tale and casts
doubts on everything that had preceded; however, because Stoker does
not use an obvious framing device like Conrad in *Heart of Darkness* or
James in *The Turn of the Screw* or employ an intrusive editor as Haggard
does in *She* and because all the narrators come to similar conclusions
about the nature of their opponent, the reader is likely to forget that
these documents are subjective records, interpretations which are
"given within the range of knowledge of those who made them."
    While Stoker's choice of narrative technique does not permit him to
comment directly on his characters, he suggests that they are particularly ill-equipped to judge the extraordinary events with which they are
faced. The three central narrators are perfectly ordinary nineteenth-
century Englishmen: the young lawyer Jonathan Harker, his wife Mina,
and a youthful psychiatrist Dr. John Seward. Other characters who
sometimes function as narrators include Dr. Van Helsing, Seward's
former teacher; Quincey Morris, an American adventurer; Arthur
Holmwood, a young English nobleman; and Lucy Westenra, Holmwood's fiancée. With the exception of Dr. Van Helsing, all the central
characters are youthful and inexperienced—two dimensional characters
whose only distinguishing characteristics are their names and their professions; and by maintaining a constancy of style throughout and em-
phasizing the beliefs which they hold in common, Stoker further
diminishes any individualizing traits.[4] The narrators appear to speak
with one voice; and Stoker suggests that their opinions are perfectly
acceptable so long as they remain within their limited fields of expertise.
The problem, however, is that these perfectly ordinary people are confronted with the extraordinary character of Dracula.
    Although Stoker did model Dracula on the historical Vlad V of Wal-
lachia and the East European superstition of the vampire,[5] he adds a

3. Bram Stoker, *Dracula* (1896; rpt. New York: Dell Publishing Co., 1971), p. 416. All future
   references will be to this edition and will be included within the text. Bracketed page numbers
   refer to this Norton Critical Edition.
4. Stephanie Demetrakopoulos addresses another facet of this similarity by showing that male
   and female sexual roles are frequently reversed in *Dracula*. Her article, "Feminism, Sex Role
   Exchanges, and Other Subliminal Fantasies in Bram Stoker's *Dracula*," is included in *Frontiers: A Journal of Women Studies*, 2 (1977), pp. 104–113.
5. Stoker could have learned of Vlad from a number of sources. Ronay adds in a footnote that
   "The Millenary of Honfoglalas, the Hungarian invasion of their present-day territory, was
   being celebrated with great pomp and circumstance in 1896—the year when Stoker was
   writing *Dracula*" (p. 56). Another possible source is cited by G. Nandris, "A Philological
   Analysis of Dracula and Rumanian Placenames and Masculine Personal Names in -a/ea,"
   Slavonic and East European Review, 37 (1959), p. 371:

   The Rumanian historian I. Bogdan, who published a monograph in 1896 on the prince
   of Wallachia, Vlad V, nicknamed Tsepesh (The Impaler), and who edited in it two
   German and four Russian versions of the Dracula legend. . . .

number of humanizing touches to make Dracula appear noble and vulnerable as well as demonic and threatening; and it becomes difficult to determine whether he is a hideous bloodsucker whose touch breeds death or a lonely and silent figure who is hunted and persecuted.[6] The difficulty in interpreting Dracula's character is compounded by the narrative technique, for the reader quickly recognizes that Dracula is *never* seen objectively and never permitted to speak for himself while his actions are recorded by people who have determined to destroy him and who, moreover, repeatedly question the sanity of their quest.

The question of sanity, which is so important in *Dracula*, provides another clue to the narrators' unreliability. More than half the novel takes place in or near Dr. Seward's London mental institution; and several of the characters are shown to be emotionally unstable: Renfield, one of Dr. Seward's patients, is an incarcerated madman who believes that he can achieve immortality by drinking the blood of insects and other small creatures; Jonathan Harker suffers a nervous breakdown after he escapes from Dracula's castle; and Lucy Westenra exhibits signs of schizophrenia, being a model of sweetness and conformity while she is awake but becoming sexually aggressive and demanding during her sleepwalking periods. More introspective than most of the other narrators, Dr. Seward occasionally refers to the questionable sanity of their mission, his diary entries mentioning his fears that they will all wake up in straitjackets. Furthermore, his entries on Renfield's condition indicate that he recognizes the narrow margin which separates sanity from insanity: "It is wonderful, however, what intellectual recuperative power lunatics have, for within a few minutes he stood up quite calmly and looked about him" (p. 133) [109].

However, even if the reader chooses to ignore the question of the narrators' sanity, it is important to understand their reasons for wishing to destroy Dracula. They accuse him of murdering the crew of the *Demeter*,[7] of killing Lucy Westenra and transforming her into a vampire, and of trying to do the same thing to Mina Harker. However, the log found on the dead body of the *Demeter's* captain, which makes only a few ambiguous allusions to a fiend or monster, is hysterical and inconclusive. Recording this "evidence," Mina's journal asserts that the verdict of the inquest was open-ended: "There is no evidence to adduce; and whether or not the man [the ship's captain] committed the

6. Royce MacGillivray explains how Stoker altered the Dracula story:

> In real life Dracula was known for his horrifying cruelty, but Stoker, who wanted a monster that his readers could both shudder at and identify with, omits all mention of the dark side of his reputation and emphasizes his greatness as a warrior chieftain.

"*Dracula*, Bram Stoker's Spoiled Masterpiece," *Queen's Quarterly*, 79 (1972), p. 520.

7. It is significant that Dracula—who is portrayed as a sexual threat—comes to England on a ship named for the Greek goddess of fertility. Furthermore, he returns to his homeland on the *Czarina Catherine*; and Stoker probably expected his readers to know the stories of Catherine's legendary sexual appetite.

murders there is now none to say" (p. 100) [84]. Lucy's death might just as easily be attributed to the blood transfusions (still a dangerous procedure at the time Stoker wrote *Dracula*) to which Dr. Van Helsing subjects her; and Mina acknowledges her complicity in the affair with Dracula by admitting that she did not want to prevent his advances. Finally, even if Dracula is responsible for all the Evil of which he is accused, he is tried, convicted, and sentenced by men (including two lawyers) who give him no opportunity to explain his actions and who repeatedly violate the laws which they profess to be defending: they avoid an inquest of Lucy's death, break into her tomb and desecrate her body, break into Dracula's houses, frequently resort to bribery and coercion to avoid legal involvement, and openly admit that they are responsible for the deaths of five alleged vampires. While it can be argued that *Dracula* is a fantasy and therefore not subject to the laws of verisimilitude, Stoker uses the flimsiness of such "evidence" to focus on the contrast between the narrators' rigorous moral arguments and their all-too-pragmatic methods.

In fact, Stoker reveals that what condemns Dracula are the English characters' subjective responses to his character and to the way of life which he represents. The reader is introduced to Dracula by Jonathan Harker's journal. His first realization that Dracula is different from himself occurs when he looks into the mirror and discovers that Dracula casts no reflection:

> This time there could be no error, for the man was close to me, and I could see him over my shoulder. But there was no reflection of him in the mirror! The whole room behind me was displayed; but there was no sign of a man in it, except myself. This was startling, and, coming on the top of so many strange things, was beginning to increase that vague sense of uneasiness which I always have when the Count is near.   (p. 34) [30–31]

The fact that vampires cast no reflection is part of the iconography of the vampire in East European folklore, but Stoker translates the superstitious belief that creatures without souls have no reflection into a metaphor by which he can illustrate his characters' lack of moral vision. Harker's inability to "see" Dracula is a manifestation of moral blindness which reveals his insensitivity to others and (as will become evident later) his inability to perceive certain traits within himself.[8]

Even before Harker begins to suspect that Dracula is a being totally unlike himself, Stoker reveals that he is troubled by everything that

---

8. Wolf comments on this characteristic in the preface to *The Annotated Dracula*:

> Here, then, is the figure that Bram Stoker created—a figure who confronts us with primordial mysteries: death, blood, and love, and how they are bound together. Finally, Stoker's achievement is this: he makes us understand in our own experience why the vampire is said to be invisible in the mirror. He is there, but we fail to recognize him since our own faces get in the way.

Dracula represents. While journeying from London to Transylvania, Harker muses on the quaint customs which he encounters; and he notes in his journal that he must question his host about them. Stoker uses Harker's perplexity to establish his character as a very parochial Englishman whose apparent curiosity is not a desire for understanding, but a need to have his preconceptions confirmed. However, instead of finding someone like himself at the end of his journey, a person who can provide a rational explanation for these examples of non-English behavior, Harker discovers a ruined castle, itself a memento of bygone ages, and a man who, reminding him that Transylvania is not England, prides himself on being an integral part of his nation's heroic past:

> . . . the Szekleys—and the Dracula as their heart's blood, their brains and their swords—can boast a record that mushroom growths like the Hapsburgs and the Romanoffs can never reach. The warlike days are over. Blood is too precious a thing in these days of dishonourable peace; and the glories of the great races are as a tale that is told. (p. 39) [35]

To Harker, Dracula initially appears to be an anachronism—an embodiment of the feudal past—rather than an innately evil being; and his journal entries at the beginning merely reproduce Dracula's pride and rugged individualism:

> Here I am noble; I am *boyar*; the common people know me, and I am master. But a stranger in a strange land, he is no one; men know him not—and to know not is to care not for. . . . I have been so long master that I would be master still—or at least that none other should be master of me. (p. 28) [26]

It is only when Harker realizes that he is assisting to take this anachronism to England that he becomes frightened.

Harker's later response indicates that he fears a kind of reverse imperialism, the threat of the primitive trying to colonize the civilized world, while the reader sees in his response a profound resemblance between Harker and Dracula:

> This was the being I was helping to transfer to London, where perhaps for centuries to come he might . . . satiate his lust for blood, and create a new and ever-widening circle of semi-demons to batten on the helpless. The very thought drove me mad. A terrible desire came upon me to rid the world of such a monster. There was no lethal weapon at hand, but I seized a shovel which the workmen had been using to fill the cases, and lifting it high, struck, with the edge downward, at the hateful face.
> (pp. 62–63) [53–54]

This scene reinforces Harker's earlier inability to see Dracula in the mirror. Taken out of context, it would be difficult to distinguish the man from the monster. Behavior generally attributed to the vampire—the habit of attacking a sleeping victim, violence, and irrational behavior—is revealed to be the behavior of the civilized Englishman also. The sole difference is that Stoker's narrative technique does not permit the reader to enter Dracula's thoughts as he stands over his victims. The reversal of roles here is important because it establishes the subjective nature of the narrators' beliefs, suggests their lack of self-knowledge, and serves to focus on the similarities between the narrators and their opponent. Later in the novel, Mina Harker provides the following analysis of Dracula which ironically also describes the single-mindedness of his pursuers:

> The Count is a criminal and of criminal type . . . and *qua* criminal he is of imperfectly formed mind. Thus, in a difficulty he has to seek resource in habit. . . . Then, as he is criminal he is selfish; and as his intellect is small and his action is based on selfishness, he confines himself to one purpose. (p. 378) [296–97]

Both Mina and Jonathan can justify their pursuit of Dracula by labeling him a murderer; and Mina adds intellectual frailty to his alleged sins. However, the narrators show themselves to be equally bound by habit and equally incapable of evaluating situations which are beyond their limited spheres of expertise. In fact, Stoker implies that the only difference between Dracula and his opponents is the narrators' ability to state individual desire in terms of what they believe is a common good. For example, the above scene shows that Harker can justify his violent attack on Dracula because he pictures himself as the protector of helpless millions; and the narrators insist on the duty to defend the innocents.

The necessity of protecting the innocent is called into question, however, when Dr. Van Helsing informs the other characters about the vampire's nature. While most of his discussion concerns the vampire's susceptibility to garlic, silver bullets, and religious artifacts, Van Helsing also admits that the vampire cannot enter a dwelling unless he is first invited by one of the inhabitants. In other words, a vampire cannot influence a human being without that person's consent. Dracula's behavior confirms that he is an internal, not an external, threat. Although perfectly capable of using superior strength when he must defend himself, he usually employs seduction, relying on the others' desires to emulate his freedom from external constraints: Renfield's desire for immortality, Lucy's wish to escape the repressive existence of an upper-class woman, and the desires of all the characters to overcome the restraints placed on them by their religion and their law. As the spokesman for civilization, Van Helsing appears to understand that the others might be tempted by their desires to become like Dracula and he warns them against the temptation:

> But to fail here, is not mere life or death. It is that we become as him; that we henceforward become foul things of the night like him—without heart or conscience, preying on the bodies and the souls of those we love best.   (p. 265) [209]

Becoming like Dracula, they too would be laws unto themselves—primitive, violent, irrational—with nothing to justify their actions except the force of their desires. No longer would they need to rationalize their "preying on the bodies and souls of their loved ones" by concealing their lust for power under the rubric of religion, their love of violence under the names of imperialism and progress, their sexual desires within an elaborate courtship ritual.

The narrators attribute their hatred of Dracula to a variety of causes. Harker's journal introduces a being whose way of life is antithetical to theirs—a warlord, a representative of the feudal past and the leader of a primitive cult who he fears will attempt to establish a vampire colony in England. Mina Harker views him as a criminal and as the murderer of her best friend; and Van Helsing sees him as a moral threat, a kind of Anti-Christ. Yet, in spite of the narrators' moral and political language, Stoker reveals that Dracula is primarily a sexual threat, a missionary of desire whose only true kingdom will be the human body. Although he flaunts his independence of social restraints and proclaims himself a master over all he sees, Dracula adheres more closely to English law than his opponents in every area except his sexual behavior. (In fact, Dracula admits to Harker that he invited him to Transylvania so he could learn the subtle nuances of English law and business.) Neither a thief, rapist, nor an overtly political threat, Dracula is dangerous because he expresses his contempt for authority in the most individualistic of ways—through his sexuality. In fact, his thirst for blood and the manner in which he satisfies this thirst can be interpreted as sexual desire which fails to observe any of society's attempts to control it—prohibitions against polygamy, promiscuity, and homosexuality.[9]

9. A number of critics have commented on the pervasive sexuality of *Dracula*. C. F. Bentley, "The Monster in the Bedroom," *Literature and Psychology*, 22 (1972), p. 28:

> What is rejected or repressed on a conscious level appears in a covert and perverted form through the novel, the apparatus of the vampire superstition described in almost obsessional detail in *Dracula* providing the means for a symbolic presentation of human sexual relationships.

Maurice Richardson, "The Psychoanalysis of Ghost Stories," *The Twentieth Century*, 166 (1959), p. 429 describes Dracula as "a vast polymorph perverse bisexual oral-anal-genital sadomasochistic timeless orgy." In *A Dream of Dracula*, Wolf refers to the sexuality of Dracula:

> His kiss permits all unions: men and women; men and men; women and women; fathers and daughters; mothers and sons. Moreover, his is an easy love that evades the usual failures of the flesh. It is the triumph of passivity, unembarrassing, sensuous, throbbing, violent, and cruel.   (p. 303)

Furthermore, Stoker suggests that it is generally through sexuality that the vampire gains control over human beings. Van Helsing recognizes this temptation when he prevents Arthur from kissing Lucy right before her death; and even the staid and morally upright Harker momentarily succombs to the sensuality of the three vampire-women in Dracula's castle:

> I felt in my heart a wicked, burning desire that they would kiss me with those red lips. It is not good to note this down, lest some day it should meet Mina's eyes and cause her pain; but it is the truth.   (p. 47) [42]

For one brief moment, Harker does appear to recognize the truth about sexual desire; it is totally irrational and has nothing to do with monogamy, love, or even respect for the beloved. It is Dracula, however, who clearly articulates the characters' most intense fears of sexuality: "Your girls that you all love are mine already; and through them you and others shall yet be mine—my creatures, to do my bidding and to be my jackals when I want to feed" (p. 340) [267]. Implicit in Dracula's warning is the similarity between vampire and opponents. Despite rare moments of comprehension, however, the narrators generally choose to ignore this similarity; and their lack of self-knowledge permits them to hunt down and kill not only Dracula and the three women in his castle, but their friend Lucy Westenra as well.

The scene in which Arthur drives the stake through Lucy's body while the other men watch thoughtfully is filled with a violent sexuality which again connects vampire and opponents:

> But Arthur never faltered. He looked like a figure of Thor as his untrembling arm rose and fell, driving deeper and deeper the mercy-bearing stake, whilst the blood from the pierced heart welled and spurted up around it. His face was set, and high duty seemed to shine through it; the sight of it gave us courage so that our voices seemed to ring through the vault. . . . There in the coffin lay no longer the foul Thing that we had dreaded and grown to hate that the work of her destruction was yielded as a privilege to the one best entitled to it, but Lucy as we had seen her in life, with her face of unequalled sweetness and purity. (p. 241) [192]

Despite Seward's elevated moral language, the scene resembles nothing so much as the combined group rape and murder of an unconscious woman; and this kind of violent attack on a helpless victim is precisely the kind of behavior which condemns Dracula in the narrators' eyes.

Joseph S. Bierman, "Dracula: Prolonged Childhood Illness and the Oral Triad," *American Imago*, 29 (1972), pp. 186–98. Bierman studies Stoker's life and concludes that much of Dracula can be attributed to Stoker's repressed death wishes toward his brothers and toward his employer Henry Irving.

Moreover, Lucy is not the only woman to be subjected to this violence. At the conclusion, in a scene which is only slightly less explicit, Dr. Van Helsing destroys the three women in Dracula's castle. Again Dr. Van Helsing admits that he is fascinated by the beautiful visages of the "wanton Un-Dead" but he never acknowledges that his violent attack is simply a role reversal or that he becomes the vampire as he stands over their unconscious bodies.

By the conclusion of the novel, all the characters who have been accused of expressing individual desire have been appropriately punished: Dracula, Lucy Westenra, and the three vampire-women have been killed; and even Mina Harker is ostracized for her momentary indiscretion. All that remains after the primitive, the passionate, and the individualistic qualities that were associated with the vampire have been destroyed is a small group of wealthy men who return after a period of one year to the site of their victory over the vampire. The surviving characters remain unchanged by the events in their lives and never come to the realization that their commitment to social values merely masks their violence and their sexuality; and the only significant difference in their condition is the birth of the Harkers' son who is appropriately named for all the men who had participated in the conquest of Dracula. Individual sexual desire has apparently been so absolutely effaced that the narrators see this child as the result of their social union rather than the product of a sexual union between one man and one woman.

The narrators insist that they are agents of God and are able to ignore their similarity to the vampire because their commitment to social values such as monogamy, proper English behavior, and the will of the majority enables them to conceal their violence and their sexual desires from each other and even from themselves. Stoker, however, reveals that these characteristics are merely masked by social convention. Instead of being eliminated, violence and sexuality emerge in particularly perverted forms.

Recently uncovered evidence suggests that Bram Stoker may have had very personal reasons for his preoccupation with repression and sexuality. In his biography of his great-uncle, Daniel Farson explains that, while the cause of Stoker's death is usually given as exhaustion, Stoker actually died of tertiary syphillis, exhaustion being one of the final stages of that disease. Farson also adds that Stoker's problematic relationship with his wife may have been responsible:

> When his wife's frigidity drove him to other women, probably prostitutes among them, Bram's writing showed signs of guilt and sexual frustration. . . . He probably caught syphilis around the turn of the century, possibly as early as the year of Dracula, 1896. (It usually takes ten to fifteen years before it kills.) By 1897 it seems

that he had been celibate for more than twenty years, as far as Florence [his wife] was concerned.[1]

Poignantly aware from his own experience that the face of the vampire is the hidden side of the human character, Stoker creates unreliable narrators to tell a tale, not of the overcoming of Evil by Good, but of the similarities between the two. *Dracula* reveals the unseen face in the mirror; and Stoker's message is similar to the passage from *Julius Caesar* which prefaces this article and might be paraphrased in the following manner: "The fault, dear reader, is not in our external enemies, but in ourselves."

FRANCO MORETTI

[A Capital *Dracula*]†

* * *

Count Dracula is an aristocrat only in manner of speaking. Jonathan Harker—the London estate agent who stays in his castle, and whose diary opens Stoker's novel—observes with astonishment that Dracula lacks precisely what makes a man 'noble': servants. Dracula stoops to driving the carriage, cooking the meals, making the beds, cleaning the castle. The Count has read Adam Smith: he knows that servants are unproductive workers who diminish the income of the person who keeps them. Dracula also lacks the aristocrat's conspicuous consumption: he does not eat, he does not drink, he does not make love, he does not like showy clothes, he does not go to the theatre and he does not go hunting, he does not hold receptions and does not build stately homes. Not even his violence has pleasure as its goal. Dracula (unlike Vlad the Impaler, the historical Dracula, and all other vampires before him) does not *like* spilling blood: he *needs* blood. He sucks just as much as is necessary and never wastes a drop. His ultimate aim is not to destroy the lives of others according to whim, to waste them, but to *use* them.[1] Dracula, in other words, is a saver, an ascetic, an upholder of the Protestant ethic. And in fact he has no body, or rather, he has no shadow. His body admittedly exists, but it is 'incorporeal'—'sensibly su-

---

1. Daniel Farson, *The Man Who Wrote Dracula: A Biography of Bram Stoker* (London: Michael Joseph, 1975), p. 234.

† From *Signs Taken for Wonders: Essays in the Sociology of Literary Forms*, Susan Fischer, David Forgacs, and David Miller, trans. (New York: Verso, 1988) 90–104. Reprinted by kind permission of the publisher.

1. Harker himself is forced to recognize this clear-headed bourgeois rationality in Dracula, after the latter has saved him from the purely destructive desire of his lovers: 'surely it is maddening to think that of all the foul things that lurk in this hateful place the Count is the least dreadful to me: that to him alone I can look for safety, even though this be only whilst I can *serve his purpose*.' (My italics). So *un*-cruel is Dracula that, once he has made use of Harker, he lets him go free without having harmed a hair on his head.

persensible' as Marx wrote of the commodity, 'impossible as a physical
fact', as Mary Shelley defines the monster in the first lines of her preface. In fact it is impossible, 'physically', to estrange a man from himself,
to de-humanize him. But alienated labour, as a *social* relation, makes
it possible. So too there really exists a social product which has no
body, which has exchange-value but no use-value. This product, we
know, is money.[2] And when Harker explores the castle, he finds just
one thing: 'a great heap of gold . . . —gold of all kinds, Roman, and
British, and Austrian, and Hungarian, and Greek and Turkish money,
covered with a film of dust, as though it had lain long in the ground.'
The money that had been buried comes back to life, becomes capital
and embarks on the conquest of the world: this and none other is the
story of Dracula the vampire.

'Capital is dead labour which, vampire-like, lives only by sucking
living labour, and lives the more, the more labour it sucks.'[3] Marx's
analogy unravels the vampire metaphor. As everyone knows, the vampire is dead and yet not dead: he is an Un-Dead, a 'dead' person who
yet manages to live thanks to the blood he sucks from the living. *Their*
strength becomes *his* strength.[4] The *stronger* the vampire becomes, the
weaker the living become: 'the capitalist gets rich, not, like the miser,
in proportion to his personal labour and restricted consumption, but at
the same rate as he squeezes out labour-power from others, and compels the worker to renounce all the enjoyments of life.'[5] Like capital,
Dracula is impelled towards a continuous growth, an unlimited expansion of his domain: accumulation is inherent in his nature. 'This',
Harker exclaims, 'was the being I was helping to transfer to London,
where, perhaps for centuries to come, he might, amongst its teeming
millions, satiate his lust for blood, and create a *new and ever widening*

2. Before Dracula there had been another literary character who had lost his shadow: Peter
Schlemihl. He had exchanged it for a purse full of money. But he soon realizes that money
can only give him one thing: more money, still more money, all the money he wants (the
purse is bottomless). But *only* money. The only desire Peter can satisfy is thus the abstract
and immaterial desire for money. His mutilated and unnatural body denies him access to
tangible, material, corporeal desires. So great a scandal is it that once the girl he loves (and
who loves him) finds out, she refuses to marry him. Peter runs away in desperation: he can
no longer love. (Just like Dracula: ' "You yourself have never loved; you never love!" . . .
Then the Count turned . . . and said in a soft whisper:—"Yes, I too can love; you yourselves
can tell it from the past. Is it not so? . . . " ') Chamisso's story is a fable (*The Marvellous Story
of Peter Schlemihl*); published in 1813, the same period as *Frankenstein*, it too revolves around
the conflict between the spread of capitalism (Peter) and feudal social structures (Mina and
her village). As in *Frankenstein*, capitalism appears in it as a fortuitous episode, involving just
one individual and lasting only a short time. But the underlying intuition has an extraordinary
power; it stands on a par with the punishment of Midas, for whom gold prevented
consumption.
3. Marx, *Capital* Volume I, Harmondsworth 1976, p. 342.
4. '. . . the Un-Dead are strong. [Dracula] have (sic) always the strength in his hand of twenty
men; even we four who gave our strength to Miss Lucy it also is all to him' (p. 183). One
cannot help recalling the words of Mephistopheles analysed by Marx: 'Six stallions, say, I can
afford,/Is not their strength my property?/I tear along, a sporting lord,/As if their legs belonged
to me.' (quoted in 'Economic and Philosophical Manuscripts', p. 376).
5. Marx, *Capital* Volume 1, p. 741.

circle of semi-demons to batten on the helpless' (my italics). 'And so the circle goes on *ever widening*', Van Helsing says later on; and Seward describes Dracula as 'the father or furtherer of a *new* order of beings' (my italics). All Dracula's actions really have as their final goal the creation of this 'new order of beings' which finds its most fertile soil, logically enough, in England. And finally, just as the capitalist is 'capital personified' and must subordinate his private existence to the abstract and incessant movement of accumulation, so Dracula is not impelled by the *desire* for power but by the *curse* of power, by an obligation he cannot escape. 'When they (the Un-Dead) become such', Van Helsing explains, 'there comes with the change the curse of immortality; they cannot die, but must go on age after age adding new victims and multiplying the evils of the world'. It is remarked later of the vampire that he 'can do all these things, *yet he is not free*' (my italics). His curse compels him to make ever more victims, just as the capitalist is compelled to accumulate. His nature forces him to struggle to be unlimited, to subjugate *the whole of society*. For this reason, one cannot 'coexist' with the vampire. One must either succumb to him or kill him, thereby freeing the world of his presence and him of his curse. When the knife plunges into Dracula's heart, in the moment before his dissolution, 'there was in the face a look of peace, such as I would never have imagined might have rested there'. There flashes forth here the idea, to which we shall return, of the *purification* of capital.

If the vampire is a metaphor for capital, then Stoker's vampire, who is of 1897, must be the capital of 1897. The capital which, after lying 'buried' for twenty long years of recession, rises again to set out on the irreversible road of concentration and monopoly. And Dracula is a true monopolist: solitary and despotic, he will not brook competition. Like monopoly capital, his ambition is to subjugate the last vestiges of the liberal era and destroy all forms of economic independence. He no longer restricts himself to incorporating (in a literal sense) the physical and moral strength of his victims. He intends to make them his *for ever*. Hence the horror, for the bourgeois mind. One is bound to Dracula, as to the devil, for *life*, no longer 'for a fixed period', as the classic bourgeois contract stipulated with the intention of maintaining the freedom of the contracting parties. The vampire, like monopoly, destroys the hope that one's independence can one day be brought back. He threatens the idea of individual liberty. For this reason the nineteenth-century bourgeois is able to imagine monopoly only in the guise of Count Dracula, the aristocrat, the figure of the past, the relic of distant lands and dark ages. Because the nineteenth-century bourgeois believes in free trade, and he knows that in order to become established, free competition had to destroy the tyranny of feudal monopoly. For him, then, monopoly and free competition are irreconcilable concepts. Monopoly is the *past* of competition, the middle ages. He cannot believe it can be its *future*, that competition itself can *generate* monopoly in new forms. And yet 'modern monopoly is . . . the true synthesis . . . the negation of feudal monopoly insofar as it implies the system of competition, and the negation of competition insofar as it is monopoly.'[6]

Dracula is thus at once the final product of the bourgeois century and its negation. In Stoker's novel only this second aspect—the negative and destructive one—appears. There are very good reasons for this. In Britain at the end of the nineteenth century, monopolistic concentration was far less developed (for various economic and political reasons) than in the other advanced capitalist societies. Monopoly could thus be perceived as something extraneous to British history: as a *foreign threat*. This is why Dracula is not British, while his antagonists (with one exception, as we shall see, and with the addition of Van Helsing, born in that other classic homeland of free trade, Holland) are British through and through. Nationalism—the defence to the death of British civilization—has a central role in *Dracula*. The idea of the nation is central because it is collective: it coordinates individual energies and enables them to resist the threat. For while Dracula threatens the freedom of the individual, the latter alone lacks the power to resist or defeat him. Indeed the followers of pure economic individualism, those who pursue their own profit, are, without knowing it, the vampire's best allies.[7] Individualism is not the weapon with which Dracula can be beaten. Other things are needed—in effect two: money and religion. These are considered as a single whole, which must not be separated: in other words, money at the service of religion and vice versa. The money of Dracula's enemies is money that *refuses to become capital*, that wants not to obey the profane economic laws of capitalism but to be used *to do good*. Towards the end of the novel, Mina Harker thinks of her friends' financial commitment: 'it made me think of the wonderful power of money! What can it not do when it is properly applied; and what might it do when basely used!' This is the point: money should be used according to justice. Money must not have its end *in itself*, in its continuous accumulation. It must have, rather, a *moral*, anti-economic end to the point where colossal expenditures and losses can be calmly accepted. This idea of money is, for the capitalist, something inadmissible. But it is also the great ideological lie of Victorian capitalism, a capitalism which is ashamed of itself and which hides

6. Marx, 'The Property of Philosophy' (1847) in Marx and Engels, *Collected Works*, Volume 6, London 1976, p. 195.

7. This is the case with all the minor characters in the novel. These (the stevedores and lawyers, sailors and estate agents, porters and accountants) are always more than satisfied with their dealings with Dracula, for the simple reason that Dracula pays well and in cash, or even facilitates the work. Dracula is one of them: an excellent master for wage-earners, an excellent partner for big businessmen. They understand one another so well, they are so useful to each other, that Dracula never behaves like a vampire with them: he does not need to suck their blood, he can buy it.

factories and stations beneath cumbrous Gothic superstructures; which prolongs and extols aristocratic models of life; which exalts the holiness of the family as the latter begins secretly to break up. Dracula's enemies are precisely the exponents of *this* capitalism. They are the militant version of Dickens's benefactors. They find their fulfilment in religious superstition, whereas the vampire is paralysed by it. And yet the crucifixes, holy wafers, garlic, magic flowers, and so on, are not important for their *intrinsic* religious meaning but for a subtler reason. Their true function consists in setting impassable limits to the vampire's activity. They prevent him from entering this or that house, conquering this or that person, carrying out this or that metamorphosis. But setting limits to the vampire-capital means attacking his very raison d'être: he must by his nature be able to expand without limit, to destroy every restraint upon his action. Religious superstition imposes the same limits on Dracula that Victorian capitalism declares itself to accept spontaneously. But Dracula—who is capital that is not ashamed of itself, true to its own nature, an end in itself—cannot survive in these conditions. And so this symbol of a cruel historical development falls victim to a handful of whited sepulchres, a bunch of fanatics who want to arrest the course of history. It is they who are the relics of the dark ages.

At the end of *Dracula* the vampire's defeat is complete. Dracula and his lovers are destroyed, Mina Harker is saved at the last moment. Only one cloud darkens the happy ending. In killing Dracula, Quincy P. Morris, the American who has been helping his British friends to save their nation, dies too, almost by accident. The occurrence seems inexplicable, extraneous to the logic of the narrative, yet it fits perfectly into Stoker's sociological design. The American, Morris, *must* die, because Morris is a vampire. From his first appearance he is shrouded in mystery (a friendly sort of mystery, it is true—but isn't Count Dracula himself likeable, at the beginning?). 'He is such a nice fellow, an American from Texas, and he looks so young and so fresh [he *looks*: like Dracula, who looks it but isn't] that it seems almost impossible that he has been to so many places and has had such adventures.' What places? What adventures? Where does all his money come from? What does Mr Morris do? Where does he live? Nobody knows any of this. But nobody suspects. Nobody suspects even when Lucy dies—and then turns into a vampire—immediately after receiving a blood transfusion from Morris. Nobody suspects when Morris, shortly afterwards, tells the story of his mare, sucked dry of blood in the Pampas (like Dracula, Morris has been round the world) by 'one of those big bats that they call vampires'. It is the first time that the name 'vampire' is mentioned in the novel: but there is no reaction. And there is no reaction a few lines further on when Morris, 'coming close to me, . . . spoke in a fierce half-whisper: "What took it [the blood] out?" ' But Dr Seward shakes his head; he hasn't the slightest idea. And Morris, reassured, promises to help. Nobody, finally, suspects when, in the course of the meeting to plan the vampire hunt, Morris leaves the room to take a shot—missing, naturally—at the big bat on the window-ledge listening to the preparations; or when, after Dracula bursts into the household, Morris hides among the trees, the only effect of which is that he loses sight of Dracula and invites the others to call off the hunt for the night. This is pretty well all Morris does in *Dracula*. He would be a totally superfluous character if, unlike the others, he were not characterized by this mysterious connivance with the world of the vampires. So long as things go well for Dracula, Morris acts like an accomplice. As soon as there is a reversal of fortunes, he turns into his staunchest enemy. Morris enters into competition with Dracula; he would like to replace him in the conquest of the Old World. He does not succeed in the novel but he will succeed, in 'real' history, a few years afterwards.

While it is interesting to understand that Morris is connected with the vampires—because America will end up by subjugating Britain in reality and Britain is, albeit unconsciously, afraid of it—the decisive thing is to understand why Stoker does *not* portray him as a vampire. The answer lies in the bourgeois conception of monopoly described earlier. For Stoker, monopoly *must* be feudal, oriental, tyrannical. It cannot be the product of that very society he wants to defend. And Morris, naturally, is by contrast a product of Western civilization, just as America is a rib of Britain and American capitalism a consequence of British capitalism. To make Morris a vampire would mean accusing capitalism directly: or rather accusing Britain, admitting that it is Britain herself that has given birth to the monster. This cannot be. For the good of Britain, then, Morris must be sacrificed. But Britain must be kept out of a crime whose legitimacy she cannot recognize. He will be killed by the chance knife-thrust of a gypsy (whom the British will allow to escape unpunished). And at the moment when Morris dies, and the threat disappears, old England grants its blessing to this excessively pushy and unscrupulous financier, and raises him to the dignity of a Bengal Lancer: 'And, to our bitter grief, with a smile and in silence, he died, a gallant gentleman.' (the sentence significantly abounds in the clichés of heroic-imperial English literature). These, it should be noted, are the *last* words of the novel, whose true ending does not lie —as is clear by now—in the death of the Romanian count, but in the killing of the American financier.[8]

---

8. The finishing touch is Jonathan Harker's short 'Note', written seven years after the events have ended. Harker informs the reader that he and Mina have christened their son 'Quincey', and that 'His mother holds, I know, the secret belief that some of our brave friend's spirit has passed into him.' (p. 336) [326]. The American outsider Morris is 'recycled' within the triumphant Victorian family, not without being made to undergo a final tacit humiliation (which would delight a linguist): his name—Quincy, as appears from the signature of the only note in his own handwriting—is transformed, by the addition of an 'e', into the much more English Quincey.

One of the most striking aspects of *Dracula*—as of *Frankenstein* before it—is its system of narrative senders. To begin with, there is the fact that in this network of letters, diaries, notes, telegrams, notices, phonograph recordings and articles, the narrative function proper, namely the description and ordering of events, is reserved for the British alone. We never have access to Van Helsing's point of view, or to Morris's, and still less to Dracula's. The string of events exists only in the form and with the meaning stamped upon it by British Victorian culture. It is those cultural categories, those moral values, those forms of expression that are endangered by the vampire: it is those same categories, forms and values that reassert themselves and emerge triumphant. It is a victory of convention over exception, of the present over the possible future, of standard British English over any kind of linguistic transgression. In *Dracula* we have, transparently, the perfect and immutable English of the narrators on the one hand, and Morris's American 'dialect', Dracula's schoolbook English and Van Helsing's bloomers on the other. As Dracula is a danger because he constitutes an unforseen variation from the British cultural code, so the maximum threat on the plane of content coincides with the maximum inefficiency and dislocation of the English language. Halfway through the novel, when Dracula seems to be in control of the situation, the frequency of Van Helsing's speeches increases enormously, and his perverse English dominates the stage. It becomes dominant because although the English language possesses the word 'vampire', it is unable to ascribe a meaning to it, in the same way that British society considers 'capitalist monopoly' a meaningless expression. Van Helsing has to explain, in his approximate and mangled English, what a vampire is. Only then, when these notions have been translated into the linguistic and cultural code of the English, and the code has been reorganized and reinforced, can the narrative return to its previous fluidity, the hunt begin and victory appear secure.[9] It is entirely logical that the last sentence should be, as we saw, a veritable procession of literary English.

In *Dracula* there is no ominiscient narrator, only individual and mutually separate points of view. The first-person account is a clear expression of the desire to keep hold of one's individuality, which the vampire threatens to subjugate. Yet so long as the conflict is one between human 'individualism' and vampirical 'totalization', things do not go at all well for the humans. Just as a system of perfect competition

9. In Stoker's novel the function of Van Helsing describes a parabola: absent at the beginning, dominant at the centre, removed to the margins of the action at the end. His aid is indeed irreplaceable, but once she has obtained it, Britain can settle matters herself: it is indicative that he is only a spectator at the killing of Dracula. In this, yet again, Fisher's *Dracula* betrays the ideological intention of the original: the great final duel between Dracula and Van Helsing belongs to a very different system of oppositions from Stoker's, where there prevails the conflict between Good and Evil, Light and Darkness, Frugality and Luxury, Reason and Superstition (see David Pirie, A *Heritage of Horror. The English Gothic Cinema* 1947–1972, London 1973, p. 51 ff.).

cannot do other than give way to monopoly, so a handful of isolated individuals cannot oppose the concentrated force of the vampire. It is a problem we have already witnessed on the plane of content: here it re-emerges on the plane of narrative forms. The individuality of the narration must be preserved and at the same time its negative aspect— the doubt, impotence, ignorance and even mutual distrust and hostility of the protagonists—must be eliminated.[1] Stoker's solution is brilliant. It is to collate, to make a systematic integration of the different points of view. In the second half of *Dracula*, that of the hunt (which begins, it should be noted, only *after* the collation), it is more accurate to speak of a 'collective' narrator than of different narrators. There are no longer, as there were at the beginning, *different* versions of a single episode, a procedure which expressed the uncertainty and error of the individual account. The narrative now expresses the *general* point of view, the official version of events. Even the style loses its initial idiosyncrasies, be they professional or individual, and is amalgamated into Standard British English. This collation is, in other words, the Victorian compromise in the field of narrative technique. It unifies the different interests and cultural paradigms of the dominant class (law, commerce, the land, science) under the banner of the common good. It restores the narrative equilibrium, giving this dark episode a form and a meaning which are finally clear, communicable and universal.

The Return of the Repressed

A sociological analysis of *Frankenstein* and *Dracula* reveals that one of the institutions most threatened by the monsters is the family. Yet this fear cannot be explained wholly in historical and economic terms. On the contrary, it is very likely that its deepest root is to be found elsewhere: in the eros, above all in sex. 'Dracula', David Pirie has written, '. . . can be seen as the great submerged force of Victorian libido breaking out to punish the repressive society which had imprisoned it; one of the most appalling things that Dracula does to the matronly women of his Victorian enemies (in the novel as in the film) is to make them sensual.'[2] It is true. For confirmation one only has to reread the episode of Lucy. Lucy is the only protagonist who falls victim to Dracula. She is punished, because she is the only one who shows some

1. The story of Lucy illuminates the interrelationship of the characters. In the opening chapters, no fewer than three of the main characters (Seward, Holmwood and Morris) enter into competition for her hand. In other words, Lucy objectively turns these men into *rivals*, she divides them, and this makes things easier for Dracula who, making them by contrast be friends again, prepares her downfall. The moral is that, when faced with the vampire, one must curb all individual appetites and interests. Poor Lucy, who acts solely on her desires and impulses (she is a woman who *chooses* her own husband, without mentioning it to her mother!) is first killed by Dracula and then, for safety's sake, run through the heart by her fiancé on what, going by the calendar, should have been their wedding night (and the whole episode, as we shall see, oozes sexual meanings).
2. Pirie, p. 84.

kind of *desire*. Stoker is inflexible on this point: all the other characters are immune to the temptations of the flesh, or capable of rigorous sublimations. Van Helsing, Morris, Seward and Holmwood are all single. Mina and Jonathan get married in hospital, when Jonathan is in a state of prostration and impotence; and they marry in order to mend, to forget the terrible experience (which was also sexual) undergone by Jonathan in Transylvania: 'Share my ignorance' is what he asks of his wife. Not so Lucy, who awaits her wedding day with impatience. It is on this restlessness—on her 'somnambulism'—that Dracula exerts leverage to win her. And the more he takes possession of Lucy, the more he brings out her sexual side. A few moments before her death, 'She opened her eyes, which were now dull and hard at once, and said in a soft voluptuous voice, such as I had never heard from her lips: . . .'. And Lucy as a 'vampire' is even more seductive: 'The sweetness was turned to adamantine, heartless cruelty, and the purity to voluptuous wantonness . . . the face became wreathed with a voluptuous smile . . . she advanced to him with outstretched arms and a wanton smile . . . and with a langorous, voluptuous grace, said:—"Come to me, Arthur. Leave these others and come to me. My arms are hungry for you. Come, and we can rest together. Come, my husband, come!" ' The seduction is about to work, but Van Helsing breaks its spell. They proceed to Lucy's execution. Lucy dies in a very unusual way: in the throes of what, to the 'public' mind of the Victorians, must have seemed like an orgasm: 'The Thing in the coffin writhed; and a hideous, blood-curdling screech came from the opened red lips. The body shook and quivered and twisted in wild contortions; the sharp white teeth champed together till the lips were cut and the mouth was smeared with a crimson foam.' Surrounded by his friends who goad him on with their cries, Arthur Holmwood Lord Godalming purges the world of this fearful Thing; not without deriving, in distorted but transparent forms, enormous sexual satisfaction: 'He looked like a figure of Thor as his untrembling arm rose and fell, driving deeper and deeper the mercy-bearing stake, whilst the blood from the pierced heart welled and spurted up from around it.'

Dracula, then, liberates and exalts sexual desire. And this desire *attracts* but—at the same time—frightens. Lucy is beautiful, but dangerous. Fear and attraction are one and the same: and not just in Stoker. Much of nineteenth-century bourgeois high culture had already treated eros and sex as *ambivalent* phenomena. Their rhetorical figure is the oxymoron, the contradiction in terms, through which Baudelaire sings the ambiguity of amorous relations. Among the condemned poems of *Les Fleurs du Mal*—a title which is itself an oxymoron—is 'Les métamorphoses du vampire', where the irresistible female seducer is described 'writhing like a snake over charcoal'. And Stendhal noted in the margin of the first page of *De l'Amour*: 'I undertake to trace with a mathematical precision and (if I can) truth, the history of the illness called *love.'* Love is an illness: it entails the renunciation of man's *individuality* and *reason.*[3] For Stendhal, the devotee of enlightenment, this means denying one's very reason for existing: love becomes a *mortal* danger, and only a *greater* danger (Dracula!) can cure the person who falls victim to it: 'The leap from Leucates was a fine image in antiquity. In fact, the remedy for love is almost impossible. It requires not only that danger which sharply recalls a man's attention to his own preservation; it also requires—something far more difficult—the continuity of an enticing danger.'[4] *An enticing danger,* just as that of love is *a dangerous enticement*: fear and desire incessantly overturn into one another. They are indivisible. We find this confirmed in Sade, in Keats' Lamia, in Poe's Ligeia, in Baudelaire's women, in Hoffmann's woman vampire. Why is this?

Vampirism is an excellent example of the identity of desire and fear: let us therefore put it at the centre of the analysis. And let us take the psychoanalytic interpretation of this phenomenon, advanced for example by Marie Bonaparte in her study of Poe. Commenting on Baudelaire's remark that all Poe's women are 'strikingly delineated as though by an adorer', Marie Bonaparte adds: 'An adorer . . . who dare not approach the object of his adoration, since he feels it surrounded by some fearful, dangerous mystery.'[5] This mystery is none other than vampirism:

> 'the danger of sexuality, the punishment that threatens all who yield, is shown, as in *Berenice*, by the manner in which Egaeus is obsessed by her teeth. And indeed, in psychoanalysis, many cases of male impotence reveal, though more or less buried in the unconscious—strange as it may seem to many a reader—the notion of the female vagina being furnished with teeth, and thus a source of danger in being able to bite and castrate. . . . Mouth and vagina are equated in the unconscious and, when Egaeus yields to the morbid impulse to draw Berenice's teeth, he yields both to the yearning for the mother's organ and to be revenged upon it, since the dangers that hedge it about make him sexually avoid all women as too menacing. His act is therefore a sort of retributive castration inflicted on the mother whom he loves, and yet hates, because obdurate to his sex-love for her in infancy. . . . This concept of the *vagina dentata* and its consequent menace is, however,

3. For Hegel too love originates from 'the surrender of the person to an individual of the opposite sex, the sacrifice of one's independent consciousness'. But then Hegel dialectically resolves and pacifies this self-negation from which love originates: 'this losing, in the other, one's consciousness of self . . . this self-forgetfulness in which the lover . . . finds the roots of his being in another, and yet in this other does entirely enjoy precisely himself.' (*Aesthetics*, 1820–29, Oxford 1975, pp. 562–3.)
4. Stendhal, *De L'Amour* (1822), Paris 1957, p. 118.
5. Marie Bonaparte, *The Life and Works of Edgar Allen Poe. A Psychoanalytic Interpretation*, London 1949, pp. 209–10.

also a displacement (in this case downwards) of a factor with roots
deep in infantile experience. We know that babes which, while
toothless, are content to suck the breast, no sooner cut their first
teeth than they use them to bite the same breast. This, in each of
us, is the first manifestation of the aggressive instinct, . . . later,
when the sense of what 'one should not do' has been instilled by
ever severer and more numerous moral injunctions . . . the memory, or rather the phantasy of biting the mother's breast must have
become charged, in the unconscious, with past feelings of wickedness. And the child, having learnt by experience what is meant
by the law of retaliation when he infringes the code . . . begins,
in his turn, to fear that the bites he wished to give his mother will
be visited on him: namely, retaliation for his "cannibalism".'[6]

This passage identifies with precision the *ambivalent* root, interweav-
ing hate and love, that underlies vampirism. An analogous ambivalence
had already been described by Freud in relation to the taboo on the
dead (and the vampire is, as we know, also a dead person who comes
back to life to destroy those who remain): 'this hostility, distressingly
felt in the unconscious as satisfaction over the death . . . [is displaced]
on to the object of the hostility, on to the dead themselves. Once again
. . . we find that the taboo has grown up on the basis of an ambivalent
emotional attitude. The taboo upon the dead arises, like the others,
from the contrast between conscious pain and unconscious satisfaction
over the death that has occurred. Since such is the origin of the ghost's
resentment, it follows naturally that the survivors who have the most to
fear will be those who were formerly its nearest and dearest.'[7]
   Freud's text leaves no doubt: the ambivalence exists *within the psyche
of the person suffering from the fear*. In order to heal this state of tension
one is forced to *repress*, unconsciously, one of the two affective states
in conflict, the one that is socially more illicit. From the repression
arises fear: 'every affect belonging to an emotional impulse, whatever
its kind, is transformed, if it is repressed, into anxiety'.[8] And fear breaks
out when—for whatever reason—this repressed impulse returns and
thrusts itself upon the mind: 'an uncanny experience occurs either
when infantile complexes which have been repressed are once more
revived by some impression, or when primitive beliefs which have been
surmounted seem once again to be confirmed.'[9] Fear, in other words,
coincides with the 'return of the repressed'. And this brings us perhaps
to the heart of the matter.
   The literature of terror is studded with passages where the protago-

6. Ibid., pp. 218–9.
7. 'Totem and Taboo' (1913) in Freud, Volume XIII, p. 61. See also the essay 'The "Uncanny". '
   (1919): 'Most likely our fear still implies the old belief that the dead man becomes the enemy
   of his survivor and seeks to carry him off to share his new life with him.' (Ibid., XVII, p. 242).
8. 'The "Uncanny". ', p. 241.
9. Ibid., p. 249.

nists brush against the awareness—described by Freud—that the perturbing element is *within them*: that it is they themselves that produce the monsters they fear. Their first fear is—inevitably—that of *going mad.* 'Remember, I am not recording the vision of a madman.' (*Frankenstein*). 'God preserve my sanity . . . there is but one thing to hope for: that I may not go mad, if, indeed, I be not mad already.' (*Dracula*, Harker's words). '[Dr Seward] says that I afford him a curious psychological study' (*Dracula*, Lucy). 'I have come to the conclusion that it must be something mental.' (*Dracula*, Seward, who is also the director of a mental hospital). Jekyll has to defend himself from the suspicion of being mad, just like Polidori's Aubrey a century earlier. In these novels, reality tends to work according to the laws that govern dreams —'I wasn't dreaming', 'as in a dream', 'as if I had gone through a long nightmare'.[1] This is the return of the repressed. But *how* does it return? Not as madness, or only marginally so. The lesson these books wish to impart is that one need not be afraid of going mad; that is one need not fear one's own repressions, the splitting of one's own psyche. No, one should be afraid of the *monster*, of something *material*, something *external*: ' "Dr Van Helsing, are you mad?" . . . "Would I were!" he said. "Madness were easy to bear compared with truth like this." ' *Would I were*: this is the key. Madness is nothing in comparison with the vampire. Madness does not present a problem. Or rather: madness, in itself, *does not exist*: it is the vampire, the monster, the potion that creates it.[2] *Dracula*, written in the same year that saw Freud begin his self-analysis, is a refined attempt by the nineteenth-century mind not to recognize itself. This is symbolized by the character who—already in the grip of fear—finds himself by chance in front of a mirror. He looks at it and jumps: in the mirror is a reflection of his face. But the reader's attention is immediately distracted: the fear does not come from his having seen his *own* image, but from the fact that the *vampire* is not reflected in the mirror. Finding himself face to face with the simple, terrible truth, the author—and with him the character and the reader —draws back in horror.

1. Mary Shelley claimed to have 'dreamt' the story of Frankenstein. And one of the passages that stands out in the text is Frankenstein's dream, which takes place immediately after the creation of the monster. At the moment when, in the dream, he is about to kiss Elizabeth, she changes into his mother's corpse. Frankenstein wakes to find the monster by his bed, in an unmistakable maternal pose: 'He held up the curtain of the bed; and his eyes . . . were fixed on me . . . a grin wrinkled his cheeks . . . one hand was stretched out.' Other things about the monster suggest a reworking of the mother figure: the fact that he is a dead man who comes back to life; his physical 'bigness'; his language, improbably more 'archaic' than Frankenstein's. The analogy, however, rests mostly on the *function* of the monster within the plot: he kills Elizabeth, punishing Frankenstein for having married her and thereby avenging his mother, killed by the scarlet fever she had caught from Elizabeth, with whom her son is now getting ready to 'betray' her. The situation recalls many of Poe's tales.
2. Think of Renfield, Seward's patient who is given considerable space in *Dracula*. Seward examines his case with the utmost care, draws on all the known psychiatric techniques, even forms new hypotheses, and calls Van Helsing for a second opinion: nothing—they draw a blank. Then, all of a sudden, the penny drops: Renfield is the servant of Dracula.

The repressed returns, then, but disguised as a monster. For a psychoanalytic study, the main fact is precisely this metamorphosis. As Francesco Orlando has remarked of his analysis of Racine's *Phèdre*, 'the relationship between the unconscious and literature was not postulated according to the presence of contents, whatever their nature, in the literary work . . . perverse desire could not have been acceptable as content in the literary work without the latter's also accepting *the formal model capable of filtering it.*'[3] This formal model is the monster metaphor, the vampire metaphor. It 'filters', makes bearable to the conscious mind those desires and fears[4] which the latter has judged to be unacceptable and has thus been forced to repress, and whose existence it consequently cannot recognize. The literary formalization, the rhetorical figure, therefore has a double function: it *expresses* the unconscious content and at the same time *hides* it. Literature always contains *both* these functions. Taking away one or the other would mean eliminating either the problem of the unconscious (by asserting that everything in literature is transparent and manifest) or the problem of literary communication (by asserting that literature serves *only* to hide certain contents). Yet while these two functions are always present in the literary metaphor, the relationship between them can nevertheless change. One can stand out more than the other and win a dominant position within the overall signification of the work. These observations have a direct bearing on our argument, because the metaphor of the vampire is a splendid example of how the equilibrium of literary functions can vary. The problem can be posed thus: what is the sex—in literature, naturally, not in reality—of vampires? Vampires, unlike angels, do have sex. But it changes. In one set of works (Poe, Hoffmann, Baudelaire: 'elite' culture) they are women. In another (Polidori, Stoker, the cinema: 'mass' culture) they are men. The metamorphosis is by no means accidental. At the root of vampirism, as we have seen, lies an ambivalent impulse of the child towards its mother. To present the vampire as a *woman* therefore means to make relatively little distortion of the unconscious content. The literary figure still retains the essential element—the sex —of that which is at the source of the perturbation. The defences that

3. Orlando, pp. 138 and 140; my italics.
4. That a desire or a fear underlie the uncanny is entirely secondary for Freud. The terror is caused by the sudden re-emergence of something repressed: having established this, 'it must be a matter of indifference whether what is uncanny was itself originally frightening or whether it carried some *other* effect.' ('The "Uncanny"', p. 241). This ambivalent unconscious origin confers a peculiar function on the literature of terror. The distinction suggested by Freud in his study of jokes—'Dreams serve predominantly for the avoidance of unpleasure, jokes for the attainment of pleasure'—and extended by Orlando to literature (which also functions for the attainment of pleasure, for the manifestation of a repressed desire), becomes highly uncertain. In the literature of terror the two functions—avoidance of unpleasure and attainment of pleasure—seem to balance each other perfectly. Indeed the one exists for the other: a terror novel that doesn't frighten doesn't give pleasure either. In this respect, and not just because of its contents, the literature of terror seems to be that whose workings approximate most closely to those of the dream: and like the dream it 'imposes' an obligatory context of enjoyment: alone, at night, in bed.

literature puts up to protect the conscious mind are relatively elastic: D. H. Lawrence (as Baudelaire, implicitly, before him) passes with ease from the vampire theme back to Poe's perverse erotic desires.[5] But if the vampire becomes a man, the unconscious source of the perturbation is hidden by a further layer of signifieds. The link becomes more tenuous. The conscious mind can rest easy: all that remains of the original fear is a word, 'Dracula': that splendid and inexplicable feminine name. The metamorphosis, in other words, serves to protect the conscious mind, or more precisely to keep it in a state of greater unawareness. The vampire is transformed into a man by mass culture, which has to promote spontaneous certainties and cannot let itself plumb the unconscious too deeply. Yet at the same time and for precisely this reason, the repressed content, which has remained unconscious, produces an irresistible fear. Spurious certainties and terror support each other.

*   *   *

CHRISTOPHER CRAFT

"Kiss Me with Those Red Lips": Gender and Inversion in Bram Stoker's *Dracula*†

* * * Bram Stoker's particular articulation of the vampire metaphor in *Dracula*, a book whose fundamental anxiety, an equivocation about the relationship between desire and gender, repeats, with a monstrous difference, a pivotal anxiety of late Victorian culture. Jonathan Harker, whose diary opens the novel, provides *Dracula*'s most precise articulation of this anxiety. About to be kissed by the "weird sisters" (64) [51], the incestuous vampiric daughters who share Castle Dracula with the Count, a supine Harker thrills to a double passion:

> All three had brilliant white teeth, that shone like pearls against the ruby of their voluptuous lips. There was something about them that made me uneasy, *some longing and at the same time some deadly fear*, I felt in my heart a wicked, burning desire that they would kiss me with those red lips. (51; emphasis added) [42]

Immobilized by the competing imperatives of "wicked desire" and "deadly fear," Harker awaits an erotic fulfillment that entails both the dissolution of the boundaries of the self and the thorough subversion of conventional Victorian gender codes, which constrained the mobility

---

5. D. H. Lawrence, *Studies in Classic American Literature*, London 1924, chapter 6.
† © 1984 by the Regents of the University of California. Reprinted from *Representations* 8 (Fall 1984): 107–33 by permission. *Dracula* quotations are from Bram Stoker, *Dracula* (New York, 1979). Bracketed page numbers refer to this Norton Critical Edition.

of sexual desire and varieties of genital behavior according to the more active male the right and responsibility of vigorous appetite, while requiring the more passive female to "suffer and be still." John Ruskin, concisely formulating Victorian conventions of sexual difference, provides us with a useful synopsis: "The man's power is active, progressive, defensive. He is eminently the doer, the creator, the discoverer, the defender. His intellect is for speculation and invention; his energy for adventure, for war, and for conquest. . . ." Woman, predictably enough, bears a different burden: "She must be enduringly, incorruptibly, good; instinctively, infallibly wise—wise, not for self-development, but for self-renunciation . . . wise, not with the narrowness of insolent and loveless pride, but with the passionate gentleness of an infinitely variable, because infinitely applicable, modesty of service—the true changefulness of woman."[1] Stoker, whose vampiric women exercise a far more dangerous "changefulness" than Ruskin imagines, anxiously inverts this conventional pattern, as virile Jonathan Harker enjoys a "feminine" passivity and awaits a delicious penetration from a woman whose demonism is figured as the power to penetrate. A swooning desire for an overwhelming penetration and an intense aversion to the demonic potency empowered to gratify that desire compose the fundamental motivating action and emotion in *Dracula*.

This ambivalence, always excited by the imminence of the vampiric kiss, finds its most sensational representation in the image of the Vampire Mouth, the central and recurring image of the novel: "There was a deliberate voluptuousness which was both thrilling and repulsive. . . . I could see in the moonlight the moisture shining on the red tongue as it lapped the white sharp teeth" (52) [42]. That is Harker describing one of the three vampire women at Castle Dracula. Here is Dr. Seward's description of the Count: "His eyes flamed red with devilish passion; the great nostrils of the white acquiline nose opened wide and quivered at the edges; and the white sharp teeth, behind the full lips of the blood-dripping mouth, champed together like those of a wild beast" (336) [247]. As the primary site of erotic experience in *Dracula*, this mouth equivocates, giving the lie to the easy separation of the masculine and the feminine. Luring at first with an inviting orifice, a promise of red softness, but delivering instead a piercing bone, the vampire mouth fuses and confuses what Dracula's civilized nemesis, Van Helsing and his Crew of Light,[2] works so hard to separate—the gender-based categories of the penetrating and the receptive, or, to use Van Helsing's language, the complementary categories of "brave men" and "good women." With its soft flesh barred by hard bone, its red

---

1. John Ruskin, *Sesame and Lilies* (New York, 1974), pp. 59–60.
2. This group of crusaders includes Van Helsing himself, Dr. John Seward, Arthur Holmwood, Quincey Morris, and later Jonathan Harker; the title Crew of Light is mine, but I have taken my cue from Stoker: Lucy, *lux*, light.

crossed by white, this mouth compels opposites and contrasts into a frightening unity, and it asks some disturbing questions. Are we male or are we female? Do we have penetrators or orifices? And if both, what does that mean? And what about our bodily fluids, the red and the white? What are the relations between blood and semen, milk and blood? Furthermore, this mouth, bespeaking the subversion of the stable and lucid distinctions of gender, is the mouth of all vampires, male and female.

Yet we must remember that the vampire mouth is first of all Dracula's mouth, and that all subsequent versions of it (in *Dracula* all vampires other than the Count are female)[3] merely repeat as diminished simulacra the desire of the Great Original, that "father or furtherer of a new order of beings" (360) [263]. Dracula himself, calling his children "my jackals to do my bidding when I want to feed," identifies the systematic creation of female surrogates who enact his will and desire (365) [267]. This should remind us that the novel's opening anxiety, its first articulation of the vampiric threat, derives from Dracula's hovering interest in Jonathan Harker; the sexual threat this novel first evokes, manipulates, sustains, but never finally represents is that Dracula will seduce, penetrate, drain another male. The suspense and power of *Dracula's* opening section, of that phase of the narrative which we have called the invitation to monstrosity, proceeds precisely from this unfulfilled sexual ambition. Dracula's desire to fuse with a male, most explicitly evoked when Harker cuts himself shaving, subtly and dangerously suffuses this text. Always postponed and never directly enacted, this desire finds evasive fulfillment in an important series of heterosexual displacements.

Dracula's ungratified desire to vamp Harker is fulfilled instead by his three vampiric daughters, whose anatomical femininity permits, because it masks, the silently inderdicted homoerotic embrace between Harker and the Count. Here, in a displacement typical both of this text and the gender-anxious culture from which it arose, an implicitly homoerotic desire achieves representation as a monstrous heterosexuality, as a demonic inversion of normal gender relations. Dracula's daughters offer Harker a feminine form but a masculine penetration:

> Lower and lower went her head as the lips went below the range of my mouth and chin and seemed to fasten on my throat. . . . I could feel the soft, shivering touch of the lips on the supersensitive skin of my throat, and the hard dents of the two sharp teeth, just touching and pausing there. I closed my eyes in a langorous ecstasy and waited—waited with a beating heart. (52) [42–43]

3. Renfield, whose "zoophagy" precedes Dracula's arrival in England and who is never vamped by Dracula, is no exception to this rule.

This moment, constituting the text's most direct and explicit representation of a male's desire to be penetrated, is governed by a double deflection: first, the agent of penetration is nominally and anatomically (from the mouth down, anyway) female; and second, this dangerous moment, fusing the maximum of desire and the maximum of anxiety, is poised precisely at the brink of penetration. Here the "two sharp teeth," just "touching" and "pausing" there, stop short of the transgression which would unsex Harker and toward which this text constantly aspires and then retreats: the actual penetration of the male.

This moment is interrupted, this penetration denied. Harker's pause at the end of the paragraph ("waited—waited with a beating heart"), which seems to anticipate an imminent piercing, in fact anticipates not the completion but the interruption of the scene of penetration. Dracula himself breaks into the room, drives the women away from Harker, and admonishes them: "How dare you touch him, any of you? How dare you cast eyes on him when I had forbidden it? Back, I tell you all! This man belongs to me" (53) [43]. Dracula's intercession here has two obvious effects: by interrupting the scene of penetration, it suspends and disperses throughout the text the desire maximized at the brink of penetration, and it repeats the threat of a more direct libidinous embrace between Dracula and Harker. Dracula's taunt, "This man belongs to me," is suggestive enough, but at no point subsequent to this moment does Dracula kiss Harker, preferring instead to pump him for his knowledge of English law, custom, and language. Dracula, soon departing for England, leaves Harker to the weird sisters, whose final penetration of him, implied but never represented, occurs in the dark interspace to which Harker's journal gives no access.

Hereafter *Dracula* will never represent so directly a male's desire to be penetrated; once in England Dracula, observing a decorous heterosexuality, vamps only women, in particular Lucy Westenra and Mina Harker. The novel, nonetheless, does not dismiss homoerotic desire and threat; rather it simply continues to diffuse and displace it. Late in the text, the Count himself announces a deflected homoeroticism when he admonishes the Crew of Light thus: "My revenge is just begun! I spread it over the centuries, and time is on my side. Your girls that you all love are mine already; and *through them you and others shall yet be mine . . .*" (365; italics added) [267]. Here Dracula specifies the process of substitution by which "the girls that you all love" mediate and displace a more direct communion among males. Van Helsing, who provides for Lucy transfusions designed to counteract the dangerous influence of the Count, confirms Dracula's declaration of surrogation; he knows that once the transfusions begin, Dracula drains from Lucy's veins not her blood, but rather blood transferred from the veins of the Crew of Light: "even we four who gave our strength to Lucy it also is all to him [sic]" (244) [181]. Here, emphatically, is another instance of the heterosexual displacement of a desire mobile enough to elude the boundaries of gender. Everywhere in this text such desire seeks a strangely deflected heterosexual distribution; only through women may men touch.

The representation of sexuality in Dracula, then, registers a powerful ambivalence in its identification of desire and fear. The text releases a sexuality so mobile and polymorphic that Dracula may be best represented as bat or wolf or floating dust; yet this effort to elude the restrictions upon desire encoded in traditional conception of gender then constrains that desire through a series of heterosexual displacements. Desire's excursive mobility is always filtered in Dracula through the mask of a monstrous or demonic heterosexuality. Indeed, Dracula's mission in England is the creation of a race of monstrous women, feminine demons equipped with masculine devices. This monstrous heterosexuality is apotropaic for two reasons: first, because it masks and deflects the anxiety consequent to a more direct representation of same sex eroticism; and second, because in imagining a sexually aggressive woman as a demonic penetrator, as a ursurper of a prerogative belonging "naturally" to the other gender, it justifies, as we shall see later, a violent expulsion of this deformed femininity.

In its particular formulation of erotic ambivalence, in its contrary need both to liberate and constrain a desire indifferent to the prescriptions of gender by figuring such desire as monstrous heterosexuality, Dracula may seem at first idiosyncratic, anomalous, merely neurotic. This is not the case. Dracula presents a characteristic, if hyperbolic, instance of Victorian anxiety over the potential fluidity of gender roles,[4] and this text's defensiveness toward the mobile sexuality it nonetheless wants to evoke parallels remarkably other late Victorian accounts of same sex eroticism, of desire in which the "sexual instincts" were said to be, in the words of John Addington Symonds, "improperly correlated to [the] sexual organs."[5] During the last decades of the nineteenth century and the first of the twentieth, English writers produced their first sustained discourse about the variability of sexual desire, with a special emphasis upon male homoerotic love, which had already received indirect and evasive endorsement from Tennyson in "In Memoriam" and from Whitman in the "Calamus" poems. The preferred taxonomic la-

---

4. The complication of gender roles in Dracula has of course been recognized in the criticism. See, for instance, Stephanie Demetrakopoulos, "Feminism, Sex Role Exchanges, and Other Subliminal Fantasies in Bram Stoker's Dracula," Frontiers, 2 (1977), pp. 104–13. Demetrakopoulos writes: "These two figures I have traced so far—the male as passive rape victim and also as violator-brutalizer—reflect the polarized sex roles and the excessive needs this polarizing engendered in Victorian culture. Goldfarb recounts the brothels that catered to masochists, sadists, and homosexuals. The latter aspect of sexuality obviously did not interest Stoker. . . ." I agree with the first sentence here and, as this essay should make clear, emphatically disagree with the last.

5. John Addington Symonds, A Problem in Modern Ethics (London, 1906), p. 74.

bel under which these writers categorized and examined such sexual desire was not, as we might anticipate, "homosexuality" but rather "sexual inversion," a classificatory term involving a complex negotiation between socially encoded gender norms and a sexual mobility that would seem at first unconstrained by those norms.

* * * Van Helsing stands as the protector of the patriarchal institutions he so emphatically represents and as the guarantor of the traditional dualisms his religion and profession promote and authorize.[6] [Van Helsing's] largest purpose is to reinscribe the dualities that Dracula would muddle and confuse. Dualities require demarcations, inexorable and ineradicable lines of separation, but Dracula, as a border being who abrogates demarcations, makes such distinctions impossible. He is *nosferatu*, neither dead nor alive but somehow both, mobile frequenter of the grave and boudoir, easeful communicant of exclusive realms, and as such he toys with the separation of the living and the dead, a distinction critical to physician, lawyer, and priest alike. His mobility and metaphoric power deride the distinction between spirit and flesh, another of Van Helsing's sanctified dualisms. Potent enough to ignore death's terminus, Dracula has a spirit's freedom and mobility, but that mobility is chained to the most mechanical of appetites: he and his children rise and fall for a drink and for nothing else, for nothing else matters. This con- or inter-fusion of spirit and appetite, of eternity and sequence, produces a madness of activity and a mania of unceasing desire. Dracula lives an eternity of sexual repetition, a lurid wedding of desire and satisfaction that parodies both.

But the traditional dualism most vigorously defended by Van Helsing and most subtly subverted by Dracula is, of course, sexual: the division of being into gender, either male or female. Indeed, as we have seen, the vampiric kiss excites a sexuality so mobile, so insistent, that it threatens to overwhelm the distinctions of gender, and the exuberant energy with which Van Helsing and the Crew of Light counter Dracula's influence represents the text's anxious defense against the very desire it also seeks to liberate. In counterposing Dracula and Van Helsing, Stoker's text simultaneously threatens and protects the line of demarcation that insures the intelligible division of being into gender. This ambivalent need to invite the vampiric kiss and then to repudiate it defines exactly the dynamic of the battle that constitutes the prolonged middle of this text. The field of this battle, of this equivocal competition for the right to define the possible relations between desire and gender, is the infinitely penetrable body of a somnolent woman. This interposition of a woman between Dracula and Van Helsing should not surprise us; in England, as in Castle Dracula, a violent wrestle between males is mediated through a feminine form.

---

6. On this point see Demetrakopoulos, p. 104.

The Crew of Light's conscious conception of women is, predictably enough, idealized—the stuff of dreams. Van Helsing's concise description of Mina may serve as a representative example: "She is one of God's women fashioned by His own hand to show us men and other women that there is a heaven we can enter, and that its light can be here on earth" (226) [168–69]. The impossible idealism of this conception of women deflects attention from the complex and complicitous interaction within this sentence of gender, authority, and representation. Here Van Helsing's exegesis of God's natural text reifies Mina into a stable sign or symbol ("one of God's women") performing a fixed and comfortable function within a masculine sign system. Having received from Van Helsing's exegesis her divine impress, Mina signifies both a masculine artistic intention ("fashioned by His own hand") and a definite didactic purpose ("to show us men and other women" how to enter heaven), each of which constitutes an enormous constraint upon the significative possibilities of the sign or symbol that Mina here becomes. Van Helsing's reading of Mina, like a dozen other instances in which his interpretation of the sacred determines and delimits the range of activity permitted to women, encodes woman with a "natural" meaning composed according to the textual imperatives of anxious males. Precisely this complicity between masculine anxiety, divine textual authority, and a fixed conception of femininity—which may seem benign enough in the passage above—will soon be used to justify the destruction of Lucy Westenra, who, having been successfully vamped by Dracula, requires a corrective penetration. To Arthur's anxious importunity "Tell me what I am to do," Van Helsing answers: "Take this stake in your left hand, ready to place the point over the heart, and the hammer in your right. Then when we begin our prayer for the dead—I shall read him; I have here the book, and the others shall follow—strike in God's name . . ." (259) [191]. Here four males (Van Helsing, Seward, Holmwood, and Quincey Morris) communally read a masculine text (Van Helsing's mangled English even permits Stoker the unidiomatic pronominalization of the genderless text: "I shall read him"),[7] in order to justify the fatal correction of Lucy's dangerous wandering, her insolent disregard for the sexual and semiotic constraint encoded in Van Helsing's exegesis of "God's women."

The process by which women are construed as signs determined by the interpretive imperatives of authorizing males had been brilliantly identified some fifty years before the publication of Dracula by John Stuart Mill in The Subjection of Women. "What is now called the nature of women," Mill writes, "is an extremely artificial thing—the result of forced repression in some directions, unnatural stimulation in oth-

7. In this instance at least Van Helsing has an excuse for his ungrammatical usage; in Dutch, Van Helsing's native tongue, the noun *bijbel* (Bible) is masculine.

ers."[8] Mill's sentence, deftly identifying "the nature of women" as an "artificial" construct formed (and deformed) by "repression" and "unnatural stimulation," quietly unties the lacings that bind something called "woman" to something else called "nature." Mill further suggests that a correct reading of gender becomes almost impossible, since the natural difference between male and female is subject to cultural interpretation: ". . . I deny that anyone knows, or can know, the nature of the two sexes, as long as they have only been seen in their present relation to one another." Mill's agnosticism regarding "the nature of the sexes" suggests the societal and institutional quality of all definitions of the natural, definitions which ultimately conspire to produce "the imaginary and conventional character of women."[9] This last phrase, like the whole of Mill's essay, understands and criticizes the authoritarian nexus that arises when a deflected or transformed desire ("imaginary"), empowered by a gender-biased societal agreement ("conventional"), imposes itself upon a person in order to create a "character." "Character" of course functions in at least three senses: who and what one "is," the role one plays in society's supervening script, and the sign or letter that is intelligible only within the constraints of a larger sign system. Van Helsing's exegesis of "God's women" creates just such an imaginary and conventional character. Mina's body/character may indeed be feminine, but the signification it bears is written and interpreted solely by males. As Susan Hardy Aiken has written, such a symbolic system takes "for granted the role of women as passive objects or signs to be manipulated in the grammar of privileged male interchanges."[1]

Yet exactly the passivity of this object and the ease of this manipulation are at question in *Dracula*. Dracula, after all, kisses these women out of their passivity and so endangers the stability of Van Helsing's symbolic system. Both the prescriptive intention of Van Helsing's exegesis and the emphatic methodology (hypodermic needle, stake, surgeon's blade) he employs to insure the durability of his interpretation of gender suggest the potential unreliability of Mina as sign, an instability that provokes an anxiety we may call fear of the mediatrix. If, as Van Helsing admits, God's women provide the essential mediation ("the light can be here on earth") between the divine but distant patriarch and his earthly sons, then God's intention may be distorted by its potentially changeable vehicle. If woman-as-signifier wanders, then Van Helsing's whole cosmology, with its founding dualisms and supporting texts, collapses. In short, Van Helsing's interpretation of Mina,

8. John Stuart Mill, *The Subjection of Women* in *Essays on Sex Equality*, ed. Alice Rossi (Chicago, 1970), p. 148.
9. Ibid., p. 187.
1. Susan Hardy Aiken, "Scripture and Poetic Discourse in *The Subjection of Women*," *PMLA*, 98 (1983), p. 354.

because endangered by the proleptic fear that his mediatrix might destabilize and wander, necessarily imposes an *a priori* constraint upon the significative possibilities of the sign "Mina." Such an authorial gesture, intended to forestall the semiotic wandering that Dracula inspires, indirectly acknowledges woman's dangerous potential. Late in the text, while Dracula is vamping Mina, Van Helsing will admit, very uneasily, that "Madam Mina, our poor, dear Madam Mina is changing" (384) [280]. The potential for such a change demonstrates what Nina Auerbach has called this woman's "mysterious amalgam of imprisonment and power."[2]

Dracula's authorizing kiss, like that of a demonic Prince Charming, triggers the release of this latent power and excites in these women a sexuality so mobile, so aggressive, that it thoroughly disrupts Van Helsing's compartmental conception of gender. Kissed into a sudden sexuality,[3] Lucy grows "voluptuous" (a word used to describe her only during the vampiric process), her lips redden, and she kisses with a new interest. This sexualization of Lucy, metamorphosing woman's "sweetness" to "adamantine, heartless cruelty, and [her] purity to voluptuous wantonness" (252) [187], terrifies her suitors because it entails a reversal or inversion of sexual identity; Lucy, now toothed like the Count, usurps the function of penetration that Van Helsing's moralized taxonomy of gender reserves for males. *Dracula*, in thus figuring the sexualization of woman as deformation, parallels exactly some of the more extreme medical uses of the idea of inversion. Late Victorian accounts of lesbianism, for instance, superscribed conventional gender norms upon sexual relationships to which those norms were anatomically irrelevant. Again the heterosexual norm proved paradigmatic. The female "husband" in such a relationship was understood to be dominant, appetitive, masculine, and "congenitally inverted"; the female "wife" was understood to be quiescent, passive, only "latently" homosexual, and, as Havelock Ellis argued, unmotivated by genital desire.[4] Extreme

---

2. Nina Auerbach, *Woman and the Demon* (Cambridge, 1982), p. 11.
3. Roth, "Suddenly Sexual Women in Bram Stoker's *Dracula*," *Literature and Psychology* 27 (1977), p. 116.
4. An adequate analysis of the ideological and political implications of the terminological shift from "inversion" to "homosexuality" is simply beyond the scope of this essay, and the problem is further complicated by a certain imprecision or fluidity in the employment by these writers of an already unstable terminology. Ellis used the word "homosexuality" under protest and Carpenter, citing the evident bastardy of any term compounded of one Greek and one Latin root, preferred the word "homogenic." However, a provisional if oversimplified discrimination between "inversion" and "homosexuality" may be useful: "true" sexual inversion, Ellis argued, consists in "sexual instinct turned by *inborn constitutional abnormality* toward persons of the same sex" (*Sexual Inversion*, p. 1; italics added), whereas homosexuality may refer to same sex eroticism generated by spurious, circumstantial (*faute de mieux*), or intentionally perverse causality. The pivotal issue here is will or choice: the "true" invert, whose "abnormality" is biologically determined and therefore "natural," does not choose his/her desire but is instead chosen by it; the latent or spurious homosexual, on the other hand, does indeed choose a sexual object of the same gender. Such a taxonomic distinction (or, perhaps better, confusion) represents a polemical and political compromise that allows, potentially at least, for the medicalization of congenital inversion and the criminalization of willful homosexuality. I repeat

deployment of the heterosexual paradigm approached the ridiculous, as George Chauncey explains:

> The early medical case histories of lesbians thus predictably paid enormous attention to their menstrual flow and the size of their sexual organs. Several doctors emphasized that their lesbian patients stopped menstruating at an early age, if they began at all, or had unusually difficult and irregular periods. They also inspected the woman's sexual organs, often claiming that inverts had unusually large clitorises, which they said the inverts used in sexual intercourse as a man would his penis.[5]

This rather pathetic hunt for the penis-in-absentia denotes a double anxiety: first, that the penis shall not be erased, and if it is erased, that it shall be reinscribed in a perverse simulacrum; and second, that all desire repeat, under the duress of deformity, the heterosexual norm that the metaphor of inversion always assumes. Medical professionals had in fact no need to pursue this fantasized amazon of the clitoris, this "unnatural" penetrator, so vigorously, since Stoker, whose imagination was at least deft enough to displace that dangerous simulacrum to an isomorphic orifice, had by the 1890s already invented her. His sexualized women are men too.

Stoker emphasizes the monstrosity implicit in such abrogation of gender codes by inverting a favorite Victorian maternal function. His New Lady Vampires feed at first only on small children, working their way up, one assumes, a demonic pleasure thermometer until they may feed at last on full-blooded males. Lucy's dietary indiscretions evoke the deepest disgust from the Crew of Light:

> With a careless motion, she flung to the ground, callous as a devil, the child that up to now she had clutched strenuously to her breast, growling over it as a dog growls over a bone. The child gave a sharp cry, and lay there moaning. There was a cold-bloodedness in the act which wrung a groan from Arthur; when she advanced to him with outstretched arms and a wanton smile, he fell back and hid his face in his hands.
>
> She still advanced, however, and with a langorous, voluptuous grace, said:
>
> "Come to me Arthur. Leave those others and come to me. My arms are hungry for you. Come, and we can rest together. Come, my husband, come!" (253–54) [188]

---

the caution that my description here entails a necessary oversimplification of a terminological muddle. For a more complete and particular analysis see Chauncey, pp. 114–46; for the applicability of such a taxonomy to lesbian relationships see Ellis, *Sexual Inversion*, pp. 131–41.
5. Chauncey, p. 132.

Stoker here gives us a *tableau mordant* of gender inversion: the child Lucy clutches "strenuously to her breast" is not being fed but is being fed upon. Furthermore, by requiring that the child be discarded that the husband may be embraced, Stoker provides a little emblem of this novel's anxious protestation that appetite in a woman "(My arms are hungry for you") is a diabolic ("callous as a devil") inversion of natural order, and of the novel's fantastic but futile hope that maternity and sexuality be divorced.

The aggressive mobility with which Lucy flaunts the encasements of gender norms generates in the Crew of Light a terrific defensive activity, as these men race to reinscribe, with a series of pointed instruments, the line of demarcation which enables the definition of gender. To save Lucy from the mobilization of desire, Van Helsing and the Crew of Light counteract Dracula's subversive series of penetrations with a more conventional series of their own, that sequence of transfusions intended to provide Lucy with the "brave man's blood" which "is the best thing on earth when a woman is in trouble" (180) [136]. There are in fact four transfusions, which begin with Arthur, who as Lucy's accepted suitor has the right of first infusion, and include Lucy's other two suitors (Dr. Seward, Quincey Morris) and Van Helsing himself. One of the established observations of *Dracula* criticism is that these therapeutic penetrations represent displaced marital (and martial) penetrations; indeed, the text is emphatic about this substitution of medical for sexual penetration. After the first transfusion, Arthur feels as if he and Lucy "had been really married and that she was his wife in the sight of God" (209) [157]; and Van Helsing, after his donation, calls himself a "bigamist" and Lucy "this so sweet maid . . . a polyandrist" (211–12) [158]. These transfusions, in short, are sexual (blood substitutes for semen here)[6] and constitute, in Nina Auerbach's superb phrase, "the most convincing epithalamiums in the novel."[7]

These transfusions represent the text's first anxious reassertion of the conventionally masculine prerogative of penetration; as Van Helsing tells Arthur before the first transfusion, "You are a man and it is a man we want" (148) [113]. Countering the dangerous mobility excited by Dracula's kiss, Van Helsing's penetrations restore to Lucy both the stillness appropriate to his sense of her gender and "the regular breathing of healthy sleep," a necessary correction of the loud "stertorous" breathing, the animal snorting, that the Count inspires. This repetitive contest (penetration, withdrawal; penetration, infusion), itself an image of *Dracula's* ambivalent need to evoke and then to repudiate the fluid pleasures of vampiric appetite, continues to be waged upon Lucy's in-

---

6. The symbolic interchangeability of blood and semen in vampirism was identified as early as 1931 by Ernest Jones in *On The Nightmare* (London, 1931), p. 119: "in the unconscious mind blood is commonly an equivalent for semen. . . ."
7. Auerbach, p. 22.

finitely penetrable body until Van Helsing exhausts his store of "brave men," whose generous gifts of blood, however efficacious, fail finally to save Lucy from the mobilization of desire.

But even the loss of this much blood does not finally enervate a masculine energy as indefatigable as the Crew of Light's, especially when it stands in the service of a tradition of "good women whose lives and whose truths may make good lesson [*sic*] for the children that are to be" (222) [166]. In the name of those good women and future children (very much the same children whose throats Lucy is now penetrating), Van Helsing will repeat, with an added emphasis, his assertion that penetration is a masculine prerogative. His logic of corrective penetration demands an escalation, as the failure of the hypodermic needle necessitates the stake. A woman is better still than mobile, better dead than sexual:

> Arthur took the stake and the hammer, and when once his mind was set on action his hands never trembled nor even quivered. Van Helsing opened his missal and began to read, and Quincey and I followed as well as we could. Arthur placed the point over the heart, and as I looked I could see its dint in the white flesh. Then he struck with all his might.
>
> The Thing in the coffin writhed; and a hideous, blood-curdling screech came from the opened red lips. The body shook and quivered and twisted in wild contortions; the sharp white teeth champed together till the lips were cut and the mouth was smeared with a crimson foam. But Arthur never faltered. He looked like the figure of Thor as his untrembling arm rose and fell, driving deeper and deeper the mercy-bearing stake, whilst the blood from the pierced heart welled and spurted up around it. His face was set, and high duty seemed to shine through it; the sight of it gave us courage, so that our voices seemed to ring through the little vault.
>
> And then the writhing and quivering of the body became less, and the teeth ceased to champ, and the face to quiver. Finally it lay still. The terrible task was over. (258–59) [191–92]

Here is the novel's real—and the woman's only—climax, its most violent and misogynistic moment, displaced roughly to the middle of the book, so that the sexual threat may be repeated but its ultimate success denied: Dracula will not win Mina, second in his series of English seductions. The murderous phallicism of this passage clearly punishes Lucy for her transgression of Van Helsing's gender code, as she finally receives a penetration adequate to insure her future quiescence. Violence against the sexual woman here is intense, sensually imagined, ferocious in its detail. Note, for instance, the terrible dimple, the "dint in the white flesh," that recalls Jonathan Harker's swoon at Castle Dracula ("I could feel . . . the hard dents of the two sharp teeth, just touching and pausing there") and anticipates the technicolor consummation of the next paragraph. That paragraph, masking murder as "high duty," completes Van Helsing's penetrative therapy by "driving deeper and deeper the mercy-bearing stake." One might question a mercy this destructive, this fatal, but Van Helsing's actions, always sanctified by the patriarchal textual tradition signified by "his missal," manage to "restore Lucy to us as a holy and not an unholy memory" (258) [191]. This enthusiastic correction of Lucy's monstrosity provides the Crew of Light with a double reassurance: it effectively exorcises the threat of a mobile and hungering feminine sexuality, and it counters the homoeroticism latent in the vampiric threat by reinscribing (upon Lucy's chest) the line dividing the male who penetrates and the woman who receives. By disciplining Lucy and restoring each gender to its "proper" function, Van Helsing's pacification program compensates for the threat of gender indefinition implicit in the vampiric kiss.

The vigor and enormity of this penetration (Arthur driving the "round wooden stake," which is "some two and a half or three inches thick and about three feet long," resembles "the figure of Thor") do not bespeak merely Stoker's personal idiosyncratic anxiety but suggest as well a whole culture's uncertainty about the fluidity of gender roles. * * * Once fatally staked, Lucy is restored to "the so sweet that was." Dr. Seward describes the change:

> There in the coffin lay no longer the foul Thing that we had so dreaded and grown to hate that the work of her destruction was yielded to the one best entitled to it, but Lucy as we had seen her in her life with her face of unequalled sweetness and purity. . . . One and all we felt that the holy calm that lay like sunshine over the wasted face and form was only an earthly token and symbol of the calm that was to reign for ever. (259) [192]

This post-penetrative peace[8] denotes not merely the final immobilization of Lucy's body, but also the corresponding stabilization of the dangerous signifier whose wandering had so threatened Van Helsing's gender code. Here a masculine interpretive community ("One and all we felt") reasserts the semiotic fixity that allows Lucy to function as the "earthly token and symbol" of eternal beatitude, of the heaven we can enter. We may say that this last penetration is doubly efficacious; in a single stoke both the sexual and the textual needs of the Crew of Light find a sufficient satisfaction.

Despite its placement in the middle of the text, this scene, which successfully pacifies Lucy and demonstrates so emphatically the efficacy of the technology Van Helsing employs to correct vampirism, corre-

---

8. Roth correctly reads Lucy's countenance at this moment as "a thank you note" for the corrective penetration: "Suddenly Sexual Women," p. 116.

sponds formally to the scene of expulsion, which usually signals the end of the gothic narrative. Here, of course, this scene signals not the end of the story but the continuation of it, since Dracula will now repeat his assault on another woman. Such displacement of the scene of expulsion requires explanation. Obviously this displacement sub-serves the text's anxiety about the direct representation of eroticism between males; Stoker simply could not represent so explicitly a violent phallic interchange between the Crew of Light and Dracula. In a by now familiar heterosexual mediation, Lucy receives the phallic correc-tion that Dracula deserves. Indeed, the actual expulsion of the Count at novel's end is a disappointing anticlimax. Two rather perfunctory knife strokes suffice to dispatch him, as *Dracula* simply forgets the elab-orate ritual of correction that vampirism previously required. And the displacement of this scene performs at least two other functions; first, by establishing early the ultimate efficacy of Van Helsing's corrective technology, it reassures everyone—Stoker, his characters, the reader— that vampirism may indeed be vanquished, that its sexual threat, how-ever powerful and intriguing, may be expelled; and second, in doing so, in establishing this reassurance, it permits the text to prolong and repeat its flirtation with vampirism, its ambivalent petition of that sexual threat. In short, the displacement of the scene of expulsion provides a heterosexual locale for Van Helsing's demonstration of compensatory phallicism, while it also extends the duration of the text's ambivalent play.

This extension of the text's flirtation with monstrosity, during which Mina is threatened by but not fully seduced into vampirism, includes the novel's only explicit scene of vampiric seduction. Important enough to be twice presented, first by Seward as spectator and then by Mina as participant, the scene occurs in the Harker bedroom, where Dracula seduces Mina while "on the bed lay Jonathan Harker, his face flushed and breathing heavily as if in a stupor." The Crew of Light bursts into the room; the voice is Dr. Seward's:

> With his left hand he held both Mrs. Harker's hands, keeping them away with her arms at full tension; his right hand gripped her by the back of the neck, forcing her face down on his bosom. Her white nightdress was smeared with blood, and a thin stream trickled down the man's bare breast, which was shown by his torn-open dress. The attitude of the two had a terrible resemblance to a child forcing a kitten's nose into a saucer of milk to compel it to drink. (336) [247]

In this initiation scene Dracula compels Mina into the pleasure of vampiric appetite and introduces her to a world where gender distinc-tions collapse, where male and female bodily fluids intermingle terribly. For Mina's drinking is double here, both a "symbolic act of enforced fellation"[9] and a lurid nursing. That this is a scene of enforced fellation is made even clearer by Mina's own description of the scene a few pages later; she adds the graphic detail of the "spurt":

> With that he pulled open his shirt, and with his long sharp nails opened a vein in his breast. When the blood began to spurt out, he took my hands in one of his, holding them tight, and with the other seized my neck and pressed my mouth to the wound, so that I must either suffocate or swallow some of the—Oh, my God, my God! What have I done? (343) [252]

That "Oh, my God, My God!" is deftly placed; Mina's verbal ejaculation supplants the Count's liquid one, leaving the fluid unnamed and encouraging us to voice the substitution that the text implies—this blood is semen too. But this scene of fellation is thoroughly displaced. We are at the Count's breast, encouraged once again to substitute white for red, as blood becomes milk: "the attitude of the two had a terrible resemblance to a child forcing a kitten's nose into a saucer of milk." Such fluidity of substitution and displacement entails a confusion of Dracula's sexual identity, or an interfusion of masculine and feminine functions, as Dracula here becomes a lurid mother offering not a breast but an open and bleeding wound. But if the Count's sexuality is double, then the open would may be yet another displacement (the reader of *Dracula* must be as mobile as the Count himself). We are back in the genital region, this time a woman's, and we have the suggestion of a bleeding vagina. The image of red and voluptuous lips, with their slow trickle of blood, has, of course, always harbored this potential.

We may read this scene, in which anatomical displacements and the confluence of blood, milk, and semen forcefully erase the demarcation separating the masculine and the feminine, as *Dracula's* most explicit representation of the anxieties excited by the vampiric kiss. Here *Dracula* defines most clearly vampirism's threat of gender indefinition. Significantly, this scene is postponed until late in the text. Indeed, this is Dracula's last great moment, his final demonstration of dangerous potency; after this, he will vamp no one. The novel, having presented most explicitly its deepest anxiety, its fear of gender dissolution, now moves mechanically to repudiate that fear. After a hundred rather tedious pages of pursuits and flight, *Dracula* perfunctorily expels the Count. The world of "natural" gender relations is happily restored, or at least seems to be.

* * *

As offspring of Jonathan and Mina Harker, Little Quincey, whose introduction so late in the narrative insures his emblematic function, seemingly represents the restoration of "natural" order and especially

9. C. F. Bentley, "The Monster in the Bedroom: Sexual Symbolism in Bram Stoker's *Dracula*," *Literature and Psychology*, 22 (1972), p. 30.

the rectification of conventional gender roles. His official genesis, is obviously enough, heterosexual, but Stoker's prose quietly suggests an alternative paternity: "His bundle of names links all our little band of men together." This is the fantasy child of those sexualized transfusions, son of an illicit and nearly invisible homosexual union. This suggestion, reinforced by the preceding pun of "spirit," constitutes this text's last and subtlest articulation of its "secret belief" that "a brave man's blood" may metamorphose into "our brave friend's spirit." But the real curiosity here is the novel's last-minute displacement, its substitution of Mina, who ultimately refused sexualization by Dracula, for Lucy, who was sexualized, vigorously penetrated, and consequently destroyed. We may say that Little Quincey was luridly conceived in the veins of Lucy Westenra and then deftly relocated to the purer body of Mina Harker. Here, in the last of its many displacements, *Dracula* insists, first, that successful filiation implies the expulsion of all "monstrous" desire in women and, second, that all desire, however mobile and omnivorous it may secretly be, must subject itself to the heterosexual configuration that alone defined the Victorian sense of the normal. In this regard, Stoker's fable, however hyperbolic its anxieties, represents his age. As we have seen, even polemicists of same sex eroticism like Symonds and Ellis could not imagine such desire without repeating within their metaphor of sexual inversion the basic structure of the heterosexual paradigm. Victorian culture's anxiety about desire's potential indifference to the prescriptions of gender produces everywhere a predictable repetition and a predictable displacement; the heterosexual norm repeats itself in a mediating image of femininity—the Count's vampiric daughters, Ulrichs's and Symonds's *anima muliebris*, Lucy Westenra's penetrable body—that displaces a more direct communion among males. Desire, despite its propensity to wander, stays home and retains an essentially heterosexual and familial definition. The result in *Dracula* is a child whose conception is curiously immaculate, yet disturbingly lurid: child of his father's violations. Little Quincey, fulfilling Van Helsing's prophecy of "the children that are to be," may be the text's emblem of a restored natural order, but his paternity has its unofficial aspect too. He is the unacknowledged son of the Crew of Light's displaced homoerotic union, and his name, linking the "little band of men together," quietly remembers that secret genesis.

BRAM DIJKSTRA

[*Dracula's* Backlash]†

* * *

The cultural preoccupation around 1900 with the struggle of evolutionary progress against the forces of bestiality and degeneration was
dramatized most coherently and consistently in what is certainly the
masterpiece of vampire literature, the ever-popular *Dracula* (1897) by
Bram Stoker. In Stoker's novel virtually all elements of the dream of
future evolutionary possibility and all aspects of the period's suspicions
about the degenerative tendencies in women have been brought together in such an effortless fashion that it is clear that for the author
these were not so much a part of the symbolic structures of fantasy as
the conditions of universal truth. Stoker's work demonstrates how thoroughly the war waged by the nineteenth-century male culture against
the dignity and self-respect of women had been fought, and how completely the ideological implications of the dualistic struggle between the
angels of the future and the demons of the past had entered into that
semi-conscious world which nurtures the cultural commonplaces gov-
erning the average person's perceptual environment. Stoker clearly was
a man of limited intelligence, typical of the fairly well-educated, fairly
well-off, middle-minded middle class. But he had a remarkably coherent socio-logical imagination and a brilliant talent for fluid, natural-
sounding, visually descriptive prose. Together these qualities made it
possible for him to write, perhaps without ever completely realizing
what he had done, a narrative destined to become the looming twentieth century's basic commonplace book of the antifeminine obsession.

It is certainly true that Dracula, the narrative's pivotal vampire, is a
male, but the world in which he operates is a world of women, the
world of Eve, a world in which reversion and acculturation are at war.
Dracula himself is merely an updated version of the art world's vile,
unevolved, grossly bestial satyr, whose inability to control his desires is
only further illuminated by his effeminate aristocratic airs. Dracula may
not officially have been one of those horrid inbred Jews everyone was
worrying about at the time Stoker wrote his novel, but he came close,
for he was very emphatically Eastern European, and hence, like du
Maurier's "filthy black Hebrew," Svengali[1], a creature who had crawled
"out of the mysterious East! The poisonous East—birthplace and home

† From *Idols of Perversity: Fantasies of Feminine Evil in Fin-de-Siecle Culture* by Bram Dijkstra
(New York and Oxford: Oxford UP, 1987) 342–44. © 1987 by Bram Dijkstra. Used by permission of Oxford University Press, Inc. *Dracula* quotations are from the Signet edition (1965).
Bracketed numbers refer to this Norton Critical Edition.
1. George du Maurier, *Trilby* [1894] (London: Everyman's Library, 1969), p. 52.

of an ill-wind that blows nobody good" (377). Like Svengali, Dracula approaches his victims "with a terrible playfulness, like that of a cat with a mouse—a weird, ungainly cat, and most unclean; a sticky, haunting, long, lean, uncanny, black spider-cat, if there is such an animal outside a bad dream"[2]

When Jonathan Harker crosses the Danube on his way to the Carpathian Mountains, he has the impression that "we were leaving the West and entering the East" (11) [9]. He soon discovers the regressive ignorance and inefficiency of Eastern life: "The further east you go the more unpunctual are the trains. What ought they to be in China?" (13) [11] It is a hair-raising question for any efficient Britisher. To travel eastward is to travel into the past. The road to Castle Dracula is "hemmed in with trees, which in places arched right over the roadway till we passed as through a tunnel" (21) [19]. Harker has to travel into the bowels of man's past to find Dracula, and when he finds him the count has all the phrenological characteristics of the sensuous satyr: "His face was a strong—a very strong—aquiline, with high bridge of the thin nose and peculiarly arched nostrils; with lofty domed forehead, and hair growing scantily round the temples but profusely elsewhere, his eyebrows were very massive, almost meeting over the nose, and with bushy hair that seemed to curl in its own confusion." If that weren't enough, he has the "peculiarly sharp white teeth" of an animal, ears "at the tops extremely pointed," and hands which, like a monkey's, "were rather coarse—broad, with squat fingers. Strange to say, there were hairs in the center of the palm" (27) [23–24]. Centuries old, and therefore not surprisingly looking like an old man when Harker first meets him, Dracula, the personification of the past, feeds on the blood of young girls to grow young again, for the bestial past lives in the blood of woman.

Having had his fill of feminine coagulants, he becomes even more Semitic in appearance, "a tall thin man, with a beaky nose and black moustache and pointed beard" (179) [155], a virtual visual reprise of du Maurier's Svengali, who was also possessed of "bold, brilliant black eyes, with long heavy lids, a thin, sallow face, and a beard of burnt-up black, which grew almost from his under eyelids; and over it his moustache, a shade lighter, fell in two long spiral twists"[3]. Stoker felt called upon to show off his up-to-date knowledge of scientific fact in his characterization of the fiend of reversion. After he has his scholar-hero Van Helsing mumble in broken English that Dracula represents the regressive criminal type, is genetically "predestinate to crime," and has a "child-brain," he lets Mina Harker, for good measure, affirm that "Nordau and Lombroso would so classify him" (346) [296].

2. *Ibid.*, p. 83.
3. *Ibid.*, p. 10.

Once this devil of blood lust and regressive, effeminate sensuality has been transported to England, the predatory forces of atavistic bestiality symbolized by Dracula can begin their challenge to the evolutionary acculturation of British womanhood. For it is woman, after all, that the chilly count is after—a fact that soon becomes obvious. Of the truly "male" men in the novel, none, not even Harker himself, the man who ventured into the very lair of the beast, becomes a victim to the creature. Dracula, in this respect, demonstrates a very myopically heterosexual bent. The two women on whom the count sets his bloodshot eyes, Lucy Westenra and Mina Harker, represent the success and failure of modern man's arduous attempts to acculturate woman to the civilized world. They are the two faces of Eve.

*   *   *

STEPHEN D. ARATA

The Occidental Tourist: *Dracula* and the Anxiety of Reverse Colonization†

*   *   *

In many respects, *Dracula* represents a break from the Gothic tradition of vampires. It is easy, for instance, to forget that the "natural" association of vampires with Transylvania begins with, rather than predates, *Dracula*. The site of Castle Dracula was in fact not determined until well after Stoker had begun to write. As Joseph Bierman points out, Stoker originally signalled his debt to his countryman Le Fanu's *Carmilla* (1872) by locating the castle in "Styria," the scene of the earlier Gothic novella.[1] In rewriting the novel's opening chapters, however, Stoker moved *his* Gothic story to a place that, for readers in 1897, resonated in ways Styria did not. Transylvania was known primarily as part of the vexed "Eastern Question" that so obsessed British foreign policy in the 1880s and '90s. The region was first and foremost the site,

---

† Reprinted by permission of the Trustees of Indiana University. from *Victorian Studies* (Summer 1990): 627–34. Bracketed page numbers refer to this Norton Critical Edition.
1. Joseph Bierman, "The Genesis and Dating of *Dracula* from Bram Stoker's Working Notes," *Notes and Queries* 24 (1977), 39–41. For a brief description of Stoker's manuscripts and notes for *Dracula*, including a "List of Sources" that Stoker drew up, see Phyllis Roth, *Bram Stoker* (Boston: Twayne, 1982), pp. 145–146. Stoker gleaned his version of Carpathian history and culture entirely from travel narratives, guidebooks, and various works on Eastern European superstitions, legends, and folktales. Daniel Farson, one of Stoker's biographers, mentions his "genius for research" (*The Man Who Wrote Dracula: A Biography of Bram Stoker* [London: Michael Joseph, 1975], p. 148). Stoker's debt to Le Fanu is most immediately evident in a chapter deleted from *Dracula*, in which Harker, travelling to Castle Dracula, discovers the mausoleum of a "Countess Dolingen of Gratz in Styria." The chapter was later reprinted separately as "Dracula's Guest." See *The Bram Stoker Bedside Companion: Ten Stories by the Author of "Dracula,"* ed. Charles Osborne (New York: Taplinger, 1973).

not of superstition and Gothic romance, but of political turbulence and racial strife. Victorian readers knew the Carpathians largely for its endemic cultural upheaval and its fostering of a dizzying succession of empires. By moving Castle Dracula there, Stoker gives distinctly political overtones to his Gothic narrative. In Stoker's version of the myth, vampires are intimately linked to military conquest and to the rise and fall of empires. According to Dr. Van Helsing, the vampire is the unavoidable consequence of any invasion: "He have follow the wake of the berserker Icelander, the devil-begotten Hun, the Slav, the Saxon, the Magyar."[2]

Nowhere else in the Europe of 1897 could provide a more fertile breeding ground for the undead than the Count's homeland. The Western accounts of the region that Stoker consulted invariably stress the ceaseless clash of antagonistic cultures in the Carpathians.[3] The cycle of empire—rise, decay, collapse, displacement—was there displayed in a particularly compressed and vivid manner. "Greeks, Romans, Huns, Avars, Magyars, Turks, Slavs, French and Germans, all have come and seen and gone, seeking conquest one over the other," opens one late-century account (Bates, p. 3). The Count himself confirms that his homeland has been the scene of perpetual invasion: "there is hardly a foot of soil in all this region that has not been enriched by the blood of men, patriots or invaders," he tells Harker (p. 33) [27]. His subsequent question is thus largely rhetorical: "Is it a wonder that we were a conquering race?" (p. 41) [34].

The "race" in which Dracula claims membership is left ambiguous here. He refers at once to his Szekely warrior past and to his vampiric present. The ambiguity underscores the impossibility of untangling the two aspects of Dracula's essential nature, since his vampirism is interwoven with his status as a conqueror and invader. Here Stoker departs significantly from his literary predecessors. Unlike Polidori and Le Fanu, for instance, who depict their vampires as wan and enervated, Stoker makes Dracula vigorous and energetic. Polidori's Count Ruthven and Le Fanu's Carmilla represent the aristocrat as decadent aesthete; their vampirism is an extension of the traditional aristocratic vices of sensualism and conspicuous consumption. Dracula represents the

---

2. Bram Stoker, *Dracula* (1897; rpt. Harmondsworth: Penguin, 1984), p. 286. [211]
3. I have based my observations on the standard Victorian and Edwardian works in English on the region, which include John Paget, *Hungary and Transylvania* (London: Murray, 1855); James O. Noyes, *Roumania* (New York: Rudd & Carlton, 1857); Charles Boner, *Transylvania: Its Products and Its People* (London: Longmans, 1865); Andrew W. Crosse, *Round About the Carpathians* (Edinburgh and London: William Blackwood and Sons, 1878); C. Johnson, *On the Track of the Crescent* (London: Hurst & Blackett, 1885); M. Edith Durham, *The Burden of the Balkans* (London: Edward Arnold, 1905); Jean Victor Bates, *Our Allies and Enemies in the Near East* (New York: E. P. Dutton & Co., n.d.); and especially Emily Gerard, *The Land Beyond the Forest: Facts, Figures, and Fancies from Transylvania*, 2 vols. (Edinburgh and London: William Blackwood and Sons, 1888).

nobleman as warrior.[4] His activities after death carry on his activities in life; in both cases he has successfully engaged in forms of conquest and domination.

Racial conquest and domination, we should immediately add. Stoker continues a Western tradition of seeing unrest in Eastern Europe primarily in terms of racial strife. For Stoker, the vampire "race" is simply the most virulent and threatening of the numerous warrior races—Berserker, Hun, Turk, Saxon, Slovak, Magyar, Szekely—inhabiting the area. Nineteenth-century accounts of the Carpathians repeatedly stress its polyracial character. The standard Victorian work on the region, Charles Boner's *Transylvania* (1865), begins by marvelling at this spectacle of variety:

> The diversity of character which the various physiognomies present that meet you at every step, also tell of the many nations which are here brought together. . . . The slim, lithe Hungarian . . . the more oriental Wallachian, with softer, sensuous air,—in her style of dress and even in her carriage unlike a dweller in the West; a Moldavian princess, wrapped in a Turkish shawl. . . . And now a Serb marches proudly past, his countenance calm as a Turk's; or a Constantinople merchant sweeps along in his loose robes and snowy turban. There are, too, Greeks, Dalmatians, and Croats, all different in feature: there is no end to the variety. (pp. 1–2).

Transylvania is what Dracula calls the "whirlpool of European races" (p. 41) [33], but within that whirlpool racial interaction usually involved conflict, not accommodation. Racial violence could in fact reach appalling proportions, as in the wholesale massacres, widely reported by the British press, of Armenians by Turks in 1894 and 1896, the years in which *Dracula* was being written. For Western writers and readers, these characteristics—racial heterogeneity combined with racial intolerance considered barbaric in its intensity—defined the area east and south of the Danube, with the Carpathians at the imaginative center of the turmoil.

By situating Dracula in the Carpathians, and by continually blurring the lines between the Count's vampiric and warrior activities, Stoker

4. Several critics have, correctly I think, placed Dracula in the tradition of aristocratic rakes like Richardson's Lovelace, who in turn have their roots in the medieval lord with his demands for the *droit de seigneur*. This view can obscure Stoker's emphasis on Dracula's military, rather than just his sexual, prowess. In addition to Bentley, Fry, and Hatlen, see Judith Weissman, "Women as Vampires: *Dracula* as a Victorian Novel," *Midwest Quarterly* 18 (1977), 392–405. It is also possible to read *Dracula* as a bourgeois fantasy of aristocratic power and privilege; like the hereditary nobleman, Dracula is associated most closely with land (he must stay in contact with his native soil to survive), wealth (which he literally digs out of the land on the night of Harker's arrival in Transylvania), family (his name is transmitted through generations without the line being interrupted), and of course blood (which in turn is connected with the other three; remember, for instance, that when Harker cuts Dracula with his knife, he "bleeds" a "stream of gold" coins [p. 364] [266]). For the middle-class Victorian audience, the vision of aristocratic puissance embodied by Dracula would have been deeply attractive, especially given the ineffectuality of the novel's only English aristocrat, Lord Godalming.

forges seemingly "natural" links among three of his principal concerns: racial strife, the collapse of empire, and vampirism. It is important too to note the sequence of events. As Van Helsing says, vampires follow "in [the] wake of" imperial decay (p. 286) [211]. Vampires are generated by racial enervation and the decline of empire, not vice versa. They are produced, in other words, by the very conditions characterizing late-Victorian Britain.

Stoker thus transforms the materials of the vampire myth, making them bear the weight of the culture's fears over its declining status. The appearance of vampires becomes the sign of profound trouble. With vampirism marking the intersection of racial strife, political upheaval, and the fall of empire, Dracula's move to London indicates that Great Britain, rather than the Carpathians, is now the scene of these connected struggles. The Count has penetrated to the heart of modern Europe's largest empire, and his very presence seems to presage its doom:

> This was the being I was helping to transfer to London [Harker writes in anguish] where, perhaps for centuries to come, he might, amongst its teeming millions, satiate his lust for blood, and create a new and ever widening circle of semi-demons to batten on the helpless. (p. 67) [53–54]

The late-Victorian nightmare of reverse colonization is expressed succinctly here: Harker envisions semi-demons spreading through the realm, colonizing bodies and land indiscriminately. The Count's "lust for blood" points in both directions: to the vampire's need for its special food, and also to the warrior's desire for conquest. The Count endangers Britain's integrity as a nation at the same time that he imperils the personal integrity of individual citizens.

Harker's lament highlights the double thrust—political and biological—of Dracula's invasion, while at the same time conflating the two into a single threat. Dracula's twin status as vampire and Szekely warrior suggests that for Stoker the Count's aggressions against the body are also aggressions against the body politic. Indeed, the Count can threaten the integrity of the nation precisely because of the nature of his threat to personal integrity. His attacks involve more than an assault on the isolated self, the subversion and loss of one's individual identity. Again unlike Polidori's Count Ruthven or Le Fanu's Carmilla (or even Thomas Prest's Sir Francis Varney), Dracula imperils not simply his victims' personal identities, but also their cultural, political, and racial selves. In *Dracula* vampirism designates a kind of colonization of the body. Horror arises not because Dracula destroys bodies, but because he appropriates and transforms them. Having yielded to his assault, one literally "goes native" by becoming a vampire oneself. As John Allen Stevenson argues, if "blood" is a sign of racial identity, then Dracula effectively deracinates his victims (p. 144). In turn, they receive a new racial identity, one that marks them as literally "Other." Miscegenation leads, not to the mixing of races, but to the biological and political annihilation of the weaker race by the stronger.

Through the vampire myth, Stoker gothicizes the political threats to Britain caused by the enervation of the Anglo-Saxon "race." These threats also operate independently of the Count's vampirism, however, for the vampire was not considered alone in its ability to deracinate. Stoker learned from Emily Gerard that the Roumanians were themselves notable for the way they could "dissolve" the identities of those they came in contact with:

> The Hungarian woman who weds a Roumanian husband will necessarily adopt the dress and manners of his people, and her children will be as good Roumanians as though they had no drop of Magyar blood in their veins; while the Magyar who takes a Roumanian girl for his wife will not only fail to convert her to his ideas, but himself, subdued by her influence, will imperceptibly begin to lose his nationality. This is a fact well known and much lamented by the Hungarians themselves, who live in anticipated apprehension of seeing their people ultimately dissolving into Roumanians.[5]

Gerard's account of the "imperceptible" but inevitable loss of identity —national, cultural, racial—sounds remarkably like the transformations that Lucy and Mina suffer under Dracula's "influence." In life Dracula was a Roumanian (Gerard designates the Szekelys as a branch of the Roumanian race); his ability to deracinate could thus derive as easily from his Roumanian as from his vampire nature.

The "anticipated apprehension" of deracination—of seeing Britons "ultimately dissolving into Roumanians" or vampires or savages—is at the heart of the reverse colonization narrative. For both Gerard and Stoker, the Roumanians' dominance can be traced to a kind of racial puissance that overwhelms its weaker victims. This racial context helps account for what critics routinely note about Dracula: that he is by his very nature vigorous, masterful, energetic, robust. Such attributes are conspicuously absent among the novel's British characters, particularly the men. All the novel's vampires are distinguished by their robust health and their equally robust fertility. The vampire serves, then, to highlight the alarming decline among the British, since the undead are, paradoxically, both "healthier" and more "fertile" than the living. Perversely, a vampiric attack can serve to invigorate its victim. "The adventure of the night does not seem to have harmed her," Mina notes

---

5. Gerard, I, 304–305. Scholars have long recognized Stoker's reliance on Gerard. See Roth, *Bram Stoker*, pp. 13–14, and Leonard Wolf, *The Annotated Dracula* (New York: Clarkson Potter, 1975), pp. xiii–xiv and references in his annotations throughout.

after Lucy's first encounter with Dracula; "on the contrary, it has benefited her, for she looks better this morning than she has done in weeks"
(p. 115) [89]. Indeed, after his attack, Lucy's body initially appears
stronger, her eyes brighter, her cheeks rosier. The corresponding enervation that marks the British men is most clearly visible in Harker
(he is "pale," "weak-looking," "exhausted," "nervous," "a wreck"), but
it can be seen in the other male British characters as well. Harker and
Dracula in fact switch places during the novel; Harker becomes tired
and white-haired as the action proceeds, while Dracula, whose white
hair grows progressively darker, becomes more vigorous.

The vampire's vigor is in turn closely connected with its virility, its
ability to produce literally endless numbers of offspring. Van Helsing's
concern that the earth in Dracula's boxes be "sterilized" (pp. 347, 355)
[213, 220–21] underlines the connection between the Count's threat
and his fecundity. In marked contrast, the nonvampires in the novel
seem unable to reproduce themselves. Fathers in particular are in short
supply: most are either dead (Mr. Westenra, Mr. Harker, Mr. Murray,
Mr. Canon), dying (Mr. Hawkins, Lord Godalming, Mr. Swales), or
missing (Mr. Seward, Mr. Morris), while the younger men, being un-
married, cannot father legitimately. Even Harker, the novel's only married man, is prohibited from touching Mina after she has been made
"unclean." In *Dracula*'s lexicon, uncleanliness is closely related to fertility, but it is the wrong kind of fertility; Mina, the men fear, is perfectly
capable of producing "offspring," but not with Jonathan. The prohibi-
tion regarding Mina is linked to the fear of vampiric fecundity, a fecundity that threatens to overwhelm the far less prolific British men.
Thus, as many critics have pointed out, the arrival of little Quincey
Harker at the story's close signals the final triumph over Dracula, since
the Harkers' ability to secure an heir—an heir whose racial credentials
are seemingly impeccable—is the surest indication that the vampire's
threat has been mastered. Even this triumph is precarious, however.
Harker proudly notes that his son is named after each of the men in
the novel, making them all figurative fathers (p. 449) [326], yet Quincey's multiple parentage only underscores the original problem. How
secure is any racial line when five fathers are needed to produce one son?

Such racial anxieties are clearest in the case of Lucy Westenra. If
Dracula's kiss serves to deracinate Lucy, and by doing so to unleash
what the male characters consider her incipiently monstrous sexual
appetite, then the only way to counter this process is to "re-racinate"
her by reinfusing her with the "proper" blood. But Stoker is careful to
establish a strict hierarchy among the potential donors. The men give
blood in this order: Holmwood, Seward, Van Helsing, Morris. Arthur
Holmwood is first choice ostensibly because he is engaged to Lucy, but
also, and perhaps more importantly, because his blood is, in Van Helsing's words, "more good than" Seward's (p. 149) [114]. As the only

English aristocrat in the novel, Holmwood possesses a "blood so pure" (p. 149) [114] that it can restore Lucy's compromised racial identity. Dr. Seward, whose blood though bourgeois is English nonetheless, comes next in line, followed by the two foreigners, Van Helsing and Morris. We should note that Van Helsing's old, Teutonic blood is still preferred over Morris's young, American blood, for reasons I will take up in a moment. Even foreign blood is better than lower-class blood, however. After Lucy suffers what proves to be the fatal attack by Dracula, Van Helsing, looking for blood donors, rejects the four apparently healthy female servants as unsafe: "I fear to trust those women" (p. 180) [136].

More precisely, Van Helsing's distrust of "those women" marks a point of intersection between his usually covert class prejudices and his often overt misogyny.[6] That Dracula propagates his race solely through the bodies of women suggests an affinity, or even an identity, between vampiric sexuality and female sexuality. Both are represented as primitive and voracious, and both threaten patriarchal hegemony. In the novel's (and Victorian Britain's) sexual economy, female sexuality has only one legitimate function, propagation within the bounds of marriage. Once separated from that function, as Lucy's desire is, female sexuality becomes monstrous. The violence of Lucy's demise is grisly enough, but we should not miss the fact that her subjection and Mina's final fate parallel one another. They differ in degree, not kind. By the novel's close, Mina's sexual energy has been harnessed for purely domestic use. In the end, women serve identical purposes for both Dracula and the Western characters. If in this novel blood stands for race, then women quite literally become the vehicles of racial propagation. The struggle between the two camps is thus on one level a struggle over access to women's bodies, and Dracula's biological colonization of women becomes a horrific parody of the sanctioned exploitation practiced by the Western male characters.

By considering the parallel fates of Lucy and Mina, moreover, we can see how the fear and guilt characteristic of reverse colonization narratives begin to overlap. The fear generated by the Count's colonization of his victims' bodies—a colonization appropriately designated monstrous—modulates into guilt that his practices simply repeat those of the "good" characters. Dracula's invasion and appropriation of female bodies does not distinguish him from his Western antagonists as much as at first appears. Instead of being uncannily Other, the vampire is here revealed as disquietingly familiar. And since the colonizations of bodies and territory are closely linked, the same blurring of distinc-

6. A full discussion of the gender issues raised by *Dracula* is outside the scope of this essay. Many critics have discussed the thinly disguised fear of women evident in the novel. In addition to Craft, Demetrakopoulous, Fry, Griffin, Roth, and Weissman, see Alan Johnson, " 'Dual Life': The Status of Women in Stoker's *Dracula*," *Tennessee Studies in Literature* 27 (1984), 20–39.

tions occurs when we consider more closely the nature of the Count's invasion of Britain. Just as Dracula's vampirism mirrors the domestic practices of Victorian patriarchs, so his invasion of London in order to "batten on the helpless" natives there mirrors British imperial activities abroad.

As a transplanted Irishman, one whose national allegiances were conspicuously split, Stoker was particularly sensitive to the issues raised by British imperial conquest and domination. Britain's subjugation of Ireland was marked by a brutality often exceeding what occurred in the colonies, while the stereotype of the "primitive . . . dirty, vengeful, and violent" Irishman was in most respects identical to that of the most despised "savage."[7] The ill will characterizing Anglo-Irish relations in the late-nineteenth century, exacerbated by the rise of Fenianism and the debate over Home Rule, far surpassed the tensions that arose as a result of British rule elsewhere. When that ill will erupted into violence, as it did in the 1882 Phoenix Park murders, Victorian readers could see, up close and in sharp focus, the potential consequences of imperial domination. For Stoker's audience, Dracula's invasion of Britain would conceivably have aroused seldom dormant fears of an Irish uprising.

The lack of autobiographical materials makes it difficult to determine the extent, if any, to which Stoker consciously felt himself in solidarity with his Irish brethren. On the one hand, his few published essays, particularly one advocating censorship, reveal a deeply conservative outlook in which "duty to the [British] state" outweighs all other considerations, even those of a dubious freedom or self-determination. On the other hand, through Stoker's very adherence to what he calls "forms of restraint" runs a deeply anarchic streak. The attraction of forbidden, outlawed, disruptive action is evident enough in *Dracula* as well as in Stoker's other fictions; the same tension between restraint and rebellion may have characterized his relation to the ruling state. It probably also characterized his professional life. Certainly his status as glorified manservant to the autocratic Henry Irving almost uncannily reenacted, on the personal level, the larger cultural pattern of English domination and Irish subservience. Stoker's lifelong passion for Irving had its dark underside: the rumors, persistent in Stoker's lifetime, that Count Dracula was modelled on Irving suggests the deep ambivalence with which the transplanted Irishman regarded his professional benefactor. Like Quincey Morris, Stoker seems finally to stand in alliance with his English companions without ever being entirely of their camp.

Dracula suggests two equations in relation to English-Irish politics: not just, Dracula is to England as Ireland is to England, but, Dracula is to England as England is to Ireland. In Count Dracula, Victorian readers could recognize their culture's imperial ideology mirrored back

---

7. See L. P. Curtis, *Anglo-Saxons and Celts: A Study of Anti-Irish Prejudice in Victorian England* (Bridgeport, CT: Bridgeport University Press, 1968).

as a kind of monstrosity. Dracula's journey from Transylvania to England could be read as a reversal of Britain's imperial exploitations of "weaker" races, including the Irish. This mirroring extends not just to the imperial practices themselves, but to their epistemological underpinnings. Before Dracula successfully invades the spaces of his victims' bodies or land, he first invades the spaces of their knowledge. The Count operates in several distinct registers in the novel. He is both the warrior nobleman, whose prowess dwarfs that of the novel's enfeebled English aristocrat, Lord Godalming, and the primitive savage, whose bestiality, fecundity, and vigor alternately repel and attract. But he is also what we might call an incipient "Occidentalist" scholar. Dracula's physical mastery of his British victims begins with an intellectual appropriation of their culture, which allows him to delve the workings of the "native mind." As Harker discovers, the Count's expertise in "English life and customs and manners" (p. 30) [25] provides the groundwork for his exploitative invasion of Britain. Thus, in Dracula the British characters see their own ideology reflected back as a form of bad faith, since the Count's Occidentalism both mimics and reverses the more familiar Orientalism underwriting Western imperial practices.[8]

∗   ∗   ∗

TALIA SCHAFFER

"A Wilde Desire Took Me": The Homoerotic History of Dracula†

∗   ∗   ∗

May 24, 1895 was a significant date for Stoker. On that date the English government convicted Oscar Wilde, and knighted Henry Irving and Stoker's brother Thornley. *Personal Reminiscences* mentions Irving's triumph directly, but describes Wilde's tragedy only indirectly (and apparently neglects Thornley's honor altogether). Stoker inserts a strange paragraph into his account of Irving's honor. He apologizes for revealing the fact that Irving had rejected a knighthood once before 1895:

> I feel it too bad that one who in his days tried to live up to the ideal of discretion, and has regarded reticence as a duty rather than a motive, should have to speak openly, even after a lapse of

8. See Edward Said, *Orientalism* (New York: Vintage, 1979).
  † First published in *English Literary History*, Vol. 61:2. ©1994 by the Johns Hopkins University Press. Reprinted by permission of the Johns Hopkins University Press. *Dracula* quotations are from Bram Stoker, *Dracula* (Oxford: Oxford UP, 1983). Bracketed page numbers refer to this Norton Critical Edition.

years, on so private a matter, and I can only trust that I may be forgiven should any one with the power of forgiveness see the need of it.[1]

The *mea culpa* is inappropriately excessive for its assigned cause. "Discretion" and "reticence," Stoker's codes for the closet, however, alert us to the real subject of the passage: insistent, diffused, urgent repression of Stoker's homoerotic secret. The man who "has regarded reticence as a duty" is the same man, though a little more frightened, who "cannot break the habit of comparative reticence." The passage makes sense as Stoker's covert *apologia* for his silence regarding Wilde. Its first sentence coheres when we read its reference as sexuality, not knighting etiquette. It is difficult, Stoker admits, to speak openly about "so private a matter" as desire. In carefully calibrated language, Stoker asks forgiveness from those who might see that his silence is a sin—to those few nameless souls who know his secret affinity with Wilde. This passage stands as a reply to all those—Caine, Terry, Irving, Willie Wilde—who wanted Stoker's sympathy for Wilde, and to whom Stoker was able to vouchsafe no answer, unable to break from the shackles of discretion and the stony weight of reticence.

Placed anomolously in the midst of his praise of Irving, the passage is a sign of Stoker's difficulty in ignoring his regrets about Wilde's trial. Wilde's trial swims to the surface as the return of the repressed. The passage shows that the trial's greatest effect on Stoker was to sharpen his self-conflicting imperatives towards articulation. In other words, Stoker registered the trial as a challenge to his own codes of delicately ambiguous language, not as a denial of his desires' legitimacy.

But the chapter also memorializes the summer of 1895 in a more indirect way, which concerns the problem of writing. Stoker records Irving's knighthood in terms of the enormous quantity of text it produced. "Cables began to pour in from all parts of the world. . . . The letters and telegraphs kept coming in, literally by hundreds. . . . They were bewildering."[2] Just as *Personal Reminiscences of Henry Irving* is really Stoker's autobiography, this account of Irving's triumph encodes a hidden account of Stoker's triumph. The stress on writing records the commencement of *Dracula*. In *Dracula*, written one month after Wilde went to jail, Stoker solved his guilty problem: avoiding the crude binary options of openness and reticence, the cruel choice between writing and silence, he produced a text that spoke about Wilde in a diffused, hidden, flowing, distorted way. *Dracula* reproduces Wilde in all his apparent monstrosity and evil, in order to work through this painful popular image of the homosexual and eventually transform it into a viable identity model.

1. Bram Stoker, *Personal Reminiscences of Henry Irving*, 2 vols. (New York: Macmillan Company), 2, p. 242.
2. *Ibid.*, p. 239.

Though Stoker had planned *Dracula* for a long time, it was in August of 1895 that he began writing it into notebooks.[3] In particular, Jonathan Harker's experiences at Castle Dracula "were written . . . in the first vivid flow of inspiration."[4] These first five chapters read as a nightmarish meeting between Harker and Dracula, who are fictionalized projections of Stoker and Wilde. Like Stoker, whose name his echoes, Harker is a married man, a solicitor who has not practiced law, and a younger man loyally working for a beloved older man. Dracula, however, does not produce such a straightforward identification. He represents not so much Oscar Wilde as the complex of fears, desires, secrecies, repressions, and punishments that Wilde's name evoked in 1895. Dracula is Wilde-as-threat, a complex cultural construction not to be confused with the historical individual Oscar Wilde. Dracula represents the ghoulishly inflated vision of Wilde produced by Wilde's prosecutors; the corrupting, evil, secretive, manipulative, magnetic devourer of innocent boys. Furthermore, *Dracula* also carries the weight of Stoker's imaginative identification with Wilde. For Stoker writes *Dracula*'s plot to allow his surrogate Harker to experience imprisonment, just as Wilde languished in goal. Thus Stoker manages to speak both from the closet and from the open; he simultaneously explores Wilde-as-monster, and identifies with the real Wilde's pain. He writes as a man victimized by Wilde's trial, and yet as a man who sympathizes with Wilde's victimization. Within *Dracula*, this binary opposition supplants the cruder opposition between closeting and coming out.

It was probably inevitable that Stoker would rejuvenate Wilde in the specific form of a vampire. Turn-of-the-century 'inversion' theory considered homosexuals neither male nor female, but, in Edward Carpenter's phrase, the "intermediate sex," inhabiting a no-man's land like the Undead who were neither dead nor alive. Furthermore, the associations

---

3. See Christopher Craft, " 'Kiss Me with Those Red Lips': Gender and Inversion in Bram Stoker's *Dracula,*" *Representations* 8 (Fall 1984): 107–33; Elaine Showalter, *Sexual Anarchy: Gender and Culture at the Fin de Siecle* (New York: Viking Penguin, 1990); Marjorie Howes, "The Mediation of the Feminine: Bisexuality, Homoerotic Desire, and Self-Expression in Bram Stoker's *Dracula,*" *Texas Studies in Literature and Language* 30 (1988): 104–19; C. F. Bentley, "The Monster in the Bedroom," *Literature and Psychology* 22 (1972): 27–24; Anne Cranny-Francis, "Sexual Politics and Political Repression in Bram Stoker's *Dracula,*" *Nineteenth-Century Suspense: From Poe to Conan Doyle,* ed. Clive Bloom, Brian Docherty, Jane Gibb, Keith Shand (New York: St. Martin's Press, 1988), 64–79.
4. There are four biographies of Stoker available now, and all draw heavily on Stoker's semiautobiographical *Reminiscences of Sir Henry Irving.* Harry Ludlam's *A Biography of Dracula: The Life Story of Bram Stoker* (London: W. Foulsham & Co. Ltd., 1962) is the earliest biography and focuses on the early film and theatre history of 'Dracula.' Daniel Farson's *The Man Who Wrote Dracula* (London: Michael Joseph Ltd., 1975) takes a slightly more critical approach to Stoker's life and also incorporates family memories, since Stoker was Farson's great-uncle. For these reasons I have chosen to rely on Farson's biography rather than Ludlam's. Both biographies lack footnotes, bibliography, and citations. The most modern biography is Alain Pozzuoli's French work, also without scholarly apparatus: *Bram Stoker, Prince des Ténébres* (France: Librairie Séguier, 1989). Phyllis A. Roth's slim biography, *Bram Stoker* (Boston: Twayne Publishers, 1982) provides a more contemporary scholarly approach but is a summary of Farson, Ludlam, and *Personal Reminiscences* that adds no new information.

between homosexuality and anality led many writers to connect homosexuality with defecation, dirt, and decay. As Ellis Hanson argues, "To comprehend the vampire is to recognize that abjected space that gay men are obliged to inhabit; that space unspeakable or unnameable, itself defined as orifice, as a 'dark continent' men dare not penetrate."[5] The vampire figure therefore fit easily as metaphor for the love that dare not speak its name. To homophobes, vampirism could function as a way of naming the homosexual as monstrous, dirty, threatening. To homosexuals, vampirism could be an elegy for the enforced interment of their desires. *Dracula*, however, functions as both accusation and elegy. Stoker used the Wildean figure of Dracula to define homosexuality as simultaneously monstrous, dirty, threatening, alluring, buried, corrupting, contagious, and indestructible.

One scene in Castle Dracula best registers the intensity of conflicting feeling generated by Wilde's trial. In the few pages before Harker's escape, he experiences the climax of both Wilde-phobia and Wilde pity: "A wild desire took me to obtain that key at any risk" (*D*, 50) [53]. Harker's wild(e) desire leads him to feel another man's body. (After Wilde's trial, 'the desire of Oscar Wilde' became a euphemism for homosexuality.) When he lifts the covers from Dracula's bed/grave, he sees that the tall, pale, aristocratic vampire has changed appearance, and now resembles Oscar Wilde.[6] His hair is "iron-grey,"

> The cheeks were fuller. . . . even the deep, burning eyes seemed set amongst swollen flesh, for the lids and pouches underneath were bloated. . . . he lay like a filthy leech, exhausted with his repletion. I shuddered as I bent over to touch him, and every sense in me revolted at the contact. (*D*, 51) [53]

In 1895, Wilde was grey-haired, heavily overweight, and famously easily exhausted. Compare a typical description of Wilde, this one by Stoker's shady acquaintance Frank Harris:[7]

> There was something oily and fat about him that repelled me. . . . his hands were flabby, greasy; his skin looked bilious and dirty. . . . His appearance filled me with distaste. I lay stress on this physical repulsion, because I think most people felt it.[8]

5. Ellis Hanson, "Undead," in *Inside/Out: Lesbian Theories, Gay Theories*, ed. Diana Fuss (New York: Routledge, 1991), 325.
6. Salli J. Kline argues that Dracula, with his fastidious attire and goatee, his strolls down Piccadilly, and his elaborate collection of valuable artworks, is meant to satirize the Aesthete. "Count Dracula de Ville [his assumed surname] obviously stands for the dandies of London, its professional aesthetes, its self-conscious, ostentatiously extravagant 'Decadents'. " (Salli J. Kline, *The Degeneration of Women* [Rheinbach-Merzbach: CMZ-Verlag, 1992]. 188–91).
7. Frank Harris's *My Life and Loves* (New York: Grove Press, 1925) details his dealings with Stoker.
8. Frank Harris, *Oscar Wilde* (East Lansing: Michigan State Univ. Press, 1959), 53–54. Though Harris is renowned for his mendacity, I have used his account because it is the most vivid description of a common observation.

The point is not that Stoker would have found Wilde physically repulsive and drawn on this memory for the rejuvenated Dracula; rather, the point is that Stoker's Dracula is a kind of basin in which images of Wilde-as-monster float, and it makes sense that a vision of Wilde's body as repulsive, which Harris claims to be universal, would be one fluid in the Dracula solution.

After Harker "felt all over the body," he muses that Dracula might "create a new and ever widening circle of semi-demons to batten on the helpless" (*D*, 51) [53–54]. This image of a monstrous progenitor amidst a horrible circle is precisely what dominated public rhetoric about Wilde during the trial. In a widely reported comment, Wilde's judge called him "the center of a hideous circle of corruption."[9] The prosecutor introduced several young male witnesses who claimed that Wilde had 'ruined' them, which forced them to make a living by buying other boys, spreading the circle of pimping and prostitution.

Harker is properly horrified by the vampire's monstrosity—but Dracula's Medusa gaze prevents him from killing his enemy: "The eyes fell full upon me, with all their blaze of basilisk horror. The sight seemed to paralyze me" (*D*, 52) [54]. Dracula's powerful eyes shift Harker/Stoker into his attitude of stiff, stony passivity. The eyes give him a thrill of horror at his own sensations of pleasure. Though his body is strainingly retentive, Harker's muscular paralysis also prevents him from harming his employer and thereby enforces his loyal 'retainer' role. So he claps the closet door closed. The lid "fell over again, and hid the horrid thing from my sight" (*D*, 52) [54].

But by locking in Dracula, Harker imprisons himself (and Stoker incarcerates part of himself). The lid slams on the vampire as doors slam around the man. This mutuality lets Stoker atone for his orthodox hatred of Wilde, for he manages an agonizing imagination of the pain Wilde must have felt at his imprisonment. In a bewildering whirl of movements, Harker hears himself locked in.

> The door to the winding stair blew to with a shock that set the dust from the lintels flying. When I ran to push it open, I found that it was hopelessly fast. I was again a prisoner, and the net of doom was closing round me more closely. . . . There is a sound of hammering; it is the box being nailed down. (*D*, 52) [54]

The passage gives an idea of what Wilde must have felt on June 9, the date of his imprisonment.[1] Stoker had prepared for this imaginative identification. As reported by *Reynold's News*, Wilde's own clothes had been removed—just as Harker's clothes had been taken by Dracula. Wilde was detained for two years, Harker for two months. The rules of

9. *The Westminster Gazette*, 27 May 1895, 2.
1. For a description of Wilde's incarceration, see Richard Ellmann, *Oscar Wilde* (New York: Vintage Books, 1987), (note 33), 479–80.

the prison were read out to Wilde, just as Dracula told Harker where he was forbidden to explore and to sleep. Here is the final, climactic moment in which Harker, like Wilde, is left alone in his prison cell:

> Now I can hear the heavy feet tramping again along the hall, with many other idle feet coming behind them. The door is shut and the chains rattle; there is a grinding of the key in the lock; I can hear the key withdrawn; then another door opens and shuts; I can hear the creaking of lock and bolt. Hark! in the courtyard and down the rocky way the roll of heavy wheels, the crack of whips, and the chorus of the Szegany as they pass into the distance. I am alone. (D, 52–53) [54–55]

Dracula allows Stoker to enact different, conflicting parts. As in a dream, the novel's characters (especially Harker) can switch identities, virtues, and sympathies with bewildering speed. The first part of the book swings wildly between utter hatred of Wilde and utter sorrow for Wilde. The strain of these contradictory emotions nearly tears apart the plot, as logical narrative is pulled and tormented to fit Stoker's emotional needs. For instance, there is no real reason why Dracula should postpone Harker's sacrifice in order to imprison him. But Stoker wants to sympathize with Wilde: "When I found that I was a prisoner a sort of *wild* feeling came over me" (D, 27, emphasis added) [32]. Harker's intense experience of imprisonment means that the rest of the novel has to be written in order to domesticate and dissipate his 'wild' experience.

Harker's hatred of Dracula problematically hovers on the margins of self-hatred. The perverse logic of rivalry demands a resemblence: the men are alike at least in their desire and their determination to achieve it. Stoker and Wilde shared love object, nationality, university training, poetic taste, area of residence, social circle, and profession. Harker and Dracula also have a great deal in common. Dracula "would have made a wonderful solicitor" says the young lawyer (D, 31) [37]. His host's library causes Harker "great delight," since it precisely reproduces his own literary tastes; no wonder Dracula can say, "I am glad you found your way in here, for I am sure there is much that will interest you" (D, 19, 21) [25–26]. They share clothing and mirrors. Moreover, Dracula models his English on Harker's, as he asks Harker to teach him how to speak. (Dracula works to lose his characteristic national accent: "I am content if I am like the rest, so that no man . . . pause in his speaking if he hear my words, to say, 'Ha, ha! a stranger!' " [D, 20] [26]. Similarly, Wilde carefully acquired a perfect English pronunciation, in marked contrast to Stoker, who kept his Irish accent all his life.[2])

When Harker sees Dracula dressed in his own clothes, the image is

2. Ellmann (note 33), 38; Farson (note 2), 232.

profoundly disturbing. Their shared clothing implies intimacy, acquaintance with the contours of each other's bodies, ease with the prospect of each other's nakedness. Dracula had seemed to Harker "a tall old man" (D, 15) [21]. But the same clothing fits both, which proves that their bodies are the same size and shape. They act alike; both crawl on the external wall of the castle. Their sense of etiquette is the same; Dracula, leaving to harvest babies, chooses to wear Harker's traveling clothes, not only because the villagers have already seen them but also because Dracula, about to travel, knows the appropriate wardrobe. In response, Harker differentiates his own body by marking the Count's as feminine. He tears "a deep gash above the forehead," thus constituting himself as hard and impenetrable (D, 52) [54]. As in the "Censorship" articles, heterosexual masculinity is produced by repression, destruction, and reticence. Harker's escape route is a last, desperate attempt to enforce his masculinity: "The precipice is steep and high. At its foot a man may sleep—as a man" (D, 53) [55]. He imagines death amidst a masculine, phallic landscape of pointed pines and steep cliffs—falling on the censor's pen and the stony ridge.

The opposite of this deathly rigor is a sort of sublimated nonphysical pleasure associated with dematerialized texts. Harker keeps his diary in his pockets. The diary's physical weight and size disappear, for Dracula undresses Harker and folds his clothes yet somehow overlooks the prize in Harker's trousers. (Similarly, Harker magically feels all over Dracula's body without finding Dracula's key.) Harker sees himself as a woman writing a love-letter, and as a desperate conspirator penning secret shorthand epistles (D, 36) [40]. But the physical aspect of his epistolary desires seems nonexistent. Dracula holds the shorthand letter and envelope in the flame "till they were consumed" and steals "every scrap of paper" that Harker possessed (D, 42, 43) [46]. Throughout the novel characters find enjoyment in writing, only to find the material on which they inscribe—their waxen phonographic cylinders, diary books, and telegrams—burned, mislaid, or misdirected, as if Stoker needs to salvage the pleasure of writing by destroying the sensuous experience of the document itself.

This intangible text relates to Stoker's other strategies for displacing sexuality. The fiery evanescence of text maps onto other discourses associated with homoerotic pleasure: 'sensoria,' Wilde-pity, arousing stories, and emotional male companionship. On the other hand, the stony reticence of repression maps onto censorship, Wilde-phobia paralysis, and police action. These two poles should not become absolute markers of difference, but rather general ways of organizing Stoker's experiences of the closet and of openness. And the two strategies interlink at certain points, since the closet is never completely closed nor openness ever completely open; for instance, the paralysis that marks his repression easily swings into the passive receptivity that conveniently 'forces' him to hear the arousing story.

Harker's strangely unsubstantiated escape shows the difficulty of traveling the region between these two poles. He can neither come out as a 'monster' nor stay in the stifling closet. Stoker's writings on sexuality had charted the ambiguous landscape between the two border posts of closure and openness. Harker's escape moves from the locked, stiflingly closed castle to the lonely, breezily vast expanse of the Transylvanian countryside. He runs from the stone enclosure to the landscape dotted with magical blue flames. He spends months on the margins of the two—hanging out of the window, crawling on the wall—refusing (or unable) to make a crude binary choice between in and out.

The spectre of brute imprisonment is never far from Stoker's delicate, idealized forms of desire, since the police threat makes his sublimations necessary. While we don't know the content of Caine's "narrative," we do know "Eugene Aram," the climax of which is "Two stern-faced men set out from Lynn, / Through the cold and heavy mist; / And Eugene Aram walked between, / With gyves upon his wrist."[3] On hearing these last words, Stoker burst into hysteria. In his letter to Whitman, he claimed that he felt "the shackles on my shoulders still."[4] What is the status of such a confession in a love letter? His emphasis on the bonds of reticence hints that repression was as much a pleasure as a duty. And he chiefly enacts Wilde's story as a longing, lingering look at imprisonment.

'Imprisonment' punctuates not only Harker's story, where the term has a certain logic, but also Dracula's English visit, where the term has only the logic of its own interest for Stoker. In the novel's only explanation of vampirism, Van Helsing says:

> Ah, but hear me through. He can do all these things, yet he is not free. Nay, he is even more prisoner than slave of the galley, than the madman in his cell. He cannot go where he lists. . . . Only at certain times can he have limited freedom. . . . We can confine him to his coffin and destroy him. (*D*, 240) [211]

The very daylight imprisons Dracula. "That monster must retain whatever form he now has. He is confined within the limitations of his earthy envelope" (*D*, 292) [255]. As Harker's group closes in, they speak of Dracula "imprisoned" in his great coffin (*D*, 373) [322]. Dracula spends almost the entire novel as a hunted man, trying to escape from his coffin prison. When Dracula does start moving freely in London, the novel immediately produces a surrogate Dracula, Renfield, whose

3. Thomas Hood, "The Dream of Eugene Aram," in *Selected Poems of Thomas Hood*, ed. John Clubbe (Cambridge: Harvard Univ. Press, 1970), 162–69.
4. Traubel (note 8), 4:182.

painful restraint and desperate, vain attempts to escape continue Sto-ker's carceral obsession.

Harker's narrative is also a story of bondage. In fact, Stoker designed Harker's experience to encode the troubling but desirable, painful but attractive image of Wilde helplessly imprisoned. In a castle full of win-dows and doors, Harker is immobilized.

> When I had seen the view I explored further; doors, doors, doors everywhere, and all locked and bolted. In no place save from the windows in the castle walls is there an available exit. The castle is a veritable prison, and I am a prisoner! (D, 26) [31–32]

No wonder that when he found himself a prisoner "a sort of wild feel-ing" came over him (D, 27) [32]. Helplessness overwhelms Harker as he recognizes his own 'wilde'ness. In the guesswork epistemology of the closet, Harker is sure that Dracula knows that Harker knows ("He knows well that I am imprisoned" [D, 27] [32]). Being imprisoned also gives Harker a certain sexual freedom—he plays the passive victim who cannot prevent Dracula's advances. Harker reveals this strategy in an impromptu error. "I was a prisoner, and . . . if I wished it I could have no choice" (D, 32; emphasis added) [37]. Using "I" instead of "he" shows that Harker and Dracula are essentially the same, with the same 'wishes.' Dracula's declaration of homosexual desire, "This man be-longs to me," was one of the first lines Stoker wrote for Dracula; indeed, he patterned chapter 5 around this speech.[5] The Count, helplessly im-prisoned but about to spring upon an unwary populace, encodes Sto-ker's fear of Wilde's eventual release from prison; the monstrous Wilde would be free to roam among London's teeming millions. On the other hand, Harker's miserable helplessness and desperate escape show Sto-ker's empathetic pity with the prisoner Wilde, the man whose hand he had "grasped in friendship," to use Caine's words.[6]

*   *   *

Harker's imprisonment follows Wilde's model. Harker can only write letters with Dracula's permission, letters which Dracula will examine. He spends most of his time reading in the library adjoining his bed-room. Similarly, Wilde was forbidden to write anything except a quota of letters to be censored by the prison governor. He had read every book in the prison library several times. Even small details, like Harker's difficulty in shaving, tally with Wilde's ill-shaven beard and scraggly hair. After a year of imprisonment, Wilde's hair had turned white and he cried continually.[7] After Mina's infection, Harker's hair, too, turns white, and he weeps often. Wilde's mother died when Wilde was in

---

5. In notes dated 1890, Dracula has an even more direct declaration: "This man belongs to me I want him." See Stoker's original working notes, 8 March 1890, EL3.f/S874d/ MS, The Rosenbach Museum and Library, Philadelphia.
6. Kernahan (note 57), 235.
7. Ellmann (note 33), 499–500.

jail; so too, Harker's adoptive father, Peter Hawkins, dies during the fight to capture Dracula.

Images, themes, and even phrases from Wilde's trial reappear in the horror novel, barely disguised. Since *Dracula* is a dreamlike projection of Wilde's traumatic trial, Stoker elaborated and distorted the evidence that the prosecutor used to convict Wilde. In particular, the conditions of secrecy necessary for nineteenth-century homosexual life—nocturnal visits, shrouded windows, no servants—become ominous emblems of Count Dracula's evil. Wilde was tried together with Alfred Taylor, who supposedly procured him boys. Taylor's nighttime visitors made his landlady suspicious. Various witnesses testified to the state of his rooms. "He kept no servant and did his own cooking on a gas stove."[8] Similarly, Dracula cooks and cleans, for "there were no servants in the house" (*D*, 27) [32]. "The windows were never opened or cleaned," said Taylor's landlady, "and the daylight was never admitted."[9] When Harker first enters Castle Dracula, he sees a room "seemingly without a window of any sort," and Dracula lives in smelly windowless underground vaults (*D*, 16) [22]. Taylor's rooms "were furnished sumptuously," just as, in Dracula's abode, "curtains and upholstery of the chairs and sofas and the hangings of my bed are of the costliest and most beautiful fabrics" (*D*, 19) [25]. Even the peculiar odor of Dracula's rooms originates in Taylor's testimony. Dracula's vaults emit "a deathly, sickly odor" that only grows "closer and heavier"; "the long disuse had made the air stale and foul" (*D*, 47, 251) [50, 221]. Taylor's rooms have never been cleaned or aired. They are hot and stuffy, and filled with smoky perfumes. Like Taylor, Dracula has no job. As the prosecutor intoned dramatically:

> "Taylor is a man without any profession. He kept no servant in these rooms, with their heavily draped windows, their candles burning on through the day, and the langorous atmosphere heavy with perfume. Here, men met together."[1]

The origin of Dracula's vaults is best revealed by the simple statement: "Taylor . . . occupied rooms which were nothing more or less than a shameful den."[2]

Evidence against Wilde also influenced the gothic conventions of *Dracula*. One line of inquiry concerned an 'innocent' boy whom Wilde had taken to sea. Similarly, Dracula destroys the good men on two ships. Wilde owned both a house and an apartment; though Wilde claimed he needed space for writing, the prosecution argued that his second establishment was a place to bring boys. Dracula, too, has two

8. H. Montgomery Hyde, *The Three Trials of Oscar Wilde* (New York: University Books, 1948), 199.
9. Hyde (note 81), 199.
1. Hyde, 190.
2. Hyde, 165.

main abodes—the Carfax estate, and a London house on Piccadilly near the Green Park (perhaps not coincidentally, Wilde's "The Critic as Artist" is set in a house on Piccadilly near the Green Park).[3] One of the worst pieces of evidence against Wilde was the presence of fecal stains on sheets in which Wilde had slept, adduced as evidence of anal sex. Wilde's 'dirty bed' led to a rhetorical efflorescence of Wilde as a creature of the sewer, living in stinking filth. For instance, Henry James warned Wilde's supporters that he smelled "a stench," which echoes Harker's admission that "under ordinary circumstances such a stench would have brought our enterprise to an end" (*D*, 251) [221]. Sardou claimed, "This muck is too vile for me to get mixed up in it."[4] Dracula's bed is a pile of notably smelly dirt. The small fecal stains become a gigantic mound of excrement, as *Dracula* projects the trial's worst moments into monstrous, threatening images. In Hanlon's words, "The chapel has become the anal orifice of castration and death, littered as it is with Dracula's fecal/phallic coffins."[5] Finally, when the Englishmen clean Dracula's coffins, they use the term that Ellen Terry, Willie Wilde, and the *Westminster Gazette* all employed to describe Wilde's punishment: "purification" (*D*, 252) [222]. Indeed, Stoker feared that *Dracula* did not sufficiently purify itself from namelessly dirty transgressions. The British Library has a letter Stoker wrote to Gladstone, in which he claims, "The book is necessarily full of horrors and terrors but I trust that these are calculated to 'cleanse the mind by pity & terror.' At any rate there is nothing base in the book."[6]

Newspaper editorials portrayed Wilde as the modern monster, thereby inventing monstrosity for the new century. The modern monster causes moral harm by perverting cultural or religious ideas. He is associated with dirt and stench. He is artificial rather than natural. Most importantly, his sin is infectious, which marks a departure from the Gothic monster whose horror is underscored by his solitude. The Gothic's secretly depraved aristocrat removes his victim to an inaccessible abbey or castle. (Frankenstein's monster exemplifies the solitude model, for he turns evil from his great loneliness.) The rest of society is still moral, sane, and good; the victim simply can't communicate with it. But *Dracula* is among the first epidemiological horror novels, concerning involuntary physical and psychological alteration caused by something that one person can 'catch' from another. *Dracula* is the progenitor of "Alien," "The Thing," "Dawn of the Dead," and "Invasion of the Body-Snatchers," where evil infects random victims' bodies and characters. Though this horror genre may have originated from late nineteenth-century fears of infectious diseases like syphilis, and late

3. This connection is mentioned by Kline (note 70), 191.
4. Ellmann (note 33), 493.
5. Hanson (note 69), 337.
6. Letter to William Gladstone, 24 May 1897, #44525 f.221, Manuscript Collection, British Library.

nineteenth-century discoveries of undetectable omnipotent 'germs,' Stoker shaped the new horror genre according to the public response to Wilde's trial. Indeed, homosexuality was the primary object of the new epidemiology, as medical theorists asked what 'caused,' 'cured,' and 'communicated' same-sex desire.[7] Epidemiological horror fiction is thus intimately associated with homophobia. It encodes the specific fear, which seems impervious to education or reason, that homosexuals want to 'corrupt' heterosexuals into a lifetime of evil sodomy.[8]

*   *   *

To sum up: the novel's ending accomplishes three tasks. First, Stoker resolves the challenge of self-hatred posed by Wilde's villification in popular culture, as he carefully undoes Wilde's apparent monstrosity and then transfers the respectable remainder of Wilde to a 'good' character. Second, he resolves the "between men" triangle by constructing a space for a spectator within any erotic encounter, and reverses the heterosexualizing imperative by making the spectator female. Third, he finds a way to represent the fruits of his peculiarly sublimated sort of desire. The ending's final function is to produce a series of stand-ins for the pleasurable male body. Stoker performs this substitution through the martyrdom of the silent man.

The novel's conclusion exults in having apparently bleached away Caine's "foul stain." "The sunset of this evening may shine on Madam Mina's forehead all white as ivory and with no stain!" (*D*, 298) [260]. And Quincey dies proclaiming "The snow is not more stainless than her forehead! The curse has passed away" (*D*, 378) [326]. Appropriately, the novel ends by alleviating its dedicatee's concern. But the pain and danger associated with Wilde's conviction—"the most awful tragedy in the whole history of literature"—get memorialized by Quincey's death. Quincey dies in Harker's lap, fluids "spurting through his fingers" (*D*, 376) [324]. While Quincey rejoices in Mina's snowy stainlessness, his own body must be soaking Harker's lap into a sticky pool of blood.[9] This vision, made inevitable by the men's physical situation, is nevertheless excluded from the text. It is the only scene of one man's blood flowing directly into another man's body, without intermediary of woman, surgical needle, or vampiric tooth. Later, we find that Quincey and Harker have a son from this encounter. Young Quincey's birth-

---

7. See, for instance, Havelock Ellis's *Studies in the Psychology of Sex* (Philadelphia: F. A. Davis Company, 1908), which analyzes homosexuality through pathological discourse, featuring chapter headings like, "Comparison with Color-blindness, Color-hearing, and Similar Abnormalities." According to Hyde's record, the judge in Wilde's case deeply regretted the lack of medical evidence that could have "thrown light on" Wilde's dark behavior (Hyde [note 98], 335).

8. This fear of destructive infection may relate to the fact that both Wilde and Stoker died from syphilis. The disease takes about fifteen years to kill its host. Thus we can calculate Wilde, who died in 1900, contracted the disease about 1885, whereas Stoker, who died in 1912, may have been infected as early as Wilde's trial in 1895 or *Dracula*'s publication in 1897.

9. Ernest Jones, *On the Nightmare* (New York: Liveright, 1951) says that blood often stands in for semen in the context of vampire narratives.

date and name establish him as the original Quincey's continuation, and "some of our brave friend's spirit has passed into him" (D, 378) [326]. Quincey's spirit fled his dying body, swirled along in his blood, soaked into Harker and became the 'seed' of Harker's son. Harker transmits Quincey's blood to Mina, just as Mina had stained her husband's body with Dracula's blood. Instead of epidemiological worry, this new blood transmission produces thriving sons. Thus Stoker recuperates the infectiousness of the vampire myth by making it into a paradigm for homosexual procreative sex.

But like a good Victorian novel, *Dracula* keeps its hero's aristocratic parentage secret. The boy is actually the final rehabilitation of Dracula's and Harker's love, for he is Dracula's son. The logic that proves the boy Quincey's spiritual heir also proves his kinship to Dracula. Quincey and Dracula died on the same day, the date on which the boy was born. Thus Dracula's spirit could have passed into him, rather than Quincey's spirit. Physically, too, Dracula's spirit was as peripatetic as Quincey's. Dracula's spirit has certainly journeyed into Harker's character, since Harker has acquired Dracula's personality traits. We can also trace the boy's physical conception through the stream of fluids that drips throughout the novel; Dracula's blood poured into Mina's mouth, and Harker's body would be covered with Dracula's blood, both from decapitating him and from supporting the bloodstained Quincey.

Little Quincey Harker can be read as the child of Dracula's and Harker's mutual desire. He is the apotheosis of Stoker's attempt to transform homosexual 'infection' into heterosexual 'procreation.' Meanwhile, Quincey's martyrdom is a red herring as well as a red stain. The intense eroticism of Dracula's death—a passive, paralyzed figure spurting fluids—merely displaces onto a respectable surrogate, Quincey's death.

*   *   *

Bram Stoker: A Chronology

	LIFE & CAREER	HISTORICAL & CULTURAL DEVELOPMENTS
1847	Bram Stoker born in Dublin.	James Malcolm Rymer's penny-dreadful *Varney the Vampyre* serialized (1845–47).
1863	Enters Trinity College.	
1865	First sees Henry Irving act in Sheridan's *The Rivals*.	Lincoln's assassination.
1868	Enters Civil Service.	Typewriter patented.
1870	Receives M.A. from Trinity College.	Death of Charles Dickens.
1871	Assumes post as drama critic for the *Dublin Mail*.	Lewis Carroll's *Alice Through the Looking Glass*. Charles Darwin's *The Descent of Man*. J. Sheridan Le Fanu's *Carmilla*.
1872	First signed work published, "The Necessity for Political Honesty."	
1875	Publishes first horror story, "The Chain of Destiny."	Bizet's *Carmen*.
1876	Death of Stoker's father. First meeting with Henry Irving.	Battle of Little Big Horn. Twain's *Tom Sawyer*. Queen Victoria declared empress of India.
1877		England annexes the Transvaal and the Orange Free State.
1878	Marries Florence Balcombe. Assumes position as acting manager of Irving's Lyceum Theatre.	
1879	First book published, *The Duties of Clerks of Petty Sessions in Ireland*. Birth of only child, Noel Thorley Stoker.	

483

1882	Publishes first story collection, *Under the Sunset*.	Birth in Hungary of actor Bela Lugosi.
1883	Organizes first North American tour of Irving's company.	
1885	*Faust* enters Lyceum repertory; Irving plays Mephistopheles.	H. Rider Haggard's *King Solomon's Mines*.
1886	Publishes lecture, *A Glimpse of America*.	Robert Louis Stevenson's *The Strange Case of Dr. Jekyll and Mr. Hyde*.
1887	Second trip to America, to plan Irving tour.	Haggard's *She*.
1888	Lyceum production of *Macbeth*.	Jack the Ripper murders.
1890	Publishes first novel, *The Snake's Pass*. Begins research on novel, *The Un-Dead*, later to be known as *Dracula*.	Emily Dickinson's *Poems*. English Jews officially emancipated.
1891		Oscar Wilde's *The Picture of Dorian Gray*.
1894	Second novel, *The Watter's Mou*.	
1895	Publishes novel, *The Shoulder of Shasta*. Employer Henry Irving and brother William Thornley Stoker knighted by Queen Victoria.	H. G. Wells's *The Time Machine*. X-rays discovered. Trial of Oscar Wilde. Viennese publication of Freud and Breuer's *Studies on Hysteria*.
1896		Wells's *The Island of Doctor Moreau*.
1897	*Dracula* published. Dramatic adaptation given elaborate "copyright reading" at Lyceum.	Kipling's poem "The Vampire." Wells's *The Invisible Man*. Queen Victoria's Diamond Jubilee. Havelock Ellis's *Studies in the Psychology of Sex*. Freud coins term "psychoanalysis."
1898	Catastrophic fire destroys stock of Lyceum scenery. Publishes novel, *Miss Betty*.	Pierre and Marie Curie discover radium.
1899	Publishes *Snowbound: The Record of a Theatrical Touring Party*. First Ameri-	

can publication of *Dracula*, as serial and book.

1900	Lyceum signed over by Irving to syndicate.	Freud's *The Interpretation of Dreams*. Death of Oscar Wilde.
1901	Stoker's mother dies. Lyceum company tours America.	Queen Victoria dies. President McKinley assassinated.
1902	Publishes novel, *The Mystery of the Sea*.	
1903	Publishes novel, *The Jewel of Seven Stars*.	
1904	Henry Irving's final tour of America.	
1905	Publishes novel, *The Man*. Death of Henry Irving. Stoker suffers stroke.	Einstein's special theory of relativity.
1906	Publishes *Personal Reminiscences of Henry Irving*.	San Francisco earthquake.
1908	Publishes novel, *Lady Athlyne*.	
1909	Publishes novel, *The Lady of the Shroud*.	
1910	Publishes nonfiction book, *Famous Imposters*.	
1911	Publishes final novel, *The Lair of the White Worm*.	
1912	Bram Stoker dies, April 20.	Sinking of the *Titanic*, April 14.

Selected Bibliography

● indicates items included or excerpted in this Norton Critical Edition.

● Arata, Stephen D. "The Occidental Tourist: *Dracula* and the Anxiety of Reverse Colonization." *Victorian Studies* (Summer 1990): 627–34.

● Auerbach, Nina. *Woman and the Demon: The Life of a Victorian Myth.* Cambridge, Mass., and London: Harvard UP, 1982. A detailed examination of the subversive, "demonic" energy lurking behind the passive stereotypes of Victorian womanhood. In particular, Auerbach discusses *Dracula*'s veiled theme of female empowerment.

———. *Ellen Terry: Player in Her Time.* New York: Norton, 1987. This biography of the beloved English actress who was a star fixture at Henry Irving's Lyceum Theatre under Bram Stoker's management gives a detailed picture of the artistic and ideological climate that also gave rise to *Dracula.*

● ———. *Our Vampires, Ourselves.* Chicago: The U of Chicago P, 1995.

Belford, Barbara. *Bram Stoker: A Biography of the Author of "Dracula."* New York: Knopf, 1996. The best-documented of three Stoker biographies to date, tracing the origins of *Dracula* in Stoker's professional relationship to the charismatic actor-manager Henry Irving.

Carter, Margaret L., ed. *"Dracula": The Novel and the Critics.* Ann Arbor, Mich.: U.M.I. Research Press, 1988. A well-rounded collection of *Dracula* criticism, including such influential essays as Eric Bentley's "The Monster in the Bedroom: Sexual Symbolism in *Dracula*" (1972) and Christopher Craft's " 'Kiss Me with Those Red Lips': Gender and Inversion in Bram Stoker's *Dracula*" (1984).

● Craft, Christopher. " 'Kiss me with Those Red Lips': Gender and Inversion in Bram Stoker's *Dracula.*" *Representations* 8 (Fall 1984): 107–33. Berkeley: The U of California P.

● Dijkstra, Bram. *Idols of Perversity: Fantasies of Feminine Evil in Fin-de-Siecle Culture.* New York and Oxford: Oxford UP, 1987. 342–44.

Dworkin, Andrea. *Intercourse.* New York: Free Press, 1987. In this radical feminist collection of literary criticism, Dworkin includes one of the most excoriating attacks on *Dracula* ever published, revealing a misogynistic anticipation of "an oncoming century filled with sexual horror: the throat as a female genital; sex and death as synonymous; killing as a sex act; slow dying as sensuality . . . intercourse itself needing blood, someone's, somewhere, to count as a sex act in a world excited by sadomasochism. . . ."

Farson, Daniel. *The Man Who Wrote "Dracula": A Biography of Bram Stoker.* New York: St. Martin's, 1985. Written by Bram Stoker's great-nephew, this readable biography benefits from Farson's apparent access to family documents but is marred by a complete lack of citations. Farson created controversy with his speculation that Stoker's death in 1912 was due to tertiary syphilis.

Leatherdale, Clive. *"Dracula": The Novel and the Legend.* Rev. ed. London: Desert Island Books, 1993. A comprehensive overview of critical approaches to *Dracula,* including detailed discussions of the story as Christian allegory and Christian parody, the book's anxious Darwinian undercurrents, the undercurrents of grail and tarot symbolism, and so on.

———, ed. *The Origins of "Dracula": The Background to Bram Stoker's Gothic Masterpiece.* London: Kimber, 1987. A useful anthology of Stoker's direct and indirect source materials.

Ludlam, Harry. *A Biography of Dracula: The Life Story of Bram Stoker.* London: Foulsham, 1962. Like Farson's 1985 biography, Ludlam's book also lacks notes and citations, making an objective evaluation difficult. This highly anecdotal, first book-length biography of Stoker was written in cooperation with Stoker's only child, Noel Thornley Stoker, and was aided by the recollections of actor-manager Hamilton Deane, who first adapted *Dracula* to the stage.

McNally, Raymond, and Radu Florescu. *In Search of Dracula*. Greenwich, Conn: New York Graphic Society, 1973. Rev. ed., Boston: Houghton Mifflin, 1994. McNally and Florescu's unprecedented excavation of the Wallachian warlord Vlad "the Impaler" Tepes (1431–1476), also known as Dracula, lavishes far more research on the historical figure than Bram Stoker himself ever attempted and is therefore more revealing as history than as a key to Stoker's literary intentions.

● Moretti, Franco. *Signs Taken for Wonders: Essays in the Sociology of Literary Forms*. Trans. Susan Fischer, David Forgacs, and David Miller. New York: Verso, 1988.

Newman, Kim. *Anno Dracula*. New York: Carroll & Graf, 1993. Newman's complex pastiche of Stoker's novel, its literary antecedents, and its pop-culture legacy is an entertainingly postmodern meditation on the vampire in Western culture. In Newman's multilayered vision, Dracula has conquered England, married Queen Victoria, and mounted Professor Van Helsing's head on a pike outside Buckingham Palace; the prostitutes of Whitechapel are real vampires; and John Seward is secretly Jack the Ripper. The overall richness of the novel defies a brief synopsis; suffice it to say that Newman leaves no subtext unturned.

● Roth, Phyllis A. "Suddenly Sexual Women in Bram Stoker's *Dracula*." *Literature and Psychology* 27 (1977): 113–21.

Saberhagen, Fred. *The Dracula Tape*. New York: Warner Books, 1975. Bram Stoker never really gives Dracula a chance to tell his own story, but in Saberhagen's revisionist novel, the count gives a witty and plausible account of human venality and undying vampire love.

● Schaffer, Talia. " 'A Wilde Desire Took Me': The Homoerotic History of *Dracula*." *English Literary History* 61.2. Baltimore: The Johns Hopkins UP, 1994.

● Senf, Carol A. "*Dracula*: The Unseen Face in the Mirror." *The Journal of Narrative Technique* 9 (1979): 160–70.

● Skal, David J. *Hollywood Gothic: The Tangled Web of "Dracula" from Novel to Stage to Screen*. New York: Norton, 1990.

———. *Dracula: The Ultimate Illustrated Edition of the World-Famous Vampire Play*. New York: St. Martin's Press, 1993.

———. *The Monster Show: A Cultural History of Horror*. New York: Norton, 1993. Paperback reprint: Penguin, 1994. In this wide-ranging followup to his *Hollywood Gothic: The Tangled Web of "Dracula" from Novel to Stage to Screen*, the author chronicles the twentieth-century evolution of Dracula and other monsters in light of changing cultural anxieties and traumas.

● Waller, Gregory A. *The Living and the Undead*. Urbana: U of Illinois P, 1986.

Wolf, Leonard, ed. *The Essential Dracula*. New York: Plume, 1993. This revised paperback edition of Wolf's *The Annotated Dracula* (1975) lacks the elegant presentation of the original but retains Wolf's richly detailed annotations along with new commentary from contemporary horror writers on the legacy of Stoker's novel.